To: Alicia B. Lyon

MAY YOU BE BLESSED BY <u>JESUS</u> IN
THIS BOOK OF HIS LOVE, MERCY
AND MIRACLES TO US AND OTHERS!

Pastor Sid & Betsy Rigell

FIRED AGAIN AND AGAIN,

PRAISE THE LORD!

PLEASE READ SOON:
Deut.:5 & 6
Joshua 1:7-9
I Sam. 15:22-24
Psalm 1:1-6
9:17
23:1-6
33:12
100:1-6
119:105
121:4
122:1-6
127:1
Matt.:6:33
John 3 & 15
Rom.8:28-39
I Cor. 13
Rev.14:6,7,13

Let's Keep Shining For Jesus!

JOSEPH S. and ELIZABETH W. RIGELL

(SID and BETSY)

The Afikomen Company
1503 East Baltimore Street
Baltimore, Maryland 21231

ACKNOWLEDGMENTS

We wish to thank all those who have helped make this book possible.

Special thanks to Stelios Maistros for his invaluable help with the computer; to author and consultant, Marie Rice; to our proof readers: Terri Monk, Bonnie O'Brian, Jack Chapman and Mae Bochau, and to the printer's representative, Bert Messelink.

Our deepest appreciation to Beth Armiger Bryant for her thoughtful illustrations for the Chapter headings. See a special story about Beth on page 110.

To each one who has had a part, to all our prayer partners and supporters our most sincere gratitude. May the Lord richly reward each one of you!

Copyright © 1992
by Joseph S. and Elizabeth W. Rigell

All Rights Reserved

No part of this book may be reproduced in any form, except for brief quotations in reviews, without the written permission of the publishers.

Scripture quotations are from the King James Version of the Holy Bible.

Printed in the United States of America, 1992.

Library of Congress Catalog Card Number is: 92-70294

ISBN 0-9632253-0-8

DEDICATION

This book is dedicated to our precious sons: Craig, Kirby, Joe, Chris, Brian, Dusty and their families to tell about the wonderful mercies and miracles of the Lord, His love, His power and His mighty works that we have seen in our lives.

Please forgive us if you have ever felt that we neglected you. We hope you know that we love you very much, but remember most of all, *that nothing can separate us from the love of God which is in Christ Jesus our Lord* (Romans 8:39).

We would also like to dedicate this book in deepest appreciation to all those precious people -- friends, co-workers, kindly teachers and faithful saints who have played a part in helping us along this journey. There are so many we could never name all the names or tell all the stories of their encouragement and help. Eternal Thanks!

FIRED AGAIN AND AGAIN, PRAISE THE LORD

"COME UNTO ME"

TABLE OF CONTENTS

Dedication i
Contents iii
Introduction v
Preface "A GOOD NAME" vii

PART I
1 THE EARLY YEARS 1
2 FROM PEACE TO WAR TO WEDDING 21
3 GETTING ON THE LORD'S COURSE 41
4 SEMINARY GRADUATION TO CONFRONTATIONS 53
5 FROM SPIRITUAL LIMBO TO GHETTO 65

PART II
6 MCKIM DAYS - INNER-CITY CHALLENGE 75
7 THE WAR ON POVERTY AND OTHER WARS 101
8 A TOTALLY UNEXPECTED WAR - OR FIRING 115
9 RACE RIOTS TO TWO MORE FIRINGS 125

PART III
10 THE LITTLE TABERNACLE ARISES! 147
11 THE FREBURGER STORY 167
12 MIRACLE CONTRACT AND GOLDEN KEY 181
13 MOM'S HOME-GOING; SON'S HOME-COMING! 199

PART IV
14 MORE MIRACLES OF JESUS 225
15 GOD'S SOLEMN WARNING TO AMERICA 237
16 AN AMAZING YEAR-1977-CALL TO ISRAEL 249
17 THE ISRAEL CONNECTION GROWS 265
18 PREPARATION FOR OUR ISRAEL ASSIGNMENT 285

PART V
19 OUR RAMOT YEAR IN JERUSALEM 303
20 FROM CONFRONTATION TO WARS 325
21 SEARCH FOR A CHURCH AND OIL 343
22 A DREAM COME TRUE -PATMOS 355

PART VI
23 GOD'S LITTLE AND BIG MIRACLES 379
24 ANOTHER ROUGH FIRING-- FROM ISRAEL 391
25 FROM PATMOS TO A WHIRLWIND SUMMER 409
26 DANGEROUS MISSIONARIES ARRESTED 421
27 SOME YUMMY STORIES 435

PART VII
28 BIBLE PROPHECIES AND WARNINGS 457
29 THREE GREAT MEN OF FAITH 487
30 RETIRING; REFIRING; "NOT FINISHED JUST BEGUN!" 521

FIRED AGAIN AND AGAIN, PRAISE THE LORD!

"MOM RIGELL"
EXAMPLE OF DEEP & COURAGEOUS FAITH IN THE LORD!

INTRODUCTION

No doubt you may question our title, FIRED AGAIN AND AGAIN, PRAISE THE LORD! In this modern day, our polite and proper society frowns on nice well-educated ministers of the Gospel getting fired and fired and fired. No one in his right mind would want that to happen either, but it did to us! Therefore, we invite you to come along with us on a long and interesting journey in which this occurred several times in one way or another.

It almost happened to me as a husband, but God intervened! Yes, there were many happy days and many rough days in our years together as husband and wife, but God's grace was more than sufficient, through our Lord Jesus. Praise His Name!

Because our backgrounds were so different, Mother Rigell wondered if our marriage would succeed. She lasted long enough to see us through 28 years of struggles, before the angels of the Lord lifted her up to heaven. Now we are in our forty-sixth year.

So much of a family's history is lost when the old folks leave this world without ever sharing any record of their life's journey which could help others. We felt the Lord wanted us to write a careful account of how He brought us through this pilgrimage. Thus, you too, can be assured of His goodness, mercy and faithfulness, as in Psalm 23, on your own rocky paths!

In a little apartment on the Island of Patmos as we began to write this book, we asked the Lord for direction. He was faithful to answer by bringing back many, many interesting experiences to recount for you.

We are undertaking this venture with deep gratitude and humility toward God for giving us the privilege of living to see His mighty hand of mercy in so many ways. He makes it so wonderfully clear that He will never run out of miracles for those who have, or will become, His sons and daughters through faith in the Lord Jesus Christ.

John 1:12.....*But as many as received him, to them gave He power to become the sons of God, even to them that believe on his name.* See also: II Cor.12:9; Phil.3:7-14; I Peter 4:12-13; and Hebrews 13:5-6.

FIRED AGAIN AND AGAIN, PRAISE THE LORD!

MOM AND DAD - MARRIED Dec. 22, 1901

PREFACE

"Sid, you have a good name; be sure to take care of it."

Uncle DeWitt looked up with tears of love as he lay on his death-bed, to impress me of that fact, which we both had learned early in life from Proverbs 22:1:.... **A good name is rather to be chosen than great riches.** What he said to me was an unforgettable reminder!

Many times after that summer of 1976, I began to wonder more and more about our origin and history. Our oldest sister, Lois (Sissy), had been researching the family tree and discovered the possibility of a connection with the Huguenots who, after terrible persecutions in France, came over in the 1700's to South Carolina and Georgia. She apparently never was able to locate full or certain evidence of this, because so many of these records were destroyed by General Sherman's scorched earth march to the sea during the Civil War.

For a long time I had a hunch that we were of French background and had been told as much by a Spanish professor at the University of Florida. Also a doctor in Baltimore once informed me that he had been an army surgeon in Normandy, France, during World War II, and there he had come across a name like ours.

Early in 1980 while Betsy and I were living with Esther Dorflinger in Jerusalem, we attended an intensive Hebrew class (Ulpan) to learn to read, write and speak Hebrew. While groping to learn how to use the Hebrew dictionary, we came across the verb "to spy", which was exactly the same as we had learned to write our name in Hebrew, *Rigel*.

Often in our contacts we would say our name meant "to spy" but, smiling, quickly add, "Of course, we're the good spies like Joshua and Caleb. We're spying out the land for our Messiah's soon return."

We had asked a tour guide friend, Moshe Dayagi, if our name had any meaning in Hebrew, and he associated it with the Hebrew word for foot or leg, *Rigel*. He also said there was a similar word in Arabic, *Rigl*, meaning "foot".

Two dear friends in Jerusalem, Zev and Ruth Weintraub, brought us a book on astronomy which told about a star of the first magnitude called Rigel located in the left foot of the constellation Orion. (Those of you who know our story, and how we have gotten the "left foot of

FIRED AGAIN AND AGAIN, PRAISE THE LORD!

unfellowship" several times for taking a stand for Jesus and His teaching, might agree that we have a very appropriate name).

Dad's name was Starlus. We are told his mother probably got the name from a book which she read about a Roman gladiator. It's interesting that the first syllable spells star and the ending syllable could easily mean light. Whether Grandmother realized that Rigel was also the name of a star in the constellation Orion, there is no way of knowing.

In the fall of 1984, we were surprised to learn that our tour guide that year was a Jewish man named Joseph Brett, originally from England. Then I recalled that my maternal grandmother's maiden name was Brett. This name Brett has a possible connection with the Hebrew word "brit", meaning covenant. Ah, could it be our forebears were assimilated Jews? Possibly!

Although there is no absolute proof of natural Jewish connections, we believe there IS such a connection, because of the love the Lord has given us for Israel, for the Jewish people and our strong desire to return to that blessed land. All through the Scriptures, the Lord promises to bring His people back to their land. Just being grafted into the Jewish Messiah Jesus makes that connection!

One day after finding the name, Moshe Rigel, in the Jerusalem phone directory, we called the number. Moshe's wife answered. Fortunately she spoke English. Moshe was not home, as he was doing Army duty. She told us her husband's family had come from Lithuania, where the name was called Rigelis. They had fled to France where it was shortened to Rigel, and they then emigrated to Israel. We look forward to meeting Moshe Rigel and his wife in Jerusalem one day.

So Rigell is a good and honorable name, but it pales into insignificance and unimportance compared to That Name which is above every name. That Name unto which every knee shall bow, and every tongue confess (Phil.2:13)--The Name JESUS. The Name of JESUS, The LORD OF ALL, is The Name we must lift up and love and honor above all names (John 12:32)! Also whether Jew or Gentile, the most important thing is that our names be written in the Lamb's Book Of Life in Heaven (Luke 10:19-20; Rev.20:15).

Many years ago an unknown author wrote the following remarkable description of JESUS illustrating the Greatness of His Name:

PREFACE

THE INCOMPARABLE JESUS CHRIST

More than nineteen hundred years ago there was a Man born contrary to the laws of life, born of a virgin. This Man lived in poverty and was reared in obscurity. He did not travel extensively. Only once did He cross the boundary of the country in which He lived; that was during His exile in childhood. He possessed neither wealth nor influence. His relatives were inconspicuous and had neither training nor formal education.

In infancy He startled a king; in childhood He puzzled doctors; in manhood He ruled the course of nature, walked upon the waves as pavement, and hushed the sea to sleep. He healed the multitudes without medicine and made no charge for His service. He never wrote a book, and yet perhaps all the libraries of the world could not hold the books that have been written about Him. He never wrote a song, and yet He has furnished the theme for more songs than all the songwriters combined. He never founded a college, but all the schools put together cannot boast of having as many students.

He never marshaled an army, nor drafted a soldier, nor fired a gun, and yet no leader ever had more volunteers who have, under His orders, made more rebels stack arms and surrender without a shot fired. He never practiced psychiatry, and yet He has healed more broken hearts than all the doctors far and near. Once each week multitudes congregate at worshiping assemblies to pay homage and respect to Him.

The names of past, proud statesmen of Greece and Rome have come and gone. The names of the past scientists, philosophers, and theologians have come and gone. But the name of this Man multiplies more and more. Though time has spread nineteen hundred years between the people of this generation and the mockers at His crucifixion, He still lives. His enemies could not destroy Him, and the grave could not hold Him. He stands forth upon the highest pinnacle of heavenly glory, proclaimed of God, acknowledged by angels, adored by saints, and feared by devils, as the risen, personal Christ, our Lord and Saviour.

- Author Unknown.

FIRED AGAIN AND AGAIN, PRAISE THE LORD!

We are either going to be forever with Him, or forever without Him. It was the incomparable Jesus Christ who said:

Come to Me, all you who are weary and burdened, and I will give you rest. (Matt.11:28).
I am the way and the truth and the life. No one comes to the Father except through Me. (John 14:6).
This is my commandment, that ye love one another, as I have loved you. (John 15:12).
By this shall all men know that you are my disciples, if you have love one to another. (John 13:35).
Abide in me, and I in you. As the branch cannot bear fruit of itself, except it abide in the vine, no more can you, except you abide in me. I am the vine, ye are the branches; He that abideth in me, and I in him, the same bringeth forth much fruit; for without me ye can do nothing! (John 15:4,5).

"I WILL GIVE YOU REST"

PREFACE

GRAND "PAPA" WILLIAMS - FARMER

"DADDY" RIGELL - LUMBERMAN

FIRED AGAIN AND AGAIN, PRAISE THE LORD!

"THE 3 BULLS" - DAD ON THE RIGHT

MILLIGAN'S POST OFFICE 1989

LUMBER MILL AT MILLIGAN VERY NEAR DAD'S LOCATION

CHAP. 1

THE EARLY YEARS

"From a child thou hast known the holy Scriptures which are able to make thee wise unto salvation through faith which is in Christ Jesus."
- II Tim.3:15

In 1917 two years after the sinking of the British pleasureship Lusitania by the Kaiser's U-boats, our nation had gone to war with Germany.

At the age of 17 my Uncle DeWitt (Mom's only brother) had joined the U.S. Expeditionary Army to fight against the Germans in France. World War I was raging. The German armies and U-Boats were taking a heavy toll of British and French lives.

When Dad learned his young brother-in-law was to be sent overseas, he decided to try to catch up with him to let DeWitt know of his family's love and prayers.

Although Dad had the name of the camp where Uncle DeWitt was stationed, he wasn't sure of the unit. Hoping to find him, he took a train from his home in Milligan, Florida to Jacksonville then north to New York and finally reached Fort Dix, New Jersey.

With God's help and some real *chutzpah* (Yiddish for audacity, boldness) Dad was able to see Uncle DeWitt and encourage him, just hours before he was to board the transport ship for France. Uncle DeWitt forever appreciated Dad's last-minute visit. In France Uncle DeWitt's unit found World War I near its end. Kaiser Wilhelm's forces were giving up the fight for the time being. In twenty years they would be back under the mad sergeant, Adolf Hitler and his Nazis.

Dad's brother, Creech, also went off to war in 1917. Sadly, he did not return. But Grandma Munny never stopped praying. She had great faith that she would see him again. Twenty years later, just months before her death, her long lost son came home. Apparently after the war Creech went to California and married. No one ever knew why he did not return home immediately, or even write. However, he did see his mother before she died--proving that God remembered Munny and answered her prayers. How good God is to those who love and trust Him!

Dad's mother was a delight to her grandchildren. She showered them with love and affection and had a favorite trick of slipping a penny into their hands each time they came to visit. As a result they called her "Munny."

Munny was a very small woman about four feet eight inches tall. No doubt she was the source of all the Rigell shortness. She had borne three daughters: Essie, Estelle and Willie; and three sons: Starlus (my father), and Uncles Alvin and Creech. Munny lived well into her 90's in the old farm place in Ashford, Alabama.

Dad was a stocky man well versed in hunting, fishing and lumbering. He had a little sawmill in the northwest Florida village of Milligan, between Crestview and Milton, on the main east-west railroad line.

Evidently Milligan was named in the 1800's by the first Scottish and Irish settlers, who helped open up the beautifully forested woodlands to settlements for farming. It was deer, wild turkey and bear country. And good fishing, too!

Although Dad's mill was relatively small, he was doing well because of the heavy demand by the Government for all kinds of lumber for army camps and other war-time needs. Dad dearly loved his family and was a good provider and a good lumberman.

Not far from the mill, and facing the railroad tracks stood our big old house where I, Mom's eighth child, was born January 1, 1918 on a cold, snowy night.

By this time my mother had already given birth to my sisters: Ruth, Essie Lois (Sissy), Mary, and my brothers: William (Bill), Starlus, Jr., Alvin and Frank. Two more children, Ann and Judy, were to follow about two years apart.

I was named after my grandfather, Joseph Sidney Williams of Ashford, Alabama, who was a successful farmer, store owner, and Houston County Commissioner. He was also a faithful Christian in the Baptist Church.

My earliest recollections are of a very loving mother and father. It was a great honor for me to sleep in the same bed with Dad when he came home from long stays at the logging camps. There his job was to supervise the cutting and hauling of timber by huge oxcarts to the railroad spurs. Somehow he always managed to bring home a large box of fruit, a huge stalk of bananas or other special goodies for his growing brood. Sometimes it would be freshly caught fish from a fishing trip, or

CHAPTER 1: "THE EARLY YEARS"

wild turkey or venison from a hunting trip.

My mother, who was an excellent seamstress, made most of our clothes. I would sit for hours behind her sewing machine, as she patiently allowed me to help feed long seams through its sewing foot, trim thread ends, thread the needle or assist with other little sewing jobs. This made me feel very important.

I was the most freckled-faced boy in the whole family. Dad had a good tan from much time spent outdoors and also had some large freckles on his hands. One day, I observed his freckles and wanting to establish my special relationship with him, I pointed to my freckles and asked my mother, "Ain't I'm kin to my Dad?"

She laughed, "Of course you are!" That made me happy.

With such a large flock of children, Mom usually had to have a nurse-housekeeper helping daily. Voncile was a very precious black girl who helped us several years. We loved Voncile but enjoyed playing little pranks on her.

My brother Frank and I were only 17 months apart and constantly into things. One day he and I decided we were still hungry. We came to Mamma in the middle of the morning and asked if she would let Voncile fix us some fried eggs--all we could eat. Mom agreed. Voncile didn't stop cooking until she had prepared about a dozen. Yessir! We had all the fried eggs we wanted--for the next twenty years. I was nearly grown before I could look a fried egg in the face. Isn't it amazing how we can overdo things, even a good thing like eating?

One morning we found a bottle with a little whiskey in it. We had seen men drink the stuff, so we decided to take a drink ourselves. Not much, but just enough to contaminate our breaths. Ugh! It tasted horrible and burned. When Mom discovered what we had done, she was shocked, saying, "Shame on you. Now you march right down and report to your father."

Guiltily we slunk down that long wooden sidewalk to the mill office.

Dad was surprised to see us. "What are you boys doing here?"

"Mom wants you to smell our *brims*." We were not familiar with the word breath, only with the word *bream,* a fish Dad often caught.

He did his best to keep a straight face. He reprimanded us, and we solemnly promised never to do it again.

The walkway back to the house was parallel with the railroad tracks. Frank and I loved to wave at the engineer as the train rumbled by. We would race along the walk, and the train man would yell, "Run big un, run little un." When we were smaller, the train whistle in the distance was a "skeery" sound because we knew it meant a big train would soon be roaring by. We could already hear the frightening clacking of the wheels on the tracks. Terrified, we would run pell mell back into the house, down the long hall, and dive headfirst into the big clothes hamper.

Being observant little kids, Frank and I noticed there was one big old rooster constantly chasing and attacking all the hens in our chicken yard. Those dear old hens worked so hard to provide eggs for us. He shouldn't be so mean to them. All he did was strut around, crow, knock them down, and drive the other roosters away. This big bully needed to be taught a lesson. Frank and I found a couple of goodly sticks. We entered Mr. Rooster's turf and chased him all over until we cornered him in the chicken house and almost beat him to death.

Fortunately we got caught. Still unaware of the rooster's reasons for pursuing hens, Frank and I bothered him no more.

In spite of our great misapplication of justice, the poor old rooster lived to chase again.

In those days modern psychiatry and psychology were little known. My parents had only the Bible to instruct them in how to rear their children. How blessed we were!

Proverbs 22:15...**Foolishness is bound in the heart of a child; but the rod of correction shall drive it far from him.**

Their rod of correction was the hairbrush or belt, and they were unafraid and unashamed to use them. Each of us got our full share. Their discipline was given in love, and it helped to clear things up quickly and set us straight. Remember Jesus' Words:

Revelation 3:19.....**As many as I love I rebuke and chasten: be zealous therefore, and repent.**

Once Dad came home and decided that all his boys needed a haircut for the summertime, which meant shaved heads, or nearly so. Even at the age of five I hated the thought. Being the youngest boy I was hoping to be exempt. He gave each of us a quarter to pay for the haircut. I promptly went out to the back porch. With a mighty heave I foolishly let my quarter go flying out into the back pasture thinking this would stop the approaching skinhead. Instead I ended up with it, plus a skinned bottom, plus a powerful lesson not to throw money away ever again.

When I was about four, Frank and I decided to pick some of the nice ripe mulberries from the big tree out beyond the smoke house. We agreed that Frank, being the oldest, would climb the tree and begin knocking down the berries. I would pick them up and put them in a bucket. Later we would wash them.

After picking a pint or so, it became necessary for Frank to climb higher in the tree. Suddenly he slipped and fell hitting the ground with

CHAPTER 1: "THE EARLY YEARS"

a hard thud. He immediately cried out in pain, "Sid, I can't get up. I'm hurt. Call Mamma."

Hearing my frantic screams, Mom and the others who were home, came running at top speed. They carefully lifted Frank up and brought him to the house. His left leg was broken above the knee, a compound fracture with the bone protruding. The country doctor came and did his best to reset the bones. For the next six months, Frank ended up on his back with his leg in a combination sling and traction. Our playing time for that summer was badly spoiled by that mulberry tree disaster.

As a result of that fall, Frank still walks with a limp and has suffered much pain in that leg over the years. In the spring of 1990, at seventy-three plus, he had to have hip replacement surgery from that damage of long ago.

About 1923 we moved from Milligan to DeFuniak Springs, where the older children were already in the Presbyterian Palmer College Academy, and where I was to get my delayed first year in school.

Because my birthday was January 1, I had to wait until I was more than seven to start. My first grade teacher, Miss Mary McKinnon, was probably the best teacher in the school. Her teaching of phonetics gave us the finest method for learning to read quickly, and her love gave the true motivation. She was also our Sunday School teacher making Jesus and the other Bible characters very real to us. What a fine start in the realm of learning and faith!

Also important to our family was The First Presbyterian Church of DeFuniak Springs, which had an outstanding preacher, Rev. Currie, and a congregation of sturdy, Bible-believing Christians of Calvinist and Scottish roots. There at the age of seven I responded to Jesus' call on my life. From that moment I knew the Lord wanted me to be a preacher, although in later years I tried to get Him to let me do other things, such as being an electrical engineer.

I was baptized in the Presbyterian way by sprinkling and received into the Church. My life-long faith in Jesus had begun! I never regretted that little boy's decision to follow Jesus!

Our family believed strongly in the need for a good education. The Christian teachers at the Presbyterian Academy gave all of us a tremendous start.

Being small in size is often a handicap for some, but it is never a handicap for learning. My oldest sister, Sissy, almost as tiny as a doll, was graduated with honors from Florida State College For Women at nineteen. (By the way, Rev. Currie was one of the smallest men who ever preached the Gospel).

There was a classmate in my first grade whose family was

well-to-do. One Saturday morning I was invited to come to his house to join him in play. When the boy showed me his roomful of toys, I hardly knew how to act. Everything a kid ever dreamed of seemed to be in that room. I couldn't believe it.

In our house we had always contented ourselves with making our own toys out of bits of string; pieces of wood; bottles; boxes; remnants of cloth; bent nails, tacks or whatever we could find.

The lumber business had fallen on hard times by then and there wasn't any money for toys anyway; therefore, we were forced to use our wits to create our own. Frank and I made some beautiful ox-trains and wagons. We hauled make-believe logs 'round and 'round the house. We had more fun with the games and toys we invented than that little boy with all his store-bought ones.

We all thought we would live a long, happy time in DeFuniak Springs with its good school and church. However, one weekend in late spring, Dad came home from his job with the Sherman Lumber Company and announced that we would be moving soon to Bay Harbor, Florida, where he worked as superintendent of the logging operations for the two mills of the Company.

Not long before this he had bought a larger house a little closer to our school. I felt very sad at the news that we would have to leave, because I had attended that school for only a year, really liked it and loved my teacher.

That same weekend, the family planned to visit Dad's brother Alvin and wife Lila in Freeport near the coast. Some of us went with Mom and Uncle Alvin to Freeport. The rest were to join us the next day for a fishing expedition. During the night the big old house caught fire. Dad and Frank were awakened by burning boards falling on their bed. Our other brothers barely escaped, but praise God, no one was lost. The house and most of our belongings were completely destroyed.

Thus we were forced to move to Bay Harbor near Panama City as soon as possible. Dad hired a small trucker to load up most of the family and the belongings we had left to take us on that sixty-five mile trip. I can still visualize riding in that old open truck for what seemed to be a long, long distance from DeFuniak Springs. How glad we were to get there safely!

Despite our high hopes for a new, happy beginning, it was not to be, even though the new home which the Company provided for us in Bay Harbor was in the prettiest location we had ever seen. It overlooked beautiful East St. Andrews Bay with its lovely white sandy beach. The sparkling waters were full of fish and crabs, and every now and then, the old lumber dock welcomed a sailing ship or a steam boat. This was

CHAPTER 1: "THE EARLY YEARS"

early 1925.

The house had a real tiled floor bathroom, pretty fireplaces, a large kitchen and dining room. There was a picket fence around our yard and the yard of a similar house next door. Both homes were under moss-draped oak trees, which we soon discovered were full of squirrels. What an exciting place in which to grow up! Unfortunately, some real tragedies lay ahead.

In grammar school the local tough boys quickly began testing our mettle by deliberately picking fights. It didn't take them long to learn if they jumped on one brother, they would quickly have to fight the other four. Soon we had gained their respect.

We went to that school for about two years when suddenly it burned down. Another elementary school opened the next fall in the midst of the grand old oaks and pine trees of Bay Harbor where there was a company store. There the local families made their weekly shopping trips and charged their groceries.

Millville was two and a half miles away with another company store; a few shops; another old sawmill, and an old-timey movie house. If we had been good and done our chores well, Mom would allow us to hike to Millville, perhaps once a month on Saturday, to see one of the old silent films, the cowboy movies, and "Our Gang" comedies of that day. Admission price 10 cents!

In those "Our Gang" comedies they would always have a sissy by the name of Sidney dressed in a spotless, Lord Fauntleroy outfit. My older brothers enjoyed teasing me about this until it stirred up some real battles and made me greatly dislike my middle name forevermore. Even today, I prefer not to write out my whole middle name and use only the first 3 letters--Sid.

Also, back in DeFuniak Springs there was an old handyman who came pushing a wheelbarrow with his yard tools throughout the neighborhood. His name was Sidney. The same older brothers would tease, "Here comes Sidney, the trash man, with his wheelbarrow."

To me their teasing was cruel. As my first name was Joseph and I was their youngest brother, many times I felt like Joseph in the Old Testament, especially after a kind lady at church gave me a many-colored coat! Joseph's story greatly consoled me (see Gen. 37-50).

Shortly after we came to Bay Harbor, Dad was brought home from the logging operations in terrible pain. After the doctors examined him, he was rushed to a larger hospital in Dothan, Alabama, 100 miles north. His appendix had ruptured and peritonitis had set in. There were no wonder drugs in those days to stop such infections. In about three days, despite all the doctors could do, Mom's precious husband, our beloved Dad, was gone. Thus on June 23, 1925, his family was left devastated with no strong human pillar of support.

The lumber company generously permitted us to continue living in the superintendent's house for at least three more years---rent-free! Praise God! It was the Lord's special care for Mom Rigell and her large brood.

Mom was no stranger to tragedy. Their first child, Ruth, died of pneumonia when they were living in a rough logging camp in Louisiana. In Milligan about 1922 our little blond, curly-haired sister, Ann, came toddling out to where her brothers were dismantling an old wooden walkway. She was curious to see what they were doing. Little Ann came too close and was struck in the head by one of the boards with old rusty nails protruding. The nails pierced Ann's brain, and she died within hours. What a sweet treasure heaven received that day! It was a very sad loss for our family and especially for the brothers who were involved.

Now that Dad was gone everyone pitched in. The youngest ones tended the chickens; fed and milked the cow; did household chores; cut wood for cooking and the fireplaces, and the older ones helped the younger ones in their studies.

Sissy began teaching mathematics in Bay County High School. She was a math "whiz". Our oldest brother, Bill, went to work in an ice plant in Millville, and Mom applied for and was qualified to teach the first and second grades, even though she had never completed high school.

A Presbyterian preacher, Rev. Clarence Leckenby, extended great help and comfort to the family. He drove five miles each Sunday morning to pick us up for Sunday school and church.

Less than four years after Dad's death, our oldest brother, Bill, while cleaning around some heavy machinery in the ice plant, was caught somehow by a large flywheel pulley belt. He was thrown into the wheel and instantly killed. Bill was probably no more than twenty-four and had been married only a short time to a lovely school teacher, Dorothy Williams, the daughter of Ralph Williams, a snapper-boat captain.

The loss of Bill was almost too much for Mom and young Dorothy. They were in deep mourning and shock for many months, as we all were. It was so sad, because Bill was young, hard working, ambitious and full of life. He also had been my special defender from the mischievous pranks of the other three brothers. It broke my heart to know that I would never see him again on this earth, but I'm sure we shall see him in heaven with the rest of the family some day.

Depending completely on the Lord's comfort, Mom and our family

CHAPTER 1: "THE EARLY YEARS"

struggled on through this latest tragedy. We were keeping on by *grit and by grace*. In sorrow and our struggle for survival we were drawn closer together. Although terribly shaken, Mom's faith in the Lord remained strongly anchored in His Word and even grew, as we faced the bleak days of the depression, which began with the great Wall Street crash of 1929.

At times her teaching pay of $50 a month came in the form of an IOU from the County Board of Education. There were no government welfare programs in those days, only the help of friends, relatives, church members and the Good Lord. Mom's father, "Papa" Williams, offered to provide us a house in Ashford, Alabama, Mom's old hometown. She was grateful but said she and the family would try to make it with God's help in Bay Harbor. "Papa" had already supplied us with a cow, and when she went dry, he promised to see that we would get another one. We had chickens again and a beautiful collie dog named Mig. The Barrow family next door also had a collie named Jack. Whenever they could get out of their yards, the two would often tangle fiercely over some bone or other. We had a favorite expression about their fights--"Our Mig won; but Jack got the bone!"

TWO SPECIAL FRIENDS

My brother Frank and I had two good friends, Walker Savell and Custer Russ, Jr. About three miles out in the country from Bay Harbor Walker and his family lived on a small farm where they had horses and ponies. Walker's parents were loving, hospitable people who would invite us along with Custer to spend weekends on their little farm. Their place was not too far from a railroad line where the long, flat rail cars for hauling timber to the mills were sidetracked when not in use. One day we decided to hike over to this line of rail cars to check them out. (One could only find such a timber hauling vehicle in some primitive land or rail museum today). The sets of wheels on each end of these cars were coupled together by long shafts approximately thirty feet long and about eight or ten inches wide.

We began chasing each other down the long, narrow shafts, climbing over the end carriages onto the next rail car and so on to the end. While running, I lost my balance and slid down beside the coupling catching the side of my leg in the jagged end of one of the huge bolts in the carriage. Its sharp edge ripped into my leg and tore a chunk of meat out of it. (There is still a noticeable hole in my left thigh today).

The next instant I was on the tracks underneath with blood pouring out of my denim pants and making a big puddle on the ground. At that time none of us knew anything about tourniquets or staunching the flow of blood. The other guys took turns trying to help me hobble back to the farm house at least a mile away. I kept getting weaker and weaker. Before long a friendly man and his son picked us up in their model "T" Ford. They just "happened" to be on that lonely country road! He told us to put pressure on the wound, rushed us back to Bay Harbor, picked up Mom and took us to the old Adams Hospital in Panama City where my leg was sewed up with many stitches. He even waited and brought us all home again. God bless that good Samaritan. The Lord had sent him in the nick of time to save me from bleeding to death.

In another two weeks or so, we were chasing each other again, but not on railroad cars!

Eventually we would experience many adventurous "Tom Sawyer days." In the early thirties our explorations covered many areas along the shoreline of St. Andrews Bay, where we discovered evidence that early Indian tribes once camped among the oak and pine trees along its banks. In nearby beautiful coves we also found a lot of ancient Indian pottery.

While living in Bay Harbor I received my first exposure to racial prejudice. This experience was to strongly influence me for the rest of my life.

One afternoon while some friends and I were hiking along one of the railroad tracks north of Bay Harbor, we came upon a couple of Negro boys who were playing in the area. I don't remember exactly who the white boys in our group were, but the young blacks had given us no reason to harass them. However, almost immediately two or three of the whites started yelling threats, calling them bad names, and throwing rocks at the two black boys until they turned and wisely retreated to a safe distance.

I did not join in this harassment; nor did I approve of it. I felt it was terribly wrong and totally contrary to the Christian teaching we regularly received at home and in our churches. I remembered how much we had loved Voncile and other black people in Milligan. I was deeply startled by this hateful attitude springing suddenly out of my normally good-natured friends, and for no obvious reason.

Deep down it could have been the beginning of a determination in me to do something, somehow, someday to openly resist such unjust racial discrimination.

By God's guidance and grace, that opportunity would come one day in the distant future.

In the deep South at that time, it was common practice for blacks and whites to have their own separate schools, churches, socials and

CHAPTER 1: "THE EARLY YEARS"

business activities. The blacks had their own colleges. One I knew about in my boyhood was Tuskegee Institute in Tuskegee, Alabama. It was made famous by the Negro scientist, Dr. George Washington Carver, a devout man of God and Bible believer. This amazing scientist developed many very, very useful products including: peanut butter, peanut oil and a tremendous list of other uses for peanuts, as well as products from sweet potatoes, clay, cotton, wood shavings, and even dandelions!

The story is told that when this son of an ex-slave was working his way through Iowa State College of Agriculture as a janitor, he would often go out into the nearby woods and fields to pray. One day as he prayed, he asked the Lord to reveal to him the secrets of the universe, and he heard the Lord reply, "George, I will reveal to you the secrets of the peanut; that's about your size!" George realized he had asked too much, and humbly accepted God's offer.

The Lord helped him to discover and develop some three hundred products from the peanut, and one hundred and eighteen from the sweet potato. Like Tuskegee's founder, Booker T. Washington, he never let the segregation restraints of the South worry or embitter him. A true man of God he was! Every child in America can thank George Washington Carver especially for developing peanut butter.

I always had a desire to meet and talk with this beloved man but never was able to do so. He died in 1943 at Tuskegee. One day we'll see him in heaven and thank him personally for his faith in God and his contributions to the world. I've often said, "Grits and peanut butter helped save the South!" Brother Carver had a real part in that.

OUR FIRST HURRICANE

In the years we lived in Bay Harbor, we experienced two or three direct hits by big hurricanes. In those days there were no storm-watching satellites or early warning systems until the hurricane was almost upon us.

Vividly I remember the advance winds of one great hurricane coming out of the Gulf across the Bay around 1928. At that time we knew nothing about the dangers or intensity of such fierce storms. This was our first! Frank and I went to the lumberdock to watch the waves building up and the sea gulls riding those early winds with effortless grace and apparent enjoyment, then sailing off to shelter. As we made our way back toward the house in the ignorant exhilaration of the moment, the winds picked up strongly, and the straw hat that one of us was wearing suddenly went sailing off into the sky--too high to be chased after or ever found again.

Black, ominous clouds were rolling overhead. Torrential rains threatened to drown us before we ever reached home. The furious winds nearly ripped the clothes off our backs. Desperately Frank and I hung on to each other. We were afraid that like that straw hat we might go sailing into the air, or be hurled into the Bay.

The family spent that night praying in our shaking house. We were shaking, too, as we heard the limbs of trees crashing to the ground and huge branches flying through the air. The Bay kept rising. Enormous waves beat furiously against the bluff. The frightened night watchman left his shed on the dock to wait out the worst of the storm with us.

Those fishermen, who were lucky or wise, had just enough time to get their boats back inside the bayous for maximum protection. Sadly, those boats which didn't make it were battered against the docks and shores and destroyed. Then, in the midst of the shrieking winds, pelting rains and angry waves, there came a beautiful break in the clouds, and an eerie calm. The sun shone through, and it looked like the horrible battling storm was over. Then once again the sea gulls came rising and flying in the gentle and sunny breeze of the eye of the storm as it passed over. This lull is very deceptive to the unwary and uninformed. After an hour or so, the eye moved on and the other side of the storm came roaring back with as much intensity and devastation as it had a few hours before. This went on for several more hours shaking the house, tearing off roofs, and battering low lying properties once again. Finally the big one passed.

After the night of such a hurricane-beating, we went to see what damage had been done, and there was plenty. Piles of limbs, fallen trees, moss and debris around the yard and around the fences and in the road. Truck loads of it! All we had was a wheel barrow, so it took us many days to clean up around our place. Thank God, the old company house had been well-built and was able to withstand the 90-120 mph blasts of that great hurricane. How we thanked the Lord for His mighty protection through it all! His angels were guarding us, probably holding down the roof that night (Ps.34:7-8).

In later years we were to see a number of other hurricanes, some of them quite damaging, but that one in the late 20's seemed to have been the worst of all. This great storm with all its torrents of rain had finally extinguished the huge pile of smoldering sawdust left over from the burning of the Bay Harbor Mill, which happened about the time we first came to the village. The destruction of this mill revealed the economic bad times affecting the lumber industry in our region. Eventually the remaining mill in Millville would gradually go out of business. It also

CHAPTER 1: "THE EARLY YEARS" 13

burned, leaving only a tugboat and barge repair business near its place.

However, out of the demise of those two mills would come a new day for Bay Harbor and the whole region, which would mean economic salvation to the people and businesses during the worst part of the depression.

It had to be by the goodness and mercy of God! God in His heaven was looking out for that little widow who faithfully tithed and taught her sons and daughters His Way. So He sent word to His angels to have a paper mill built on that spot, which industry would become the lifelong profession of three of her sons. Starlus, Jr. eventually became a mill manager; Frank, a power plant engineer; and Alvin, a pulpwood contractor.

In 1929 we received word from Mr. Walter C. Sherman, Dad's employer before his death, that the International Paper Company would soon begin building a paper mill on the site. Its main office was to be located where our house and the Barrow's stood. We would have to move soon. Oh, how we boys hated the thought of leaving the scene of our many exciting adventures!

Rev. Leckenby found a house which was being sold for back taxes. The place needed much cleaning and repair, but it would hold our tribe. We were very happy to know that it was located right behind his house in Panama City. Somehow Mom and Sissy managed to get the necessary three hundred dollars for the back taxes, a small fortune in those days. With Rev. Leckenby's help we were able to buy the old house. After twenty years a clear deed of ownership was obtained.

This old house was located at 310 Third Court. Its east side overlooked beautiful Massalina Bayou; its north side faced the Bay County Court House with its palm trees and moss-hung oaks; its west side faced Rev. Leckenby's fig tree and back porch, and its south side, more woods.

Again the Lord had wonderfully provided safe harbor for the little widow teacher and her brood. With a wood-shingled roof and brown, lap-board siding, this house was to become a real home for Mom and her family. It would see a lot of living, working, praying and trusting the Lord for the next forty years or more.

The Leckenbys became even closer friends until Rev. Leckenby was called back to Maine with his family. We shall never forget them and their wonderful kindness to us. Mrs. Leckenby even took me into their home to care for me during my bout with measles, while Mom and Sissy continued teaching and the rest were going to school.

Our sister Mary came home to help, and got a job with Mr. B. S. Gordon, manager of the Gulf Power Company. She had been living with

Uncle Everett in Alabama, and after attending Montebello College had worked for a doctor in Tuscaloosa. Like Sissy, she became a strong support pillar.

For a long time we couldn't afford a telephone, but there was a real need for Sissy, Mary and Mom to be reachable, so those dear Leckenbys next door permitted the use of their phone.

Rev. Leckenby had a colorful parrot roosting in their big fig tree between our houses. The Reverend had visited Cuba where he bought this talking bird which soon learned to imitate Mrs. Leckenby calling Sissy to the phone. She used Sissy's given name, Essie Lois. So the old parrot became the relayer of these calls and was responsible for many an extra call saying loudly and clearly, "Essie Lois, telephone!" When Sissy would come to answer the phone, the parrot would shriek with laughter. Everybody would laugh with and at the parrot--except Sissy!

CHALLENGED!

Not long after moving to that little house beside beautiful Massalina Bayou in Panama City, we were busy with school work again. Mom continued for some time teaching in the Millville Elementary school. Sissy was teaching at the High School, Mary worked as secretary at the Power Co., and the rest of us were in the Panama Grammar or High School, except Starlus who was finishing at Palmer College in DeFuniak Springs. Only the Lord knows how Mom and the sisters financed that.

Coming from an outlying elementary school, which was considered to be a tough one, and entering the sixth grade, in Panama City, I was immediately put in the B class or lower section of the 6th grade, where I was promptly challenged by a ruling clique of boys. One of their number was chosen to beat me up to let me know that they were the big wheels in charge. During recess one day a boy named Alex was chosen to jump me. We wrestled and fought all recess. Fortunately for me, he was fairly skinny and light-weight like myself. When the recess-ending bell rang, we had fought to a draw--no conclusive winner. At lunchtime the clique decided that the fight was to start again. This was totally unexpected by me, but I had considerable experience in fighting and wrestling with the tough kids back in Bay Harbor and Millville, also with my brother Frank. Well, during the last class or two I had gotten my wind back and quickly determined to try to end this foolishness.

Using a wrestling technique learned in the Millville battles, I quickly had him pinned to the ground and held him there until the two of us agreed to a peaceable solution--no more fighting!

CHAPTER 1: "THE EARLY YEARS" 15

Interestingly enough, Alex and I became very good friends thereafter, and I got along real well with the other guys in that grammar school clique. Praise the Lord for that.

Later, during a chase and catch game that some of us were playing, I came rushing around a corner at full speed and crashed into Henry, the biggest boy in our class. He was coming from the other direction like a speeding freight train. We collided head on. He fell on me doubling me backwards to the ground. My back popped. There was terrible pain. Suddenly the lower part of my body went numb. I'm sure I cried out to the Lord for mercy, "Help me, O God."

Henry and others picked me up and carried me across the street to a teacher's house. After a time I was brought home and put to bed. Feeling soon started coming back into my legs and by evening I was able to move again. I can't remember being checked by a doctor, but it was a near back-breaking tragedy. Later I would have many problems with that area of my back.

I wasn't in the lower section of the B class very long. During the first two months my grades were all A's, (as they had been in the rural school), and I was moved up into the lower part of the A section. After another month or so my grades in that class were such that I was moved near to the top seat and battled it out for first place the rest of the way through grammar school. In 1932 I graduated at the top of the 8th grade class.

During the three years in the Panama Grammar School, always glued to the front edge of my desk, was a small hand-printed sign *In God I Trust*. With God's help, in spite of the strong competition, I had the top average and the privilege of giving a valedictory word of thanks to the teachers and encouragement to the classmates.

At our 50th High School graduation reunion in 1986, movies were shown about many events of the "ancient days" in Panama City. Near the end of the lengthy film was some interesting footage of that Grammar School graduation class of 1932. It showed me standing bashfully next to the tallest girl in the class. She seemed to be about a foot and a half taller than I! A Mutt and Jeffy situation!

We were able to obtain a video copy of that film by newsman Allen Douglas for our family archives and reunions.

LOST IN A GREAT SWAMP!

I wish there was a film to show God's miracle of my deliverance from death in a great swamp, probably in my second year in Bay High. For miles around the delta of Florida's Appalachicola River, west and northwest of where it enters into the Gulf of Mexico, there is a dangerous, snake-infested swamp region. Unwary hunters and fishermen have been lost in the jungle streams and sloughs of this region and never found. Even with today's helicopters, it would be difficult to find a lost hunter, and any one going into such an area should make sure he has an experienced woodsman or local guide with him.

When I look back on this experience of being lost in that jungle, the memory is still vivid and scary, to put it mildly.

The fathers of our two long-time boyhood friends, Custer Russ and Walker Savell, had offered to take Frank and me with several other fathers and sons on a squirrel hunting expedition there. The boys were all about 13 and 14 years old.

The whole group was to go into a hunting-fishing camp on the Brother's River which wound its way through the swamp and dense jungle in a southeasterly direction to the Appalachicola River. Most of the group were experienced hunters. We were to spend the night in an old shelter, rise before daybreak, get into outboard motorboats, then we would be dropped off in pairs down along the river bank, and picked up at that spot later on.

Frank was assigned to George McCall, the police chief, and I was put under the wing of Mr. A.M. Lewis, a well known oil business agent. We were let off at the break of dawn and quickly moved back into the jungle in search of game. Before long we found some squirrels, and Mr. Lewis was able to hit about three of them in the tops of the huge trees. Although I tried many times, I don't think I ever hit anything that day.

Soon Mr. Lewis spotted a hoot owl. Its big wide feathered eyes were watching us from its high treeperch. Bang! He shot it, and it tumbled to the ground close by. An owl seems to have a large head and thick neck. It looks like a fat bird, which is what I expected as I ran over and picked it up. I felt a bit sad, because we were hunting squirrel and the owl didn't need to be killed. Instead of a fat bird with a big neck and head, underneath those pretty fluffed up feathers was a surprisingly scrawny little body. Then I felt even sadder that Mr. Lewis had shot it.

After four hours of hunting time, we were scheduled to be picked up at nine o'clock at the dropoff point on the river bank.

However, after about three hours of hunting through the dense jungle with its interlaced canopy of tall trees, its vines, low underbrush, bogs and watery sloughs, we suddenly realized that we had no idea where the river was!

In the thickness of the dense vegetation jungle, there was no way to see the sun or tell north from south or east from west. How to get back to the river? That was the real question now. We realized we

CHAPTER 1: "THE EARLY YEARS"

were lost--as lost as could be!

We tried shouting. The only reply was the fluttering of a startled bird. The sloughs curved around in all kinds of slimy, contorted directions. A naturalist and a jungle lover would have said, "Man, this is beautiful. Look at the lush growth, the trees, bushes, algae and moss in a myriad of different forms and colors." But to us it wasn't pretty. It was life threatening! Ominous! Fearful! Suddenly all desire to hunt squirrels or anything else was gone, except the way out of there.

By this time we were trying to walk in some kind of straight line, not in circles; but that was terribly difficult because of the maze of marshes and sloughs under those big trees. We would stop and listen for human sounds, but nothing broke the stillness. Occasionally another bird would be seen flying up to the dark green ceiling over us. We were beginning to panic because we had no food and very little water with us.

Finally, in early afternoon we heard a distant sound like the old-timey skidder-whistle that loggers use when they pull in logs with steel cables from where the trees had been felled, but it seemed a long, long way off. We could only guess it was coming from an easterly direction. We kept trying to make a straight line move toward that sound by staying on the ridges between the sloughs. However it was not always possible. We also had to keep our eyes open for snakes, for this area was known to have some big rattlers, moccasins, and other wild critters like black bears and wild cats.

We had not stopped to pray, but I'm sure both of us were praying silently, "Please help us Lord," and He did!

We kept following the sound of the whistle. At times we wondered if we were following its echo. It is so easy to be deceived in a jungle. Then, it seemed that the sound was getting a tiny bit louder. Though the swamp was still the same--dense and defiant--our hopes were growing that we were nearing the logging camp!

The time was now well after 4:00 p.m., and dark heavy shadows were spreading all around us.

Suddenly, we came out on the edge of a beautiful pond. Glory to God! There were two fishermen sitting in a rowboat right in the middle. Hallelujah! Surely they knew where they were, even if we didn't. They were some distance away, but we shouted until we got their attention. Immediately they pulled in their lines, cranked up their little motor and came toward us. Found at last! Thank You, Lord!

I forgot to mention that years before Mr. Lewis had had a hunting accident in which he had lost a big toe. All day long he had been limping and must have been hurting badly. However, praise God for Mr. Lewis' special alertness at this moment, for He saved my life.

I had started to slide down the steep bushy bank, eager to catch the bow of the boat as it came in against the weedy shore. At that moment there was a tremendous blast across my shoulder. The muzzle of Mr. Lewis' gun had gone off almost at my ear. Providentially, just where the boat was about to hit the bank, he had seen a huge snake as large around as a big man's arm, and I was about to slide down into its poisonous fangs! As the boat touched the bank, the dying snake was writhing wildly at the water's edge. The Lord had saved me again and was in the process of saving us both from that deadly place!

Without another look at the ugly snake, we hurriedly climbed into the boat. Mr. Lewis explained who we were, and the fishermen took us across the pond to a deserted landing. They told us we were a good twenty miles away from our camp and showed us how to reach it. They explained their car was a good distance on the other side of the pond, and it would take over an hour for them to come back with it. They felt we would have a better chance finding other fishermen at a crossroad not far away, who would take us back to the camp. We thanked them for their help and started walking down this narrow, rutted road through what was now more like a forest than a jungle. Soon, some other fishermen came along in a car, and they were happy to take us back to our camp. We thanked them greatly, and Mr. Lewis offered to pay them something, but of course, they refused, because most folks feel it is wrong to accept payment for rescue help.

Back at the camp our friends greeted us joyously. After searching for us all day with no success, they were very worried. Now that we were back safely, we all gave thanks for the good Lord's mighty hand upon us, and thanks for Mr. Lewis' alert eyes and sharp-shooting!

A final word: "Stay out of jungles if you can. But, if you must go in one, have a good guide, be hooked up with the Good Lord Jesus, watch out for snakes, and have a good sharp-shooter with you!"

A COLD WINTER'S NIGHT DECISION

In northwest Florida the winter of 1934 was very, very cold. For about a month in February we had freezing temperatures. Some snow fell in the region--not much--but enough to stay for many days in the roof corners and eaves of the houses. An event would take place in this cold-cold month that would help steer me away from another kind of jungle, the dark jungle of Satan.

Our little Presbyterian Church on Harrison Avenue had a fine bachelor minister by the name of Howard Gould, later followed by A. Clarke Dean. Both would powerfully influence my life. They were well-educated for the ministry and very scholarly. Originally Howard had

CHAPTER 1: "THE EARLY YEARS"

started out in medicine, but the Lord led him to theology. He soon learned that I was interested in the things of the Lord, the Church and the Bible. By this time I had begun high school and was working after school in whatever jobs I could find.

Howard was very missionary-minded. He had started outposts--one ten miles north of the city, and the other some twenty miles in the northern part of the county in a CCC Camp (Civilian Conservation Corps, a program to give meaningful jobs to unemployed young men during the depression days). The adult members of his church and his young people helped in these outreach projects. Along with others I taught a Bible class at the Bayou George Sunday School. Often when I had a free night, I would go with him to the CCC Camp Bible Study and Preaching Service.

Coming back from one of these preaching services, probably 10:30 at night, Howard asked me a startling question, which no one had ever asked me before, "Sid are you saved?"

I kind of gulped and answered, "Well, I guess so, Howard, I think so."

"Well, you need to know whether you are saved or not, and you CAN know. It's not what you guess. It's not what you think. It's not what you feel. It's not by good works. It simply depends on whether you believe God's Word. Do you know what John 3:16 says?"

"Sure."

"Tell me."

He joined me as I repeated, **For God so loved the world that He gave His only begotten Son that whosoever believeth in Him shall not perish but have everlasting life.**

He quoted the next verse: **For God sent not his son into the world to condemn the world, but that the world through Him might be saved.**

He asked, "Sid, do you believe that in your heart?"

"I sure do."

"If you believe it in your heart, and you are willing to confess it with your mouth; then, according to the Word of God you are saved."

By this time he had stopped the car by the side of the road. As we talked he led me in a prayer thanking God for loving me so much that He sent Jesus to die for me that I might not perish but have eternal life through Him. We thanked Jesus for paying the death penalty for me. We also asked Him to forgive my sins and be my Lord and Saviour forever.

That cold night decision was the beginning of a much closer walk with Jesus.

Romans 10:9,10 gives full assurance of salvation in these words:

That if thou shalt confess with thy mouth the Lord Jesus, and shall believe in thine heart that God hath raised him from the dead, thou shalt be saved. For with the heart man believeth unto righteousness; and with the mouth confession is made unto salvation.

We had stopped and talked only 15-20 minutes, but these were some of the most important minutes in my life. Although having accepted Jesus at the age of seven, that recommitment prayer of WHOLLY accepting Jesus as my Lord and Saviour, and CONFESSING it with my mouth, was a new beginning for me. I would never forget nor regret that decision made at the age of 16. Praise The Name of Jesus!

Because of the cold late hour, Howard quickly started the car and soon had us back in Panama City.

FIRST LONG PANTS
BAY HARBOR, FLA. 1927

MOM IN BEACH SHELTER-1945

HOME IN PANAMA CITY

WITH CLO BUDDIES AT U.F. 1937

FROM PEACE TO WAR TO WEDDING!

Wherewithal shall a young man cleanse his way? By taking heed thereto according to thy Word. - Psalm 119:9

In those early years in the Millville and Bay Harbor schools, Edwin Williams, a quiet, even-tempered boy, and I became good friends. He and his sister, Lucille, lived with an aunt in Millville, while we were in Bay Harbor about two miles away. During my three years in the Panama City Grammar School, I seldom saw him, but when we arrived in High School in the fall of 1932, our friendship was rekindled.

He was an excellent student and quite as serious-minded as I. We would always eat our lunch together--usually peanut butter and jelly sandwiches--which we brought in a brown paper bag from home.

One day at lunch, shortly after I had recommitted my life to Jesus Christ, I began to talk to Ed about giving his heart and life to Jesus. He was very open, and on those gymnasium steps, he asked Jesus to come into his heart and surrendered his life completely to Him. What a beautiful time it was that day! We had become eternal brothers in Christ Jesus and felt a stronger relationship established between us--the bond yoke and presence of Jesus Christ. Many times during our High School days we came together to pray and share God's Word.

He continued going to his Methodist Church in Millville, while I continued worshiping in our little Presbyterian Church in Panama City. After our 1936 Bay County High School graduation, Ed and I went looking for work, while hoping somehow to be able to go to college. Ed found a job with a credit company, where he worked until the beginning of World War II, when he enlisted in the Air Force.

As during previous summers, I worked with my Uncle DeWitt as his bicycle delivery boy and soda fountain helper in his pharmacy in Marietta, Georgia. Jobs were still scarce, especially for a little guy who looked fifteen and weighed only 125 pounds soaking wet. Aunt Willie May never could fill my "food tank"! Uncle DeWitt still had his old

Expeditionary Army uniform, steel helmet and gas mask in his closet. He never forgot how Dad made that long trip to see him just before he was sent overseas.

I came back from Marietta in time to hitch-hike to the University of Florida--thanks to Sissy's sacrificial financial help of about $350.00 for the whole year. That was a lot of money in those days. I must admit academically it wasn't a very good year for one who had finished at the top of his high school class. Despite that disappointment, I was able to make some lasting friendships, including Reichardt Taylor, Dr. U.S. Gordon and others.

Friendship with some seniors in the CLO House (Cooperative Living Organization) where I stayed that year led to their invitation to be the cook for the University of Florida's YMCA Youth Bus Tour of the Eastern half of the U.S.A. that summer. The six week trip took us from Florida, to New York, to Maine, to Canada, to Minnesota, down the Mississippi, through the Ozarks to New Orleans, and back to Florida. It was a fantastic tour, and though the cooking conditions were very bad, we all gained weight!

I probably had no more than ten dollars spending money for the whole trip, but I praised and thanked the Lord for that and for the remarkable tour.

I was still dissatisfied with my freshman college year and was willing to drop out to work for a year or two so the family could help brother Frank finish at Auburn. However, a senior law student, Ed Fletcher, stuck a thorn in my psyche. Ed was one of the leaders in the CLO and he strongly warned, "Sid, if you drop out now, I doubt if you'll ever come back." Perhaps it was a good thing he said that, because it became a silent goad in my spirit for a long time, until I did come back nine years later.

In 1939 while I was working at the Gulf Power Company in Panama City, Fla., as a billing clerk, and Frank was employed in the Paper Mill power plant, Hitler's war machine was already spreading destruction over Europe. His panzer divisions were blitzing the neighboring countries. In 1940 his Air Force was pounding the cities of England, and the United States had to initiate its first draft and rush its military build-up.

Strong efforts were being made by our military leaders to train, equip and increase our fighting forces, including the Air Force. Because we had low draft numbers, Frank and I decided to volunteer for the Air Force Pilot Training Program. Despite our short stature, we were accepted and sent to Americus, Georgia.

This training was extremely intense with hardly a minute of rest throughout the long day. It included: several academic classes

CHAPTER 2: FROM PEACE TO WAR TO WEDDING! 23

concerning flying planes; aerodynamics; meteorology; aviation navigation; airplane engines, plus periods of actual instruction in flying by veteran civilian instructors. In addition there were military drills, physical training, and nightly required study periods. We had no problem falling asleep at bedtime.

It did not take the training officers long to notice that Frank had a distinct limp. He was called into the Flight Surgeon's office for a careful check-up and was soon sent home terribly disappointed that he could not keep on with the training. The Air Force wasn't aware that they had lost a tough little fighter.

The officers may have considered Frank handicapped, but he never missed a day of work at the Paper Mill. He had plenty of grit. Frank is left-handed and while in college, despite his leg limp, he became an outstanding Golden Gloves boxer. He packed a powerful punch in that left hand which I found out a few times to my regret. I never quite learned how to box a southpaw.

After seven or eight hours of instruction in the Stearman trainers I was allowed to solo. Later on I especially liked the training in aerial acrobatics which was aimed at readying the pilots for combat dogfighting.

THE TAKE-OFF CRASH

Near the end of three months of primary flight school, they were teaching us how to make very accurate spot landings on the field. The instructors had taken us up and demonstrated two or three times the type of landings they expected, then turned the planes over to the students. By this time, with some eighty or more hours of flight time we were fairly skilled in flying this particular plane.

The huge, grassy training field was hard-surfaced, long and wide enough for at least two lines of planes to be taking off and landing at the same time. Every student pilot was taught to watch carefully for his lane to clear, then take off and circle the field in a rectangular pattern. Coming in, he was to land directly opposite the point where his instructor was standing; then take off again until three spot landings were completed. After finishing the exercise, he had to land without crossing the other flight lanes and always taxi to the very end of the landing lane, then square the field to reach the instructor safely.

The plane was turned over to me. After taxiing up to the assigned take-off lane, and revving the engine while waiting for the lane to clear, it was then my turn to take off. I shoved the throttle full forward for take-off power. In a few moments I was able to push the stick forward enough to raise the tail and see over the cowl of the engine. At that moment dead ahead of me was a plane piloted by a fellow cadet. He was crossing the lanes diagonally as we had been warned not to do. I was in big trouble, and so was he!

I was already nearing flying speed. If I pulled the throttle and tried to stop, I would have crashed directly into him, perhaps killing both of us. There were no more than a few seconds to do something.

Frantically I tried to pull the plane up. It began to stall! I found myself pushing the nose back down and in the next second pulling back up. My plane almost cleared him in sort of a flying hurdle. My landing gear skidded across the tip of his right wing and ripped it off deflecting my plane in an angle toward the ground again.

Directly in my path was the smokestack of a nearby factory. Breathlessly, I was able to let the plane go downward for a second or two then pull up in a leftward bank to miss the smokestack and climb to the safe three hundred feet high landing pattern. As I came around the pattern, I felt a special peace. It had to be the Lord's presence. He had saved me once more! Thanks be to God!

To this day I believe the Lord's hand took over the flying of that plane!

As I landed, I had the feeling that this could be my last flight. I taxied over to the hangar parking apron, filled out the plane's log, climbed down to the ground and was unbuckling my parachute when a fellow cadet approached me. "Rigell, our instructor says you are to report immediately to the Base Commanding Officer. Capt. Gurr wants a verbal and written report of the accident."

About this time a mechanic came walking by with part of the other plane's wing. I asked him for a small piece as a souvenir. He grinned and gave me one. When I reported to the Commanding Officer, I described what happened and was told to fill out an accident form which I proceeded to do. In it I said it was probably a lack of sufficient caution by both pilots. This wasn't exactly so, but I didn't want to hurt the other pilot as he was my friend.

I was then sent to the flight surgeon for a clinical check and was told to climb on the examining table to wait for the doctor. While waiting I fell asleep. After twenty minutes the doctor awakened me and asked how I was.

I said, "Sir, I'm feeling just fine." He grinned and told me to get back to duty.

On one of those crucial days when my hide was hanging in the balance, word got back to me that all the instructors had seen the accident about to happen and had been amazed at "my" flying maneuvers. The Lord had saved me again!

My instructor asked if I had thought about damage to my plane's

CHAPTER 2: FROM PEACE TO WAR TO WEDDING!

landing gear.

"Well, Sir, it was not as hard a blow as some of the landings I've made."

The instructor grinned slightly. He also told me at the graduation picnic that he was always surprised at how well I had learned to fly--being so small. But, he was an excellent teacher and also small.

In the Secondary Flight School in Macon, Georgia, only a week or so after we arrived we were already flying the larger training planes. I had had a couple of hairy experiences in flight and had seen another student and his instructor killed in an accident.

One day while playing volley ball as part of our physical training exercises, I somehow twisted my left leg in such a way that the cartilages popped loose and the knee swelled badly. If I remember correctly, I went ahead and flew that day, but by the next day it was hurting so badly that I asked permission to go to the Base Hospital to have it checked. After several weeks there was no change. The leg stayed swollen and the cartilages remained loose. The doctor disqualified me from further flying and eventually sent me home. I was one sad sack, because I loved flying.

Disgusted, I went home. I worked for a winter for a contractor building Tyndall Air Field east of Panama City, then tried to get back into the Air Force but was turned down. Next I worked for a summer at Larkway Villa and in the winter worked in the Wainwright Shipyard helping to build Liberty ships. Then another summer at Larkway on the Gulf Beach. Finally, in the fall of '43 I was able to get back into military service. As a volunteer I could choose which branch. This time the Navy was my choice.

I never got over my disappointment for being washed out of the Air Force, but apparently the Lord was saving my life again as He had done so many times in the past. Probably less than half of my flying buddies made it through the war. Some fought in the South Pacific; some in Europe; some flew the hump in Southeast Asia. One, Joe Wilkinson, lived to become a top pilot for Delta Airlines. Sadly, my boyhood friend, Edwin Williams, didn't make it.

In 1941 he went into the Air Force, a short time after Frank and I did. Ed went on to become an outstanding navigator leading four-engine bomber groups over Nazi Germany. These planes were called Flying Fortresses. Ed flew about one hundred and twenty very dangerous missions. I know it was totally against his nature and faith, but like all of us, he felt it was something he had to do to help put a stop to this terrible Nazi curse.

No doubt Edwin had finished enough missions to come home. He had reached the rank of Major and earned all the medals a man could receive in battle, but he stayed beyond the necessary tour of duty. In spite of all these extremely dangerous missions, I know Ed never lost his kind, mild-tempered disposition.

During the months before his final flight, Edwin and his Christian friends, calling themselves The Twelve Disciples, kept active in a little church near London where one of them was always there praying!

On April 12, 1944 his bomber was caught by anti-aircraft fire after crossing the English Channel into Germany. Not long before he gave his life to end the Nazi scourge, Ed had written his precious sister, Lucille, these amazing words: "I've never known fear in all these missions, except when I have let something come between God and me."

No doubt Ed was immediately welcomed into heaven with these words from his Lord Jesus, **Well done, good and faithful servant** (Matt.25:23). He gave his life to help put an end to that awful war, and perhaps unknowingly, to stop the slaughter of the Jews, because of his love for his Jewish Lord and Saviour--The Messiah Jesus.

Six years later in September of 1950, after I was already in the ministry, his family was notified that his body was being shipped back for burial to his little hometown of Millville, Florida. His sister wrote asking me to officiate at the funeral of my best friend. What a sad and difficult day it was! But something I knew for sure--Edwin was in heaven with Jesus and all the saints who had gone on before.

From that time on I felt that I needed to do some extra work in ministry for our Lord Jesus on his behalf. "Help me, Lord, to be as faithful and courageous as Edwin Williams was in Your service" (See I Cor.15:57-58 & Hebrews 12:1-3).

THE OTHER KNEE BLOWS UP!

In the two summers of operating the Larkway Villas, which had some thirty summer cottages, I had time to do a lot of swimming and running, and the left leg seemed to have recovered nicely. When I volunteered for the service, I was in excellent physical condition.

My orders came to report with a group the following Thursday. On Wednesday an old friend from Dothan, Alabama came to visit me. He was a paratrooper recovering from wounds he had received somewhere in the European theater.

He warned, "Sid don't go over there. Those people are crazy. They'll kill you."

This was early October 1943. That wasn't the most cheerful news, but I already knew that war was no picnic. We went off to the beach to swim in the beautiful Gulf waters, and when we came back on the soft, snow-white beach, we began some physical horseplay. He sailed

CHAPTER 2: FROM PEACE TO WAR TO WEDDING! 27

me over his shoulder and I landed askew on my right leg. Out went the cartilages in THAT knee! Oh no--not again! By the time he dropped me off at Mom's house late that day, the right knee was swollen and the cartilages were wandering around.

I spent the night praying that the knee would go back to normal and that the cartilages would go back to their proper places. I was determined to be classed physically fit--not 4-F again. I felt I could serve my country in the war effort somehow and not be classified as a draft dodger.

When I arrived at the Draft Assembly Point I still had a swelled, gimpy knee, which I managed to hide while reporting in and climbing on the bus for the nearly three hundred mile trip to the Induction Center in Camp Blanding, Florida. Upon arrival we were fed and put into barracks to await the medical examinations the next morning. Fortunately, this gave another night for the swelling to go down.

The next day when we reported for the examinations, my left leg was doing fine, but my right knee was still painful. As military guys know, such examinations are not based on modesty. We had to go from doctor to doctor buck-naked. At long last came the test I was dreading. How was I going to pass the knee bends? By putting most of my weight heavily on my left knee (the one that had been injured in the Air Force), I was able to do them. That knee came through with flying colors.

When the final doctor checked through all the reports, he said, "Fine! I see you're a volunteer. What branch do you want?"

I answered, "Navy," and he stamped my papers NAVY!

As I started to walk away from him he called me back. "I find in your papers that you were given a medical discharge from the Air Force because of "osteo chronditis dissecens" of the left knee. How's that knee now?"

I lifted my left knee up and down several times, while my right knee was still hurting and said, "Captain, I've been swimming and running a lot since then and that knee is in good shape now."

"OK, Son, I'll give you trial duty in the Navy."

Thus I was off to the Navy boot camp in Bainbridge, Maryland. The trial duty would go from that October 1943 until the war's end and my discharge on February 2, 1946.

BOOT CAMP--MUSTARD GAS--FACING DEATH--TOTAL COMMITMENT

At the age of 23, I had gone into the U.S. Air Force and soon found myself wondering if I would live to be 25. The daily papers were filled with pictures and stories about Great Britain fighting tenaciously against the masses of German planes and bombs. Heroes were being made, but they were also dying. Air aces were chalking up their kills and were then being killed. The future did not look bright.

For quite awhile I had a longing to find the fine Christian wife that God had for me. I had met a number of very nice Christian girls and had been close friends with several. Each probably would have made a good wife for someone, even me, but I knew the Lord had that special one for me at the right time.

Now having reached the ripe old age of 25, I was going into the Navy still wondering and looking for that special helpmate that God's Word speaks about. I suppose I had wasted a lot of time looking for her.

Because of previous military training in the ROTC at the University of Florida and the Air Force, I was soon made the Petty Officer in charge of marching and drilling one of the platoons in our Navy training company. Later I was given honorary Chief Petty Officer's stripes. At the end of this intensive, rough boot camp I had a two-week leave to go home to Florida to visit Mom and the family, to date girls a little bit and then back to the Navy Outgoing Unit at Bainbridge.

On my return to the base, a notice went around calling for volunteers for a week-long experiment with gas suits and masks at the Anacostia Naval Base in Washington, D.C. Volunteers would receive two weeks additional leave. ....REALLY NOTHING TO IT.....SAFE AS PIE. That sounded real good to me. Stupidly, I signed up and was sent the next week to Washington, D.C. with the new batch of guinea pigs.

There were classes on various types of poison gas and different ways of facing poison gas situations--even working in those situations using special suits and masks. One objective was to train a nucleus of men for such hazardous duty, but also to continue testing various types of suits and masks for use in this kind of warfare, if such should arise.

On one of the final days our group was outfitted and marched into a large chamber that then was filled with mustard gas, one of the deadliest of warfare poisons. The group was to spend about forty-five minutes there. It didn't take long to regret ever coming on this little "safe as pie" experiment. It looked awfully deadly to me, and my mask didn't seem to be working right. I'm sure I got enough whiffs of the mustard gas to burn my lungs. This is one of those situations where forty-five minutes seems like forever.

Finally, the men in charge who had been watching the group through observation windows, let us come out. The suits and masks were removed, and we returned to our quarters. The next day we were all given careful physical exams by the doctors to see if any of the mustard gas had penetrated the suits enough to burn the skin.

Mustard gas is horrible. It killed thousands in World War I. More

CHAPTER 2: FROM PEACE TO WAR TO WEDDING!

recently it was used in some of the modern wars, such as the Iran-Iraq war and Iraq's war against the Kurds. People without protection would have horrible disfiguring burn blisters on their skin and faces. They would quickly die of body fluids released into the lungs. In our group there were a few light burns on the arms, wrists, and shoulders. I had light burns across my shoulders, but apparently they were not deep, because after a few days they had faded away. At that time, neither I nor the doctors realized that my lungs had been seriously affected.

Very happily we went back to Bainbridge to receive our two-week leave papers. Believing I was in the pink of health, I headed back home to Florida.

It was wintertime, probably late January. I never will forget traveling from Washington, D.C., to Jacksonville. The train was so crowded; there was absolutely no sitting room left. Way into the night I was still standing. As we were passing through South Carolina, a nearby seat was vacated next to a large, well-dressed black lady, who was wearing a wool coat with a big fur collar. I quickly asked if the seat was available, and she said it was. In no time at all, I was sound asleep leaning on that dear lady's fur collar. Bless her heart! She didn't seem to mind at all.

A few days after arriving in Panama City, I found myself developing an unusual and unexpected cough. I didn't seem to have the normal cold or flu symptoms, just this hacking cough. By the time I was to go back to Bainbridge, Mom was getting quite concerned and so was I, but I felt that being in such good physical shape, I would throw it off in a few days.

Naturally while I was home, I had kept my eyes open for that special girl. No success. Back at Bainbridge I checked into the Outgoing Unit and immediately found myself coughing throughout the night. This went on for two or three days, until the Chief Petty Officer noticed and urged me to go to the sick bay. I still looked quite healthy, but I knew something was happening inside my chest which was not right. After almost being turned down at the sick bay, I was able to persuade the doctor there to put me in the Regimental Sick Bay over the weekend to try to discover why I was coughing so much.

Saturday went by. Now I was coughing in the daytime also. Early Sunday morning I began having chills and high fever. My temperature, which had been almost normal until now, shot up quickly to 104 degrees. It was becoming very painful to breathe. The corpsmen immediately knew they had a sick man on their hands. After a couple of hours, they were able to get the duty officer to authorize an ambulance to take me to the Main Base Hospital.

On arriving there, I was already feeling half dead and in great pain.

The ambulance boys turned me over to other corpsmen, who quickly stood me up, naked and shaking badly, in front of an x-ray machine, then took me to a bed in an open ward. No doubt their x-ray picture was blurry!

Not long after, I was examined by a chief physician who diagnosed me as having acute lumbar pneumonia. The ward doctor was ordered to tape my chest down and put me in an oxygen tent in a room reserved for oxygen patients.

Before the doctor left, he asked if I needed anything. I told him I sure would like a large glass of fresh Florida orange juice. He replied, "I'll see what we can do. Now, don't worry, son, you're going to be all right."

At that moment those were the most encouraging words anybody could have said, because I was feeling like everything was all wrong and getting worse. Just before they put me under the oxygen tent, the orange juice came. It looked so very good, and it was GOOD! By this time, although the doctor's words were indeed encouraging, I was in such pain that I wasn't sure of the outcome. Maybe this was the end of my road. As they gave me pills or shots, I vaguely remember praying a special prayer.

I believe I started with the Lord's prayer. Then I said, "Heavenly Father, I know I haven't been living for You completely. Please forgive me for that. I know I've been into worldly things and wasting a lot of time looking for a wife. Please forgive me, Father, and let me live--if its Your will. If it IS Your will, Lord, with Your help I'll live it all for You. I'll do all my work as unto You, and I won't spend any more time looking for a wife. Lord, when You want me to have a wife, please show her to me. Now, Lord, I commit my life into Your hands. In Jesus' Name, Father. Amen."

Under sedations I slept and slept. I was in that tent for about a week. The nurses, corpsmen and doctors were very kind and attentive. By the end of that week the pain began to recede, but my chest still was taped up for some time, and I was still not out of the woods.

In that second week, I needed oxygen only part of the time. I knew I had to somehow get word to Mom. She would be terribly worried. I got a nurse to bring me a writing pad to let Mom know that I did have to go to the hospital, but the doctors and the Good Lord had things under control. I should be fit as a fiddle soon. That "soon" would be nearly two months before they would let me go back to duty.

When Mom got my letter, she called the Commanding Officer of the base, the Commanding Officer of the hospital and the Officer-In-Charge of the Pneumonia Ward until she pinned down what was going on. She probably assured them they would have a lot of help, because she would be praying for them and for me.

CHAPTER 2: FROM PEACE TO WAR TO WEDDING!

The Good Lord and the Navy nurses and doctors did get me back to active duty after fifty days or so. However, the doctors never admitted to me that there was any connection between the pneumonia and the poison gas, but they knew, and I knew, that it had been caused by that mustard gas experiment in Washington, D.C.

(Note: Articles in the Baltimore Sun newspaper in November 1990 and on June 13, 1991 describe the lingering effects of exposure and the "battles" of some of these injured "volunteers" to gain recognition and help from the V.A. Eventually in 1991 the V.A. doctors, after examining me, concluded there was a 10% breathing loss from the mustard gas burns.)

On my return to the Outgoing Unit, I started looking for my personal gear. Finally, I found my seabag and a few things, but my locker had been cleared out and the stuff sent to a ship's store locker. Some of it I never found. But, praise the Lord, I was back in business and waiting for my first assignment which was to the Wright Junior College, then a Navy Basic Electronics School in Chicago for six weeks. Earlier I had taken aptitude tests for Aviation Radio-Radar Technician training and had passed. Now the Navy was sending me to school for basic training in the electronic fundamentals. I remember the bunks there were three-deckers--almost skyscrapers.

The next school was to be a large Navy Radio School in Gulfport, Mississippi. We arrived in May still dressed in winter blues that were needed in Chicago. The Navy base was several miles outside of town and, we had to march there in the hot blistering sun. Several companies of us, including a company of Marines, made it--soaking wet with perspiration.

The next day we were formed into platoons. Volunteers were called to compete for the job of platoon leader and assistant. Several in our group including myself and a big 6'4" guy from Oregon tried out. He and I ended up competing against each other in briefly drill-marching the platoon before the barracks. The Chief Petty Officer chose me to be the platoon leader. The big guy, Norm Sholseth, was to be my assistant. A special room was assigned to us and we became fast friends.

No doubt many of the men resented having such a small "squirt" as their platoon leader, but with Norm's backing they accepted me.

We got along quite well during the three months there, except for one maverick, who couldn't get along with anyone. He, no doubt, was looking for an early discharge paper.

It's a bit ironic that I'd been in two branches of our military service, sustained injuries to both knees and almost died from burns from poison gas; yet, I had not left the country or faced our major enemies.

I was my own foolish enemy in that poison gas episode, but our God

THE GREAT SURPRISE IN GULFPORT

is so merciful. He used the long delays and great danger to bring about a full rededication to Him, which I needed badly, and a special meeting!

We were beginning to adjust to the heavy training routine on the base as well as to the extreme heat and were looking forward to the third weekend and our first shore leave. I had been doing everything I could to re-establish regular attendance at Sunday worship services.

When that first liberty arrived, I invited my friend, Norm, to attend church with me, and afterwards we'd go swimming somewhere. He accepted my invitation. We went to a Methodist Church then picked up a quick lunch. On our way to the shore we passed the Hotel Markham's pool which was very tempting.

"Why not swim here?"

"OK." (A window of heaven was about to open briefly!)

We paid the entry fee, changed to our swim shorts, then brought our wallets to check with the bright young lady at the check-room window. As she smiled pleasantly, I noticed her light brown, wavy hair and beautiful, expressive blue eyes.

We were walking toward the pool when I turned around and looked again at this girl. Suddenly in my heart, I distinctly felt the Lord was saying, "There she is--the girl I've chosen to be your wife!"

I could have shouted with surprise and delight. It had been over four months since I lay on that hospital bed asking the Lord to spare me and find a wife for me. Now, He was saying, "There she is!"

Norm had quite a reputation for being a ladies' man. I turned to him, "Norm, get acquainted with that girl and introduce me properly." If this was really of the Lord, I had no intention of wasting any time.

Norm was agreeable. He went to the window, spoke to her briefly and learned her name was Betsy White. As they were talking I took a picture of them. He called me over and introduced me as his good friend, "Leetle Jose Rigell."

We explained that we were at the Navy Base training as radio technicians, and she explained that she was with her father and mother in nearby Long Beach. Her father was an instructor in navigation for the Air Force Crash-Boat crews--the Army's "Navy."

After finishing our swim and talking more with Betsy, we invited her to dinner. She thanked us but said she could not go without her parent's approval.

That was OK by me.

We went into the Hotel lobby and I wrote a note on its stationery:

CHAPTER 2: FROM PEACE TO WAR TO WEDDING!

"Dear Miss Blue Eyes,

We hope to be back for a swim on Saturday and want very much to see you again. Please, please arrange for us to meet your parents.   Joseph Rigell"

When Betsy received that note signed Joseph Rigell, her Dad (Pappy), having seen Regal beer in New Orleans, asked, "Is that sailor Jewish?"

Betsy replied, "Well, his nose did look a little Jewish."

For a long time the hotels in Atlantic City were mainly Jewish or Quaker. Betsy's family was in the hotel business there, and they were Quakers. Living in Atlantic City had made the family somewhat prejudiced because of business competition. However, before long, their prejudice was destined to disappear.

Betsy arranged for us to come to their home for a late breakfast on Sunday morning. While her father, not a religious man, was out pursuing his favorite pastime of fishing, we all went to the seawall to watch him casting his throw net. Then, we went to the house for breakfast.

I was feeling a little guilty for not being in church, but if the Lord had said Betsy White was to be my wife, and we didn't have much time left in the Gulfport Navy school, I figured it was all right with the Lord for me to be with her.

At some point in the morning, Betsy demonstrated her expertise on the piano by playing the two or three pieces that she knew well. I thought,"Hum-m, this is great. Every preacher needs a wife who can play the piano," but Betsy wasn't yet aware that God was calling me to be a preacher.

At 2:00 p.m. Betsy had to be back at work. Norm and I rode with her on the bus into Gulfport to the Hotel Markham. On the way I explained to her that I felt the Lord wanted me to become a preacher after I finished my time in the Navy. There were other things we talked about, but this was the most important, because if she was to be my wife, I felt she needed to begin thinking in the direction of the things of the Lord. She was politely interested.

The following Saturday night on our only date, we went to the USO (a club for servicemen). It turned out to be a very pleasant evening.

The weekend before my class was to ship out to Corpus Christi, Texas, for advanced training in Aviation Radar Equipment, her parents brought her to the Base for a picnic. During that precious picnic time, Betsy and I read some of the Gospel of St.John together and had a quiet time before the Lord in which it seemed He was sealing our relationship for the future.

At that time I was unaware that Betsy's mother had warned her,

"Don't make any promises which you'll regret later. You're still very young and you have college ahead of you."

No promises were made other than to write each other, which we both did faithfully--every day for the next year and a half, with phone calls or special delivery letters on Sundays.

Betsy still knew very little about my background, except that I was from a large Presbyterian family who lived in Florida, and that my widowed mother was a teacher. I knew very little about the White family except they were from Atlantic City, New Jersey. Her mother was a very genteel lady, and her father was a Warrant Officer teaching navigation. My first impression of him was, "Man, what a grouch!" At that time no one knew he was under stress because he was facing a very dangerous O.S.S.(Office of Strategic Services) assignment which he could not reveal.

ANOTHER SURPRISE - IN CORPUS CHRISTI

After Gulfport Norm and I were sent to the North Island Navy School in Corpus Christi for intensive training in Aviation Radar which was a secret operation. The base was surrounded by the beautiful Corpus Christi Bay waters with the bright sunshine of deep Texas, and the salty air of the Gulf of Mexico constantly breezing in from the south. One of the outstanding things about the place was the high barbed wire security fence around it. There was a main guard gate. Inside were many barracks, administration buildings, and hundreds of Navy and Marine men in various stages of training.

Each morning we were up at 6:00 a.m., had chow by 7:00, cleaned the barracks and assembled in company formation by 7:30. Then, with a student marching band leading us, we marched to the heavily guarded school compound behind more barbed wire fences. Promptly at 8:00 a.m. we were in classrooms furiously taking notes on some of the most complex technical equipment and operations one could have. I loved it, because we were getting not only theory but also practical operational experience with the gear. This went on for three months, until our heads felt overstuffed with radar formulae and instruction.

Norm would quote several technical formulas and then joke, "But how in the world do you turn this thing ON? Where's the 'blankety-blank' switch?"

One weekend while on shore leave, I went into town and walked out to the harbor area to take some scenery snapshots of the yachts and sail boats tied up in the marinas. Suddenly, a twangy voice called, "Hey, Sailor!" A Navy pilot standing with a young lady motioned to me. He extended his camera and asked me to take their picture, which I did.

CHAPTER 2: FROM PEACE TO WAR TO WEDDING!

"Where are you from, Mate?"
"Florida".
"Where in Florida?"
"Panama City."
"Panama City? That's where I'm from! What's your name?"
"Joe Rigell. Middle name Sid."
"Sid Rigell? Hey, I know that name. I'm Sam Davis. I grew up on the Bay and went to Bay High with your brothers."

Now I remembered. I had heard that twangy voice before.

From that meeting a life-long friendship was born.

At that time Sam was a Navy flight instructor. His specialty was PBY planes which the Navy called flying boats. A number of times after our meeting he took me with him on training flights. This greatly pleased me, because I still loved to fly.

He later married that young lady in the picture and was sent to the South Pacific not long afterward. There he and his crew flew many extremely dangerous rescue missions right into the jaws of the Nipponese Tiger, for which they received the highest Navy decorations for valor.

It was here in Corpus Christi that my big friend, Norm Sholseth, also met a WAVE--a Navy girl--who was to become his future wife.

After graduation day at Corpus Christi, Norm was sent to the Pacific fleet. And, surprise-surprise, I was assigned to the secret Counter-Measure School on California's San Clemente Island, which the sailors nicknamed "Goat Island". Years would pass before Norm and I would see each other again.

We reported to a Navy boat in San Diego and rode about 70 miles west through choppy seas to the rocky island, where we began work immediately in the techniques of radio and radar jamming. There was a small airstrip on top of this mountainous island where the Navy had some classroom training planes. But, to me, there hardly seemed to be enough in-flight training for the deadly missions for which we were being trained.

Often while sitting in the chow-hall or class rooms, we would hear sounds like distant thunder; then we'd be jarred almost out of our seats. Upon investigation, we learned that the other end of the island was used by Navy warships and planes for their bombardment practice before heading off to war.

One day a beach swim party was announced for a certain afternoon. I thought, "Oh boy! We get to go swimming at a nice warm California beach." How naive I was! Even in the summertime the weather on San Clemente Island was rather cool and often foggy.

It didn't take long for the old Navy bus to get to the beach, which was quite narrow and rock strewn. Huge rock formations jutted up out of the nearby waters, and fairly large waves were rolling in, but I didn't worry about them for I was a good swimmer. Without stopping to test the water I dashed into the ocean. The shock was almost too much! The water was so cold that in seconds my legs felt like two frozen ice sticks. My teeth were chattering, but to show what a courageous fellow I was, I quickly dunked myself in that icy water. Only then did I notice the seals playing around on the near-by rocks. It seemed they were having a good laugh at my expense. Stiff as a board and trying not to show my embarrassment, I came out of that ocean as quickly as I could. What a surprise that was! This Florida boy swore he would never again swim in those famous California waters. But, he did.

HAPPY DAYS AHEAD - PRAISE THE LORD!

After San Clemente, with a week's leave and a special diamond ring in hand, I was off on a flying trip to Philadelphia to visit my pretty little blue-eyed girl, Betsy White, who was then a freshman at Swarthmore College.

When I first saw her I was amazed. In eight months she had gained about 20 pounds!

She saw the look on my face and timidly asked, "I hope you don't think I've changed too much?"

"Of course not, Honey. Maybe a little," I teased.

With a pounding heart I put my arms around her and kissed her. Slowly we strolled hand in hand under the big trees near her dorm. Enjoying every precious moment of our reunion, we sat on a bench admiring the beauty and the sweet aroma of the springtime flowers.

"Betsy?"

"Yes?"

As I fumbled for the ring, beads of perspiration dotted my forehead. What if she would refuse? Oh, what was I worried about? For weeks our letters had been moving in this direction. Taking a deep breath, I asked "Betsy....Dearest.... will you....be my wife?"

She blushed. Softly and shyly she answered, "Yes." Then she hesitated and looked quizzically at me. "By the way....how do you pronounce your last name?" (We'd gotten to know each other mostly through letters, and she had always called me Sid.)

Thinking our engagement was a big secret, I asked, "Whom shall we tell first?"

Betsy replied, "I promised to tell my cousin, Nancy Steward, first!"

Why, it was no secret at all! Betsy knew all the time that I was going to propose. My brother Frank's wife had let the cat out of the

CHAPTER 2: FROM PEACE TO WAR TO WEDDING!   37

bag in a "welcome to the family" letter.

Many of us in the San Clemente School were now shipped to Minneapolis for the final stage of our Counter-Measure training. We would be attached there to the Navy's big four-engine planes especially equipped for Counter-Measure assignment in the Far East. From there we would be sent to the China Theater to fly jamming missions against Japan.

The Lord was sending me from one school to another, where I was getting more technical training and flying experiences than I ever dreamed, but never again in that special role as a pilot which I had loved doing so much.

In May of 1945 the German forces had surrendered. Now in August, because of the atomic bombs dropped on Hiroshima and Nagasaki, the Japanese were surrendering. Was it right to use those A-bombs? Yes, I think President Truman did make the correct decision. Although some 75,000 Japanese died then, millions of Allies and Japanese would have been killed through surface invasion.

The city of Minneapolis, together with the peoples of the world, were ecstatic over the War's end. The streets erupted with people celebrating everywhere. Wondering how soon I would get out of the Navy, I went to bed and got a good night's sleep. For a few days I toyed with the idea of continuing on in the Navy because of its many benefits, but deep down I knew the Lord wanted me to finish college and go on to Seminary and become a minister. My Navy mission was over. Praise the Lord!

We finished our work at Wold Chamberlain Field in Minneapolis and were ordered to San Diego, where I was shifted to several Navy bases in that area; then I was to go to Jacksonville, Florida for my Navy Discharge, which would take place February 2, 1946.

Before going to Florida, I met Betsy in Atlantic City and went to visit her parents and make plans for a June wedding. Pappy's only question after I asked for his daughter's hand was, "Do you have any insurance?"

Fortunately I still had the $10,000 Military Insurance plus a $1,000 New York Life policy. He didn't want his daughter marrying an "irresponsible sailor", and he let me know it.

Pappy, had been teaching navigation to Air Force Crash Boat crews in Biloxi Mississippi, had just been released from his O.S.S. (which we called "Oh, So Secret") assignment. This would have taken him, his crew, and several others, into the Japanese waters in crash boats loaded with high explosives to be sunk and detonated over the tunnels between the Japanese islands to greatly disrupt the Japanese war effort. Pappy and his men were to be disguised as fishermen and would abandon the crash boats just before reaching the tunnels. Airplane controls would then guide these floating bombs to their targets. Pappy had lost many pounds preparing for that dangerous secret mission about which he could tell no one--not even his wife. Now, thank God, that mission was not to be.

During the war the Atlantic City hotels had been taken over by the Army for training schools and hospitals for the returning wounded. The White family's Marlborough Blenheim Hotel was used as a cooking school. By January of 1946 most of the hotels had been returned to their owners. Much renovation was needed in these businesses after the wear and tear of the Army schools.

Pappy and Gin (Betsy's mother, Virginia) would be in Winter Haven, Florida celebrating their 24th wedding anniversary on Saturday, March 2nd. Betsy's grandparents (Pop and Tata) would be there, and it would be fairly easy for my family to come to Winter Haven from Panama City. So, why not have a double celebration on that same day?

We chose our rings in a little jewelry shop in Atlantic City, had them engraved, went through the required blood tests, and began notifying friends and relatives about our up-coming wedding set for March 2, 1946, not June.

While Pappy and Gin were helping Betsy with all the necessary wedding preparations, I reported to the Jacksonville Naval Discharge Center Feb. 1, 1946 and was honorably discharged the following day. I immediately headed for Gainesville, Florida, where Betsy and I would live while I continued my education at the University of Florida. We would be assured of two and a half years of regular financial help through the recently passed GI Bill of Rights.

Nearly nine years had passed since I had worshipped at the Presbyterian Church with the beloved Pastor, Dr. U.S. Gordon, who had led his University flock for so long. I shall never forget that first Sunday I went back to worship there. The church sanctuary was overflowing with returning service men, all of us grateful to God to be alive and starting our careers anew, most still in uniform.

"Preacher" Gordon had a very encouraging message, "Letting God Help You Pick Up the Broken Pieces." Then he came down in front of the pulpit to greet the congregation and his long-absent servicemen. It took quite some time for me to get close enough to speak to him. When he saw me coming, he hesitated, then reached out his hand and exclaimed happily, "Bo Sparrow! It's so good to see you! Welcome back!"

"Preacher" Gordon came from Mississippi where the name of the spunky little sparrow was always "Bo-Sparrow." Nine years ago he had given me this nickname. Reichardt Taylor, my best college friend at the time, he named "Cypress".

CHAPTER 2: FROM PEACE TO WAR TO WEDDING!

Thirty-eight years later, while Betsy and I were attending a conference in Montreat, North Carolina, someone slipped behind me and whispered, "Bo-Sparrow!"

I turned around and shouted with surprise, "Cypress!" Here was my good friend of long ago, who had spent 35 years as a missionary in Brazil.

The next day, after seeing Preacher Gordon at Church, I beelined it to the University Electrical Engineering Department to register for that college and to search for an Electronics Technician's job. I was referred to a scientist, Mr. Tedder, head of some government research projects who immediately put me to work.

Then began the discouraging hunt for an apartment or room. Gainesville was packed out! No vacancies! It seemed that thousands of already discharged veterans had beat me there. I was desperate. "Lord, we need your help to find a place to live! Our wedding day is almost here."

Just before the wedding, I put a want-ad in the local paper for a room with cooking privileges. I added "Husband and wife willing to help with chores."

Early Saturday morning, March 2nd, I left Gainesville by bus for Winter Haven. We were to be married that afternoon. Pappy and Betsy met me at the bus station, and we went immediately to the Bartow Court House to pick up the marriage license. Fortunately for us, the Court House was open on Saturday mornings.

Since our meeting and courtship had all taken place during my Navy service time, we had decided that I might as well be married in my Navy uniform.

The families had already gathered for this great event. It was a gorgeous day and so wonderful to have our loved ones all together.

My brother Al's wife, Eugenia, had come from Alabama. Mom, Sissy, Judy Beth, Judy, Frank and Sally arrived from Panama City. They had spent the night in nearby Ft. Meade with Mom's sister, Ose Aunty.

My brother Frank was my best man. At 2:00 p.m. at the First Presbyterian Church, we took our places with Dr. Woods who was to officiate. As we stood there for quite awhile, I nervously wondered what was causing the delay. Had Betsy changed her mind? Was I going to be left standing at the altar? Later I learned that Nancy Steward, the maid of honor, had broken a bra strap and was frantically looking for a safety pin. Although we only waited a few minutes, it seemed hours before her red-faced cousin, came down the aisle followed by my beautiful bride escorted by her proud father. Now that Betsy had lost those 20 pounds, she looked like a dream in her beautiful, borrowed wedding gown.

After we had repeated our Holy Vows to God and each other, it was time for the exchange of rings. Frank's hand was shaking so much, I had to grab it and hold it still enough to get the ring. At the end of the ceremony I kissed my beautiful bride and arm in arm, as the wedding recessional played, we turned and marched happily into the future. At last I had the wife the Lord had promised me. I'll praise and thank Him forever!

Later Frank growled at me out of the corner of his mouth, "How come I was the one that was nervous? You're the one that's supposed to be nervous."

Back at Aunt Laura's house on Lake Lulu there was a lovely reception amidst the orange groves and the sweet fragrance of the citrus blossoms.

Before Betsy went to change into her honeymoon traveling outfit, she stood on the porch and tossed the wedding bouquet to the happy onlookers. Great Aunt Laura, who had practiced medicine for 50 years in Connecticut, joyfully caught the bridal bouquet, but, at the age of 80, her hopes of being the next one to get married were not too good.

While I was waiting for Betsy, Pappy called me over to where he was standing with her Grandpop and some other kin. All of them congratulated me. Pappy then handed me an envelope. I quickly glanced into it and saw a number of checks from different White family members. Some of the checks were larger than anything I had ever seen. Immediately I wondered if Betsy's kin-folks doubted my ability to support her in a proper way. We certainly didn't expect any such gifts. Pappy noticed my astonishment and rather negative reaction. He took me aside and whispered,

"Take them, son; they can all afford it!"

The Lord had blessed us that day by making us ONE and giving us financial blessings that would help us in the lean days ahead.

As we drove off in Aunt Bert's car decorated with "Just Married" signs and streamers, Grandpop pretended to hitch a ride on the running board, which Pappy recorded with his movie camera.

On the way to the Manatee River Hotel in Bradenton, we stopped and cleaned off as best we could some of the "Just Married" signs. The next morning, as I opened the car door for Betsy, some strangers were smiling and wishing us good luck in our marriage.

I walked around the back of the car and noticed two old shoes still tied under the bumper--the clear give-away of our newlywed status. Smiling happily, we thanked them, took the old shoes off, waved "goodbye", and motored off into our married life with high expectations! And deep thanksgiving to God for His goodness and mercy to us--as in Psalm 23:6!

CHAP. 3

GETTING ON THE LORD'S COURSE

Trust in the Lord with all thine heart; and lean not unto thine own understanding. In all thy ways acknowledge Him, and He shall direct thy paths. — Proverbs 3:5,6

On our day and a half honeymoon, we drove from Bradenton to Lake Wales to visit Cypress Gardens and the Lovely Bok Tower to hear its famous carillon bells in concert. We took pictures, of course. By the way Pappy made a movie of our wedding which still can be seen forty-five years later. After a quick visit to introduce Betsy to some dear relatives in Lake Wales, we headed back to Winter Haven and another ancient hotel by a lake.

The next morning, nearly two days after the wedding, we returned the car to Aunt Bert and departed for Gainesville by bus. There we stayed in a lovely little antique hotel set among moss covered oaks.

We were delighted, when after a week of searching, we finally received a response from the newspaper ad. The lady had only one room with kitchen privileges available. She also needed help for an aging mother. Having no choice, we rented it. First we had to clear out huge piles of newspapers and junk before we could set up a bed. In spite of this, we were glad to have a place of our own.

Through some church members, Betsy and I found two secondhand bicycles for transportation. I went back to work at the Research Lab where there was talk about a team being recruited for the U.S. A-bomb tests on the Eniwetok Island in the middle of the Pacific Ocean. I had been assigned to work with an engineer on a certain project which would be needed for the Eniwetok tests. He was signing up to go there and asked me to come along as his assistant. It sounded like a great idea to further my engineering education. He told me I would be away only four to six weeks, and I would be back in plenty of time to start summer school.

I talked it over with Betsy, and she was very agreeable. "Go ahead,

Honey! I'll hold down the room for us. It will be something special to tell our grandchildren."

Little did she realize the work which would be involved--taking care of the elderly mother, cleaning for her, trying to stay on the right side of the daughter while sharing the kitchen. It was very difficult. Having been brought up in a hotel, where everything was done for her, this was to be a whole new, undesirable experience.

Two weeks after our happy marriage, I left for Fort Monmouth, New Jersey, with the engineer to enlist with the Eniwetok Task Force. We were enrolled as Research Engineers in government service at good salaries. All seemed well at this point.

The engineer was a married man with children. In less than 48 hours he was already the most homesick man I ever saw.

Knowing I needed to discuss my decision with Betsy's parents, I went to Atlantic City on the weekend to inform them of my intentions and hopefully get their approval.

Fortunately for everyone, a Presidential decision intervened. Pappy showed me the head-lines stating that President Truman had decided to postpone the A-bomb tests for three months. Immediately I realized this would interfere with my college plans. I had to get out of the whole thing as quickly as possible.

By the time I got back to Fort Monmouth, my homesick boss was already in the process of resigning, and I followed. Our train fare was paid back to the University of Florida, and we were compensated nicely for our few days with the aborted mission. After an absence of only a week we were greatly elated to be back with our respective wives. Betsy met me tearfully. She had been feeling very deserted.

Thank God, it was not His will for us to go on that mission. I should have been more careful and checked with Him before deciding to take that step--or any step.

So, it was back to work for me at the Lab. Betsy was able to start a secretarial course in a nearby business school, which would soon open the door for her to work as the secretary for the Lab Director, Mr. Tedder.

Shortly after my return, she was asked to help in the Primary Sunday School Department at "Preacher" Gordon's church although she was not yet a member; nor had she been baptized. Her Quaker background did not require baptism.

While preparing the Sunday School lesson one day, she realized the teachings of Jesus were the truth. She accepted Him as her Savior and was baptized by Dr. Gordon as a follower of the Lord Jesus Christ. Bells were ringing as all heaven rejoiced.

That summer I began full-time classes on my way to an engineering

CHAPTER 3: GETTING ON THE LORD'S COURSE 43

degree in electronics, or so I thought. Eighteen months later I was informed that an extra year of courses would be required. Suddenly, I was faced with the grim fact that this would cause us to run completely out of the G.I. Bill support, and we would have a very rough time financially getting through the Seminary years. We took it to the Lord on our knees in prayer. Immediately I was impressed to check out the requirements for a degree in the College of Arts and Science. When I did this, they had very good news for me. If I transferred from Engineering to Arts and Science, I would receive credit for a number of Navy courses, which the Engineering College wouldn't credit. By finishing the courses I was taking that spring and the ones I could complete in the second Summer School, I could graduate in June 1948, at least a year earlier than expected, and just two years after returning to the University. This was great! Thank God for His leading!

I transferred immediately and was on my way to a degree in Arts and Science without having to sweat out two more years in Engineering. Gone was my dream to be a Missionary Communications Engineer. The Lord had other more interesting plans!

During the first nine months of our marriage I was very disappointed that Betsy showed no signs of pregnancy. Because I had expected to start a family immediately and have maybe a dozen children, I jokingly threatened to take out adoption papers if something didn't happen soon.

However, the Lord heard our prayers, and Betsy soon became pregnant. On August 6, 1947 we were blessed with the arrival of our first son, Craig! We were now living at Flavet II, temporary housing for veterans, on the University campus. Nancy Steward had come by for a visit. She had so many funny stories to tell about various events in her life that our baby son was laughed into the world.

About 10:30 p.m. Betsy began the early stages of labor. A kind neighbor drove us to the Alachua County Hospital. Four hours later we became proud parents. What a great night that was! Betsy and our son were just fine. After Betsy and the baby were released from the hospital, I rode ahead of the ambulance on my trusty bike to show the driver where to take his precious cargo.

The job at the Research Lab ended when I switched out of Engineering, so to help supplement our limited income from the G.I.Bill, I found work in the grounds-keeping department. My job was to clean streets, clip hedges and trim the ivy on the walls of the University buildings. We used long, double-type ladders--no "cherry pickers" in those days. Often I ran into hornets' nests, so I became quite expert at sliding speedily down the tall ladders, usually without a sting. The night of Craig's birth had left me somewhat tired and sleepy so the next day I was excused from climbing ladders. This gave me time to go back to the hospital, take a nap, then continue building a baby crib. We had bought a mattress to use with a spring which I'd found. It just needed a frame! Well, eventually, the crib was quite pretty and served our first two sons nicely.

We named our first child Craig DeWitt after a friend, Craig McKinnon and my Uncle DeWitt. We dedicated him to the Lord in a christening service by Dr. Gordon at the Church. Betsy and I were so proud of our little one; we expected him to be a genius immediately.

Craig was a sweet-tempered little guy, but so solemn; we often called him "the little judge." When he was about a year old, we were visiting in Panama City and had asked Mamma Rigell and Janie Hall, her star boarder, to be our baby sitters while we slipped off to a "once-in-a-great-while" movie.

The little judge must have thought we were deserting him forever. He created such a fuss that Janie Hall finally put him in her car and drove to town looking for us. Late that evening, just as Betsy and I were leaving the theater, she drove by with Craig standing up in the front seat intently searching for his Mommy and Daddy. Much to the relief of all, Janie spotted us and took us home. We discovered our son didn't like being left with baby sitters--even if they were his dear Grandmamma and our family friend, Janie.

Encouraged by a friend who was running for Student Body President I tried my hand at student politics. He won the election, and I won a seat on the Student Body Executive Council, receiving a beautiful Executive Council key at the end of my term. My one piece of successful legislation had to do with requiring all political candidates to clean up their posters tacked everywhere after an election. The street cleaners needed help!

Not long before graduation from the University of Florida, I was taken under the care of the Suwannee Presbytery as a candidate for the Southern Presbyterian Ministry. Something interesting happened that day. To me, it was a most solemn moment. After giving my statement of faith and the reasons why I believed the Lord had called me to His ministry, a motion was made that I be accepted under the care of the Suwannee Presbytery. It was passed unanimously. (I never knew to what degree that "care" meant, since I never heard from them again.) As I was returning to my seat, "Preacher" Gordon whispered, "Sid, for heaven's sake, develop a sense of humor!"

I'm still trying to work on his advice. Perhaps my humor quotient has improved a little, especially after learning Proverbs 17:22......*A merry heart doeth good like a medicine, but a broken spirit dries up the bones.*

In June 1948, I graduated from the University of Florida with a Bachelor of Arts and Science Degree, excellent grades, and majors in

CHAPTER 3: GETTING ON THE LORD'S COURSE 45

Math and Philosophy. At the exercises in the stadium that day any newly-born child of a graduating veteran received an honorary degree with his name properly inscribed. Craig, not quite a year old, received his certificate also. Exactly 11 years had gone by since I left the University of Florida after my first year. By His amazing mercies the Lord had brought me back to finish--on course with Him!

My mother had prayed us through the Great Depression, World War II, and now another of her sons to a University graduation. We were so glad to have her with us for that happy occasion.

A SUMMER OF SHARK FISHING!

Several days after "our" graduation, we packed and moved our things to a Veterans Apartment Complex at Columbia Seminary in Decatur, Georgia, an eastern suburb of Atlanta. Since we were not scheduled for classes until September, Betsy took Baby Craig to Atlantic City to visit her family for several weeks. Meanwhile I went to live with Mom in Panama City, to work for our brother-in-law, Walter Anderson, with his deep-sea shark fishing crew on the old "Barbara Jo" snapper boat. My job was to be the cook and deck hand.

It was an interesting summer of fishing for huge sharks! We would set out quarter-mile-long-chain lines with big buoys with a flag at each end. Very large baited shark hooks on three foot long chains were spaced every fifty feet or so on the main chain line. Baiting the hooks with large fish heads and setting those lines from a rocking boat was rough, back-breaking and hazardous work. Early each morning, weather permitting, we would pull up the line from buoy to buoy with a powerful, ratcheted pulley deck engine, and with a crane arm, hoisting up huge battling sharks along the way, until there was a pile of them stacked nearly four feet high in the middle of the deck. We had a healthy respect for these biggies whose mouths were lined with many rows of teeth as sharp as razor blades.

The crew soon began the dirty work of slitting the sharks open to obtain their huge livers, which were then put into large steel barrels. In the summer heat the livers quickly melted into liver oil, which later would be sold to large milk companies for fortifying condensed milk and other products with Vitamin D. The shark carcasses were hoisted overboard; the deck was washed down, and the rebaiting process begun for the next night's catch.

Because of the war with the Japanese, their fish oil supply had been cut off completely, so our Gulf Coast fishermen had gone into the shark liver-oil business and were making a very good profit. Shark fins were also in demand. These were carefully cut and dried for the Chinese restaurant market in the U.S.. By the end of 1948 the Japanese fishermen were busy again supplying the American market; hence, this was the last summer of that type of shark fishing. Needless to say, I was happy to be in the operation--for only one summer!

The lives of the "Barbara Jo's" crew were far from easy. Besides the rough work, almost daily they faced some dangers from terrible storms. We had to wait out several squalls that summer by facing into them with the engine running powerfully to keep from being overturned or driven from our long shark lines.

Suddenly, one came upon us while we had a steadying sail raised on the aft mast. Blinding rains encased us. While we were all in the shelter of the wheelhouse, something raged across our stern...."Whoomph!" The winds quickly abated. The sun shone again. Praise God we were safe! But, that aft sail was never seen again. Several huge waterspouts had been spotted that day not too far away from us and we realized the "Whoomph" was one of them. (A waterspout looks like a seagoing tornado.)

One of my friends on the boat, a weather-beaten old fishermen, had very thick callouses on his feet from working barefoot in all kinds of weather. I really admired him and loved to hear his stories. He had many interesting tales to tell. One of them was about the courage and sympathy of porpoises in protecting their young and wounded, or net-trapped mates, and even humans endangered by sharks. They drive the sharks away by high-speed ramming! Another was about a tough snapper-boat captain, who had found far out in the Gulf a great school of red snapper fish. His crew was beginning to make a tremendous catch of this valuable fish when, in an instant, one of those squalls blew them off the spot.

This captain was well-known for his blasphemous temper. In the midst of the storm the captain angrily climbed the rigging to the top of the mast, shook his fist at God and cursed Him. The curses were barely uttered when a lightning bolt knocked him off the mast to the deck below. He eventually recovered from his injuries--but he never cursed God again.

That story was told in 1948. Forty years later, national newspapers told a similar story. A proud, hot-headed lawyer, fishing in a lake near New Orleans without success, stood up in his boat and shook his fist at God and cursed Him. Lightning struck again. His stay on planet earth was over! The lesson is clear, isn't it? Read Hebrews 10:30-31 and Psalm 14:1.

CHAPTER 3: GETTING ON THE LORD'S COURSE

THE MAYOR'S BOATHOUSE DISAPPEARS

Mom, an early riser, had for many years regularly sat at the kitchen table looking out through the large kitchen window during the lovely sunrise and her quiet time with the Lord, praying and reading God's word before preparing breakfast for the family. She always enjoyed that picturesque view of Massalina Bayou framed by oaks, palm trees and magnolias with their gray beards of moss and wild grape vines. This beautiful scene brought joy to Mom and everyone who visited this humble home of faith, love and courage. That view was a special treasure which was about to be stolen from her.

It was probably in January 1944 while I was on a brief leave from the Naval Training Base in Bainbridge, Maryland that I noticed Mom seemed unhappy. Sitting by that window, she explained how the mayor, who was also the major bank president, and his bar-owner friend, had decided to build a boat dock and a monstrous galvanized boathouse for their deep-sea yachts directly in front of Mom's window. These ugly eyesores would obscure the beautiful view of the Bayou and the glorious sunrises. Mom was in tears and rightly so.

When she called on the mayor, he said the dock would go out from the street right-of-way. It and the boathouse would be out far enough in six feet of water--beyond her lot's riparian rights. Arrogantly he told her that everything was legal; she had absolutely no grounds for action. They definitely would not stop building it.

She went to see a Christian friend and neighbor, who was a retired judge, for advice. He confirmed their legal rights. "Bess, I guess the best thing you can do is pray." And pray she did!

When I learned of the situation I said, "Mom, you know God defends widows and orphans and delights to bring down those that do them injustices (Proverbs 15:25). Let's agree and ask Him for a miracle."

Four years passed and that infamous boathouse was still intact, but Mom never stopped praying and believing that the Lord would do something to remove it. Neither did I!

One day in August, 1948, the "Barbara Jo" had just returned from a trip off the coast of Ft. Walton. I needed to see a doctor because of an infection in my left hand from handling rotten bait. Red streaks were going up my left arm already. Something needed to be done about it quickly. The infection was leading to serious blood poisoning. The doctor gave me a preventive shot and some pills.

About 4:00 p.m. I came back home and went to my bedroom. Before lying down, I noticed a very dark storm cloud formation stretching all across the Bay. We had been in storms many, many times before, so I didn't feel too concerned about it, even though one had overtaken us at sea and ripped the large steadying sail off the stern mast of the boat, as told earlier.

About an hour later the sky grew very, very dark as the storm clouds rolled in from the Gulf. Very heavy torrential rains began falling. I got up thinking to close the windows. Suddenly, that dreadful sound of roaring winds like twenty freight trains engulfed us.

Realizing a tornado was upon us, I dived under the dining room table and called to Mom, who was trying to close the windows in the kitchen, "Quick! Get under a table! Leave the windows alone!"

Papers and magazines went sailing horizontally through the house, lifted as by a magnet! Loud, banging, clattering noises were frightening. In less than two or three minutes the rains had ended; the clouds moved over; the darkness passed, and the winds stopped. Praise God we were still there! Not one window had been broken. Cautiously we went outside. For at least a block away the oak and palm trees were sprinkled with the crumpled tin siding and roof of that boathouse. Its broken timbers were smashed against the bank and trees. With all the fury of God, that twister had hit the boathouse, smashing it to smithereens. Amazingly the tail of the tornado missed the five story Court House two hundred feet in front of us. Not a single shingle or window on Mom's house, the Court House, or our neighbors' house was broken. Not one!

The next day workers came and began cleaning up the rubble. The boathouse was gone and never rebuilt! Thanks to God's mighty hand of justice for a widow who loved and served Him with all her heart!

"Don't mess with God's humble and faithful widows" is surely a strong lesson we all must learn; for, God's Word tells us in Psalm 146:9....*The Lord preserveth the strangers; He relieveth the fatherless and the widows: but the way of the wicked he turneth upside down*. Proverbs 15:25....*The Lord will destroy the house of the proud but He will establish the border of the widow.* Praise His Holy Name!

THE FIRST LESSON AT SEMINARY

One would think that on arrival at Seminary a lovely red carpet would be rolled out (perhaps by angels!)--especially for a number of war veterans coming back from years of service in the Military. Our first contact at the Seminary was in the main office with a spinster lady who looked as if she fed on bitter herbs and carpet tacks. She seemed to delight in displaying her authority and superior knowledge of the operations and seemed to enjoy putting down new seminarians. Way down!

She had been there a long time and was an established fixture in the

CHAPTER 3: GETTING ON THE LORD'S COURSE 49

administration. As we did with the drill sergeants in the service, we quickly learned to grin and bear it. She was probably the most prayed-for member of the Seminary staff. (Maybe that's the reason she had lasted so long.) We asked the Lord to show us some way to develop a friendly relationship with her, and He answered our prayers.

We learned that she was a great baseball fan who knew more about baseball than most of us. She even knew who hit the home run that won the World Series in the last of the ninth inning years before. From then on, before anything else, we would ask her who won the big game the previous day. That was her Achilles' heel. After that we were able to stay out of trouble with her. Yes sir! She was part of the training--a powerful instructor in humility and prayer! No doubt we all needed it!

One might think the Lord would smooth the path for His men in training for service in His Church. But the Lord knows there are battles ahead, and He wants His servants to be able to take the hard knocks, survive the battles, endure the storms, and know the rudiments of how to be overcomers. He wants them to solve their problems His way.

During the week the men (no women then) studied Theology; Homiletics; Church History; Old and New Testament Scriptures; Greek;, Hebrew;, Soteriology (Salvation), Eschatology (study of end-time things). We also had to study The Major and Minor Prophets, Evangelism, Church Administration and much more. My favorite course was Old and New Testament Scriptures taught by Dr. Manford G. Gutzke, a former pastor who, in his early life had been a farm boy and soldier-boxer in Canada - a grizzly-bear of a man with the bright light and love, wisdom and humor of Jesus shining through.

In his teaching he emphasized the importance of having a sensitive wife and appreciating her. He told of how things weren't going too well in one of his early pastorates. The session members (the ruling elders) were resisting some progressive moves which he thought were needed. The membership seemed complacent and unwilling to wake up and get on with the battle for souls.

One Saturday after hours of working on his message for Sunday morning, he told his wife quite vehemently, "Honey, I've finally got a sermon that's going to blast them right out of their pews!"

Her sweet reply was gentle and effective, "Now Manford, is that really what the Lord wants you to do?"

Sheepishly, he went back to his study to take out the explosives and replace them with love.

Betsy and the seminary wives met once a week for special instruction on the duties of a good pastor's wife: on teaching the children, helping their husbands, and making ends meet on the usually very low pastor's salary--all ably taught by Mrs. Sarah Gutzke, a Jewish

Christian. During this class the husbands were baby sitters.

Instead of Christmas cards for 1948, we decided to do something different. We'd dress little Craig in diapers and a banner saying, WELCOME TO THE NEW YEAR! He would be shown coming out through curtains waving and smiling. Our neighbor, Bob Bullard, who was also a professional photographer, did a beautiful job in taking his picture, which we sent out as our Happy New Year card. Craig proved to be a fine model for the "Happy New Year Baby" welcoming 1949. Needless to say, we've always cherished that photo.

January of '49 was very cold in the Atlanta area. Our apartment had plywood walls without insulation, and our natural gas heater couldn't put out enough heat to keep out the sub-freezing cold. We began insulating the windows with newspapers. That seemed to help a little. Betsy was soon to have our second child and I joked, "Maybe it will be frozen and we'll have to thaw it out." My lousy humor!

On January 19, at Emory Hospital in Atlanta our second son, Kirby, was born "warm" and perfect in every way. He was somewhat longer than Craig and turned out to be a happy baby also. We dedicated him to the Lord and Dr. Gutzke christened him in the seminary chapel. During Betsy's recovery Grandma Gin came to help out. Later Pop and Tata came by and noticed our need for a large baby carriage. They promptly provided one large enough to hold baby Kirby and Craig plus the groceries when necessary. One day this all-purpose carriage, top heavy on one end, tipped over. The handle struck Craig's thumb and his screams let the whole countryside know what happened. He still carries the scar of that wound.

The summer after Kirby's birth we were asked to serve a little country church in beautiful farm country about thirty-five miles southeast of Atlanta. The Hopewell Associate Reformed Presbyterian Church was a great learning experience for us. It was made up of some wonderful people, unpretentious, mainly farm families, staunchly Presbyterian, with a very conservative custom of singing only the Psalms set to music. There were some very fine elders and deacons.

Not long after we arrived, the little manse received its first indoor toilet. Up until then we had to use the outdoor facilities! There was no telephone. Weekday communications had to be made by car. Through my brother, Al, the Lord earlier had provided us a nice little four-door Chevrolet.

The old-time white wooden church building and its one hundred-year-old cemetery sat directly across the county road from the manse. On each side of us were small dairy farms operated by elders of the church, who kept us supplied with milk and summer vegetables. Often on Sunday afternoons they also provided ice cream--much to

CHAPTER 3: GETTING ON THE LORD'S COURSE

Betsy's joy, which turned into chagrin when she realized she had regained those twenty pounds again that summer.

One of the elders gave us a live chicken, so we invited the Bullards from Seminary to have a chicken dinner with us. Then began the problem of getting that tough old hen ready for cooking. I knew how to catch and dispatch the old bird and dip her in boiling water to remove the feathers. Much to Betsy's great consternation, she had most of the plucking to do. Unfortunately, we didn't start to kill the bird until that morning. Instead of stewing the old hen for a few hours (or days), Betsy tried to fry it! The Bullards arrived for lunch. The meal with "fried" chicken was served. The meat was so tough that a tiger would have had a hard time with it.

We never did hear much of the Bullards after that!

It didn't take long to discover the congregation had an intense disagreement about a proposed Sunday School building. Some wanted a separate structure; some wanted an add-on building attached to the sanctuary.

Using some mechanical drawing training, I was able to construct cardboard scale models of each type. Thus, they were enabled to view the models objectively and take another vote on the design. By the end of the summer they had made a near-unanimous decision and could get on with the erection of the much needed Sunday School rooms. They chose the separate building and had it completed by the next summer.

To God be all the glory and thanks for whatever good we were able to do that summer in the ARP Church. And for the lessons learned!

EXTRA WORK AND ANOTHER CLOSE CALL

In my first two years at Columbia Seminary I had developed a great liking for Greek and wanted to become proficient in the reading and use of New Testament Greek. However, I kept sensing the Lord's quiet inner voice saying, "I want you to concentrate more on Hebrew, for one day you will need it!"

Little did we know that thirty years later the Lord would have us in Israel studying Hebrew again and encouraging His people there.

Early in that second year, an old friend, Cook Freeman, asked me to take over his dry-cleaning route for the seminary which required about five hours a week to pick up the clothes, take them to the cleaner and return them. It paid about twenty "bucks" a week, which was a real help to us.

In the fall of 1949 I was asked to serve the Acworth and Mars Hill Presbyterian Churches as student pastor. Acworth was a little textile mill town about thirty miles north of Atlanta with a beautiful little ivy-covered church building and a number of faithful old-line Presbyterian families. The Mars Hill Church was about four miles southwest of Acworth with a typical white, wooden, country church building and a congregation of staunch Presbyterian farm families. But many of them were now also engaged in industrial work at the Lockheed Aircraft Factory near Marietta, where the famous B-51 bombers were produced. These two little churches were already planning to call me as full-time pastor upon my graduation and ordination.

For several years, I had felt a dull pain in my lower right side. It would bother me even in my sleep, and the only way I could get relief was by drawing up my right leg toward my abdomen. Suspecting that I could be developing a bad appendix but not wanting to interrupt school or work time for an operation, I put off getting a medical examination until the end of my second year in seminary, when we learned of a fine surgeon in Atlanta who did appendectomies. He checked me out and advised me to have the operation even though it wasn't urgent.

Since we didn't want a repeat of my Dad's fatal experience with appendicitis and peritonitis, I agreed to have the operation soon. The Doctor checked me into the Piedmont Hospital. Preliminary tests were to be that afternoon, and the operation would follow the next morning.

In the room with me was an older Jewish man who had just had a hernia operation. He was in the first very painful stages of recovery. We spoke briefly, and I prayed silently that the Lord would ease his pain and quickly heal him.

My turn came the next morning. After the operation they rolled me into the room with the breathing tube still in my mouth and throat. Betsy was waiting in the hall but they would not let her in. Providentially, the Jewish man was observing everything from his bed. According to him, I was left alone for several minutes and began turning blue. The breathing tube had become totally clogged. The Jewish man began shouting for help, "Hurry! This man is dying!"

The doctors and nurses rushed into the room in time. Very quickly they had me breathing again.

At the age of seven I was saved forever by my Jewish Saviour Messiah Jesus. Thank God, He had another Jewish man sound the alarm 26 years later when I was dying in that hospital room! Thank You, Jesus!

CHAPTER 3: GETTING ON THE LORD'S COURSE   52A

GOODBYE NAVY, FEB. 1946   BRIDE-TO-BE BETSY, 1945

MARCH 2, 1946 - WINTER HAVEN, FLA.

MY LOVELY BRIDE   CUTTING THE RECEPTION CAKE

52B   FIRED AGAIN AND AGAIN, PRAISE THE LORD!

HAPPY MOM AND CRAIG, 1948

INDIAN POTTERY FOUND IN THE COVE, 1934

"ME READY GO NOW!"

CRAIG AND KIRBY, DEC. 1951

CAPT. ANDERSON'S SHARK CREW, 1948

CHAP. 4

SEMINARY GRADUATION TO CONFRONTATIONS

All scripture is given by inspiration of God, and is profitable for doctrine, for reproof, for correction, for instruction in righteousness.
II Timothy 3:16

Dr. J. McDowell Richards, the President of Columbia Presbyterian Seminary, had a pet project called "COLUMBIA FRIENDSHIP CIRCLE." Its purpose was to raise money to build apartments on the beautifully landscaped Seminary grounds for missionaries home on furlough.

Mom had become interested in this endeavor, and for years she continued to raise money in our home church in Panama City to support it. Due to her enthusiasm, she usually received very generous donations from her former students who were now successful businessmen. If she didn't have what she felt was a good gift to send, she would go back to these men for more--and get it. Dr. Richards was very grateful and always sent her a warm personal letter of appreciation on behalf of the Seminary. When I graduated in early June 1951, Mom was able to attend and was graciously received by Dr. Richards. We were very happy to see this recognition given her.

Also, we were pleased that our dear friends from the Acworth Church, Elder Fred Hull and his wife Bess, were able to attend the graduation program. He was the Clerk of the Church Session (the Board of Elders), a man with a delightful sense of humor, who knew where he stood with Jesus. Brother Fred had a little jewelry store from which he also did the Acworth City Clerk's business for many years.

Thirty-three years later we were privileged to visit them in a nursing home. Both were blind but still sweetly in love at the ages of 99 and 98. Before we left I inquired, "Brother Fred, how long have you and Bess been married?"

He chuckled, "I really can't remember ever being single!"

As a farewell gesture Betsy and I sang the last part of the 23rd Psalm. He put his arms around our shoulders and said with tears in his eyes, "Kids, Bess and I have repeated that Psalm as a prayer together every night before going to sleep--for 79 years."

After graduation I had to be examined and approved by Cherokee Presbytery for ordination and to receive the Call to be installed as pastor of the Acworth and Mars Hill Churches. The Call and Installation plans were approved and set for two weeks later.

Dr. Manford G. Gutzke of Columbia Seminary brought the Ordination and Installation Message and Charge. It was a beautiful ceremony which ended with the Ordination Committee ministers and elders laying hands on me as I knelt for the Ordination Prayer. A very solemn and holy occasion!

One of the last subjects we had at Seminary was a Practical Theology course in Outreach Evangelism, teaching Jesus' own method of sending the disciples out two by two to tell the Good News about salvation and reconciliation with our Heavenly Father. I'm sure the Seminary fathers were hoping we would go out into the Southern Presbyterian fields and build up a strong evangelistic outreach in the churches.

Having already worked with the precious folk of the Acworth and Mars Hill Churches for two years as student supply pastor, I now felt the urge to assemble the elders and deacons from both of them to propose and discuss the outreach program which the whole denomination was undertaking.

On a designated Sunday afternoon seventeen or eighteen men from both churches gathered in the Acworth Church's Sunday School Assembly Room. After an opening prayer for God's guidance and the Holy Spirit's inspiration to fill us with evangelistic zeal for lost souls, I began an introduction to the outreach plan which required us to establish clearly where we ourselves stood with the Lord Jesus. Were we saved? Did we know the Gospel? Could we really call ourselves Christians? Did we believe that Jesus is **THE WAY, THE TRUTH AND THE LIFE** (JOHN 14:6)? Did we believe **THERE IS NONE OTHER NAME UNDER HEAVEN GIVEN AMONG MEN WHEREBY WE MUST BE SAVED** (ACTS 4:12)? Did we believe **EXCEPT A MAN BE BORN AGAIN HE CANNOT SEE THE KINGDOM OF HEAVEN** (JOHN 3:3)?

I emphasized that, before we can persuade anyone else, each of us must be completely sure that Jesus Christ is our Lord and Savior. With my hand held high I asked, "How many of us can say right now, 'I am a Christian! Jesus has saved me and I am following Him?'"

Immediately Brother Fred Hull's hand shot straight up. The Sunday School superintendent next to him hesitated for a moment, then slowly raised his hand halfway. Of the group, those were the only hands raised. I was crushed with disappointment. Instantly I knew that much hard work would be needed within these two little churches before we

CHAPTER 4: SEMINARY GRADUATION TO CONFRONTATIONS. 55

could reach out seriously and successfully. If I had asked the less penetrating question, "How many of us here today can say we are Presbyterians?" probably all of them would have held up their hands.

Without a serious commitment to Jesus Christ, church membership becomes a religious club without any real eternal meaning. A personal, passionate love for and devotion to Jesus is an absolute necessity to the Christian and to His true Church.

No wonder the good Lord gave Brother Fred and Bess Hull long lives here on earth. Goodness and mercy followed them all their days, and we know they will surely dwell in His house forever (Psalm 23:6).

Even though we didn't get far with the evangelistic program through the officers of the churches, we did have some good special speakers and revivals, particularly in the Mars Hill Church where the Gospel singing by those farm folk was something very special. The Lord blessed, and souls were saved.

I tried to persuade one rugged farmer to accept Jesus as His Lord and Saviour and become a member of the Lord's Church. I told him, "Your little sons already want to accept Jesus as their Savior, but they are not coming because you won't. But the moment you do, they will be right behind you. Please don't block their way to heaven by your stubbornness and unbelief."

Praise God! At an August revival meeting this farmer, followed by his two little excited sons, came forward to receive Jesus as their Lord and Savior.

During one of those meetings the Lord also marvelously saved a local bootlegger. After that wonderful night service in which he gave his heart to Jesus and was born-again, he just had to tell somebody. He got into his car with his wife and drove into the mountains of northwest Georgia to let his startled relatives and old bootlegging friends know that the Lord had saved him and had put him out of his old business into a new one--serving Jesus! Bootlegging had long been a backwoods private industry in those parts. Years later we saw him in Marietta and he was still serving the Lord.

In the days before these summer revival services, I would try to make house calls along the country roads to invite people to come. I would leave a mimeographed announcement with them or, in their mailbox, if they weren't home. Not too far from the church was a house where many unchurched people gathered every Sunday. One day I stopped, introduced myself and extended an invitation to the meetings and regular services at the Mars Hill Church. The mother or grandmother of the family spoke up, "Well, we don't know whether we will be here or not."

"Are you visiting?"

"No, we live here, but we don't know for how long."

"How long have you been here?"

"Oh--about seventeen years!"

I grinned as I began leaving. "I sure hope you will get around to attending church soon. We never know when our time HERE will be up."

Hopefully some of them eventually came to the Lord. Most people don't realize that it's not just the preacher who is knocking on their door but also the Lord Jesus.

Revelation 3:20....**Behold I stand at the door and knock; if any man hear my voice, and open the door, I will come in to him, and will sup with him, and he with me.**

In the Mars Hill Church there was a faithful, loving member who had been a school teacher for many years. She was a widow whose aged mother and brother lived with her. One summer afternoon I stopped by to visit them. Daisy brought me into the living room where her mother was sitting in her favorite rocking chair. In spite of her age, the old lady had a spunky twinkle in her eye as I greeted her.

"Good afternoon, Mrs. Nix, how are you today? Have you been behaving yourself?"

With a bit of flint in her expression she began shaking a bony finger in my face and said, "Young man, I've been behaving myself for 94 years; I want you to know." After that I was more careful in asking that question!

Many good things occurred in the Acworth Church: some new members added; some baptisms; some drop-outs returned; some young people encouraged in their walk with Jesus (two of whom eventually became preachers); some mistakes made; some renovations and some problems solved.

The church was not a fully tithing church. Apparently, about all it ever gave to missions was the interest income of a small endowment left by one of the grandfathers---amounting to perhaps $250.00 per year.

At that time there was a campaign to increase tithing and giving to missions. The elders and deacons, after careful deliberations, finally agreed to call on the members to tithe carefully for three months as a challenge. After all bills were paid, the Church would give any remaining balance to home and foreign missions. Some of the men seemed to think that the amount would be relatively small and could easily be given without serious pain. So, why not?

After three months, to everyone's surprise, the surplus amounted to just over $500.00! At that time this would pay the pastor's salary for two months. However, as there was no way out of the promise given,

CHAPTER 4: SEMINARY GRADUATION TO CONFRONTATIONS. 57

the whole amount was sent to the Mission Boards--a miracle indeed!

Tithing continued to be much improved after that.

One day I was on visitation in the Mars Hill area. As I was leaving one family they asked me if I would be interested in adopting two small kittens which they had found in their barn. They wanted to get rid of them, because they were both infected with leech worms. In spite of the infection they were very cute. Thinking we could help them to recover, I agreed to take them.

When Betsy and our two little sons saw the pitiful creatures, they too wanted to help care for them. We remembered Dr. Laura's powerful oily antiseptic containing pine tar, camphor, probably alcohol and a few other unknown ancient ingredients. We had used it on ourselves successfully for all kinds of scratches, bug bites and bruises. We were sure it should be safe and therapeutic for the kittens. Indeed it was! Overnight the parasites had turned over and died. The kittens were delighted, and so were we.

They grew and loved our family and their life in the church manse, until they and the manse somehow became infested with fleas. Something had to be done! The flea battle began! The cats were the main carriers of these vicious, biting critters.

Betsy took our plight to some of our church ladies and someone suggested a kerosene dip, without giving exact directions. Betsy got a bucket, filled it with kerosene, and proceeded to dip the teenage cats in the UNDILUTED kerosene. She took them out, dried them off with old rags and felt pleased that she had followed their advice. It was the end of the fleas on the cats, all right, but it was almost the end of the cats! They immediately lost use of their hind quarters and could only move their front legs. Soon all their fur fell out. Those two little hairless cats, dragging themselves around with their front paws, were truly a pitiful sight. After a remorseful Betsy, with the help of our little boys had carefully fed and nursed them, life gradually came back into their rear quarters, and their fur grew out again. Once more they were able to walk, and look, and act like cats. The second time they were let outside, they kept going and never came back! So much for our ministry to country cats!

It became a family fun story that Betsy, although she loved cats, was somehow hard on them. Many years later a young Jewish girl named Esther became our spiritual daughter. When in the United States, she often stays with us and is terribly allergic to cats and homes where cats live. We are very glad we never became cat keepers.

A COUPLE TO BE MARRIED?

Late one Saturday night a loud demanding knock on the manse door disturbed us. I wondered who on earth could be there at this time of night. I turned on the porch light and opened the door. A very disheveled couple stood smiling at me. "Good evening. We're looking for the Pastor. We want to get married--tonight."

"Tonight?" I was in no mood to discuss a marriage service with anyone that late at night. A bulletin and Sunday message were waiting to be completed and I was feeling a bit grumpy because of interruptions. However, a pastor has to be polite, so I invited them in.

As they entered I noticed there was something familiar about these two. I stared intently at them. They just stood there looking at me. Then.... "Joe and Kat Wilkinson! What in the world are YOU doing here?"

Kat giggled, "We pulled a good one on him didn't we, Joe?"

Laughing, we hugged each other. I called Betsy and we had a glad reunion. Joe and Kat were long-ago friends from my Florida and Alabama bachelor days. They had already been married for several years. Kat's best friend, an attractive redhead, had been a dear friend of mine before the War.

During World War II Joe had piloted transport planes carrying supplies to the Allied Forces in the Burma-China war theater. They were now living in Atlanta where he was a top pilot with Delta Airlines. They heard we were pastoring the little Presbyterian Church in Acworth, and while on a fishing trip on nearby Lake Allatoona, they decided to play a practical joke on us. What a nice surprise!

This began a renewal of a loving friendship that has become eternal. Joe and Kat became members of a Presbyterian Church in Peachtree City, Georgia. While still flying regularly, he studied and became a lay minister and special servant of the Lord in a number of outreaches. He helped establish the Chapel and Chaplaincy at the Atlanta Airport, also the ongoing lay chaplaincy and special care for the Alzheimer's homes in Christian City near Atlanta.

Toward the end of his flying days Joe had become the chief instructor of pilots and was greatly loved by the entire Delta airline personnel.

In 1988, Joe graduated from this earthly life to his heavenly home, after a courageous battle against cancer. His last flight ticket was paid in full, for he had loved and served the Lord Jesus Christ faithfully.

Kat called and requested that we come. I was given the great honor of giving the last-flight message. How blessed and privileged we were to know this brave pilot whose chief instructor was Jesus!

CHAPTER 4: SEMINARY GRADUATION TO CONFRONTATIONS.

We still continue our close contact with Kat and her family and will see Joe one fine day in Heaven!

MORE ABOUT MOM

In retirement my mother spent her spare time in growing flowers, writing her children weekly, and studying her Bible. She was often the teacher for the Ladies Circle or Bible Class and was very interested in working the daily crossword puzzle, which helped to keep her mentally alert and her vocabulary well-honed.

Mom was the kind of person who would stop whatever she might be doing to welcome unexpected visitors or neighbors, showing them great hospitality--however long it might take. No doubt she entertained many angels unawares, as Hebrews 13:2 instructs us to do.

Never would she allow an ill word to be spoken in her presence about her pastor or any other pastor, for they were the servants of God, no matter how poorly they might be doing the job. She remembered always the verse from Psalm 105:15.... **Touch not mine anointed, and do my prophets no harm!**

To supplement her meager pension she usually had a lady school teacher stay with her for the winter school term. Most were very congenial, but there was one green apple in the barrel.

This thoughtless woman tested to the "nth" degree Mom's patience. No matter how Mom fixed her breakfast, lunch or dinner, made her bed or cleaned her room, baked her a cake or wrapped a Christmas present, or any other kindly thing she tried to do for the woman, nothing, but absolutely nothing, seemed to please her.

When this old-maidish teacher finally left, Mom gave her a sweet "Goodbye" but was greatly relieved to see her go. The only word that Mom would ever allow herself to say about her unhappy ex-boarder was, "She didn't even like vanilla!" As far as Mom was concerned that seemed to cover everything in a fairly nice way.

For a long time this saying became a family favorite when referring to some hard-to-please person.

Since all her children were grown, married and living elsewhere, my mother wonderfully served as our family's center of communication. Wherever we were, she kept us lovingly informed about what was going on in the other branches of the family. This helped to keep us knit together no matter how far away we were.

Betsy, the children and I always loved being with her. As often as we could, we would invite her to join us on our vacations.

One time on a trip to Montreat through the mountains of North Carolina, teacher Mom invented some special little "territory" games to keep Craig and Kirby from getting too rambunctious on what seemed to them was a never-ending journey. We spent much time searching for that special picnic place--a nice table under good shade trees, beside a cool babbling mountain brook, with no crowd of people. With these specifications such a place was a little hard to find but, once in a while, we discovered such a lovely spot. Usually there were uninvited guests--picnic bees! Then we made a mad dash and gladly relinquished our table to them.

Once, on such a trip, as we were winding through the mountains on those hair-pin curves, the Lord wonderfully saved our lives! Just before reaching the next extremely sharp, wrap-a-round curve, the Lord seemed to command, "Quick! Move over to the very edge! Right now!"

Without question I obeyed. Immediately around that curve came a speed demon in a sports car taking half my lane. He missed us by inches! Had the Lord not warned us to hug the edge of the cliff, that car would have wiped us all out.

As we drove slowly on, we thanked and praised the Lord for delivering us from being knocked over the edge. I hate to think what might have happened if I had not listened to the Lord's voice.

OUR MOVE TO CHESTER AND THE SECOND FIRING!

One of my Seminary classmates working in the South Carolina area, had recommended us to the pastor of the Chester Presbyterian Church. This large church had been establishing a Chapel Ministry on the edge of the town in a textile mill community and had a very capable ministerial candidate working in the field. The young man had done an excellent job, and the Chapel group had grown to where it could be fully organized into a separate church congregation. An ordained minister was needed to do this.

Soon after the tithing miracle in Acworth, perhaps the middle of '53, we were invited to help establish the new church in Chester. Should we or shouldn't we? After all we had spent five years at Acworth and Mars Hill and it would be very difficult to leave. We prayed about it and felt the Lord would have us accept this new challenge. We received reluctant approval to move from the two churches and the Presbytery. We left with five years of precious memories and the well wishes of the congregations.

There was no warning about the spiritual and social tornado that lay just ahead!

The Chapel congregation with the help of the mother church had already built the pastor's home and the Church Sanctuary, with Sunday School rooms adjoining. It was a real lively group of Southern

CHAPTER 4: SEMINARY GRADUATION TO CONFRONTATIONS. 61

Presbyterians with quite a lot of young people and children. A group of old-line textile mill-workers were ready, it was thought, to be ordained as elders and deacons.

With bright hopes we arrived in Chester, confident the Lord would give us His guidance and help in organizing this new little church, nicely situated on a red clay road off the main highway. It was interesting to see that black and white families were scattered throughout the community, and their children were often seen playing together. Although they went to separate schools and the little black church was just down the road, there was a friendly atmosphere and people got along very well.

Not long after arriving, we had Open House at the manse for the church members, friends and neighbors. In late afternoon, just before the guests were to come, a near catastrophe took place. Downstairs there were still many unpacked moving boxes which needed to be stored in the partly finished attic directly over the living room ceiling. While hurriedly trying to place the boxes in this storage area, I slipped and fell. My left leg went through the ceiling, knocking out a tile. My shin-bone hit the joist. I almost panicked and cried, "Oh Lord, help me! It's my fault. The ceiling is badly damaged. The guests will notice it. My name will be mud. My leg is killing me. Please get me out of this jam!"

Little Kirby, about four and a half years old, happened to be sitting in an arm chair in the living room, directly below me. He heard my cry and saw my plight. With indescribable nonchalance, Kirby leaned back in that comfortable chair, looked up at my dangling leg and said, "Well Dad, all you have to do is just take your foot and ram it back up there!" That added some curative humor to this very painful situation.

Despite my badly bruised shin-bone and spirit, I was able to quickly replace the broken piece of ceiling tile with glue and some kind of filler that made it almost unnoticeable. It wasn't a good beginning and may have been prophetic of a future fall-out.

Not long after that episode, the Presbytery sent its commission to officially organize the Chapel into the St. Paul's Presbyterian Church. They ordained the necessary elders and deacons and installed me as the Pastor. Everything seemed to be going well. Before long, there was a lovely wedding, a Boy Scout Troop organized, and other good things taking shape.

About this time one of the elders, whose wife had died recently, asked if I would marry him and his new lady friend--also a member of the Church. I said I would be glad to do so, but first I wanted them to stop by to talk about it, because I needed more information.

One evening after his little store was closed for the night, they came, and I learned that his lady friend was a divorcee. I explained our denomination would permit a marriage only for the "innocent party", so I would need to see the divorce papers.

When I learned the woman had been married twice before without benefit of a divorce, I told them as kindly as I could that I could not marry them. This began the build-up of strong anger and opposition against me. In only a few months the water had heated up, but it would soon get much hotter.

After the 1954 Supreme Court ruling against segregation in schools, I was led to preach two sermons on the Mind of Christ and what our Lord Jesus would want in our relationships to blacks--especially as Christians.

The Lord led me to point out carefully that forced integration, like forced religion or politics, was not His Mind or Will. A program of voluntary acceptance, working together, schooling together, yes, worshipping together IN LOVE, was His desire. To say such things at that time was Southern heresy! Even in the Church!

The Supreme Court ruling and such preaching were totally contrary to the mores and traditions of the South. Anyone proposing such a break would instantly incur the wrath of the traditionalists as well as the Ku Klux Klan.

Some of the elders and deacons arranged to meet secretly with Presbytery leaders. They brought all kinds of false charges against me and asked that I be removed. The Church congregation met and, by a large majority, voted against me. They didn't like my position of quietly calling the Church to follow Christ in this matter of desegregation and civil rights. At that point I realized we were in a no-win situation and resigned. There was even a rumor that the KKK was seriously considering showing me the "tarred and feathered" way out of town! Somehow, the good Lord stopped that.

One bright spot in this whole stormy situation was a statement made one night by an old elder who knew what was going on behind the scenes and wanted to let us know we had at least one friend left. He said, "Preacher, I'm with you; I may not agree with you in everything, but I'm with you. It's like with my wife. We don't agree with each other in everything, either. In fact, if she agreed with me in everything, I'd run her off! There are times when I am wrong and she NEEDS to disagree with me."

After we had left, the Presbytery appointed a commission to investigate all the charges, which were proved totally false. I was fully exonerated. The whole vendetta was turned around and some of those same officers were removed.

The Jewish writer in North Carolina, Harry Golden, wrote in his

CHAPTER 4: SEMINARY GRADUATION TO CONFRONTATIONS. 63

book, JOHN F. KENNEDY AND THE NEGRO, the names of two ministers, who were the first to be booted out of the South for their stand against segregation. I had the unexpected and unsought-for honor of being one of them!

That first church-firing was also unexpected and undesired. It was most traumatic. We soon found we had become "persona non grata" in standard church circles in most of the South. However, we have to believe that the Lord has truly made it all work out for our good, and also the good of many dear believers in that church.

Romans 8:28..... *And we know that all things work together for good to them that love God, to them who are the called according to His purpose.*

ACWORTH PRESBYTERIAN ← CHURCH

64 FIRED AGAIN AND AGAIN, PRAISE THE LORD!

"OUR FIRST FRUITS,"
CRAIG AND KIRBY,
MARCH, 1950

3 GARDNERS! 1953
CHESTER, S.C.

SHELTERED BY GRANDPAPPY
ATLANTIC CITY,
SUMMER 1949

CHAP. 5

FROM SPIRITUAL LIMBO TO GHETTO

I will never leave thee, nor forsake thee. So that we may boldly say, The Lord is my helper, and I will not fear what man shall do unto me.
-Hebrews 13:5b,6

Wondering if we should continue in the ministry, we ended up in Panama City at Christmas of that same year. Totally rejected and discouraged, we felt as if we were untouchables. Until a new direction could be determined, my sister, Sissy, and her husband, Walter Anderson, took us in with our two boys. And Betsy was pregnant again. How we bless their memory for accepting us in love, caring for us and not condemning us!

During this time I was able to build a little marine paint barge for the painting and repair of Walter's boats. We named it "The Little Joe". Also we were able to encourage them to undertake the purchase and development of their marina and their famous restaurant, "The Captain Anderson" on Grand Lagoon.

At first Walter hesitated, because the water-front property next to the old wooden bridge required a rather large initial loan, and a lot of dredging would be needed.

I went with him to visually check out the land. After seeing the possibilities I strongly urged him to go ahead with it and had a deep inner feeling that it would be very blessed of the Lord. He needed a docking place near the pass to the Gulf of Mexico for several deep-sea fishing boats. This would be just right.

But, here we were in spiritual limbo and Betsy was expecting a baby! At this point we didn't know where we would be going, or what the future held for us. We were still trying to hear from the Lord whether we should continue in the ministry or not. Bravely we tried to "Praise The Lord Anyhow," as we're told to do in Psalm 34:1-4 and Phil.4:4.

For a while it seemed no one wanted to touch us with a forty-foot pole. We hadn't received any invitation to minister anywhere. Finally, in February a surprise call came from an elder in a Pensacola Presbyterian Church inviting me to preach there for a Sunday service.

No doubt this invitation had been a result of Sissy's urging, because at that time she was a key worker in the local and state organizations of the Presbyterian Women of the Church.

Very prayerfully I drove those long, lonely 106 miles along the Gulf to the Westminster Presbyterian Church on the west side of Pensacola where the membership was made up mainly of Navy personnel. And, they invited me back! This was a great encouragement to us. I continued supplying there each Sunday for about the next 3 months. Having been a Navy man, I felt at home with these people.

March 27 was a cold, snowy Sunday morning which was unusual for that area. Instead of going to Pensacola I was free to take Betsy to the hospital. Having previously lost two sons at birth and advised not to have any more children, how happy and thankful we were for our healthy baby Joe's safe arrival!

The next Sunday he was taken to church for his christening with Mamma and all the family present.

Two weeks later I preached at the Beach Presbyterian Church near Panama City with our three sons and my wife in the congregation. On the way home, five year old Kirby made a very important statement which was the turning point for our whole family. "Dad it sure was good to see you up there preaching again!"

Out of the mouth of a babe, the Lord was confirming that we were not to quit but continue in His ministry. Sissy's famous Sunday dinner of roast, rice, rolls, fresh vegetables, gallons of iced tea never tasted so good!

Another big encouragement was the invitation from the Pensacola Church to become their pastor. Indeed, I wanted to do it very much.

However, deep in my heart, I felt the Lord wanted us to go to Princeton Seminary for a year of graduate study in counseling with juvenile delinquents. For some years the Lord had been showing me there would be a great increase in such problems during and after World War II, because of the serious relaxation of Biblical moral standards. With all the strikes against us and with very little income during these months, we were wondering how in the world we could possibly do it.

Next I found myself doing a very "crazy" thing, seemingly. Toward the end of our limbo in Panama City, I suddenly felt that the Lord wanted us to find a little water-front lot, something like Mamma's, somewhere on the Bay. I thought, "Maybe in the future we could build a little retirement cottage there. The prices will be going up each year, so we'd better to find one now. Surely the Lord would want us to have a place to come home to." I had not fully learned that "Wherever we are in the world serving the Lord, that's home!" After all, our final home is not even on this earth, but in heaven, where He has prepared us a

CHAPTER 5: FROM SPIRITUAL LIMBO TO GHETTO! 67

mansion (John 14).

I had about a week to find this important lot. The ones along the main part of the Bay were too expensive for poor folks like us. Then I heard about a man selling lots in the old College Point development on a bayou north of Lynn Haven. There we found a nice lot, 100 by 165 feet which we could buy for a little down and $25.00 a month.

Betsy and I agreed to buy it and somehow over the next four years, the Lord enabled us to keep up those $25 a month payments until we were the happy owners of a beautiful "retirement" lot. It would be so nice one day to come back to beautiful St. Andrews Bay where I grew up. Our future spot among the pines, palms, palmettoes and sand spurs was assured, or so we thought. Seventeen years would pass before we knew the "rest of the story!"

By early June, 1955, with our ten week old baby, our two other sons and a dog, we headed to Key West, where my sister Judy, and her husband, Navy Commander Dick Gaunt, were living and had arranged for me to preach in their little Presbyterian Church.

HEADING NORTH

Something like Abraham of old, we were leaving our home country and heading toward a distant land with only the promise of our Lord Jesus that, if we would go forth in His name to do His bidding, He would be with us even to the end of the world (Matt.28:20). That was enough!

We stopped in southern Maryland where we stayed with Betsy's parents in their retirement home. While in those few days at "White's Bight" (as they called it), a letter came addressed to Betsy from her Great Aunt Fanny in Swarthmore. It contained a note with a check saying this gift was a distribution from her estate to her great nieces and nephews while she was still living. With her love and best wishes to each.

With surprise still written on her face, Betsy looked up from the check, her eyes brimming with tears and said, "Honey, this is the Lord's provision for our year at Princeton. It's a gift of $2,000.00." That gift, with the money carefully saved from the wedding gifts, would be enough to get us through most of a year, if we were admitted to the Graduate School at Princeton Seminary. We quickly wrote Aunt Fanny our deepest thanks and told her what it would be used for.

When we passed through Baltimore, Maryland, in the midst of the snail-like traffic, through that congested city with its miles and miles of row houses, I said, "Dear Lord, please don't EVER send us to a place like Baltimore!"

Praying or telling God what not to do was most foolish! For one year later, beginning with the summer of 1956 we would be serving almost 24 years in that city before He would allow us to go anywhere else.

On our way to Atlantic City to see Betsy's grandparents, we stopped by Princeton Seminary and found that my credentials and transcripts would be acceptable for enrollment in their graduate school. Then we asked about housing and they laughed. "That's going to be a real problem. We doubt you'll find a furnished apartment within 25 miles of Princeton for $90.00 a month."

I replied, "That's all we can budget for rent. I'm sure the Lord will lead us to one."

Happily assured that we could enroll in Princeton Seminary the last of August we visited Betsy's brother Kirby and his family in Margate just south of Atlantic City. Brother Kirby was now part of the family management team for the Marlborough Blenheim Hotel. They were happy to see us and put us up in their home for a few days.

It was there that one night our little wire fox terrier, "Connie", got an unexpected and scary run for her life. One of the boys had taken her out for a walk with the other children and, while playing, they had hooked her to the bumper of Uncle Kirby's car. Kirby came out to go on an errand. About two blocks down the street he heard people screaming for him to stop. He discovered he had been dragging poor Connie for two blocks. Her little paws were already bloody. After some hasty first aid, she quickly recovered from her unplanned "skiing trip" on the pavement.

We visited with Pop and Tata in their lovely home on Harrisburg Ave. Our boys were very interested in hearing their great grandparents speaking their Quaker "thees and thous" in quiet conversation with their mother Betsy.

From there we visited Betsy's sweet old nurse, Nanan, and her sister Ethel. We were able to see and smell their English wall-flowers and admire their lovely English water-colored paintings. Nanan was a faithful church-goer and had been a constant nurse and caretaker for Betsy from her earliest childhood. She and her sister both still had clear remnants of their British accent, and we always were served proper English tea on those visits. All the while, our little boys along with Connie, strained at their leashes for us to get on with our trip.

The next journey was to see Betsy's sister Cindy's family in Mt. Tabor, New Jersey. Through their kindness we stayed with them for a week or more. They had boys about the age of ours, and together they had a great time participating in the Mt. Tabor 4th of July celebration with a community parade and prizes for the best floats and costumes.

CHAPTER 5: FROM SPIRITUAL LIMBO TO GHETTO!

Little did we dream that one day some twenty-five years later we would be blessed to see the Biblical Mt. Tabor and view northern Israel from its round top!

Quickly the time flew by and something had to be done about living quarters in or near Princeton for the coming seminary year. One early morning, leaving Betsy and the boys at Mt. Tabor, I drove to Princeton to fill out the necessary admission papers and pay the required fees. I then asked again for any suggestions on finding a furnished apartment. The answer was the same, "You'll not likely find anything within 25 miles." I leaned on the steering wheel of the little old Chevrolet and prayed, "Dear Lord, you know our need for a furnished apartment and surely You know if there's one close by. I have only about two hours left before I need to head back to Mt. Tabor, so please Lord, direct every turn and stop I make. They mentioned nearby Lawrenceville, so Lord, I'll head that way. Thank you Lord, In Jesus Name."

I started the car and turned southwest on the road leading to Lawrenceville. I stopped at a real estate office there. They had nothing to offer but told me to go north a couple of miles to another village and ask. Nothing there! Someone directed me to a little place called Hopewell to look for a bakery shop where they sold a county paper. Maybe it had something.

I stopped at the little German bakery and asked if they had a county paper. The baker wiped his hands on his flour-dusty apron and said in somewhat broken English, "Young man, ve are all out of der county paper. May I ask vot are you looking for?"

I said, "I'm coming to Princeton Seminary to study with my family and we need a furnished apartment for this winter."

"Oh, you don't say?" he replied, "Vell let me tell you, yust around der corner, up der steep bank, dere is a lady, a Mrs. Ackerman. She go to Florida every year and she like to rent her apartment for der vinter. You go round and see her. Tell her I send you."

I walked around the corner and found the apartment. It was a quaint little two story duplex under some lovely trees. I walked up the very steep flight of steps and knocked on her door. Praise God! She was home.

I told her who I was and what I was looking for. She invited me in. Yes, she was planning to rent her side of the duplex. She didn't mind having children. She didn't mind our keeping a dog. In fact, Mrs. Ackerman pointed to the oil painting on the mantelpiece. It was a picture of one of her beloved cocker spaniels. Yes, she would let us have it for $90.00 a month, instead of the $100.00 she had hoped to get. Yes, we could move in around the first of August when she left for Florida. Yes, the apartment would be left completely furnished.

Everything we needed would be there. Everything!

Glory to God in the highest! In just about ninety minutes the Lord had led me straight to this little lady and her fully furnished, spic-and-span apartment which was only eight miles from Princeton Seminary. I was so excited I could hardly wait to tell the good news to Betsy and the boys. I praised the Lord all the way back to Mt. Tabor. The Lord was putting things together in His own miraculous way!

Finally, we were nicely established in the little apartment. Craig and Kirby, eight and six years old respectively, were in the Hopewell Grammar School.

One day after I had returned home from my studies at Princeton, Betsy met me at the door with a very distressed look on her face. In her arms, she held a battered and bruised little Joe, who was crying his heart out. He had a huge lump on his forehead and was barely able to breath. At the time he was only about nine months old and still nursing. What in the world had happened to little Joe?

She had called doctor who was expecting us to bring Joe right away. We jumped in the car and rushed the baby to the doctor's office. On the way Betsy explained what had happened.

After returning from grocery shopping she had pushed the stroller up the hill to the back door. While unloading the groceries she had left little Joe in the stroller with the brake on. Because the little back porch was level, Betsy thought it would be safe to leave the stroller there. The phone rang and she went to answer it.

Seconds later she heard someone pounding on the front door. A black lady was standing there holding little Joe, who was screaming, and his face was covered with blood. "Is this your baby?" she asked.

Betsy took our frightened child in her arms. "My God! What happened?"

As the woman was coming around the little curve, she saw the stroller flying down the hill. It hit the sidewalk and went over a four foot drop onto the busy narrow road and dumped the baby out. Frantically the woman stopped her car in the middle of the highway blocking traffic. She picked up the baby, and climbed up the steep steps to our door. All this Betsy was blurting out between sobs, as we approached the doctor's office.

In the duplex next to us was an intellectual couple with all the modern ideas of non-discipline for child-rearing. Their three year old, was already a mean little menace. Seeing the stroller with the baby in it, he took the brake off, pushed the stroller around the side of the house and let it go. By God's great mercy, Joe had not been killed, only seriously hurt.

After a thorough examination, the young doctor felt we could take

CHAPTER 5: FROM SPIRITUAL LIMBO TO GHETTO!

Joe home, but we had to watch him carefully through the night. If he had a problem breathing because of his nose continuing to swell, we were to call a neighbor-medic who would bring oxygen if needed.

Little Joe had a terrible time trying to nurse. Betsy and he took turns crying as she held him in her arms and rocked him most of the night.

Still looking like he'd been kicked between the eyes by a mule, our baby finally began to mend. Many prayers had gone up for him. The Lord had heard them all.

Earlier we had heard of a two-unit work in Baltimore at McKim Center and McKim Boys Haven which dealt with delinquents in more of a Christian context. We felt led by the Lord to check it out during the Christmas holidays.

At the Seminary I had some interesting courses in individual counseling, some practical field experiences in dealing with emotionally disturbed older people in a New Jersey mental hospital, and in group counseling at Highfields with tough youth offenders from northern New Jersey. The Highfield Center was especially interesting because it was the former estate of Col. Charles Lindberg. It was from this large mansion that the Lindberg's first child was kidnapped in the early 30's.

After taking Betsy and the boys to see Pappy and Gin at "White's Bight" in southern Maryland, I came back to Baltimore the day before Christmas. I hoped to contact the leaders to learn about their work. However, I could find no one at either place and had to leave that very cold day for the eighty mile drive back to the family somewhat discouraged.

Sometime in January, a notice appeared on the Seminary bulletin board about a Presbytery Executive from Baltimore coming to Princeton to interview men concerning a job opening with the McKim Association in Baltimore. Being quite busy with my seminary courses and counseling research, I almost let this interview date slip by. But, at the last minute, I saw the notice again and came in to meet with Dr. Walter Cremeans, who was a retired minister called back into service to do the General Presbyter's work in Baltimore. He was a most likeable man. When he learned of my background he promptly invited me to look into the work and the possibility of taking the job as Executive Director of the McKim Association. I agreed to take a look.

Because of the South Carolina firing, up until this time I had no ministry assignments at Princeton. The prospect of finding work in Baltimore lifted our spirits. Maybe in its slums I would have a chance to preach God's Word.

I made two trips by train from Princeton to Baltimore to meet Dr. Cremeans and then Dr. Lloyd Ice, the President of the McKim Board and the longtime minister of the Govans Presbyterian Church.

They showed me the Community Center and The Boys Haven and told me about the little Church that the McKim executive would serve as pastor. They spoke about the small Pre-School program and the Rummage Center. I was introduced to the workers. Some of them were conscientious objectors, Quakers and Mennonites, doing alternative service rather than military duty. The Korean War was going on then (1956).

While we were leaving, walking across the Center's basketball court, Dr. Cremeans stated, "Joseph, I believe if you take this job, you really can make a name for yourself."

I was startled and troubled by this approach and quickly said, "Dr. Cremeans, if I take this job, it will not be to make a name for myself; it will be for one reason only, to lift up the Name of Jesus Christ."

I do not remember if there was a response, but I meant what I said to him that day. It must have touched his heart, because as long as he was in Baltimore he was a faithful supporter of our work. Even after he moved to Florida in full retirement he continued to support us to the end of his life.

I caught the train back to Princeton late that day and told Betsy that it seemed to be too much for one man. It probably would be the toughest assignment we could ever have. Not only that, it would be very dangerous due to the area in which we would be working. We might even have to live in a dingy apartment right opposite the Center. Praise God! She was willing.

Not long afterwards, I was asked to come back to meet with the McKim Board Committee. I prayed, "Lord, the job is too big for one man," and the Lord kept saying, *My grace is sufficient, I will be with you. I will be with you all the way.* (Matt.28:20; II Cor.12:9; Hebrews 13:5-6).

At the meeting I was questioned intensively by a retired social worker. Finally, they gave me the news that the job was mine as the Executive Director of the Association if I would take it, and they would have an apartment for us.

Little did I know then, that the job had been turned down previously by five or six capable men. This I learned a year later in Chicago, when I met one of those men who said that after he had been interviewed for the job in Baltimore, he had refused it saying they were foolish to expect any man to do such a monstrous job. They expected one man to do the work of five. Fortunately, the Lord was with me. Just as He showed Moses, He directed me to put good men in charge of each unit and, if necessary, I would train them myself.

Since I did not have time at Princeton to develop a thesis in summation of my studies and work in the area of counseling in

CHAPTER 5: FROM SPIRITUAL LIMBO TO GHETTO! 73

delinquency problems, it was decided with my advisor at the Seminary that I would write it after a time of field work at McKim.

(Perhaps this book may serve as my final thesis and dissertation! We'll see!)

Before leaving Princeton, I had the privilege of meeting a couple of times with that great servant of God, Dr. John MacKay, the highly esteemed president of the Seminary. Hearing that we needed three or four hundred dollars to finish paying our expenses for that year, he immediately approved a loan of that amount from the Student Aid Funds to be repaid within the next year, which was done.

In earlier years Dr. MacKay had been a missionary in South America. In spite of his considerable scholastic achievements, which sometimes dampens the compassion of some leaders, Dr. MacKay never lost his zeal for the Lord Jesus. You could sense his deep love and compassion for souls as well as for his brothers and sisters in Christ.

He would pay close attention to whatever one might be saying, and in his inimitable way reply, "Good-good-good!" May he rest in peace.

THE HAPPY RIGELLS
ATTENDING POP 'N TATA'S 60TH WEDDING ANNIVERSARY
IN ATLANTIC CITY, OCTOBER 1956
(LITTLE JOE ON THE LEFT)

74　　FIRED AGAIN AND AGAIN, PRAISE THE LORD!

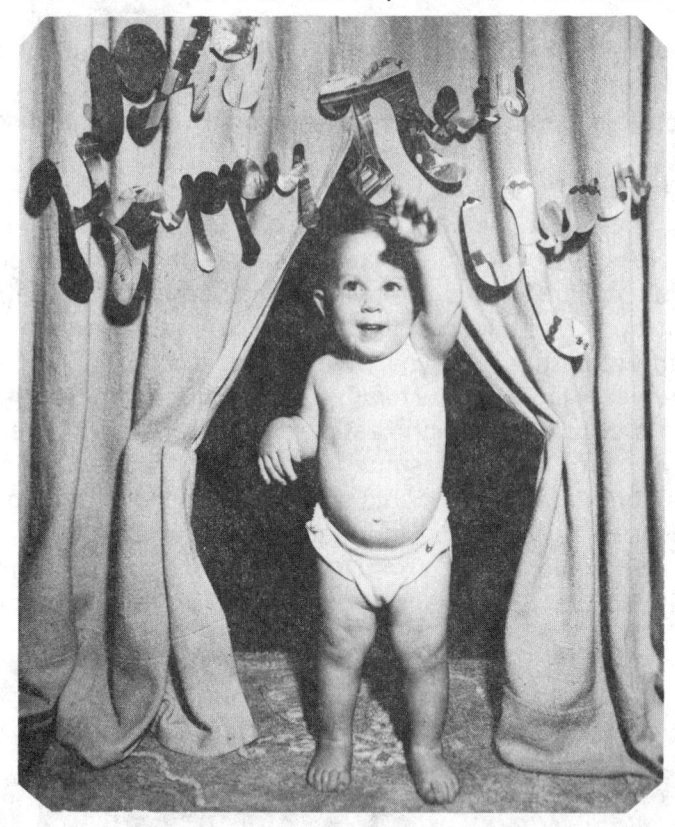

HAPPY NEW YEAR GREETER CRAIG
A cherished photo (see page 50)

HOW MOM RIGELL'S BROOD GREW BY 1956
PRAISE THE LORD

CHAP. 6

MCKIM DAYS (OR DAZE)
GREAT INNER-CITY CHALLENGE!

"....If any man will come after Me, let him deny himself and take up his cross, and follow Me. For whosoever will save his life shall lose it: and whosoever will lose his life for my sake shall find it."
-Matthew 16:24-25

I had to report to Baltimore on July 15, 1956 to begin work. Betsy would stay with the boys at White's Bight with her parents in Southern Maryland until the apartment in Baltimore was available. This apartment on Deepdene Road belonged to a McKim Board member who was going to England for some time. Our household furnishings had been in storage in Panama City since December 1954 and would have to be brought by a moving van to Baltimore.

From July 15th into August, I slept on a little cot set up for me in the staff apartment across the street from the Community Center. So I began "digging in," meeting members of the operating staff and familiarizing myself with all phases of this inner-city mission. I tried to reassure everybody that I was there to help in every way and would not be making any major changes right away.

It seemed that both the Community Center and the Boys Haven were already being managed by intelligent and effective young men and, with some other believing staff members, were also doing their best to keep the Little Church of the Saviour alive.

The one remaining elder, Ted Shaw and his capable wife Sarah, plus a dear Sunday School teacher, Miss Amelia H'Lavacek, were the key and faithful members in the church. Miss H'Lavacek was also helping to keep the Free Nursery School operating.

For 134 years this McKim building had housed the historic Free School, one of the first in the United States. (King William's school in Annapolis, established in 1696 was the first free school in America. Its purpose included the propagation of the Gospel and the education of the youth of the Province in good letters and manners, and its success led to an extension of the free school system in other parts of Maryland. As a boy, Quaker Johns Hopkins attended the South River branch in the early 1820's).[1] The McKim Free School was founded by Quakers John and William McKim in 1822. They had made a fortune in the clipper-ship far-eastern trade of that day. Since the early 1920's that little Greek temple-like building had also housed the Community Center, the Nursery School, the Church on Sunday, and the main office, which was about the size of three or four postage stamps side-by-side. It contained three small desks and one telephone. There was no air conditioning--just God's ---via a high window! The office was usually so crowded with the wide-ranging activities of the personnel that I usually operated out of my brief case and shirt pocket. Back in those days, it would have been nice to have one of the new-fangled, walk-around phones attached to my belt.

The Boys Haven, with its staff and its tough, troubled, teenage boys, was in another location many blocks away at 1701 Park Ave.

Before coming to Baltimore, the Lord had directed me to wear full-time a clerical collar and vest. (Many of the kids called it "Rev's bullet-proof vest.") However, it helped to identify me as a Christian minister on the streets and in the courts.

I never will forget that first Saturday at the Center when I accompanied a bus-load of neighborhood kids and Center staff to a free Oriole baseball game at Memorial Stadium. I knew I needed to get acquainted quickly with the youth and families of the neighborhood, and this was a good way to begin. Returning to the Center after the game, suddenly the kids started shouting, "Mr. Bob's car is running away!"

Quickly I turned around to see that our staff member Bob Russo's car was rolling slowly toward the intersection. I jumped out of the bus and was able to run, catch the car and dive in to hit the brakes with my hands and then climb all the way in to secure it. Apparently the emergency brake had given way just as we arrived back at the Center. Mr. Bob had his keys with him and soon had his little car back in safe parking.

This piece of action helped the kids and staff realize that their new "Preach" was no "Wimp."

As we were unloading, I invited the kids to come to the church services the next day. One little black boy called out, "Mr. Preach, can colored chillun come to yo church?"

---

[1] From "Johns Hopkins A Silhouette" by Helen Hopkins Thom, copyright 1929 by Johns Hopkins Press: Used with permission.

CHAPTER 6: MCKIM DAYS (OR DAZE!)

I answered, "Sure thing. Everybody's welcome. Come and see." Many did.

Eventually some of them would be saved and become young staff leaders in the Center and the Church. My age at this time was 38 yrs.

Betsy and the boys joined me the day our furniture arrived from Florida. It was a happy time. We immediately set up the beds in the duplex apartment. No more army cot for a while!

Our "new home" was the very last house on Deepdene Road. It was a tree-lined, dead-end street, near a good grammar school for our little boys and only about 15-20 minutes through city traffic to the McKim Center. Betsy and I were happy there was a small fenced-in back yard where the boys and dog could play.

The old "Ma & Pa" railroad, an ancient short-line from Baltimore to York, Pennsylvania, ran right by the east side of our house. Early in the morning its friendly engineer and fireman waved to children along the way. What a thrill for our boys, who could stand on our couch by the window returning their waves! Near sundown, it would come chugging back into Baltimore. It ran perhaps another two years before closing down. Later the tracks were pulled up, and the high railroad right-of-way became a hiking path through those beautiful woods.

At this point of time we had three living sons: Craig, Kirby and Joe. Earlier, two babies, Knox and Kenneth, who came between Kirby and Joe, died at birth. We were still hoping and praying that the Lord would give us more children even after the doctors had told us not to have any more. And in 1955 the Lord had given us Joe! Now two years later, Betsy was expecting again! The Lord had smiled on us again!

By God's mercy all went well with Betsy's pregnancy. On October 4, 1957, the day the Russians launched their sputnik, our "little sputnik" Christopher was launched in good condition with a good set of lungs to prove it. Like our others he was quickly christened and dedicated to the Lord in the Church of the Saviour.

When about a year old, Chris had a close call caused by an intussusception (a dangerous and painful telescoping of the intestines), which the pediatrician diagnosed properly with x-rays, and which the Lord corrected without an operation! Praise His Holy Name!

SOME MCKIM HISTORY

The McKim Association Board was a coalition of Quakers and Presbyterians. The Quakers started the McKim Free School around 1822, and the Presbyterians founded the Mission Church of the Saviour among Italian immigrants around 1915, under the leadership of Dr. John and Edna DeBenedetto and Miss Emma Johnson.

A cooperative working agreement had been achieved in the early 1920's to help continue the Free School, the Church and the Community Center programs for the neighborhood children and families. Near the end of World War II, the joint Presbyterian-Quaker Committee was organized into a Board of Directors for incorporation as The McKim Community Association, Inc. They brought in some new staff leadership and retired the old.

At that time the McKim Board was made up of twelve Presbyterians and six Quakers, most of whom were living in suburban areas of the city or beyond, none from the area served.

In the mid-40's they employed as Minister and Center Director a young man who not only was just graduating from Princeton Seminary, but also had experience in YMCA work. This man and his wife came to take over the operation of the Free School, the Church and the Community Center.

About 1951 they began a recovery home for delinquent boys, calling it "The McKim Boys Haven." With camping and athletic programs at the Center, this man enlarged the work with slum kids. To publicize this seemingly successful slum work in Baltimore, a Saturday Evening Post reporter was invited early in 1955 to do an article which he called "The Angel of the Slums."

Behind the scenes at that time, as I was told, the police had begun to uncover a web of homosexual activity led by this so-called "angel of the slums." The Courts and a judge ordered this "minister" to get out of town in 24 hours, or he would be charged with sexual crimes with children. He was gone the next day!

According to a staff member who was closest to the situation, the public reason given by Board officials for his sudden departure was that he had suffered a heart attack and had to leave for a long recuperation.

Sadly, this was a deception that God could not bless, ever. **Cursed be he that doeth the work of the Lord deceitfully....** Jeremiah 48:10.

In the past the true Angels of Baltimore Street had been those three leaders who had been forced into retirement: Dr. John and Edna DeBenedetto and Miss Emma Johnson, three of the most dedicated and effective church workers ever to walk these streets. Their quiet, humble, faithful service to God bore much good fruit!

Under their ministry they guided young people in that early Christian Center to become key leaders in suburban churches and in other vocations. Little Miss Johnson operated an ongoing boys club of "toughies" through the 20's, 30's, and 40's, based on the motto of the Knights of the Round Table from "The Idylls Of The King," by Sir Walter Scott:

CHAPTER 6: MCKIM DAYS (OR DAZE!)

Live Pure, Speak True,
Right Wrong, Follow the King;
Follow Christ the King,
Else Wherefore Born!

Interestingly, the DeBenedettos were to long outlive those who forced their retirement. Dr. John lived to the age of ninety. Mrs. DeBenedetto went to be with the Lord in early 1990 at the age of 102! Miss Johnson lived into her 80's before going to her heavenly home to see King Jesus! These were the true "Angels of The Slum!"

That counterfeit preacher, who took their places, apparently knew nothing about their work or their Lord, nor what damage he did to the youth in the community. Many of the kids knew he was a sex-pervert. In their minds every minister they would ever meet would be considered one also. God's Word, in no uncertain terms, thoroughly condemns all sexual perversion as open rebellion against God, as an abomination; worthy of death.

The courageous, dedicated, underpaid staff had to pick up the pieces and carry on the work in the devastating wake of that false and fallen "angel." They were doing a remarkable job under the circumstances.

After about two months I felt strongly from the Lord that I must recommend Bob Russo, the Acting Director of the Community Center, to be made Full Director, and that Jim Elmore, should become the Full Director of the Boys Haven. This was quickly approved by the Board, as both of these men already were doing these jobs effectively. There were still many weak areas, which we all endeavored to strengthen.

An unusual number of requests by churches and civic groups came in that first year for speaking engagements about the work. Some were filled by Bob and Jim. I filled over 100 myself besides a weekly church service and countless other duties.

My first McKim speaking engagement was a Sunday morning service in a little country Presbyterian Church not too far out of Baltimore. For the Scripture, I read Jesus' words in Matt.25:31-46....***In-as-much-as ye have done it unto one of the least of these, my brethren, ye have done it unto me***.

At the end of the message, an elder of the congregation presented me with a check as a gift to the McKim work. Having heard strong criticism about the previous director's handling of money and the accounting mess he left, I thanked the elder and the church and asked him to please mail the check to McKim's treasurer. I went home thinking everything was fine and dandy, but it seems I had made a capital mistake.

A few days later while I was in the company of our Board President and his friend, they let me know how seriously I had "goofed."

Dr. Ice said, "Joseph, from now on, when anybody offers you anything for McKim, take it. Bring it back to McKim yourself! Ok?"

"Yes sir, Dr. Ice. I sure will."

In days to come there were a few horrible rummage items I did refuse to take--worn-out stoves and refrigerators-- but never again a check!

Come to think of it, I was never invited back to that little church. I wonder why? Another firing? Oh well, Praise the Lord anyhow!

Getting time away from the work became a perpetual problem. Maybe at Thanksgiving and Christmas, the whole family could slip down to White's Bight for a little respite. Grandma Gin could never understand why I had to spend the first twelve hours sleeping and waiting for my soul to catch up. Thank God for that woodsy hideaway. We always were refreshed and could go back into the McKim battles with renewed vitality. The "Bight" became a "Retreat Center" for us.

Sometime in the Spring of 1957, Jim Elmore told us that he and his wife, Betty, desperately needed a week off. Would we please substitute for them at the Boys Haven?

"Sure, we'll be glad to, Jim."

We didn't realize what a hornet's nest we were getting into.

Jim was one of the finest Christian men I had ever known. He was quiet, easy going, not easily ruffled. He had been a tough, mean, burly, h-raising Army sergeant during World War II and had fought all the way from Bastogne to Berlin with his outfit.

Thanks to a praying mother back in Lumberton, North Carolina, Jim met JESUS in Berlin and, like Paul in the Bible, his life was totally transformed. The Lord told him to go home, sell his considerable property, repay anyone he had ever cheated or owed and give what was left of his earthly wealth to the Lord's work. Then he was to search out a way to devote the rest of his life in serving the Lord. Jesus said He would lead him all the way.

While living near Baltimore at a place called Koinonia, he heard about McKim Boys Haven needing houseparents. One day he went to the Haven and said to the startled staff member, "The Lord has sent me to work here." Sure enough they needed him!

Now he was a very tired director needing a week's vacation!

The twelve delinquents at the Boys Haven were in various stages of schooling and deliverance from rebellion against family, society and their own defiant natures and ugly habits. With the help of several other staff people, Jim had things pretty well under control, so he and his family left for their vacation.

CHAPTER 6: MCKIM DAYS (OR DAZE!)

Well, the cat was away, and the mice did surely play! Testing our mettle, those boys pulled almost every dirty trick in the book. Also during that unforgettable week, a Juvenile Court clerk called to ask if we had room for one more boy, a 17 year old named Peter who, the clerk thought, would respond to the Haven program. He was at the court at that moment. They didn't want to keep him locked up but had no other place to send him.

Knowing we had a spare bed, I went to the court and brought him back. Everything seemed to be going well, except for the escapades of the other boys.

The semi-retired social worker who came two days per week discovered that I had taken in a new boy without clearing with her. This greatly angered her, and she didn't stop until she had made a capital case against me for breaking the established procedures. She took her case to her friend on our Board. Together they complained to the head of the City Welfare Department.

Very soon our Board President and Directors received a demand that I be removed immediately from any relationship with the McKim Boys Haven; otherwise, they would stop all welfare payments for the boys. Fired again! Praise the Lord!

Finally Jim came back after that long, long week! Of course we were more than happy to turn things back to him. All of us had survived at the Haven. No serious damage had taken place. Those boys had developed a real measure of respect for me and Betsy and love for our children. Moreover we had come to love each one of them.

The lad we had taken in stayed on at the Haven until he reached the Home age-limit of eighteen. Having nowhere else to go, he then came to live with us while working or looking for work. He stayed with us about a year until he moved to another state. Peter, who was always respectful and helpful, accepted Jesus Christ as his Saviour and Lord. May he still be walking with JESUS!

Because some of the Board members feared that I was much too religious and too upsetting to the social-work officials, they made their first attempt to have me fired. They had me "called on the carpet" by the Presbytery Executive or General Presbyter.

The General Presbyter asked my thoughts on the matter. I told him truthfully how the whole thing had come about. He listened, then kindly offered his considerable influence to help me find another position far, far away. Basically, he was suggesting that I resign quietly. Feeling considerably wronged in the whole situation and knowing that the Lord had brought me to Baltimore, I looked him squarely in the eyes and said as firmly as I could, "Sir, I know with all my heart that the Lord Jesus brought me to this place, and I'm not about to leave it until He tells me.

At this point, He hasn't told me to leave!"

"Sid, you're trying to make yourself a martyr," replied the General Presbyter.

"No, I'm not, but in the Lord's service martyrs are needed from time to time. And if that's what He wants for me now, I'm ready to be one."

"That's not needed," he replied.

Surprisingly after that, the whole affair quieted down and I heard no more about it. The Lord had intervened as He promised.

I stayed in frequent touch with Jim to encourage him in every way, but I kept hands off of the Haven. Jim endured the Haven's part-time, overruling, overbearing social worker for several more years. Finally, after many hours of intense prayer, he announced to her, "Mrs.Z., either you resign today or I resign. I've had enough!"

She resigned immediately. Needless to say, there was "peace and joy in Mudville" that day.

Later he found an outstanding, Spirit-filled social worker to carry on those duties. She was capable, effective and a pleasure to work with.

Many, many people were touched by this ex-army sergeant. He was the man who prayed for Harold Hill to receive the Baptism of the Holy Spirit at Koinonia. Mr. Hill was a well-known engineer and scientist who wrote "How To Live Like A King's Kid" and other books. (In writings and speeches, Harold Hill described the Bible as the Manufacturer's or Engineer's Handbook!)

In spite of all my education, training in three seminaries, and years in the ministry, Jim knew Jesus and the written Word far better than I. Because I wanted others to know him and receive the spiritual refreshment that I got as he talked about the Lord, I would often invite him to go with me to an occasional Presbyterian Health and Welfare Conference which was usually a spiritual Sahara, sprinkled with liberal religious double-talk.

In a Chicago conference one night Jim asked me, "Where is the Scripture which starts off *If my people who are called...?* These folks need to hear it."

I couldn't think of it at the moment. Around 4:00 a.m. he awakened to pray and read the Bible as was his custom. On his knees before the Lord, he held the Bible closed in front of him on the bed and prayed, "Lord, You wrote this Bible and You know exactly where that Scripture is. Please, Lord, find it for me. In Jesus' Name I ask."

He slowly let the Bible fall open and his eyes fell on:

II Chronicles 7:14.....*If my people which are called by my name, shall humble themselves and pray, and seek my face, and turn from their wicked ways; then will*

CHAPTER 6: MCKIM DAYS (OR DAZE!) 83

I hear from heaven, and will forgive their sin, and will heal their land.

That morning my thankful friend Jim was able to share it with the National Missions Committee. It touched the heart of the chairman, Dr. Alex Sharp, who later came to Baltimore and warmly commended us because we were keeping Jesus and the Bible central in our work.

As we boarded the jet to fly back home from Chicago, the stewardess welcomed us at the door of the plane. While waiting a few moments before we could move on to our seats, she asked what kind of work we did.

"I run a Christian Recovery Home for delinquent kids," Jim said.

"I operate a Christian Community Center in inner-city Baltimore," I replied.

The little stewardess was impressed. "Oh, I was a "sosh maj" (sociology major) in college. May I come talk with you about your work?"

"Sure thing."

The flight to Baltimore would be just over an hour, and she sat with us most of the way. As usual when with Jim, I would do the listening while he talked. That day the young stewardess did the questioning.

Jim explained our approach to helping delinquents.

When the flight was almost over, she asked with renewed interest, "Mr. Elmore, tell me again. Just what is it you do?"

He repeated, "We try to help them know JESUS, that JESUS is The Way, The Truth and The Life. That He can always help them. That He is real and can deliver them. That He can save to the utmost, if they will let Him come in and take charge. That He can make them new creations through the new birth experience. We also teach them to follow Him through regular Bible study, prayer, worship and daily obedience."

"But, how can you know Jesus is so real?"

Jim reached across me (in the middle seat), put his hand on her's and said, "My dear young lady, JESUS is more real to me than you are."

Her mouth dropped open in amazement. She hesitated and slowly remarked, "I must get the passengers ready for landing."

While descending the steep steps of the big jet, Jim nudged me and said with a grin, "Sid, I bet she'll never be the same!"

"That's for sure! After that, how could she?!"

Jim lasted at that job from 1955 to 1967. One day in the Spring of '67, a massive heart attack sent him home to be with His Blessed Lord forever. What a loss to us all!

After their first attempt to send me packing to "Timbucktu," or wherever, I kept knocking myself out, working night and day to get various units moving soundly, trying to keep up with the speaking engagements, and writing letters to increase financial support for the work. Hearsay criticism often was brought before a Board meeting and it was taken seriously. The Board would agree that some kind of action should be taken. Only two or three of these members ever had any meaningful working contact with the units or staff. I was amazed that such unfair criticism was even considered.

I was very angry at the willingness of some Board members to believe such lies and asked permission to respond to the ugly charges. I had spoken only a few sentences when one of the leading Presbyterian ministers, an influential member of the Board, began calling me down for my "angry and intemperate remarks." By this time I was biting my tongue to keep from saying anything further.

There was an awkward pause which was broken surprisingly by an old Quaker who had been on the Board for years and had a reputation of almost never saying a word. That day he made a statement I shall never forget. Quietly he said:

> *"I believe that everyone in this organization should have the right to speak his honest feelings and thoughts and we should hear him out!"*

That was all, but it was enough. Hallelujah! That dear old Quaker spoke with such finality that it totally stopped the attack of my detractors. "Olivah Sholem!" (May he rest in peace.)

DUSTY ARRIVES

"Dusty" Miller was a tall, bright young lad who had been a resident of the Boys Haven. Just before we got to Baltimore the Haven staff and social worker made arrangements for him to go on to the West Nottingham Academy in Colora, Maryland. The hope was that he could catch up with his schooling and eventually go on to college.

This lad had shown some leadership ability even when running the streets of Central Baltimore. At the age of thirteen he had become the leader of a gang which did all kinds of mischief in their struggle for survival. It was said, "he outfitted his boys from the best shops in Baltimore!"

He seemed to have a good attitude and a dry sense of humor. After Jim Elmore had taken him to a Christian Camp in North Carolina, Dusty came back asking, "What's happened with everyone around here? Everybody seems to have changed. You're not mean and grouchy like

CHAPTER 6: MCKIM DAYS (OR DAZE!)

you used to be. How come?" Dusty didn't realize at that moment that he was the one who had been changed by accepting Jesus as Saviour and Lord at that camp. He had become a New Creature in Jesus Christ (II Cor. 5:17)!

During the school year he would be at the Academy, but on vacations he stayed at the Haven. In June of '57 he was reaching the age limit for boys at the Home and would have to leave.

After the farewell party at the Boys Haven, his married sister, Sandy, took him in, but that didn't work out satisfactorily. When vacation-time came that summer, we invited Dusty to live with us when not in school. And he did!

Dusty adopted us and we've been family ever since. We've seen him through two trips as a Marine to Vietnam, through college, through some years of teaching at West Nottingham Academy, and through work with the National Security Agency. More recently he has been in the Army Ready Reserves with paratrooper training. So far he has not married. Perhaps he feels he's had enough combat already!

Along with our own boys and their school friends, different clubs from the Center, church groups, visiting ministers and their families, our little home seldom had a dull moment, first on Deepdene and then on Colorado Ave.

GOD PROVIDES A HOME!

For a long time Betsy had been dreaming of having our own house. We could look out of our tiny kitchen window and see a separate little house on the next street at 615 Colorado Avenue. Like our duplex, it was located on a dead-end street next to the old railroad bed facing north. We would think how nice it would be to have one like that.

Early one Sunday morning in the spring of '58, Betsy saw a "for sale" sign go up in front of that little house. She asked if we could go over and look at it that afternoon.

I said, "Yes, we'll take a look. Maybe the Board will let us use the rental allowance for the payments."

After the morning Church services, we were both eager to see the house. The real estate man showed us through and we liked it. The part brick-faced bungalow had three small bedrooms, a full basement, nice front and back yards. It even had a dish washer! That, no doubt, was the selling point for Betsy.

We asked how much they wanted for it and how much would be required down.

He gave us the figures and we said, "Sold!"

"That's good, but you'll have to put down a deposit for me to hold it."

"It's the Lord's day," we answered. "We can't put down money today. Just take our word for it."

"Sorry, but I will have to have a binder deposit."

"We'll bring it first thing in the morning." That was not good enough for him.

"Well, that's too bad. We can't do any buying business today, but we believe the Lord wants us to have it."

The next day he did call to say that two other people had put up deposits, and he would know in a few days whether the first or second would be the new owner. We called back Tuesday morning. The number one person had decided their furniture was too large for the house. He had not heard from the other. Tuesday night he called to say the second family had dropped out. "Come in Wednesday morning, The house is yours!"

Well, praise God, the Lord had held the house for us and was making it possible for it to be our home--and His for a long time!

With the use of the old McKim Rummage truck and the help of volunteers, we were able to make that round-the-block move in very short order. The Board had approved our use of the housing allowance for the monthly payments, and the Lord had helped us come up with the down payment. So we were happily on the way to being homeowners with an assured roof over our heads. We truly gave the Lord all the praise and thanksgiving as we dedicated the home to His use and purposes.

Over the years with the Lord's guidance and help, we had an unofficial boys haven at that little house on Colorado Avenue. The Lord greatly blessed!

THE HELL BOUND FLAGS

Besides being Executive Director of the McKim Association, I became involved with the Boys' Clubs and Betsy with the Girls' Clubs program at the Community Center. Each leader was assigned to work with neighborhood friendship groups--black, white or mixed. There were about twenty groupings. Many of the club leaders, who were church and college volunteers, normally worked with five to ten boys or girls in each group at least once a week.

Staff and volunteers sought to provide sound Christian leadership and activities with these individual groups. Hopefully and prayerfully they would be led in a sound healthy Christian direction. The more mature staff worked with the older and tougher groupings. The majority of the kids were from broken and very poor homes, most often with

CHAPTER 6: MCKIM DAYS (OR DAZE!)

welfare support. In a year's time several hundred youngsters were registered in some program or other.

I worked closely with the Explorer Club. We did a lot of camping in the countryside around Baltimore. In the early years a number of the boys came to church. The Lord saved a few of them who went on to good things. Sadly, some of them didn't.

Baltimore's notorious "Block" was only a short distance from the Center. Every kid knew about the wicked activities that went on there. Two, in particular, secretly organized their own separate gang and called themselves the "Hell-Bound Flags" with home-made tatoos on their arms to that effect. They lived in the low-income, highrise housing project called Flag House Court.

The Flag House name refers to the nearby home of Mary Pickersgill, where she made the famous flag, "The Star-Spangled Banner", that flew over Fort McHenry during the war of 1812 when the British sailed in to take Baltimore after burning Washington, D.C.

At the Center there was a staff member who was very much interested in athletics: judo, weight lifting, body building and that sort of thing. In our meetings we all agreed that he was to try to make constructive contact with these young gang members and guide them in a positive direction; hopefully, to dissolve the gang by redirecting individuals in it to go God's way. We called it, "Peeling them off, one by one."

In spite of McKim's financial problems this man was getting a comparatively good monthly salary. However, his work with the gang was not succeeding. Because of this it became necessary to end his employment at the Center.

THE GANG ATTACKS

Almost immediately word came back to me through the neighborhood grapevine that the gang was very angry about my discharging their friend, and they were coming to kill me. I knew it was no idle threat and began asking the Lord for direction. "Should I carry a gun? Should I ask for police protection? Should I post guards?"

The Lord impressed that I was simply to trust Him; show love to them when they came, and He would move in a mighty way.

We had developed a good Junior Staff program at the Center. That evening the regular Senior and Junior Staff workers were there supervising the weight-lifting, ball playing, ping-pong and whatever else was going on at the moment. A large group of youth were in the building participating or watching the activities.

Suddenly the gang of about six or seven tough guys came bulldozing in. They looked mean and were itching for a fight. Obviously they were high on something. I met them face-to-face. "Fellows, you're all hopped up on something. As your long-time friend, I'm asking you to leave quietly before there's trouble. Some of you are already on probation. If something bad happens here tonight, you'll be put away for a long time. Don't do whatever you have in mind. Leave now before I have to call the police."

Several of them melted into the crowd of onlookers. Two of the more belligerent ones kept jostling me. One tried to hit me but couldn't do it.

I repeated, "Guys, please leave; otherwise, I'll have to call the police right now."

They didn't move.

I opened the dutch door to the office and began dialing the police.

The gang member who had been chosen to kill me followed and tried once again to hit me. He couldn't bring himself to do it. Something was restraining him!

The police dispatcher took the call for help and said they would be there in a few minutes.

"Please hurry."

He answered, "Right!"

I grabbed the arm of the struggling "enforcer" and urged him to get out before the police arrived.

Suddenly, two huge policemen with night sticks in hand came rushing through the front door. (What a blest sight that was !)

"What's going on here?" they growled.

"Officers, we don't want any trouble. We just want these guys to leave."

The "enforcer" was already known as a police hater, especially when he was "goofed up" on something. When the policemen tried to lead him out peacefully, he began resisting violently. More policemen arrived to help. It took about six policemen to take him bodily out of the Center and place him hand-cuffed in a patrol car. By then, police cars were jamming the street.

We learned from the first policemen that their two patrol cars were just passing the Center when the emergency call came! All they had to do was put on their brakes and flashers! So off to Central Police Station went this completely subdued tough guy, to be charged with resisting arrest and disturbing the peace. I wasn't about to place attempted murder charges against him, although I learned later he had a large knife in his jacket, intending to use it on me.

All through this episode I could not show anger or fear--only love. I felt as if I was encased in a wall of love. Praise the Lord, the gang

CHAPTER 6: MCKIM DAYS (OR DAZE!)

member was bound by God's mighty power--LOVE!

Around 11:00 p.m. the other members of the gang came back to the Center and demanded, "What are you going to do about JR?"

I replied calmly, "Let's go down to the police station and see."

When we got there the lock-up sergeant wouldn't let me near JR, because he was too "high" and incoherent. However, he was mumbling something about food. At that, the gang all piled into my old Chevy and we went over to Lombard Street where I bought a corned-beef sandwich for JR.

The next morning I came back to the municipal court. Based on my promise to help him find some kind of work, I was able to persuade the judge to let him go.

The judge gave JR a strong warning, "If you ever come back again, I'll take you off probation and make you serve all your time in prison, plus more years for any new offenses."

After that JR came to work at the Center as our maintenance man. He was a good one. Another gang member peeled off! Glory to God!

Very soon after JR began working with us, the gang decided to wipe him out because he knew too much and had gone over to the "enemy." One night they trapped him in an alley. When he refused to come back with them, they attacked. The gang leader's knife aimed for his throat but missed it leaving a large gash across his jawbone.

A little while later they enticed him to a party and got him drunk. Then they all came to the Center and started throwing their knives into the front door. Thump, thump, thump! In the office I could hear the noise of their knives hitting the double front doors which had crash bars. Standing behind one of doors until the last "thump", I kicked the other open and picked up a handful of their knives. I gave them a friendly wave and went back in the Center locking the door behind me.

A few minutes later there was a commotion out back on the basketball court. I went out to find drunken JR lying on the pavement bleeding. The gang had knocked him down and were viciously kicking him. I ran into the midst of them and began shoving them off as hard as I could. At that very moment, a police patrol appeared. It stopped and called for more help. The gang scattered in all directions. Of course JR would not squeal on his old buddies.

He got married not long after. I officiated at his wedding which took place at the Center. The wife had two children by an earlier marriage and later she and JR had three other children.

JR worked with us for awhile, then he found employment in two or three industrial jobs. Worldly connections kept pulling him back into his old ways until he was again heavily addicted to alcohol and drugs.

Several years later JR died in his early 30's from the effects of a drug overdose.

JR had been a real tragic figure. In spite of all the mean and foolish things he had done, he had a warm and tender heart, especially towards children and old people. No doubt he felt they would accept and love him. He had come from a broken home. His mother worked. The father had gone off with someone else. He learned to "hook" school and run the streets at a very early age, surviving by "hook or crook!".

Although we had tried to get him to sit with tutors after he came to work with us, he never really learned to read or write. Nevertheless, he could repair almost anything. We still weep inside when we think of what a fine engineer or builder this capable young man could have become, if he had completely committed his way to the Lord Jesus. His death was a real heartbreaker for all of us.

It's not whether a kid comes from a broken home or not. What matters is what kind of home he has left. If the parents are not loving and God-fearing, the child is left on the waves of immorality and wickedness with no real anchor for his soul and no solid rock to build on (See Matt.7:24-27).

JR's was another sad funeral that I had to do. As I looked at the people in the crowded funeral home, I knew most of them were headed toward Hell. My heart ached for them, and I tried to present a plain message that they would understand. I told them of the abundant life and Heaven they would gain through Jesus, and by rejecting Him they would have nothing but a ruined life on earth and an eternity in hell. I went on to tell them that Jesus is now and always....*The way, the truth and the life. No man comes unto the Father except by Jesus* (John 14:6). *There's no other Name under heaven given among men whereby we must be saved* (Acts 4:12). Repent and believe the Gospel. Receive Jesus. *Believe on the Lord Jesus Christ and Thou shalt be saved, and thy house* (Acts 16:31)!

Then I stated that we have a choice as to which way we will go. Jesus tells us in Matt.7:13-14....*Enter ye at the narrow gate: for wide is the gate, and broad is the way, that leads to destruction, and many there be which go in there. Because narrow is the gate, and narrow is the way which leads to life, and few there be that find it.*

At least they heard there was another and better way. I tried to plant good seeds. I prayed someone else would come along and water them, and I knew God would give the increase. With Jesus there is no fear of death--or Hell!

CHAPTER 6: MCKIM DAYS (OR DAZE!)

GANG LEADER INVADES OFFICE

One day as Marge Nuckolls, our Center secretary, was working in the office alone, one of the gang leaders reached over the dutch door, unlocked it and walked to my side of the big double desk. Then he brazenly started going through the desk drawers looking for money.

Marge said quietly, "You shouldn't be doing that."

Just then I came into the building and found this rascal in the office searching my desk and arguing with the secretary. Quickly opening the door wide, I grabbed him by the belt and jacket, wheeled him around and, keeping him off balance all the way, I shoved him out the back door.

He kept screaming, "What do you think you are doing? You can't do this to me!"

I just pushed him into the arms of his waiting gang.

They were furious and shouted, "Let's get him!" and began threatening moves toward me.

I was angry as a hornet but remained fairly calm as I said, "OK fellas, knock it off! I've been a good friend to you guys. I went to court with you and took you on camping trips. Whenever any of you were in trouble, I helped you. Now go ahead and jump me if you like, but I'll guarantee you one thing, if I ever find any of you rummaging in that office again, even if you are ten feet tall and could stomp me through this pavement, I'll throw you out as I did Norm.".

The leader turned to the others. "Come on, let's get out of this lousy place." Sheepishly they followed him without looking back.

A REAL MIRACLE FOR JR'S LITTLE BOY

When JR's little boy Timmy was four years old, he began having a hearing problem in one ear. At that time he was enrolled in the nursery school. After the doctor's examination, the mother came to us in great distress wondering whatever she could or should do for him. Somehow the little bones in his ear had been shattered and he would never hear again in that ear. No operation could fix it.

As she finished her description of his condition, I reached over, drew little Timmy to me and sat him on my knee. I called on the adults in the office to join me in prayer.

Following the Lord's teaching in James, chapter five, we anointed his forehead and ear with oil, laid hands on him and prayed, "You're our Healer, Lord, and we thank You right now for healing Timmy's ear and restoring his hearing. We ask this in Jesus' Name, in faith believing, and we give You all the thanks and glory in Jesus' Name. Amen."

92 FIRED AGAIN AND AGAIN, PRAISE THE LORD!

Nothing happened immediately or so we thought. They left for their nearby apartment in the high-rise. A few days later, we received great news.

On a scheduled visit back to the doctor, both ears were checked. Amazingly, Timmy was hearing perfectly in both ears! Whatever was needed, the Lord had provided. The doctor marveled, because Timmy still had no bones in the hearing mechanism, but the child could hear! HE HAD RECEIVED A MIRACLE FROM GOD!

WONDERFUL COMMUNITY CENTER WORKERS

We would be remiss in not giving a big word of appreciation and commendation to the many outstanding Christian workers who helped make the Community Center the tremendous success it was during the '60's. This book would be filled for a score of pages of names of these outstanding workers; like the Friends, Mennonite, and Brethren alternative service workers, the local Presbyterian Church volunteers, the scores of college students from Goucher, Towson State and Morgan State. Each year in the late Spring we would have a Volunteer Awards Banquet and do our best to recognize and express our deepest appreciation for these dear people. How we loved them then and still do. May the Lord bless and keep every one of them in His very special care. Special words of appreciation go out to Maurice and Norma Horst, Clyde and Edna Weaver, the late Ted and Sarah Shaw, Beth Armiger (now Bryant), the late Marge Nuckolls, Christian social worker Bonnie Harmon, Linda Requard (Thatcher), Jim Mack, Ray Tillery, Bob Robinson, Bob Kemp, Miki Moto, Dovie Croft, and Mr. Blizard, and a multitude of faithful prayer partners and supporters.

THE HOME-GROWN FUTURE DIRECTOR

Another beautiful and specific evidence of the Lord's powerful work in all of this is seen in the life and witness of the present Director of McKim Center, Dwight Warren, whom we still see from time to time at the local bank. There we get to hear from Dwight the news of McKim's ongoing work with the youth and community. As a boy, Dwight came to the Center and Church while we were there, participated in the clubs, camping and athletic programs of the Center and regularly in the worship services of "The Church of The Saviour". Later he became a member of the Junior Staff, maintenance man, wrestling champion, assistant wrestling coach, staff member and on to Morgan State College about the time we had to leave in 1970.

One of the last recommendations we made to the McKim Board of

CHAPTER 6: MCKIM DAYS (OR DAZE!)

Directors was that they consider Dwight as Assistant Director and later as Director of the Center. This he has become, over the last 16 years, and he has been doing an outstanding job of it.

Soon after coming to Baltimore, I was led by the Lord to make a study of other centers, and in one I visited in New York City, the lady director urged me to concentrate on building up the staff with local leadership by having a strong Junior Staff training program. She said, "To have a good staff, you must GROW your own!" It made good sense and fit into our own philosophy of helping youngsters to learn how to work responsibly at an early age--basic to God's Way of sound growth and fulfillment.

The Lord helping, we were able to build up an outstanding Junior Staff program involving up to 20 youngsters each year. Most of these young people have successfully climbed out of the "ghetto." We always sought to impart to them "The Faith Factor." (A real faith in and obedience to God through His mighty son, Jesus.) This is the key factor that brings divine help throughout life's pilgrimage.

In the 14 years that we were at the McKim Center, we dealt with literally hundreds of youngsters, and we trust that the Christ-centered influence of the Center helped many to get on God's track and stay on it. Perhaps we should mention a few more of those who have succeeded:

Ralph Dusty Miller, mentioned earlier.

Charles Dickens, after finishing high school, went into the Army and became a military policeman. Eventually he came back to Baltimore to begin a career in the Baltimore City Police Department where he has risen to be one of the top-ranking officers on the force.

Only Heaven knows how many more have gone on to real success since we were at McKim.

Probably the most outstanding wrestler ever to come out of the McKim wrestling program, was Robert Franklin. Bobby, as we all called him, went on to obtain a Bachelor of Science degree in Criminal Justice at the University of Baltimore and later a Master of Public Administration at the same school, and presently is pursuing a Master in Business Administration at another college in his spare time.

After his early college days, Bobby spent the next five years in the Baltimore police headquarters division, and had some rare experiences in the special weapons unit. Once, he faced an armed fugitive in an alley who had his gun already raised to fire. Bobby had just rolled out of his police car and had not had time to draw his weapon. All he could call out was the Name, "JESUS!". At the sound of that name the gunman began weeping and lowering his gun, then willingly handed it over. Another time a criminal drew his weapon and began firing it at

Bobby right across the hood of his police car, only a few feet separating them. Again all Bobby could say was, "JESUS, JESUS!" None of the bullets hit him!

After the police department, Bobby moved in the direction of labor and employee relations with General Motors Chevrolet division in Flint, Michigan. For the last eleven years he has been with Solorex Company, a subsidiary of Amoco in Rockville, Maryland as manager of employee relations.

Recently Bobby wrote us that he and his wife, Deborah, met at McKim and have been married twenty years, have three fine children and one granddaughter. He ended his letter with this beautiful statement: "And still love the Lord! Keep in touch, Bobby."

OUR ITALIAN RESTAURANT FRIEND

Early in the 60's an Italian family operated a little delicatessen-restaurant on Baltimore Street directly across from McKim Center. It wasn't long before we became friends with Augie and his family.

He had been a paratrooper in the Italian theater the latter part of World War II and had some bad experiences there which still caused deep emotional stress in his life. He was a hard worker and a good restaurateur, but maybe a little too hot-tempered at times.

Each week drifters of all kinds stopped at the Center asking for hand-outs--mainly money to feed their drinking habits. We had a policy that everybody had to work for his bread. This meant food, not money. The drifter was asked to do some small chore, like picking up paper and trash in the street around the Center. Then he could come in and receive something to eat.

Earlier I had asked Augie if, once-in-awhile, I could bring one of these fellows over to get a bowl of soup and some crackers. He was very agreeable. "Why sure!"

One afternoon I took one of the derelicts to the restaurant.

In a high-minded way the drifter asked,"Is your soup greasy?"

Angrily Augie pointed toward the door and shouted, "Get Out!" And he meant OUT! No bum was going to ask him if his soup, the best in town, was greasy. No way! His "OUT" included me too!

On another occasion a salesman, who had been a long-time customer of the little restaurant, came in toward the end of a busy day and told our Italian friend that he was hungry for something very special.

"What would you suggest, Augie?" he inquired.

"I'll fix you something super-special--one of my Italian club sandwiches," and he began to create his masterpiece. He brought it out

CHAPTER 6: MCKIM DAYS (OR DAZE!) 95

with a great flourish and set it proudly in front of the salesman.

"Man, that looks great! Now, please bring me the catsup."

"WHAT!" Augie stepped back in shock. He quickly grabbed the long plate with the club sandwich and shouted, "Nobody's going to put catsup on my Speciality. Get out of here, you bum!"

Augie had a very tender heart. One summer as we were about to leave on vacation to visit my family in Florida, he and his wife asked us to please stop by before we left town. We went there in early afternoon and they had prepared sandwiches, spreads, and foods of all kinds--all neatly labeled. Much of it was already packed in coolers for safe keeping on the journey, enough for the whole trip.

They were such dear people. We surely hated to see them move to southern Florida a couple of years later. Since then, we have tried to keep in touch.

TWO SPECIAL STREET FRIENDS

One is bound to become friends with a large variety of people in this kind of inner-city church work. Sometimes strange, most always needy, lonely, yet often lovable. Many people became regulars in our work-for-food program for the hungry. We would try to get to know them and help them in other ways too.

I never will forget the day there was a knock on the front door of the Center. When I went to answer it I was startled, even shocked! The scariest face I had ever seen peered at me from the darkness inside the vestibule. The man said his name was Eugene and he was hungry. I motioned him to come in.

After getting him to do a little work, I gave him some food. When I questioned him he explained about his scarred face. He had been working as a handyman in a filling station down south. There was an explosion at a gasoline pump, and the fire almost burned him to death. He was left with a mass of scars and incredibly wrinkled skin grafts.

Eugene became a regular visitor and would sometimes come to church.

One Saturday morning I came to the Center to do some maintenance work. I had a tool kit in my hands and was dressed in some old coveralls. As I climbed out of the old VW van at the back of the Center, Eugene was waiting. He was hungry and hoping to find the Center open.

Surprised to see me dressed as a maintenance man, he said, "Why Rev. Sid, I didn't know you could work!"

That morning he helped me do some odd jobs.

Apparently he grew real fond of this preacher guy, for shortly thereafter I had to go to the hospital for a hemorrhoid operation. Lo and behold, while recovering, a special visitor was brought in--my old friend, scar-faced Eugene! The young resident doctors took special interest in him. They were amazed at his extensive facial surgeries.

Jimmy, another street friend, had once been a merchant marine radioman. During World War II he had been riddled with machine gun bullets and survived. However, he could never get rid of his addiction to alcohol.

Like Eugene, Jimmy was a good-natured fellow always wanting to help out somehow. One day he heard me talking to someone about the old Friends Meeting House on the corner behind the Center. It was wrecked inside and loaded with all kinds of junk. The Board had promised to renovate it ten years before but never got around to it.

Glibly, I made the remark, "The best thing in the world for that old building would be a big fire. To just burn it down."

Wanting to please, Jimmy "went to work" that very night. He got into the old building and set it on fire. To his great disgust that fire was quickly extinguished by the city firemen. After waiting a few days for the building to dry out he tried again. This time he got picked up by the police. After explaining he was just trying to help clean up the neighborhood, he didn't stay in jail very long. However, his effort did gain the attention of certain officials, including the Mayor, who began the pressure that led to the rebuilding of that old Quaker Meeting House which had been built in 1781.

Mayor McKeldin came by the Center one day and found me sweeping the street around it, "Here, let me help you." He swept a little bit, then asked me, "Rev., what are we going to do about the old Meeting House over there?"

I answered, "I've been trying for 10 years to get the Board to keep their promise about the place. Maybe you'll have to *build a fire under them* from your side, and I'll do what I can from mine."

At the next Board Meeting, our Board President announced that the Mayor had sent word that we either renovate the old Meeting House or completely lose the opportunity to make use of it. Very soon architectural plans were completed, $50,000.00 raised, and a contractor was hired.

Our two oldest sons, Craig and Kirby, had summer jobs with the contractor. They helped with the tearing out and the early stage of rebuilding it. The city added more money for a special playground for our nursery school groups, another basketball court, and a small tree-lined park area with benches.

More about Jimmy. He had come from a devout Christian family in

CHAPTER 6: MCKIM DAYS (OR DAZE!)

South Carolina. After he was charged with arson and minor theft, he called a sister for help. His family wondered where he was and what had become of him. When his sister learned he was in Baltimore she came hoping to pray him out of his alcoholic condition. He did go home for a little while, but soon he was back in Baltimore with his drinking buddies.

Sometime later the newspapers reported a fire that killed a derelict, a very tragic ending for my friend Jimmy, whose last name--was Christian.

The big cities are so full of these sad stories. What a shame! But, praise God, many are set free by Jesus and get to live out their lives for Him!

Mayor McKeldin soon ascended the political ladder and became Governor of Maryland. We thought it might be a good idea to enlist his backing for a Jobs-For-Youth Program for Baltimore. Staff member Bob agreed. So we invited the Governor to have lunch with us at Haussner's, a famous East Baltimore restaurant. The Governor promised to see what he could do. Eventually the idea caught on and good things came of it, for which we were grateful.

In the middle 60's we also made an effort to establish a Baltimore Committee on Equity Housing. The plan was to rebuild the eastern corridor of Baltimore with decent townhouses instead of more high-rises. Then progressive area families could begin buying and making real homes for themselves. This would be a stabilizing force in the community.

After many meetings with key leaders of Urban Renewal and Housing, and pleading with them for help, they agreed to put several million dollars into the effort. Several years later the funds became available, and today the whole corridor is filled with town-houses, which hard-working people have bought.

Yet without strong connections with the Lord and His church, no neighborhood can become truly wholesome and stable.

Psalm 127:1...*Except the Lord build the house, they labour in vain that build it: except the Lord keep the city, the watchman waketh but in vain.*

During these two efforts, and as a result of giving Bob additional responsibilities at the Center and opportunities to represent McKim in speaking engagements, it seemed that Bob began maneuvering for my job.

When he first came to McKim, he was out of work and had no qualifications for the job. However, he had a convincing story of having surrendered his life to Jesus, and he wanted to do something for the

Lord in this field. He said he would work for "peanuts" in order to learn the work. At that time we had no money for taking on extra workers. I told him maybe we could find a few peanuts somewhere. He quickly grabbed at the chance and said, "I'll take it."

Bob became most dependable and knowledgeable in the work, until eventually he became Program Director for the Center. At this point he got a good case of "VA" and "GE" ("Vaulting Ambitions and "Galloping Ego", origin unknown). With the help of one or two Board members, his next move was for my job. This was a firing for me that didn't succeed. The Lord was still with me, and I was able to help him find a position with the city at much better pay. After that he went on to greater things, including super balloons for national parades!

THE DAVID YANKELOV STORY

Whenever possible I liked to walk down East Lombard Street, between Albemarle and Central Avenues, to greet and pass the time of day with the people I knew. On this particular sunny day I came near a kosher poultry shop operated by a very chubby Jewish man and his equally chubby sister.

David Yankelov was standing outside his store awaiting customers as was his habit. He was a very friendly person, and after we greeted each other, I asked, "What's new, David?"

He replied, "Rev., if you have a moment, I want to tell you a special story."

"Go ahead, David; I would like to hear it."

"Well for a long time, Rev., I had been suffering with hemorrhoids and was afraid to go to the doctor. Finally, I was in so much pain that I agreed to go to a specialist and he told me I had to have an operation right away.

"Because I was scared, I asked him if there was some kind of medicine I could take, but he said my only hope was surgery--immediately."

"Did you go?" I asked.

"Wait, Rev., let me tell you. I pleaded with the Doctor to give me a little time to think about it and he gave me two weeks. But I was so afraid I didn't know if I would go back.

"That night I got down on my knees by my bed and I began to pray like I'd never prayed before. 'Dear Lord, You know me, I'm David Yankelov, and I've got a terrible problem with hemorrhoids. The Doctor says I need a very serious operation right away. Lord, You know that I'm terrified about operations. I'm supposed to go back to the surgeon in two weeks, and, Lord, I'm almost scared to death right now. So I'm coming to You to ask that You do something for me. You made me, and I understand from Your Holy Word that You can fix things. So, Lord, I'm asking right now, while Your David is asleep, You send down an angel in the night and let him do the surgery--without any pain! Please Lord! Amen.'

"And you know, Rev., He did it! He sent His angel in the night to remove the hemorrhoids and when I awoke the next day, the hemorrhoids were gone. THEY WERE REALLY GONE! Praise The Lord!"

"David, that's wonderful. What did the doctor say?"

"He was dumbfounded and asked, 'David, where did you get the operation? I have never seen such a beautiful hemorrhoid operation!'

"I told him what had happened and I guess the surgeon is still shaking his head in amazement."

Many years later, on a Sunday after church, several of us decided to go over to a nearby Roy Rogers restaurant for some fried chicken. While sitting at our table, we noticed some old-time pictures of Baltimore scenes on the walls of the restaurant. A separate sign said these pictures were on loan from the Peale Museum. As our eyes moved from picture to picture, we were quite surprised to see one of David Yankelov's Kosher poultry shop on Lombard Street. Proud as a peacock, David was standing outside his establishment holding one of his choice birds. It brought a nostalgic smile to my face, and memories of his miracle.

This David Yankelov story was one with which I could fully sympathize. Two years before his miracle operation, I had to have a second one which I underwent without too much trouble. It was nothing like that earlier time in the Navy. I still cringe when I think of the pain I underwent after that first Navy operation.

At that time, the military surgeons cauterized wounds with a silver nitrate solution. That particular treatment was like having my southside set on fire for hours. I lay on my stomach shaking and crying and wondering what on earth I had done to deserve this. One can now understand why I especially liked the David Yankelov story, and his special prayer, and how the Lord healed him!

100 FIRED AGAIN AND AGAIN, PRAISE THE LORD!

MCKIM CENTER RENOVATION - EARLY 60'S

MCKIM CENTER GROUP - EARLY 60'S
Future Director of McKim, Dwight Warren dirctly behind Mr. Sid

MCKIM FREE NURSERY SCHOOL GRADUATION LED BY "MISS BETSY"

CHAP. 7

THE WAR ON POVERTY AND OTHER WARS

Except the Lord build the house, they labour in vain that build it; except the Lord keep the city, the watchman waketh but in vain.
                                                                     -Psalm 127:1

1960 saw young John F. Kennedy inaugurated as President of the United States and begin his "Great Society," with Lyndon Johnson as his Vice President. They and the Democrats began their immense plans to re-do America after the Eisenhower years, based on Keynesian economic theories, which had taken root during F.D. Roosevelt's presidency.

America was never told that Britisher Lord Maynard Keynes was a Fabian socialist and his ideas were pre-determined to engender this system in the U.S.A. Years later Socialist party head, Norman Thomas, said he no longer had to seek the U.S presidency because the Democrats were doing his party's work. The Fabian Socialist plan was to take over a nation by careful deception and gradualism, the wolf-in-sheep's clothing technique--as revealed by that inner-circle symbol back in England.

During the Roosevelt years, when their father Joseph was Ambassador to England, the Kennedy boys had studied at the London School of Economics, the center of Fabian Socialism. Early in the '30's, President Roosevelt had brought Lord Keynes, over to a Chair of Economics in one of the Ivy League Universities to further indoctrinate the future economists and leaders of America in Fabian Socialism. One of the perverted ideas behind this socialism is simply that a nation should not worry about debts and deficits; it can simply spend itself rich, into prosperity for all! What a devilish lie!

Worst still, Keynes was a sophisticated homosexual. According to God's Word, and practical observation, nothing truly good can ever come from such a person, for they are in absolute rebellion against God and His Word. They are under God's curse and can in no way be fruitful in a worthwhile sense.

Karl Marx and his God-denying followers (including Lenin, Mao,

Gorbachev, Castro, and Ortego et al) are in the same fix, under the same curse! Russia's miserable slave state and cursed collective farming system are super examples of God's preventing men and nations, who deny Him, from succeeding and prospering. They turn it into a collective state without serious belief in God or acceptance of God's way revealed in His Word and commandments and face failure after failure. Man by his own intelligence cannot collectively make a Great Society. They can all make it sound good by saying we'll take the wealth from the idle rich, eliminate them, divide it up among the workers--"from each according to his ability, to each according to his need"--then we shall have the collective Utopia of man. Bible students will quickly remember The Tower of Babel, another socialist collective effort without God of long, long ago in Genesis 11.

Psalms 9:17 tells the story...***The wicked shall be turned into hell, and all the nations that forget God.***

God's First Economic Law was "Keep the Garden." After Adam's Fall, the law became: ***..In the sweat of thy face*** (from now on) ***shalt thou eat bread...***(Genesis 3:19). Man has been dodging that Rule for ages! To his own hurt!

The Fabian socialist founders also had a slick trick in order to secure financing for their secret machinations and propaganda. They agreed among themselves to marry into money, each one to find himself a rich mate if he could. Then they would be free to devote themselves full-time in selling their perverted brand of economics, secretly seeking footholds of power in every field.

Intellectually, what may come out of such a homosexual mind may look good, sound good, and simulate good, but it "ain't" good, and can't bring good in the final analysis. Such people can be delivered by God if they will repent of their perversion, like a thief or a murderer, renounce it and turn to Jesus Christ to obey and live for Him. He will save them to the utmost - and is saving many today.

Early tragedy came to the Kennedy situation when he and others in his administration allowed Cuba to be taken over completely by the Communists under Fidel Castro, who brought in his Soviet comrades to make Cuba a communist missile, airplane and submarine fortress 90 miles off the shores of Florida. Also, it would be the launching pad for the Soviet-backed revolutions in Central America as was done in Nicaragua and other Central American republics.

Of course the assassination of Kennedy was a terrible tragedy for the nation on November 22, 1963. It's hard to forget the scenes of that day. How the nation almost stopped functioning in total shock and mourning, watching the funeral, the swearing-in of Lyndon Johnson, the capture and public murder of J. Harvey Oswald seen on T.V. All these

CHAPTER 7: THE WAR ON POVERTY AND OTHER WARS 103

years were filled with Civil Rights marches under the leadership of Rev. Martin Luther King Jr., setting fires of discontent everywhere he went, with his "Ghandian non-violent" tactics to bring about social change.

Dr. Ralph E. Abernathy in his book,[1] "AND THE WALLS CAME TUMBLING DOWN" (pp.125-126) tells about Rev. King's first visit to his home in Montgomery, and how they sat around after dinner discussing the "1954 Brown vs The Board of Education" Supreme Court decision ending segregation in American schools. He said the law now seemed to be on the side of the blacks, and that the federal government now might be helpful in their "fight for freedom." Even though Rev. King was a stranger to them, he uninhibitedly advocated "An active program to force the issue and to bring about freedom more rapidly." He said he was fully committed "To the preaching of a social gospel that would awaken the Christian churches and mobilize them in the fight against segregation." He indicated that he had been working on plans to do just that and when the time came to do battle, he hoped the churches would be ready.

Rev. Abernathy then asked Rev. King, "How long do you think it will be before we can make a move?"

He replied, "Not for a long time, at least several years. We must move slowly and carefully, so that when the time does come, we will be sufficiently prepared."

Rev. Abernathy's book is an excellent account of the Civil Rights struggle as he served as Rev. King's chief aide throughout. However, both he and Rev. King seem not to recognize that there's no lasting power in the social gospel! It's a fact: the social gospel never has saved a single soul nor does it save a society. Look at the Soviet Union!

Frankly, I had deep misgivings about the character and morality of both Kennedy and King. Later written revelations of constant infidelities by both men proved my distrust of them was well-founded.

The NAACP had some communist foundation roots (in W.E.B. Dubois and others), with long-range intentions of using black-white frictions and animosities to abet the eventual communist-socialist revolutionary take-over of America. This was a typical communist technique, as is being done right now in 1990-91 in South Africa, where the ANC is working to bring down the white government from their headquarters in Zambia. Few Americans know that the African National Congress is made up of 9/10ths communists in its directorate and one is a white KGB agent named Joe Slovo. This is Nelson Mandela's "Party."

---

[1] "And The Walls Came Tumbling Down" by Ralph D. Abernathy, copyright 1989, Harper & Ro, publishers, 10 E. 53rd St., N.Y., N.Y. 10022

So the racial and ideological fires were growing in those early '60's, which would explode violently, just before Palm Sunday in 1968, in Washington, Baltimore, Philadelphia, New York, Detroit, Chicago, and Los Angeles when Martin Luther King, Jr. was assassinated in Memphis by a man whose motivation never has been pinned down. The Baltimore riots of '68 would explode all around McKim Center.

The "great" socialist thinkers like Margaret Meade, Gurnar Myrdol, and Schlessinger were busy with their books and "great" ideas on how to eliminate poverty in the U.S.A. So President Johnson and his Democratic-controlled Congress undertook the "great" War on Poverty. Never once was it mentioned that children of all races, in order to get out of poverty anywhere in the world, must love and obey the Lord, work hard to gain a sound education, learn how to perform a good vocation, and then work hard at it six days a week and honor God all week, and especially on the seventh day of each week. Please check: Joshua 1, Deuter.5-6, Psalm 1, Proverbs 1, Matt.5,6:33,7:21-27, I Thess.5, II Thess.3:10-13, II Timothy 3.

We began saying in our talks, and to our Board, that unless there was an all-out war on Spiritual Poverty in America, the so-called War on Economic Poverty was doomed to failure. Pouring huge amounts of money, billions in fact, on poverty conditions, is like trying to save people by sprinkling water on them. It won't work!

We had found out that we can't social-work the devil and "hell" out of delinquents or anybody. But if we'll bring them to Jesus, He has the power to change the very hearts of boys and girls, men and women and make new creatures out of them. HE has the power to get the devil and "hell" out. (II Cor.5:17). This is the age-old GOOD NEWS of the GOSPEL. As Jesus tells us in John 3, to have a truly blessed life here and hereafter, people must be BORN-AGAIN by God's Holy Spirit. This NEW BIRTH comes through FAITH IN JESUS! John 10;14:6!

People have to be persuaded that they must turn away, by JESUS' POWER, from wickedness, immorality, self-indulgence, greed, hate, unbelief and disobedience to God, to go GOD'S WAY by receiving and following JESUS CHRIST. Most early Americans were doing or trying to do this. This is WHY America became great! Read "The Light and The Glory" by Peter Marshall Jr. and David Manual.

It was interesting to observe that some of the outstanding and successful black athletes never seemed to approve of the NAACP & Martin Luther King Jr's tactics. Maybe they gave lip service to them, but that famous 5 ft. 4 in. tall half-back for the Washington Red Skins football team, Buddy Young, would always say that he belonged to the NAALP (the one I've always belonged to) The National Association For Advancement of Little People - Going God's Way. This Way advances

CHAPTER 7: THE WAR ON POVERTY AND OTHER WARS

every person no matter what color! We were seeing it happen at McKim.

In the Fall of 1964, after hearing of possible grants for Inner-City programs, the Staff and Board of McKim wondered if we could secure such grants for our work -- since we were working with the under-privileged -- with two homes for recovery of delinquents, a successful interracial Pre-school Program, and a Community Center.

There was strong pressure from part of our Board to do so, but I felt that with the recent Earl Warren Supreme Court rulings in '62 & '63, against Prayer and Bible Reading in the schools, such federal grants would have undesirable strings attached. They sure did! After discussing it with the then Board President, Mr. Walter Lohr, a perceptive layman, I went ahead and applied to the Federal agency in Washington for consideration for grants for three major areas of our program: the Pre-School program, the Community Center program and The Boys Homes. After perhaps a month, a huge, official brown envelope from Washington came containing many newly written forms, pamphlets and instructions concerning proper applications for grants. The cover letter indicated that we seem to be working in areas they would want to help.

If we would fill out the 30 pages of details and return it with a special form that the Board itself must fully agree to and sign, then they would be happy to consider us further. The special form, designated the "001" form which we must agree to, contained the absolute requirement of the elimination of all religious teaching, religious artifacts, and religious requirements for the staff. After I got over my shock at this blatant exclusion of God and His teaching, and support of His workers, I called the Board president to tell him what we had received from the much publicized War On Poverty main office in Washington. I said that neither I nor any of our staff of nearly twenty-five could approve working under these restrictions. "We are Christians and we're not about to exclude God, His teaching, His Bible, His Son Jesus, or His servants from any area of the work."

Mr. Lohr, head of a large telephone answering service, said, "I fully agree. We don't need their money if that's what they require. Tell them, 'No Thanks.'" His partner, Mr. Bruce Danzer, also a Board member and fine Presbyterian layman, said, "We will not eliminate the Christian Emphasis." That was that for a time.

We wrote back saying "Thanks a lot but no thanks. We can not accept such terms." We reminded them of such scriptures as Psalm l; 33:12; 127:1; Matt.6:33; 7:24-27; II Tim.3:14-17.

Some on our Board and the upper echelon liberal leaders of the Presbyterian Church, then in power, kept pushing us to secure the grants. So early in 1965, a national Presbyterian conference was arranged for executives in the Presbyterian Homes, Orphanages, Schools, and Hospitals to be instructed on grant applications and fund raising in general. Jim Elmore and I went to the conference in Chicago. The most important speaker ended his instructions and comments by saying, "Don't mutilate your programs just to get federal or other grants, for it is still true that 'Whoever pays the piper will call the tune.'" We returned and told our Board this, and it seemed to take the pressure off for a time.

Our support from the local churches had grown considerably over the years, and the former Director of Presbyterian National Missions, Dr. Alex Sharp, said that our McKim work in Baltimore was probably the best of its type in the country, and that he fully supported it, especially with its Christian emphasis.

Having heard of McKim, some research workers from the Washington Office of Economic Opportunity, came to McKim to observe it's pre-school program. We were having at that time two sessions a day dealing with some 40-50 children, and having excellent contacts with the homes and families and good results with the children. God and Jesus, prayer and the Bible were key parts of the program. We pleaded with these researchers to keep these Faith Ingredients in any Head Start program, for the children's and America's sake. Education without God, the Bible and Jesus is doomed to failure, as all the great American leaders have said in the past until this century. The Psalmist puts it in these words in Psalm 127:1..***Except the Lord build the house they labour in vain that build it: except the Lord keep the city, the watchman waketh but in vain.***

Needless to say they didn't heed our appeal. I would dread to analyze the actual results of the so-called Head Start program, most of which have proved remarkably futile and pagan! May God have mercy on America! It had such a good beginning. All the early Colleges and Universities (over 100 of them) were founded to produce highly trained and dedicated ministers of the Gospel and teachers of the Bible.

The liberals on our Board, the Presbytery and the National Mission office in New York arranged for an official survey of our situation in the Spring of '68. They reported back to our Board that it would be wise to pursue federal grants for our work, even to agreeing to eliminate all explicit religious emphasis. Of course this meant removing all those who stood in the way--me in particular! Had our friend, Dr. Alex Sharp, still been the Director of the Board of National Missions this would not have happened. Apparently he had been swept aside by the same liberal movement in the Church in the late 60's.

Education without divine guidance is a fraud! The story is told that

CHAPTER 7: THE WAR ON POVERTY AND OTHER WARS

one day President Theodore (Teddy) Roosevelt was in his special train car waiting to leave Washington for a brief trip. As he and some friends were sitting there, they watched a repair crew working on another track nearby. Someone began commenting on what a shame it was that these men had such poor prospects for life because of their meager education. "They would be restricted always to this hard physical labor. No doubt they would be forced, when no one was looking, to break into boxcars and steal. Surely we must greatly improve our secular educational system so this won't be necessary, so their future can be bright."

Teddy looked at his education-minded companion and said, "It's true that without powerful moral controls working in a man's life, and no police control nearby, when you turn your back on him, he will break into the boxcar to steal. However, if you give them all kinds of secular education without careful instruction in God's Word to give him moral restraints, he or they will end up stealing the whole railroad! We must not try to educate our people without God's Word and His requirements for a good life here and hereafter." (These may not be his exact words but are similar and befitting this God-fearing President.)

It should also be noted here that one of the early proponents of free education in America in the 1840's, Horace Mann, a Quaker, strongly pushed his views throughout America in those days saying "Give us in this great land free public education for all our children, and in 100 years we will have eliminated all poverty and crime."

Education for all has been achieved, but because education in the things of God and His Word has been removed from all, our nation is bogged down in crime, drugs, pornography, and plagues from immorality such as AIDS and other deadly sexually transmitted diseases. Marriage and marital fidelity are mocked; over 27,000,000 first degree murders of babies have been committed in the United States in the last 17 years; street violence and murders are endemic across our country. Yes, there is a Heaven to gain Going God's Way, but a fiery Hell to pay if we don't! If America doesn't stop its slaughter of unborn babies soon (a horrible holocaust worse than Hitler's), and turn back to God and His Word, the Bible, America will face a most terrible, fiery judgment from God soon! May God have mercy on our nation and help us to turn back soon to Him and His Word, His Way.(Ps.33:12, Ps.127:l and Ps.2)

CAST-IRON STOMACH, SPECIAL AUDIT
AND THE GREAT PSYCHIATRIST

Over the years, through some of the college student workers and our growing Junior Staff, McKim Center had developed an outstanding wrestling team and a fine weight-lifting program. In the wrestling league we were always near to winning the championship. But our mats were so ancient, patched, and resewn, they were ready for the trash truck.

That winter, knowing the funds were available, we arranged to buy some new mats without first getting the Center Committee or the full Board to approve the expenditure of several hundred dollars. When my unfriendly friends on the Board heard about it, they immediately demanded an explanation plus an internal audit by a retired C.P.A. member of the Board.

From the beginning the Lord had warned me to always be able to account for every penny that ever came in. So we had kept a very accurate accounting system going and had given accurate financial reports during the years. When the demand by the Board for an audit came, we were happy to comply. Not only had we been one of the major money raisers for the Association, but also one of its best contributors, making sure always that more than our tithe went back into the work. (Another reason why the Lord had been blessing, as in Malachi 3:10-12.)

The day came when this elderly board member came to begin his audit. We had a friendly preliminary conversation at the office desk, at which time he seemed quite pleased to tell me that the last minister that he had audited in a large local church ended up with a serious case of stomach ulcers. No doubt he was quite surprised when I chuckled and told him that he could not possibly do the same for me because, "the Lord has given me a cast-iron stomach."

Our secretary then was asked to show him all our records and answer all his questions. He searched for a couple of hours but lost interest. Apparently he could find nothing wrong. And there was no more "flak" from the Board about it!

During our entire 14 years, we did our best to lift up the Name of Jesus, somehow, daily. Maybe sometimes we didn't do it well or wisely, but we tried. Yet it seemed I never lacked for detractors or resistance or actual efforts to eliminate me, from time to time, from the organization. Also I never lacked real friends, especially One named Jesus! What A Friend He is!

The liberals on the Board agreed that I was a good money raiser, and perhaps effective and energetic in the operations, perhaps even grudgingly admitting successful achievements, but that "religious stuff" got on important people's nerves, theirs and some of the non-religious staff, and certain Church leaders. It was completely unnecessary as far as they were concerned. To them what was needed was just non-religious social work. (I repeat: Non-religious social work never saved

CHAPTER 7: THE WAR ON POVERTY AND OTHER WARS

a single soul!). Therefore about every two years, like in politics, an effort would be mounted to remove me from the organization.

During this time my unfriendly friends on the Board decided that I needed psychiatric counseling, supposedly to develop better working relationships with the Board and staff. It seemed there were some serious disagreements on both sides of the picture (and naturally so). The love of Jesus was not the key motivating factor in their lives. So a Board member suggested that his big company had access to the services of a highly placed psychiatrist from New York, who was coming from time to time to counsel his key people on personnel relations. He would be glad to arrange for him to interview me in their conference room when he came again. At the meeting where this was being discussed, I was asked if this would be okay with me, and I said, "Sure, No problem. Perhaps he can help."

On the way home to tell Betsy what was about to happen, I was fussing a little bit with the Lord and saying, "Lord, you know better than I what they are up to. This group wants very much to find some psychiatric flaw or missing link by which they can hang me or finally ship me off to 'Timbuktu,' that proverbial place of exile."

The Lord answered, "It's ok. Go ahead and take his examination or counseling and don't forget, I'm still with you." I don't remember what Betsy's reaction to this was. With all my battles, she may have been wondering about my sanity too.

The very next evening the Lord gave me great assurance when He brought me to the Scripture in II Tim. 1:7.... **For God hath not given us the spirit of fear, but of power, and of love and of a sound mind.** Also II Tim.1:12 ...**For the which cause I also suffer these things: nevertheless I am not ashamed: for I know whom I have believed; and am persuaded that He is able to keep that which I have committed unto him against that day.** "That day" in the Scripture means the future Judgement Day, but "that day" was about to come to me, right then.

Soon I was alerted by the Board member when to come meet with this psychiatrist. I asked the Lord what I should do in preparation for it, and He told me, "Just relax. You know I'm with you."

I went into that examination, as we used to say, relaxed as a "hound-dog", enjoyed meeting the psychiatrist, enjoyed taking the battery of tests he put me through, and came back the next day for more. We had a final discussion at his hotel that night. I believe he was a Jewish man and probably was intrigued by my faith in Jesus. We had a good talk. I remember telling him that I had an idea for a book, which would present a strong case that every man and woman has been created by God, not only with a soul and spirit to be in touch with Him, but also with a mind to be in touch with practical life and to be creative in the world. Even our hands were designed by God, not just to feed ourselves, or twiddle our thumbs, or to scratch, but also to be guided by our minds in creative work, however lowly. I felt that no person could ever be spiritually, mentally and physically adjusted and happy unless he was using his hands in some kind of productive work for the Lord such as: gardening, knitting, sewing, painting, farming, building or driving trucks, tractors, planes, etc. But certainly not smoking, dice rolling, or nail biting!

He replied, "Don't bother, I've already written the book."

I forgot to ask him the name of his book. Before I left him, he agreed to send me a copy of his official report to our Board of Directors.

About a month later, his report arrived with a brief cover note. Oh yes, during his examination, often when I couldn't recall certain answers, the Lord would give me special recall and the answer would come flying in. Praise His Holy Name. In the report the psychiatrist said, in a nutshell:

> "That their Executive Director ranked in the upper two or three percent of the intelligencia of the nation. That they were fortunate to have him working for them. That he could easily be making a much, much higher salary somewhere else. That there were a few minor problems which could be worked out with a bit of patience on all sides."

I do not recall ever hearing the slightest mention of this report in later Board meetings. The Lord had won another big battle. To Him be all the praise, glory, and thanksgiving! Yet there were other more dreadful storms ahead, and storm clouds still unseen at least by me.

I would be a rank ingrate if I didn't mention an amazing defense the Lord raised up for me in a Board meeting about this time. The Board had ordered several of the Center Staff to come to a meeting at a Board member's home. After I had given my regular report, I was told that I would not be needed any further that evening. One of the staff who had been asked to appear at this meeting to give such evidence as she could concerning my faults and failings was the young secretary for me and the Center. Beth Armiger was one of the finest Christian girls we had ever known and had been working with us intermittently at the Center since her high school days. She was a very sweet, attractive and mild-mannered young lady, one with deep Christian convictions and strong character, but could react with fiery indignation if pushed too far.

Well, that night at the Board meeting, apparently all that she heard set her off into a fiery defense of me. When that meeting was over the attacking forces were left demolished on the battlefield. When seemingly no one else would defend me, the Lord raised up this lovely, mild-mannered Joan of Arc to single-handedly wipe the enemy out with His holy fire! Hallelujah. Glory to God! Thank you, Jesus! And Beth!

THE DEAD-END CONFERENCE IN CINCINNATI

It was about springtime 1966 that another Health, Education and Welfare conference of the church was being held in Cincinnati. Two men from the nearby Presbyterian Hospital planned to go, as well as Jim and I from the McKim Association. Just before we left an interesting phone call came from Doctor Chalfonte, who had been years before a medical missionary to China. He said, "Sid, I hear you are going to the Cincinnati Church Conference on HEW."

"Yes, I am, Dr. Chalfonte."

"Well I have something I want to ask you to do for me."

"You name it, Doctor. I'll be glad to do whatever I can for you there."

"I'm sure you know how things have been going in these areas of the church recently. Will you please put in a good word for JESUS verbally at that conference?"

"Dr. Chalfonte, I fully intend to do just that. I wouldn't be going if I didn't plan to do so. Jim Elmore is going with me, and together we should be able to get a good word for the Lord in, one way or the other."

"Good, May the Lord bless you. Have a good trip."

"Thanks and God bless you, Doctor Chalfonte."

In a very real way it was a dead-end conference, a complete waste of time and money. But before I tell you how it came out, let me tell you briefly about our meeting with a famous comedian in the elevator of that hotel. We were having dinner at the hotel with our hospital friends from Baltimore, and suddenly one of them said, "Hey, isn't that the famous comedian, Henny Youngman, eating at a nearby table?"

Well, Jim and I didn't know Henny Youngman from Adam at that moment, but we were told he was one of the top one-line, stand-up comedians in the country, "squeaking out" a little violin music in between jokes, like the more famous Jack Benny of that day.

Well, the next morning after finishing one of the "blah" meetings, Jim and I headed for the elevator to go to our room for a few minutes rest before lunch. We moved to the back side of the elevator, after pushing our floor number, and in walks this tall comedian. In a very friendly way he looks down on us and says, "Well, hello again. Didn't I see you before?"

We nodded.

He then grinned and asked, "What do you guys do? Where are you from?"

Jim replied in his drawl, "We're from Baltimore, and I run a home for delinquents."

He looked at me, and I said, "I'm also from Baltimore and run a community center for gangs."

He raised his eyebrows as if about to ask another question.

Jokingly, I smiled up at him and quickly asked, "By the way, what do you do for a living?"

He answered, "I just ignore it!"

Apparently his night club act was not going well, so as we were leaving the elevator, over the heads of the people we heard a falsetto voice projecting a plaintiff cry, saying, "S-e-n-d- -p-e-o-p-l-e".

We went on through that day and the next to other listless, aimless meetings. At the final summation meeting by a panel of experts on what was happening in all these areas of Church work and what positive direction could be given for the future, there was still no real agreement. The final expert read one of his favorite humorous poems, or one written for the occasion, which was all about the existential blessings and joy of confusion! So the conference was ending on the note of confusion, confessing that we don't have the answers.

There were a couple of microphones in the aisles for people to ask questions of the speakers or to respond in some way. These were the waning moments of the conference. Up to this moment we had heard absolutely NOTHING about the sure ways of JESUS nor about His Word, nor about the guidance of His Holy Spirit, nor anything about God's solutions or answers for life's problems or difficulties. Nothing about God's wisdom for human life!

Saying a quick prayer, "Help me Lord," I jumped for the nearest mike and said, "Ladies and Gentlemen, I want to make a brief statement. We've all been here for some time as representatives and leaders in various units of Church work across the nation, and I've yet to hear any discussion or presentation of God's Biblical answers to man's confusion, problems and dilemmas. There have been no references to JESUS or GOD'S WRITTEN WORD, and to what HE can do in our time to give people abundant, joyful lives, victorious lives, unconfused and holy lives. Nothing about His power to give life meaning and worth and to spiritually and powerfully solve every problem of those who love and follow Him. I've heard no references to the LOVE OF CHRIST constraining us to serve, to love, to make HIM known, Who is the Way, the Truth and the Life; without Whom no man can come to the Heavenly Father.

CHAPTER 7: THE WAR ON POVERTY AND OTHER WARS   113

"Let me say finally that it's like a husband and his wife. If the husband doesn't tell his wife he loves her at least once a week, he's in real trouble. And the same with our relationship to Jesus Christ. We've got to be expressing our love to Him at least once a week or we're in terrible trouble. Thank you for listening."

I could sense a slight rise of sentiment against what I was saying at the beginning, but at the end there were so many people at the conference who had been hoping for a Word from the Lord, and for the Lord, that there was a strong spontaneous applause for my remarks. Thank God that I didn't fail in my promise to Dr. Chalfonte and in my commitment to Jesus Christ.

My statement concerning love for the wife and the Lord, however, was woefully inadequate! Our expression of love for each other and for the Lord needs to be a DAILY ONE! That's the truly blessed and fruitful way of walking together, living together, working together in VICTORY!

PRAYER AND THE BIBLE WERE ESSENTIAL
TO THE MCKIM NURSERY SCHOOL AND CENTER!
WITHOUT THESE KEY INGREDIENTS EDUCATION IS A FRAUD!
"BRING THE LITTLE CHILDREN UNTO ME" - JESUS

114   FIRED AGAIN AND AGAIN, PRAISE THE LORD!

MCKIM CENTER
AND CHURCH
SUMMER BIBLE SCHOOL
← PARADE IN '60'S

DWIGHT WARREN
FINE YOUTH LEADER IN '60'S
FUTURE CENTER DIRECTOR

MCKIM CLUB-WORK CREW -60'S

↓

TOP YOUTH LEADER
RAY TILLERY

GREAT COLT LINEBACKER
FRIEND DON SHINNICK - 60'S

CHAPTER 7: THE WAR ON POVERTY AND OTHER WARS   114A

"EXPLORER" CLUB CAMPING
AT MILLERS' FARM
WITH OUR GREAT FRIEND
JIM ELMORE,
DIRECTOR MCKIM BOYS HAVEN

TIME FRAME THE 60'S

MCKIM WRESTLERS

CHAMPION WRESTLERS

THE BIG CATCH IN PANAMA CITY
MCKIM BOYS JERRY & JIMMY WITH KIRBY & CRAIG

AWARDS NIGHT
& TROPHY TIME

114B FIRED AGAIN AND AGAIN, PRAISE THE LORD!

MCKIM SEWING –
CLUB LED BY
MRS. SARAH SHAW

MCKIM'S "BIG" OFFICE
MARGE, BOB & MR. SID

RIGELLS WITH 4 SONS
CHRIS, JOE, CRAIG & KIRBY
FAMILY REUNION, 1958

"JESUS
LOVES
ME,
THIS
I KNOW
FOR
THE BIBLE
TELLS
ME SO!"

CHAP. 8

A TOTALLY UNEXPECTED WAR -- OR FIRING

And Jesus said unto her, "Neither do I condemn thee, go and sin no more."
— John 8:11

MY BETSY LEAVES ME

A totally unexpected and most devastating event occurred in July, 1966. Late one Saturday afternoon, I shook one of our boys as he was telling a lie. Out of that shaking came some shocking truths! For I heard my wife of 20 years angrily blurt out, "I don't love you any more, I want a divorce. I'm in love with someone else."

With all I had put her through perhaps she had ample reason from the world's view-point, but I was not prepared for this. I was shocked beyond words. There had been two awful dreams showing me something terribly wrong in Betsy's life and so with our marriage, but I couldn't believe them. So I put them aside as foolish nightmares.

My breath and heart seemed to stop when she spoke those words! "This just can't be possible," I kept thinking. I walked in a daze but silently began looking to Jesus for His guidance on what to do. "Lord, please help me." Then I found myself saying to Betsy, "I'll take you and the boys far away from here. That will stop this horrible mess."

Betsy was shaking her head and bluntly replied, "I won't go!"

Then, as I calmed down, I seemed to begin hearing the Lord saying, "Easy does it. No harsh words, no threats. Let her go. Let Me handle this. Trust Me." We sat on our little back porch talking calmly for a quite a while. I felt led to urge Betsy to go to her parents at "The Bight" and pray diligently about her desire to leave me, to get a divorce, and to marry someone else. Who it was, I had no idea.

As the sun set and twilight surrounded us on that tiny porch, I was able to say, "Betsy, Dear, you know I love you and want you to be my wife always. Because I love you I will not make a fight over anything. The Lord is leading me to say very carefully that if you come back it will have to be according to God's Word, to me alone!" Obviously there was a secret affair of which I knew nothing---'til now.

How I lived through that night, I'll never know. Only God's grace kept me alive. It seemed my breath and heart stopped many times! There seemed to be no remorse on her part--and certainly no repentance. How could this be happening to us? To my Betsy? Who had no guile in her, so I'd always thought. I never dreamed I would be fired by my own wife. But it was happening!

As usual we got up that Sunday morning and went on to church together. I preached. What? I don't remember. We felt we must keep this bad news from the boys, and from the church at this point.

After church, Betsy and the boys left for the "Bight" to be with her parents. I did not know if I would ever see them again. I had to drive to a summer camp to pick up some McKim campers that afternoon.

Through that week I was fasting, weeping, and praying constantly and working in that dazed shock, thinking no one else knew, except the Lord. One other person did though, our secretary Marge Nuckolls, who had become a close friend of Betsy's.

Through my nights at home alone that week I began doing some needed repairs Betsy had wanted for some time. Our little part-Dachshund dog "Nickel" kept me company as I worked and prayed. Each night I would call Betsy at the "Bight" briefly to see how they were and share any Word the Lord had given me---for us. One was Psalm 73!

Miraculously, the Lord brought her back the following Friday, her love for me still missing and not restored, not for a long time. But He brought her back and eventually restored her love completely. Praise His Holy Name forever! Only by grace, God's Amazing Grace, were we delivered from that miserable mess and deadly folly. She will tell you how God did it in her own words. First, she wants to describe something of her early years.

BETSY TELLS HER BACKGROUND

Much different from my husband's background, I grew up in the Marlborough Blenheim Hotel on the corner of Park Place and Boardwalk in Atlantic City, N.J. I was very fat as a baby. One of the first old family movies shows my sister Cindy feeding me ice cream! So fat that I didn't walk until age two. A kiddy car was my means of transportation, and, oh yes, pushing along on my seat with my legs from side to side. Before moving to the apartment at the hotel, I pushed the kiddy car, with me in it, down the basement steps, probably just bounced around a bit, but gave my mother a fright.

Life at the hotel was so different. We ate most of our meals in the children's dining room, with Nanan our governess, while our parents ate in the main dining room with the guests, keeping a watchful eye on the

CHAPTER 8: A TOTALLY UNEXPECTED WAR--OR FIRING

service. If I had been a good girl, not playing dirigible with my spinach, Nanan would take me to the hotel lobby to hear the chamber music. I would try to dance to the music and the hotel guests would ask,

"Why do they keep that little boy in dresses so long?" (My parents kept my hair in a boyish bob.)

One particular Jewish family who visited the hotel regularly during those years used to bring special gifts to me. Amazingly, 45 years later this was to be one of the Lord's miraculous connections with their granddaughter in Israel!

We attended Friends Grammar School and my sister Cindy, 4 years older than I, and my brother Kirby, 3 years older, disliked having to walk with me the ten blocks on the Boardwalk to school. I would keep having to cry out, "Wait for me!"

Although of Quaker background (my Dad's folks, Pop and Tata, used the familiar "thee and thy" when they spoke to members of the family) my family was not very religious. Sunday was a day for ice skating at the Convention Hall, or picnics in the pine-barren woods of south Jersey. We used to have some special softball games at a favorite picnic spot called "Lost Farm". I can remember one outing when we were skipping smooth stones on a lake, and my brother, Kirby, threw a stone that hit Pappy on the head. It made a lasting impression on me, as well as on Pappy.

Tata did not think Atlantic City, the World's Playground, was the place for us children in the summer. So from the age of nine through sixteen, for eight summers, I attended Ragged Mountain Camp in Andover, New Hampshire. This was an Episcopal camp. As well as learning to swim (with coaches from the Princeton swimming team), ride horses, cook out and crafts, we learned about camp spirit, and every morning began with prayer. On Sundays we participated in a church service in which we sang hymns like "Ode To Joy of Man's Desiring," These were just a mumble of sounds to me until I became a believer and their meaning about Jesus became alive. I thank the Lord for those eight precious summers at Ragged Mountain Camp.

The only other Religious experience I remember was attending Friends First Day School in the seventh grade. After hearing stories about Jesus as a good man and singing hymns like "I Would Be True" and "Dear Lord and Father of Mankind" (Tata's favorite), we would attend Quaker meeting for the last half hour. There, the elders of the meeting would sit on the facing benches in the front, women on one side, men on the other. All would sit in silence unless "The Inner Light," (which we would call the Holy Spirit), prompted someone to get up and share his thoughts. Otherwise, the meeting was silent and would end by the men on the facing benches shaking hands. (Back in the beginning of the Quaker movement in the 1700's with George Fox being truly led by the Spirit and meditating on God's Word, it must have been a real Spirit-filled worship experience.)

I have a vivid memory of Pearl Harbor Day, December 7, 1941. I was 14 years old. It was Sunday afternoon, we were walking home on the Boardwalk from the Figure Skating Club (my parents were the presidents of the club) at the Convention Hall. When we arrived at the entrance of the Blenheim, the windows of the Japanese shop had been smashed in. Here this Japanese family was as American as we were, and it didn't make sense to me. The hotels were soon taken over by the Army and we moved in with Pop and Tata on Harrisburg Avenue.

By this time, in the eleventh grade, my weight was above 160 pounds (I had been taking thyroid medicine since age nine), and my girl friend was dating my boy friend, Henry, who later became a mortician. So it was time to do something about my weight. I sent away for a diet, beauty and exercise program called the "DuBarry Success Course." Part of the program was thumping exercises to bounce the fat off your hips and arms. Now, it so happened that my bedroom was directly above Pop 'n Tata's sitting room and when cracks appeared in the living room ceiling, I was speedily relegated to the basement for my exercises!

Praise the Lord, the program was fairly successful! After my senior year of High School in New Orleans, where Pappy was stationed in the Army's "Navy", training crash boat crews for rescuing downed pilots at sea, we lived for the summer in Gulfport, Mississippi. I had a job at the Markham Hotel swimming pool (making $80 a month). By then my weight was 135 pounds, and a sailor named Sid came in swimming and you know the story from there.

During my freshman year at Swarthmore College, as we were writing daily to each other, I can remember asking my roommate, Zell Hall, "How can I be a minister's wife, when I don't believe in Jesus?"

To which Zell replied, "Don't worry, you will."

During the few visits we had together when Sid had Navy leave, we would read together the Gospel of John, and Sid would patiently answer my questions about Christians and Jesus. As we looked at the beautiful nature around us, who could doubt there was a creator God?

I'll never forget the time in June of '45 when I was to meet Sid in his hometown of Panama City, Florida, to be introduced to his family. The war was still raging. My Dad and Mom and Mary were living in St. Petersburg where Pappy was preparing for his secret mission in Japanese waters. My sister Cindy's husband, Freeman, was in the Seabees in the Japanese theater and brother Kirby was in the Navy. So Cindy accompanied me on the all-night train to Jacksonville, Florida. While she went on to visit our folks, I transferred to the New Orleans

CHAPTER 8: A TOTALLY UNEXPECTED WAR--OR FIRING

train to see Sid. But, it wasn't that easy! The train was delayed leaving Jacksonville a couple of hours (waiting for some politician), so by the late afternoon when we reached Cottondale, Florida, the connecting Bay Line train had already left. There I was, 18 years old in a seemingly deserted, tiny northwest Florida town; Panama City still 50 miles away, and it was dark already! Fortunately, there was another girl trying to get to Tyndall Airforce Base in Panama City to visit her husband. So we went together and for $7 apiece, hired a cab to take us to Panama City. We arrived at the train station, but no Sid. At the Railway Express office I found a phone to call his home. His younger sister, Judy, came to meet me in a cab. It seems Sid was with a man meeting my cabmate to tell her the terrible news her husband had been killed in a flight training accident that morning. Both were hitchhiking up to Cottondale to meet us.

Judy, Mamma Rigell and all the family made me feel so welcome and there were a dozen red roses in my room from my dear fiance. Soon he returned and we had a wonderful visit with the family much of it on the lovely white sands of the Panama City Beach, the family staying altogether in one of the Larkway cottages. I do remember attending church with them at the old Wallace Memorial Presbyterian Church and wondering if I should take communion with them or not. I had so much to learn! I took the communion, and I believe the Lord honored that step of faith.

Sid had to return to Minneapolis, where his Navy electronics countermeasure group awaited orders for China. I traveled by bus to join my Mom and Dad and sister, Cindy, in St. Petersburg, Florida before returning to Atlantic City for the summer, to help care for my niece and nephews. We didn't see each other again until the following January 1946, when Sid, on his way to be discharged from the Navy, came to see me at Swarthmore. Of course, we were in contact by daily letters, special delivery on Sunday and phone calls.

During our January visit when we set the wedding date, for March 2, I can remember wondering, "What will we talk about all these years ahead?" But when you're in love it doesn't really matter!!

A VERY DIFFICULT STORY
(As told by Betsy)

This is a difficult part of our lives to share, and oh, how I wish it had never happened, because of the devastating pain and anguish I caused my husband. Yet if it will give hope to any couples who feel their marriage is "on the rocks", we want to share this almost tragic part of our lives! Praise God, we know The Lord can save and heal marriages,

He has done it for us, and He can do it for you. So we share this hateful chapter in our lives.

As St. Paul says in II Corinthians 1:3b-4 **Blessed be the God of all comfort; who comforteth us in all our tribulation, that we may be able to comfort them which are in any trouble, by the comfort wherewith we ourselves are comforted of God.**

We had been living in Baltimore several years, with a happy home and four fine sons! Sid was busy with the McKim work, morning, noon and night. One night a week I would attend classes at the University of Maryland night school working toward a degree in Early Childhood Education. The Nursery School at McKim was going full blast with two sessions and we wanted to be accredited by the State Board of Education, but needed a "certified" teacher! It was a vicious circle. My practice teaching didn't count because the school was not accredited. So, I was going to night school while Sid baby sat one night a week. I know I was still deeply in love with my husband, because for one of the assigned papers for an English class, I wrote about my husband and my love for him in such glowing terms, the professor couldn't believe it.

I was not firm enough with the rearing of our boys. Most of our disagreements came about the discipline of the children, when I would take the side of the "little darlings," making excuses for them while they got away with "murder." Sid was real busy with the five phases of the McKim work and trying to keep the Board happy. So with the housework, care of the kids, the Nursery School, Sunday School and the Church Bulletins, I became president of the "Poor-Little-Me-Club." My Mother unknowingly fed my "Pity Party," saying "Poor Betsy"...So---I let Satan in and he had a "field day", almost wrecking our marriage completely!

In 1966, I made the terrible mistake of trying to witness to one of the opposite sex, even making a date for coffee. One thing led to another and, before I knew it, I had let Satan trick me into believing I was in love with this other man, into breaking the 7th commandment, and of course, lying to cover up. It's truly God's great mercy that we were never caught, me a minister's wife. I became so hardened to things of the Lord, and only seldom would I feel any warning from the Holy Spirit, as when hearing Jesus' Words: **You cannot serve two masters.** I knew I was leading a double life.

My poor dear husband, trusted me completely. He was struggling through these battles at McKim, while I was doing my own thing. We had two cars and a part-time baby sitter. I had started smoking secretly and was "going down the tube," and didn't care or see what I was doing. I was truly going to Hell!

The one bright light in the situation was the Center's Spirit-filled

CHAPTER 8: A TOTALLY UNEXPECTED WAR--OR FIRING

secretary, Marge Nuckolls. (We had met her and the part-time social worker, Bonnie Harmon, through the Spirit-filled Director of the Boys Haven, Jim Elmore). I could confide in Marge and she knew what I was doing. She did not condone it, and yet did not condemn me, but would pray with me, and sometimes in this strange language. She would just say, "Jesus is so wonderful that we just run out of words in English to Praise Him with!"

So one night in early July when the two older boys, Craig and Kirby, were working for the summer with their Aunt Sissy and Uncle Walter in Panama City, Florida, Sid and I had a disagreement over disciplining the children, and I told my husband I wanted a divorce, that I was in love with someone else. Poor Sid was devastated, and I had no compassion. The next day was Sunday, and he had to preach! With God's grace he got through two services and then suggested I go with the two younger boys to Grandma Gin's and Pappy's to decide what I was going to do. He stayed at home fasting, praying, and weeping with "Nickel," our faithful dog. All the time he had to continue the work at McKim.

Marge Nuckolls, my "forever sister," called me at the "Bight" to give me the Scripture, Romans 8:13 **The suffering of the present time is not worthy to be compared with the glory which shall be revealed in us.** I thought I was suffering, not having an inkling as to what I was putting Sid through. After about four days, I realized for the sake of the Church, of Jesus and of the children, I needed to go back to Sid and keep a proper home. Sid had made it plain that, if I came back, there must be no more double life and I agreed.

So back we went to 615 Colorado Avenue. Sid had put up big signs to welcome us home, and bent over backwards to make us feel at home and loved. We started having "vitamin breaks," telling each other we loved each other every few hours. Of course he was afraid to let me out of his sight, and it was a long while before he could trust me again, a long while before the bond of trust was healed. Did he forgive me? Yes, he did, with all his heart!

That fall the FGBMFI sponsored a free dinner for ministers and their wives with special Spirit-filled speakers, such as Dr. Dennis Bennett and Dr. David Duplesse. Of course Marge, Bonnie and many others, like Pastor Jim Mulholland from Randallstown, were praying that we and other Presbyterian ministers would go. Amazingly, we did go, and we can remember having our defenses up: "Tongues" were divisive, that was for the early church, etc. But the speakers seemed to have a living relationship with Jesus that we didn't have! And needed!

After the meeting at their booktable, I picked up a book called "Aglow With The Spirit" by a geologist, Roger Frost, since I was studying Geology at night school. Then, early in the mornings when I would try to have a quiet-time with the Lord and read the Bible, I read this little book. There was still something I hadn't released to the Lord. Even though I was not seeing this man anymore and was trying to be a good wife to Sid, I still felt I loved this other man and made the mistake of calling him once a week during the break at school, which he said he couldn't live without. (Sid would bring me to school and pick me up again.)

So early in the morning on January 21, 1968, as I was praying in the kitchen, looking at the morning star, all of a sudden I was praying in one or two syllables I didn't understand, just worshipping the Lord. Immediately such peace came into my heart, such joy, and such a new love for my Lord Jesus, and for my husband. The most amazing thing was the power to get things straight in my life. If Jesus was so wonderful, certainly He was all this other man needed, he didn't need me. At the Center that morning with Marge, I called him and told him all he needed was Jesus and that was the end of the phone calls, and any more double life! Hallelujah, I was free! The whole world looked brighter, the grass greener! It was truly a fresh new beginning! I couldn't wait to get alone with the Lord to pray to Him in my new syllables which soon became a prayer language.

That wonderful morning when I had gone in to wake Sid, I had told him about the miracle in my life and the couple of sounds in a new language and soon he could see the change in me! It was so wonderful to have a renewed love for my husband. The Lord truly does give us the desires of our hearts, even when we don't know them! Only then could I truly feel remorse for what I had put Sid through. The Holy Spirit brought true repentance for the terrible things I had done. John 16:7b,8....**When the comforter is come, he will reprove (convince) the world of sin, of righteousness and of judgment.**

It wasn't until almost a year later that I prayed in tongues in front of Sid. We were driving to Florida and watching the most beautiful sunset and praising the Lord together for His wonderful works, and for His goodness unto the children of men, and I just burst into the Heavenly language the Holy Spirit gives us to praise Him with.

How we, how I, praise and thank the Lord for His stopping me from the awful acts I was doing, for stopping me from bringing disgrace to His Name, from destroying my husband, my family. Oh, I praise Him for His forgiveness and for my husband's forgiveness, and for the wonderful new life He has given us together in Christ Jesus. We know that the Lord can save marriages. He has done it for us!

The Scriptures say in Job 4:8....**They that plow iniquity and sow wickedness, reap the same.** I want to ask forgiveness, not only of the Lord and of my husband, but also from you, our children, for not having

CHAPTER 8: A TOTALLY UNEXPECTED WAR--OR FIRING

a truly united loving home and for the sinful life I was living during some of your most important formative years. Praise the Lord, we have a God who comes after us, a "Rear Guard," who can correct our mistakes, heal the wounds and use them for His glory! "What a Mighty God we serve!"

I remember the first time we shared this testimony openly. It was at a small Full Gospel Business Men's meeting at Koinonia. After sharing I sat down in my seat near a Presbyterian Elder and asked, "Will you ever speak to me again."

He replied, "What God has cleansed, let no man call unclean." (Quoted from God's words to Peter in Acts 10:15).

Still I needed to renounce completely and be set free totally from a spirit of adultery and of lying. After doing that in Jesus' Name, my mind was set free to concentrate on things of the Lord. Truly as Psalm 40:2,3,5 says...

> **He has brought me up also out of an horrible pit, out of the miry clay, and set my feet upon a rock and established my goings. And He hath put a new song in my mouth, even praise unto our God: Many shall see it, and fear and shall trust in the Lord...Many, O Lord my God are thy wonderful works which thou has done and thy thoughts which are to us-ward....**

Yes, Oh Lord, may You truly be magnified in our Lives. I'll thank You and praise You and serve You forever in Jesus' Name!

MARLBOROUGH BLENHEIM HOTEL
ATLANTIC CITY, N. J.
WHERE BETSY GREW UP

124 FIRED AGAIN AND AGAIN, PRAISE THE LORD!

66 YEARS HAPPILY MARRIED!

"POP"-BETSY'S GRANDFATHER

"TATA"-BETSY'S GRANDMOTHER

"PAPPY"-BETSY'S DAD

"GRANDMAGIN"-BETSY'S MOM

BETSY- ABOUT 9 YRS. OLD

50 YEARS HAPPILY MARRIED!

CHAP. 9

FROM RACE RIOTS TO TWO MORE FIRINGS

Whether it be right in the sight of God to hearken unto you more than unto God, judge ye. For we cannot but speak the things which we have seen and heard.   Acts 4:19,20

PALM SUNDAY RIOTS - 1968

During the previous year our beloved and trusted co-worker, Jim Elmore, the Director of the two Havens, had suddenly gone on to be with the Lord. In his early 40's, heavyset, Jim was doing a "boot camp" physical training program with the Haven boys, and his heart couldn't take it. What a tremendous loss to all of us. Some of the key staff were persuaded to stay on until a new Director, house parents, and other staff could be located.

The Community Center program was going well, because the Lord's plan for gradual voluntary integration and the training of mixed Junior and Senior staff was working beautifully. City community centers that had announced instant and total integration, had instantly found themselves segregated the other way. The whites abandoned those centers immediately. We were the only Center that continued during those years with a good mixture of races: Blacks, Whites, Indians, and Puerto Ricans. This Christian Center and Church were coming through these volatile days of civil rights unrest, marches and demands with almost a model of race relations and integration. Sure there were racial spats here and there, and criticisms of our approach, which the Lord had shown us would work, but nothing of really serious dimension.

Betsy and I were moving along together in the restored harmony, especially after she received the Baptism in the Holy Spirit which greatly effected her life and mine too. Thank God for the flooding of His Holy Spirit in both of us!

However, two days before Palm Sunday, 1968, something else happened that would effect the whole country--the assassination of Martin Luther King, Jr. We deeply regretted this tragic event, though many had felt that such a thing probably would happen if he kept up his intensive drive for total integration through confrontations and strong civil rights legislation. To some it seemed that he was intent on making it happen---his own martyrdom.

Betsy and I, with the boys, were attending special revival meetings at the Belvedere Baptist Church. At the Saturday night meeting there was much prayer for the nation, for the King family, for the finding of the murderer of Rev. King, and for peace between the races. Suddenly the evangelist, overcome with emotion, began weeping before the Lord and the congregation, over this tragic death and no doubt for the impending tragedies that were soon to follow. He told the congregation that during that weeping time the Lord had given him a vision of Baltimore burning! It began that very night!

We woke up early the next morning (Sunday) to the shrieking sounds of police and fire truck sirens wailing all over the city. Later investigations showed that left-wing, hate-filled inciters had come in from Washington the night before to begin setting the torch to inner-city Baltimore. Revenge would be had through looting and burning!

The first fires were only a few blocks from the McKim Center, where we were to be having the Palm Sunday worship service that morning. It seemed to us that there was a lull in the storm, so to speak, during the Church services. But as we began taking some of the blacks and whites home after the service, we suddenly found ourselves engulfed in wild-eyed rioters, carrying stolen goods in every direction from shops and stores that had been broken open. One of our white helpers in his car just ahead of us had his car window smashed and was slightly cut by flying glass, but he got through. As we tried to move slowly through the same rioters, we were not hit, probably because we had some black youngsters in our car with our own boys.

Liquor stores seemed to be favorite first targets of the rioters. In the midst of a large group of blacks that almost climbed over our car to get into a newly broken open bar, we were saddened to see one of our teenage boys with his McKim jacket on, rushing to rip off whatever he could. We got through the worst of the rioting safely, Praise God, and at home we began listening to radio reports. By phone we canceled the evening meeting. During that night the Governor had to call in the National Guard to seal off an area of approximately 25 blocks square, maybe two miles square, in the inner-city and begin patrolling it, as wild break-ins, fires and attacks continued throughout the night. Policemen, firemen and many "white" cars were being stoned. However, orders had been issued to the police and National Guard to exercise total restraint in the use of their weapons.

On Monday morning, with the riots in full sway, after taking food to one dear old black grandmother and her family, and also to two elderly

CHAPTER 9: RACE RIOTS TO TWO MORE FIRINGS! 127

white sisters, all members of the Church and all afraid to come out of their homes, we began riding through the main riot streets in our McKim area and through the housing projects. We saw a huge gang of people vengefully stoning white people as they tried to drive through to work, not realizing the city was on fire. With my "bullet proof vest" (clerical collar) on, I stopped our car, leaving Betsy and our two little boys in it, and jumped out into the street with a commanding voice shouting "In the Name of Jesus Christ, stop this terrible thing you are doing. It is not of God, it is of the devil."

Most of these people knew me and many stopped. At this moment a big black man came up beside me, obviously fortified with some of the stolen liquor, and stood with me saying out of the side of his mouth, "Rev., you're right, but this ain't no place for you to be right now; you'd better get out of here before you get hurt." At this moment police and national guard patrols came rolling through and the rioters rapidly disappeared, only to reappear somewhere else.

So we got back in the car, drove to the next block where there were Italian and Jewish food and poultry shops. Actually a well known block - "Corned-Beef Row." We stopped again to see the anxious shopkeepers behind their plate-glass windows, some of them holding shotguns ready to defend their shops. As I came out of an Italian shop, I heard a crowd of teenage rioters moving across the street farther up the block to break into a little old Jewish couple's shop.

Regular traffic had stopped in that area, so I began walking up the middle of the street toward this bunch of about 15 black teenagers. They were still some 150 feet away when they saw this solitary figure marching down the middle of the street toward them. Later it reminded us of that memorable scene in the "Shoot-out at OK Corral"---only I didn't have any guns. Suddenly they saw me, and one of the teenagers shouted, "Here come Rev. Sid! Here come Rev. Sid!" The whole group disappeared as if by magic into the nearby alleys. Praise God, another shop was spared for the moment. It was heart-breaking to see so many people caught up in this senseless, hate-filled violence.

From there we moved over two blocks to Baltimore Street. Passing the McKim Center, we began slowly driving toward Broadway, especially to check on our Rummage Shop in the 1400 block, which at that time was being operated by a tough little West Virginia woman. Wisely, she and her husband had stayed home that day. But just as we passed the alley next to the Rummage Shop, we saw another large mob of teenage and older black men pouring out of the alley, the ring leaders carrying pieces of bricks and clubs. Again we stopped quickly and I rolled out to confront them saying, "In the Name of Jesus Christ, I order you to stop this foolishness. It is of the devil, not of God. Please for

God's sake and your own stop it, and give me those bricks right now."

At that moment they saw the National Guard jeeps coming and two hired guards with pump shotguns outside the pawn shop they were about to break into. Instantly I found myself with a load of "brickbats" in my arms, the guys fleeing down every nearby alley, and the patrol racing by.

Amazingly, here again a big black friend came alongside of me, standing with me against this evil, like a protector saying, "Rev., this ain't no place for you and your family to be. Take my advice, and get out of here!"

I assured him we would be on our way shortly.

We checked again on McKim Center and headed for home out of the riot area and began calling some of the Center workers and Junior staff to meet us the next morning to decide whatever else we could be doing. The riots and fires raged on through that night. On Tuesday morning we met at the Center to set up an area patrol of our own, to dissuade our members and neighbors from getting involved in the rioting.

After that meeting, I walked back through the Lombard Street Flag House Court area and was amazed to find a small group of little kids searching through the area for whatever they could steal from shops already broken into. I stopped them and spoke to the little leader of the group and asked him, "Don't you know this is wrong? It's of the devil! In Jesus' Name I tell you to stop it. Are you a Christian?"

"No, I'm a Catholic," he said.

"Well go ask your priest, Father Joe, to tell you whether stealing is right or terribly wrong. He'll tell you it is very wrong. Christians don't steal." Sheepishly they left, hopefully going home.

I walked around the block and saw some policemen I knew who were trying to catch several teenage rioters, but they were easily escaping. One policeman was so frustrated that he had drawn his gun and was about to fire in the direction of the teenagers. When I yelled a warning to the nearest one, the policeman thought better of it and dropped his gun.

I moved on up Exeter street thinking I might see some of these young guys to talk to, most of whom I probably knew, when suddenly, out from a vandalized bar on the right came a large group of older young men and women with their arms filled with unopened beer cans, turning toward Baltimore street, devilishly wild-eyed, heading toward a dry cleaning shop on the corner.

As before, I called out, "Stop this! It's not of God, it's of the devil! Stop it!"

They poured past me, without the slightest indication that they had heard or even seen me, as I stood there obviously a minister of God. In

CHAPTER 9: RACE RIOTS TO TWO MORE FIRINGS! 129

seconds they had broken the windows and doors of the shop, and moments later were carrying out arm loads of clothing, anything they could grab off the racks. That shop was never used again. Only an empty lot remains. It was killed by fire in that moment! Something about this group kept ringing in my mind, until I'd finally realized that I'd seen some of them on the streets before. They were known homosexuals and lesbians. No wonder they didn't hear me. According to Romans 1, they had rejected all things concerning God.

The rampaging and burning continued on into the night with more injuries to firemen as they courageously sought to extinguish the fires while being bombarded with bottles and stones by the rioters. Surprisingly, there were only a few deaths, but a huge number of arrests, maybe 5 or 6 thousand. So much devastation, like a war zone, was visible on every block that many years would pass before the signs of "that war" would disappear through urban renewal programs. Even today, 22 years later, one can still find sad evidences of that awful riot. Did these people have a right to riot, steal and burn? No way. The great majority of the blacks knew better and didn't participate.

By Wednesday the worst was over. Damages and losses in Baltimore alone ran into scores of millions. The wreckage in lives was beyond estimate. The lost ground in race relations would probably not be repaired fully for decades, no matter how many laws were passed. The whites, still in the area, began moving as far away as they could. Who could blame them?

In more recent years (1985-90) due to many urban renewal projects in the area based on our equity housing idea, or home ownership for the poor, that we had promoted with the city officials in the early '60's, some whites have begun moving back. There is new hope springing up that peaceable, mixed neighborhoods are now possible.

By the grace of God, we had come through these awful experiences without a scratch on our bodies, but with some deep scars in our memories.

THE LOUISVILLE SHOUT-DOWN

Not long after the riots of '68, the Presbyterian Church leaders called for a conference in Louisville on what could be done to help the "disadvantaged" by its Health, Education and Welfare workers across America. Knowing that Betsy and I needed to be together as much as possible, and with her important work as director of McKim's Free Nursery School program, we arranged to attend this three-day Presbyterian conference in Louisville.

After a few sessions of lectures and discussions in our areas of concern, it became clear that we were again not attending a very religious conference. Although the big Church leaders were there from seminaries and Church headquarters, there was little or no reference to God's principles, to the Bible, to Jesus Christ, or any desire to speak forth the Gospel, or to win anyone to Jesus Christ as THE REAL SOLUTION for social problems, for our nation's malaise.

There was much talk about liberation theology, (the clenched-fist type), about feeding the multitudes with Government hand-outs, about militant social workers demanding rights for minorities, and much about our looking on ourselves as the real agents of great social change. In one of the seminars, after standing the militant, demanding, covetous jargon as long as I could, I asked for the privilege to speak. "We are all here supposedly, as representatives of the Church and thereby representatives of the GREATEST CHANGE AGENT of them all, JESUS CHRIST, and of HIS MIGHTY LOVE and SAVING POWER." Before I could fully verbalize that nothing is being said here at all about bringing the minorities and underprivileged to know JESUS as the GREAT CHANGE AGENT and INSPIRATION for THEIR LIVES, I was being shouted down and told to shut up!

"We don't want to hear that junk," someone screamed at me.

Betsy and I were deeply grieved over what obviously was a complete take-over of these fields in the Church by gravely deceived and often totally "unsaved church leaders".

A luncheon was to follow that day where a key conference leader was to speak. He hardly had begun his talk before some of the militant social workers and seminarians began to express objections and ridicule. Shortly they began shouting back at the speaker and shaking their fists demanding control. "Cut out this nonsense. Give us 'the bread', or we are going to come and take it."

Thus the speaker was shouted down. The so-called change agents were taking over, the dinner was ending in total disarray and dismay for many. We were absolutely convinced that these fist-shakers were not working for the Lord! This also applies today. In the final analysis fist-shaking change-agents, whether in Iran, Iraq, South Africa, or America are working for the Lord's great enemy, Satan!

Betsy and I hurriedly made our way to our room and called the airport to request an early flight home. With bags in hand as we passed through the lobby, we noticed one of the noted church leaders from Chicago waiting for an elevator in friendly conversation with some of the "change agent" seminarians, apparently all very happy, at their success in getting their ungodly threats across.

As we walked down the steps toward the entrance doors of this hotel to find a cab to the airport, I suddenly heard a strange mournful song being sung by a sobbing voice, "Is there anybody here who knows

CHAPTER 9: RACE RIOTS TO TWO MORE FIRINGS!

my Jesus, anybody here who loves My Lord." I turned to look at Betsy. There she was by my side, tears rolling down her face, sobbing out those words, led by the Holy Spirit! She was giving an apt conclusion to this conference, something like Jesus had said on Patmos to the Church at Ephesus, **You've lost your first love, repent and come back.** Rev. 2:4,5.

On our flight home I promised Betsy never to take her to another such conference. We would find one to attend where the Name and Way of Jesus would be magnified. Soon we found such a conference, a Full Gospel Business Men's conference in New York City, where we also could take our children. What a blessing it was to all of us to go to that one, where Jesus was being lifted up and souls saved!

CARL'S FUNERAL

Two other special events took place during this time. One was Dusty's little nephew, Brian, coming to live with us late in 1968, and the other a special trip to Atlanta for the funeral of a very dear friend, Carl Presley, a deacon in the Acworth Presbyterian Church.

Carl had a lung cancer operation while we were pastoring there, and the Good Lord had given him 17 years more. The Church had prayed earnestly for him and he was ever grateful to God for those extra years. Now his widow, Mattie Lou, wanted me to come to conduct his funeral service and I agreed to do so. At the same time I asked the Lord to please help me see our son, Kirby, a freshman at Georgia Tech., my Uncle DeWitt in Marietta, and another dear teacher friend of ours, Fern Armstrong, near Acworth. Fern's husband, Mac, whose funeral I had held not long before, was once a soldier of fortune and had come back to the Lord in our ministry. All of this in one day's flying trip to Atlanta, Marietta, and Acworth, was an awful lot to ask in the six or seven hours I would be in that area! But the Lord did it! With amazing ease! There was no time for me to notify the others I was coming.

After landing in Atlanta about 10 a.m. from Baltimore, I obtained a rental car and drove directly to Georgia Tech. Kirby was not in his room and his roommate did not know where he was. As I was leaving the campus, I noticed a group of students gathered around an old model car decorating it like "the rambling wreck of Georgia tech." I pulled up beside them and called out, "Do any of you know Kirby Rigell?

Guess what? One young man at the front of the "wreck" raised up and said, "I do, I'm Kirby."

Sure enough it was! We made a date to have supper together that evening on my way back to the airport. # 1 miracle timing of the Lord.

Marietta was 25 miles away, so I decided to head straight for Uncle

DeWitt's house there. The expressway got me to his house quickly but no one was home. As I started to back out of the driveway, Uncle DeWitt drove into the driveway, explaining he was on the way to lunch, but had forgotten something and had to come back. What a delightful # 2 coincidence from the Lord. He asked me to come have a quick lunch with him at his favorite restaurant, which was on the highway toward Acworth.

About two hours left before the funeral service. It was noon time and the restaurant was fairly crowded. After we were seated and gave our order, I excused myself to go to the restroom, passing a group of ladies at a large table as I went. On the way back I passed them again and thought I heard a voice calling my name and turned to look. "Lo and behold" the Lord was answering the # 3 miracle meeting: Fern Armstrong, a teacher, was having lunch with several other teachers and just happened to spot me! Praise God! I had a few moments to share our love and concern for her. She was so pleased and so was I! I knew that the trip was in the center of God's will and right on His incredible timings.

After that delightful lunch with Uncle DeWitt I was able to make it in plenty of time for the funeral service for Carl at the First Presbyterian Church in Acworth. We knew, too, that Carl had graduated right on God's schedule and we will see him again one day; his widow too.

Kirby and I had a very special supper together near the University that evening before I caught my plane back home to Baltimore, arriving before midnight. What a wonderful and mighty God we serve. He had put it all together in one "short" day. Be sure to be on the look-out for God's miracle timings! You'll find them along the way, everyday, as you love and serve Him with all your heart.

BRIAN'S ARRIVAL

The pre-Christmas days during December 1968 were about to bring us an unexpected special surprise. Chris was now 11, Joe 13, Kirby 19 at Georgia Tech, Craig a 21 year old senior at Maryville College, and Dusty after two Marine hitches in VietNam was back in college at Maryville, too.

Since my salary was never large enough to send a flea off to college, our boys were being greatly helped by their grandfather, Betsy's Dad, and Dusty was on the G.I. Bill.

But what was the surprise? Dusty's only living relative was a sister named Sandy, whom we had met, but did not know very well. Sandy had become very sick with cancer and her little boy, Brian, was being cared for by friends. Our boys and we began praying that the Lord

CHAPTER 9: RACE RIOTS TO TWO MORE FIRINGS! 133

would provide a good home for Brian, should his mother die, not realizing that he would soon be a member of our family! Ours was to be the prayed-for home!

Shortly we heard from Dusty that his sister had died. Would we help take care of seven-year-old Brian? Dusty was to be the guardian but could not undertake that and go to school at the same time. So we applied to the orphans court to get approved for guardianship of Brian just before Christmas 1968. Since Sandy's special friends had already planned Christmas for Brian, we arranged for him to stay with them and come to be with us a week after Christmas. Brian was a fine young lad and quickly became a younger brother for our boys. Two years later we were permitted by the orphans court to adopt him. So the Lord had surprisingly and providentially given us six sons, counting his Uncle Dusty. Praise The Lord forever!

THE NEAR SELF-MASSACRE ON MEMORIAL DAY

Craig was to graduate from Maryville College on June 2, 1969 and the President of the College had invited me to have a prayer at the Graduation service.

We arranged to have a few days off that weekend to drive to Tennessee with the younger boys via Betsy's mom and dad (GrandmaGin and Pappy) at their beautifully located home called "The Bight" on St. Leonard's Creek in Southern Maryland. While there Pappy mentioned his need of having a large limb cut off a sycamore tree down near his dock; this limb interfered with getting his little sailboat into the water each summer.

Knowing how to operate a chainsaw and without discussing it with anyone, I quietly decided to go down and lop off that limb as a favor to "Pappy" before we left for Tennessee.

I secured an extension ladder and tied it in place against the limb 15 ft. up. Then I cranked up the small chainsaw and let it idle as I climbed up the ladder to the limb. Everything was going according to plan. In only a few more moments that limb would be down, or so I thought! To steady myself on the ladder, I had to use my left hand to hold onto the limb next to the saw and try to operate and control this small chainsaw with my right hand-- something no one in his right mind should ever do! The next thing I knew the saw had bucked out of its cutting channel over onto my left wrist. I turned off the switch instantly but the chain kept turning enough to cut up my left wrist badly, including nerves. I quickly lowered the saw and grabbed a paper towel I had in my pocket and jammed it on my wrist to stanch the blood. I know I got the ladder down and the saw put away, but I don't remember exactly how.

I went up to the house, called Pappy, and explained what had happened. He called Betsy and since the nerves were cut we felt we should phone our family Doctor, Dr. John Nesbit, in Baltimore to find a specialist. He was able to contact Dr. Wilges, a hand specialist, who just happened to be home cutting his grass, but would meet us at Union Memorial Hospital in two hours. With Betsy driving and me holding pressure on the wrist, we made the journey back to Baltimore in record time. On the way I was not feeling a great deal of pain because the nerves were cut, but I felt the Lord saying that He would show us a miracle by restoring the feeling in the hand again.

Dr. Wilges was there and immediately had me put on an emergency operating table with my left arm stretched out. After giving me local anesthesia in my arm and wrist area and thoroughly cleaning up the jagged wound, the surgeon began the slow careful sewing job, from where I lay it looked like he was sewing up some hamburger! I was still quite awake. Betsy nearby was trying to keep from passing out. I asked Dr. Wilges if he was going to sew my nerves back, and he said he would. Then I asked if the feeling would ever be restored in my hand. He asked me how old I was, and I said, "50".

He then said, "If you were a child I would say you'd have an excellent chance of feeling again, if you were half your age you would have 50% chance, but at your age there's not much hope."

Then I screwed up my faith-courage and repeated what the Lord had said to me on the way to the hospital, "Doctor, I believe the Lord is saying that He is going to restore full feeling to my hand."

He replied, "I hope so. We shall see."

So this fine young doctor very carefully sewed up the upper part of my left wrist including the nerves (fortunately no tendons were cut) and bandaged the hand and wrist until it looked like a huge white boxing glove and sent us on our way, back to the "Bight" that night.

The next day Betsy drove us the 500 miles to Maryville, Tennessee, in time to help our son Craig graduate, by giving the special prayer dressed in a clergy robe and my "white gauze boxing glove!"

At the end of August that same year, 1969, Craig and his college sweetheart, Ann Little, were married in a small Presbyterian Church near Maryville. Mamma Rigell and Pappy and GrandmaGin all came to the wedding. Craig's brother, Kirby, was his best man. Ann's sister, Trudy, her maid of honor. It was so good to have both families united in this way. Ann's parents, also Presbyterians in Jackson, Mississippi, had long supported our inner-city work in Baltimore.

But the Memorial Day wrist massacre did not end there, nor did our son Craig's education end there. The Vietnam War was still going on,

CHAPTER 9: RACE RIOTS TO TWO MORE FIRINGS! 135

sad to say, and Craig, having a low draft number, had the delightful option of being drafted or volunteering. He chose the latter and became an honored soldier in his basic training and served in the medical corps, where he spent three years teaching anatomy to the x-ray students and helping with the burn units in San Antonio, Texas. During his last years at Maryville he had served as a surgical orderly in the Blount County Hospital to help pay his way through school and had developed a tremendous interest in medicine and hoped to go on to medical school after his army tour. That was not to be, but after further training at University of Tennessee, he became a biology teacher at an Oak Ridge Middle School, then an outstanding Vice-Principal of Robertsville Junior High. He is now the Principal of Willow Brook Elementary School in Oak Ridge, and with his dear wife, Ann, who is in personnel work at Oak Ridge Associated Universities, is guiding his home flock: Ginny 16, and Allen 12.

One summer when Craig and Ann were stationed in San Antonio, Texas, they invited our three sons, still at home, Joe, Chris and Brian, to fly down for a visit and then join us, Mom and Dad, later in Panama City. Ann remarked how listless Brian had seemed, but figured it was the extreme heat. We all met in Panama City and later, back in Baltimore, Brian's doctor diagnosed his problem as diabetes and insisted we rush him to the hospital. There began his and Mom's lessons in giving insulin shots. For several following summers Brian attended Camp Glyndon for diabetic children which was a big help to him. It's been no picnic for Brian and we greatly admire the way he has faced it. Today he is a college graduate, working in a bank in Maryville, Tennessee, and is our best letter writer! We'll catch you up with the other four sons later.

Now as for my chopped-up wrist, did the nerves ever grow back? Just as the Lord had told me, the nerves did grow back even more sensitive than before! Little by little in the next two months, a slight tingling pain indicated the gradual new life of the nerves. Frequent checks by Dr. Wilges confirmed the restoration. He was amazed and just as delighted and thankful as I was. He had done his job well, and the Lord had kept His promise to do His!

Right after returning from Maryville, our secretary, Marge Nuckolls, a Spirit filled saint, had placed on my desk a scripture card promise from Exodus 15:26...

If thou will diligently hearken to the voice of the Lord thy God, and will do that which is right in his sight, and will give ear to his commandments, and keep all his statutes, I will put none of these diseases upon thee, which I have brought upon the Egyptians: for I am the Lord that

healeth thee. Jehovah Rapha! Thank You, Lord!

On another occasion when the "firing fires" seemed about to engulf me, Marge greatly encouraged me with another of God's great promises from II Chronicles 20:15b:

Thus saith the Lord unto you, Be not afraid nor dismayed by reason of this great multitude; for the battle is not yours, but God's.

OUR FIRST JOSHUA MARCH--JULY 1969

With Jim Elmore gone on to Heaven from directing the Boys Haven, and the rest of his team gradually moving out to other work, the problem of finding staff and keeping the place running became more and more difficult. The McKim pay was always minimal, so any worker had to be dedicated to the Lord and satisfied to help kids in trouble have a chance in life to succeed at something besides crime!

Jim had been the mainstay of the Haven work for our first ten years there. Because of my efforts to keep lifting up Jesus in the Community Center work and refusal to eliminate the explicit Christian emphasis, I was often under attack by the liberal elements of our Board and denomination. For example, each year there were scores of speaking engagements throughout Baltimore and Maryland to tell about the work. Most of them in Churches, but often there were civic club invitations. Sad to say, one of our Board members admonished me strongly to lay off the religious element in speaking to such groups. I did not agree, remembering Peter and John's statement to the Pharisees when they were told to shut up about Jesus and they said...

Whether it be right in the sight of God to hearken unto you more than unto God, judge you. For we cannot but speak the things which we have seen and heard. (Acts 4:19,20).

During those years at least six major efforts had already been made to have me fired and sent to "Timbuktu!" In fact behind the scenes the seventh and final effort was already underway to effect my removal. A Board committee was formed to oversee the selling of the Riall Home and the closing and selling of the Boys Haven on Park Avenue.

In the face of the great need for such homes, our "fearless" Board was ordering the closing of our two homes for boys, within 30 days. This involved the dismissal of the remaining staff and the relocation of all the boys, some eight or ten at the time. I had been directed to concern myself only with the Community Center, the Pre-school program, the small mission Church and the Thrift Shop, all of which

CHAPTER 9: RACE RIOTS TO TWO MORE FIRINGS!

indeed was a handful. But we had a good staff, and I was still deeply concerned about the Boys Home, especially the one on Park Avenue, where our dear friend, Jim Elmore, had worked his heart out and for which he literally had given his life.

About this time the Lord had me reading about Joshua's march around Jericho, how Joshua was told to march around the city at dawn, every day for six days and on the seventh day, seven times around: and the walls would fall down. The Haven closing was taking effect the week after our Vacation Bible School at the Community Center. I began sensing from the Lord, that, if He could bring down the walls for Joshua, He could keep up the walls of that Boys Home, if we would march around it like Joshua and the Israelites, and also fast for that week.

I felt sure at least some of the Church family and Center staff would join us in the effort to keep the home alive.

When I told Betsy I felt the Lord wanted us to go on a "Joshua March" the following week, she reacted with considerable alarm. There were fist-shaking protest marches in Washington and all over the country in the days before and she wanted no part of a march. However, by the work of the Holy Spirit, she had come to believe God's Word about submitting to the desires of her husband (at least in Godly things), so she silently resolved to take it to the Lord in prayer.

A couple of hours later, Betsy called me at the Center and said, tearfully, that the Lord had specifically shown her that we were to do it. She was on her knees praying with the Bible before her on the bed, asking the Lord for His confirmation in this "march" matter. Slowly she opened the Bible to Ezra 10:4.... **Arise; for this matter belongeth unto thee; we also will be with thee; be of good courage and do it.**

In tears she thanked the Lord. This was indeed a tremendous confirmation to me too. We felt further from the Lord, that the Board President and members must be informed of our objections to closing the home so quickly, and of our proposed fasting and "Joshua March" appeal to God to prevent it. We got special letters off to them immediately about it.

At dawn on Monday morning about nine of us assembled outside the Haven, and silently made our first march around it. Seven small white wooden crosses, about a foot high, had been made, and we each carried our Bibles. To march around the Haven required marching around an area that would be a distance of about seven blocks. We completed that first march, got back in the two cars, and went over to the Community Center on Baltimore Street to begin the first day of Bible School.

The next morning, in the middle of the Bible School, I was called outside to the basketball court parking lot to talk with the Board President, Mr. Harry Cole, a long-time contractor friend, whom I had recommended to be on the Board years before. Harry said, "Sid, we received your letter about this so-called march and at an executive committee meeting last night we unanimously concluded to tell you to call off the march immediately."

I replied, "Harry, we will call off the march if you folks will stop the closing of the home."

He answered, "The decision to close the home is final; it won't be changed."

"I'm sorry, Harry, but we believe the march must go on, too."

No doubt that ended our friendship, I regret to say, and no doubt, "Cooked my goose!" But I knew it was pretty much already cooked, and the Lord had told us to march.

Before the day was out I was able to contact a newspaper reporter we knew, who seemed interested. The next morning he had a photographer on hand to catch the march as it began, in front of the Boys Haven, crosses and Bibles lifted high. The picture and article appeared shortly in one of the papers. It didn't win us any "brownie points" with the Board members as one dear board member told me later. But on through that busy week we went, praising God, fasting and carrying out the Bible School and Community Center work. It was a beautiful week, the fasting got easier toward the seventh day. We were taking some liquids each day, but no regular foods. (I took a glass of milk and a spoonful of honey each day.)

On the seventh day there were about fifteen of us assembled at dawn for the seven times around. It took us altogether about two hours to finish all that seventh day march, in total silence as all the others had been, with our crosses and Bibles lifted high. Finally at the end of the seventh time around, we stood in front of the near empty Haven and began singing as loudly as we could:

> "To God Be the Glory, Great things He has done,
> So loved He the world that He gave us His Son,
> Who yielded His life an atonement for sin,
> And opened the life gates that all may come in.
> Praise the Lord, Praise the Lord,
> Let the earth hear His Voice,
> Praise the Lord, Praise the Lord,
> Let the people rejoice,
> Oh, come to the Father through Jesus the Son,
> And give Him the glory, great things He has done."
>   (Fanny J. Crosby).

CHAPTER 9: RACE RIOTS TO TWO MORE FIRINGS!

We closed the march with a brief prayer of thanksgiving to God for His bountiful care and for keeping the home alive and intact. We went on over to the Center for the Church services that day with much rejoicing in the Lord.

You might be wondering how we were feeling after seven days of fasting. We had each lost several pounds of weight, but were feeling just great, thanks to the good Lord for His sustaining strength. To Him be all praise and thanksgiving and glory, too!

THE AXE FALLS AT MCKIM!

During those years the Lord had led us to concentrate on growing up and training our own Center and Church leadership, almost all of whom have gone on to successful careers in other fields. One of them, Dwight Warren, who came to us as a boy, is today carrying on as the highly regarded director of the Center. We have fond and grateful memories of those young people who dug their heels in and learned to love the Lord, and became men and women of fine Christian character.

Following that "Joshua March," the Board began acting pretty much as if I no longer existed and I kept wondering when the "axe would fall." It did on April 1st, 1970, about a month after the Board almost doubled the Director's salary, hoping to attract someone as a replacement. The new President of the Board, a very fine black Christian man, Leonard Wilmore, asked me to have lunch with him on April Fool's Day, 1970. His assignment, no doubt difficult for him, was to inform me that my discharge had been set for June 15. I don't think either one of us enjoyed that lunch, but inside I was much relieved that my battles against the unfortunate liberal trends in those circles were over. We shook hands and parted, both sincerely regretting this sad ending.

There were never any thanks or commendations from the Board for those fourteen years of trojan work that Betsy and I had given McKim. A local newspaper carried a small notice of my "resignation" as announced by the Board. However, the beautiful Staff at the Center, Church, School and Thrift shop got together and presented Betsy and me each a desk plaque expressing their appreciation for our devotion to them, the community and the Lord. Nothing could have been better than that! And we praise the Lord for it.

Oh yes, you are wondering what happened to the Boys Haven? Very sadly it was closed down in thirty days as the Board had directed, everyone went their separate ways, except for one asked to live in as a night watchman while efforts were being made to sell it. A year went by and they could find no buyer. During that time when other empty places in the area were being badly vandalized, not a single window was broken in the empty Haven building!

Finally, at the end of the year, a Youth Home group leased the place and reopened it with Christian leadership as a Boy's Home! The Lord had kept the walls up. How long it lasted as a boys' home we don't know. But, eventually we heard that it was sold for private use again.

We should not leave the story of the old Boys' Haven without telling you that it once was the large town house of a Doctor, with many, many rooms and fireplaces on three floors and a carriage house and a servant's quarters behind it. It had curved windows on the front corner, a huge living room, billiard room, library and kitchen on the first floor, a dumb-waiter going up to the other floors and a laundry in the basement, parquet floors, beautiful paneling throughout. The library fireplace had a mantelpiece with the words beautifully carved in oak in Olde English letters, "WHEN YOU SIT BY MY FYRE TO KEEPE YORESELFE WARME, BE SHURE THAT YORE TUNGUE DOTH YORE NAYBORE (NEIGHBOR) NO HARME." Isn't that what the Lord wants us all to do?

We were not to see any of the Board members again officially after that. We did see Mr. Leonard Wilmore perhaps once more at a Presbytery meeting and once outside the Post Office where he worked, and Mr. Cole one more time some six years later in 1976. At that time the General Assembly of the United Presbyterian Church was meeting at the Baltimore Civic Center and being asked to approve the ordination of homosexuals by the Presbytery of New York City. They didn't.

One evening on our way to pass out leaflets warning against such approval to the delegates at the Civic Center, we passed Harry Cole on the street and stopped to exchange brief greetings. Suddenly I felt compelled to tell him, "Harry, we just want you to know how much we appreciate your firing us! We have no hard feelings toward you."

With sort of a downcast look he muttered, "I didn't do it, the Board did it." Harry was a good man but apparently did not grasp the extent of apostasy undermining the Church today.

We wished him and his companions well and went on about the effort to warn the Church against another deadly move, feeling something like John the Baptist, "A voice crying in the wilderness." Or a Jeremiah!

THE OLD FACTORY BECOMES A CHRISTIAN CENTER

Early in 1970 a well-to-do Presbyterian businessman, who knew about the efforts to eliminate the Christian emphasis at McKim Center, talked with us about opening a real Christian Center in the area.

CHAPTER 9: RACE RIOTS TO TWO MORE FIRINGS!   141

Perhaps the old Belfort wartime factory building that was for sale nearby on the corner of Baltimore and Central Avenue could be renovated for this purpose.

He arranged for us to tour the building with him. Actually, it was two large buildings joined together, three floors, more space than we had ever had before, with separate large rooms that could serve as a gym and chapel, office and classrooms. It could be converted nicely, without a huge expenditure. So we began serious talks, knowing that my firing from McKim was only weeks away.

Through longtime loyal friendships which the Lord had given us we were able to recommend two other men to make up the Board: an outstanding college coach, and a retired minister friend of strong conservative beliefs. So by the time the firing came from the McKim Association, the new Christian Community Center was ready to roll. The businessman had the money to close the purchase of the old factory and within two weeks after our firing, by July the first, we were moving into the old factory office and were having Church services there in an "Upper Room."

Back in the spring the Presbytery of Baltimore had decided to dissolve the mission Church of the Saviour, no doubt in further efforts by the liberals to sever all connections with me as the pastor of the Church and a "thorn in their flesh." It would also free the McKim Community Center from the "albatross" of the Church connection. We requested the General Presbyter and his committee to officially release the little Church from the Presbytery and to allow me to continue as its pastor, as an Independent Community Church. I believe both requests were approved in that year. Other churches were also desiring to be released during that period.

Eventually the Presbytery placed me on their retired roll, but I was never more active in the work of the Lord. For the Baptism of the Holy Spirit early in 1969 had set me on fire for the Lord Jesus as never before and Betsy and I were to see some amazing years ahead in the U.S.A. and abroad.

At the newly formed Christian Community Center the following agreement had been much discussed with the businessman Board president:

I) It was to be a Christian Community Center, unashamedly. Everything to be done in the Name of Jesus and to the Glory of God. The Bible would be the textbook of the Center.

2) We were to slowly build a Christian staff. I would have authority to hire staff and discharge them as needed, with approval of the Board.

3) Betsy and I were to be full members of the Board of Directors. No decisions would be made by the Board in any way circumventing us.

4) I was to be the Executive Director of the Center and Pastor of the Church.

5) We were to have a direct part in fund raising and financial matters.

6) We would never be looked upon as hired staff, but be full partners in the establishment and functioning of the Center.

7) The Church would be able to have full use of the facilities. The Upper Room to be devoted completely for Christian Services.

Unfortunately we never put this agreement in writing to be signed by him and the other Board members. We would later greatly regret not doing so. However, even that would not have made any difference.

The fledgling Center did get off to an excellent start: the needed renovations were quickly completed, an athletic and club program was begun for neighborhood youth. The Church was meeting regularly, a weekly neighborhood and supporters luncheon was initiated, a nursery school was begun; the staff had the best office space ever, everything seemed to be moving toward good success, Praise The Lord!

But the first warning of trouble came when we decided to get our longtime maintenance friend to paint the main entrance doors a bright red. We soon learned this had greatly displeased the businessman and his second wife. Strike #1.

Next we ordered a case each of paper towels and toilet paper for the rapidly growing center and for long-term savings. That came close to upsetting the "apple cart" and became Strike #2.

We were working with neighborhood youth, most of them pretty good kids, but we felt we also should keep a door open to the tough kids. Before long we found the Lord was sending us some real tough ones, including several young drug addicts who needed help. One of them later would become a minister, and another one almost. We put them to work helping us around the Center for a bed and food at our house. This was probably Strike #3 against us with the businessman, who wanted us to work just with the good ones and not with the bad ones. We kept thinking, "But the Lord came also for the bad ones, didn't He?"

We got through that winter nicely. Then came a Board meeting at the Board President's house in the late spring, in which he totally denied making any of the above agreements, that we would be Board members, and so forth.

We were quite upset by these denials. At one point I said to him and the Board, "None of what you are saying is true."

He turned angrily to me and said, Are you calling me a liar in my own house?"

I looked him in the eye and said, "I just reckon I am."

CHAPTER 9: RACE RIOTS TO TWO MORE FIRINGS! 143

His face flushed red, and immediately he pointed toward the door hollering, "Out, Out, Out of my house."

We were glad to go! That had to be Strike #4 and Firing No.?!

We continued to operate the Center and Church through that summer and when the Board came back together again that September, they ordered me to report back to them in writing the following Monday that I would submit every move and need in writing for prior approval, even to the smallest item. This was an almost unbearable straight-jacket they were putting us in, but they said, if we agreed to it, we would continue in the work as Director.

So again we went to prayer and fasting for that weekend.

We did contact the other Board members to discuss the whole situation with them trying to calm the disturbed waters. By Sunday night the Lord had given us two Scriptures for guidance, but we just could not understand how they fit together.

The first was Isaiah 51:21-23....*Therefore hear now this, thou afflicted, and drunken, but not with wine: Thus saith thy Lord the Lord and thy God that pleadeth the cause of His people. Behold I have taken out of thine hand the cup of trembling, even the dregs of the cup of my fury; thou shalt no more drink it again: But I will put it into the hand of them that afflict thee; which have said to thy soul, Bow down, that we may go over, and thou hast laid thy body as the ground, and as the street, to them that went over.*

The second was Isaiah 52:11-12....*Depart ye, depart ye, go ye out from thence, touch no unclean thing; go ye out of the midst of her; be ye clean that bear the vessels of the Lord. For ye shall not go out with haste, nor go by flight: for the Lord will go before you; and the God of Israel will be your rereward.*

Both are tremendously meaningful Scriptures, but seemingly contradictory, one saying lie down and be run over, and the other saying depart slowly!

So Monday morning we had our typewritten "straight-jacket" acceptance letter ready. We went into the meeting and presented our letter to the Board President, which he promptly read. After a moment, he turned to me and said curtly, "This clears that up," Then he proceeded to belittle my work and business ability openly, saying, "Therefore I must handle all the business details myself. By the way, since last Thursday I have rechecked our finances, and instead of keeping you on as we promised, we must let you go at the end of this month."

Just two weeks remained!

The meeting was ended and we could scarcely control our joy, for now we saw how those two Scripture verses above fit together. They were so true for our situation! No way could we continue in a place where promises were meaningless.

We did ask if the Church could continue meeting in the Upper Room for a time and he agreed to allow us one month to be out. That's when we quickly wrote a letter to our supporting friends and family:

FIRED AGAIN, PRAISE THE LORD!

Dear Beloved Friends in Jesus: Oct.5, 1971

Yes, its's true. I've been fired again and we're praising our mighty Lord!

On the pink slip attached is the main paragraph of the amazing letter of dismissal to me, dated Sept. 14, from the Board of Directors of the Christian Community Center. As you will see, we (Betsy and I) are no longer with the Christian Community Center as of September 30, 1971. But, praise the Lord with us, we believe it's all for the best! It's the goodness of the Lord even now!

Another key worker in establishing the Center, Mrs. Sarah Shaw, resigned and was dismissed as of Friday, Sept. 24th. She will continue with the Church full-time, and with such pay as the Lord provides.

What's happened? We believe God is moving us ahead! (Purging, cleansing, regrouping, reequipping!) He does truly guide those who put their complete trust in Him and diligently seek His guidance. Praise His Name! After we fasted, prayed, and wept before Him, He showed us in His Word, (Isaiah 51:21-23; 52:11-12) exactly what we were to do in this crisis situation.

By this guidance, given us on Sept. 10 and confirmed several times since, God shows that He also wants us to come out. He wants the rejected, castaway, inconsequential (to some in high places) Church of The Saviour, to be separate, to continue in HIS ministry in this ghetto area, free from bondage, to do ALL the witness and work He wants us to do in these troubled days. Praise His Name every breath!

Soon, God willing, this little throw-away Church will open nearby, a Spirit-filled, powerful "Jesus Center," reaching out to all whom He sends, or sends us to, with the redeeming and healing of Jesus - even to young drug addicts!

Yes, we believe it is clear that God wants us to move the "Little Tabernacle" (The Church) to another location in the immediate area. At the moment we are not sure where. But the Lord will lead us by the

CHAPTER 9: RACE RIOTS TO TWO MORE FIRINGS!   145

Light of His Fire, His Holy Spirit. He has promised! The Church meetings must be transferred elsewhere by October 15. Not much time, but, praise God, with Him the impossible is wonderfully possible!

You will wonder if the Little Tabernacle Church of The Saviour can possibly finance such a moving out and the cost of a pastor and other workers for its continuing ministry for Christ. The answer, of course, is clearly, "No, not by itself. But God can and, we believe, will. "The Little Church has never had an income over $3000 per year, so, praise God, we're being called by faith into a hostile "desert" where God must be all in all - our Supply - our Strength - our Everything. We believe He will fully provide all the Manna we'll need, together with many other miracles in the precious Name of Jesus! (Phil.4:19) *But my God shall supply all your need according to his riches in glory by Christ Jesus.*

Many of you will be moved by the Holy Spirit to share in this continuing ministry of Jesus in this little ghetto Church. Please address all such gifts to The Church of The Saviour and be assured of God's great blessing to both you and your gift as we serve our risen and mighty Saviour together in His Amazing Mission in a very dark corner of this rebel world.

We move on with great confidence and joy in the Lord. We've seen so many miracles the past 15 months, we know greater blessings are ahead. Oh, how our Lord has blessed and is blessing us! Praise Him evermore!

Keep us in your prayers. Keep in touch. Keep praising Jesus with us!

With deepest regards in our Wonderful Saviour and Lord.

Yours in Him,

JSR/bwr   Joseph S. Rigell, Pastor

P.S. The Church is having to change its name slightly in order to incorporate under state laws. The Lord has led us to add "Little Tabernacle" as an apt prefix to Church of The Saviour. The incorporation was completed on Sept. 30, 1971! Praise God!

Please know we are so grateful for your faithful prayers and gifts in the past rough years. You know we are not quitters, and we know you won't quit us now. God hasn't fired us; He's giving us a tougher job to do!

PPS: Here is the main paragraph of the Dismissal Letter to Joseph S. Rigell from the Board of the Christian Community Center dated September 14, 1971:

"A schedule for the Fall and Winter seasons has been set up which will permit the Center to operate programs that can be financed within the income that may reasonably be expected. This program and schedule will not warrant the proportion of management with relation to staff as

it now stands. Because of this we regretfully must discontinue your connection with the Center as of September 30, 1971.
Yours very truly,
Christian Community Center. Inc.

Perhaps you may wonder how long the Christian Center lasted after the loss of the three key full-time staff. (Mrs. Shaw resigned 10 days later). Not long is the answer!

The elderly Board President tried to operate it on into that Fall and Winter, but found it too much for him to handle. Soon he was negotiating to sell the place to a Christian Rescue Mission, which was having to leave its quarters on the west side of Baltimore. After additional renovations, it became the "new" home of the fine "Baltimore Rescue Mission" for "homeless men and women."

- - - - - - - - - -

So we praise and thank God for this Firing too! To be fired at age 53 without any prospect of future income is not easy to take--unless the Lord has told you to trust Him and take it! And rejoice in Him! So He told us in His Word! He has wonderfully taken care of us, as He promised, and you will see as you read on. His promises are sure; they never fail!

**CHRISTIAN COMMUNITY CENTER
1970-71
J.R. AND HELPERS**

CHAP. 10

THE LITTLE TABERNACLE ARISES

But my God shall supply all your need according to His riches in glory by Christ Jesus.   - Philippians 4:19

Up to this time the little mission Church of the Saviour had been operating under the corporate umbrella of the United Presbyterian Church, but now, from every angle, it was being put out on the waters, to sink or swim by itself. So we quickly asked a lawyer friend to help us become incorporated under its own name, Church of The Saviour.

Shortly he told us that another church corporation had that name in the state of Maryland, and we would have to change it. After serious prayer we were led to propose the name of The Little Tabernacle Church of The Saviour. Mr. Pettit, our lawyer, quickly cleared this name with the state authorities, and soon had us officially incorporated in the State of Maryland by Sept. 30, 1971, our last day at the Christian Center.

We asked Mr. Pettit to proceed with all speed in helping us obtain federal tax exemption. Our application papers went in by November and were approved in about 90 days, an unusually short time for such a federal clearance. Praise the Lord forever, for His goodness and mercy.

We knew the Lord wanted us to stay in the community and were searching every block for some place for the Little Tabernacle to meet. Of course we didn't have any money to buy a building, but we knew the Lord would wonderfully provide when it was needed. How wonderfully He did! But first, let us tell you about a miracle that took place on the day we were fired; and another miracle during the last worship service in the Upper Room.

GOD'S LONG DISTANCE CALL VIA FLORIDA

An amazing thing happened in the evening of the day we were "fired" from the Christian Center and were rejoicing over God's remarkable Scriptural guidance concerning that situation, which we described earlier.

Naturally we were greatly disappointed at the turn of events. All of us had worked almost night and day for the previous fifteen months to get the Center established, to encourage participation and support, and to enlist volunteers for the work. Probably over $25-30,000 worth of free labor had been contributed. It had been a remarkable year of progress. Yet, we were not discouraged. Our eyes were on the Lord, and if this was what He wanted, it was what we wanted. He had something better ahead. Even with my pay ending in two weeks, we knew the Lord would provide!

During the 14 years at McKim we were always on "peon pay", but the Lord always made the ends meet. We never failed to tithe and give extra offerings to His Work. We sensed we were about to go into a new and exciting venture with the Lord, and we would see His mighty Hand of mercy and miracles in the days ahead, beginning this very same evening of the firing!

Almost no one knew it, except Betsy, but for over a year I had been suffering from a slipped disc in my lower back; at times it felt like a piece was missing from my spine. We had prayed much, but still no healing or relief. X-rays and treatments made by doctors and chiropractors had brought no relief.

In the evening of that same firing day there was a FGBMFI meeting to which Betsy especially wanted to go. Dr. Samuel Doctorian was the speaker, and I wanted to hear him too, but preferably from a prone position, like on a bed. He told how a highly placed lady in Egypt had asked him to pray for her unsaved husband to be saved and he did, but the Holy Spirit led him to warn her that things would get a lot worse before they got any better. And sure enough things got worse, but eventually the husband surrendered his heart to Jesus. At one point in the meeting, I whispered to Betsy not to be surprised if I slipped out to the car to lie down to relieve the pain. About this time one of the leaders came over and asked me to join the men in praying for the sick, which I did in spite of my own pain.

Afterwards, on our way out, suddenly here comes a little grey-haired woman up to me who says, "Are you the Rev. Rigell that works down on Baltimore Street?"

I said, "Yes, Ma'am."

We had never met before. She immediately plopped her things on a table, and said, "I've been looking for you all over and praying for you for the last three days. The Lord has shown me a vision of you and told me to pray earnestly for you, for Satan is trying to kill you."

I said, "Well, I can believe that."

At this she said, "Let me pray for you now." She boldly clamped her right hand on my head and began praying one of the most powerful prayers I had ever heard. Obviously she was one of the Lord's strong intercessors, sometimes called prayer warriors. When she got through, I knew I had been prayed for as never before. She had bound Satan and

CHAPTER 10: THE LITTLE TABERNACLE ARISES! 149

all his demons by the power of the Name of Jesus. She had bound the spirit of poverty and infirmity and had prayed for healing, renewing and abundant provisions in the Name of Jesus. She had commanded Satan and all his demons to take their hands off us and off God's provisions for us, we were God's servants, bought and kept by the blood of Jesus, the Lamb of God, and in the Name of Jesus they were to get out!

That little lady, Thelma Forest, who became a dear friend, was right on God's perfect timing. Not long before this we had been led to give the few hundred dollars which were left in our savings account to help an evangelistic campaign in Baltimore, so on this firing day we were facing a bad case of poverty. How grateful we were for this little God-fearing woman. No, my back was not immediately healed, but we knew it would be soon.

We headed for home, arriving about 11 p.m. The phone was ringing, long distance from Florida. The caller said he was a real estate man, had been trying to reach us for some time, to ask if we wanted to sell a lot we owned on a little bayou outside of Panama City, Florida, my old home town. This was September, 1971. We had almost forgotten about buying that lot in June 1955, for $25 a month, with the idea that perhaps someday the Lord would let us come back and have a little retirement home near the water. Once a year we got reminded when a small tax bill came.

I said to him, "Well, after what has happened today, I guess we should think about selling it."

He said, "I have two people who would like to buy it. How much do you want for it?"

I replied, "I don't know exactly how much to ask. I do know that such lots have gone way up in price during the past 16 years." So, I screwed up my courage and said, "We are probably going to have to ask at least $10,000 for it."

He cheerfully replied, "Oh, I think I can get that for you. Maybe more, maybe even $12,000."

I told him that we had just gotten fired that day, so he went to work and got $12,500 clear for us, and his commission over that, with a down payment of $2,500 to come in before Christmas and the rest in equal payments the next four years. The Lord is a good Business Man and a Good Provider! The Best! On that firing day He was clearly showing us that *He would truly supply all our needs through His riches in glory by Christ Jesus* (Phil.4:19). *That nothing could separate us from His Love in Christ Jesus* (Romans 8:39). And that *His Grace (Mercy) was more than sufficient* (II Cor.12:9); and that *He would make all things work out for our good as we loved Him and followed His purpose.* (Rom.8:28, Matt.6:33)!!!

THE TRAFFIC LIGHT HEALING

The painful back problem continued on for several weeks. I had been wearing a wide elastic back support with a small folded towel on the left side of my spine where it was most painful and seemed to have a missing link. This improvised back support gave me some relief, but the problem was still there, the disc missing from its proper place. After that little lady's anointed prayer, surely the Lord's healing would come soon, for hadn't she prayed for many people and the Lord had healed them?

One day I lost an old filling in one of my teeth and had to make an appointment with our dentist for repairs. He was an excellent dentist with three treatment rooms and patients in various stages of treatment. He put me in a contour dental chair. It was an early appointment and I was still a bit sleepy, so I promptly dozed off. He came in and repaired the tooth quickly, without using novocaine, barely waking me up. I paid the bill and said, "Thanks, Dr. M.. Have a nice day." Then I walked about a block to where our car was parked. I drove slowly back toward our house to pick up Betsy and had to stop at a long traffic light at Charles Street. While sitting there waiting for the stoplight to change, I felt the Lord saying, "Hold on to the steering wheel, but start leaning slowly toward the seat."

It seemed HIS hand was on my left shoulder and HE was saying slowly, "Farther, farther, farther," until my right shoulder was almost on the seat.

Suddenly, just as the light changed, I felt a distinct "pop-pop" in my back and an incredible sense of relief! HIS hand was gone from my shoulder. I straightened up, drove through the green light and slowly made it to the house, savoring that beautiful relief in my back all the way, and full of joy and desire to tell Betsy what the Lord had done at the traffic light. All pain was gone! He had healed me! Together we praised and thanked Him!

Now, some 16 years later, my back is still healed, thanks to the Good Lord's miraculous traffic light "Adjustment!" Not long after this wonderful healing at the traffic light, I was telling a doctor friend about it, and he asked that specific question, "Was there a distinct 'pop-pop' sound and feeling at the time?"

I told him, "Yes, that's exactly what it was." Obviously he knew precisely what was needed to get a slipped disc back in place. Thank God it's still in place!

CHAPTER 10: THE LITTLE TABERNACLE ARISES!

ANOTHER TRAFFIC LIGHT MIRACLE

Let me tell you about one other little traffic light miracle some years before this. While I was heavily engaged in the McKim Center work, I would take turns helping with the night program at the Center where we had basketball games, wrestling, weight lifting, ping-pong, and punching bags. This was to bring the teenagers in off the streets at night by giving them something positive to do and giving the staff the opportunity to have some directive influence with them, demonstrating by example the Lord's Better Way. Very often some of the old seamen, waiting for their next ship in a little rooming house next door (which we called the "Heart-Break Hotel") would come in to talk about their troubles, usually from drinking, and we would be able to have prayer with them and point them to the Lord.

Normally we would close at 10 p.m., but for some reason I was kept on until 11 p.m. talking with one of those seamen. Finally, dog tired, I got into our old Chevrolet and started for home, some 20 minutes away through town. About a half mile from the Center, I came to another stoplight at a heavily used intersection. A light changed overhead and being half asleep, I began moving across the intersection. The next thing I knew cars were blowing their horns madly at me, and I just narrowly escaped being hit by them. The lights on the corner beer sign had changed! Not the traffic light! Moving when beer signs change colors is not the best way to cross a very busy inner-city intersection. So far it hasn't happened again!

On another of those nights, a skinny little policeman from West Virginia, a newcomer to Baltimore's fine police force, stopped by to chat a few minutes. He told me about a couple of recent "close-calls" that had happened to him on his beat. How he got on the police force was a wonder; he was so skinny. He always looked as if his gun belt was going to slip down around his knees. Well, one night at a bar about a half a block away, as he passed by, the bartender came to the door and called him for help. There was a big drunk sitting at the bar in the back, who was getting rowdy because the bartender wouldn't serve him any more liquor. He'd had too much already. Would the policeman come and convince him to leave. So Joe, the skinny policeman, came in to do his duty. The drunk was on the bar stool in the back, hunched over the edge of the bar, glowering in all directions and shouting. "Bartender, give me another drink, before I really get mad."

Skinny Joe, the policeman, walked up behind him and put his hand on his shoulder and said in a kindly way, "Mister, the bartender says you've already had too much; come on out and go home quietly."

The drunk, with no more than a slight glance, casually shoved the policeman's hand off his shoulder and growled, "You go away. I want another drink, bartender."

At this, skinny Joe, the policeman, knew his authority was being challenged and he must get firmer. So now he lifted his night stick and tapped the drunk on the same shoulder and said, "Sir, I'm a Baltimore policeman. You've been asked nicely to leave, you've had too much to drink already, the bartender will not serve you any more, so I am ordering you to get up and leave quietly, right now or face arrest."

The policeman told me that he wasn't quite ready for what was about to happen. Sure enough the drunk started standing up, and up, and up, and up, until finally he towered over Skinny Joe, it seemed something like three feet, looking down on him with a sneer, like the giant he was, and said, "Who's gonna make me?"

Joe mustered all the courage he had and looked up to say in a strong voice, "I am", but his voice had changed to a shrill falsetto and all that came out was a little high pitched, squeaky, "I am!"

His knees were knocking together about 100 times per minute and he thought the drunk was going to pick him up and shred him, but, when he heard that high pitched, "I am", the humor of it broke the drunk up! Laughing as hard as he could, he threw his arm around Skinny Joe and walked out, laughing all the way.

That same night, policeman Joe told me about another incident a few days before on the other side of us. Some blacks had a big fight going inside this bar, and he was called to come in and stop it. Well, he went in and hardly said a word before they all grabbed him and threw him through the plate glass window, and went back to fighting. No doubt other policemen came quickly to his aid, and miraculously he was not injured.

I didn't see policeman Joe much after that. I suspect he found a job in a more peaceful state far, far away from Baltimore. Maybe he became chief of police in a quiet West Virginia town. I hope so. May the Lord bless him, wherever he is. I do hope he got out of Baltimore alive.

THE LAST UPPER ROOM SERVICE IN THE OLD FACTORY

We had been told to get out by the 15th of October and this was the 14th, our last Sunday in this Upper Room. Almost all the members who had stuck with us through the trying events of the past two years were present for this final worship service. Perhaps some 30 people, counting children and teenagers. After all our hard work, of course we were deeply saddened to have to leave, but our faith was in the Lord. We would not weep or bemoan our fate. It was a hot, muggy October

CHAPTER 10: THE LITTLE TABERNACLE ARISES! 153

day. Not a breath of air was stirring. The lower windows were all up, and the old stand-up fan was silent; it had burned out a few days before. So after the opening prayer of thanksgiving for God's mercies to us in the past and sure promises for the future, we announced the next meeting would be in a nearby park if no other place was found before next Sunday. Unknown to us, God was about to give us two fantastic reassurances of His love and power and presence with us, even as we sang the first hymn:

"HOW GREAT THOU ART!"[1]
by Stuart K. Hine
1) *Oh Lord My God when I in awesome wonder,*
Consider all the *worlds Thy hands have made.
I see the stars, I hear the *rolling thunder,
Thy power throughout the universe displayed.

(At that very moment heaven's mighty thunder began rolling across Baltimore and continued through the chorus. Most of our hands were lifted up in adoration and thanksgiving!)

Chorus:
Then sings my soul, my Saviour God to thee,
How great thou art, How great thou art. (2 times)

2) *When through the woods and forest glades I wander,*
And hear the birds sing sweetly in the trees,
When I look down from lofty mountain grandeur,
And hear the brooks and feel the gentle breeze.

(At that very moment the sweet breeze of God began blowing through the windows, lifting up and waving the newly made curtains back and forth on both sides of the room. Now we knew that God was hearing us and reassuring us! We sang on through the chorus and the last two verses at the top of our lungs, very excited that God was saying He really was with us!)
Chorus....

---

[1] Author's original words are "works" and "mighty". Copyright 1953 S.K. Hine. Assigned to Manna Music, Inc. Renewed 1981 by Manna Music, Inc. 25510 Avenue Stanford, Suite 101, Valencia, Ca 91355. International Copyright Secured. All rights reserved. Used by permission.

*3) And when I think that God His Son not sparing,
Sent Him to die I scarce can take it in,
That on the cross, my burden gladly bearing,
He bled and died to take away my sin.
Chorus....
4) When Christ shall come with shouts of acclamation
And take me home, what joy shall fill my heart.
Then I shall bow, in humble adoration,
And there proclaim, My God How Great Thou Art.
Chorus....*

We can't remember much else that happened that day, but it was a very happy worship time before the Lord, and a very happy Little Tabernacle family who left that Upper Room for the last time, ready for God's next move!

The next Sunday we did meet in a park nearby and one of the young men, whom the Lord had delivered from drugs, was officially accepted into our Church-care to go off to Bible School. He was to serve the Lord for several years after that in the middle West. We pray that he still is walking with and serving the Lord Jesus.

THE SEARCH BEGINS FOR ANOTHER HOME FOR THE LITTLE TABERNACLE

With our eviction only days away, it became our very urgent task to search for another meeting place for the Little Tabernacle. We had been praying for guidance and the Lord was already telling us He wanted us to stay in the community, ministering to the little Church family, and many other people we had known through the Community Center work. We knew the Lord had a place for us, but it seemed it would be up to us, to ask, seek, knock and find just as He tells us in His Word in Matt.7:7. So we set out asking, seeking, and knocking.

There was a little chapel on Caroline Street, just south of Baltimore Street which even had large stained-glass windows. There was some Hebrew writing in the cornerstone, and carved in the white stone peak of the facade inside a Star of David were the Greek letters IHS for JESUS. All this interested us very much, giving us a rise in our spirits, but we would drive on by saying, "Surely we could never have anything that nice." So we would look elsewhere.

We did find a small place, a tiny building on Eden Street in terrible disrepair, which was for sale for $2,000. But our dear lawyer friend, Rosser Pettit, saved us from moving in that direction, as there was no

CHAPTER 10: THE LITTLE TABERNACLE ARISES!   155

clear title.

One afternoon, before finally leaving the Center, during the last week of September, I felt from the Lord that Betsy and I needed to go meet the people who were operating a Messianic Jewish work in a nice looking building at 1503 E. Baltimore Street, called the Lederer Foundation. I'm sorry to say that in all our years on the Street we had never met Dr. and Mrs. Henry Einspruch. They turned out to be most hospitable and kind when we rang their doorbell. We must have visited with them for at least an hour, and they shared with us about their Messianic literature and Bible ministry to Jewish Believers around the world, including their New Testament in Yiddish, translated by Dr. Einspruch and which is still considered the finest ever produced. Their work was sponsored by the Lutheran Church.

Patiently they showed us throughout the building, mentioned the new gas furnace in the basement, took us to a back room on the first floor where they had their typesetting and printing-plate machines, to his large library on the second floor, and most amazing of all, at the end of the long hall on the first floor the door opened into their very large shipping room, lined all around with large bookshelves, holding thousands of copies of their Messianic books and pamphlets. Over by its front door, which opened on Caroline Street, were many packages stacked and ready for shipping to all parts of the world.

Our eyes were quickly drawn above the door to the beautiful stained-glass windows which we immediately realized were the ones we had seen from the outside. That lovely little Chapel on Caroline Street was actually joined to the 1503 building on Baltimore Street at their back sides and was the packing and shipping room for the Lederer Foundation Messianic Ministry, directed by the Einspruchs. Surprise-surprise! It was like discovering a very special jewel in a downtrodden ghetto. They told us their work had been started around 1920, and this was their chapel for Messianic worship services back when they first built it in 1925 for only $15,000. But when the Jews moved to the suburbs, they converted it into a shipping room.

At least three times during our guided tour through the buildings I tried to mention our need for a meeting place for the Little Tabernacle. But each time the Lord seemed to be saying not to do it. Back in their office we told them how much we appreciated what they were doing, and how much we were concerned for Israel and the Jewish people and how often we told people our own boss was a Jew named Jesus.

After words of encouragement to them and a brief prayer, we said goodbye. Out on the sidewalk, Betsy quickly "hopped" on me for not mentioning our need for a meeting place, and I told her the Lord kept saying, "Not now, don't do it."

So back home we went, still wondering about that visit and also about what next to do. A dear little neighborhood woman named Miss Kitty, who was desperately ill with cancer in a hospital, and whom we were visiting as often as we could, had invited us to use her row house for a meeting place. So for the next two or three Sundays we accepted her offer until another place, a vacant, old Barber School store-front, was made available to us for $50 per month!

Miss Kitty's place was fine in an emergency, but most of our little group suffered great anguish, because Miss Kitty was a cat and dog lover and her row house was so saturated with these odors, we could hardly stand it. Elder Ted and Sarah Shaw, two faithful long-time members, had two lovely daughters, Faith and Mary, and little Mary said, "If Jesus could stand a stable, surely we could stand Miss Kitty's cat and dog house." But you can be sure we all were glad to be able to move into the old Barber School store-front. No doubt Mary and Joseph were also very happy to move Baby Jesus out of that stable as soon as possible. Remember how the Heavenly Father sent the Wise Men with gold, frankincense and myrrh to help finance their flight to Egypt, not to be in luxury, but in safety while old King Herod did his massacre of babies trying to wipe out the King of Kings at His very beginning on earth.

About two weeks after our first visit with the Einspruchs at the Lederer Foundation, we were at home getting some mail out, and the Lord distinctly spoke to me and said, "Now, go call Dr. Einspruch about your need."

This was still while we were meeting in Miss Kitty's house. On the phone I greeted Dr. Einspruch and thanked him again for such a delightful visit with him and his wife, and for the tour of the Lederer Buildings. Then I said, "Dr. Einspruch, at this time our Church has just lost it's place of meeting. Would it ever be possible to rent or lease your beautiful little Chapel?"

He immediately replied, "Oh, no, no, no! That's impossible! We require it for the packing and shipping of our materials around the world to Jewish Believers in many, many nations. It's an important part of our work."

I was led to say, "Dr. Einspruch, we certainly understand that and are very thankful for your important work, and do not wish to hinder it in anyway. But, perhaps if you ever consider moving out of the area, which so many Jewish and Gentile people have done recently, would you be willing then to talk about letting us use your Chapel for our Church?"

And he said, "Why, yes, we would. In fact we are looking at a place now to move to, out in Park Heights, and in two weeks we will know

CHAPTER 10: THE LITTLE TABERNACLE ARISES!   157

if we can secure it."

"Then could we call you back in two weeks concerning this?" I asked.

"Oh, yes, please do," he replied, "That will be fine."

We told each other goodbye, and I quickly shared with Betsy and Mrs. Shaw the possible good news.

We were in for a big surprise the very next day. Our phone rang and it was Mrs. Einspruch asking to speak to "Dr. Rigell." (She had given me a quick D.D.--"Donated Doctor of Divinity!").

She immediately said to me, "Dr. Rigell, you spoke with my dear husband, Dr. Henry Einspruch, yesterday about the possible use of our buildings for your Church. Well, Dr. Einspruch is a very outstanding scholar and leader in this field, but it has become my part to handle business matters. And I must say that we cannot hold any talks about these buildings any time soon because it will be at least a year before we can move, if we decide on another place."

I said, "Mrs. Einspruch, we can understand that and we can surely wait a year if necessary. The Lord will provide us a temporary place to work until you move."

She immediately replied, "Well if you are willing to wait a year, perhaps we can arrange to talk with you about it."

I said, "We are certainly willing to wait." Then, screwing up my courage again, I asked her, "Mrs. Einspruch could you tell us just how much you may be asking for the buildings if you decide to sell?" (My mental computer had already gone over $75,000 or $80,000 as I waited for her answer.)

She replied, "Oh my, we've done so much, new furnace, new roof, new this and new that. We will have to ask at least $10,000."

I gulped silently and asked, "For which building?"

"Oh," she said, "for BOTH!"

I could hardly believe what I was hearing, but quickly asked, "Mrs. Einspruch, when do you think we can begin our talks?"

She answered, "Will next week be all right?"

And I said, "It sure will be. Praise the Lord! Mrs. Einspruch, would Thursday at 10 a.m. at your office be OK?"

She said, "Yes."

And I almost shouted, "Thank you, Mrs. Einspruch!"

By the next week we had had the funeral service for the grandfather of a dear young drug addict named Carmen, whom the Lord had delivered in an all-night prayer watch. At the funeral service we would receive a special gift from the grandfather's brother which was to become the downpayment on the Little Tabernacle's new home. Here is how it happened!

THE AMAZING FUNERAL HONORARIUM

Carmen had been one of the young drug addicts whom we were able to help for a short time through the love and power of Jesus, back at the Christian Center. But she had dropped out of sight for a while. We didn't know where she was. Somehow she got in touch with our Elder friend, Frank DiMattei, saying that her Grandfather had died and her Grandmother needed a minister to hold his funeral and they wanted me to do it. We called them back that night to let them know that we would help, with a family prayer-time at the funeral home the night before, and the funeral service there the next day.

At the family prayer service that night, after reading appropriate Scriptures for the family concerning salvation through Jesus Christ, and assurance of eternal life through His death and resurrection, and a brief prayer time, we were invited to come to the family home for refreshments, which we agreed to do. Suddenly, there was a lot of commotion--noisy running in and out of the funeral home by relatives. It turned out that one or two children momentarily had been lost. They were soon found and calm returned. We've always remembered Brother Frank's comment during that flurry of activity and excitement: "I decided to stay by the casket; it was much more peaceful there!"

At Carmen's grandmother's home we found ourselves sitting next to the deceased grandfather's brother from Atlanta. He was a distinguished looking, grey-haired businessman, head of his own large company in Atlanta. After further conversation we found that he was a key member of a Baptist Church in Decatur, and his Pastor was a former classmate of mine, President of our Senior class, at Columbia Presbyterian Seminary in Decatur. (Don Aderholt was the only Baptist in our class.) After a brief time at the grandmother's, we offered to take Mr. D. and his wife to a new motel near John Hopkins Hospital, which was on our way home.

The next morning before the main funeral service, I was waiting in the undertaker's office when this dear gentleman quietly handed me a small folded piece of paper, saying on behalf of the family he wanted to express their appreciation for our help.

I assumed it was a funeral honorarium and said, "Thank you very much, Mr. D," and put it in my pocket.

Immediately, I sensed the Lord saying, "Take it out and look at it."

I opened it and saw the figure 20 and nodded my thanks again. "Nice. Thank you sir."

Again, I felt the Lord saying, "Look at it carefully."

There was no decimal point, but another zero. I looked again, still another zero, $2,000--from a man we never saw before the previous

CHAPTER 10: THE LITTLE TABERNACLE ARISES!   159

night and might never see again! I wanted to hug his neck. Hallelujah, the Lord had provided the full down payment on the Little Tabernacle's "New buildings" for which the purchase talks would begin very soon.

Later we wrote to thank him and tell what his generous gift had done for the glory of God. We'll thank him again "up there!"

The rest of the service went fine, no more lost children. We hear from the widow, Lucy, and from Carmen infrequently. Apparently Carmen had urged her great Uncle to do something real nice for us! He certainly did! Bless his memory. Another Wise Man!

THE CONFERENCE WITH THE EINSPRUCHS

On the following Thursday, as agreed, Betsy and I went to meet again with the Einspruchs. They received us cordially and began telling us about the renovation work that would have to be done at the new place they were buying out on Park Heights Ave., indicating that it would take nearly a year to complete. We reassured them that the Lord was working out a temporary place for us to meet only a half a block away, and that He had just in the past few days provided a good down payment, should the sale be approved. We proceeded to tell them the amazing way it came to us from a man we had never known before. No doubt this encouraged them to have more confidence in dealing with us.

Again they took us through the building, to show us the things they would be taking, including his library book cases upstairs, the office equipment, and the special type setting and printing plate machines, which they would be selling. They would be leaving in the building a piano, over a dozen captain's chairs, and a number of large Biblical pictures in beautiful frames, plus drapes, and a large quantity of book-shelving in the "shipping room Chapel", which later we were to use for shelves and counters throughout the building. The final agreed on price for the two beautiful buildings with all these extras was $10,500.

Our conference probably lasted an hour and a half until we had covered the necessary points for a contract to be drawn up, which they said their lawyer would do. When it was ready, they would contact us for a closing meeting with their lawyer and ours present. With a deep sense of thanksgiving to God and appreciation to this dear couple, Dr. and Mrs. Einspruch, who had been faithfully and courageously carrying on this beautiful work for Jesus for more than 50 years, we left this meeting as if on a miracle-cloud of God's mercy and love.

FIRED AGAIN AND AGAIN, PRAISE THE LORD!

JESSE'S PART

During this time a very interesting side-light was taking place, which we learned later on from Mrs. Einspruch.

For many, many years in the next block, directly across from the old barber school, which we would be renting for the next year, was a little grocery store called "JESSE'S." Everybody in the neighborhood knew about "JESSE'S." It was one of the last little "Ma and Pa" Jewish stores in the area and one of the few to survive the riots of '68. Jesse Hermanson and his wife were tiny people, even smaller than I, but were the kindest and friendliest of people. No doubt this had helped them to survive.

They were also close friends with the Einspruchs, and each week would get together for the Erev Shabbat (Friday evening) meal and afterwards play a little canasta. So after our first contact with the Einspruchs, they asked their friends, Jesse and his wife, if they knew anything about us.

And Jesse replied, "Oh yes, I know them. They have been doing a good work in the area for a long time, helping the kids through a little Church down the street at McKim Center. Pastor Rigell was head of it for a long time. You ask me should you sell your place to them? Oh, yes, they are good people; they will take care of it. You sell it to them, and be sure to **Leave A Little Wheat in the Field for them.** An ancient Jewish custom, noted in the book of Ruth in the Bible. (Ruth 2:16)

- - - - - - - - - -

Glory to God! They practically left the whole field for us! No doubt both buildings were worth 10 times more than what they were selling them to us for! Praise The Lord forever! And bless the memories of these dear Jewish friends.

During the next ten months the Lord did send in more than enough to make the final payment. By June first it was up to $6,029, and by Sept. 2, 1972 the full amount was on hand! It was like buying a twin mansion when you only had two cents to your name. God knows how to take care of His kids! (Matt.6:33) Hallelujah!

We are the ones who once rode by this stained-glass windowed chapel with the Star of David carved in the stone capital, and the actual Hebrew words from Psalm 118:43 inscribed in the cornerstone and said to ourselves, "We could never have such a nice place as that, could we?" That Hebrew inscription reads: **The stone that was rejected by the builders, is become the head of the corner.** Little did we know what the Lord had in store for us. (See I Cor.2:9).

CHAPTER 10: THE LITTLE TABERNACLE ARISES!

OUR NEXT TENT, THE OLD BARBER SCHOOL

One couldn't argue over the price of $50 a month for a meeting place plus another pigeon hole office with a sink and commode closet. With all the old barber chairs out of the barber school room, it made a fairly nice Christian meeting room. The move from Miss Kitty's was almost across the street. From the Christian Center which we'd just left, we were about two blocks away. From McKim Center, we were 3 blocks away; so we were still very much in the old neighborhood, and a whole bunch of people in the area were still going to Hell with great persistence, refusing to believe and receive and follow JESUS. (See John 3:16-17, 34-36 and Acts 4:12.)

You may have wondered why we have stayed on in "the impossible mission"--trying to keep our lights on for God in the growing darkness of the inner-city--seeking to win souls to Christ in the devil's backyard--preaching the Gospel of Jesus Christ in the face of mounting apostasy and opposition. Kitty's Dream will explain part of the reasons why.

Kitty was a tiny woman living on East Baltimore St., who fought a terrific battle against throat cancer, probably from heavy smoking. In her late sixties, widowed, alone, except for her dog and cats and a few friends. The doctors performed drastic surgery on her face, throat, neck. She battled to live, and prayed, and cheered up the nurses, and her pastor and his wife (Bets and me). We visited her often in her final days in the hospital. During this time, Kitty urged us to use her row house for the Church meetings in October when we had no other place.

Although the Lord had already told us to stay on in the area with the Church ministry, seeking to win these dear people to Jesus, Miss Kitty's dream was a tremendous confirmation. Here's the way she told it from her hospital bed:

KITTY'S DREAM
Feb. 25, 1972

From her hospital bed, struggling to be understood (half her tongue was gone), she told us how the Lord Jesus had just appeared in a vision to let her know He loved her and was with her. Another time she told us of a dream: "I was in a bus which was sliding backwards down a steep hill, at the end of which was a bottomless fiery pit, with all my friends and neighbors in it. I was headed toward it too! You and Rev. Sid were on the sidewalk watching. I called out to you through the bus window, 'Don't leave. These people need you.'

"Rev. Sid replied, 'We've been trying to help them find the Way for so long, it's no use.' But you caught my hand and held on and said you would stay. Somehow Jesus stopped the bus and saved me. Then I saw a restaurant window with such high tables and chairs I couldn't see the top, and with legs so wide around I couldn't grab hold to pull up to see..."

Praise God, Kitty was saved at the last moment and was enabled by Jesus to begin feeding at God's Big Spiritual Table, to know she was ready to go to be with Him, to know the deep joy of communing with Him right here, to know that He was keeping her pastor and his wife in the battle for the lives and souls of her neighbors, to know that many of them also were going to be saved!

Sixteen years later, Miss Kitty's long-ago neighbor, desperately sick in Church Home hospital, finally accepted Jesus as her Saviour and happily gave up her long-time addiction to cigarette smoking. Today she openly confesses her faith in Jesus and is apparently recovered from her sickness which she and her family thought was her last. Praise God for Miss Kitty's dream and for her neighbor's salvation, at long last. May the Lord grant that all her family will turn to JESUS and be saved, too. Many times it takes coming face to face with Death and Hell to wake a person up and help him turn and go God's way through Jesus, to Heaven not Hell! You know JESUS is still saying what He said to His first disciples just before He died on the cross, **I am the Way, the Truth, and the Life, no man cometh unto the Father but by me.** (John 14:6). And rough-tough Apostle Peter repeated this same thought right after that first Pentecost when he preached, **That there's no other name under heaven given among men, whereby we must be saved.** (Acts 4:12).

MIRACLES IN THE STORE FRONT

During this transition time, each day we kept seeing miraculous timings and provisions of the Lord. It was almost as if we could just look up to heaven when there was a need and in a few minutes it would be provided. As mentioned, there were a lot of repairs and fast improvised renovations necessary to make the former "Barber School" at 1437 E. Baltimore St. usable by the Little Tabernacle. We remember the walls were all beat up in the main room where they had taken down mirrors and fixtures. Just a few days before we rented it, a dear retired engineer, a Presbyterian Elder by the name of Herb Wilhelm, had insisted that we come out and pick up some used, heavy-duty curtains that could be quickly tacked up and serve as wall coverings.

This elder had a remarkable sense of humor, very much like the comedian Bob Hope. At his house there was an evergreen bush at the entrance that almost every month "bloomed" a different kind of flower!

CHAPTER 10: THE LITTLE TABERNACLE ARISES!   163

After a period he would go out in the evening and change the blooms; they were all artificial! When you visited him he would keep you rolling with laughter with his dry humor and twinkling eyes! Once we told him we'd just come back from New Jersey and had met a man and his wife in a certain town who had the same last name as his.

We asked, "Are you kin to them?"

Without batting an eye, Wilhelm asked "Are they rich?"
If they were, he'd be glad to claim them as kinfolk. Actually he didn't know them. Well that station wagon load of curtains dressed up the old barber school walls and made that long room quite usable.

At the same time, we needed a polaroid camera to take some black and white pictures to let our friends know that we were still alive and well on Baltimore Street. Within about an hour, an old friend who worked at City Hall and often came to have lunch with us, arrived for another lunch-break bearing a polaroid camera he had just purchased at a downtown pawnshop. Irv Lennon said, "Something told me you might need this, when I saw it in that pawnshop window."

After much hard work, cleaning, scrubbing, repairing, we were ready to have our first Thursday "Praise-The-Lord-Luncheon" in the Old Barber School. We saw we needed a tape recorder for the special speaker, Linda Requard, who would be giving a teaching series on "The Baptism of the Holy Spirit." A number of outside guests would attend. Well, who should show up for lunch that day, but Irv again holding a tape recorder under his arm? As before he said he had passed that pawnshop, and something had told him we might need one of these gadgets. So here it was! Well, Irv not only kept us supplied with various items like these, but also with news from City Hall.

Linda's teaching series on the Baptism of the Holy Spirit was a powerful one, and many people from near and far received The Holy Spirit Baptism in that "scroungy" place on Baltimore Street, which quickly came to be known as a "Spiritual Filling Station," or an "Oasis For Spiritually Hungry People."

Someone brought a little Catholic sister by the name of Sister Felix to hear this series by Linda, and she asked for prayer to receive this Blessed Baptism of the Holy Spirit. She did! Later this precious little nun, originally from England, with still a trace of a British accent (reminded us of Nanan, Betsy's childhood English governess) would testify with a glow on her face that, "Once I was only interested in the things of the past, but now I am only interested in the things of the future." And when asked why she was not wearing the nun's black dress or "habit," she would reply, "My Spouse is very much alive. I'm not in mourning!" When asked at the convent where she was going as she left for the Thursday luncheon she replied, "To have lunch with the

Lord!" How she would radiate His joy when we would sing Psalm 30:11-12! *Thou hast turned my mourning into dancing for me, Thou hast put off my sackcloth, and girded me with gladness, To the end my glory may sing praise unto Thee, and not be silent. Oh, Lord my God, I will give thanks unto Thee forever.* Sister Felix went to be with her Spouse on Christmas 1986 at the age of 94 years!

There were many healings, renewings, deliverances and salvations during our year-long sojourn in that Old Barber School storefront! To God be all the praise, glory, honor and thanksgiving! Almost hated to leave it!

A group from a Full Gospel suburban church came one night a week to operate a coffeehouse and street ministry and had many decisions for Christ. The place was ideal for this type of ministry since there were big plate glass windows outsiders could see through and doors they could walk straight in from the street. Many a curious youngster came in for refreshments and received Jesus and a new way of living. Many others came and went away mocking, as in JESUS' own day.

In one of Linda's last teaching sessions, she ended it with a very wonderful prayer, and then the Holy Spirit gave her the following amazing message in tongues with the interpretation. The message came forth with great clarity and shows clearly that the Lord still speaks by the Holy Spirit to his followers today, to guide them and to show them things to come. Here is this amazing prophetic message which is still being fulfilled today. All praise and glory to the Holy Name of Jesus forever! (I Cor. 12: 1-11; I Cor. 14:3; John 16:13-15).

AMAZING PROPHECY GIVEN BY THE HOLY SPIRIT

At The Little Tabernacle through Linda Requard, March 2, 1972

"I would speak a word of encouragement, saith the Lord, to the body of Christ in this place. I know your works and I have tried you, saith the Lord, sorely. But I know thy works and I know thy patience and I know thy endurance, and I see that you have not departed from your first love. And I will vindicate you, saith the Lord, and I will show Myself strong in this place, saith the Lord, and I will lay your needs on the hearts of other members of My body. And I shall rally around you other brothers and sisters, at the sight of which your hearts will be glad and rejoice. But know this, saith the Lord, that this work is not yours but it is Mine; therefore, stand still and see the salvation of the Lord. The battle is not yours, be not overwhelmed, be not overcome, but stand still and see the salvation of the Lord. For the battle is Mine, saith the Lord; I have stripped the powers and principalities of darkness of their power at the Cross. And as you stay true to your vision of the

CHAPTER 10: THE LITTLE TABERNACLE ARISES!   165

Cross, and as you take up your cross daily and deny yourself and follow Me, I say I will reward you in this world, as well as in the world to come.

"And I will lift up the standard of the Cross, and though the enemy has come in like a flood against this place, he shall not prevail, for I say I shall send forth signs and wonders to follow the Word of God, if you will but speak it in faith.

"Therefore, take unto you the full armour of God, take unto you the full armour of God, and after you have done all, stand, stand, stand against the wiles of the enemy, for I will give you the Sword of the Spirit with great power. And if you will but pray in the Spirit and wait upon Me, for praise waiteth upon Me, saith the Lord, I will show you great and mighty things that you do not know. I promise you, saith the Lord, I do not know how to say it in a way that would truly arrest your attention and make your hearts respond. But when it shall come to pass, you shall remember that I have promised you, saith the Lord. Just stand fast, do not compromise what I have given you. Pray in the Spirit is my command. Test me, prove me, and I will open up the windows of heaven and pour out a blessing that you will not have room to receive. Oh, I will call those from many places, and they shall stand with you, and the Name of the Lord Jesus Christ shall be glorified in this area."   - - - - - - - - -

Linda and her parents had been long time friends, having been introduced to the deeper life in the Holy Spirit in the middle 60's. Linda had spent one of her summers home from College (ORU) working with us at McKim Center in the Vacation Bible School and Youth Club programs. The effectiveness of her work with the young people was absolute proof of the power of Jesus Christ through the Holy Spirit in a person's life. We still keep in touch with this beloved family and have seen Linda and her preacher husband, Jim, a couple of times in Israel, on tours from their parish in Louisiana. Not long ago her parents, Lou and Louise Requard, sent the Little Tabernacle a station wagon load of food supplies.

We still are amazed at the Lord's prophecy through Linda and have seen already many incredible fulfillments of it both here in the U.S. and overseas. Praise The Lord forever!

GIN'S REQUEST GRANTED!

It is interesting to note that this prophecy was given on March 2, 1972, at one of our free-for-all "Praise-The-Lord" Thursday Luncheons. That date was the 26th wedding anniversary for Betsy and me, and

166   FIRED AGAIN AND AGAIN, PRAISE THE LORD!

Betsy's father and mother's (Pappy and Gin, for Virginia) 50th wedding anniversary. They were hoping to celebrate this anniversary later in the year with a family reunion, but in May of that year, while working among her beloved flowers outside the house at the "Bight", after complaining of a terrible headache, she suddenly collapsed and was gone. It was a terrible shock to Pappy and the family, but such a "going" is one of God's most merciful ways of ending our earthly journey. Praise His Holy Name forever! Grandma Gin was a most loving and thoughtful wife, mother and grandmother, and friend of many, many people. A real treasure, and a lovely lady always. She had never wanted to be a burden to anyone, and the Lord granted her request! "Baruch Ha Shem!" --- "Bless The Name of The Lord!"

"THE BIGHT" - PAPPY & GRANDMA GIN'S HOME IN SOUTHERN MARYLAND, BUILT LARGELY WITH THEIR OWN HANDS-1951-52

CHAP. 11

THE FREBURGER STORY

Though He slay me yet will I Trust Him. - Job 13:15

EXCITING ADVENTURES AHEAD

After the separate incorporation of the Little Tabernacle Church and relocation to the "store-front" old Barber School, and the initial agreement on the purchase of the "new" buildings, we felt from the Lord that great things were ahead, that surely the Little Tabernacle Church should rededicate itself as a Body to the service of the Lord. This special service took place on December 5, 1971, and was followed by increased participation by a group of young believers led by Mr. & Mrs. Bob Freburger.

To be correct, we should say led by Mrs. Freburger with her husband Bob, at that time, aiding them with transportation, but still not confessing his need of Jesus for salvation. He was a gruff, tough, red-headed, top-notch welder at that time in a major industry in Baltimore, the Lever Bros. His pride and joy was a nice, big second-hand Cadillac.

Bob and Phyllis had four children, two boys and two girls. In the following pages Phyllis will tell her heart-touching story of how she met JESUS, received the Holy Spirit Baptism, and took a miracle and trial-filled "Journey Into Faith."

"A JOURNEY INTO FAITH"[1]
by Phyllis Freburger

God had a call on my life a long time ago. Not understanding the spiritual things happening at the time caused me to run in fear.

For example: I often saw a figure standing in my room at night as if just watching over me. Also, I would sing and talk in a strange language

---

[1] Used with permission of the author.

while working and playing. It felt so good, but someone dear to me overheard me and really laughed. I felt ridiculed and embarrassed.

Frequently in dreams other spirits warned me not to follow my Pentecostal grandmother up the steps she was climbing. I longed to be good but found myself falling deeper and deeper into sin. After trying and failing so many times, I made several suicide attempts. Only the Lord's mercy prevented my death. Finally, I cried out to God in utter despair.

One night the Lord gave me a dream. A long line of people were going up a sandy mountain side. They were rushing and falling, pushy and panicky. No one looked familiar. I was scared and confused. I tried to get in front of someone to ask what was happening. They wouldn't stop to answer. They ignored me. At last, I fell to my knees exhausted. Someone gave me their hand. I looked up and saw a long white garment. Then I looked at this person. It didn't seem possible, but I recognized Jesus. I felt something deep inside my mind say, 'But that was just a story wasn't it?' But at that moment I sensed that He was real and personal. He said nothing, but began walking again. He was not rushing. He was walking in a different direction than the crowd. I couldn't figure out why they weren't walking with Him. After a brief struggle, I decided to follow Him. As I took those first steps in the direction he had gone, a sureness and a peace gripped me. For the first time in my life I knew everything was all right.

Because of my desire to be a good parent, we started attending church. My husband, Bob, generally worked on Sunday, so it was just the four children and I. A Lutheran Church was conveniently nearby, so we attended there. (As a child, I attended the Pentecostal Church with my grandparents until I was 15 years old. I hated all the emotionalism and had no understanding of their beliefs. So for the following 10 years I did not attend church.) In the fall of 1969, our ladies prayer group in the Lutheran Church had a visitor. He shared strange things with us. Strange, yet somehow exciting. He talked about I Cor.12, and the gifts of the Spirit. Even though I came from a Pentecostal background, I heard things that, by then, were foreign to the beliefs I accepted. As he told about Jesus healing today in the same miraculous ways as when He walked the earth, something was stirred deep within me.

A few months later another visitor came. A Catholic lady who talked about the baptism of the Holy Spirit, healing, prophecy, speaking in tongues....speaking in tongues? I knew that could not be of God. I remembered people saying so when they were questioned about the Pentecostal Church. Or could it be? I longed for the truth that I was soon to find out. I ran home in the rain crying. I got on my knees and asked Jesus and He showed me in His Word. Acts 1 & 2. Especially

CHAPTER 11: THE FREBURGER STORY

Acts 2:39 saying, *for as many as the Lord God shall call.* That's me, I thought. If it is in the Word of God that's good enough for me.

A few months later, I received the Baptism of the Holy Spirit. As I started being open and bold for Jesus some misunderstanding arose among my relatives, church, and friends. But though the dealings of the Spirit I realized what the enemy was trying to do, which made me more determined to follow my Lord Jesus and claim victory for others, too.

Through some trial with our oldest son (16 at the time) the Lord dealt with my heart to invite young people into our home and share the love of Jesus with them. After struggling with the Lord about what I lacked and my hang-ups about having my home messed up, we started meeting in January 1971. The Lord was faithful to His word to supply all our need. One surprising thing to me was that Bob agreed to let them come in. He was angry and uptight every time I even spoke about Jesus but, nevertheless, he agreed. During the meetings, he either tinkered in the basement or watched TV in our bedroom.

About this same time, Bob, a welder by trade, became interested in painting oil paintings. The subject that seemed to be heavy on his heart? Jesus! The Lord's Supper, the Garden of Gethsemane, and then a painting of Matt.7:13,14 were among his first works. Praise the Lord! He never read the Bible. He didn't even know Scripture, and yet he painted Scripture. Whenever he was questioned about it he got very uptight. He was gruff and would mumble, "I don't know why I painted it." - But I did. Praise God!

Also at this time God sent a precious sister on the scene, Judy Reamer. What do you suppose her occupation had been? An art teacher! Bob fell "in love" with her, and as she was sharing about painting, she was also sharing the love of Jesus, and Bob was soaking it up.

Also on the scene was Mother Pace, the spiritual mother the Lord gave me. Sometimes as she was getting out of our car, she would touch Bob on the shoulder and say, "I claim you for the Lord." This guy who was cursing me for talking about the Lord would say to her, "Keep praying for me." Bob wasn't very good at hiding his hunger. Thank God!

In December 1971, one of the young people, Connie, came home from a meeting and had a brochure about a Christian rally--Explo '72--in Dallas, Texas. The young people started making plans to go and one of the parents offered to watch my younger children if I could take the young people. "Impossible," I thought, then quickly remembered *'with God all things are possible.'* But how could I leave Bob and my children for 2 or 3 weeks? One night I mentioned it to Bob and the kids at the dinner table and waited for him to thunder. But instead, Bob amazed me with his reply. "We can sell our Cadillac (1967 model, but very important to him), buy a bus, take our three weeks vacation, and take the young people to Texas."

The Lord started sending us large sums of money. When Bob witnessed this, tears came to his eyes. I knew something deep was happening, because he just never cried. He made the statement that if that starts happening, it would make a believer out of him. And praise God it did! On March 3, 1972, the anointing of God fell in our prayer group and four Lutheran youths were baptized in the Holy Spirit. It was so precious and my heart ached that Bob was missing it. But the overflow must have saturated the bedroom where Bob was sleeping. In the night the Lord awoke him and told him he would need a Bible if he was to go to Texas with the young people. The next day Bob found himself in a Christian bookstore buying one of their best Bibles.

At the leading of the Lord, I invited Brother and Sister Rigell (Sid and Betsy) to dinner on March 7. Little did I know these were the ones chosen by God to stand with us through a terrific crisis in our lives. Sid shared with Bob about his painting and the true meaning of salvation. We knew Bob believed in his heart by now, but he had not made open confession (Rom.10:9).

The 13th of March on our way to a prayer meeting Bob made open confession of Jesus as his Saviour. Praise the Lord! He came home from work the next day and threw the ash tray away. He was a three-pack-a-day cigarette smoker. He said the Lord spoke to him at work and said, "You don't need them anymore." He was completely delivered! Praise God! The next evening at mealtime he announced he was going to pray the blessing. Bob never prayed with us before. Yet, now, he prayed and cried, thanking God for so much and holding others up to be saved. Our three oldest children began to cry and raised hands to God, praising Him. The youngest, eight years old, just sat looking from one to the other. All I could do was laugh, tears streaming down my face. I never imagined anything this wonderful. Our home was full of love, joy and peace. Thank you, Jesus!

Two days later, we had a positive leading on the bus. It cost just the amount God had sent us by that time. In the process of Bob settling things about the bus, Bill, the owner, gave his heart to Jesus. Since then Bill's wife, mom and dad, and many others in the family came to Jesus. On that very first visit to their home, Bob found himself witnessing for three hours and then getting on his knees with them to pray. One beautiful thing was that our son (12) was there taking it all in. Praise God!

Since we had about 200 young people come through our home, we were trusting God to pick the crew to go with us to Dallas. Isaiah 55:8

CHAPTER 11: THE FREBURGER STORY

says *His thoughts and ways are not like ours.* When the Lord sent me into the prison ministry I met another volunteer, a mother with two backslidden daughters who were chosen of God to go with us. The Lord also gave me names of kids who I wasn't even sure of their salvation. I called them and told them what the Lord put on my heart and left it between them and the Lord. I even made reservations for some before talking to them. The Lord told me there were going to be some going with us whom we had not yet met. A call came from Washington from two young people who wanted to go and, immediately, I got the okay from the Lord. The Lord worked out every detail with school, as we were leaving two weeks before the close of school. He also dealt with parents (some unsaved) to let their youths come. One parent called me a week before departure and said her husband was concerned about finances. He thought we should have at least $1000 when we left. I told her not to worry; we had $83.50 and God's promise-note big enough to supply all our needs. By departure time, we had nearly $1500. Praise Him!

One week after Bob's salvation, he received the Baptism of the Holy Spirit. It was after the prayer meeting and he took some kids home. Bob returned home and as he tried to open the front door, it was as though a vacuum kept it closed. We were not aware Bob was at the door because we were still praying over some of the young people. Bob waited, thinking someone was trying to prevent any interruptions during prayer. After a few minutes he tried again, and suddenly realized the enemy was trying to keep him out. In Jesus power, Bob pulled hard and the door opened. No one was near the door. Our eight year old asked to receive the Baptism of the Holy Spirit and afterwards Bob sat in and asked to receive. Praise God! And so he did.

On Monday, June 5 at 7 a.m. we boarded the bus. Sixteen young people, Mother Pace, our four children, Bob and me.

The night before, during communion at church, I realized Bob was flushed and I asked Brother Sid, calling him aside, to pray for Bob. That evening Bob was feverish with cold symptoms starting, but insisted on maintaining the schedule.

Several times before we left Mother Pace had a vision of someone mighty sick in Texas. "Honey," she would say, "It will take a miracle to save them. Whoever it is they are really sick."

Bob and some of the young people had worked hard to fix up the old school bus and it was a beautiful sight to see. Across the front was printed "Disciples of Jesus" and the sides proclaimed bold Bible messages.

We boarded the bus with thanksgiving, prayer, and praise to God, asking His protection and guidance. We rode for hours singing praises to Jesus, and a spirit of love and unity took hold. Stopping at a gas station to share the love of Jesus, eat and gas up, we saw our first convert come to Jesus. Forest, a young gas station attendant, has continued the fellowship through one of the young people.

Later that afternoon, we had trouble with the tires. During the three hour wait to get them fixed we walked around sharing the love of Jesus and sang and praised God. When we pulled out of the garage, Bob handed me a pink copy of the bill. It cost $146.15, and the owner donated that to us. We shared the news as we drove out, the praises almost lifted the bus in the air. God blessed again that night by putting it on the hearts of the campground owners to give us half price at the camp.

The next morning at 6 a.m., I took a walk in the morning dew to seek the Lord for guidance. I walked a short distance from the camp and sat on a ledge in a gully. Looking up, I saw in front of me large hills with the words "Only Believe, Only Believe" shooting across the hills and heard a choir of angels saying it over and over in unison, "Only Believe, Only Believe." Praise God!

We started our days in the Word and God fed us richly. Everyday He gave us Prov. 4:22 - "They are life to them that find them and health to all their flesh." We traveled much and shared as the Lord led. By early evening, we pulled into a campsite anxious to get our clothes washed and dried. Spirit-filled Baptist people ran the camp. We soon found out the dryer was broken. As we began to wash clothes and put up lines, a storm came up. I suggested we pray and ask God to stop the rain. It rained all the harder. Lightening was hitting all around us and stung a couple of us in the ankles. We started dancing and praising God in the rain. God spoke and said not to worry, we would have our clean clothes when we needed them. The presence of God was so mighty and so real. As I looked around I saw figures of men in navy blue suits standing arm in arm in a complete circle around us. I felt fearful until the Lord told me they were His angels, Ps. 91:11. Praise Him! Thank you Jesus! The owners of the camp joined our campfire service, and afterwards gave us $80, saying they were led of the Lord. Also the wife insisted on washing and drying our clothes and brought them back to us by morning. Praise Jesus! God is faithful.

Bob was resting much between driving. His fever broke but his right eye was swollen. We kept praying and believing God to heal him.

We had many opportunities to share in food stores, gas stations, shopping centers, etc. One day in a laundromat a young negro fellow expressed a real hunger to know Jesus better. Mother Pace and I shared with him about the baptism in the Holy Spirit and he received. Praise the Lord!

CHAPTER 11: THE FREBURGER STORY

One day while driving along praising the Lord, our spirits were low. Then a tremendous anointing fell as we sang over and over, "I want more of Jesus - More and More and More." We started rejoicing in the Spirit, and prophecy came forth for many. I don't know how Bob kept on driving, but I believe the Holy Spirit was in full control and our spirits were certainly lifted.

Of course the enemy was very upset with us and was pressing in hard. A spirit of heaviness would crowd us and the Lord would stress the importance of His Word and keeping fully armoured. As we shared in the Word, praised God and stayed in the Spirit, the love and unity grew among us. I was falling in love with these kids more each day. They were real troopers for Jesus. God was dealing with us in a mighty way, teaching us to share one another's burdens and pray for one another as we confessed our faults to each other. We were eaten up with insect bites. It was hot and sticky and we were hungry and very tired. But we had to keep pressing on to accomplish what God was sending us for. There were many trials and tribulations which made us more determined to be bold for Jesus.

We reached Texas on June 10, and went to the home of an aunt and uncle of one of the youths. The Crawfords offered to open their home to us when we reached Texas. We prayed and asked the Lord for His will and He said go. They had two sons on drugs, worshipping satan, really messed up. Before it was over they were saved and baptized in the Holy Spirit. The Crawfords also received the baptism of the Holy Spirit before our two week visit was up. And Mr. Crawford had poured down the drain gallons of the other kind of spirits!

June 12, we went to our campsite near Dallas. During our prayer time, an anointing fell, and the Holy Spirit began to rebuke the enemy. A tremendous deliverance took place in our camp for many that night. After that, I believe everyone realized in a fuller way the mighty power of God.

On June 13, we went to the Cotton Bowl and saw a tremendous sight. Some of the young people sat, in order to form a cross, in the middle of the field. They were clapping and lifting holy hands to God and worshiping in great unity.

For a few days Bob's eye was clear and he seemed fine. But now at the Cotton Bowl, Bob was flushed again and said he had a headache. I was exhausted and prayed for strength to go on and for divine guidance.

Before we could get out of the parking lot, our bus broke down. We had to split up. Bob stayed on the bus with a few young people and our eight year old daughter, Lisa. Mother Pace and I took the rest back to camp on a bus provided by someone there. Numb from exhaustion,

Mother Pace and I climbed in one of the tents half torn down and flooded by the rain. Lying on a damp sleeping bag with water dripping in, we praised the Lord and managed to get a few hours sleep. The kids were super. Some had stayed up all night helping others in the camp to get their tents in order--all the while sharing their testimonies and the love of Jesus. What troopers for Jesus. I knew this was all of the Lord for we were spent of ourselves.

One of the young boys, Mark, woke up with a scorpion on his arm. They brushed it off and killed it. God was with us all the way.

God lifted our spirits that day as a group of Christians marched and praised God around the campground. Then making a big circle in the middle of the grounds, we all sang, praised and danced before the Lord. Thank Jesus.

Bob was feeling worse again and our son Tim (13) and Cathy got sick. We anointed them with oil and prayed the prayer of faith, (James 5:15). Tim and Cathy were healed almost immediately. Bob was still plagued by headaches. The Lord put it on my heart to fast a couple of days. Some of the others who had never fasted had the same leading. I kept saying, "Pray, and pray much in the Spirit." I didn't know why, but I felt a terrific battle ahead. I also felt led to call Brother Sid in Baltimore and ask for prayers.

Late in the night of June 15, I climbed in my bunk, totally exhausted. We had another flood tearing down our tents. I noticed Bob's bunk was empty. I felt a warning but decided Bob was in the men's room; so I waited a few minutes for him to come back. My son Bobby(18), and another young man found him in the showers, half-dressed, half-delirious. Shortly afterwards we took him to the hospital and found out he had spinal meningitis. He went into a coma the afternoon of the 16th.

The next weeks are hard to put on paper. We went through many deep and troubled waters, and we had many fiery places to tread, but we were not alone (Isaiah 43:2). Jesus went before us and walked very close beside us. We found His Word to be dependable and firm as a rock. We had many deep communications, saturated by His love in the hours of standing to see the salvation of the Lord for many souls. Praise Him!

The Crawfords received us back in their home, 22 of us by now. Brother Sid and Mother Pace were led of the Lord to stay with us in Texas. Brother Ed Schmidt came down to bring the bus and young people back home. On the way back several got saved and blessed. The Lord strongly impressed Brother Ed to keep moving. Unknown to him hurricane Agnes was right behind them all the way.

I wasn't sure how God wanted me to pray, so I prayed much in the

CHAPTER 11: THE FREBURGER STORY

Spirit, waiting for God to give me word about what He desired me to do. On June 18, the Lord sent word from the saints in Baltimore that He was going to do a complete healing. The next day, God told me He was going to bring Bob out of the coma on the eighth day (Ezekiel 43:25-27). I told the doctors so they would know what to expect. In the intensive care waiting room, the doctors said they admired my faith, but told me I would have to be realistic. I don't know any other reality than Jesus and His Word (Ps. 103:3; Is.53:5; Mark 11:24; Matt. 9:29; John 14:14).

The doctors and nurses were very evasive, but finally, on the seventh day of Bob's coma, I cornered the doctor. He said, "Sorry, Mrs. Freburger, we have done all we can do. He has contracted the worst kind of pneumonia, convulsions, abscess on the brain, and he is not responding to treatment. It is only a matter of time."

I said, "Thank you, but the Lord has said tomorrow is the day of awakening." The Lord had told me to see and see not, to hear and hear not. Only to look to Him and hear only what His Word says. I was determined to do that, but it was only by the grace He was giving me hour by hour. I was amazed at the total peace He gave me.

That same afternoon of the negative report, Mike, the breathing therapist, stood at Bob's bedside. With tears in his eyes he said, "I thank God for sending your husband here, it has brought me back to the Lord."

From the 19th of June, Brother and Sister Sherwin McCurdy were on the scene daily ministering support in every way. Brother Sherwin McCurdy was president of the FGBMFI in Dallas, Texas and God had used him to pray a man back to life who had been dead 45 minutes. I thank God for the body of Christ, joined together to manifest the power and love of Jesus. Many people were seeing a witness of God's miracle power. The body of Christ had united and was believing God for that miracle for Bob. Thank Jesus!

On June 23rd at 7:30 p.m. a young man from the intensive care waiting room found me at the phone and said, "Come quick; your husband's awake!" Tears were coming from the eyes of nurses, and doctors who were awe-struck. The doctor said, "It is a miracle!"

For the next four days Bob did not recognize me as his wife. Because of the throat operation needed to keep him alive the first night in the hospital, he could not talk. He pointed to my wedding ring and scribbled on paper, barely understandable, "W I F E?" I tried to convince him I was his wife, but he insisted I wasn't. When I jokingly asked him who I was, "A friend?"

He shook his head, "Yes."

I said, "I'll settle for that. It is the first time we have been friends since we've been married!" I didn't realize it then, but we were to remain friends from then on. Praise God!

Late in the afternoon of the third day after Bob came out of the coma, Mother Pace, Brother Sid and I were once again praying before the Lord in the Chapel. God spoke to both of them about a Joshua March around the hospital. I thought, "I'll never make it. I am so tired and it is 105 degrees outside." Besides, there was construction work going on to build a new part to the hospital which meant additional distance around the building. But the Lord gave us strength. And in complete silence, except to praise Jesus, we walked around the hospital seven times; then, stood outside the door with hands raised and sang, "We'll give the glory to Jesus." As we marched around once, twice, then three times, one construction worker looked at the other and said, "Hey, I am getting dizzy." We went home and forgot all about the walk. And the next morning, Bob was sitting up and he recognized me as his wife! Praise God! And the walls came tumbling down. We believe the walls came down for many others in that hospital, too.

Before we left, I had a chance to share my testimony with a 17 year old girl who tried to poison herself because she was lonely. She and her mother listened and were very open. She said she knew some Jesus people and wondered if it was for real. They were so grateful for my visit. I am believing God for a miracle in their lives, too.

The doctors sent us home on July 4 with tests showing clear. No need for surgery was the word. It felt so good to walk into our home and be reunited as a family. Praise the Lord!

But this exciting journey into the 'Promised Land' was not over yet. We still had some giants to destroy (Deut. 7).

By July 6, Bob was back in the hospital in a coma. The doctors reported a mass on the brain and immediate surgery was needed. The surgeon got upset when I asked for five minutes to pray, saying he told me Bob was dying and I was asking for precious minutes to pray. I told him I needed to connect with the higher power to find out what He wanted to do. I wasn't expecting talk of surgery for I had prayed it would not be necessary. However, as we turned to Jesus, He said go ahead with surgery so we did. I earnestly prayed for the doctor during the operation. Afterward the doctor said that Bob's life was entirely in the hands of the Lord.

It was amazing how God hid the mass on the reports and tests in Texas yet let the mass be detected back in Baltimore. God was finished with the miracle in Texas and now wanted to continue it to reach people here. Praise Him!

In Texas we were told that if Bob lived his left side would be paralyzed. Nevertheless, the morning following Bob's surgery, the

CHAPTER 11: THE FREBURGER STORY 177

doctor's associate came out of intensive care and asked for me. "It is a miracle," he said. I told him that a miracle is what we prayed for. He said, "No, really, he is supposed to be dead, but he is sitting up talking."

I smiled and said, "I know, it is the Lord."

Bob's recovery amazed everyone, even our doctor. Bob came home in two weeks and very rapidly recovered. When he went in for his check up a few weeks later, the doctor smiled and clapped his hands when he saw Bob raise his left hand above his head. He said he was proud of us and admired our faith and quickly added with his hands in the air, "I know, I know, it's the Lord." He then opened up and started asking questions about our faith. We were able to share some of what God has done for us, and what Jesus means to us. Upon our next visit, as we entered, Bob said, "Praise the Lord."

The doctor looked up at Bob, strangely, and said, "I'll go for that."

Six weeks after Bob came home from the hospital, Bob was released to return to work full time. During recuperation, before Bob returned to work, the Lord blessed us in our home in tremendous ways. Times were set up by the Lord for confessions and forgiveness, for healing old wounds, and for learning what true submissiveness and unity in the home means. I praise and thank the Lord for helping Bob to pray with me and for me. Something wonderful and powerful happens whenever we pray together. I had asked the Lord for two things when He saved Bob: to do a quick work, and to make him tender. Bob was always so tough and hard. God answered my prayers. Praise Him!

Bob's paycheck is smaller since he now works five days a week instead of seven. Phil. 4:19 has been proven over and over in our life. Like the night a man dropped a white envelope in Bob's lap. (We believe it was an angel.) Amen! -- Or, like when our insurance company overpaid us but wouldn't believe it. --Or, like the times the Lord put it on our son's heart to give us extra money. Praise God!

Satan tries to make us doubt God in every way, but when the enemy comes in like a flood, the Spirit of God takes a stand against him. (Isaiah 59:19). There is never any victory for satan, if we live by the standards of God. Only victory in Jesus!

God started calling Bob away from his medicine. The doctor said Bob needed it for two years because of seizures. We asked it he could cut it down and he said, "No." So Bob continued and became increasingly depressed. We were both becoming bound by the medicine, fearful about taking it and fearful about not taking it. We called out to God and said, "Help, Lord, help! We don't want to run ahead or be impatient."

After being heavily attacked by the enemy one day, Bob went

upstairs and threw the medicine away. The enemy tried to scare us through several attacks by seizures. Bob had seizures even while taking the medicine so he decided to stand and trust the Lord. I decided to stand with Bob whatever he decided. And the Lord decided, at the beginning of time, to stand with us if we trust Him. We have had word from the Lord: "No more seizures." Praise God! He is truly a wonderful Lord and Saviour.

We thank God for the struggles and for the places that seem impossible (Luke 1:37). Knowing that God can do the impossible is an exciting revelation, but seeing Him do the impossible is a tremendous experience in Him, never to be forgotten. Amen! Praise His Name Forever!

Isn't Jesus wonderful? I believe my grandmother was praying for me many times when I found her on her knees. Even though she didn't live to see the fruits of her prayers, I believe God is tuning her in on our journey, and she is rejoicing along with the angels.

My earnest prayer is for us all to become more like Jesus everyday. May you too find that sweeter gets the journey everyday. His richest blessings be on each of you.

OTHERS SHARE THE JOURNEY

All the Little Tabernacle and many more praying people in Baltimore were in constant prayer during the weeks of this odyssey of Faith Under Trial. Trials did arise in Texas, and the Lord sent Ed Schmidt and me early on to Texas to help them in every way we could. Betsy came a little later. Absolutely everything that Phyllis tells is true. We know because we were there.

When Mrs. Freburger called for urgent prayer help, (Bob was dying in Texas of meningitis). We quickly searched out the McCurdy name from a Voice Magazine as a FGBMFI director in the Dallas area. Ed Schmidt and I arrived in Dallas that Saturday night with their phone number in my pocket. Someone met us at the airport and took us straight to the hospital. As ministers we were able to gain admission even to the isolation room in Intensive Care, dressed in the required cap, mask and gown, to anoint Bob for the Lord's healing. At that moment he was in a total coma, convulsing frequently, which condition continued and worsened through the following Thursday night. After anointing him and praying earnestly for his healing, Ed and I were taken to the Crawford's home for a few hours sleep, before moving to get the bus and kids on their way back to Baltimore with Ed in charge. We phoned the Sherwin McCurdys in Dallas some 30 miles away to ask them to come to the Arlington hospital to join us in prayer for Bob, and

CHAPTER 11: THE FREBURGER STORY

they did, every night thereafter, sometimes as late as midnight they would come. We also called the Doctor in charge of Bob's case to determine whether the group of young people had been exposed to the contagious meningitis virus. Being assured by him that they were not, we felt clear to get the bus packed and rolling. Hurricane Agnes was in the Gulf moving northward toward Louisiana and we needed to get the bus ahead of that if possible. According to the weather map there was another huge low pressure area in the center of the country and the Lord was showing us that if these two lows got together there would really be some rough weather ahead.

Well, Ed and the kids finally got moving real early the next morning, thinking they might camp again, but with the help of a young driver, Ed and the group were led to keep driving, stopping only for fuel, all those 1,200 miles back to Baltimore. They were one jump ahead of reinforced hurricane Agnes which was wreaking havoc just behind them. Again God's special timing and protection! Mother Pace and I and the Freburger oldest daughter, Terri, and her friend, Cathy Plummer, stayed on to help Phyllis and Bob, and Betsy came a little later.

I was there in the Arlington hospital when the doctors told Mrs. Freburger there was no hope for her husband, Bob, and she replied, "I hear what you are saying, Doctor, but the Lord has said He will raise Him up on the 8th day..."

During the Joshua March around the hospital, to help bring down the "wall" that was keeping Bob from recognizing his own wife, Mother Pace, in her late 60's, found walking in that 105 degree heat too much, so she sat down after the first half turn around the hospital. And when Mrs. Freburger and I reached the sixth and a half turn, Mother Pace joined us to finish the Joshua March with us. She had sat in the hot Texas sunshine all the time. Someone had stopped and tried to get her to go in the shade and she, discerning the person might need a little warning replied, "It's a lot hotter in hell!"

What an inspiration Mother Pace was then and throughout her life! In March 1988, she graduated to "Heaven". Talk about a Graduation Celebration! Her church and family and friends gave her the most anointed send-off any saint has ever had. It looked as if over one half the congregation gathered around her coffin in the Praise Time, wanting to go with her! Her Home Going was a Great Celebration! Praise the Lord forever!

While we were still in Texas, after things took a turn for the better, Betsy and I arranged to fly down to San Antonio for the day to see Craig and Ann, where they were stationed and Craig was teaching in the Army Medical School. On the way down we saw a beautiful double rainbow, which reassured us of God's great promises that are all *Yea*

180   FIRED AGAIN AND AGAIN, PRAISE THE LORD!

and Amen in Christ Jesus. (II Cor.1:20). After a pleasant day, with lunch in the rotating tower, we flew back to Dallas. Shortly we were all back in Baltimore, battling some more!!

An unforgettable song the Lord gave Phyllis during those trials:

WHERE'ER I GO[2]
By: Phyllis Freburger

1) Where'er I Go, You're always right there with me.
   Where'er I go, You always can be found.
   Where'er I go, I look to You to cling to,
   Where'er I go, You always are around.

Chorus:
   Oh, help me, Lord, to crucify my self-life,
   And help me, Lord, to stand against the foe.
   By the grace You give,
   I will to live for You, Lord;
   Your servant waits for Your command to go.

2) In suffering, You're always right there with me.
   In paths unsure, Your footsteps can be heard.
   In darkest times, Your hand is always leading,
   In things undone, You follow from behind.

3) You take me thru the valley of despair,
   You take me thru and show You really care.
   You never leave nor do You e're forsake me;
   My Lord, My God, on You I can depend.

4) I've seen Your hand of mercy and of miracles.
   I've known Your voice which comforts and sustains.
   I've looked around and seen the unforgivable
   Washed by Your blood; You remember their sins no more.

---

[2] Used with permission of the author.

CHAP. 12

MIRACLE CONTRACT AND GOLDEN KEY

And I will give unto thee the keys of the kingdom of heaven: and whatsoever thou shalt bind on earth shall be bound in heaven: and whatsoever thou shalt loose on earth shall be loosed in heaven.
— Matthew 16:19

From the time we met Dr. and Mrs. Einspruch and had verbally agreed on a contract for the two buildings, all of us at the Little Tabernacle continued feeling confident that the Lord would put all the agreement, legal work, and finances together by His wonderful power and mercy. But not until one arrives at the meeting, where the down payment is paid and signatures are signed and notarized do you begin breathing easier. Further, not until the last payments are paid and the title and keys in hand does one begin breathing totally at ease, but there was never any need for any anxiety at all, for the Lord was going to make both of these events come to pass right on schedule, the first in January and the latter at the end of September 1972.

In a letter written January 22, 1972, under the heading "By My Spirit Saith The Lord," from the "Storefront," giving news of what was happening, we wrote family and friends the following: "By God's Spirit, The Little Tabernacle has now a firm contract, since January 3rd, for two attached buildings nearby in beautiful condition, one a small Jewish-Christian synagogue, which will be available later this year. We believe that by the moving of God's Spirit, the balance needed on these buildings will come in this year. We want all of you, who are sharing in this ministry of 'Lifting Up The Wonderful Name and Gospel of Jesus' in the heart of Baltimore, to see these buildings God is providing, to hear first-hand of His wonderful works here and now, and to praise Him with us!"

AT LONG LAST THE GOLDEN KEY

We'll call it the Golden Key because it was basically a gift from the Lord from Heaven. Betsy and I with our lawyer, and long-time church worker Mrs. Sarah Shaw, met with the Einspruchs in their lawyer's office for this final settlement. The precious Golden Key was gently handed to us in an envelope by Dr. Einspruch as his wife watched and we handed him the final check for $9,500, giving our deepest thanks for their trust and great favor. The transfer title would be duly recorded by the lawyers and sent on to us shortly. This was done on Friday morning, the 29th of September 1972. To conclude this momentous meeting, I asked if we could have a thanksgiving prayer to God and petition for His continued mighty blessings upon both ministries.

Dr. Einspruch died a few years later and Mrs. Einspruch finally retired early in 1988, after carrying on the Lederer Foundation work for 16 more years, bless her heart. There will be great rewards awaiting her in heaven, for her untiring devotion and service to the Lord. The work of these two precious saints of God continues beautifully under the direction of Barry Rubin.

It was now Friday noon and there was a monumental task awaiting us in "Our" (The Lord's) "new building" at 1503 E. Baltimore Street. We had announced that we would meet in the Chapel on Sunday for the first worship service and have Communion on this World Wide Communion Sunday, October 1, 1972. There was a lot of work to be done, and only about 24 hours to do it in. All those large, tall book shelves that nearly filled the Chapel had to be crowbarred from the floor, sawed into manageable sections and removed from the Chapel, and temporarily placed somewhere else in the other building.

At that moment our manpower was quite limited and the Lord knew it. As in many other times, He somehow got word to our former maintenance man, J.R. Bell, and brought him by that Friday afternoon. He agreed to join us early the next day, Saturday, and work with us and our sons Chris and Brian. We brought from home the necessary tools: power-saw, hammers, crow bars and began working with all our might and didn't stop until about 10 o'clock that night, after having swept and mopped the floor, cleaned the wainscotting and set up some 30 folding chairs, a small lectern, and a communion table.

If I remember rightly, the walls and ceiling looked dark and dingy but it wasn't too noticeable because the long fluorescent lights were hung quite low (later to be raised about 8 more feet). We were extremely weary but wonderfully happy in the Lord! The Lord had again given the Little Tabernacle a working home with its own "Golden Key" to it. The larger dedication service was being planned for the last Sunday in October, the 29th, in the afternoon, so that friends from many churches could attend. But that little Communion Service with the Little Tabernacle family, meeting in a kind of makeshift way on that first Sunday in that potentially, and eventually, beautiful Chapel, was one of the sweetest and happiest services in our lives. We praised and thanked

CHAPTER 12: MIRACLE CONTRACT AND GOLDEN KEY

and worshipped God with all our hearts, singing again, "How Great Thou Art" and the song "We'll give the Glory to Jesus."

To conclude this service we were led to take our Bibles with those seven white crosses lifted up and do a Joshua March seven times around the one quarter block that we could circle, claiming it all for the Lord's work, as in God's promise to Joshua when he entered the Promised Land at Jericho. (Joshua 1:3; 6:16). We ended the march and the service singing "To God Be the Glory, Great Things He Has Done."

Always in the past someone or some other group held the key of control and authority over the facilities used by the Church, and could tell the little Church when it could stay or when it must get out. Now the Little Tabernacle was the happy owner of its own facilities by the Grace of God. In the final analysis the Lord owned these facilities. He had given them to us for His purposes only. He was in direct control! May we ever remember this and hear His Voice and obey Him. "Trust and Obey" was still the song to sing, if we want His guidance and blessings. The "Golden Key" was His Key!

DEBBIE COMES TO WASHINGTON

Betsy's only brother, Kirby White, was still involved with the family's Hotel business in Atlantic City, the rather famous "un-twin," victorian Marlborough Blenheim at Park Place and Boardwalk. Atlantic City was changing and so was the hotel business, and the family members still in management were doing their best to keep the hotels going, but the oil crunch of '73, when oil prices shot sky high, would eventuate in heavy losses for many old line hotels and cause many to be sold in the next three to five years. The big gambling interests already were searching out an East Coast area to become the center for their Las Vegas-like gambling operations. Like vultures they began pouncing on and buying up struggling hotel properties for their future gambling casinos.

Kirby and his attractive wife, Debbie, had a nice family with two boys and two girls, Stuart, John, Shirley and Linda, and Debbie was engaged in the normal civic club interests of their Margate community. Later they moved to Ocean City, New Jersey. Debbie had found life, at its best, so full of deadly problems and few good solutions that she thought, "Surely God had better answers." Her search for God's best led her to Jesus and in Him her own life's puzzle began to fall into place. She found new life and hope. Still many tough problems persisted. Her sister-in-law, Betsy, talked of greater power for the Christian walk through something called the Baptism by Jesus in the Holy Spirit and invited her to attend with us a Full Gospel Convention (FGBMFI) in

Washington, D.C. in early January 1973.

Debbie attended and was gloriously filled by the Holy Spirit, praising God in a new language--about three hours after arguing through a lunch with us and our dear friend, Thelma Forest, in a little Washington cafeteria near the conference hotel, that she had all she needed without that particular gift. In that very afternoon meeting she was strangely moved to go up for prayer by Dr. Hilton Sutton. That's when new spiritual things began to happen. Oh, the change, the glow, the spontaneous lifting up the hands to God now. The following "Little Thank You" letter came to us a few days after she arrived home. To God be all praise and glory! Now problems are God's opportunities and tests for our faith. All thanksgiving and praise to Him in all things! (Col.3:15-16; I Thess.5:15-18-24).

DEBBIE'S LETTER

January 19, 1973

Dear Bets and Sid,

I could never repay you for your support in helping God to set the scene for me to have had this beautiful experience with Him--Praise God!! I had no idea of the magnitude of His love for each of us! I am writing you another letter--much longer--and it is still in the process of becoming--hope to complete it this weekend!

So this is just a pause for basics in my still total involvement in loving and praising Him because I am still agog with the awareness of His love for me and for each one of us!   "The Things of Earth Will Grow Strangely Dim!" "His Amazing Grace!" "Tongues" alone can express the rapture--it has bypassed words in its magnitude! I am "in love" again and all else is pale by comparison! Hope you understand all this. He has made me one of His "peculiar people"--Hallelujah!

Love to you,
Debbie

P.S. And I thought I knew all there was to know about Him!!

Praise God she has continued in her walk with Him in spite of many difficulties and has seen great miracles and victories.

THE UNEXPECTED INVITATION

Out of the same conference was to come a very special and totally unexpected invitation to me to be interviewed on one of Pat Robertson's CBN TV programs then at Portsmouth, Virginia.

We had been greatly delighted at the Washington convention to meet and visit again with those two wonderful prayer warriors in the

CHAPTER 12: MIRACLE CONTRACT AND GOLDEN KEY

battle for Bob Freburger's life down in Texas, Sherwin and Leah Mae McCurdy. So we invited them to come over to Baltimore to speak to our group and to see the Freburgers. They agreed to come.

Before the FGBMFI conference closed, Sherwin came to me and asked if I would be willing to go with him to CBN with a group of men flying down to Portsmouth. One of the businessmen selected at the conference for interview on CBN TV had had to drop out. Would I take his place? He thought he could arrange it. Sherwin had heard one or two stories of how the Lord had wonderfully delivered us at McKim Center and he thought it would be good to testify about the Lord's power in a TV interview. I told him I would be honored and glad to do it.

We would all go down by a small chartered plane and be brought back to the Washington National Airport the same day. Sherwin made phone calls to Ruth Egert, who made the arrangements at CBN, and the next morning we were on the little plane heading for the interviews led by Harold Bredesen on CBN's "Charisma" Program. I spent most of the day at CBN in their prayer room praying and fasting for the Lord's guidance and blessings on these interviews. My turn came last, late in the day, and naturally I was a bit nervous. But Harold Bredesen, a veteran host, quickly put me at ease, and as we talked, I felt a tremendous anointing of the Lord as I shared about the gang who had come to kill me and how the Lord had given me a three-foot-thick armor of Jesus' love and power surrounding me which they couldn't penetrate. One or two of the cameramen came up and thanked me for sharing, as did Harold Bredesen. Funny thing: I'd completely forgotten that they had put makeup on my face for the TV interview and back at the airport I kept wondering why people kept giving me queer looks, until I went into the restroom and saw myself in the mirror. Then I knew why, and quickly washed my face! I was soon heading back to Washington and Baltimore praising God for this special opportunity to lift up the Name of Jesus. Special thanks to our dear friend Sherwin McCurdy, in his heavenly home now!.

Sherwin and Leah Mae came over to the Little Tabernacle and spoke that Sunday and on the way back to the Washington airport we remember them sitting in the back seat of our car, sharing many of their experiences in the Lord's service and teaching us one of the songs they love to sing, "My Lord is Able":

> "My Lord is able, He's able, I know He is able,
>   I know my Lord is able to carry me through. (2 times)
>   He heals the brokenhearted,
>   And He sets the captives free;

He healed the sick, and He raised the dead,
And He caused the blind to see.
My Lord is able, He's able, I know He is able,
I know my Lord is able to carry me through."

Sherwin and Leah Mae later were to serve full-time with FGBMFI as convention coordinators and also as special fund raisers for CBN, until the Lord called Him home. Leah Mae was still courageously serving the Lord in an intercessory group in Dallas and visited us in the fall of '87 before she too went to be with the Lord.

Perhaps some might wonder if we got to meet Pat that day. The answer is yes! Just after we arrived he came out to meet us and thanked us for coming. Years later we were to meet his wife, Dede, at an Aglow meeting, where Betsy would be leading the praise and worship with her autoharp and lovely voice.

THE BIG PICTURE OF JESUS FINDS A HOME

Years earlier, a church had given us a large (5 ft. by 8 ft.) oil painting of Jesus standing on a rocky surface looking down at you with His arms outstretched. Behind him were mountains and rolling clouds. A truly beautiful old painting that had been kept over the entrance door at McKim, high up, with desperate hope that it would not be hit by a basketball or any other flying missile inside the Center during its daily use as a school room and gym, plus Church on Sundays. Since McKim was moving in a non-religious direction, we felt when we left McKim in June 1970 that the picture should go with the Church to the Christian Center. But we never could find a suitable place there to hang it. It somehow survived the months in that Community Center in a small room, and upon leaving there, our friend Hugh Eagan, who owned a nearby foundry, agreed to store it in his loft if we would cover it well. From October 1971 until October 1972, it remained in Hugh's foundry loft. If the old painting could have talked, it probably was wondering if we'd ever be back, or was it to be lost forever? Well, we remembered it right after getting the Golden Key to the new home of the Tabernacle at 1503 E. Baltimore Street. We could see in the Chapel a beautiful arched wall recess on the south side facing the hallway entrance, into which we immediately felt the picture would fit perfectly, and be at home. Since the congregation would be facing toward the east and where the altar, cross and communion table and pulpit were, they would not be facing the picture, preventing the idea that we were worshipping or bowing down to a man-made picture or icon. The Lord's Second Commandment strongly forbids this. (Exodus 20:4,5; Deut.5:8,9).

CHAPTER 12: MIRACLE CONTRACT AND GOLDEN KEY

With the help of J.R. and others, we retrieved the old painting, dusted it, and placed it carefully on metal brackets attached to the wall at the top and bottom. By the time we had the walls and ceiling beautifully painted yellow gold, and the long fluorescent lights raised some 6 to 8 feet higher, the painting and the whole room seemed to fit together in a remarkable way, just as if that arch had been waiting since 1925 for that picture. It had found its home, just as the Little Tabernacle had!

Anyone coming into the Chapel through the door at the end of the hallway will immediately be arrested by this winsome painting of Jesus reaching out to them, just as He reached out in compassion to his disciples that time in Galilee, probably at Capernaum, when He said, **Come unto Me all ye that labor and are heavy laden, and I will give you rest. Take my yoke upon you and learn of Me: for I am meek and lowly in heart: And ye shall find rest for your souls, For my yoke is easy and My burden is light.** (Matt.11:28-30). Reminds us of that famous statue at Hopkins Hospital.

THE HUGE STATUE OF JESUS AT JOHNS HOPKINS

As many of you know the Little Tabernacle is only about five or six blocks from the famous Johns Hopkins Hospital in Baltimore, within easy walking distance, and we are often visiting sick members or friends there or in the even closer hospital, Church Home.

Everyone familiar with the old entrance to Johns Hopkins will remember the very high domed foyer with a giant size statue of JESUS right in the center, carved out of one piece of Italian carrara marble. As with the painting at the Little Tabernacle, JESUS' head and eyes are looking down and His arms are compassionately reaching out to the sick and wounded that come into the hospital. In the pedestal beneath His feet are the large carved letters, **"Come Unto Me..."** with the Scripture reference. You can see the nail prints in His hands and His feet and the spear wound in His side, only the hardest of hearts could pass this statue without being touched. This statue is a replica of the original standing in Christ Church in Copenhagen, Denmark done by the famous Danish sculptor, Albert Bertal Thorvaldsen.

A very touching story is told about the artist's desire to produce a great statue of Jesus with His arms lifted up to His heavenly Father. With this conception in mind he went to work constructing a model out of wire and plaster. The last thing he added one night were the wire arms lifted up to the Heavenly Father, and then covered them with wet plaster. At last he felt he had the statue of the Christ that he wanted.

He asked a dear friend to come with him the next morning to see it and give his opinion. On arriving they found that the arms had cracked and fallen down to an outstretched position toward the floor. He was in great anguish at this failure of his model and he grabbed the heavy hammer used in his work and started to demolish his model in anger.

Quickly his friend grabbed the hammer and hand and said, "No, no, no, don't do it. This is the true Christ reaching out to the world to be saved, healed, delivered and loved."

So Thorvaldsen went on to produce this famous statue of Christ calling the world to Himself to be saved, healed, delivered and loved. To receive abundant and eternal life through His death and resurrection, through the shedding of His blood as the final sacrifice for the sins of mankind. All who come do find rest for their souls and their burdens are lightened.

As often as possible we try to take our special guests to the Johns Hopkins foyer to see this anointed work of a sculptor who loved the living Christ.

Amazingly, interestingly, appropriately, right today hundreds of doctors, nurses and technicians go about their duties in this hospital seeking to heal the sick with modern techniques and medicines, all in the shadow of JESUS' statue.

Until recently the Lord had a humble little housekeeper working there for forty years who knew how to pray and get through to the Lord in Heaven. Almost daily as she went on her housekeeping rounds, she was asked to pray for someone desperately ill or dying. In the most loving way, she would pray for their healing, or lead them in a salvation prayer before they died. Most of the time they were healed quickly, and no telling how many were saved under her quiet housekeeping "ministry" in this hospital. This precious faithful, courageous, humble, loving, little black servant of Jesus Christ has been a member and trustee of the Little Tabernacle since McKim days, has a deep love for the Jewish people and for Israel, and has been to Israel five times with us! Dorothy Felton is also President of an Inner-city Women's Aglow Chapter and is truly one of the Lord's special saints.

Don't miss the later story of a little girl named Jennifer, dying of cancer, who dearly loved JESUS and His statue!

JOHNS HOPKINS READ OUT OF MEETING

Once I was in a downtown Baltimore office, waiting to keep an appointment with a Presbytery official and I noticed a book about Johns Hopkins on the side table next to me. I picked it up to find out more about this illustrious Quaker. Six Quakers and twelve Presbyterians

CHAPTER 12: MIRACLE CONTRACT AND GOLDEN KEY

made up the McKim Board of Directors. I should learn more about them. Quakers built the Greek Temple-like building around 1821 to house the Quaker McKim Free School, perhaps the earliest free school in Baltimore.

Many years later we found another book called "Johns Hopkins A Silhouette," by Helen Hopkins Thom which gave us the following insights into his youth and success:

PAGES 10-13:[1]

South River School was a branch of King William's school in Annapolis, the first <u>Free</u> School established in America. In 1696 a petition for a free school in Maryland had been addressed to his Most Excellent Majesty, King William. "The act explained the needs of the Province for the establishment of free schools and asked the royal permission for such a school in Anne-Arundel-Town, upon the Severn River, to be named after the King and to be under the special guidance of the Archbishop of Canterbury. The Royal permission was obtained, and certain lots of land in Annapolis, together with the "Kentish House," an ample brick building still standing in the shadow of the State House, were given for this school. Its purpose was, "to prepare both English and Indian boys for his Majesty's Royal College of William and Mary, in Virginia" and for the "propagation of the Gospel and the education of the youth of the Province in good letters and manners."

The school was finally conveyed, with its property, funds, masters, and students to St. John's College in Annapolis, whose beautiful colonial buildings still greet the visitor entering this quaint old town.

The success of King William's school led to an extension of the free school system in other parts of Maryland; and in 1723 free schools were located in the twelve Counties of the Province. It was that branch, or extension, of King William's school at the head of South River which Johns Hopkins attended, and to which his young brother, Gerard, became what was called a "visitor," in 1823. Gerard is spoken of as a "Planter whose home lay among the hills but a mile from the school building." He must have been a remarkable boy, for at this time he seems to have been not more than sixteen years of age. The visitors to these free schools were chosen from among the best men of the counties and were conscientious in maintaining a high standard. When chosen for the position of visitor, each man had to serve the public in this capacity or forfeit one hundred pounds of tobacco. The influence

---

[1] From "Johns Hopkins A Silhouette" by Helen Hopkins Thom, copyright 1929 by Johns Hopkins Press: Used with permission.

of Gerard Hopkins was immediately felt. He advocated abandoning free scholarships, substituting the paying of a small tuition fee for each pupil, and urged the using of such fees for improvements upon the school lands and buildings. These suggestions were adopted.

The South River school was built on a tract of 150 acres of land "purchased from Mr. Richard Snowden" and known as "God Wills" and "Iron Mine." The building was of two stories, seventeen by twenty-five feet. The first story consisted of one large school-room with a great fireplace. Two rooms upstairs, with a fireplace in each, constituted the residence of the Master. The masters were required to be: "of the Church of England and of pious and exemplary lives and conversations and capable of teaching well, Grammar, good writing and the Mathematicks, if such could conveniently be got at twenty pounds sterling ($100) a year and the free use of the school plantation."

Such, however, could not often "be got," and most of the schools suffered in consequence. South River school, however, was most fortunate in this respect. The great prosperity of the colony brought many Englishmen of education to Maryland in search of their fortunes. They often met the fate of most adventurers and were quite frequently obliged to resort to teaching. This master at South River was no doubt one of these.

Among the group of country boys who filled up the main room of that little South River school, the master soon came to look for "Johnsie Hopkins," a blue-eyed, long-legged boy whose eager, intelligent face showed the deep interest he felt in his studies. Johns loved History and English Literature, and it was his delight to recite long passages from his favorite poems.

The time came, however, when he was sorely needed on the farm, and when he must put his shoulder to the wheel as his brother Joseph had done. School must be given up. No more meeting with the other boys at the cross-roads in the early morning; no more friendly days in the school-yard; no more loitering along the road with school-mates in the long afternoons. Stern necessity beckoned and the boy had to take on the ways of the man.

It was arranged that Johns should study his lessons at home from time to time through the day, as he was able, and on Saturday evenings the Master of the School came to dine with the Hopkins family and heard Johns recite his lessons. The whole family looked forward to this as the most delightful part of the week. The schoolmaster was a very interesting man, who would stay and talk after the lessons were over. It is partly to the inspiration of this English man of letters that we may attribute the later founding of the famous seat of learning in Baltimore. He implanted a love of learning which, thwarted in Johns Hopkins's

CHAPTER 12: MIRACLE CONTRACT AND GOLDEN KEY

early years, found compensation later in giving to others that for which he himself had longed.

In the hard school of necessity the young Johns Hopkins was shaped into habits of self-denial, industry, and thrift. This early training, added to his natural ability, fitted him when opportunity offered later on, not only to assume the responsibilities of a man of wealth, but also to occupy many positions of trust. In later life he used the great fortune which he had accumulated to help youths who were anxious as he had been for a wider education.

(Johns' mother, realizing her son's business-like abilities, arranged for him to go to work in Baltimore with his Uncle Gerard. Johns was quick to "catch on" and became a great asset in the business. He also fell in love with Uncle Gerard's daughter, Elizabeth, but their hoped-for marriage was forbidden. Neither ever married!)

The cordial relations which for seven years had existed between Gerard Hopkins and his nephew had been interrupted. Following upon the unfortunate love affair with Elizabeth, there came other disagreements and finally a breach.

Gerard Hopkins was devoted to the work of preaching and went on many visits to Quaker meetings in various parts of the neighboring country. His nephew spoke very frankly to him on this subject telling him that if he did not stay at home and pay more attention to his business affairs the results would be disastrous.

The older man disregarded this advice, and Johns Hopkins was not one to allow things to interfere with his purposes. He felt that he had given his best efforts to his uncle, and that the firm had flourished in consequence; he did not propose now to let it suffer while he was connected with it. Also, there were certain questions upon which the older man and his young nephew did not agree. Times had become very hard, yellow fever was raging, and money was scarce. Out-of-town customers, who found it hard to pay cash, proposed that they should pay for goods by shipping whiskey in return. Johns Hopkins felt that this was legitimate, and was willing that they should do so; but his uncle felt differently and declared that he would never consent to thus "sell souls into perdition." They decided to separate and Johns Hopkins withdrew from the firm.

This break, which did not seem to affect the friendship existing between the young man and his uncle's family was, however, very significant in its consequences. Johns Hopkins was now in a position to develop his business genius unhampered, and he did so in a swift, sure, and brilliant manner. After a short partnership with a certain

192 FIRED AGAIN AND AGAIN, PRAISE THE LORD!

Benjamin Moore, which almost immediately dissolved, he decided to go into business for himself, and taking his three brothers, Philip, Gerard, and Mahlon, as salesmen, he formed the wholesale Provision House of "Hopkins Brothers." This house soon did a large business, especially through North Carolina and the valley of Virginia, where they had important connections. The new firm took whiskey in return for goods and sold it under the brand of "Hopkins' Best."

This action on the part of Johns Hopkins offended the Society of Friends and he was temporarily turned out of Meeting. He continued to sell whiskey, never-the-less; but he went regularly to meeting, continued to contribute and was later reinstated. In his later life, however, he felt that he had been wrong in the stand he had taken; and he told his nephew, Joseph Hopkins, that he wished he had never sold liquor, and that in so doing he had made the greatest mistake of his life.

Meanwhile (Uncle) Gerard Hopkins was not ungenerous, and as a token of confidence in the new firm of Hopkins' Brothers he indorsed for it to the extent of ten thousand dollars...

PAGE 90: From the Letter of Instructions given by Johns Hopkins to the Hospital Trustees, Baltimore, March 10th, 1873.

"It is my special request that the influences of religion should be felt in and impressed upon the whole management of the hospital; but I desire, nevertheless, that the administration of the charity shall be undisturbed by sectarian influence, discipline, or control."[2]

Apparently Johns Hopkins' fame and wealth earned him a way back into the Society of Friends. His deep concern for the education and medical care for poor children and youth led him to leave most of his fortune to establish The Johns Hopkins Hospital and also The Johns Hopkins University. Also it seems he was thoroughly convicted by the Holy Spirit about bottling the "moonshine" liquor and selling it as "Hopkins' Best!" No doubt, too, since the Bible was the top literature of those days, he knew well Jesus' teaching on true Salvation and the dangers of great wealth as in Mark 8:34-38:

"Whosoever will come after me, let him deny himself, and take up his cross, and follow me. For whosoever will save his life shall lose it; but whosoever shall lose his life for my sake and the Gospel's, the same shall save it. For what shall it profit a man, if he shall gain the

---

[2] End of Selections from "Johns Hopkins A Silhouette," by Helen Hopkins Thom, copyright 1929, Johns Hopkins Press. By Permission

CHAPTER 12: MIRACLE CONTRACT AND GOLDEN KEY

whole world, and lose his own soul? Or what shall a man give in exchange for his soul? Whosoever therefore shall be ashamed of me and of my words in this adulterous and sinful generation, of him also shall the Son of man be ashamed, when he cometh in the glory of his Father with the holy angels."

And see Jesus' parables on Three Rich Men: (Matt.19:16-26; Luke 12:16-21; 16:19-31). None of these were saved because they would not be rich toward God.
But it seems Johns' heart was both right and rich toward God.

THE UNEXPECTED CALL FROM THE BUS STATION

One night after prayer meeting we were about to load up our cars to take people home when, as often happened, the phone rang and someone was calling for help. This time it was a young man calling from the bus station (not the police station as sometimes). A young man named Joseph with an Italian last name was saying that he had just come in from Albuquerque, was without money or a place to stay, but someone had given him our name that we might help him out. He was on his way to Connecticut where his adoptive parents lived. I was bone weary at the time, but the Lord seemed to be saying "Help him." So we went and picked him up and took him home with us.

He was about 20 years old, maybe 21, very nervous and mixed up, but not a bad looking kid. We gave him an empty bed in the basement and told him to try to get some sleep, that we would talk more in the morning. After our boys got off to school, we had time to hear more of his story. He told us that his adopted parents were well-to-do, had given him a good home, but he didn't really think they loved him or he them. And he was always wanting to find his Mother, a woman of "the streets" who had given him up for adoption at birth. He was angry about that, and hated her. He was always having some kind of strange attacks that felt like Satan had a vise around his head, and ever tightening it. Sometimes it was so painful he would fall down and beat his head on the floor to try to break this tightening band.

With the Holy Spirit's leading, we realized that this was evidence of demonic attacks and probably indwelling evil spirits which needed to be cast out. We also realized by the gift of discernment, quite early, that he had a spirit of homosexuality and perversion in him. These spirits, often not hard to detect, are almost impossible to get out unless the person recognizes the reality of them being in him and wants to be set free to live a holy life for Jesus. Jesus is still setting many homosexuals and lesbians free today when they really want to be free to live a clean and holy life for Him.

Joseph was with us several weeks and at every service he was wanting prayer for deliverance for the binding torture he was having in his head. In this condition at other times he was so preoccupied that he was not much good helping at anything. One day he came in the office begging for prayer relief for his head pains and we felt from the Lord to confront him about the unclean homosexual spirit that we had discerned. He finally admitted that he had been so involved. We asked him if he was ready to confess this as a grievous sin against God and God's plan for man, a sin which God's Word totally forbids, and he said he was willing to confess it as horrible sin and to turn from it completely, with Jesus' help. We led him in a prayer confessing this as a terrible sin against God and against himself, asking God's forgiveness, and for total deliverance in Jesus' Name.

We said, "Joseph you must say, 'I renounce this foul homosexual spirit in Jesus Name.'"

As he said this he fell on the floor almost in convulsions, beating his head on the floor.

I said, "You foul unclean homosexual spirit, I bind you by the power of the Name Jesus, and by the power of the blood of Jesus I command you to come out of Joseph and to touch no one as you go. You are to get out of Joseph now." We sensed the power of the Lord Jesus was present and setting him free.

In a few moments he relaxed and got up saying, "Praise the Lord, I believe I've been set free. Thank you, Jesus!"

We don't believe the head binding problem ever came back and Joseph, at the next meeting, much brighter and happier, was asking for the Baptism of the Holy Spirit. After the morning and evening Sunday services, the Elders prayed for him. Still no success, but still he wanted it.

So on Wednesday night, again he wanted prayer for the Baptism of the Holy Spirit with the evidence of the gift of speaking in tongues. (See again I Cor.12 & 14.) By this time I was a little frustrated with Joseph. We knew something must still be wrong with him, but didn't know what. So at the close of that meeting he asked the Elders and congregation again to pray with him to receive. At least four men surrounded him, laying hands on him to pray, and somehow I was led to just stand in front of him with my hands lifted up praying in the Spirit. Suddenly my raised right hand came swinging down across his face with a resounding slap, the Lord was showing me what was wrong in that moment. Joseph must forgive my slap, and must forgive his Mother who had deserted him.

As Joe, reacting to the slap, stared at me in anger, the Lord led

CHAPTER 12: MIRACLE CONTRACT AND GOLDEN KEY

me to put my right hand out as if to shake his hand, and say, "Joseph, you must forgive me. The Lord had me do that, to show you that you must forgive your Mother right now in the Name of Jesus, absolutely forgive her, it must go, and you must forgive me and love me."

While I was still holding my hand out to him, with tears pouring down his face, he said, "I don't want to shake your hand, I want to hug your neck." He hugged, tears pouring out of my eyes too, and in the next moments, Joseph had been filled to overflowing, not only with the spirit of forgiveness, but the fullness of the Holy Spirit, and he began speaking in the most beautiful Holy Spirit language I had ever heard before or since. He came on into the office looking like he wasn't even on earth. He kept speaking this wonderful new language in the back seat of the car during the 20 minute drive home and continued speaking in his beautiful heavenly language for at least an hour on the couch in the living room at home.

Not long afterward Joe went home to Connecticut, was reunited with his adoptive parents, and soon married his childhood sweetheart. About a year and a half later at a Youth Camp in Pennsylvania, probably Jesus '74, lo and behold, we met Joe, his wife and little baby all bright and happy. They were living nearby in a little Pennsylvania town. He was working regularly, and they were part of a Church fellowship. Praise God forever!

During those days we saw others, including lesbians, totally set free from this foul, unclean homosexual bondage, completely free. It's a lie of the devil to say anyone is born that way, at least not genetically, no matter what the homosexual experts may say. It's a learned, seduced and induced, unnatural sexual conduct which is absolutely of the devil, not of God. A total perversion of God's plan and a total rebellion against His will. For more on such deliverances read books by Marie Rice, Don Basham, and many others. Also read how it comes about in the first chapter of Romans and how it is totally condemned. (Genesis 19:1-25; Leviticus 18:22; 20:13; Deut.23:17-18; Romans 1:18-32; I Cor. 6:9-10; Rev. 21:8, 22:15;)

A REBEL BOY DELIVERED

Not long after this we had a call from the Christian parents of a young lad with whom they were having a lot of trouble keeping him in school and getting along with him, and he with them. He was getting into a pattern of thievery, which is somewhat typical of rebelling youth for they have need to finance their rebel desires and plans as they grow older, desires and plans which right-thinking parents won't approve or finance.

We suggested to them that if the son really wanted to get rid of that rebellious attitude, and get straightened out, then we felt it would be good if they brought him by for special prayer for deliverance. We had known the family and the lad for a number of years, and he knew we were not in a sweet, patty-cake, superficial ministry.

Praise God. They brought him down to the Tabernacle the next week, and we were able to pray for the Lord's help to show him from the Bible that rebellion is as the sin of witchcraft and totally opposite of what God wants; that the Lord commands us to love, honor and respect our parents that our lives may be long in this land which the Lord gives us, the one commandment with a special promise of long life. We showed him that Satan and his demons were all rebel angels cast out of heaven and that these rebel demons delight in persuading the sons of men to join them in rebellion against God, their parents and anyone else in authority, including school teachers and policemen. Spirits of rebellion and lust for power, money, and sex are behind almost all the wickedness in the world. Adam and Eve's sin was basically rebellion. Listening to Satan and rebelling against God, they lost their very favored condition. So do we, if we go that way, the rebel way!

We spoke a little bit about the results of the spirit of rebellion--what horrible destruction it would bring, and how we need to renounce it and ask the Lord to deliver us.

"Mike, are you willing," I asked, "to confess you have the spirit of rebellion and ask God to forgive you and deliver you in the Name of Jesus Christ, and help you live in obedience to your parents and teachers and minister in the days to come?"

He nodded his assent.

Together we prayed the prayer of confessing the sin of rebellion, renouncing the spirit of rebellion and asking the Lord to forgive and deliver him, in Jesus name, from the foul spirit of rebellion.

And The Lord did it!

Then in the name of Jesus (in a strong vocal way), I commanded that spirit of rebellion to be bound and cast out forever from young Mike. I asked Mike to tell it to get out and stay out in Jesus Name and he did.

Soon after, they moved to Maryland's Eastern Shore. Many months later, perhaps a year, the parents wrote us that Mike was doing just great in school and at home. Praise the Lord forever for His wonderful deliverance power through His Name and blood. His parents still send love gifts to help the Little Tabernacle ministry.

CHAPTER 12: MIRACLE CONTRACT AND GOLDEN KEY

JESUS '73 CAMP AND THE TORNADO TURNS AWAY

In January '73 remembering the special march we had had seven times around the quarter block claiming it for the Lord's ministry, by faith we began negotiating for the empty dilapidated corner building 1501, though knowing that it would take an awful lot of money to renovate it even if we could get it for a low price. The owner was glad to get rid of it for $2,987. Thank the Lord! And before the year would be over the Lord did send in enough money to get the rebuilding done, though more costly than we had originally thought.

Bob and Phyllis Freburger and their young people kept coming and participating in a very meaningful way in the ministry of the Little Tabernacle. About this time a policeman, Bob Schloer, got saved and baptized in the Holy Spirit, in his patrol car out in the county, and brought his nephew down for deliverance from alcoholism. His nephew had made a deal with satan so kept falling back into his old ways, but Bob, the policeman, became a real servant of the Lord and a minister of Jesus Christ, an Elder and Trustee of the Little Tabernacle. Eventually he was to operate the LTC Book Shop in the renovated 1501 building next door doing an excellent job, after retiring from the county police force.

That year the Freburgers led the young people to the "Jesus '73" camp on a large farm in Pennsylvania near Lancaster. Betsy's sister-in-law Debbie wanted to come. Because of Bob Freburger's still unsteady condition, some of the older ones of our group stayed in a nearby motel close to the camp. Between 15,000-20,000 young people were spread out in the farm valley, attending some great evangelistic, praise, and teaching meetings at an open stage, and under large open-sided tents, led by many outstanding Christian teachers, evangelists and Gospel singing groups.

A remarkable event took place on the second day of the camp-out. We were with our group at their camp-site on the side of the hill overlooking the main tent area, when the sky began darkening from heavy rain clouds and soon there were ominous gusts of wind, and rain began pelting down. Our campers and others scurried to get their camp gear in the tent or inside the old Texas Trip Bus alongside the tent. Some of us were already praying, recognizing signs of a tornado. Suddenly there were heavier gusts of whirling wind, tearing down tents and knocking down part of one of the main meeting tents. Debbie, Bob Freburger and myself turned toward the southeastern corner of the encampment, climbing toward higher ground, and in the Name of Jesus we spoke to the wind and the storm that were rapidly approaching the camp. In the Name of Jesus we commanded it to turn and go another way! Usually in a dark-clouded storm there is a lot of lightning, and being on the hilltop is not a safe place to be. Soon I looked around and found I was alone. Bob and Debbie had gone back to shelter. I am sure I was not alone however. Probably everybody in that camp was praying with all their might to God to turn the storm, and Praise God, at the very last moment before striking the camp with its heaviest winds, this tornado-like storm did turn 90 degrees and went up into the mountains. Two Pennsylvania state patrolmen were on duty on a road nearby and saw it turn those 90 degrees just before reaching the camp with its worst fury. They became believers that day and many others did, too. If it had hit the encampment with its full force, the camp would have been a disaster area, but by God's grace and power it was spared, except for a few downed tents, no injuries and a number of people really saved. Praise God forever! His mercy and truth endureth to all generations! To ours, too! Another mighty miracle from the Lord!

The turning of a tornado away might seem impossible or foolishness to some or as some nut's imagination, but this event was recorded in the Lancaster, Pa. newspaper. It is not unlike the stilling of the storm on the Sea of Galilee by Jesus, who tells us that He gives us the authority to do such things in His Name and by His power. (Luke 10:18, Jn.14:12; I Cor. 12:9,10). Among the gifts of the Holy Spirit are Faith, Healing and Miracles! ANOTHER JESUS MIRACLE! Praise God!

We've told you earlier about the tornado that the Lord sent in answer to prayer to correct the boathouse injustice against my Mom, and the literal turning away of hurricanes in answer to humble prayer by God's people in Florida. God sent miracles to Gen. George Washington, a devout praying man, against the vaunted British redcoats and navy. Also there were miracles for the British at Dunkirk in W.W.II and for U.S. forces in bringing down Hitler. Satan may gain a lot of power and advantage, but God rules and overrules with His mighty miracles and power. Our God Reigns!
(Isa.52:7; Psalm 148:8).

CHAP. 13

MOM'S HOME-GOING; SON'S HOME-COMING!

Precious in the sight of the Lord is the death of His saints.
                                                    -Psalm 116:15

LIFE WITH PAPA AND THE NO-GOOD FARM MIRACLE

My grandfather, Joseph S. Williams, whom I dearly loved and respected, lived to the age of 75 and went to be with the Lord on February 4, 1937. Aunt Eunice said that, as he was dying, he was praying the Lord's Prayer and asking the Lord to forgive all his sins, and expressing forgiveness toward all those who had wronged him in any way. After praying that prayer, he peacefully passed into Heaven.

Papa, as we all called him, had lived a long honorable life, mainly in Ashford, Alabama, in the southeastern corner of that state. He had grown up helping his own father in a tiny general store just east of Ashford in a little place called Pansy. He was a faithful member of the Baptist Church and a faithful student of the Bible. His interest in farming led eventually to his owning three farms, one of which was not productive at all, and never thought worth the price he paid for it. He also became a county commissioner for the eastern district of Houston County, and hated and refused to participate in the mud-slinging battles of political elections. He always did his very best for the people, as God gave Him wisdom to do, but no doubt found that no one, however good and wise, can or will please everybody.

After Dad died, Mom had to "farm out" her children to relatives in the summers of the early '30's, while she attended Florida State College for Women (FSCW), to keep up her teaching certification. Al would go to Uncle Alvin and Aunt Lila in Freeport, Florida; Frank would go to Uncle Everett and Aunt Essie in Fayette, Alabama; and I would go to Papa and Mother Williams, with Eunice and Uncle Wister Cook in Ashford, Alabama. We kids thoroughly enjoyed being "farmed out" to our kinfolk! Mom was deeply grateful!

We boys always got various work assignments such as cleaning yards, feeding the cows and chickens, hoeing and picking cotton, and helping to harvest peanuts. One of the great treats for me was Papa asking me to get up early and go on the rounds of his farms with him, and also the road building projects in his part of the county. He would usually have some other man sitting with him in the front seat of his little open Chevrolet, and I would always sit behind him as he drove, especially to watch how he shifted gears and drove his car. That's how I learned to drive. He was a Chevrolet man and Uncle Everett was a Ford man. Of course Papa liked to smoke a cigar now and then, but mainly he would chew it and spit the tobacco juice. Sitting behind him in the car, I had to be very watchful to duck when he spat or I would get some of the tobacco juice spray. I became pretty adept at ducking! Eventually, as I got older, he would let me back the car out of the garage, and later drive a little out on the farm roads. My driving ceased somewhat after I once backed one wheel into a ditch! But it was all part of a boy growing up, whose Grandfather had become like a Dad to him. As you know my Dad had died when I was 7 in 1925.

There were other summer treats, like picnics with Aunt Eunice and her friends, fishing with Uncle Wister, and making ice cream mixed with fruit (peaches and strawberries) with him late on summer Sunday afternoons. This came only after regular Sunday School and Church worship services in the morning at the Baptist Church across the street, and after a big Sunday dinner. What a great joy for a skinny, ever hungry little boy!

As for those Sunday afternoon ice cream treats, my"job" was to crack the ice and pack the old-time freezer, and take turns cranking it until the ice cream was made, an arm-tiring job. Then Eunice and Wister would serve up large saucers of ice cream for each one.

Uncle Wister would insist on my getting an eye-bugging portion, stacked as high as the dish would hold. No doubt he realized that we seldom got such treats, or as large a one, in our big family back home. Well, before the strawberry season was over that summer, I had developed a strong dislike for strawberry ice cream, never wanting to see any of it again!

Not until our first pastorate in Acworth, Ga., some 20 years later at Elder Hull's Sunday dinner table, did I learn to like strawberry ice cream again! His dear wife, Bessie, came bringing out the desert--strawberry ice cream. Foolishly, I had just told the story about my boyhood allergy to strawberry ice cream. The Lord sure can change our tunes and tastes quickly!! If we'll let Him!!! He did mine right then!

At Papa's Baptist Church, the sermons were long, and the large bladed ceiling fans did little to cool the sultry summer air. Hand fans, with the name of a funeral home prominently written on them, were for

CHAPTER 13: MOM'S HOME-GOING; SON'S HOME-COMING!

individual use. But using them either worked up more heat or more appetite! The important thing was they preached the Gospel and people were saved and strengthened in their walk with Jesus and their heavenly Father! Those country folk "meant business" with God! Their hymn singing showed it!

At that time the blacks had their churches, and the whites had theirs, and there was much good-will between the races because Jesus and the Bible were basic to both churches. The Great Depression was on, and everybody was working hard to keep, as they would say, "body and soul together." Saturday of course was the big shopping day in the little farm town. There were as many wagons and buggies as there were cars in those days. This was before Franklin Roosevelt's New Deal Fabian socialist programs began bankrupting the work ethic of the Christian foundations of America. (See chapter 7).

Well, it seems we've digressed somewhat in telling the background of life with Papa in those difficult days. Of real family history interest is the fact that when Papa married his childhood sweetheart, Tabitha Brett, (a name with Jewish roots), at the wedding there was a pretty little six year old girl, a member of the Coe family. Papa sat her on his knee at the reception and looked around and said (no doubt jokingly),"If I ever need to get married again, this little girl will be my choice."

Actually it was a true prophecy. For some years later, Tabitha, after having two girls, Mom and "Ose Aunty" and one son, DeWitt, developed a serious infection and blood poisoning which caused her death.

After a proper period of mourning, at least a year in those days, Papa did indeed ask Lillian Coe, that grown-up little girl, to be his second wife. Together they had one child, Eunice, who is in her early 90's now, and still living in the old family home in Ashford. Eunice and Wister had one child, Wister Jean, who eventually became a Doctor of English Literature, and a professor in the English Department at Georgia Tech for many years.

"Mother", as we knew her, Papa's second wife, became a real mother to all the children, a true grand-mother to all of us grandchildren, and lived many years after Papa's death until age 94! She never lost her somewhat mischievous sense of humor, and also was faithful to the Lord Jesus in that little Baptist Church across the street. But it was said of her that she thought that "there would be more Baptist preachers in hell than any other group!" How she arrived at that conclusion, no one knows today! She, too, faithfully managed Papa's farms and store building rentals over the years. But that one farm on the north side of town never was profitable at all, for anything!

So we're back to the subject of this chapter, "The Miracle of The No-Good Farm". After "Mother's" death in 1969 the heirs of hers and Papa's estate were now the four children and a division had to be made by the executors.

Once when we came home to see Mom in Panama City, I found her at that old kitchen table, overlooking "her" beautiful Massalina Bayou, but this time again she was distressed and tearful as she leafed through some legal papers concerning the disposition of Papa's estate.

I asked her, "Mom, what's the matter? Why are you so upset?"

She said, "These papers show a division of Papa's estate. Sister (Ose Aunty) and I, the two oldest heirs, are being asked to take as our share that worthless old farm, and to sign these final settlement papers." (Maybe there were some other things added, I don't know. I didn't read the executor's report, but nothing more of real importance was mentioned. This is the way Mom saw it at that time.)

Immediately, the Holy Spirit brought to my mind the separation that took place between Abraham and Lot. Genesis 13 tells how both tribes and flocks had grown greatly until serious frictions had developed between their herdsmen.

So the Lord led Abraham to say to his nephew Lot, "Let's go different ways and you take the first choice."

Lot's choice was southward, the rich low lands, including Sodom and Gomorrah, and Abraham took what was left, the mountainous country to the North. But there was now peace between them, because Abraham had obeyed the Lord.

So I quickly said to Mom, "Mom, you remember the story of Abraham and Lot, how Lot got the first choice, and chose what he thought was best for him and his family, and Abraham took the second choice obeying the Lord, and was wonderfully blessed by God in that second choice? Leave it in the Lord's hands, Mom, leave it in His Hands!"

And she did and her sister did, too. She never discussed it again and continued to love her brother and sister with all her heart. And do you know what happened? God blessed that old farm beyond everybody's imagination, but not as a farm! Eventually, we were told, the government built a large dam not far away, and local speculators began buying up farm land for building sites. That old farm became worth a large amount of money and was sold by the sisters giving them a greater inheritance than they ever imagined!

Mom had always wanted to leave a small inheritance for each of her children and thought how wonderful it would be if she could leave each one a thousand dollars. By God's mighty blessing, she left about twelve thousand to each one of us!

CHAPTER 13: MOM'S HOME-GOING; SON'S HOME-COMING! 203

That's the story of God's miracle for "The Old No-Good Farm" and for Mom and her children!! How great and good God is! All glory, praise, and thanksgiving to Him forever!

THE LORD'S WARNING MESSAGE TO A POPULAR MINISTER: "STOP QUENCHING THE HOLY SPIRIT!"

In August 1973, we made our annual vacation trip to Panama City, Florida and nearby Lynn Haven. Sissy was still in Panama City; Mary and Charlie, Dick and Judy had built homes side by side facing Anderson Bayou in Lynn Haven; Starlus, Willy and Nancy were also living in Lynn Haven.

Mom's heart had weakened so in the past two years that she could no longer live by herself at 310 Third Court, but had her own room now with Mary and Charlie, and was bedfast most of the time, with the sisters looking after her during the day and a night-nurse at night. She needed almost constant help and at times special oxygen. Judy prepared meals next door and brought them over for Mom. Thank God that Mom could be so tenderly cared for in her last two years with us. She was quite cheerful, alert, and both her good humor and her courageous faith were constant!

Many of her old friends would come to Lynn Haven to visit, and she always received them, thoughtfully and graciously. They went away encouraged in the Lord. One little retired Scottish couple came frequently to share their love with her. The husband began calling Mom his special girl friend, and always leaned over and kissed her and afterwards uncovered a little gift of wine that he had brought for her. She seemed to enjoy both the nips of wine (which her Doctor encouraged for her heart) and the Scotsman's kiss (which his wife permitted!). From what she said, she looked forward to their visits very much. Mom was known to be a teetotaler, but she would use a little rum in her fruit cakes, and her famous lane cake at Christmas time-- made them tastier.

We were there for about two weeks, and had use of Mom's old brown shingled-house at 310 Third Court, and would daily go out to Lynn Haven to see her. One Sunday after Communion Service her pastor asked us if we would join him in serving Communion to her that afternoon. When he arrived about 4 p.m. at Mary and Charlie's house, we brought him to her room, but at that moment Mom began having a hard-to-breathe spell and needed oxygen, so we were asked to go into the living room and wait until she recovered.

As he, Betsy and myself sat down in the living room to wait, the Lord spoke to my heart at that moment and said, "Now tell him."

We must digress a moment here to explain the message the Lord had given months before to give to him. During the previous two years each time we visited his church, we would meet precious Presbyterians who had found out about the Baptism of the Holy Spirit from Full Gospel people and had been wonderfully blessed by the Lord with this Baptism, including the gift of tongues, as Paul writes about in I Corinthians 12 and 14. Almost always they became the brightest lights in the Church, the liveliest and boldest witnesses for Jesus!

We were delighted to see this happening in this rather staid Presbyterian Church. It would mean more power and life and light in the Body of Christ there. However, we learned that these people were not being encouraged, were being put down, put aside, quenched, or pushed out when possible.

There began building up in me a strong word from the Lord by the Holy Spirit that if he did not stop quenching the Holy Spirit by repressing these the Lord was filling in his church, that his "successful ministry" of 25 years in that church would come collapsing down on him. I believe the Lord had wanted us to give that message to him the year before, but I hesitated, thinking "Who am I to bring such a message to such a successful minister in that area?" But here we were again, soon to give Communion together to Mom, and the Lord is saying, "Now, tell him!" Hesitantly, I said, "Brother, I believe the Lord has given me a special message for you and He wants me to tell you now."

He said, "Yes, what is it?"

I replied, "It is this: the Lord is saying if you don't stop the quenching of the Holy Spirit in your Church by repressing those whom He has baptized in the Holy Spirit, your ministry will soon come collapsing down on you."

He said something like: "I cannot believe this or accept it for I have much understanding of the Holy Spirit's work and I don't believe I am quenching it. My concept of the Holy Spirit is the same as E. Stanley Jones'."

I said, "I don't know too much about the E. Stanley Jones' position, but am just giving you what the Lord by the Holy Spirit has given me to tell you."

At that moment we were called back into Mom's bedroom.

Now this man was highly trained, personable, active in civic and civil rights affairs, as well as denominational matters. His well prepared messages were broadcast each Sunday. He was highly thought of in the official circles of the city and seemingly quite capable in the affairs of the denomination. No doubt he was in line for higher offices in the Presbytery. But here was a strong warning from God through a lowly, "fired" many times servant, which he was not receiving.

CHAPTER 13: MOM'S HOME-GOING; SON'S HOME-COMING!

We were then ushered back to Mom's bedroom, and proceeded in a quiet and loving way to have brief prayers and Bible reading, and the Bread and Grape Juice of Communion. No doubt Mom was deeply blessed in the remembrance of the suffering and death of Jesus for her salvation, and her eternal home with Him in Heaven.

We bade goodbye to the Pastor in a warm and friendly way, thanking him for his coming, yet deeply concerned for him because he had not received the message the Lord had sent us to give to him.

Soon we were back in Baltimore, keeping almost weekly touch by long distance phone with our Lynn Haven family concerning Mom's condition, and praying daily for her. That Fall she was in and out of the hospital two or three times until she was calling the ambulance drivers "her boys." Mom's condition worsened, but she made it into January, the month of her glorious home going, which we will tell about later.

It was not long after her funeral in January that we began hearing through the family that the Church and the Pastor were having problems over changes being proposed by the denomination in a new Confession of Faith. The majority of the Church officers were quite conservative, and were strongly opposed to any changes. By the end of Spring the minister suddenly resigned. His ministry there was ended, just as the Lord had warned it would.

Even so, many of the people loved him and his family so much that they gave them a sabbatical leave as a parting gift from the Church. Not only should this be a strong warning to all of us not to quench the Holy Spirit who is the Spirit of Truth, and the living communication of the Lord's voice, messages and truths to His people, but also a strong warning against even the slightest deception in God's work.

The story of Ananias and Sapphira (Acts 5:1-11) in the early church when they lied about the selling of their property and giving supposedly all of it to the Lord's Church, and both of them dropped dead because of the lie, should be a sufficient warning to all of us about being truthful at all times.

Another warning in God's Word that is seldom known or remembered is the one that the prophet Jeremiah gave: **Cursed be he who doeth the work of God by deception.** (Jer.48:10a).

God is merciful and will forgive us our sins and cleanse us if we will truly confess our sins and turn away from them (I John 1 :8-9). May this be true of each one of us, including this Pastor, and some famous preachers since then.

THE LORD'S MIRACLE METHOD OF ARTIFICIAL RESPIRATION

We promised earlier to tell how the head injury Little Joe received that day in Hopewell, New Jersey could possibly effect him seriously many years later, and did. For about the time he was in the tenth grade in Polytechnic High School in Baltimore, he began having migraine headaches and one or two brief periods of disorientation.

In the Fall of the next school year, he and Chris were invited to go regularly to a Charismatic prayer meeting with a young minister on Friday nights. One Friday night after Joe had received prayer for the Baptism in the Holy Spirit, he and Chris came home and went straight to bed, everything seemingly fine.

As usual, being the late bird, I was reading in the dining room on past midnight. Suddenly I realized there was a strange sound coming from near the bathroom, like the sound of water gurgling down the drain. I got up and looked in the bathroom, but there was no water running in the sink or in the tub. So I sat down again, still wondering and listening, and there it came again.

Joe and Chris' room was next to the bathroom and the door was partly open, so I went a step or two into the room and quickly realized the noise was coming from Joe's bed. I flipped on the light and found that Joe was in a near death situation, already turning blue from lack of oxygen and the gurgling sound was as if he was being choked to death, his natural breathing almost completely shut off.

Immediately I called out to Betsy to call a rescue ambulance and then said over Joe, "In the Name of Jesus, I command you Satan to get your hands off my son. In the Name of Jesus you spirit of death get out of here." And while I was saying that, I grabbed Joe up, one arm behind his neck (he was a big boy by now) and under his right arm, and my left arm reaching around his ribs in front to grasp my right hand. I was saying, "Help me Jesus! Help me Jesus!" And I began pumping him like an accordion, squeezing hard and then releasing, squeezing hard and releasing. I could hear the air come out and the air go into his lungs. After a few minutes of pumping his lungs like this, the color began coming back. By the time the ambulance came, in about 10 minutes, he was again breathing on his own, Praise God forever! Through all this he still was not conscious at all.

The ambulance men took over, giving him oxygen and rushed him to Union Memorial Hospital. In the emergency room, about half an hour later, he became conscious, and the doctors began asking him questions about where he'd been, what he'd been doing that evening, apparently thinking he'd gotten into some drugs of some sort. We knew he'd been with this trusted young minister at the prayer group, so the drug idea did not apply.

They gave him a shot of phenobarbital and a prescription for dilantin and told us to contact a physician soon for a brain scan, which we did.

CHAPTER 13: MOM'S HOME-GOING; SON'S HOME-COMING!

The next morning he seemed quite normal, but stayed home from school, and we went to get the brain scan which showed some slight abnormality but nothing really serious. He continued taking dilantin and we had much prayer for him and fasting before the next brain scan about a year later. This one showed no abnormalities at all! The dilantin was stopped and Joe has been okay ever since with no more seizures or migraines. The Lord had healed him completely. Praise His Holy Name!

Today, 18 years later, you will be happy to know that Joe is in good health, a graduate of Maryville College in Tennessee, and has been serving as Director of Admissions for St. Andrews Presbyterian College in North Carolina, after working well in this capacity in other colleges.

It sure was a good thing that I was on the "late shift" that night--and our God never slumbers nor sleeps, but guards His own around the clock! Including Israel! Psalm 121:4. Also it is good to know that He can give instant and miraculous guidance in crisis situations when we cry out to Him--in Jesus' Name! (Jeremiah 33:3; John 14:13-14; John 16:23-24).

NEWS EVENTS FOR 1974

In our first days in Baltimore from 1956 on we had to write to the Board of National Missions a monthly report of the program activities, the problems and plans for the McKim Association work in which the National Missions Board was investing $7-8000 a year. This report would be converted by us into a Newsletter to all our other supporting friends. Later on at the Christian Center and then at the Little Tabernacle for the last 16 years, we have felt that less frequent reports would be appropriate, and certainly a saving of finances. Since our first day at the new Little Tabernacle location we have been under God's specific guidance not to be sending out financial appeals, with the attached return envelope, even though funds were needed and we were fully approved for tax-exempt gifts.

Looking back over the newsletters of the year 1974 we surely see that the Lord was blessing His Little Tabernacle then with His wonderful provisions, guidances and protection! How we praise His Holy Name! All His promises are still "Yea and Amen" in Christ Jesus!!

We want to share several of these tremendous stories with you now. The first was the coming of the Rev. Harold Wallace family into our lives sometime in '73, intertwining their family with ours in a continuing ministry over the last 17 years and the Wallaces coming back early in '74 for an evangelistic series. It was during that series of meetings that we had to leave Baltimore to fly down to Panama City to be with Mom Rigell during her last hours on earth. That magnificent story will follow, plus a few others, including how God got into Betsy's brother-in-law's hospital room to minister hope and salvation to him in the last few days before his death, even though we were told he didn't want any religious fanatics to visit him. Also the golden story of how our own son met Jesus in the Sangre de Cristo (Blood of Christ) mountains and was wonderfully saved.

A TINY TASTE OF A NEWSLETTER

"HE HAS ANOINTED MY HEAD WITH OIL"

276-2317	OUR LORD IS RISEN!	Jan-Feb-Mar-1974
1503 E. Baltimore St.	LITTLE TABERNACLE NEWS	Box 2415, 21203

"Anointed With Oil" - God's sheep are going to get bruised and bumped, cut and scratched, in the normal run of living - but there's always the healing touch of our Master's hand, the balm of His love and presence, the oil of gladness at His nearness and mighty care, the warming of head and heart by His Holy Spirit's anointing. Praise God, He anoints His sheep faithfully with His healing oil of gladness - even when His sheep are persecuted and reproached for Him. (Ps.23:5; Matt.5:1; I Peter 4:12-14; John 15:11). We know this is true, for our Lord has prepared a good table before us in the presence of our enemies, and anointed our heads with His oil of love, healing, renewal and gladness. We will praise Him at all times! This is for you too, dear friend, if you are hearing Jesus' voice and sincerely following Him. Our Great Shepherd, JESUS, gives LIFE, eternal life, anointed, abundant life, and nothing can pluck us out of his hand! (Jn.10:10,27-28)

God's Miracles Are For Us Today! We cannot believe that the miracles of God ended with the last Apostle's departure into heaven. God's miracles of birth and life, re-birth and new-life through JESUS, natural and supernatural healings, physical and Holy Spirit gifts, timings and deliverances are continuing today! Jesus' words: "HAVE FAITH IN GOD," were not just for then but for now! (Matt.18:18-20; Mk.9:23;11:22-24) JESUS IS FOR NOW! FOR YOU! FOR US! HE MAKES GOD'S MIRACLES REAL FOR OUR LIVES TODAY!

THE ANGELS CAME AND LIFTED MOM UP TO HEAVEN
Luke 16:19-31

Yes, we emphatically say that the angels came and lifted Mom up to heaven about 10:30 a.m., January 19, 1974. No doubt there are many folks who cannot believe this about angels, and maybe there are some that don't even believe in angels, but we do. The Bible is full of stories about angels. Several dear friends have seen them. Israel's modern enemies have seen them, and fled from them. So we believe this story will bless you.

As reported earlier, Mom's weak heart condition had continued to worsen through the fall months, requiring several trips to the hospital, bringing a friendly relationship with the young ambulance drivers because she was becoming one of their regular and favorite customers. Her light of love and friendliness was as strong as ever, even though her

CHAPTER 13: MOM'S HOME-GOING; SON'S HOME-COMING!

heart was getting weaker and weaker.

The family members at Lynn Haven were keeping us posted in Baltimore regularly. Our ministry at the Little Tabernacle was keeping us busy. During the third week in January we had a series of meetings scheduled with a visiting evangelist which we were hoping to complete before going back to Florida for Mom's last few days. However, about Wednesday of that week we received word by phone that we should come on quickly. At least by Friday. So we arranged for a flight out of Baltimore on Friday noon, but had been warned that because of wintry conditions on the northwest coast of Florida, the whole coast was blanketed in fog and many small airports were shut down. We called the family and said we were coming. They mentioned about the foggy conditions and the probability that the airport would be closed. But we said, "We'll believe the Lord will roll the fog back for us to land."

Finally, after delays in Atlanta, we were on a smaller plane for Panama City, and sure enough about 10 p.m. that evening, after the plane captain had warned that we might have to land in another place, he found that the fog had rolled away from Panama City and we were able to come in. Then the fog rolled back in, an opening of about 30 minutes. The Lord had done it! Praise His Holy Name!

My brother, Frank, and his wife, Sally, met us and took us straight to the hospital some six miles away. We were allowed to go directly in to see Mom, and as we took her hands and began talking to her, she quickly realized that we had arrived from Baltimore, and her face brightened up. She could see and her hearing was better, but she couldn't speak. So we told her about our trip and how her grandchildren were, and how we had been praying for her, and we had been keeping in touch with the family, and how on the plane the Lord had given us Psalm 116 for her, especially verse 15: **"Precious in the eyes of the Lord is the death of his saints."** Mom was not one to call herself a saint, although in the eyes of the Lord and according to His Word she was one. Earlier, as the nurse was bringing us to Mom's bed, she told us that while Mom could still talk she told her that she had some unfinished business she needed to complete before leaving. The nurse said she seemed to be holding on with all her might in order to get whatever it was finished.

So after reading this Psalm to Mom and talking about how wonderful it soon was going to be to see Dad and Mother and Bill and Al and all who had gone on before, she brightened up. We talked with her for quite a while and then prayed in Jesus' Name a thanksgiving prayer for Mom and for all the wonderful help she was receiving, and we asked the Lord, in the next few hours, to roll back the curtains of Heaven and show Mom that everything was all right, that her business was completed, that she could come home.

By this time it was after mid-night, and we needed some rest ourselves, so we told her good-night, we would be back. Some of the family stayed on in the hospital, but we went on to Mom's house and slept a while, and were able to get back to the hospital about 9 a.m. that Saturday morning.

All the family members had gathered again at the hospital, taking turns to go in pairs to stand by her bed, holding her hands. Mom was still with us, but only for about two more hours. Around 9:45, Frank and our oldest brother, Starlus, were on each side of her bed holding her hands when suddenly Mom looked up as if she were seeing into Heaven. A bright smile came on her face.

Someone asked, "What do you see Mom? Are you seeing Dad?"
She shook her head, "No."
"Papa?"
Headshake, "No",
"Are you seeing little Ann"?
She nodded, "Yes", and then she looked at these two sons the most loving look of forgiveness and love, for everything was all right with little Ann. These two sons had unintentionally caused the tragic accident that had taken little Ann's life when she was just three years old. Mom wanted them to know that they were completely forgiven by her and by the Lord. They didn't have to carry any guilt burden anymore. Business # 1 completed!

Mom seemed to rest a moment, and then again her expression changed to a very worried look.

Someone said, "What is troubling you, Mom? All the family's here, Mom."

She still looked troubled.

"Oh, is it about Uncle DeWitt, you haven't heard from him?"
She nodded.

Her only brother, whom she dearly loved, had always come when she was sick or in a crisis situation. We knew he had not been able to come because of a heart problem himself. But we were able to get him on the phone in Marietta, Georgia, and held the phone up to her ear, so he could reassure her that he was okay. Peace came back upon her face and Business # 2 was finished.

A few moments after this call and this special concern in her heart was satisfied, she looked up again through the open-curtain of Heaven and saw another sight that brightened her face.

Someone asked, "What is it Mom?"

But before there could be any answer, there was a distinct fluttering in the room (at least to me). The Holy Spirit spoke to my heart and said,

CHAPTER 13: MOM'S HOME-GOING; SON'S HOME-COMING!

she was seeing Al, and the angels are lifting her up to Heaven. She was gone in the arms of the angels! Al had been one of her precious sons who had been successful in the pulpwood business and had given generous gifts to her, but had ruined his life with alcohol, until the last three months of his life when he renewed his faith in the Lord Jesus. Mom had said she wasn't sure she wanted to go to Heaven if Al wasn't there. In her last moments here, the Lord had shown her in His great mercy that Al was there, that all of her business was taken care of, she could come home with great joy--and with her faithful angels! Business # 3 all done!

This wonderful Mom of ours had gone home to be with her Lord and those beloved family members who had gone on before. What a great reunion day that was by the grace and mercy of God through the precious atoning blood and saving power of His Son, Jesus. Mom had fought a good fight! She had been a faithful follower and servant of Jesus all her life and there was laid up for her a crown of life eternal in the heavens. ...*be thou faithful unto death, and I will give thee a crown of life.* (Revelation 2:10b). We all came and stood by her bedside. There were many prayers of thanksgiving for Mom, going up with her during that quiet Goodbye-time at her bedside.

I shared with some of the family about hearing the angels lift Mom up to Heaven, but the responses were mainly respectful disbelief, out of their tolerance for their "nutty" preacher brother's strange ideas.

Because I didn't have any Scriptural proof at that moment, Satan began bugging me, accusing me of not telling the truth, or misrepresenting the things of God. Imagine that guy bugging someone about truth, when he's the father of lies! It was not until we were back in Baltimore the following Wednesday night while I was sitting on our couch reading the Scriptures, that the Lord brought me to the passage that I needed. You'll find it in Luke 16:19-31. I found myself reading in Jesus' own words:

> *There was a certain rich man which was clothed in purple and fine linen, and fared sumptuously every day; and there was a certain beggar named Lazarus which was laid at his gate, full of sores, desiring to be fed with the crumbs which fell from the rich man's table. Moreover the dogs came and licked his sores. And it came to pass, that the beggar died and was carried by the angels into Abraham's bosom (Heaven); the rich man also died, and was buried, and in Hell he lifted up his eyes being in torments...*

The whole story is recommended reading. IF JESUS SAID IT, I BELIEVE IT AND THAT SETTLES IT! That was all the proof I needed! (Actually there are many modern stories of angels lifting God's servants to Heaven, and also demons taking wicked men and women in chains, screaming in terror to the place of torment, in other words, HELL!

So the angels of the Lord, who had encamped around Mom all of her 89 years, as Psalm 34:7-8 says, were there to give her their personal lift and escort her to her Heavenly home with Jesus and her loved ones! (See also John 14:1-6, and I Cor.2:9-10.)

A REMARKABLE STORY TOLD AT THE FUNERAL HOME
(I Peter 5:7)

The final funeral plans for Mom were initiated that Saturday afternoon which called for Mom's casket to be on view for one day--that Sunday at the Smith Funeral Home. Mourners were requested to visit there or with the family at Mary and Charlie's home in Lynn Haven, where Mom had spent the last two years of her long, fruitful, and courageous life. Betsy and I felt the Lord wanted us to attend worship service that Sunday morning with other members of the family and then, very soon after lunch, go directly to the funeral home to stand near Mom's casket to receive and thank the many old friends that came to say "Goodbye." It was a very special time for Betsy and me to see the love for her and the sympathy of so many friends who came to share their special words of appreciation for her. Having been a longtime second grade teacher, she had become a beloved mother figure for hundreds of now grown people in Panama City, many now leaders in the affairs of the city. The funeral service the next morning was packed with such leaders and longtime friends. In fact they had chosen her as "Mother Of The Year" for that area of the state back in the late '60's.

But on that Sunday afternoon and evening many of these dear friends came for a last visit with her. One couple whom we did not recognize, but who had known her for a long time, came and told us a startling and amazing story out of their past, which seemed out of place at that moment, having nothing to do with Mom. But it was to become a miracle help for a distraught mother in southeast Alabama the following afternoon, when Mom was laid to rest beside Dad and other members of the family who had preceded her.

What was that startling story? The man telling it was perhaps in his early 60's who said he had been an insurance man in northern Alabama many years before. His name we can't remember, but he said he had a monthly circuit in which he would travel for his company collecting the small insurance premiums from his customers. One of his customers was a little wrinkled and worn black grandmother who scraped together 25 cents a month for her burial insurance policy.

One day he came by to collect her premium and she said to him:

CHAPTER 13: MOM'S HOME-GOING; SON'S HOME-COMING! 213

(We'll call his name, John), "Mr. John, you got a few minutes to spare me? I wants to tell you a story."

He said, "Yes, Mam, I've got the time to spare."

So she took him through her clean little yard with some chickens running around it into her little one-room, weather-beaten shack, lovingly cared for as her home.

Inside she said, "Mr John, my story goes like this. Years ago I had a baby boy, and he was a beautiful little boy. He grew up in this little house at my knee and I taught him to love the Lord. When there was preaching at the Church house, we went everytime. He learned about Jesus, he was a good little boy, he minded his Mammy and Jesus. But when he got up to about 12-14 years old, he began running with some bad boys, and began doing bad things with them and getting in trouble with the law. Up to this time I had been able to hold on to the little farm out yonder that my husband had worked so hard to buy and farm before he passed on.

"At first the Sheriff and the Judge would warn my boy, because they knew he had a good Mammy and a good Pappy, but after a while came fines that had to be paid, and bail money, and lawyer money, and I had to start selling off my little farm, until everything was gone, 'cept this little shack of mine. You see there ain't much left, just my ramshackley bed and his little bunk, this table, those two old chairs, and the little wood stove over there that I cook on and keep warm by in the winter.

"Finally one day the Sheriff come and said, 'Mamie, we've got your boy again and it looks real bad. It looks like we're going to have to put him away for a long time.'

By this time there was nothing left, so I said, 'Mr. Sheriff, I've done all I can for that boy; you're going to have to just put him away, but tell him I love him, and the Lord loves him still.'

"Mr. John, I came back to this table and to this chair, and I got down on my knees and prayed: 'Dear God,' I said, 'You know me, Mamie, and you know that little boy you gave me, how I did all I could to help him know Your way, to know Jesus, and he was a good boy for a long time. But now he's turned into a bad boy, and I sold everything I had to help get him out of trouble. But, he's in more trouble now, and I ain't got anything else to help him with except this little shack, and I knows you want me to have a place to live in. So, dear God, I've done all I could for that boy, and I can't do no more. From now on he's YOUR BOY, YOU'VE got to help him somehow. Thank you, dear God, for doing something for YOUR BOY. In Jesus Name, Amen.'

"Mr. John, maybe you ain't going to believe what I'm going to tell you. But you know, something began happening to dat boy. He began writing me from prison and telling that something special had happened to him. The Lord had done saved him in prison and he was going to be a good man when he got out. You know, Mr. John, they let him out early cause they see that born-again change in him. Today he's out, has a good job, he's married to a good believing woman and they have their own little boy, and they's helping me and looking after me all they can. They's going to Church today, Mr. John. My boy has become a good man. That's a good story ain't it, Mr. John?"

"Yes, Mamie, that's a very good story, and thank God for it."

Mamie had done all she could to honor the Lord and, in childlike faith, she had fallen on her knees and put it all in God's hands. And God wonderfully rewarded her faith in Him.

This was the amazing story which this dear man told us beside Mom's casket that Sunday evening, while other people came, prayed and left. We wondered why we were hearing it just then. The answer came quickly!

The next day in Ashford, Alabama, after the final grave-side services in the old cemetery, we went back to Papa's old house, and Aunt Eunice asked us to sit down and talk with a very distressed mother in the living room. This nicely dressed mother of a well-to-do-family began telling us about her 16 year old son who also had once been a good boy, but now was in total rebellion. It seemed he could cost them everything before it was over, even their business. Would we have any advice for her and her husband?

Now you see why the Lord had given us Mamie's beautiful story of faith. We quietly shared it with her for her own son's deliverance, and in prayer she turned him over to the Lord as Mamie had done. We believe she received the same miracle for her son. Jesus said, *"If any two of you agree on anything that they shall ask, it shall be done for them of my Father."* (Matt.18:19)

Cast all your cares on Him for He careth for you. (I Peter 5:7)

And we know that all things work together for good to them that love God, to them who are the called according to His purpose.

(Romans 8:28)

OUR OWN MISSING SON RETURNS!
HALLELUJAH!

We certainly knew what Mamie had gone through, for our talented second son had left college (Georgia Tech), and family, and God, and "disappeared" in total rebellion into the drug world for nearly 4 years without any trace or contact with us or any member of our family that we knew of. But we and Mom and many others of our believing friends kept him lifted up to the Lord daily the whole time. We knew with so

CHAPTER 13: MOM'S HOME-GOING; SON'S HOME-COMING!

many people praying, somehow everything would work out wonderfully for him. The Lord would bring him back! We were able to assure Mom of this before she moved to her Mansion in Heaven! (John 14:2). In that same year he was to come home as a new creation in Jesus Christ!

Would you like to hear that story? How the Lord worked it out is another one of the miracle stories of His love, power and mercy, and illustrates the fact that there's no way we can hide from God (Psalm 139:1-12). There's nothing too hard for Him (Luke 1:37). We did a lot of praying, a lot of believing, and a lot of singing songs like:

"I Believe God! I believe God!
Ask what you will and it shall be done.
Trust and obey, believe Him and say,
I believe, I believe God!"

This all happened in the late '60's and early '70's during the worst of the USA involvement in the Vietnam War. Kirby, a tall, bright young man finished Baltimore's Polytechnic High School hoping to become an architect. So he applied to Georgia Tech and was admitted. With the help of his grandparents and a small scholarship from his high school, he would be able to attend. So off he went to the world of higher education with our blessings and prayers and the Church's too, where he had served as a junior deacon for a number of years.

His first year at Tech went by fairly well, but then he began asking for an O.K. to join a fraternity. We were reluctant to give our consent, but finally relented and gave it, after carefully warning of the dangers and temptations of such groups. Before that year was out, he was failing in some of his subjects, had gotten into pot smoking and drinking, and soon dropped out of college. Our relationship with him was growing more distant all the time. Then he had to submit himself to the Army draft, taking six months active duty and six years Reserve enlistment. He did the six months and was trained as a medic. He returned to Atlanta where he began trying to support himself doing carpentry work in road building. Soon some conscientious objector "friends" were urging him to drop out of the military altogether and be a war resister with them. All this time he had stopped communicating with us. In effect OUR OWN SON HAD "FIRED US"! We learned all these things later. We were notified by the Army that he had dropped out of the Reserve program and was AWOL. This too was a heart-breaker!

We made two searches for him in Atlanta, and found him once, but after he dropped out of Army Reserve, we could no longer find him. So for 3 years he was missing from us, but not from our God! In the summer of '71 when Mick McNichols, an ex-drug pusher, was still with us, we arranged for him to go down to Atlanta to search out the haunts of lost kids, hoping that Mick could persuade him to come back to the Lord, and get out of the drug culture before it destroyed him, as it was doing to so many fine young people.

Mick did find him, but didn't get to first base in persuading Kirby to turn around. Mick had been a big drug dealer in the South at one point, had been cleaned out in a crooked deal earlier that year in Baltimore, and ended up in Court on a minor charge. I was in court for a companion of his. Fortunately, his charges were dismissed that morning, but Mick asked if he could come to the Center with me. He did come, and stayed with us in our home for a time, and best of all he came to his senses. He gave his heart to Jesus, and went on to Elim Bible College to become a minister. That day he came back from Atlanta with sad news about Kirby, but at least we knew he was alive and one day he would come to his senses like Mick had! Praise the Lord!

Our Lord knew where He was! From here on let him share how the Lord made Himself known to him in a wonderful way on a special mountain in New Mexico.

Cordova, N.M.   Jan. 21, 1976
"JESUS IS REAL!"
By: A. Kirby Rigell

Jesus showed me His reality when i was far from seeking Him. For over 25 years i rebelled against God. My "hang-up" with Christ, for i was in church with my parents every Sunday for nearly 18 years, was the "no other way" of John 14:6 -- Jesus said: **"I am the Way, the Truth and the Life. There is no other way unto the Father but by Me."** i feel many other young people are also hung-up on this "stumbling stone". i pray now that the Lord will show them, as clearly as He has me, that He is The Way"! II Peter 3:9 - **The Lord is not slack concerning His Promise, as some men count slackness, but is long-suffering to us-ward, not willing that any should perish, but that all should come to repentance.** He gives us all the slack we need! He'll let us run our own show till we foul up the whole thing, and finally turn to Him! You'll notice it says: "all should come." That doesn't leave anyone out! I Timothy 2:4 - **Who (God our Saviour) will have all men to be saved, and come to the knowledge of truth.** He calls us all, Praise Jesus! Let me tell you a little of how i realized He came to call me.

My Father, Reverend Joseph S. Rigell, a minister of the Lord some 27 years, raised me and my brothers (all 6 of us!) in the "way we should go." As far back as i can remember, through southern-country churches to down-town Baltimore mission churches, i don't think any of us missed a Sunday, except perhaps for illness. It felt that our

CHAPTER 13: MOM'S HOME-GOING; SON'S HOME-COMING!

Christianity was force-fed, although i thank God now that my family is and was God-fearing. i was confirmed in the church at 12 - but i can't recall it meaning much to me then. Shortly after, my rebellion and doubts grew, till i couldn't wait to be out on my own.

After graduating from High School, i chose the farthest institution from home (Georgia Tech in Atlanta, Ga.) that my folks would allow me to attend, and almost immediately began drinking and doing everything i felt i had been denied for so long. Soon my grades were bad and i was in financial trouble, because of my prodigal living, but i wouldn't repent. After two and a half years of this, i had spent all of the money my folks had provided for my education and had to drop out of school and take a job with the city of Atlanta Traffic Engineering Dept. to earn some money to finish school.

The Vietnam War was in full swing by this time (1970) and my student deferment was up! My draft lottery # was 12! i wanted to apply, because of religious beliefs, for a conscientious objector's status, but i wasn't even sure what those beliefs were! Confused and alienated, i turned to drugs and marijuana. Shortly after i received my draft induction notice, i freaked out, copped out, and ran down to a local Army Reserve Unit to enlist as a medical corpsman. During my subsequent training, and indeed for the next four or five years, i stayed "high" on pot, hash and acid, etc. Let me say to those who believe they are seeking God on these trips - "Friends, you don't know what 'high' is till you've found Jesus!"

Anyway, shortly after my release from training, facing five and a half years monthly service in a V.A. hospital, i copped out again. i was extremely "lucky" not to have to go to Vietnam. (Blessed - there's no such thing as "luck" with the Lord!) But at the time, i transferred units, saying i wanted to go to school in Lexington, Ky., and never signed up in another unit. After 90 days i was declared AWOL and in 30 more a deserter! Now i was really a rebel, on the run. For more than two and a half years i hitched, drove and worked across this country.

It seemed the nation was insane, that i was caught in a web of circumstances, and i felt i was seeking truth through it all. Actually i was still the rebel, trying to run my own show my way. Friends, that just gives the devil the chance to call the shots, no matter what we think we are doing!

"Somehow" i stayed AWOL just long enough to get tossed out with the other "bad apples" at the switch to all volunteer Army at the very tail-end of the War. i got caught at 3:30 a.m. one morning in Missouri, sleeping with two friends in a picnic grounds, on our way cross-country. After 3 days in Ft. Leavenworth, Ky. army guardhouse (i think i may have tried to do some praying there) and 24 days at Ft. Riley, Kansas, i was discharged as undesirable. Now, i could have gone (by regulations) to military prison and hard labor! Did i give thanks? No - i was feeling "lucky" and still going my own way. To make a long story short - it took almost 3 more years of "going my own way" to end up in the mountains of northern New Mexico (Cordova, N.M.).

What do you think those mountains are called? - "The Sangre de Cristo" - The Blood of Christ Mountains! Here and now - as i write this, i can see and feel the Hands of my Lord Jesus in my life, longsuffering through all my rebellion. He took a peyote trip of mine (still doing drugs) 15 months ago in September '74 and turned me to a realization of His salvation. As i walked up into The Blood of Christ Mountain that bright moonlit night, i felt as if i was going to be "blooded" - in the sense that i was going to meet a mountain lion or wrestle a spirit-power or something. But, Praise God, i met my Saviour instead! When i got to the canyon where the river runs down from the mountains, i felt a command in my heart, "Get into the water." i obeyed and, brother, that water was COLD! As i felt that icy water over me, it seemed like i saw Christ on the Cross, dying for me! The sensation, this water is colder than death (it wasn't) made the realization: Christ went through much worse for me! i came out of the water Praising Jesus for the first time, saying, "Praise you, Jesus! Thank you, Jesus!" knowing He died for my sins, that i might live!

The Lord Jesus seemed to say, "Put on your clothes, build a fire, and stay here through the night as I have something to tell you." i did so and one of the things He told me that wonderful night, was that i was to go home, and tell my Dad that everything he'd taught me about the Lord was right. About 6 weeks later i hitchhiked east to Baltimore and had a tearful and beautiful reunion with Dad and Mom. i told them then that i felt the Lord wanted me to go back to New Mexico to live and serve Him there.

From the moment of my water baptism into Jesus in that cold mountain stream, i would tell my friends i was a Christian and i began to study the Bible, especially the New Testament. But, like so many, i was unable to surrender my will completely to Him. So for another 14 months here in New Mexico, i still walked my own way, smoking pot and doing peyote, out of my Lord's Perfect Way.

An incident this past spring ('75) showed me how wide-open my door still was to the devil. My pride (that is of the devil) led me to confront a fellow who ripped off a pair of boots from me. Several times i spoke to his wife about getting them back and she insisted he hadn't stolen them and that he wasn't home. One day, as i stood at the door of their trailer-house, i heard a bellow from a back room and here he came with a knife, right for me, slashing and stabbing! i almost lost my

CHAPTER 13: MOM'S HOME-GOING; SON'S HOME-COMING!

nose trying a judo hold, then turned and ran. Since he was right behind me, in desperation, i picked up a heavy board and hit him in the face, causing him to drop the knife. As his wife was screaming from the porch, some neighbors rushed out to pull us apart. i then got in the truck with a friend and left. The next day that fellow died from an overdose of barbiturates and alcohol. And his family said they blamed me for the pain i gave him when i hit him. My friends all tried to reassure me of my innocence, but i know what the Bible says, and know that, if i had been following the teaching of Jesus, i never would have gotten into that situation. i felt very guilty. But God had spared me again!

My folks wanted all the sons home for Christmas 1975, but we were not able to get together until the week after Christmas. The night after i arrived by plane from New Mexico, i felt led to accompany Mom and Dad and a young minister and his wife to a Full Gospel Business Men's Fellowship Meeting in Hagerstown, Md., where Dad and Mom were to speak. We spent most of the trip, of some 80 miles, just singing praises to the Lord. Not far from Hagerstown, with a heavy anointing of God upon us, Dad asked if i would like to receive the Baptism in the Holy Spirit, and i said, "Yes, i would, Dad." (When i was home the year before, i stood right next to a big, brawny young man, named Bob, when he received his baptism and i knew there was something to it, and i needed it.) Dad asked the young minister, John, to lead me in receiving the Holy Spirit Baptism, and before we got to Hagerstown, i had received a deep touch of the Holy Spirit, but something seemed to be blocking me from the fullness. Later i realized that it was my guilt concerning the young man who died after the fight and overdose. i did give my first public testimony for Jesus that night - a brief one, but real!

Back in Baltimore the next night, on New Year's Eve, in John's apartment i felt led to confess this sin that had been weighing on my mind. John shared from his own past how the Lord had delivered him from a similar guilt, and then suggested i ask the Lord's forgiveness, and I did, down on my knees. At that moment a beautiful, indescribable peace went right through me. Thank God, Thank You Jesus, for Your long-suffering to us-ward! He washed me in His precious blood and that same evening, after a midnight Communion Service in His Church, He baptized me in His Holy Spirit! What a New Year! If i could only tell you what this means, to be born again and filled with God's Holy Spirit! In Jesus! Joy unspeakable and full of Glory! Peace that passes understanding! Miracles and Guiding from that hour on! If you have Jesus, you know. If you haven't, dear friends, i pray that you will! i will never turn back on Him. In fact, i believe He will have me telling His

Good News the rest of my life on this earth--for JESUS IS TRULY REAL!

After all those months and years of weeping and praying and believing and praising God, the first we finally heard from Kirby directly was a letter from New Mexico in early September 1974, saying things that startled, yet thrilled us:

"Dear Mom and Dad,

How are you? Hope everything is okay with you. I'm working in a bridge building job as a carpenter and earlier I planted and God grew a little crop of pinto beans. My goat is giving milk, and Praise the Lord the chickens are laying. I have many things to tell you and hope to come home soon.

Love, Kirby"

About a month later, Mom Betsy being the early bird, heard a knock on the kitchen door about 6 a.m. There he was, big, brawny, bearded Kirby in cowboy boots and a huge pack on his back. I heard the commotion, but slept a little longer while he told his mother much of what had happened. When I got up about 7 a.m., he came and gave me a big hug. And I said, "Well, the prodigal son has finally come home; let's kill the fatted calf and celebrate." I think he said, "Aw Dad,"...then he told me the story of how he had met Jesus on the Sangre de Cristo mountain and Jesus had told him to go home to tell his Mom and Dad that everything we had taught him about God and Jesus was true.

There was great rejoicing in the home, among family, friends and Church. Our long lost son had come home! But only for three days. He felt the Lord wanted him to go back to New Mexico and work among the Mexican Americans there, and too, he still had a job, and goats and chickens and a little shack on a tiny plot of land in Cordova, New Mexico. We hated to see him go again, but had seen how wonderfully our Lord had saved and delivered him! So we again put him in the Lord's hands, confident that the Lord would make everything work out for his good and ours too, now that he was solidly in the yoke of Jesus! To God be all the praise and glory forever for His mighty works!

Christmas of '75 he came home to be with the rest of the family for a few days. Through the help of a young minister, John Warrington, he received the Baptism of the Holy Spirit and again went back toward New Mexico. On the way he met someone from the Tulsa Christian Fellowship, and was invited to come back and live at the JESUS INN, which he did in a very short time. There he made some tremendous Christian friends, attended a summer discipleship training program and

CHAPTER 13: MOM'S HOME-GOING; SON'S HOME-COMING! 221

met his wife-to-be, Carol Briggs. Then he began a two year Bible College program in a fine school, supporting himself all the while in carpentry and home-building work. But more about his story later. Again to God be all the Praise, Glory and Thanksgiving in the mighty Name of Jesus for his miraculous deliverance BY JESUS on the Sangre De Christo Mountain, the "Blood of Christ" Mountain, in New Mexico.

YOU CAN'T BLOCK GOD OUT!
OR HIDE FROM HIM!

Psalm 139 contains some incredible knowledge and wisdom about God and man; every one should know that Psalm. It goes on to say: *Where shall I go from Thy Spirit or where shall I flee from Thy presence? If I ascend up into heaven, Thou art there; if I make my bed in hell, behold, Thou art there; if I take the wings of the morning and dwell in the uttermost parts of the sea, even there shall Thy hand lead me and Thy right hand shall hold me* (verses 7-10). For a man of faith, that's good talk, knowing God is always with you, knowing none can hide from Almighty God! The Psalm closes with these words: *Search me, oh God, and know my heart: try me, and know my thoughts: and see if there be any wicked way in me, and lead me in the way everlasting* (vs.23-24).

ANOTHER REBEL CALLED HOME!

Another man who seemingly tried to hide from God, or say there was no God to hide from, was Betsy's brother-in-law, Freeman Lohr. I personally believe that Freeman, in his boyhood days in a little Methodist Church in East Orange, N.J., had met and given his heart to Jesus. I think the story we now tell really proves it. Freeman grew up there, went off to a very liberal college, graduated as a civil engineer, married Betsy's sister, Cindy, served honorably in the U.S. Navy Seabees in the South Pacific in W.W.II, came home to build his family and his career in engineering, living and working some years in Nicaragua and Mexico. He had become a hard-nose religious objector; somewhere along the line his faith in God and Jesus had been left behind, probably in college where so many young people's faith gets demolished by modern-day godless professors.

In August '73 while working as a Project Engineer for the Baltimore Inner Harbor Renewal, he had to go into Johns Hopkins Hospital for an operation for stomach cancer. That's when we, only about five blocks away, were told to stay away. Our prayers and ministry were not needed. The following January he had to go back to another hospital in Annapolis, near his home. A few days before we went to Florida to be with Mom in her last hours, Betsy had been allowed to go to the Annapolis hospital to see Free for the last time, and she told him we were praying earnestly for him.

Betsy and I redoubled our prayers for him, praying earnestly that God would still send him somebody who could talk to him about Jesus and salvation and being saved from what seemed to be hard-nosed unbelief. God did just that in a very remarkable way!

It was cold, snowy, icy winter-time, as Baltimore almost always is in January, a time when a person needs to watch his step constantly to keep from slipping. Well, the Lord had just the right man to send into that hospital to see Freeman. He was a very well known engineer-scientist, Christian author, and speaker by the name of Harold Hill.

About a year before, our sister-in-law, Debbie, had tried to get Freeman and his wife, Cindy, to attend a Full Gospel meeting where Harold Hill was the key speaker. She gave him one of Harold's taped messages, but no one knows whether he ever listened to it or not. On one of those cold 1974 January nights, Mr. Hill was having a men's meeting in his basement, and apparently they had entered through a basement door, tracking in some snow and ice. Suddenly Brother Hill found himself slipping on that hard basement floor in such a way that he ended up with a terribly broken ankle, in great pain and needing immediate hospital care. The men prayed earnestly for him, and the pain dissipated quickly, but the ankle still needed to be set and put in a cast. He was rushed to the same hospital in Annapolis where Freeman was, the x-rays were made, the ankle reset, and a full leg-cast put on. He was ready again to get on about the Lord's work in a wheel chair. A connection was needed! So while visiting Freeman in the Annapolis hospital, his death only a few days away, Betsy's brother, Kirby and his wife Debbie saw Mr. Hill and Debbie introduced herself and urged him to visit her brother-in-law, Freeman, in a nearby room.

Freeman's wife, Cindy, knowing Brother Hill through AA meetings, was surprised to find him also in the hospital. He inquired about her husband, and right away, this outstanding engineer, scientist, author, Harold Hill, in cast and wheel chair, was visiting Freeman, the hard-nose engineer, in his last few days on earth.

We saw Brother Hill not long after, at another meeting and we asked him if he felt his visits with Freeman were successful, and he replied, "What do you think? Does God's Word return void?" We knew the Scripture in Isaiah 55 which plainly says *His Word does not return void or empty handed.*

Let's never think that we can ever hide from or lock God out of our lives! Let's be filled with His Word, obeying it, and bearing good fruit for His Glory!

CHAPTER 13: MOM'S HOME-GOING; SON'S HOME-COMING! 223

Many years later in 1989, we were visiting Freeman's mother in a nursing home near Annapolis. She confirmed to us that Freeman had had a sincere faith in Jesus as a little boy, and how she had prayed and longed for him to come back to Jesus. She had never heard of Harold Hill's special miracle visit with her son Freeman which we shared with her. Oh the tears of joy that flowed down her cheeks as she realized her own son had made it Home to Jesus at last--by God's Amazing grace and love!

FAMILY REUNION CHRISTMAS 1976

224 FIRED AGAIN AND AGAIN, PRAISE THE LORD!

DEAR SISTER FELIX AT PTL LUNCHEON
IN OLD BARBER SCHOOL- 3\72

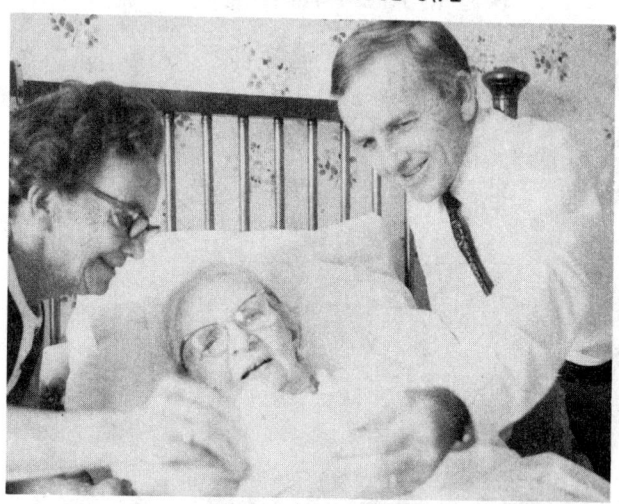

WITH SISSY AT
MOM RIGELL'S BEDSIDE- 8\73

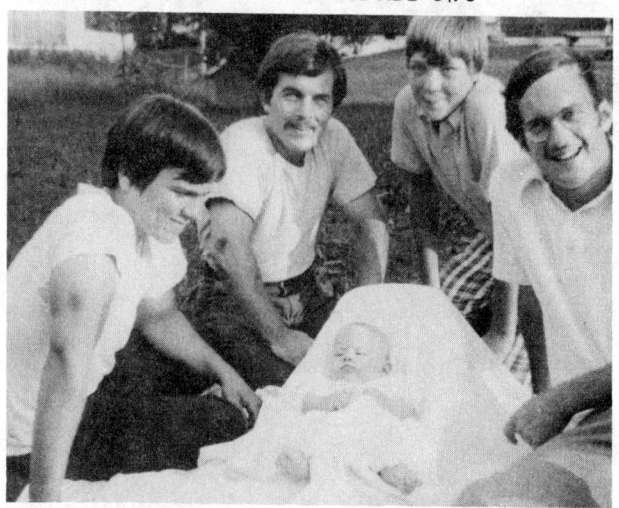

SON CRAIG PROUDLY INTRODUCES HIS LITTLE GINNY
TO 3 UNCLES: CHRIS, BRIAN, & JOE- 8/75

CHAP. 14

MORE MIRACLES OF JESUS

Eye hath not seen, nor ear heard, neither have entered into the heart of man, the things which God hath prepared for them that love Him.
- I Corinthians 2:9

"DASHING THROUGH THE SNOW"

Christmas 1974 was rapidly approaching. We were all busy at the Little Tabernacle with the newly filled Youth Home and opened Bible Book and Gift Shop, and trying to get things lined up for the Church's Christmas programs and celebration. Real winter snows still had not arrived in Baltimore, so the reference here is to words in that familiar Christmas song of "Jingle Bells".

Chris was a junior at Poly, Brian was in the 8th grade at Roland Park, Bernie was our chubby, jovial foster child, about Brian's age. We were extremely happy approaching this Christmas since we knew our son Kirby had found the Lord and was all right and back in New Mexico.

The Turn-Around-With-Jesus-Home was full with John Warrington leading the Youth Home group and being a great help in the Church services in teaching and preaching God's Word. Just recently we held a dedication service for the home and bookshop in which we recognized everyone involved, especially the good Lord whose hand had made it all possible!

For years we had been purchasing hardware items at a little neighborhood hardware store called Ritterhoff's. Every few days we would need nails, screws, locks, keys, paint or something from them. Paul and Charles Ritterhoff had operated the hardware store for many, many years as their father had before them. They had survived the riots fairly well and were continuing in business, for which we are most thankful.

On this particular day, I walked the two blocks to the hardware store, and was immediately drawn aside by a young clerk named Joe Macus. Joe was a new immigrant from South America and was trying hard to get adjusted to life in America. He always had a question or

FIRED AGAIN AND AGAIN, PRAISE THE LORD!

two for me when I came in.

It was about December 18th or 20th. Joe said in broken English, "Rev, on the way to work I heard on de radio da song Jingle Bells. You know da song?"

I nodded, and he continued, "But in a few moments, instead da words dey were singing, I hear utter words like:

'Praise de Lord, Praise de Lord,

Praise His Holy Name,

He's so good----'

And dat's as far as I got. Would it be okay to change de words like that?" asked Joe.

"Yes, Joe, that's great. It sure would. Let me take these words back to the Little Tabernacle. We have ladies there who know about music and I'm sure they will be able to fill it out and make it praise Jesus for His Birthday."

Back at the Little Tabernacle office with the thoughts of Jingle Bells in my head and trying to remember Joe's words, I found Betsy, Sarah Shaw, Ann Thomas and her daughter, and I told them about Joe Macus' inspiration for new words to the tune of "Jingle Bells". Sure enough, these dear ladies excitedly went to work on the idea and in less than 20-25 minutes they had it all worked out. It truly was a work of inspiration by the Holy Spirit to fill this lively familiar tune with Praises for Jesus.

Here are the words they quickly put together that day in the Little Tabernacle. They have not been changed since, and have literally flown around the world, to many nations of the world, including Jerusalem, Israel, Europe, England, Australia, New Zealand, Hawaii, etc. We trust you will bless the Lord at your next Christmas by singing these precious words to that old, old tune, "Jingle Bells." We call this version the:

"Jesus Jingle Bells Song!"

"Dashing through the snow
With Jesus on My Mind,
Telling the Good News
To everyone I find
Going where God leads
To every life forlorn
Spreading forth the Word of God
That Jesus Christ is born."

Chorus: "Praise The Lord, Praise The Lord,
Praise His Holy Name,

CHAPTER 14: MORE MIRACLES OF JESUS

He's so good! He's so kind!
He's everyday the same!" (Repeat)

There you have it! Just add a heart filled with the love of Jesus and sing with great joy and gusto!

A CHRISTIAN TELEVISION STATION FOR BALTIMORE?

Before we leave '74, a mention needs to be made of efforts by some Christian ministers and lay-people to obtain a full-time Christian TV station in Baltimore. At LTC we had felt the growing need for decent Christian TV and had even made a trip to South Bend and Indianapolis, Ind. to check into Dr. Lester Summerall's Christian radio and TV operations out there. Lester was very kind and encouraging to us, and amazingly, we found out in our talks with him that he had spent some of his boyhood years in St. Andrews, Florida (a suburb of Panama City), and had made his boyhood commitment to Jesus there beside the St. Andrews Bay, where I had made mine.

In '74 a Baltimore TV station was available for purchase and also the FCC had opened the possibility of a Channel 20 being made available for Baltimore. We soon learned that Father Phil Zampino of St. Timothy's in Catonsville was heading up a group seeking to establish a Christian TV station. Father Phil asked us to defer to them so, having only "3 nickels to our name," we urged them to proceed with all speed, the need was so great. We would help in any way we could and we did just that.

A Zampino-led Christian TV Rally, seeking to raise the interest of the Christian Community in Baltimore and to obtain the large financial backing that would be needed, was held in one of the main churches in Baltimore. In this particular meeting, suddenly, I felt the leading of the Holy Spirit to tell Father Zampino and the group, that the Lord would raise up large financial backing for the project within two weeks after the meeting. I really felt this was a Word from the Lord.

After two weeks when no announcement came about large financing available for the TV station, I was soon being called, by some, a false prophet.

Much later Father Phil was to tell me, when I asked specifically, that, in truth, a Christian financier had offered sufficient funds within those two weeks to get the station going, but because of certain strings attached, the offer was turned down. Father Phil's statement of what happened in those two weeks greatly relieved me and confirmed I really had heard from the Lord!

Some three or four years went by without any great success and apparently the whole project was to die a slow death. With the "garbage" coming in on TV today, even in primetime, Baltimore's need for a fulltime Christian TV station is greater than ever. Some used to call much of the U.S.TV a "wasteland". It's become worse than that today! A "Garbage Dump" is too good a name for it. "Satan's Sewer Line" might be better!

To this day, I wonder if a serious mistake wasn't made in rejecting that man's offer of finances. There's still no separate Christian TV station in Baltimore! It's a pity and a shame! It should be said that the Zampino TV group did make a commendable effort toward establishing a Christian TV station in Baltimore, but could not bring it about.

THE STRANGE SNOW FALL

Can God control snowfalls? Earlier in this story we mentioned Psalm 148:7,8 in connection with the last worship service in the Upper Room when we all sang "How Great Thou Art" in praise to God --after that sudden "firing" from the short-lived Christian Community Center!

We now want to share with you another strange coincidence of nature during a FGBMFI meeting in Atlantic City, N. J. at a special hotel there, on April 12, 1975. Betsy and I were leading the group in singing that same song "How Great Thou Art" and other praise choruses. But before we describe what happened, let's fill in some pertinent details.

On that special day, Betsy and I, our three boys, Chris our high school senior, Brian our adopted 8th grader, and Bernie, our foster son also an 8th grader, all were in Atlantic City for the Full Gospel Business Men's Meeting at the Hotel Marlborough Blenheim. (We had long prayed to see such a meeting in this particular hotel--it was founded by Betsy's Quaker great-grandfather.) We were about to see our prayers answered, having arrived the night before for a weekend-after-Easter Retreat from our own busy life at the Little Tabernacle in Baltimore. Betsy's brother Kirby White, one of the hotel's managers, and his wife, Debbie, both active supporters of the FGBMFI effort in Atlantic City, had invited us to come as their guests.

The invitation to lead the praise service came as a surprise to us; however, when the time came, we gladly undertook to do so. It was a sizable group, now reassembled after breakfast in a beautiful domed meeting room, all happy to sing the praise of our mighty God and Saviour Jesus Christ. We sang verses from the Psalms, such as "I Will Bless The Lord At All Times," "The Angels of The Lord Encamp..." (Ps.34), and "Bless The Lord, Oh My Soul" (Ps.103), plus the choruses, "He Is Lord," and "Lift Jesus Higher."

Then we asked the assembly to join us in singing "How Great Thou

CHAPTER 14: MORE MIRACLES OF JESUS

Art." As preface to singing it, we told the amazing experience we had in mid-October 1971, when we were singing this same hymn on the 3rd floor of an old factory, in a room we called "The Upper Room." (See page 153). Our little band of Christians were worshipping there for the last time, because we were being evicted on very short notice, with no known meeting place in sight except, perhaps, outdoors in a nearby park. We told how we believed we were in God's purpose and time, and so on that last day, we had boldly begun to sing this great hymn to God!

Something wonderful happened that hot, sultry, day as we sang to God from our hearts! Exactly at the moment we sang, "I hear the rolling thunder," all of Baltimore was shaken by waves of God's mighty rolling thunder. Then in the second verse at the precise moment we sang the phrase, "and feel the gentle breeze," the beautiful new curtains in that "Upper Room" began lifting high and waving back and forth in a very strong, but gentle breeze of God. Oh, what a time of praise to God that was, as we realized that God was telling us through the very elements of nature, that He was with us, that He controls it all, that we had naught to fear as we went forth, like Abraham of old, not knowing where we were going. Glory to God! That Sunday He rolled His thunder and blew His wind precisely on time to powerfully confirm it!

So here in Atlantic City, we began to sing this truly inspired hymn. Every voice was joined together in a great joyful union of praise and adoration to God. We sang three verses, and the presence and power of God was sensed by all. Again amazing things happened by the hand of God! As we finished, the Chapter president, Jess Martin, began sharing a word of knowledge by the Holy Spirit that God was doing a great healing work among the people assembled. And He was! Praise His Holy Name! Many were being healed as we all sang His praise! Then something else! Outside on that bright April 12 in Atlantic City, it was snowing, for just the time we were singing that great hymn! Hallelujah, the snow was singing "How Great Thou Art" with us! And bringing a warning message from God as seen below!

That evening after dinner with Debbie and Kirby, the Hills and the Martins, Debbie handed us a brief article titled "See What's Coming", by Charles Gardner of Forest Park, Ga., dated May '74, which she had been reminded of by the Holy Spirit during that morning's Miracle Snow. She had located it, believing there was a real timely connection.

THE VISION OF CHARLES GARDNER:

"Recently I had a vision I would like to share. The Lord showed me what looked like millions of people in little groups. And the Lord said this is my church. Some groups glowed like a light, while others were only people grouped together in activity. The Lord said those that glowed had come together in love. Then it began to snow or what looked like snow on all the people. The Lord said this is the tribulation that has begun to fall. The groups that glowed began to grow brighter, and the other groups only seemed to come closer together, glowing only slightly. Then the Lord said, "IF MY PEOPLE WILL NOT COME TOGETHER IN LOVE, THEY WILL COME TOGETHER IN TRIBULATION." As the snow continued, those that came together in Great Love continued to shine brighter; those who wouldn't, disappeared under the snow. Then the trumpet sounded and the vision vanished."

May this story about God's "Miracle Snow," "Rolling thunder," "Mighty But Gentle Breeze," and "The Snowfall Vision" of Charles Gardner, be a strong encouragement to you in your walk with Jesus. May this story help us all to grow and glow in Jesus, in His Love for one another. "Make us one, Lord, in You and in Your Love! Even with the snows of tribulation if necessary! Keep us ever Praising You!"

"JESUS' PIGGY-BANK MIRACLE"

Can Jesus multiply the loaves and fishes today? Many people would lift a very skeptical eyebrow if they heard such a question. But He can! Let us tell you the miracle story of how Jesus multiplied, in October, 1975, the small piggy-bank gift of a little boy over a thousand-fold and turned it, in a week and a half, into an all-expense paid 10-day trip to Jerusalem, for a specially chosen "ambassador" to Israel and to The 1975 World Conference on the Holy Spirit there.

This Holy Spirit Conference for 1975 in Jerusalem was planned for over a year for Oct. 29--Nov. 6, by Logos International Fellowship in New Jersey with internationally known speakers and singers invited. One of the most anointed, Spirit-filled singers we knew was a beautiful young woman by the name of Loretta Young who lived with her husband Don and daughter Rehya in Washington, D.C., at that time, and her parents lived in Baltimore. Loretta had studied to be an opera singer, but now was singing for the Lord in schools, churches and conventions. In her heart she felt God wanted her to sing at the Jerusalem Conference--but no invitation-- and no finances.

Some eight months before, after being one of the singers at the Jesus Youth Easter Rally in Baltimore, she had heard the Lord speaking in her spirit to get ready to go to Israel. She readily said, "Yes, Lord," but wondered, "How can we do it?" She knew in her heart that, with the obligations she and her husband had, there would be no way for them to finance the trip. About this time she visited the Little Tabernacle and sang at one of the Thursday PTL Luncheons, and the Holy Spirit

CHAPTER 14: MORE MIRACLES OF JESUS

confirmed, by a word of prophecy through one of the brothers, that she was to get ready and that the Lord would provide all that was necessary. So she began getting her passport updated, and her "traveling shoes" ready. She waited on The Lord. By mid-October, still lacking funds, she found reservations closed for flights and groups going to the Conference.

Had she missed God's voice and purpose? She remembered:"God is always faithful to His Word!"

Now less than two weeks before departure time, her spirits no doubt sagging near the bottom, but still convinced that the Lord wanted her to go and would somehow make a way where there was obviously no way, she came to the Little Tabernacle to praise the Lord with the Thursday Luncheon group. A few moments after her arrival and warm greetings, she reached in her pocket and pulled out a handful of coins which she said the four year old son of a close friend had asked her to bring to Jesus when he found out she was coming to the Little Tabernacle. He had literally opened his piggy-bank and poured out everything he had to give to Jesus. Just like the little boy of long ago, beside the Sea of Galilee, had given his five loaves and two fishes--all he had---to Jesus.

Immediately the Lord seemed to be saying to us, "This is how I will send Loretta to Israel. I will show you that I can still multiply the loaves and the fishes today. Lift up his 89 cents to me, let me have them, and I will show you. Confidently dedicate them to this purpose for I have chosen Loretta to be a special ambassador to bless my people and my land Israel." So together with the group at the luncheon that day, we lifted up the 89 cents to Jesus and set them apart as the little boy's loaves and fishes in His hands. One week later the 89 cents had grown to $890, and on the following Sunday grew to over $1200. Praise The Lord! Jesus had done it again!

Completing the miracle on the Thursday before the air-lifts departed, Logos found a way to include Loretta in a special group out of Canada, and on the Tuesday morning of departure, all the funds she needed were in her hands---by the wonderful and mighty hand of Jesus. Praise His Holy Name! His Miracles will never cease!

Hallelujah! The Lord did send Loretta to Israel and had both Pat Robertson and Jamie Buckingham ask her to sing at the Conference. He sent her to bless Israel and she did through her singing which was broadcast! *And I will bless them that bless thee!* (Genesis 12:3) Praise God for His singing ambassadors for Christ!

Praise God for little boys who have loaves, fishes and piggy-banks to give to Jesus, to bring His miracle blessings to His people and His Israel today. YES! JESUS DOES MULTIPLY THE LOAVES AND FISHES

TODAY FOR HIS "ABIDING-IN-HIM" DISCIPLES!

Today for all those teenagers and adults, whatever age and place, who will give JESUS their all, He will enlarge and increase their lives with great abundance right here on earth, and in eternity to come. Here are just a few of His great Promises:

But seek ye first the Kingdom of God and His righteousness and all these things shall be added unto you. (Matt.6:33)

And everyone that hath forsaken houses, or brethren, or sisters, or father, or mother, or wife, or children, or lands, for my name's sake shall receive an hundredfold, and shall inherit everlasting life. (Matt.19:29)

Eye hath not seen, nor ear heard, neither has entered into the heart of man, the things which God hath prepared for them that love Him. But God hath revealed them unto us by His Spirit: for the Spirit searcheth all things, yea, the deep things of God. (I Cor.2:9,10)

Bring ye all the tithes into the storehouse, that there may be meat in mine house, and prove me now herewith, saith the Lord of hosts, if I will not open you the windows of heaven, and pour you out a blessing that there shall not be room enough to receive it! And I will rebuke the devourer for your sakes, and he shall not destroy the fruits of your ground. (Mal.3:10-11a)

The thief cometh not, but for to steal and to kill, and to destroy: I am come that they might have life, and that they might have it more abundantly. (John 10:10)

A VERY SPECIAL CHRISTMAS - 1975

The Piggy Bank miracle was just completed and we began praying for another miracle - the full reunion of our immediate family for the first time in six years. We so longed to see our sons all together again and, wonderfully, the Lord did bring us together, not exactly on Christmas day, but in the week following between Christmas and New Year.

The group now included a new little baby by the name of Ginny, brought at the age of 7 months, by her parents, Craig and Ann, to see her Grandparents. Joe and Dusty came from college. Chris and Brian were still with us. Kirby flew by air from New Mexico, tall and tanned, still wearing his beard, boots, construction man's clothes, a large knapsack, and best of all carrying a well-worn New Testament in his shirt pocket.

As he told earlier in his story, he had had a rough and dangerous year, but the Lord had brought him through. Naturally, we all were full of joy and thanksgiving. Kirby and John Warrington had become good friends the year before, and John immediately sensed that Kirby had

CHAPTER 14: MORE MIRACLES OF JESUS

something heavy on his heart, and still wanted and needed the Baptism in the Holy Spirit. Brother John helped him confess everything to the Lord and receive forgiveness, and on New Year's Eve he came to the midnight watch service and was gloriously filled with the Holy Spirit. What a tremendous Christmas for all of us, and what a way to begin the New Year! All thanks and Praise to our Lord Jesus and to our heavenly Father!

On the way back to New Mexico, Kirby was detoured by the Lord to the "Jesus Inn" in Tulsa. A whole new chapter in his life was begun which would lead him to Bible College, to finding his future wife, and eventually to come back in October, 1979 to take our place at the Little Tabernacle as we left for Israel.

Another note about the young minister, John Warrington, whom the Lord had sent with his wife, and the six young disciples he had led to Jesus. He and they had pitched in and done all kinds of jobs, and given themselves to much prayer for the strengthening of the ministry. John's early life had been troubled by angry rebellion, drugs, occult practices, even imprisonment, but the Lord Jesus had transformed him into a calm, humble, wise, courageous, servant of the Lord. We will be forever grateful for his and their coming to be the first residents of The Turn-Around-With-Jesus Home, and to greatly strengthen the work and witness of the ministry at the Little Tabernacle.

It was during this time that I was forced to withdraw from the scene for a time due either to a mild heart attack or exhaustion. Dr. Nesbit's cardiogram, however, did not show anything serious. But one day during these "laid-up" days there was a knock on our door, and there was young John Warrington asking if he could come in and pray for me. He was welcome to come in. He immediately said the Lord wanted him to get a pan of water and wash my feet as he prayed for me. As he ended his prayer he was moved by the Holy Spirit to speak a prophetic word saying, "Fear not, my son, for I am healing you and you shall serve me many more years and your feet will travel to many, many places for me and the Gospel's sake." What an encouragement!

Not long afterwards, early in '76, they headed back toward the upper California region where most of them had come from. We would deeply miss them and pray to see them again.

(In 1989, John Warrington returned to the Little Tabernacle right out of the blue! He is preaching Jesus on the street corners of America and, when in Baltimore, is making the Little Tabernacle his home. His own marriage had been ripped apart by Satan. We are believing with him that the Lord will restore what has been stolen.)

Before John left in '76, he brought to the Little Tabernacle a young black minister, with his large family (seven children, little stair-steps). The sweetest group of Jesus lovers you ever saw. John recommended that they be allowed to use the TAWJ Home after he and his group left. We all agreed. They had been staying in the back of an old theater building, hoping and praying to get a successful evangelistic ministry going in Baltimore. Bro. Ware was quite an evangelist and musician, and his whole family made up a choir and orchestra! With their amplifying equipment they had some of the boldest music you've ever heard. Often, on Saturday, he would set up his equipment on the corner next to the bookshop and begin his music and testimonies and powerful preaching. However, A. Ware was preaching the real-repentance-and-obedience-and-hard-work-and-love-everybody-Gospel straight down the line, and not the social welfare gospel that so many were wanting to hear. He and his family (wife, Carol) helped in every way they could and spent about a year with us.

At one point he seemed to be disgruntled toward me, so we sat down in the office one day and went over the Gifts of the Holy Spirit as outlined in I Corinthians 12, and I was led to ask him, "Bro. Ware, do you see in this list a 10th gift?"

He looked at the Scripture again and said, "Pastor Sid, there is no 10th gift here, I only see nine."

I said, "But there are some folks around here right now thinking there's a 10th gift."

He asked, "What is that?"

I answered, "The gift of criticism."

This answer struck his funny bone and he said, "Bro. Sid, you're right, you're absolutely right. We don't have any business with that gift, that one's from the devil."

We remained fast friends and co-workers until eventually they moved back to his home country in Texas. That dear brother, like John Warrington, had had some hair-raising adventures and heaven-sent miracles of deliverance. May the Lord bless A. Ware and his big beautiful family wherever they are and give them many, many souls for His Kingdom.

It was about this time that a few people in the Church had become somewhat upset with the pastor (me) and had cast about for ways to replace me. However, one young Jewish believer was not in agreement with them at all. Wanting to cheer me up, she brought in a humorous poster which we tacked up in the office. It read: "When people come to run you out of town, get in front and make it look like you're leading a parade!" It helped cool things too!

One of the really sad things in the ministry and Church today is that so-called brothers spend more time cutting each other up with criticisms, true or not, rather than building each other up in love. It does great damage to the cause of Christ. It reminds me of my Mother's rule concerning ministers. "Never say anything bad in her presence about her minister, no matter how inept he might be. He's God's servant." In other words, don't touch God's called servant with bad remarks in her presence --- or the fire of her wrath would fall on you! And God's, too!

We could write a long chapter on the beautiful ministries and servants of God whom the Lord sent our way to help in those years. We think of the tremendous help that James and Judith Hathaway gave at the Little Tabernacle in wonderful praise and worship and Bible teaching and preaching and loving friendship that continues today even though they have been many years in Odessa, Texas. As we are writing this in 1988 on Patmos, each day, we are playing one of their tapes of Scripture Songs. These tapes are some of the best ever made and are still blessing God's people across America and on Patmos! Write them at 4641 Oakwood Drive #69, Odessa, Tx. 79761, for copies of their Praise Tapes.

Then there was the teaching and deliverance ministry of police Sgt. Stelman Smith and his wife, Sue, which brought many blessings. Fondly we remember Dr. Jerry and Ginny Kirchner from Aberdeen, who came for several years with their dental technician, Betty Angelilli, to help the Church. They sold their flourishing dental practice and for several years now have been in full-time, very courageous ministry in the Far East. Betty and her husband Paul McDowell lived for several years in Israel, having three of their own little Israelies (three of the cutest little believers you'll ever find). Paul worked in Hadassah Hospital, but now they are back in Pennsylvania.

A dear nurse named Judy Ross came and lived in the third floor apartment of 1503 with her little dog and was a special help in the spring and summer months of 1976. After Judy, the Elsberries came to live in the third floor apartment and train in practical ministry. They then went on to an Episcopal seminary, and service in that denomination. How blessed we've been to know and work with these devoted servants of the Lord Jesus. May the Lord continue to bless them richly above all they could ask or think, according to His promises.

236 FIRED AGAIN AND AGAIN, PRAISE THE LORD!

DEDICATION SUNDAY,
OCTOBER '72
REV. SID INTRODUCES
MRS. DEBENEDETTO

LITTLE TABERNACLE CHAPEL
ON CAROLINE STREET
CORNERSTONE IN HEBREW
PSALM 118:22

VBS PARADE LED BY
SARAH, TERRI,
DOROTHY AND BETSY - 1973

THE LORD'S CORNER -
BALTIMORE & CAROLINE STS.
(L to R) THE VICTORY HOME,
LITTLE TABERNACLE OFFICE
& BOOK SHOP

CHAP. 15

GOD'S SOLEMN WARNING TO THE CHURCH

Sirs, what must I do to be saved? And they said, "Believe on the Lord Jesus Christ and thou shalt be saved and thy house.
- Acts 16:30b-31

THE SOLEMN WARNING TO THE PRESBYTERIAN CHURCH
A TOUGH ASSIGNMENT

In May of 1976 the Lord was to give us one of our toughest assignments ever, an assignment that hopefully could influence the entire United Presbyterian Church for years to come. "The Presbyterian Layman" is a conservative paper that has for years been trying to prevent terrible apostasies from creeping into the Church and trying to maintain faithful allegiance to the Word of God, to the real gospel of Jesus Christ and the true calling of Christ upon His Church. Through this Journal we were keeping track of unholy and unfaithful trends in the Church, such as approving the removal of the Bible and Prayer from the schools of America, approving abortions, approving ordination of many who did not believe in the Bible as fully God's Word and who could not believe in the divinity of Christ and His Virgin Birth, nor His sacrificial death for our sins. The Church had been winking at these forms of unbelief for some time.

And now in this year a strong effort was being made by a Presbytery in New York to obtain approval by the General Assembly for the ordination of homosexuals into the Presbyterian ministry. Anyone in his right mind and with any knowledge of the Holy Scriptures and of the Will of God for His Church and ministry should know in a minute that this life style is clearly proscribed as an abomination in the eyes of God, subject under the Levitical law to the death penalty, not to be approved in any way, shape or form by God's people and true ministers.

Biblically it would be on par with ordaining an unsaved, unrepentant thief, murderer or whoremonger. It was and forever will be an abomination in the eyes of God. It is total rebellion against God as He clearly describes it in Romans 1. Such people can repent, be saved and delivered completely from this demonic and ungodly life style, as we've told you before. So the projection for this General Assembly meeting in the Baltimore Civic Center was that it could very well approve this New York Presbytery overture asking permission to ordain homosexuals to the ministry. In fact a so-called homosexual caucus would be attending the General Assembly and having its own suite of rooms in the key convention hotel, ready to button-hole all the commissioners with their unbiblical and deceptive arguments on behalf of this issue.

Just the weekend before the General Assembly was to meet in Baltimore, there was to be a large Presbyterian Charismatic Conference in Montreat, N.C., with Dr. Brick Bradford, one of the conveners. Betsy and I wanted to go. My brother Frank and his wife, Sally, were coming up from Mississippi and our Elder Frank DiMattei and his wife Sally were planning to go. How we were going to attend this conference and be back in time to compose a strong warning that would penetrate the General Assembly Convention, we didn't know. But we knew the Lord would help us. At that time my relationship with the local Presbytery was very tenuous and "left-fieldish". I was not eligible for any official pass into the convention. We would be strictly on the outside hoping to get a powerful warning inside!

The Montreat Conference was very special, strengthening and renewing us in faith and courage for the days ahead. It was a marvelous blessing for us to be with the two Franks and Sallies and, Praise God, Frank DiMattei's wife at long last received the Baptism in the Holy Spirit, which changed her heart and attitude toward us.

On the way back from Montreat that Sunday afternoon, Betsy and I took turns driving, pressing to get back to Baltimore before midnight. The Assembly would be getting underway on Monday. We arrived about 10 p.m. that night and, with the ideas the Lord was already putting together in my heart and mind, I immediately began writing a "Solemn Warning" to our fellow Presbyterians which we would mimeograph in hundreds of copies on Monday. On the back of this warning we were to place an amazing story by Demos Shakarian, the International President of FGBMFI. Demos' family had been Presbyterians back in Armenia around 1875 before fleeing to America. We plan to include this story with permission from Demos and his organization.

By the end of that Monday we had some 600 copies of the warning ready and with Judy Ross accompanying us, we headed for the Civic Center. We were hoping to be able to stand outside before the evening session to distribute these warnings. Praise God, it went off smoothly, like clockwork (after a prayer for the Lord's timing, blessing and success

CHAPTER 15: GOD'S SOLEMN WARNING TO THE CHURCH 239

in distributing the warning).

We stood outside the entrance doors and as the delegates (called Commissioners) approached, we would smile a "Good evening, may we share something very important with you? Please read it as soon as you can." One Elder commissioner, when handed one of these by Betsy, asked "Why Little Tabernacle, where have you been? I've been looking all over for you." He very quickly caught what the warning was about and said to Betsy, "Hey, there goes one of the leaders of the gay caucus, give her one." Betsy caught up with her and gave it to her. Truly, she was one who needed to hear the warning. Dear Betsy, Judy and I worked like busy vendors at a baseball game distributing our "hot cake warnings" and continued until there were only a few left and apparently all the delegates were seated inside the Center.

The next day we ran off additional copies of the Solemn Warning and brought them back Tuesday night to pass out and we reached many that we had missed the first night, and we got rebuffed by a number of the liberal commissioners who angrily or smugly disagreed with us. We saw our Elder commissioner friend again and he invited us to come have breakfast with him at his hotel the next morning, the last day of the General Assembly. We happily agreed to come. There, another one of God's special miracles in this whole business would take place!

After our distribution was finished, we slipped up to the upper balcony to observe that night's proceedings, part of which involved electing an important officer of the General Assembly, called the Stated Clerk--like a chief executive. Several men had offered themselves for this office including the long-time incumbent, a Presbyterian lawyer by the name of Wm. Thompson. It just so happened that about 13 years before I had attended a General Assembly meeting in Buffalo, N.Y. and Mr. Thompson was also attending. On leaving Buffalo to return to Baltimore, I found myself sitting next to Mr. Thompson on the plane as far as Pittsburgh, and was able to share with him a little about our work with the Presbyterian National Missions at McKim. Well, that night in the balcony we prayed for something that I felt the Lord wanted us to do: "Get one of these warnings into Mr. Thompson's hands personally." So as he was being re-elected to this influential office in the Presbyterian Church, we prayed: "Somehow, Lord, make a way for us to get a copy of this Solemn Warning into his hands, personally. In Jesus' Name, Amen!" Then we left the Center, sadly feeling like we had been watching a political convention on TV.

The next morning we were at our new friend's hotel for breakfast and soon were seated at a booth in the restaurant asking him to tell us the story of how he had come to know the love of the Lord so much. He shared with us about his rocky road in marriage and faith to a victorious Spirit-filled life in Jesus, a rather unusual testimony for an active Presbyterian layman and Elder. Well, praise God for it and may there be many more!

Just as we were finishing our breakfast, and his story was drawing to a close, we heard a group of people rise from tables and move down the aisle toward us. The group stopped so that the leader could talk with someone at the table right next to us! Were we ever surprised! In the next moment I was looking up at the tall man standing within inches of me and saw it was Mr. Wm. Thompson! In my coat pockets were the Warnings, and all I had to do was catch his sleeve to get his attention. He looked down, and I said, "Mr. Thompson, you and I sat together on a plane out of Buffalo on the way to Pittsburg after the 1961 General Assembly. I shared a little bit with you then about our work here in Baltimore. The Lord has given us a special message that He wants you to have." I handed him the Solemn Warning. He received it and said he would read it. The Lord had done it again - timed everything just right to answer our prayer and to fulfill His will perfectly! Praise Him!

We heard from our breakfast friend later that the move to ordain homosexuals had been tabled until an official committee could study the situation for the next two years. Can you imagine that! Studying for two years what God very plainly calls gross sin, an abomination today? We learned later that Wm. Thompson did resist strongly further efforts to get approval for ordaining homosexuals. Praise God!

As we've said, just like murderers and thieves, they can be saved if they will truly repent of this evil lifestyle and turn away from it completely. They must receive full deliverance, by the power of Jesus, from this unclean and rebellious demon that controls them and live holy lives serving the Lord Jesus Christ.

Now in the 80's the plague of AIDS should cause anyone with a grain of sense to realize that this lifestyle is absolutely cursed by God. No cure will be found for it in the future. The only cure is true repentance and pleading for mercy like the thief on the cross!

The following is a copy of THE SOLEMN WARNING we were handing out to the delegates of the General Assembly:

LITTLE TABERNACLE CHURCH OF THE SAVIOUR
1503 E. Baltimore St., Balto. Md. 21231
301-276-2317   May 25, 1976

Dear Fellow Presbyterians: "A SOLEMN WARNING!"

The United Presbyterian General Assembly ends its visit to

CHAPTER 15: GOD'S SOLEMN WARNING TO THE CHURCH

Baltimore on a very sad note for the Bible-Believing Christians. This heartbreaking note is its inability to speak God's Plain Word concerning the gross evil of sexual perversions, and the incredible situation of such evildoers seeking ecclesiastical acceptance and even ordination.

The Bible, which true Christians fully believe to be God's only rule for faith and life, states clearly that such conduct is sin, is evil, is abomination to God, is worthy of death, and sends to hell. It excludes those who practice such acts from the Kingdom of God and from the Church of God, unless there is full repentance, and deliverance from this evil life pattern. Yes, Jesus can save even lesbians and homosexuals, just as He can save drunkards, thieves, drug addicts, and the rest of us from our sins, by His amazing power and love, through faith in Him and repentance. (Heb.7:25).

The moderators and leaders of all church assemblies should know already (without further study) that God has no place in His Kingdom, here or hereafter, for practicing murderers, adulterers, thieves, liars, idolaters, homosexuals, etc. (I Cor.6:9-10, Lev.18:22; 20:13, Deut.23:17-18, Gen.19:1-25, Romans 1:18-32, I Tim. 1:10, Gal.5:19-21, Rev.21:8, 22:15.)

A SOLEMN WARNING: There will be far greater losses in denominational membership if church leaders do not stop compromising what God plainly condemns. (Revelations 2 & 3). There also will be great losses if the church leaders and members continue to resist the great move of God's Holy Spirit in this day. (See Isaiah 59:19, Acts 2, Eph.5, and the "Moment of Truth" story inside.)

Eternal best wishes in Jesus, our Mighty Saviour and Lord!

In His Saving Love,
Joseph S. Rigell,

Inside the Warning was this story:

"MOMENT OF TRUTH"
By: Demos Shakarian, President FGBMFI

Our people came to Los Angeles from the old country in 1900, before the great massacre in Turkey, when a million and a half were wiped out during the first world war. The Shakarians were originally Eastern Orthodox, but by 1875 they had embraced the PRESBYTERIAN faith. Then Spirit-filled believers came from Russia, prayed for the Armenians and laid hands on them, and many received the Baptism in the Holy Spirit. As nearly as I can remember, over one million Russians had previously been baptized in the Spirit, and were terribly persecuted as a result. Many of them were driven across the border into Finland as well as into Armenia, and carried the message of Pentecost into that land also.

My great-grandfather, a died-in-the-wool Presbyterian, simply refused to believe the news of the Holy Spirit outpouring in Russia. "The things you are talking about," he said, "such as the gifts of the Spirit and miracles--those were done away with at the end of the apostolic period. They were necessary to get the church started, but we don't need them anymore." No matter what was said, he refused to budge from his doctrinal position.

One day some Russians came in a caravan and asked if they could hold a week's camp meeting on my grandfather's farm. Grandfather agreed and then he and his father decided they had best go out and kill a beef in order to feed all these people. Walking out into the pasture they found just what they were looking for, a nice fat beef. Nice, that is, except for one blind eye. "That's the one we ought to kill," said my great-grandfather. "But it is blemished, blind in one eye," said grandfather, "and I think these Christian guests should have the best." "Oh, they will never know the difference," said his father. "We'll just bury the head somewhere and they won't know anything about it."

So they killed the beef and cut off the head which they then put into a sack and buried in a stack of threshed wheat located about three hundred yards from the house, intending thereby to keep it cool until the end of the camp meeting, at which time they would bring it out and roast it (in the old country that was a great delicacy).

It was the custom in those days to gather in the living room before the meal for a time of singing and waiting upon the Lord. So when the Russian caravan arrived, our family hosted the members in this manner. The meal was set out on the table, and they all began to sing softly. As the Holy Spirit began to fall, ever so gently, some lifted their hands and commenced to dance, a very beautiful and graceful folk dance in the Spirit. The custom was to then take the Bible and hold it about the head of the family as he knelt before them, and lay hands upon each member of the family and bless them. Then the Bible would be opened and bread placed upon it, and in this manner they would bless the food. The food was never blessed until the Spirit fell, even though they might sing for an hour before this would occur. As they were singing and the anointing was beginning to come, the leader of the Russian group (they called him "Prophet") walked out of the house, and as though the Holy Spirit had him by the hand, went straight to the wheat pile and stopped-- then suddenly shoved his hand right into the pile! Feeling something, he pulled out the sack and looked inside it. In that dreadful moment the Lord revealed to him what had happened!

My father told me that when the Prophet strode into the living room

CHAPTER 15: GOD'S SOLEMN WARNING TO THE CHURCH 243

with that sack in his hand (the people were still singing), my great-grandfather--who had said, "This Holy Spirit business passed away with the early church"--let out a scream and began to cry. "Don't blame my son: I did it! Is there any hope for me? Will God forgive me for the things I have said, and for this terrible thing I have done?"

The Russians assured him that there was forgiveness. And as they gathered around and prayerfully laid hands upon him, in that moment he was baptized in the Holy Spirit and there was great rejoicing as the blessing of God came down.

Thus was the Shakarian family initiated into this wonderful experience called the Baptism in the Holy Spirit! I for one am thankful that they brought it with them when they came to America!"[1]

1776 - 1976 - 200TH BIRTHDAY OF OUR COUNTRY!

This being the 200th Birthday Anniversary for our nation, we would like to put in a plug for a book about America's true beginnings, very carefully researched and written by Peter Marshall, Jr. and David Manuel. We were privileged to hear Peter Marshall, Jr. at the Montreat conference which we attended just before the Presbyterian General Assembly which met here in Baltimore in late May. When we eventually got copies of it and had read it, we began a two person publicity committee to get everybody in the nation to read it, and gave away a number of copies to help the "campaign" to get rolling.

Most Americans in the secular schools will never hear of the Biblical and true Christian foundation of our nation, about how Columbus was a devout Believer in Jesus Christ, having daily prayers on his ships, or that George Washington was a devout believer in and servant of Jesus Christ. No wonder God chose him to lead this nation into being. Nor will they learn in the modern history books how all the original Ivy League Colleges were founded to train ministers and teachers of God's Word, that this nation might truly be one whose God is the God found in the Holy Bible and through His Holy Son Jesus, our Saviour!.

Someone pointed out recently that in the modern school history book there were only about 7 brief references to George Washington, and 8 or 9 full pages devoted to Marilyn Monroe, the tragic sex symbol in the early 60's.

We would urge all those who read this to find a copy of "THE LIGHT

---

[1] The above story is quoted with permission from the Voice Magazine of The Full Gospel Business Men's Fellowship, International for October 1975.

AND THE GLORY" and read it and share it with others.[2]

DR. KARL BARTH'S REPLY

One of the most notable theologians in this century was Dr. Karl Barth, a Swiss Theologian, who was much sought after as a speaker and lecturer in America during the mid-Century years. The basic derivation and meaning of the Greek word theology is the study of God (Theo - God, logia - study). At the time Dr. Barth was considered number one in this field by many of his colleagues and students.

The story is told that he came to one of America's top Seminaries to lecture to the student body (perhaps Princeton Seminary), all of the students being college graduates, doing graduate study in theology. After his lecture, Dr. Barth would have a question and answer period for the young theologians. At one session one of the young men rose to ask the question, "Dr. Barth, would you tell us what is the greatest, single piece of theological wisdom you have ever learned in all your many years of study of theology?"

Dr. Barth smiled and said, "My dear young man, that is a question I am happy to answer. It is simply this: *'Jesus Loves Me, This I Know, For The Bible Tells Me So.'*" I don't know whether Dr. Barth received a standing ovation for that answer, but he should have. For it was the Love of Jesus for and in those early Apostles and disciples, and the empowerment of the Holy Spirit filling them with that love (Romans 5:5) that turned the world upside down, or right side up and gave us, eventually, this nation, founded on the Word of God and the Love of Jesus that made it so great.

BUT AMERICA THROWS OUT THE BIBLE AND PRAYER!

It was the elimination of the Bible, God's Word and the Love of Jesus, and Prayer in His Name in 1962-63, from our public schools, instigated by atheist-communist Madeline Murray (now O'Hair), backed by an atheist lawyer, both of Baltimore, that greatly accelerated the disintegration of America as a moral nation.

Equally startling and reprehensible were the testimonies of so-called religious leaders, several from Baltimore, at the Supreme Court, aiding and abetting this crime of the century. It was the greatest blow to the faith and moral roots of our nation ever to take place, undermining the

---

[2] See special section called "Three Great Men of Faith" at the end of our book.

CHAPTER 15: GOD'S SOLEMN WARNING TO THE CHURCH

educational system, the moral values, the faith in God and in His Word foundation of the nation when our highest Court ruled none of it was necessary by official decree. The same day in '62 that this ungodly Court ruled out prayer for school children, it approved printing pornography for homosexuals! This officially opened the flood gates of immorality, pornography, crime, delinquency, murders, abortions, disease, adultery, drugs, divorce, perverted sex such as lesbianism and homosexuality, all of which are abominations in the eyes of God and totally condemned by the Word of God. The Bible was removed in "63!

It is most interesting that Mrs. O'Hair's oldest son, William, who was in our son Craig's class at Baltimore Polytechnic High School when all this happened, who was used in the Supreme Court case against the Bible and Prayer in our schools, has become a Born-again Believer, a Preacher of God's Word, a servant of Jesus Christ, and an author of several Christian books! He denounces as total evil and anti-Christ what happened in the early '60's. Praise God, William Murray finally found Dr. Barth's great truth that, "JESUS LOVES ME (AND SAVES ME), THIS I KNOW FOR THE BIBLE TELLS ME SO!"

However, Madeline and her organization, American Atheists, are still very active at their nearly 2 million dollar headquarters near Austin, Texas. They boast a membership of 38,000 and a budget of $750,000, plus a monthly magazine, plus a TV program called American Atheist Forum. The Forum deals with Church-State separation problems. By the way, she was born into a Presbyterian family in Pittsburg, became interested in atheism in the fourth grade, became an atheist and a communist and has devoted the last 60 years to this cause, having written eleven books along the way.

Their three main goals now are: 1) Removing "In God We Trust" from the U.S. money; 2) Barring the use of churches as polling (voting) places; 3) Removing all granite blocks engraved with the 10 Commandments from the front of all courthouses and other public buildings in the nation. She now calls her son William, "The rotten apple in the barrel." That figures for someone the Bible calls "a fool!" (Ps.14:1 and Ps.53:1) *The fool hath said in his heart there is no God..* May God save her soon!

ANOTHER GODLESS AND SUBVERSIVE ORGANIZATION

As mentioned earlier, Mrs. O'Hair was not alone in her efforts to save her sons and America from the "Terrible Perils" of Prayer and Bible reading in the Schools. She was being assisted by communist lawyers similar to the communist-front organization called the A.C.L.U. (American Civil Liberties Union), a secret membership organization of some 250,000 members with a $15 million budget today. This organization was founded in 1920 by Roger Baldwin and three other men, who became leaders of the Communist Party. In 1935 Baldwin, the ACLU's long-time director said: "I am for socialism, disarmament, and ultimately for abolishing the state itself as an instrument of violence and compulsion. I seek the social ownership of property, the abolition of the property class, and the sole control of those who produce wealth. Communism is the goal."

The ACLU put on a more decent front in the 1950's due to one of its founders, Louis Budenz, bolting the Communist Party, and becoming a militant anti-communist. By 1969 it had turned radically left again, and today the Communist party, USA is merely a decoy. The ACLU is the real communist party in America, and it has successfully deceived the public into thinking that it defends "civil liberties."

"ACLU is a communist-front organization which, among other things, works actively to abolish anti-obscenity laws, capital punishment, prayer in schools, Christmas displays on public property, right to bear arms, and now blood tests for AIDS. It is for gay rights, abortion, legalizing ALL drugs, inflexible racial quotas, protecting criminals, child pornography and other nonsense."[3]

One almost trembles in his boots when he remembers that the leading Democratic candidate for President in 1988 was a card carrying ACLU member, and his campaign manager was a director of the national board of the ACLU. Makes one wonder who's running the Democratic Party?

Also reminds us of a quote from the long-time socialist party head, Norman Thomas, who was a perennial candidate for the Presidency, when asked why he stopped running, he answered, "I don't need to run anymore, the Democrats have taken over all our goals!"

THE VON TRAPP FAMILY

When you are serving the Lord with all your heart, one of the ways you get especially blessed is to meet along the road some of God's really beautiful people. These special saints of God often have lost or given up everything for the sake of Jesus Christ, have been through heavy trials, and even suffering, have seen many victories, griefs and joys, and have much to share, many lessons to teach--if you can slow them down long enough to teach you.

---

[3] Letter--Western Legal Institute, Fort Collins, Co. 8/88 in Human Events 7/2/88.

CHAPTER 15: GOD'S SOLEMN WARNING TO THE CHURCH

A special friend of the Freburgers was one of those servants of the Lord, by the name of Agathe von Trapp, who visited the Little Tabernacle a few brief times with Phyllis. This eventually led to our meeting her sister, Rosemary, and later her Mother, Marie von Trapp, the dauntless mother and leader of the famous Von Trapp Family Singers, about whom the famous movie "The Sound Of Music" was made. The movie as you remember was a really excellent movie with extraordinary music and songs featuring Julie Andrews.

One of the saddest things about the movie, was that not one cent of the multiplied millions of dollars of profit made on that movie ever came to the Von Trapps! When first shown, they were invited to the Premier in New York City, but had to pay for their own tickets! Can you believe that?! Yes, an unbelievable rip off, probably one of the century's biggest, next to the tripling (or more) of the oil prices in 1973 by the Middle East oil producers! - The recent S & L frauds! - The recent Senate night pay raids! All reprehensible!

A special sidelight about Marie von Trapp. One day her daughter Rosemary asked us to take her to Washington to pick her mother up for a visit. Of course we were honored to do so. On the way home we stopped for lunch at a famous Greek restaurant, called the Carriage House, run by some dear friends, the Petrides. After lunch, Marie gave me a little gift of money and said "Now, that's to buy something special for your wife, Betsy." And unknown to me, at the same time she gave Betsy a similar little gift, and told her, "This is to buy something special for your husband!" That was just like Marie!

Anyway, the oldest daughter, Agathe von Trapp was a teacher in a Catholic kindergarten in Glyndon, outside of Baltimore, a deeply dedicated and Spirit-filled Christian who was daily in touch with the Lord.

Late in '73 the Lord gave her a message, a warning for America and she sent it to as many people as she could. We helped in a small way. Keep in mind after you read it that 1973 was the year that the infamous Roe vs Wade case came before the U.S. Supreme Court, resulting in a ruling that each woman could legally abort (kill) her unborn baby if she desired. It has come out recently that the case was based on a total lie: the woman claiming to have been raped was not, and did not even have an abortion but gave birth to her child. But that spurious case and ungodly Supreme Court decision opened the gates to what has become a HOLOCAUST OF BABIES, the pre-meditated murders of over 27 million babies by year 1991. This once God-fearing nation, that still says on its coins and currency "In God We Trust," had gone mad!

Agathe von Trapp's message of warning of destruction to come and judgment ahead for this nation was right on time.

EARLY WARNING THROUGH AGATHE
Little Tabernacle Church
March 15, 1974

Dear Christian Friends:

God Is Calling Us! In many ways God is warning His people in America to wake up, clean up, pray up, and pay up our vows to Him!

On January 26, 1974 God gave Agathe Von Trapp this message: "TELL THE PEOPLE THAT THE LORD HAS ORDAINED DESTRUCTION UPON THE LAND FOR THE SAKE OF THOSE WHO DO NOT LISTEN TO THE WORD OF GOD, BUT THAT HE WILL RELENT IF ENOUGH PEOPLE WILL FAST AND PRAY AND PRAISE THE LORD IN THEIR THOUGHTS, WORDS AND DEEDS. THIS IS THE WORD OF THE LORD."

We believe God is sending prophetic warnings today, that He chooses whom HE will to receive the warnings, that this message bearer is a holy servant of God, that these calls to fast and pray are from God, and that we must heed them. The future of this nation hangs in the balance. The obedience of God's people to His warnings will decide the fate of our country. Lets obey God! See II Chron.7:14...

If my people, which are called by my name, shall humble themselves, and pray, and seek my face, and turn from their wicked ways; then will I hear from heaven, and will forgive their sin, and will heal their land.

In Jesus Name, J.S.R. & L.T.C.

OUR FAMILY WITH DR. & MRS. GUTZKE - 1965
ONE OF THE GREAT BIBLE TEACHERS OF SOUTHERN PRESBYTERIAN CHURCH

CHAP. 16

AN AMAZING YEAR--1977-- CALL TO ISRAEL

Let us now go even unto Bethlehem, and see this thing which is come to pass, which the Lord hath made known unto us. - Luke 2:15b

THE CHRISTMAS THAT WOULDN'T TURN OFF

So Christmas 1976 was rapidly approaching. As always we were looking forward to the joy and delight of preparing for and celebrating Jesus' Birthday, of singing the old and new Christmas Carols, of going over the Scriptural details of the prophecies of His coming, of the Annunciation, of His actual arrival at Bethlehem, of Mary and Joseph, of the Angels, Shepherds and Wise Men moving on the stage at the precise moments. Of the prophecies concerning His future, of why He had to come and die on a cross and, yes, rise again from the dead. It was for us, that we might be saved, and delivered from Satan's grasp, and from sin and self, from misery and hell. His coming was the greatest event in all history, and the great water-shed in time, separating time into B.C. and A.D.

Indeed, we always thoroughly love to celebrate Jesus' Birthday with the Church and the family. It is so rich in meaning and beauty, so spiritually enriching! Some would add it makes an awful lot of merchants rich, too. A great number of our Jewish friends should be annually saying, "Baruch Ha Shem bishvil Yom Christmas, o bishvil Yom HaHoledit shel Yeshua."--"Bless the Name (of the Lord) for Christmas Day, or for the Birthday of Jesus!"

That Christmas we wrote the following letter to our family and friends:

"HAPPY BIRTHDAY, JESUS"

"Dear Jesus,   December 25, 1976

It's Your Wonderful Birthday we're celebrating. Yours is so Special! We greet You this happy morning with "Happy Birthday, Dear Jesus!" We want to thank You for coming down to earth to bring love, joy and peace to millions upon millions of lives. We cannot thank You enough for all You've done for us, for all the gifts You have given us all year long. We bring You our hearts full of love this day and always.

As You look down from Heaven and see the world You made and visited 1976 years ago on Your Great Mission to Planet Earth, to save us from our sins, to restore our fellowship with our heavenly Father, You see so well how confused things seem to be going. Like a perpetual earthquake, everything seems to be shaking and quaking, unstable and unglued. Government leaders issue bold, but unconvincing pronouncements about the world's troubles. Religious leaders do the same. At a time when man thinks he knows so much and can do so much, he appears to be more and more confounded. World planners seem to be looking for a "One World Leader" to solve the mess. Said one former U.N. official, "Be he man or devil, it matters not, but give us someone to lead and unite us before we destroy ourselves and we will follow him."

Jesus, we wish they would choose You. You're the One we need; You've done so much for the world since You first came to Your manger-birth at Bethlehem. You have all the wisdom and love and power to make this old world a Heaven on earth. We've seen Your power to heal, to save, to make all new! Lord Jesus, we know You're the ONE this world needs to find peace and goodwill.

But as we have walked downtown streets recently inviting thousands to the Jesus TV Rally, we found so few interested in You. So few wanted You or Your Good News. So few even knew You or cared at all as they rushed by - on their way to destruction (Matt.7:13-14). Our hearts were grieved for them, Lord, and we remembered how You wept over Jerusalem. We remembered that the crowds, and leaders denied You, reviled You, spat on You, killed You within three years after You began Your ministry of miracles, of love, of warning the world to repent and turn back to God. This old world still doesn't like Your "Repent, Believe and Be Saved" message, Lord. It still doesn't care for Your "Bloody Cross Religion". It still loves darkness more than light and man still thinks he can save himself somehow without You. How sad, Lord, how sad!

But, Lord, there are millions in this old world who believe in You, love You, and will follow You all the way--who are singing with the angels and shepherds and saints: "JOY TO THE WORLD THE LORD IS COME, LET EARTH RECEIVE HER KING! You did what we could not do!

> "You paid a debt You did not owe,
> We owed a debt we could not pay,
> We needed someone to wash our sins away,
> And now we sing a brand new song, 'Amazing Grace'
> Christ Jesus paid the debt that we could never pay."

CHAPTER 16: AMAZING YEAR-1977-CALL TO ISRAEL

Thank You, forever, dear Jesus, for Your miracle Birth that brought miracle rebirth to us. We know You want us to share our rejoicing with other members of Your big family, Lord! So Happy Birthday Dear Jesus, and "A Happy Jesus' Birthday" to all!

With All our Love,

Your L.T.C. Family

P.S.: Lord, we pray You'll be coming back soon. We need You more than ever!

- - - - - - -

This Christmas however was to be like none we'd ever celebrated, all the others have tended to turn off rather quickly after The Day. Very seldom do you find Church-goers wanting to sing Christmas carols in the first Sunday of the New Year. We should, but we don't. For real Christians the "Joy of Jesus" should be year-round. (By the way the title of the first sermon I ever preached was, "Year Round Christmas Joy").

The Christmas "switch" seems to get turned off by New Year's Day. On this particular Christmas it didn't. Amazingly, into the New Year, we kept hearing the Shepherds saying "Let us go unto Bethlehem and see this thing which is come to pass," and the Carols still were singing and ringing over and over in our hearts 'til we began asking ourselves, "What is going on, what is happening? Does the Lord really want us to go to Israel, to Bethlehem?" In the past we'd helped others to go, but had never felt the need to go to Bethlehem ourselves! Couldn't we serve the Lord just as well without having to go to that dusty land so far away?

As soon as we really prayed together, looking to the Lord seriously about what He wanted, we began hearing Him say, "Yes, I want you to go!" "But how, Lord?" "Go with a tour group. Remember, I have great things in store for you as you are obedient to Me." "Yes, Lord, we will go." (There was no audible voice, but this is what we sensed by the Holy Spirit, that the Lord wanted and was saying.)

As soon as we agreed to go the Carols and Shepherd's voices began to fade into the background, but we had that special peace in our hearts that this was truly the Lord's will for us. Very soon after this, a letter of invitation came from George Otis and Pat Boone in California, asking us to recruit some Baltimore pilgrims to go with them in March. This was much too soon we felt, so we wrote them thanking them for the invitation, but it would not fit in with our rather full springtime schedule. So we kept busy, waiting on the Lord to show us the group we were to go with. We didn't have to wait long. Another offer was just 'around the corner'.

On the recommendation of a friend, we had invited an evangelist and Bible teacher by the name of Ray Solomon, to come up from North

Carolina for a series of meetings at the Little Tabernacle in the latter part of January. Ray was a very tall Trinidadian, who had a strong evangelistic ministry there before coming to the States under the auspices of Gerald Derstine, whose ministry we knew and respected. The Lord had given Ray a very special song called **"I Believe I'm Going To Make It."** He loved to sing it and teach it to new groups. Here are the words of the Chorus first:

"I Believe I'm going to make it, Jesus put it on my mind,
To reach that city, New Jerusalem, one step at a time,
Though the devil wars against me, to hinder my climb,
I see the lights in the distance, it's just a matter of time.

1st verse:

"I stood at the bottom, looking up at the hill,
The hill was so tall, and I was so small,
Each step that I took, I thought I would fall,
But He kept holding me still.

2nd. verse:

"At first I would worry, but He gave me courage,
To go all the way up the hill.
And each step that I climb, new contentment I find,
He has shown me the top will be mine."

We made quite a "Mutt and Jeff" pair singing that song together.

At this time he announced to us that he was leading his 6th tour to Israel in the fall, Oct. 23 - Nov. 2nd. This sounded just right to us, and we quickly announced that we would like to enlist a group from the Little Tabernacle and Baltimore to go with him. In a very short time, we were to have about 15 people signed up to go on our first tour to Israel. Signing up about 8 or 9 months away is not hard at all, but as you come closer to the time of the tour, you have to have most or all of the money sent in--that's the hard part. Several of our young people who had signed up would need some real financial miracles to pay for the cost of the round-trip tour ticket. Well, the Lord didn't let any of them down. They all worked hard and ended up on the tour to Israel. Even crippled Mary Fitze had believed the Lord for her tour money, and went just a short while after a hip operation. The Lord even sent a young nurse in our group to help look after Mary. But more about that great trip later.

BEFORE ISRAEL, MEET EDGAR BAILLIE

Another special speaker was to follow soon after the Solomon meetings. We were to be privileged to have a remarkable man of God

CHAPTER 16: AMAZING YEAR-1977-CALL TO ISRAEL 253

by the name of Edgar Baillie and his wife Charlotte, out of California. These meetings would be marked with a number of special miracles of healing, since Edgar himself had been miraculously healed by the Lord. If we can fit it in, we'd like to share with you part of that story. He and his wife Charlotte just happened to be Presbyterians! The story of his own desperately needed miracle of healing will follow, as printed in a news account in California. It amply proves that God has not run out of miracles for His people, even for Presbyterians, or Baptists or others!

GOD FILLS IN FLESH AND CREATES NEW HAND
by Chris Loeffler

It is the opinion of our editors and publisher that the following story should have made the headlines of every newspaper in San Diego County back in 1973 when it happened. We publish this story in detail today in honor of the celebration of the birth of our Lord Jesus Christ. Ed Baillie's enthusiasm for our Lord is an inspiring thing to behold. He has every reason to be excited about what God has done for him...physically as well as spiritually.. ..and there is a long line of witnesses, starting with his pastor and other members of the church, to verify what I am going to report to you today. This is his story as told to me - Chris Loeffler.

"Although we were members of the Presbyterian Church, my wife, Charlotte, and I were also attending the North County Christian Center at the time they were building their church back in 1973. The congregation was building the church with their own hands, and believe me, it was built by God.

"We had decided to help work on the church that Saturday. After a call from Roy Wyman (a fellow Presbyterian at the time) it had been decided that we would drive out to the church with Roy and his two sons. Quite a few people were working on the church that day including three sailors off the U.S.S. Sperry. The building was in the framing stage and one of the jobs being done was putting hot tar on the roof, a normal building procedure where the tar is "on fire" when it is applied, which enables it to sear into the wood and etch it. Then tar paper is put down which seals it, insuring a leakproof roof.

"By about 3 o'clock in the afternoon, we were getting ready to quit. I was on a scaffold two stories high. Roy's son, Ralph was there bent over some plywood. Unknown to us there was an open knothole in the roof just over our heads. I had turned around to talk to one of the sailors and was pointing with my left arm outstretched towards a stack of plywood when I got the shock of my life. Burning tar came through the roof and hit my arm! A big 3 inch glob of tar landed just below my elbow joint, another big glob all over my watch and wrist, another on the back of my hand!

"The minute it hit I let out a giant yell, 'God!!!' I turned back and saw another ball of fiery tar falling, and I could see that it was going to hit Roy's son in the back of the neck. He didn't have a hat on. I reached out and caught it like a baseball (it was sheer instinct). When I did, my hand shut and tar burned the flesh more seriously than third degree burns. I could smell the meat, and so could everyone else, so they knew that it was serious.

"Writhing in pain, I climbed down off the scaffold. My hand was sealed shut...I couldn't open it. I shook my head and kept saying, 'Oh GOD!!!!!! GOD!!!!...WHY?????'

"I was HURTING!...and I was crying because I was hurting! I couldn't even swear! What was I going to do? I looked at my hands and my arm in tormented agony and I was conscious of physically shaking like a leaf. Then something stopped me right in the middle of the church. I wasn't hearing anything...It was a feeling. As unnatural as it may sound, all of a sudden I felt led to give praise to God.

"I looked up right into the roof of that building and I said, 'God, you have allowed this to happen to me in this house, and you sure as heck aren't going to let Satan in here. God, I accept this burn because it's part of your plan. I love you for it, and I praise you in the name of Jesus Christ. AMEN!'

"Still trembling, I then proceeded to walk up the stair to the back. One lady exclaimed, 'Oh-h-h-h LOOK at him!'

"I asked my wife to take off my watch. Charlotte took it off even though my flesh was stuck to it, and she could see how badly I was hurt.

"Another lady walked up and said, 'I couldn't figure out why we stayed, but there was a reason for us to stay. We have ice tea!' She grabbed a chunk of ice and said, 'Let me put this on, it will help.' The ice made the tar really hard.

"Without knowing what would happen, I said, 'Please pull that tar off of there.'

"The ladies gathered around me. Roy Wyman, the three sailors and some other people were all there. They started to take the tar off me and one lady cried out in anguish. "Oh NO!" I looked down and there were just holes. When she tried to pull off the tar, the flesh came with it.

"I cried out, 'Man! That HURTS!!!...You better not do it. Roy, you'll have to take me to the hospital.'

"Roy saw the pain that I was in and the sweat running off me and the tears, and he turned to the Pastor and said, 'Pastor, please, you

CHAPTER 16: AMAZING YEAR-1977-CALL TO ISRAEL

have to pray a healing prayer for him. I know it...RIGHT NOW!'

"Fifty-four years a minister of God, and the co-pastor of this congregation, Vernon couldn't wait. That was right up his alley. (This was the first time I ever had anyone lay hands on me. I had heard about it, but it had never happened to me before). The women laid hands on me, and THE BOSS came running up with his hard hat still on and got on his knees. (The three sailors and my wife stood back watching me). They all laid hands on me and Vernon prayed a prayer like I had never heard before in my life. While he was praying, I said to the Lord. 'God, I know that you'll hear this...if you would just stop the hurt...if you'd just take away the pain...that's all I ask, God, and I thank you for it in Jesus' name.'

"Just then Vernon's voice was ringing out with authority as he prayed with a loud voice, 'I don't want a scar, I want all of it healed. We know that you are going to do it in Jesus' name AMEN!'

"My right hand opened up. The tar was curled up and the whole palm of my hand was stuck to it. All the flesh was gone, a real mess. My first thought was that I would have to go to the hospital and get a skin graft...since my hand was gone. Then I realized there was no more pain!

"I cried out, 'It's gone!'

"Roy quickly asked, 'What's gone?'

"I joyfully replied, 'The pain!...there is no more pain!'

"And everybody started saying, 'Oh, Praise the Lord!...Praise the Lord!'

"I exclaimed, 'WOW! Pull the rest of that tar off!'

"Mrs. House asked, 'But won't it hurt?'

"I replied, 'I just told you it's healed...its completely healed!'

"She pulled it off and the flesh went with it, and there was no pain. It was bad looking and there I was grinning and exclaiming, 'Hey, it doesn't hurt!'

"Then my hand and arm started to burn intensely, and the burn was much worse than the burn I got from the hot tar. As it burned, Mrs. Fowe's eyes grew wide with an incredulous look and then she gasped, 'Look LOOK! He's got a whole new hand!'

"It just grew right back...just like that, all the holes filled up ...brand new baby pink skin...the darndest thing I ever saw in my life. I looked at it and started shaking. All three sailors had fallen on their knees and accepted Jesus Christ right then and there. I shook violently. I shook so badly I didn't know what was holding my body together. The tears were flowing. Everyone was getting blessed. They were crying, too. I've never seen anything like it in my life.

"All one lady could say was, 'PRAISE THE LORD, ...OH, PRAISE THE

LORD!' over and over again.

"The boss jumped up and down with his hard hat in his hand exclaiming, 'WOW! God is good!... Praise GOD....I've never seen anything like it.' What a time of praise and thanksgiving!

"After seeing the holes in my hands and my arm...then witnessing the filling in of my flesh in an instant of time, I don't waste any time wondering whether God is capable of creating man from the dust, or the earth and the heavens with all that they contain, in six days. I know He is.

"Afterwards, when we got back to Roy Wyman's house, Roy wanted to take another look at my hands and arm. For some reason, one area of my left hand had not been healed. It wasn't very pretty. Everything else looked absolutely normal, completely healed with no scars. I kept asking the question, 'God, how come this didn't heal? There's a reason for it.'

"When we got into his house, Roy suggested that he put solarcain on the part of my hand that hadn't healed. I replied, 'Roy, don't you understand?' And with that I hit my hand hard 'There's no pain, and I don't want any solarcain.'

"Then God spoke to me, 'don't worry about your hand, Edgar. Tomorrow you'll be in the Presbyterian Church. I left that for a witness. After church, I'll take it away if you wish.'" Just like that.

"'Praise the Lord, Roy, do you know why this is here?' I asked pointing to the unhealed area of my hand. 'I'm going to testify in church tomorrow morning.'

"Roy was surprised, 'In the Presbyterian Church?'

"'You can bet your life on it, if God wants me to. I know it,' I replied.

"I had never testified in a church in my life. That's exactly what happened. I stood in front of a large prayer group in the Presbyterian Church to which we belonged and told them exactly what had happened. That night I went home and thanked the Lord so much. When I looked down, my hand was almost all healed. After another meeting Tuesday night where I shared the story of my healing again, the healing was completed. Believe me, God is great...and God is good. Praise His Holy Name."[1]

Later there will be another amazing story about Edgar's praying for a young Jewish woman at the Little Tabernacle and the manifestation of another Miracle of God!

---

[1] From the San Diego Church News, December 1975, page 20.

CHAPTER 16: AMAZING YEAR-1977-CALL TO ISRAEL

BEFORE ISRAEL COMES
DON ODON'S SCHOOL OF THE PROPHETS
In Early March

You remember the singer, Loretta Young, who went to Israel to the Holy Spirit Conference just a few months ago? Getting there via that amazing Little Piggy-Bank Miracle? Pat Robertson, who had asked her to sing, had apparently invited her to come testify and sing at his CBN station back in the States in Virginia Beach. While at the station Loretta met the Hungarian-English Evangelist Don Odon, and had urged us to invite him to the Little Tabernacle, which we did.

He had come in '76, and now he was coming back in 1977 to undertake his School of the Prophets, teaching practical ministry courses. The Lord was surely looking after us by enlivening the Little Tabernacle's family and outreach. Nearly 25 young adults had signed up for the school, some of them even leaving good jobs to come to it.

To make a long story short, many amazing good fruits were borne out of those teaching sessions, and afternoons spent in practical witnessing and ministering the gifts of the Holy Spirit on the streets in our area and further downtown.

We've found a "thank you" letter relating to the Little Tabernacle's very busy oasis ministry at that time which we want to share with you.

LITTLE TABERNACLE CHURCH
1503 E. Baltimore St., Baltimore, Md
"YOU ARE PART OF GOD'S LTC MIRACLE"

You are part of a mighty miracle of God - a continuing miracle of God. Left to man or the devil, this ministry would not be, but it is! And very much alive by the hand of God. Praise the Name of Jesus!

As we think of your gracious gifts and prayers for us, our hearts well up in praise and thanksgiving to God continually for you. And because you are having a part in this miracle of God, we are praying and believing that you will be daily blessed with His special miracles of love, protection and provisions. (Ephes. 3)

What is this miracle we speak of? It is an around-the-clock miracle lighthouse for Jesus in a very dark place, a miracle outpost of witness to Jesus in the devil's backyard, a miracle example of blacks and whites (and all races) loving each other in Jesus in worship, work and communion, a miracle channel of love and help to hundreds of lost and hungry souls, a miracle oasis for Bible study, prayer and fellowship in an arid locale. It is a miracle place of refuge from the storms of life for many, where souls find holy contact with God and miracle help from

Him. It is a miracle meeting place with Jesus, and with the Father and with the Holy Spirit! Praise God forever!

Why do we talk this way? It is not to blow the horn of human endeavor! It is simply to tell you what we see our Lord doing here as we lift Him up always. (John 12:32) This mission is His miracle ministry to a broad cross-section of people, both Jews and Gentiles. (Romans 1:16) To Him be all the praise and glory and thanksgiving!

Every Oasis is God's miracle, and so are His spiritual ones, such as His LTC! God is reaching and changing many lives through His Little Tabernacle Church, the Jesus Youth Home, and the PTL Book & Thrifte Shoppe ministries. Each one is a mighty miracle of God's love and power through Jesus. We thank God for your part in His continuing miracle oasis in Jesus here.

May the Lord continue to bless you with His abundant life blessings now and His forever blessings in Jesus. Keep on keeping on with Jesus!

> Deepest Thanks and Love in Him,
> Joseph S. Rigell and LTC Family

P.S.: We hope soon to be able to write you news of the many events of recent weeks and months concerning 2 great series of meetings by Ray Solomon, 3 exciting days with Ed Baillie, 3 weeks of miracle meetings with Don Odon from England and his School of the Prophets, visits by other precious servants of God, and our approaching trip to Tulsa for our son Kirby's wedding, and the Israel trip in October, plus some prophetic insights the Lord is giving His people for these days. Until then -- John 15!

P.P.S: There are a few more places left in Ray Solomon's October tour group to Israel. Come, go with us!

The P.S. at the close of the letter gives a rather startling summary of what had been going on, and what was soon to come. Betsy, Brian and I did get to fly down to Tulsa for Kirby and Carol's wedding.

Craig, Ann and little Ginny and our other Tennessee sons at that time, Joe and Chris, drove from Oak Ridge, Tenn. to the wedding. It was held at the Bible College where Kirby had recently graduated and he had asked the President of the school, Dr. Wuertch and Gordon Wright from the Jesus Inn and myself to take part in the service. Kirby and Carol had asked that I include in my part a strong evangelistic appeal that day, since a number of the attending friends and kin were far from being believers, at least not committed followers of Jesus. Gordon Wright had lent his camper to the newlyweds, and after a beautiful reception at the college they were off on their honeymoon, and the rest of us were on our way back East.

CHAPTER 16: AMAZING YEAR-1977-CALL TO ISRAEL   259

One interesting little event that evening, when Craig was driving the rest of us out to see the ORU campus, and after going through a red light he was stopped by a police officer for doing so. Craig got out of the van and walked back to talk to the policeman and shortly came back chuckling and without a ticket. He had told the officer the truth, at the moment of the red stop light his little daughter was on her potty in the back of the van, and the policeman said "That's the best one I've ever heard, I can understand, you may go."

- Dear Reader, Those of you, who are not overly religious and have gotten this far--our special appreciation and congratulations! Just hang on a little while longer, we have only about 10 more years to go before the end! End of the book only, we hope! Like the fellow in the cartoon we just read about in the newspaper your "Pappy" used to call "The Daily Worker," his nickname for "The Wall Street Journal," a copy of which occasionally finds its way to this Island. Anyway, the cartoon has one of these old bearded long-robed Doom prophets walking along the street toting a sign saying "The World will End as soon as the Paper Work is done."

"THEY THAT WAIT UPON THE LORD"

We must admit that as we go over the newsletter file, with our notes and memories of those days, we are almost immediately exhausted by the thought of everything that was going on. I guess when you are 70 that's the feeling you tend to get when looking back at your younger days, such as 11 years ago when I was a youthful 59, and Betsy many years younger! Surely the Lord was renewing our strength as He promises in Isaiah 40:31. *But they that wait upon the Lord shall renew their strength; they shall mount up with wings as eagles: they shall run and not be weary, and they shall walk and not faint.* "Waiting" here connotes trusting in the Lord completely and serving Him faithfully. Another key scripture adopted by the Little Tabernacle was Isaiah 58: which ends with verses 13 & 14: *If thou turn away thy foot from the sabbath, from doing thy pleasure on my holy day, and call the sabbath a delight, the holy of the Lord, honourable; and shalt honour him, not doing thine own ways, nor finding thine own pleasure, nor speaking thine own words: Then shalt thou delight thyself in the Lord; and I will cause thee to ride upon the high places of the earth, and feed thee with the heritage of Jacob thy father, for the mouth of the Lord hath spoken it.* Being of child-like faith, Betsy and I were believing this and teaching it. Also we were believing that God has never repealed His promises.

OUR FIRST RIDE HIGH UP TO ISRAEL

So we were about to ride on some high places of the earth and feed on the heritage of Jacob, with mighty praise and joy and thanksgiving in our hearts. To prepare our group for the pilgrimage to Israel, we invited a dear Messianic couple, Stan and Betty Grodnitzky, to come and teach us some Jewish songs such as "Hevenu Shalom Allechem" ("We Bring Peace To You"), and "Henay Ma Tov" ("Behold How Good and How Pleasant," Ps. 133) and "Awake, Oh Israel," and "Stand By Israel," and "The Shema," ("Hear, Oh Israel" Deut.6:4) and "Pray for The Peace of Jerusalem" (Ps.122:6), and from Gen.12:3, "I Will Bless Those Who Bless Thee." And the young Jewish Believer in our group, "Laurie" helped us to learn how to say, "Todah Rabah" (Thank you very much) and "Bevakasha" (You're welcome), and that great Hebrew word "Savlanut" (Patience). So off we went as every good first-time pilgrim would do with prayer and our cameras at ready.

After our flight from Baltimore we assembled in the New York Kennedy Airport for the non-stop El Al flight to Israel. Altogether nearly 100 pilgrims mainly from the east coast made up the Solomon tour group. Little did Betsy and I know that this was just the beginning of many, many flights to and from Israel in the next ten years, and that many new, undreamed of adventures lay ahead of us, including another war with guns and rockets, another riot, on a mountain this time, and another firing!

Normally pilgrim flights to Israel arrive at Ben Gurion airport in the afternoon and the group goes immediately to a hotel in Tel Aviv or Jerusalem to begin touring the next day, after a good night's rest. But somehow on that first tour we arrived just before dawn in Israel, and saw a fantastic sunrise as our bus took us through the Judean mountains up to Jerusalem. Of course we had been sleeping fitfully through the 12 hour flight, but were surprised when our Jewish tour guide, Zev Gill, announced, as we arrived at the Diplomat Hotel in Jerusalem, that we would have about one hour to wash our faces, get some breakfast, and be back on the bus for the first day's tour. Zev was a paratrooper reservist and a tough "Sabra", which we were quickly to learn is the word for the cactus and also for those born in the land of Israel. They would explain, "Yes, Israelis are like the cactus fruit: prickly on the outside, but very sweet inside! (That's true of a cactus pear. If you can get underneath the porcupine-like surface you find a sweet and tasty fruit inside. True also of the Israelis, generally speaking!)

We won't try to recall every detail of that wonderful first tour, the words inspiring, exhilarating, enlightening and exciting would all fit. From your first view of the ancient Temple Mount from the Mt. of Olives

CHAPTER 16: AMAZING YEAR-1977-CALL TO ISRAEL   261

to the Garden of Gethsemane, from Caiaphas' house to the Upper Room, from the Via Delorosa to the Western Wall of the ancient Jewish Temple, from the Kennesset (Parliament building) to the Garden Tomb, from Bethlehem's Church of the Nativity to the Shepherd's field, to Jericho, to the Dead Sea to Massada, on north to Caesarea, Haifa, Megido, Nazareth, Cana, passing Mt. Tabor, the Sea of Galilee, to Tiberias, To Tagba, the Mt. of Beatitudes, to Capernaum, the Baptism in the "Mighty" River Jordan, and the wonderful boat ride on the Sea of Galilee, then north through the Hula Valley through Kiryat Shmona to the Good Fence at Metulla. Seeing a blooming and blossoming Israel and the young Israeli soldiers on and off duty, having to guard every inch of the borders, the towns, villages and farms. An Israel that is very much alive, fulfilling many, many prophetic Scriptures, no matter what the enemies of Israel are constantly saying.

One Scripture that needs to be understood and taken to heart by all Christian people around the world is found in Psalm 102:12-18. Verse 16 says: **When the Lord shall build up Zion, He shall appear in His Glory.** Despite incredible odds, the Lord has built up Israel today, largely using unbelievers to do it to the consternation of many so-called Jewish and Christian religious thinkers. We were all so happy to be in the Land, seeing what the Lord is doing, remarkable evidence of His soon return in glory! We were seeing the places where Jesus lived and humbly fulfilled His heavenly Father's plan of salvation for sinners by the blood of the Lamb of God, the only begotten Son, to deliver us from Satan's hands and reconcile us to the Holy God of Heaven; seeing the place where His blood was shed, the prayers were made, the sick were healed in multitudes, the stormy sea was stilled. These events and the Bible itself all come alive and one is never the same again.

Inside the Garden Tomb, Betsy knelt near the stone resting place where Jesus' body was laid. I tried to take a picture of her kneeling inside the tomb, and the flash didn't go off. But praise God, the picture somehow took, showing the tomb in a golden glow, the silhouette of Betsy kneeling. An impressive, holy scene!

In Northern Israel we were to stay in a Kibbutz called Nof Ginossar, which means a lovely view of the Sea. It was right by the Sea of Galilee. But as we approached it after dark that first evening, our guide, Zev announced, " You know in kibbutz life men are in one tent, and women in another, and everyone will have to take turns in the kitchen and waiting tables, and men standing guard at night. Lee Nelson, you will have first night watch." He was saying this as we rolled up to this fine looking building ostensibly to "get the keys to our tents"! Actually, it is one of the nicest motel accommodations in Israel.

We said, "Look, Zev, we have only one tube of toothpaste!"

Grinning he gave us our key to our tent, which was the corner room on the 2nd floor of a well-built set of motel rooms.

Betsy and I will never forget a special miracle which took place outside that room. We'd forgotten our alarm clock, yet we wanted to get up at sunrise to walk the shore as Jesus did, and we prayed that somehow the Lord would wake us up just before dawn. Guess what? He did it! By sending the loveliest little alarm clock turned on loudly right outside our window. He sent a little song bird to perch in the tree right next to our window, and to sing with full volume the most beautiful bird song you can imagine, which woke us up right on time! You can't beat that! Praise the Name of the Lord forever.

At the Sea of Galilee, at the southern end, where it flows into the Jordan River, some 47 of our total group of 100 went down to be baptized by the five ministers in the group, on that cool cloudless day. A real dove began circling the group there on the bank and in the water, reminding us of the Dove that came down and sat on Jesus when He was baptized, and a Voice from heaven said, **"This is My beloved Son in whom I am well pleased."** (Matt.3:17) After the last person was baptized, I alone was left in the water, actually thinking about swimming across the narrow river and back, when I looked up above the point of land where the Sea of Galilee poured into the River, and there was a small cloud floating in over the scene which had the distinct shape of a "Dove Cloud." I quickly called up to Jackie Martin, who was taking pictures for us and said, "Jackie, get the cloud." She turned her camera around getting a beautiful picture with the cross-like stair railing showing in the foreground. For all our group this was probably one of the most significant and memorable events of the entire tour, for we felt that our heavenly Father was also saying to us, "These are my beloved children who are following my Son in whom I am well pleased." But there was one more side event that took place at the other end of the Sea of Galilee which was to have a tremendous effect on the future of our lives, and make a connection with some bread cast on the waters 45 years before! (Ecc.11:1)

There at Capernaum, amidst the ancient ruins of that city where Jesus did so many of His mighty miracles, Betsy and I found ourselves being introduced, by two of our group, to a young-looking Jewish woman by the name of Esther Dorflinger.

Jackie and Laurie were saying, "Esther, we want you to meet our Pastor and his wife, Betsy."

We said, "Esther, it's nice to meet you".

And at that very moment the Lord spoke to our hearts and said, "You're to help this Jewish woman in every way you can, tell her."

So in the next moment I found myself saying to this woman,

CHAPTER 16: AMAZING YEAR-1977-CALL TO ISRAEL

"Esther, when you come to the States, please get in touch with us, we will help you in every way we can. The girls will give you our name, address and phone number."

In the next moment Betsy and I were being called with our bus group to the boat landing and Esther to her bus. We didn't learn anything further about Esther at that time, other than she must be in some kind of trouble with the authorities in Israel because of her faith in Jesus. (Some two months later she did come to the States and we were able to help her in surprising ways.) So that first tour to Israel ended with some truly happy memories and experiences, and a sense with many of us, because of Jesus, that we had finally found our ancient home! Certainly our spiritual roots and home!

Oh, yes, back in New York at the Kennedy Airport on a little motel bus, we were told to shut up about Jesus! All along the journey in Israel we had sung the songs of Jesus and no one had objected, but on our return to the States this brash young woman bluntly shouted "Shut up" when we started to sing thanks and Praise to the Lord. The devil tried to dampen our spirits, but didn't succeed. It only emphasized the job needing to be done for Jesus in the U.S.A.!

Seven years would go by before we learned there was a remarkable and direct connection between Esther's Grandfather and Betsy when Betsy was a little girl living in her family's hotel, the Marlborough-Blenheim in Atlantic City, N.J.

WE MEET ESTHER DORFLINGER IN ISRAEL, 1977

264 FIRED AGAIN AND AGAIN, PRAISE THE LORD!

"THE DOVE CLOUD" AT JORDAN RIVER BAPTISM, 1977

GOD'S OLD OLIVE TREE AND 2 BRANCHES OF YESHUA ON TEMPLE MOUNT 1977

JESUS' SERVANTS: DON ODON, BOB GARRETT, AND SID RIGELL

CHAP. 17

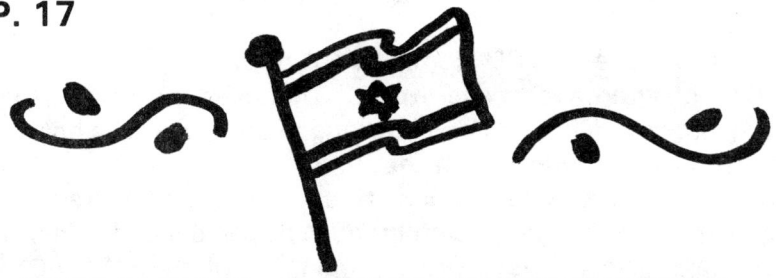

THE ISRAEL CONNECTION GROWS

Come and let us go up to the mountain of the Lord, and to the house of the God of Jacob; and He will teach us of his ways, and we will walk in his paths; for the law shall go forth of Zion, and the word of the Lord from Jerusalem. — Micah 4:2

ESTHER COMES TO BALTIMORE

By January of '77 Betsy had become Vice-President of the West Baltimore Aglow Chapter, leading the praise and worship at the monthly meetings on the first Friday of each month. During the first week in February a sizeable snowfall snarled traffic in the Baltimore-Washington region causing a week's postponement of the Aglow meeting. The scheduled speaker, Judge Helen Dodge, an outstanding federal Judge from Washington, D.C., had to cancel because of other commitments for the next week.

Somehow we'd heard that Esther had come to the States and was at Stoney Brook, Long Island. We understood she was coming to make a speaking tour, wherever she could in the States. Perhaps she could come to the postponed meeting. Finally, we got through to her by phone at Stoney Brook and she said she would come. She arrived by train the day before the meeting, having borrowed the train fare, and having $1 left to her name. After clearing with the Aglow officers, we took her to the Friday meeting as the substitute speaker, where she gave a very heart-touching account of how she, a Jew, came to know Jesus as her Messiah and the subsequent difficulties that followed, including having her Israeli citizenship withdrawn, being deported from Israel because she was following Jesus and the teachings of the New Testament. She told how, because of her own physical sickness, after being kicked out of Israel, she had had to give up her own two sons, to go to live with their father, who had remarried, and how she had been rejected by her parents. She ended with a challenge to this large group of women to make a 100% commitment to Jesus as Lord of all - their marriages, children, work, everything. The anointing of the Holy Spirit was truly present in her talk and challenge, and there was not a dry eye in the restaurant meeting room that day!

From there we took her to make two weeks of radio interviews with Sid Roth for his Messianic Vision broadcasts, all done in a few hours in a recording studio. This was the beginning of her "WE LOVE YOU ISRAEL SCROLL" in which she asked people across America and around the world to sign a sheet of paper with their name and country and to send a love gift for the welfare needs in Israel, to be presented to Israel's Prime Minister later that year in honor of Israel's 30th Birthday--or year of Independence. She did travel around the nation and the world and eventually took $50,000 in Bank Checks to present to Prime Minister Begin in Israel with the Love Scroll containing some 30,000 names from America, Europe, Scandinavia, South America, Australia, and New Zealand and Malaysia. It was quite a journey of faith to put it mildly. And the "LOVE SCROLL", in which Sid Roth had a real part, made a tremendous impression on the Prime Minister and his key deputies and many in the Knesset. In fact the scroll was kept in a cabinet in the Prime Minister's office to be shown often to visitors, and a picture of it hung on his wall while he was Prime Minister. We'll tell later how we got to see it there ourselves! The Lord surely blessed this young Jewish woman's bold faith in her Messiah Yeshua (Jesus).

Esther was with us about a month, and before she was to leave, she asked if we could take her down to Charlotte, N.C. to PTL and then over to CBN in Norfolk to see if she could interest these two leading Christian TV stations in presenting this call to American Christians to express their love to Israel on Israel's 30th Birthday.

It was late February 1978 when we arrived in Charlotte to begin looking for the TV station. We went out to find the place first, and talked with the gate-keepers about what time the program would begin the next day, and we introduced Esther to them. Some of the guards had already heard her on the Sid Roth broadcasts and were delighted she had come to PTL. This seemed like a good start. We found a motel, had supper and got a good night's rest, and were back the next morning in plenty of time for the morning TV program. We found seats in the balcony to observe the whole program. Just as we were about to sit down, someone coming into the balcony caught our attention. It was our dear Evangelist friend, Harold Wallace, who had met Esther earlier at the Little Tabernacle. Bro. Harold had worked with many of the key people at PTL when they all were working at CBN. We didn't know that he would be there, nor he, that we would be there. He said the Lord had told him to come, and he would go to work to contact key

CHAPTER 17: THE ISRAEL CONNECTION GROWS 267

people he knew to try to get Esther interviewed on the next day's program. Before the day was out it was agreed that Henry Harrison would interview her and specific seats were set aside for us in the audience for the next morning with Esther sitting on an aisle seat. Ah, it looked like the Lord was moving everything to get this Jewish girl on a nationally viewed TV program.

But we must tell you something here at this moment that troubled us deeply. As we watched that TV program that first day, Betsy and I began feeling a little sick to our stomachs, or in our spirits; we began sensing that we were watching a program called Christian, but one that was aping shows like Johnny Carson's. We were deeply grieved in our hearts, and, after it was over, we went back to a prayer room set aside for visitors who felt the need to pray. We fell on our knees and prayed and wept for about an hour. And now 10 years later, we understand why we needed to do it. The downfall of the key PTL leaders early in 1987 showed that they were living extravagantly and in almost shameless disregard of the basic principles of the Christian faith. May God have mercy on them, and bring them all to a humble, penitent, obedient walk with the Lord.

Well, what happened the next day? We were at the station bright and early and in our assigned seats; Esther on the aisle for easy interviewing. Henry Harrison was already on the stage, greeting the audience, the cameras were already focussed in, musicians and singers were all ready, the telephone counselors were in their places. Henry opened the show and greeted everyone and said they had some special people to interview and was about to announce the name of the first interviewee, when Jim Bakker came up and said, "Henry, I'll do the interviews today." He took the mike and began coming up the aisle.

He came to Esther and said, "Now who are you, young lady?"

Esther plainly said, "Esther Dorflinger from Jerusalem."

He immediately moved the mike over to Betsy asking the same question.

Betsy answered saying, "Betsy Rigell from Baltimore."

Mr. Bakker then lifted the mike and said, "I'm looking for a little grandmother who has ridden motorcycles and lives on a pig farm." He found the dear little grandmother farther up the aisle and talked to her perhaps 15 minutes about her motorcycle riding and pig farm and he told how they were planning for plastic-pig-trash-containers in their future Heritage village. (Quite uninspiring to say the least!)

After it was all over, all of us hurting inside, suddenly we looked around for Esther and she was missing from her seat. Then we looked toward the stage and there she was talking face to face with Jim Bakker, saying, as she told us later, "Mr. Bakker, if you could spend 15 minutes talking about pigs, surely you could spend 5 minutes talking about Israel."

At that moment he abruptly turned away, leaving her standing, and told an assistant to tell Brother Wallace that his Jewish girl had just "blown it!"

We were all mystified by this turn of events and very disappointed. Ten years later we were to learn why! About three months before this, Jim Bakker had had 2 or 3 Messianic Jews on the program and afterwards he was approached by some rabbis in the area and threatened with much opposition from them if he ever did it again. It seems that unfortunately, Jim caved in to their demands, as proven by events of this day. Jim should never have capitulated to these threats. Here was a Jewish girl with every right as a Jew to believe in Jesus as her Messiah, and also to call other Believers throughout our land to pray for and stand by Israel. If anybody "missed the boat" that day, Jim Bakker surely did! But that did not end our visit to PTL.

Both Brother Harold Wallace and Esther had been promised the interview and we all felt we needed an explanation. Brother Harold went back to his friends in the main office seeking to talk with Jim Bakker to find out what happened. We went back to the outside Gazebo to pray and sing "Stand By Israel." In time we felt, from the Lord, to begin another "Joshua March," this one around the PTL headquarters, seven times around silently, and at the end of it, stand in front of the main office entrance to sing again quite strongly the song, "Stand By Israel". So we started marching, the distance about a small block around. I led with my Bible held high, all in silence. Around and around we went, still silent, 3, 4, 5, 6, (fortunately it was just around this one building!). Then came the 7th and last time. By this time a lot of eyes had seen us. Someone was about to order the gate guards to come pick us up and throw us out of the place. The last turn ended in front of the main office entrance and we began to sing "Stand By Israel". About halfway through, one of the top officials came out of the door and down the steps to watch and listen. Apparently he decided we weren't dangerous and joined in singing the last chorus, and then invited Esther to come up for a private interview. (Not for TV of course). Her story and mission were heard, and she was told that their rules did not permit them to allow such appeals as her's to be broadcast. They were sorry and wished her well.

After what we have seen in the last year or so, it's doubtful that Esther was told the truth that day. On the way out of the gate, we stopped to let Esther go in to speak with and thank the guards for not coming to arrest us, and for their concern for her. We said "Goodby" to Brother Harold, and headed eastward toward CBN, where Esther got very much the same treatment and came out of their administration building weeping, at which moment there was a definite earth tremor in the Norfolk area, perhaps of God's anger at another rejection of His servant.

That evening, as we were eating supper in a restaurant next to our motel, we were recognized by friends on the previous year's tour to Israel, and Esther was invited to come to a large meeting room where a group of Full Gospel Men were meeting. Here she was given 15-20 minutes to share and most of them signed the "We Love You Israel Scroll". It was God's way of assuring her, and us, that He would get the job done without the help of the big TV personalities.

As we said earlier the "LOVE SCROLL" that Esther took around the world did bring much love and encouragement to the Prime Minister, to his Deputy Yechiel Kadishai, and to Israel, and gave Esther ready access to that high office as long as Mr. Begin was prime minister. A very coveted privilege that few others would be granted.

"BROTHER SID NEEDS AN OPERATION AND BETSY'S DIAMOND DISAPPEARS"

So Esther went on her wandering journey around the world with her "ISRAEL LOVE SCROLL," and we went back to the busy life at the Little Tabernacle with a special Easter program, special speakers, those wonderful "Praise The Lord Luncheons" and the intense efforts to recruit a good group for our second tour to Israel in the Fall.

But somewhere along the line I had developed what appeared to be a serious hernia condition which would require surgery before that next tour. How it came about I could not really explain, unless it was from trying to help too many people with their luggage on that first tour, and then bringing back from Israel a carry-on bag with several pounds of souvenir rocks picked up all over Israel. Psalm 102:14 says: *For thy servants take pleasure in her stones and favor the dust thereof.* I was one of His servants and since Israel has trillions of stones for the picking, I thought a bag full of these would make nice gifts for our friends. Surely everyone would want a little piece of the "Promised Land," wouldn't they?

So it may be that both the luggage and load of stones together gave me the hernia. No matter how hard we prayed, the Lord was not giving me a direct healing. So off to Dr. Finney, a surgeon who had helped me before, and the operation was underway.

As we were waiting in the admitting office of Union Memorial Hospital, Betsy looked down at her ring-finger, and realized the little diamond was missing from her engagement ring!! Could it have fallen out as we were getting out of the car, or walking into the hospital. We quickly went back and examined every inch of the way, but no sparkling gleam shined up at us as we examined the walkway to and from the car. No sign of it anywhere. We were both saddened to think that this little diamond that announced our engagement 33 years before might be lost. We prayed about it and put it in the hands of the Lord. Then I checked into the hospital for the operation, which took place the next morning and supposedly went quite well.

A few days later, despite what I had been told about painless hernia operations, I was being sent home to recuperate, still very much in pain. So much so, that I asked Betsy to let me sleep in a single bed in the boys room that I could get out of without doubling up in pain. Apparently there was some sort of lesion in the way the lining was sewed up that was causing the problem. Eventually it subsided and stopped altogether. Praise God!

Betsy had searched and searched and searched the house and driveway for her diamond, and still nothing. She got someone to check the sink traps. Nothing!

Finally, the day after I got home, she dumped her purse out on the other single bed next to me. Still nothing. But praise God, the next morning, as she was making up that same bed, she suddenly noticed a starry twinkle in the covers, and looking closer, she had found the missing diamond! Praise God forever! The Lord had saved the diamond for her, and us. It was finally found, and would soon be solidly reset to continue proclaiming our "plighted troth" (old English for pledged love and fidelity) to each other. Praise the Lord forever for His goodness and Mercy! He helps us get over painful operations and painful losses!

OUR SECOND TOUR TO ISRAEL

The hernia operation over and my recovery moving along as quickly as possible, we continued the intense efforts to enlist a sizeable group to go with us again to Israel, to bless them and to bless Israel. We know of instances where leaders have been able to make considerable profit for themselves, but we can assure you that we never made a nickel for ourselves on any of our tours. If there were any free passes, they always went to help someone else to go. We were delighted to see it happen that way.

On our second tour (1978), we were going with the Ray Solomon group again, 40 of us in all, about 12 from the Baltimore area. We remember with real joy most of the names of those in our group: Mary Faulkner, Fred Panzer, Dorothy Felton, Delores Dellospedale, Pam Failes, George Moore and his wife, Ike Butner and Ethyl Jolleston. The Lord

FIRED AGAIN AND AGAIN, PRAISE THE LORD!

A) ST. ANDREWS BAY. B) NORTH BAY BAYOU. C) GULF OF MEXICO DUNE & SEA OATS.

FIRED AGAIN AND AGAIN, PRAISE THE LORD!

TOP: PAPPY'S ANCHORAGE AT "THE BIGHT"
MID: THE FAMILY AT CHRIS & JULIE'S WEDDING IN MARYVILLE, TENN. MAY '89
BOT: 7 GRANDCHILDREN, PTL! MATTHEW, LUKE, BETSY, PETER, GINNY, ALLEN & LAURA

FIRED AGAIN AND AGAIN, PRAISE THE LORD!

THE WARNING #2 OVER THE SEA OF GALILEE - 1978 (P.273)

BETSY KNEELING INSIDE JESUS' TOMB IN THE SHEKINAH LIGHT - 1977 (P.261)

LTC TEAM FIGHTS ABORTION IN ANNAPOLIS - 1990

FIRED AGAIN AND AGAIN, PRAISE THE LORD!

BETSY AND ESTHER RESTING ON TOP OF MT. HORA

THREE FRIENDS MEET OVERLOOKING THE PATMOS HARBOR

WELCOME TO THE LORD'S BEAUTIFUL PATMOS

Baltimore, Md.
April 25, 1992
- 1995 -

Dear Friend,

It's a real joy to send you our book, "FIRED AGAIN AND AGAIN, PRAISE THE LORD!", <u>as a love gift</u>. It's a faithful record of God's mercies and miracles in our life-pilgrimage (so far) on the way to that city which hath foundations whose builder and maker is God, a "New Jerusalem!" (Hebrew 11:10; Rev.21:1). We do hope you will enjoy and be blessed by it. We believe the book will be helpful, instructive and encouraging to many, especially to those who have had or will face similar "firings" or fiery trials!

Should you wish to order more for family or friends (or enemies!), you may do so <u>for free</u>, by letter, or phone to Rev. Sid & Betsy Rigell at 615 Colorado Ave., Baltimore, Md. 21210. Phone: (410) 435-9009.

Please let us hear from you!

Yours in Jesus' Mighty Love,

Pastor Sid & Betsy Rigell

Pastor Sid and Betsy Rigell

August

CHAPTER 17: THE ISRAEL CONNECTION GROWS

blessed mightily everyone in that precious group for it was going to have a great tour of Israel, and would see an extraordinary sight over the Sea of Galilee.

On the flight overseas to Israel, one of those amazing heaven-sent coincidences occurred. We were on another El Al jumbo jet, one that has 3 seats on each side by the windows and 4 in the middle, and aisles between the middle and the side seats. You feel like you are in a plane a block long and you're in the midst of a sea of people. Betsy and I finally found our seats in the middle row. Both of us were wearing, as usual, our Stars of David, mine with a cross in the middle. We soon discovered that the other two seats in our row were taken by a very nice Jewish couple, somewhere near our age from Long Island. The husband was a builder of shopping centers, they were Morris and Katie Sosnow. After introductions, Betsy, right away, began learning how to make some Jewish dishes from this pleasant Jewish lady. We had introduced ourselves as being in a Church ministry in inner-city Baltimore, with special love for Jews and Israel, and working with a number of young people, like kids in trouble.

Morris leaned toward us and said, "Isn't it a real shame, what is happening to our young people? So many are turning away from the traditions of their families and getting into strange cults. You said you were from Baltimore, and we know of a dear young Jewish girl who has gotten mixed up with some cult in Baltimore. We know her Mother and Dad real well. This girl used to work for me in my business."

Betsy responded, "Well there are some good groups that the kids are getting into, like Messianic fellowships."

Mr. Susnow replied, "Oh no, it is something much worse than that."

Being quickened by the Holy Spirit as to who this girl was, Betsy asked, "Do you remember her name?"

Morris said, "Not at this moment."

Betsy asked, "Could it be Laurie, Laurie Rendler?"

"Yes, that's it! How did you know?"

"Well, we are the crazy people she is mixed up with!"

Talk about surprised people - they were! Betsy went on to say that Laurie had gone with us to Israel the year before, and was already thinking about making Aliyah (immigrating) to Israel. We just "happened" to have some pictures of Laurie and our first tour to show them. So the next 10 - 12 hours, Laurie's old boss and his wife would have to sit next to the "crazy people" she was mixed up with!

Morris and Katie were on their way to Israel to see his elderly Mother who was having eyesight problems. We spent much of the time talking about Old Testament Scriptures that pointed to Jesus and showed that He would be the Light and the Saviour for both Jews and Gentiles. Just as we were descending into the Ben Gurion Airport, outside of Tel Aviv, Morris leaned toward us and whispered, "You've almost persuaded me to believe!" May God grant that he did. That statement immediately reminded us of King Agrippa, who said the same thing to Paul (Acts 26:28).

Our tour guide that year, Moshe Dayagi, was a very rugged veteran of all the wars from his youth, probably a captain or major in the reserves, a man whom we thoroughly appreciated, loved and enjoyed. He had been commander of a company in the Sinai campaign that lost over 100 men and his company had been given the honor of being the last company withdrawn from the Egyptian side of the Suez Canal, as the Israel Army withdrew to cease-fire lines at the close of the Six Day War in 1967.

Later we were to see him many times, meet his whole family, visit in his home, know his lovely wife, Beatrice, and his jet pilot son, Gil, his lovely daughter, Ronet and 2 younger sons, Eran and Yaron. This time we were to stay in the Holy Land West Hotel, on the west side of Jerusalem. The visits to the Holy sites were greatly blessed by the timely readings from the Scripture by our dear brother from Warrenton, Va., Dick Overgard, and Moshe's guide lectures were outstanding throughout.

But the highlight of the trip truly was the afternoon that we reached the Mount of Beatitudes. Our group moved quietly from the bus over to the lookout point under the huge shade trees, they looked something like magnolias, perhaps banyan. Just behind them was the Franciscan sisters' convent. (These nuns keep the grounds spotless.) We sat at the overlook and had a brief prayer and it had been decided to just read the full Sermon on the Mount. Brother Overgard would read the 5th, 6th, and 7th chapters of Matthew. After his quiet reading, he had a brief prayer, and the group slowly rose and walked down to the beautiful Chapel of Beatitudes, built at that spot in the '30's by the Roman Catholics.

However, Betsy and I felt constrained by the Holy Spirit, to stand at the overlook looking southward over the Sea of Galilee and slowly begin singing softly with our eyes closed and hands joined and lifted up, "The Lord's Prayer". As we sang the A-men, we opened our eyes and looked up into the sky to see an amazing sight. There written in the sky, as by the finger of God, was a perfect, white, vapor-trail-like number "2", covering nearly half the width of the Sea. There had been no airplane activity that afternoon, and jet pilots have told us that it could not have been written by a jet or a skywriter in exactly this form.

Looking with great wonder, we immediately said, "Lord, what does it mean?" And by the Holy Spirit, the Lord spoke to our hearts and said,

CHAPTER 17: THE ISRAEL CONNECTION GROWS

"IT MEANS MY SECOND COMING IS VERY NEAR, TELL MY PEOPLE EVERYWHERE." After alerting the others to look, we got our camera and took a picture of it at the overlook spot where we had first seen it. The sun was now setting in the west, already painting the sky with its multi-colored hues. The Number "2" remained perfectly shaped and visible for at least an hour, drifting slowly east toward the Golan Heights.

About 3 years later, while living in Israel, we brought a Jewish Believer with us to the Mount of Beatitudes. As we walked to the overlook he glanced down on that normally spotless gravel walkway saying, "Isn't this where you saw the #2 in the sky?"

We said, "Yes,"

"Well," he said, "Here's another one!" and he picked up the only piece of paper on the path, and on it was a lone printed number "2" in the same shape as that first # 2 we had seen in the sky.

We felt the Lord was saying, "Hey, Fellows, Get Busy Telling My People, MY SECOND COMING IS VERY NEAR!"

Since that time there have been at least 6 other # 2's in widely different places to remind us of His Soon Coming. This book is being written partly in Antonios Vamvakos' #2 apartment on Patmos. Today we believe that His Second Coming can easily be within the next ten to twenty years! Please, please get ready and stay ready for His Return!

Jesus Himself urges such readiness in Matthew 24:42-51, where He speaks of the good steward and the bad steward. The good steward stays ready for His master's return.

We never saw a tour guide at the end of a tour get so many hugs as did our guide, Moshe Dayagi, at the end of this tour. He had made us all want to stay!

So we say, Shalom, Shalom, and Lehetraot (which means, "Peace, Peace, and hope to see you again soon.") And off we go into the "Nice Blue Yonder" to the United States.

OUR MACEDONIAN CALL

On that last tour we did get to see Esther in the apartment complex on the Northwest side of Jerusalem, called Ramot, where she had moved recently. We arrived with a whole bus load of pilgrims for a quick "Hello" that day, finding that she had only a small desk and a pad on the floor for a bed. So we had prayer for her, asking the Lord to guide her through the final days of the court case and provide her with some better furnishings, which He did. We left her that day, thinking it would be way in 1979 before we would see her again. Little did we know!

Christmas 1978 was coming up for us and the Little Tabernacle and again we were quite busy. One morning about one week before Christmas, a long distance call came to us from Jerusalem, from Esther, asking us to come back to Jerusalem for the big final day of her case before the Supreme Court on December 27th. She said she needed us to be there with a group of friends, praying for her as she gave her oral defense in her case seeking the restoration of her citizenship, which had been withdrawn because she believed in Jesus as the Jewish Messiah.

We said, "Esther it's a week before Christmas. We have Church programs and the end of the year duties and our boys are coming home for Christmas. We don't see how it's possible for us to come."

Then she added an expression that has become almost a trademark with her. "Well, pray about it."

We said we would and let her know.

Immediately after I hung up the phone and looked up to the Lord for His guidance, I saw a vision of that Macedonian (Acts 16:9) of long ago saying to Paul, **Come over and help us.** And Paul did! I hadn't thought of that Macedonian in quite a while, but there he was and I knew instantly that the Lord was calling us to "our Macedonia" to help Esther.

But we needed some real miracles to get it all together, to get to Jerusalem in time for this High Court case on the 27th. As well as Christmas, it was also the Jewish holiday of Hanukkah, the eight days of lighting lights in commemoration of the miracle cruse of oil that lasted 8 days when the temple was cleansed after it's desecration by the Greek Invader, Antiochus in 165 B.C. So the Israeli planes, El Al and several others were already booked and full.

Finally Betsy was able to find two seats left on the British Airline plane leaving Dulles Airport outside of Washington on that Christmas night. This made possible our being with the Church and our sons through Christmas Day. We had already had a good visit with Chris, since he had come home from Maryville College earlier in the month. Craig and Ann, Kirby and Carol were busy with their first children far away, so only four sons were home, Dusty, Joe, Chris and Brian and they drove us to Dulles late that afternoon. We had a nice Christmas visit with them after all!

At this time something heavy on our hearts was the condition of my oldest sister, Sissy, who was battling a serious recurrence of cancer and undergoing chemotherapy in Panama City. Sissy had been like a second mother to all her younger brothers and sisters, and a main support of the family for many years after our father died.

We had seen her some months before and prayed with her in Panama City, but now certainly didn't want to be out of the country if she were near death. We were quite torn between the two desires, but

CHAPTER 17: THE ISRAEL CONNECTION GROWS

knew we had a Macedonian call to answer. Finally, just before the plane departure at Dulles, we were able to get a call through to Sissy and talk with her about her condition and let her know of our concern and prayers, and also what we were being called to do by the Lord. She told us the chemotherapy was rough, was driving her up the wall at times, but at times bearable. She then urged us to go ahead. Sissy always had an understanding heart concerning the Lord's Hand on our lives. She along with two other members of our family had been baptized in the Holy Spirit two or three years before when we had prayed for them there. It had made a precious difference in their lives, as it had in ours. We told Sissy how much we loved her and appreciated her and with some misgivings in our hearts, we said "Goodbye", assuring her we would be in touch as soon as we got back. We never talked with her again on this earth, because she went to be with the Lord before we got back. But we were to receive a special telegram about her death while spending a night in Nazareth, Israel, some 10 days later. "Alavha-Sholem!" (A Yiddish expression used by an old Jewish friend, Brother Louis Gold, which he always said, when mentioning some friend or family member who had passed on. It apparently means, "May he or she rest in peace.") More about her in a little while.

Another communication which we needed to make before leaving the States was a special telegram addressed to Esther in Jerusalem, saying only, "Please pick up your Christmas presents on Dec. 26th at Ben Gurion Airport, B.A. flight #744, arriving at 4:35 p.m." We had not told her otherwise that we were coming!

Later she would tell us that when she got the telegram, she began wondering what in the world are they sending, and how do I go about picking up the items on the arrival of the flight to the airport. The year before in '78 she had had a real "bollygon" (a mixup, a messy problem) trying to pick up an air express letter we had sent to that same airport. After wrestling with it for a time, she heard the Lord say, "Esther, it's them, Dummy; you're to pick them up!"

"Oh!"

Just before the plane was to land at Ben Gurion Airport, after a good flight from D.C. by way of London, Betsy and I pulled out of our carry-on luggage two big Red Christmas Bows, the kind you see on large packages, and tied them around our necks, to look like walking Christmas gifts. There were some startled looks around us, but we grinned and with great "hutzpah" carried on the charade, through passport control, the baggage area, wishing everyone Happy Holidays, then down the long exit walkway with our luggage cart to a big happy greeting from Esther and another friend, Jackie. First we took some pictures and then pushed the baggage cart to a "Sherut," which in Israel is not a long black Cuban cigar, but a large taxi that can hold up to 7 passengers, and will take you and your luggage to your exact destination. The word "Sherut" is also Hebrew for "service." From the airport to Jerusalem is about an hour's ride or less.

At Esther's apartment in Ramot that night, we were pleased to find that the Lord had provided her with additional furniture including a single and a double bed. Esther lent us her double bed and went back to sleeping on a foam pad in the living room; her other visitor had the single.

At the airport she had given us quite a surprise shock by telling us that the final hearings at the High Court had been postponed for a month, to allow time for her to produce a written defense, rather than an oral one before the Court which could have been stopped in mid sentence. It was a wise decision, but nonetheless, a real blow to our expectations, and seemingly knocking the props out from under the reason for our coming. On Dec. 27th, the supposed day of the High Court hearing, guess what we were doing? You've no idea? Well, Mom and Dad Rigell were carrying the dirty laundry on an Israeli bus to a laundromat in Ramot Eschol (on the north side of Jerusalem.)

However, we quickly learned there was another problem, a mean one, taking place in Jerusalem among some Christian leaders which needed to be confronted. We had some inkling of this back in the States shortly before coming, when we received a registered letter from a Messianic big shot on Long Island, warning other leaders across the country about this notorious Esther Dorflinger who was in all kinds of error. Apparently the key Church Elders in Jerusalem at that time, had gotten this strange and damning letter, too. Having been with Esther earlier that year at many speaking engagements, hearing her state her beliefs in Jesus as the Son of God, and calling thousands to whole-hearted commitment to Him, made us know that the letter was not in anyway based on facts, or from the Lord. We were told that these elders in Jerusalem had had a meeting, heard the charges against her by one or two men, had accepted them, and without ever talking to her in any way, had basically ruled that she was a heretic who was causing serious danger to the true Messianic Believers in Israel with her Court case.

What startled us was that they had not come to see her, nor asked her to come to face them--which is what our Lord Jesus calls for us to do in Matthew 18:15-17. Here Jesus tells us that if a person has offended us in any way, we are to go to them privately to clear up the problem in love and forgiveness. If that doesn't succeed, then we are to go again with one or two elders with us. If that doesn't succeed,

CHAPTER 17: THE ISRAEL CONNECTION GROWS

then the Church is to hear it and decide what should be done. Then if the person refuses to hear the Church, Jesus says then let him be as a heathen man and a publican.

Also Paul writes this in Galatians 6:1, **Brethren, if a man be overtaken in a fault, you who are spiritual restore such a one in the spirit of meekness, considering yourself, lest you also be tempted.** Well, we immediately began sensing from the Lord that we must spend time on this trip talking to these elders and asking them why they had not talked with Esther, individually or collectively, before making such a damaging decision. We did get to see three of the men.

One of them did come to see Esther personally and to read her written defense for the High Court, which totally disproved all that was being said against her.

Another looked upon us as "nobodies", without any right to question their authority or decision. He had no answer when we asked why he didn't talk to Esther personally, or have the group talk to her collectively, as the Lord has directed us to do. That was an icy cold meeting!

The next one we saw was highly angered by our coming to question why they had not bothered to invite Esther to speak in her own defense, and ended up so angry that we almost expected to be thrown out bodily. It didn't happen though. It should be said here that when we came back to live in Israel, after some time, we were able to re-establish a friendly and loving relationship with these men. And thank God, Esther's name was fully cleared, too, after the publication of her written defense before the High Court. Even though the High Court ruled against her for citizenship, because she believed in Jesus as the divine Son of God, had been baptized, and was following the teachings of Paul (that "terrible traitor" to Judaism). Later the court was to grant her permanent residency which is nearly the same as citizenship with all tax-paying privileges, but without full voting rights.

Esther arranged for us to meet many of her dear friends in Jerusalem, among whom were Zev and Ruth Weintraub, who invited us all to their apartment on Shimoni Street for dinner, a couple and street that we would later get to know quite well! The Weintraubs were to become very precious friends and neighbors. That night we did learn that Zev was from Baltimore, and had moved to Israel in 1960 after completing his U.S. military service in the Airforce. Now in Israel he was a regular in the Israeli Army Reserve, still serving one or two months on active duty each year as all able-bodied Israelis do up to the age of 55. The Weintraubs had been most faithful friends of Esther's during all her difficulties, and had helped her in many, many ways. They thought nothing of hiking the many miles out to Ramot on their day off to see her, an undreamed-of feat for us spoiled Americans!

The first draft of Esther's written defense had been completed before we got to Israel, but Esther felt it needed to be gone over, word by word, again with the several Jewish Believers who had helped her in the formulation of it, all 29 typed pages of it. The group was to meet in Nazareth, on a certain day during our stay, to do the final reading, and corrections, if any. They wanted us to be with them. So we caught buses back to the airport, rented a little Autobianchi, and were on our way northward to Nazareth along the coastal road to Haifa, then northeast to Nazareth. That night at Arieh's apartment the final reading of Esther's defense presentation was made, and approved with only the slightest changes. It was ready for its final typing and handing into Esther's lawyer for delivery to the High Court.

During that evening a telegram came from Ruth Weintraub in Jerusalem for us to call our son Craig in the States. We were to spend the night with the Baptist Pastor in Nazareth and, finally, the next morning we were able to get through to Craig in Oak Ridge, Tenn. He told us that Sissy had died suddenly; the chemo was too much for her. We all knew that Sissy was surely a saved servant of God, and was ready to meet the Lord, but the loss of this precious sister was coming as a tremendous shock to us and to the whole family. How terribly she would be missed, this tiny little 4 ft. 10 in. sister, who had graduated from college at the age of 19 and had helped to support our big family as a high school math teacher and vice principal. Later she and her husband, Capt. Walter Anderson, would establish the famous Capt. Anderson's Restaurant in Panama City at the Grand Lagoon. Along the way she would become an outstanding women's leader in the Presbyterian Church, locally and statewide. This little "Big Sister" surely was going to be missed! We were able to ask Craig to please go and represent our own family at her funeral in Panama City, since there was no way for us to get there in time. He did, admirably. We were also able to get a call through to Sissy's only child, a married daughter, Judy Beth, to express our sorrow and sympathy. Then we knelt down by that telephone table, Betsy and I did, and gave God thanks for Sissy, for her love and devotion to the Lord and to her family, and to untold numbers of others in her lifetime. And suddenly as we prayed, our eyes being closed, the Lord began showing me a beautiful vision inside of Heaven, with beautiful trees and flowers and mansions, and He said distinctly, "Her mansion was ready!" Praise Ye the Lord!

After taking care of the phone charges and thanking the minister and his wife for their hospitality, we went back to Arieh's to pick up Esther and Jackie, for our plans called for us to drive further north above the Sea of Galilee to see some other dear friends of Esther's. Before leaving

CHAPTER 17: THE ISRAEL CONNECTION GROWS

Arieh's however, we asked his cute little 3-year old daughter, Sarai, to sing again her favorite chorus based on Romans 1:16 which says: *I am not ashamed of the Gospel for it's the power of salvation to all those who believe, to the Jew first and also to the Greek.* How lovely to see and hear this pretty child's love for Jesus!

About then Arieh and Mary said, "Why don't you return to Israel and live here and be Grandma and Grandpa to our children and Mom and Dad to us and go on circuit from time to time to visit with us and other Believers?"

We said, "Thanks for the invitation, it sounds good, and we sure would like to do it. Perhaps we can some day." (Thinking, after "retirement" some 5 years away!) Little did we know what was soon to happen.

Here it was the very beginning of 1979, and in the year before, several times, I had mentioned to Betsy that I felt the Lord was saying there would be a big change in our lives in 1979. Now I'm thinking is this the change that He was talking about? They had all expressed their sincere condolences concerning my sister's death, and I had been able to share with them about the vision of her mansion being ready.

So we headed north to visit the other friends before returning to Jerusalem. Some of the friends lived and worked at a Horse Ranch called Vered HaGalil, (which literally means "Rose of The Galilee"), a sort of dude ranch with bunk houses, a few cottages, and a very good restaurant, where Esther knew she could get a fine hot fudge sundae, one of her special delights. Jackie had been hoping to find some kind of work in Israel, and had been praying that perhaps she could find something at Vered HaGalil. So while we were eating, she was interviewed by the manager and was hired on the spot, subject to agreeing to taking a Hebrew course, which she wanted to do anyway. She was to report back the following week.

At Vered HaGalil, we met a very special older couple, Ray and Virginia Cornwell, who had fallen in love with Israel, and had come back about a year before and offered themselves to help on the Ranch without pay, maybe room and board. Back in the States they had many years working in camps and on ranches until retirement. Yudah, the owner gave them a little cubby hole out near the barn to live in, and they went to work eagerly. Before long, they were the most trusted and valuable workers and, after a time, would have their own separate house and be considered as almost indispensable. They also became like foster parents to Jackie while she worked there. The last time we saw them was in the Fall of '90 and they both were into their 70's still working hard, still a blessing to Yudah and Yona, the Ranch owners, and many more. Thank God for these two precious older Christians who had come to Israel to help build up Zion for the Lord (Ps.102:16). We still think of him as the unofficial Bishop of Northeast Israel, because they were constant pillars of faith, love, wisdom and encouragement to all the Believers in that region from Tiberias to Metulla.

A light rain was falling as we left the horse farm that day, and as we looked back we saw a rainbow, with one end reaching right down upon this ranch. The Lord was showing us that His work was being done, His blessings were there! We had prayed for a back injury that Ray had and for Jackie's job, and we felt the Lord was saying that He was taking care of these matters! Praise His Holy Name!

We drove westward to Nahariya on the Mediterranean, spent the night with more of Esther's Jewish friends, and then back south to Jerusalem and Ramot. A trip marked with deep sadness, yet with a vision of Heaven's Mansions, a song of love, a rainbow of God's sure promise, and an invitation to return to Israel!

ON FINDING EMMAUS

Earlier in our stay we had called our dear friend, Moshe Dayagi, the guide, at his home in Ashkelon, some 30 miles south of Tel Aviv, to find out when we might come down to see him. He and his wife decided it would be okay to come with Esther and Jackie on Shabbat morning about 11 a.m. So when Shabbat (Saturday) morning arrived, thinking that Esther would know more about how to get to Ashkelon from Jerusalem, I asked her if she would like to drive our rented car.

And she replied, "Okay, I'll drive if you put away your maps and let me follow the precise guidance of the Holy Spirit."

Somewhat surprised by this lack of practical interest of following the map we had in hand, we said, "Okay, go ahead and do it," and climbed into the back seat. Jackie sat in the front with Esther as driver. And off we went in the wrong direction (to our great consternation in the back seat!) Esther had taken a turn heading us north, instead of southwest where we knew we should be going. After a time we were in the heart of Ramallah, north of Jerusalem, practically hanging off a cliff. We were spared by God's mercy from falling into this chasm and were still trying to keep our "cool" and our mouths shut, but it was getting much harder!

Finally, Esther was on a road heading West, which helped our feelings a great deal. At least we were heading toward the Coast, not the Jordan River. On the coast there was a large highway running north and south. Surely we would have a 50% chance of taking a turn southward there. We not only had just visited Ramallah, a stronghold of the Palestinians, but we were riding through other rural roads in the

CHAPTER 17: THE ISRAEL CONNECTION GROWS

West Bank, where, even then, Israelis were not at all welcome, nor their cars. Israeli cars have yellow tags, like the ones on our car. West Bankers have cars with blue tags. The time was well past 10 am, and we were still a long ways from the coast, and Ashkelon!. At the rate we were going, we couldn't possibly get to Ashkelon before 12:30 pm.

Finally, we came to a place that had a big sign on it, saying "The Canadian Israel National Forest." No doubt that sign meant forest one day in the distant future, because at that moment by usual standards for forests, this wasn't one. Although there were a large number of small trees planted, "This forest needed a lot of prayer to be one!" Israel has planted over 50 million trees since her nationhood was announced in 1948. And by the grace of God a lot of them have survived the low rainfall and are a credit to Israel's determination to reforest the land and to God's mighty help.

Next we took a turn to the left, following a sign toward a spring. This was an interesting turn we thought because there are not many springs available in these parts. By this time our teeth were gritting themselves pretty hard. Our jaws were firmly set and our eyes were looking off into the distance for some way out of this. There is a heavy cloud of silence in the car. And Esther drove on. Now we are off the macadam road entirely and circling on a narrow gravel road around a small mountain, all part of this scraggly forest. (Forgive me, Lord!) Now the road goes sideways down the hill toward a gully which we bounced through and made a sharp turn to the left continuing along the edge of a hill going down into another gully. Soon, just ahead, we see another Park sign. Surely this will give us some help on how to find our way out of this lost state we were in. As we stop in front of this park sign in this rocky scrub forest, we have a big, big surprise!! The sign reads "This is The Ancient Site of The Spring of Emmaus, that fed water to the village of Emmaus, just below here in ancient days." So we had gone in a strange circuitous direction from Ramot to Ramallah, to the forest, to the Spring of Emmaus!

Several times we had asked our guides, "Just where is Emmaus?" They would wave their hands to the side of the big highway and say over there. On this day, in a very special way, the Lord had guided Esther by the Holy Spirit to bring us to Emmaus! We had always wanted to find Emmaus! This was an "EXTRA" from the Lord!

We dismounted from the little Autobianci and wandered off toward the narrow ancient aquaduct, walking among the ancient pottery chards, trying to collect ourselves and find the presence of the Lord at The Spring of Emmaus. Betsy found a little cave to hide herself in for a few minutes, and I picked up pottery chards!

Soon, we were back in the car, now able to speak to each other, and heading out toward the road again, we hoped. When we got there, we found a sign, at last, a sign pointing straight ahead to Ashkelon! To arrive there two hours late, we thought! Finding the Dayagi's house took a little time too! When we knocked on the door, they gave us the warmest welcome and said they were so glad we came at that time. Their little son had been sick during the night, keeping them awake a good bit and they needed to sleep late. So what seemed to be late to us, was being right on God's time for the Dayagi's. Isn't the Lord good! His mercy is everlasting and His truth endureth to all generations! (Ps. 100)

RETURN TO ISRAEL CONFIRMED IN ENGLAND

The second week in January, we were again on our way to the Ben Gurion Airport, the car loaded to the roof with ourselves, Esther, and two other passengers. Esther was making a tape for the Little Tabernacle saying, "Dear Little Tab, thank you for loaning Pastor Sid and Sister Betsy to us. We need them here; they've been a big help to us. Please help them to pack; because we are praying them back. Don't try to keep them, because we will out-pray you."

So we were saying "Shalom" to Israel and Esther again. This time we were on our way back to the U.S. via British Air, with a one night stopover in England, and directions to Deale near Dover on the southeast coast for an overnight visit with Don Odon and family. It was c-c-cold in England, with snow and ice all the way to Dover. You would look out the train window and see flocks of sheep and think how blessed they are to have on their heavy winter coats.

Don met us in his left-hand-driven British car, and shortly had us in his nice home, with his big beautiful family. (Remember now, we had just left Israel that morning.) After a delightful dinner-time, we all gathered in their small living room where there was a coal fire gleaming in the fireplace, keeping the place warm. We shared some of the interesting events of the Israel trip with them, and they all brought us up to date on the latest events in the Odon family life. Some of the children had homework to do, but after a while they all came back for their nightly Scripture reading as a family.

A big surprise was about to come to Betsy and me! The family was reading in the book of First Samuel at the time, and began reading in the 6th chapter, after a prayer for understanding. The youngest one read a few verses, then the next, right on up the age steps to the older sisters and brothers, then the parents, then Betsy and finally me. We were now in the last of the 7th chapter and I found myself reading verses 15-17: ***And Samuel judged Israel all the days of his life. And he***

CHAPTER 17: THE ISRAEL CONNECTION GROWS

went from year to year in circuit, to Bethel, to Gilgal, and Mizpeh, and judged Israel in all those places. And his return was to Ramah, for there was his house, and there he judged Israel, and there he built an altar unto the Lord.

Just the previous Sunday we had tried to hike from Ramot to the Prophet Samuel's burial place on a mountain just north of Ramot, and had been turned back by an Israeli soldier saying in Hebrew, "It was not safe." Fortunately a little Israeli boy was with us who spoke Hebrew and understood the warning. But the Holy Spirit was quickening certain words in this passage as applying specifically to us: "Going on circuit, his return, and having a house and building an altar unto the Lord there." We had left Israel just that morning with the words still ringing in our ears and hearts, "Come back, return soon, go on circuit to encourage us, make your home with us, worship the Lord with us." I immediately felt those words were meant for us, and this was really to be our next assignment from the Lord. And what a change it would be for us! How would we ever work it out? And who can we find to take our place? No wonder I was thinking on those verses for sometime afterwards, but now we were certain that God was saying He wanted us to go to Israel and live there for a time with His people. A big change, indeed! The Lord wouldn't listen to me when I thought, "But Lord, I'm 61 years of age." He rebuffed me, saying, "Look at Abraham and Moses, and many others who went out at much older ages at My bidding."

So back to America the next day, after that happy visit with the Odons, assured that we had some big "getting-ready-to-move" work to do! We reported back to the Little Tabernacle and gave them Esther's message and, soon after, asked the officers and congregation if they would approve an invitation to our son, Kirby, and his wife, Carol, to come take our place the next Fall, to release us for a time in Israel. They did, and we wrote an official letter from the Church inviting Kirby to come serve as Pastor beginning in October. He had been ordained when he graduated from Bible College, but was continuing in home building work in Tulsa. There was no immediate answer!

Finally, some 6 weeks later, we received a call one Sunday night after the evening worship service from Kirby in Tulsa, saying, "Sorry, Dad I haven't answered, but the Lord told me this morning in a Communion Service that we are to come and take your place for you and Mom to go to Israel."

"That's great, Kirby. We know the Lord will bless you for it. Thanks so much for letting us know."

Kirby told us later that he didn't want to make the same mistake that I had made, way back before we ever came to Baltimore to live. We had been working in the South, and Betsy's family was living in Atlantic

City, N.J., so we would have to drive through Baltimore on the way to see them during vacations. My big mistake was made as we drove through Baltimore each time, by saying, "O Lord, Please don't ever send me to a place like Baltimore. It's so big and crowded. Anywhere but Baltimore." You'll need only one guess to tell where the Lord eventually sent us, giving me a sentence of 23 ½ years in Baltimore before He would "parole" us to go to Israel for a time.

So we learned the big lesson, like Jonah, that when we are serving the Lord, our happiness depends upon being exactly where the Lord wants us to be, without complaining! He'll make a difficult place enjoyable. We must never tell the Lord where not to send us, for He will send us there to prove that His grace is entirely sufficient for us right there. So Kirby told us that he told the Lord he would be willing to go anywhere, even to Baltimore!

Neither Betsy or I knew the tremendous amount of work that lay ahead of us before October when we finally could make the change. Our plans at that moment involved enlisting another tour group for a Fall tour, to tour the land with them, to come back to the Ben Gurion Airport with them, and wave goodbye to them. We would stay on in Israel for the rest of the 3 months visa, or visitor permit, which is normally stamped in your passport when you come with a U.S. tour group, and then request visa extensions.

Esther would make a room available for us at her apartment in Ramot. Big problems would arise before all this came to pass, but the Lord would amazingly work things out for us. Bless His Holy Name!

ESTHER & JACKIE PICK UP "CHRISTMAS GIFTS"
AT BEN GURION AIRPORT, DEC. 1978

CHAP. 18

PREPARATION FOR OUR ISRAEL ASSIGNMENT

Fear thou not; for I am with thee: be not dismayed; for I am thy God; I will strengthen thee, yea, I will help thee; yea, I will uphold thee with the right hand of my righteousness.   *Isaiah 41:10*
I can do all things through Christ which strengtheneth me. - Phil. 4:13

THE GREAT HOUSE MOVING OF '79

As we sit here on "our little writing porch" on Patmos (with Betsy sunning herself, pen in hand, and me trying to stay out of the sun as best I can), we have been rereading a three-page LTC newsletter for that long-ago summer of '79. It tells of many visiting speakers at the Little Tabernacle, many beautiful blessings and miracles to God's people from the Lord that summer, and many young people being blessed in the "Turn-Around-With-Jesus-Home."

There's the story of precious little "BJ", who had been a drug user and pusher down South. How wonderfully the Lord changed her life and began giving her beautiful songs and a good job and business school training. There was the excellent completion by our son, Chris, of his college courses, graduating with highest honors in both Chemistry and Math. That certainly warmed the cockles of our hearts. Then, of course, there were the enlistment efforts going on for another special October tour to Israel.

But a super problem was arising that needed immediate attention, and monumental work (Honest!), before we could leave the States for our stay in Israel. Down in Florida the Bay County Commissioners had decided Mom's old house, right behind the Courthouse, and the tiny lot it was on next to the Massalina Bayou, would be bought by the County (whether we liked it or not) to make space for enlarging the Court House parking area. Well, that old house was full of precious memories for

Mom's family for over 50 years, and had seen a lot of hard work by us in repairs and improvements since I was a boy. But now the county wanted the tiny lot and would destroy the house if we didn't do something with it.

It had become ours, as part of the division of Mom's estate. It wasn't fancy in any way. In fact most modern folks would say it was sadly substandard. But we had loved living in that old house, which had been built out of virgin pine lumber and cypress shingles probably around 1915, and, if the Lord willed, we'd live in it again. If not, we could rent it to help support us in the Lord's work. The floor joists and beams were so tough and full of pine rosin that the termites wouldn't touch it. If they did, they went away complaining of dental problems and indigestion!

Well, we must admit we couldn't stand the idea of seeing that old house torn down and thrown away. Having been warned by our brother-in-law, Charlie Abbott, that it was about to happen, we hurriedly found the name of a well-known house mover in Northwest Florida, a man named "Ducky" Johnson. Apparently he and his big tough crew, all built like short Samsons, were not afraid of moving anything including houses, schools, and banks (legally, that is). So we called and asked him if he would take a look at the house at 310 Third Court in Panama City and let us know if he could move it to a new lot 7 miles away that our niece Judy Beth would sell us. He said he would be glad to do it, and the price would be about $5,000. We thought that was a good price for this really tough job. But we didn't realize what a tough job lay ahead of US!!!

When we got to Panama City in September, we learned that "Ducky" Johnson was in the area moving a schoolhouse and we also learned, to our dismay, that the house he had looked at, thinking it was ours, was not ours! "Gulp!" So we quickly persuaded him to take a look at the real one down by the bayou. We could see the headlines, "Preacher has house-mover move the wrong house!" Boy, would we have been in trouble, and in jail, too, probably. He came with us in his big car, saw the right house and told us what we had to do, or get done, before he could move it. Because of the size of the old house the big front screened porch would have to come off. The little back porch would have to come off, and the roof would have to be lowered about six feet. Wow! We could get it done or he could get it done, but it would run up the cost several thousand dollars. We said we would get it done, since I knew how to use hammer, saws and crowbars and we had a powerful son who was in the business and hopefully he could come help us, since he was coming on to Baltimore shortly anyway.

So we called Kirby and he agreed to come with Carol and the two

CHAPTER 18: PREPARING FOR OUR ISRAEL ASSIGNMENT 287

little boys and be with us through this mammoth house moving project. And mammoth it was!

First, the lot in Lynn Haven had to be cleared of many big trees and much underbrush, mainly the famous ground hugging plants called palmettos. Now and then an underground nest of yellow jackets or hornets had to be dealt with the native way: gasoline carefully poured into their holes, followed with a match. What happened? There would be a small "baloom", a small underground explosion, and no more hornets! With chain saws, and axes, and extra hired help we were able to clear the lot in a few days, to make it ready to receive the house, doing everything we could to save as many of these beautiful pines and oaks as possible. Brian and Chris came to help. Our sister and brother-in-law, Dick and Judy, gave us all kinds of help, and so did our niece Nancy.

As soon as the lot was cleared in Lynn Haven some of us went to work on dismantling the porches back at 310 Third Court in Panama City. When Kirby arrived, he was put in charge of disassembling the roof with old Dad's "expert" help, carefully laying the rafters down on the attic floor joists. Hot, sweaty, thirsty, and weary was the rule in those Florida September days! We worked and prayed. Weather could be a problem. Any heavy rains could ruin the inside of the house. We obtained huge rolls of plastic to cover and help prevent damage.

Finally, the day of the movers came. They began bulldozing a path down the slope to the house and shovel-digging paths for huge steel beams to slide under the house, with connecting huge wooden beams crosswise to form a platform. The steel beams were jacked up to receive wheels, and steel matting was then laid out in front of the wheels while the steel beams and wheels were jacked up further. Other steel beams were laid down with other cross beams to support the house during the move. This is a rough picture of it!

Then came the big pull by the powerful moving trucks, using cables to pull it up the graded bank, out of the lot. The whole rig and house had to be moved up to the street level, a rise of at least 12 feet in the short horizontal distance of about 100 feet. It was an extraordinary feat of power and moving ingenuity, taking at least three days to achieve, by that team of 10 - 12 tough, good-hearted men. They really knew their job! And earned their pay!.

At last, the roofless house was sitting up on the old Perritt house-lot (now empty too) at sort of a precarious angle, and had to be left there for the weekend, with news already coming about a low-pressure storm system building up in the Gulf. It meant a hurricane was about to head our way! "Lord, please give us a few more good days before it gets here," was our prayer. After spending much of Saturday making a temporary covering of plastic which might stop some rain, but not heavy winds, on Sunday we all tried to relax and attend worship services at our old home church, The Wallace Memorial Presbyterian Church.

Well, the good weather continued into Monday, praise the Lord, and the movers were back for the first leg of the move through Panama City along Third Court to Magnolia, north to Airport Road, right on 22nd. to the Lynn Haven Road with brother-in-law, Dick Gaunt, taking pictures all the way. Because of traffic hours the house had to be left on an empty corner lot until after the morning rush hour. Then the moving caravan was underway again with one of their men on top to see that no wires were struck, Dick taking pictures, and this time our dear oldest brother Starlus (a retired paper mill manager) followed in his car. We arrived at the lot on Missouri Ave. in less than an hour without incident, and the movers rolled the house into it's position on the lot and readied it for lowering. The weather man said the hurricane should hit the panhandle area (ours) by Tuesday afternoon or evening only 24 hours away!

Kirby felt the old rafters were too irregular and warped to try to use again, so he went to a lumber company and ordered new rafters and ridge beam. We cut those rafters to size and with Betsy's help, and a few others, we got them on the roof and began nailing them in place. By 8 or 9 o'clock that evening, with flood lights rigged up by Dick, we were still working, nearing the completion of the new roof framework. But no covering, only the temporary planks we had nailed on for climbing.

The week before, Betsy and I had attended a Full Gospel Church where a challenge had been made in a Word from the Lord through an elder, to drop everything to give assistance to a brother in emergency need. There was another meeting of that same Church group this night, and Betsy felt pressed to go request some emergency help for enough strong young people to come help us put on at least a plastic covering for that night. Before we knew it she was back with about a dozen young people with their own hammers and raring to go. By midnight the roof had, at least, a plastic covering on! Praise God for those young people and for the help of family and friends and Kirby's extraordinary work on that project! What a grimy bunch we were as we knocked off after midnight! We hoped to get a few hours sleep before the last big push to get plywood sheets and roofing tar-paper on before the hurricane came the next day. The storm seemed to be stalling a bit out in the Gulf! Could the Lord be doing it?!

In Dick's old truck, Kirby went for a load of plywood "sheeting" early, and soon he and another carpenter who had come to help were

CHAPTER 18: PREPARING FOR OUR ISRAEL ASSIGNMENT

nailing the sheets in place as we pushed them up. "Ducky" and his crew were back to finish, at least partly, the new foundation for the house. Due to the weather forecast, he and his men hoped to leave for their homes (about 70 miles away) around noon that day. Everyone was working with all their might. Nancy had to go for more plywood, Betsy was going for this, that and the other ("a good gopher"), and the clouds were busy forming an ominous overcast.

With forerunner gusts of storm winds beginning about 11:30 am, and the plywood sheeting on both sides of the V roof down, we began sending up the rolls of roofing tar paper. A light drizzle had begun. "Ducky" Johnson, standing next to me on the ground, said in a slow drawl, "You folks could use a little help, couldn't you?"

I said, "Ducky, we sure could."

In less that 2 minutes he had all 10-12 of his men with hammers up on the roof, rolling and nailing tar paper with Kirby and our friend Hutchinson. And, Glory to God, Praise His Holy Name, by 12:30 pm with the forerunner rains of that hurricane coming down steadily, the roof was sealed in! We got all the men in a big circle around the peak of that roof and joined hands and asked Kirby to give a prayer of thanksgiving to God for all the men and all the work in His perfect timing! Since it was quite normal for all of us to be soaking wet from perspiration in those hot days of hard work, none of us were minding the rain as it came pelting down. It was feeling good!

We'll never forget nor cease thanking the Lord for "Ducky" Johnson and his tremendously hardworking crew, and for our crew. In no time they were heading to their homes and we to Judy and Dick's. As for the hurricane, the full force of it came ashore some 60 miles west of us, but there were some heavy rains and winds that afternoon and evening. Praise God for turning the worst of that hurricane away!

We had to head back to Baltimore shortly, but Kirby and Carol stayed on with their boys another two weeks or so, finishing the roof with shingles, building new porches, and an open carport with Mr. Hutchinson helping. Finally, they finished as much as they could and then went back to Tulsa to pack up for their move to Baltimore to relieve us for the soon coming tour and stay in Israel.

By the grace of God and the marvelous help of a lot of people, that old house had been spared the wrecker's ball to serve the Lord some more. What the county had paid us was not enough to complete the moving and rebuilding. It took a loan of an extra $10,000 from our brothers and sisters to finish it. We are so grateful to them. Future rents also would help Kirby and the Little Tabernacle, thanks to the careful management by our brother-in-law, Dick Gaunt.

FINDING FISHING WORMS - THE OLD TIMEY WAY!

About where that hurricane went ashore, in the area of Destin, there is a fairly large creek that flows into the Choctahatchee Bay near the long ago site of a turpentine still. Unlike moonshine, distilling turpentine in my boyhood days was a fairly large industry in the South, legal that is! Distilling moonshine probably was large too, but not legal, and not done at that turpentine still.

My Uncle Alvin, Dad's one-armed brother, who lost his arm in a saw mill accident, was in charge of the turpentine operations. There the collected gum from the huge pine trees was brought in barrels, dumped in huge vats, was boiled with the vapors collecting in the still to form the product called turpentine, and rosin; the turpentine being poured off again into barrels. These products were much in use in the shipping and paint industries, and other ways.

My brother Frank and I were privileged to live with Uncle Alvin and Aunt Lila for a couple of summers, while Mom was taking her summer school courses at Florida State College For Women. Those were some idyllic days for a couple of "twin-like" boys, roaming that plantation-type setting, doing chores for Uncle Alvin and Aunt Lila, watching the big still in operation, and going fishing up Black Creek.

Uncle Alvin was an avid hunter, as was our Dad, and was quite a sharp-shooter, even with his one arm. But Aunt Lila was the special fishing expert in the family and seemed to know exactly where to find beds of worms and beds of fish called "brim" (officially bream), a hand-size, fresh water fish that is especially "good eating." The main idea of this story is to share my amazement in how Aunt Lila filled up her bait cans quickly just before we rowed up the creek to catch those yummy fish.

She would go outside the house, under some trees where the earth was rich, and with an axe she would drive a 2 foot long stake down into the ground till about 6 or 8 inches were left above the ground. Then she would begin rubbing the side of the axe blade across the top of the stake. This would immediately set up deep vibrations in the earth. And almost before you knew it, nice fat worms would begin popping up out of the earth as far as 10 or 12 feet all around you. In no time you could fill up a couple of bait cans, and stuffing a bit of wet moss in the top of the cans, you were ready to go. Getting your bait this old-fashioned way would beat "by a mile" digging for them. I believe they called it "grunting" for worms back in those olden days.

Somehow Aunt Lila also had learned there was a special scent in the water over a bed of "brim", and could always spot this tell-tale sign! She never failed to bring home a nice mess of these tasty fish.

She was quite an amazing self-taught naturalist, and a very kind and loving Aunt to two adventuresome boys.

Many years ago when Craig and Kirby were little boys, while on vacation, and driving through old Lynn Haven, I spotted someone in an open area near the road doing what seemed to be "grunting for worms". We stopped to observe and sure enough the man's little boys were walking in a circle around him, picking up worms as they crawled out of their vibrating homes in the ground as if someone had shouted, "Fire! Run for your life!" Perhaps this old fashioned technique of fetching worms is still practiced in rural woodland regions in the South. Modern bait farms have nearly taken all the fun out of finding worms for a bream (brim) fishing trip!

In this modern day almost no one will believe this "grunting for worms" story, but it really is true. Really!

IT WASN'T EASY BEING A PREACHER'S KID!

We are hoping our boys will write their remembrances of the difficulties of being a Preacher's kid, but here are a few incidents we remember! Many of them have to do with our rides back and forth to Church from our home in the Wyndhurst area by the old "Ma and Pa" (Maryland and Pennsylvania) Railroad route.

When we first moved to Baltimore, on our way to Church at McKim Center we would drive by the statue of Martin Luther, his Bible in his hand, and our boys would call out "Hi, Martin", and we'd add, "Keep Standing on God's Word, Luther!" Well, with all the new highways, the Jones Falls Expressway, etc., Martin got moved to Lake Montebello, but he is still standing lifting up God's Word!

Not far from Lake Montebello is Clifton Park, where Old Poly played their baseball games. When Craig was about a sophomore in High School and on the baseball team, he was hiking with a friend from Poly on North Ave. to baseball practice at Clifton Park. When they neared the old Sears building, they were jumped by some bullies. One of the guys had a knife and began swinging at them, slicing up their book bags which Craig and his friend were using as shields. Somehow by God's mercy they were able to escape! When Craig told us about it, I tried to get the police to better patrol that area and arranged with Craig to walk the same route again, as I followed him on a bicycle. Our angels must have been around that day too, because there was no more attack. From then on he rode the bus. It wasn't easy growing up in the inner-city! No wonder all of our sons fell in love with Tennessee!

Then there was "Expressway-Willie!" One Sunday morning we were driving down the expressway on our way to Church, and as we rounded a curve near Druid Hill Park, there was a drunk staggering right out in the middle of the expressway!! It was a good thing it was Sunday and not much traffic. We pulled over to the side and backed up to help. When I got out of the car, the drunk thought we were a taxi. I told him we could act like one and helped him get into the car. (Our boys never knew whom we might be picking up!) So still-drunk "Willie" gave us directions, as best he could in his condition, to his home. As we drove up his street near Druid Park, he said, "I own this house, and that one, and that one." We stopped in front of a big brownstone house with many steps and I helped him stagger up those steps and rang the doorbell. Soon this tug-boat Annie of a wife, big, towering, battleaxe, opens the door slightly, looks down on us, and yells angrily, "Come in here Willie, you bum." She reaches out to grab him and says to me, "Mister, don't believe a word he says. I own it all." One could see at least one reason why Willie turned to drink! Earlier he had insisted on giving us $2 for the ride, and we used it to buy a city map. For many years we called it, "Expressway Willie's Map!"

Then there was the lady with the cough syrup! We were waiting in the car by the house when this woman comes by, wanting bus fare to go to town. Since we were going that way, we offered her a ride instead. She was obviously disheveled so the boys scooted as far away as they could as she got in the car. On the way we had to stop at Miss H'Lavacek's. Our rider looked in her bag for her "cough medicine" and pulls out a miniature bottle to take some gulps of "4 Roses," or something similar, all the while alleging to the boys, it was needed "cough syrup!" We were glad to get her to town!

Once during the coffee house at the barber school Jerome Brown had bought a muskrat at the market for his Dad. We hung it outside during the meeting, since we didn't have a refrigerator. When he went to get it to take it home, all that was left was the skeleton. The alley cats had thoroughly enjoyed the muskrat!

Then there are some way back memories at the Bight: when Craig fell into the Creek in his blue jeans and all, right off the dock, and screamed "bloody murder", not because he would drown, he could swim, but because of the jelly fish! When Kirby was little, GrandmaGin's Pastor called him "Sugar Crisp" because of his love for that cereal, and we called him the "deeper of the dookies," because he liked to be appointed guard over them and had a problem with the "k" sound!

We've written of Joe's stroller dive off the hill in Hopewell, N.J., and his later close call with death as a teenager, when his Dad heard this sound like a sink being emptied of water, and it was Joe gasping for breath.

CHAPTER 18: PREPARING FOR OUR ISRAEL ASSIGNMENT 293

Once when Chris was about 5 years old, he was attending the McKim preschool nursery with his Mom as his teacher, along with 20 other children from the neighborhood housing courts. His Mom would take him with her on visits to the children's homes to encourage the mothers. On one occasion a teenager we knew, offered to watch the kids while we visited, and playfully put Chris in this big garbage dumpster at Flag House Courts. To this day Chris can remember his state of terror as he ran over the garbage on the inside from one end to the other trying to get out of that stinking dumpster. His screams of terror soon secured his rescue!

Then there was the Church picnic in Western Maryland when Chris was about 10 years old. He was with a McKim group, fishing around a small lake and somehow ended up with a fishhook stuck in the end of his thumb. On the spot surgery was needed or a hospital trip. Before leaving home that day his Dad fortunately had honed his pen knife to razor sharpness and was able to remove the hook quickly. We had other first aid supplies with us, so Chris soon had a bandaged thumb soaked with Merthiolate and a few tears on the side. He stood it all quite bravely; his Dad was very proud of him. His Mom couldn't watch and probably hurt the most.

Brian, Bernie, Faith and Mary Shaw used to make quite a "gang." We remember their super help at News Letter time. And doing the bulletins each Sunday morning, they became real pros!! We're sure glad computers came along in time to help with mailing labels, etc, now that all of them are grown and moved far away!

Oh yes, we remember the paper routes! Those Sunday mornings stuffing papers! Then there were the "guests" we would have! Like dear Ben Goldstick, who stretched out on the kitchen floor, while drunk, feeding ham to our frowzy dog, Peaches. The Lord Jesus lifted Ben out of his miry clay, set his feet on the Rock, and made him a highly esteemed counselor in alcohol and drug addiction rehabilitation programs. Some of the others didn't make it. We remember one young man we had picked up somewhere but didn't really trust him. So when we had to go to a meeting, we told Chris not to have anything to do with him. So Chris didn't. And while we were away, he moved out of the basement, taking a carload of our things with him!

There was the time when Dusty played the Green Dragon, and when Mick McNickols told how he would offer new or used air, if a lady wanted her tires checked at the filling station?

Yes, there were a lot of good memories. We praise the Lord for each one of our boys, and for bringing all of them through for Him. Through it all!!

Probably for most preacher's kids, in all times, the "worst" thing that happened to them was that their Moms and Dads, like good Jewish parents, always insisted on taking their children with them to the worship services, all of them. At least we did with ours, trying to bring them up in the way they should go as Proverbs 22:6 instructs us. Also Deut. 5 and 6. When all their worldly friends were doing their own pleasure on the Lord's day, they were being constrained to follow a religious way and Satan began telling them that their parents were cruelly "cramming religion down their throats." This can be heard often from college professors and social workers. We profoundly hope that our children have realized that their parents were trying to be obedient to the Lord Himself Who tells us:

1) *To bring up your children in the nurture and admonition of the Lord.*
(Ephesians 6:4)
2) *To help them from childhood to know the Holy Scriptures which are able to make them wise unto salvation through faith in Christ Jesus.*
(II Tim.3:15)
3) *To help them to delight in keeping the Sabbath as holy unto the Lord, not as a fun day in the world.* (Isa. 58:13,14; Exodus 20:8-11)
4) *To help them know the TEN COMMANDMENTS and the Love commandments and to keep them.* (Deut. 5 & Exodus 20)
5) *To seek first God's kingdom and His righteousness and know that all else will be added unto them.* (Matt. 6:33)
6) *To bring your children to Jesus, and forbid them not, to come unto me: for of such is the kingdom of heaven.* (Matt.19:14)
7) *To take His yoke and learn of Him to find salvation.*(Matt.11:25-30)

The world has mocked this approach in recent decades, making it very hard for children to accept, and for parents to persist in teaching these God-given and Bible-centered concepts. We know that it's been very hard for our own children, but we will forever believe that we did what God wanted and that He will make the end of the story a good one for each one.

THE HEAVENLY ANOINTING OIL MIRACLE

As already shown, these were days of considerable pressure and hard work and excitement in the Lord's work as we pressed on to have the tour group members all lined up for the trip to Israel, to have our house in Baltimore ready for Kirby's use, or to rent; to have the Little Tabernacle affairs in good shape to turn over completely to Kirby and Carol and the Elders, and finally to complete a special three day series of meetings at the Little Tabernacle with our good friend, Edgar Baillie, who had been with us the year before. How good it was to see him and

CHAPTER 18: PREPARING FOR OUR ISRAEL ASSIGNMENT

his wife Charlotte again.

The services went extremely well. There were a number of healings, including one to an elderly little man by the name of Commander Ernest Green, who said he had been a merchant marine ship's captain in World War II. (He confided that his ship was the one that rescued John F. Kennedy in the South Pacific when his PT boat was sunk by the Japanese.) He came to these meetings because he badly needed a healing on his left leg and knee. That night Brother Baillie anointed him with some very special oil the Lord had given him, and Brother Green was marvelously healed. For the rest of his days, he was over-flowing with gratitude and praise to God and regularly attended the Little Tabernacle services as often as he could. He was about 79 at that time. (He died in 1988, at the age of 88, from a heart attack, but had attended Church up to two weeks before, always insisting that when he died, he wanted to die in the Little Tabernacle. We had the sad privilege of helping with his funeral and helping his widow, Teresa, during those days.) How he loved to sing "How Great Thou Art!"

While Edgar was with us, we had a surprise call from the Baltimore airport! It was Esther Dorflinger, just in from Israel. We had promised our tour group we would see her in Jerusalem! Here she is in the States, but she says she'll see us all at the New York airport as we are leaving for Israel! We went to the B.W.I. Airport and brought her home, fed her, and said, Esther, "Come, go to the last Edgar Baillie meeting with us."

Being very tired from traveling, she at first said, "No, I'm too tired to go." But with a little pleading and arm twisting, she finally decided she would. An unforgettable experience awaited her!

Toward the end of the long service, Bro. Edgar came over to where she was wearily sitting on a front seat, sat down beside her and asked, "Esther what hand do you use in praying for people?"

Surprised Esther said, "Well, I'm left handed, so I guess I use my left hand." So Bro. Edgar took her left hand, holding it open and laid his right hand over it and began praying for her, for her life and children, and work as God's servant around the world, and for God's anointing on her for a Special Mission the Lord was about to send her on.

Now Edgar's very special anointing oil was at least 15 feet away on the Communion table. It was a bottle of fragrant oil the Lord Himself regularly re-filled! (Believe it or not!)

When he stopped praying and took his hand off her hand, the palm of her hand was filled with the most aromatic oil one could imagine. We all looked at it in amazement, even leaned over to smell it. What a lovely scent! Suddenly Bro. Edgar, led by the Holy Spirit, lifted her left hand and placed it on her head and forehead to seal God's Holy

Anointing upon her for the coming very Special Mission she was to be sent on, about which neither she or Bro. Edgar knew a thing at that moment. How happy we all were that she did not miss that meeting, because she was going to need that anointing in the very near future.

At the J.F.Kennedy Airport with our '79 tour group, we learned of Esther's special mission! We arrived at the "jump off" point with about 18 people in our group joining up again with the Solomon pilgrims, making a total of about 45 people. Betsy and I, planning to stay at least a year, if possible, had six bags, two over the allowed limit. Fortunately, we had people with only one bag who could carry one of ours. A lady taking one of ours had trouble at the security check, because we had forgotten to show her how to open it, but was allowed through after we explained and showed her. We were very busy gathering together our pilgrims as they came in from all parts, and getting the main part of our own luggage checked through the security. Suddenly Esther appears beside us "out of nowhere" saying, "Brother Sid and Betsy, I've got to talk with you right away. Give me 5 minutes please!"

"Esther, where did you come from?"

"Connecticut, but never mind, I've got to see you!"

"Okay, just as soon as we get some order out of this chaos!"

In a few minutes we were all gathering in a large waiting room to await the call to pass through the hand luggage security and to board the plane. Now, we could go aside with Esther to see what in the world she had on her mind; her tone seemed so urgent. We stepped out in the hallway to get her story and this is what she poured out!

"During my Bible reading this morning before catching the plane here, I was reading in Acts how the Lord told Paul that as he had been His witness in Jerusalem, he would also be His witness in Rome. And the Lord said to me, 'Esther, this applies to you, I want you to go to Rome to speak to the Pope.'"

Esther then said, "I pulled the covers over my head and hid for a moment, saying, 'Not me Lord.' 'Yes, you Esther.' 'You've got to confirm this, Lord, please.'

"So at the Hartford Airport in the ladies room the cleaning woman asked me about my coat. When I told her it came from Jerusalem, she was very interested and, although a Catholic, she ended up really giving her heart to the Lord Jesus." (A lot of Catholics, as well as Protestants have made head confessions without full commitments of their hearts to Jesus.) Esther went on saying that after this confirmation, of a Jew leading a Roman Catholic to Jesus, on the flight from Hartford to J.F.K., the Lord gave her another word: "I want Sid and Betsy to go to Rome with you! Tell them to meet you there after their tour of Israel on Nov.

CHAPTER 18: PREPARING FOR OUR ISRAEL ASSIGNMENT 297

19th." We both looked at Esther with amazement and some consternation! Here we are helping to lead a large tour group to Israel, with further plans to stay on with Esther in Israel for a year. "Wasn't that enough? We were thinking!" As we went back to the meeting room it began dawning on me that if we were serving God by coming to help Esther and others in Israel, we should be willing to help her in Rome as well.

But Betsy still didn't get a clear witness and we certainly needed to be all in agreement (Ecc.4:12). This is a special Scripture that Dick Mills gave to Betsy and me, the last part of which speaks of the strength of a 3-fold cord, and we were beginning to apply it to our relationship with Esther. (There would be many, many times when the devil tried to ruin our spiritual bond.)

So back in the large room, our group was still waiting; we introduced Esther and she had a few minutes to greet them and tell them a bit about life in Israel. She apologized for meeting them on the wrong side of the ocean, but this is the way the Lord had worked it out! She did request special prayer, but did not mention the soon coming Special Mission to Rome. That was not to be divulged by any of us until after it was completed.

Then Betsy began playing on her autoharp and singing, "Henay Mah Tov" ("How good and how pleasant for brothers to dwell in unity." Ps.133) and "Stand By Israel." Suddenly, with tears in her eyes, she nodded, "Yes, we would go to Rome." (Even if it took a "Joshua March" around the Vatican!)

At that moment Betsy and I did not know how we would finance the trip of going to Rome, but began hoping that our return tour tickets (to the U.S.) would get us at least to Rome. We were in for a big surprise, because the moment we didn't come back with the tour group our return tickets were null and void.

Someone may be wondering about our responsibility to see our group all the way back home, which we think a tour leader should do, or make very sure he has adequate back-up leadership to carry out this responsibility. Fortunately the Lord had given us two fine ministers to lead the group home: Ed Schmidt and Bill Bass. They did the job quite well!

So off to Israel we go again. Our guide, Moshe Dayagi, met us with a great welcome and took us to a hotel in Tel Aviv to begin another outstanding tour of Israel. After all the recent work and activities that Betsy and I had been through, we probably were working entirely on "automatic" during this tour.

One thing that we found helpful on some of the long drives was to get different ones of the group to share a song or a miracle story, or how they came to know Jesus as their Saviour. One of the most moving ever heard on such a tour was the testimony that Ed Schmidt gave. He told on the bus mike how he as a drug addict for 16 years in and out of prisons and hospitals, had found Jesus and had been wonderfully transformed. We especially wanted Moshe and our Jewish driver to hear this testimony. Maybe the driver heard, even though busy driving that big bus. But Moshe, in the guide's special seat, had a Hebrew newspaper open in front of him the whole time, acting like he was busy reading. Frankly, I think he was busy listening.

Another sidelight was the hot sulfa baths at the Dead Sea, which many of us enjoyed, including Ed Schmidt. He shouldn't have, because a sign warned people with heart problems to avoid the baths. Also there, several of us walked around on the Beach, Betsy with the autoharp, singing Hebrew and Christian songs as sort of balladeers, to the delight of a number of the Israelis.

All too soon these precious tours end and we were back at the airport tearfully hugging and kissing and waving goodbye to the tour group. By this time Betsy and I were feeling like two lonely, little people about to be left far, far behind in a strange land. But as usual when that spirit comes around, we quickly kick it out and head for the next step the Lord says to take. Esther had given us a key to her apartment, so we found a sherut (or taxi) and headed for Jerusalem and out to her apartment in Ramot. We knew we had to find some food for the weekend coming up and find out some way to get round trip tickets to Rome on the 19th, the coming Tuesday.

The money we had saved to help us in the living expenses while in Israel was in a bank check which could only be deposited in a dollar account, taking some two weeks to clear. So we went to The Ambassador Tours, Mrs. Sarah Fetterman in charge, who began reservations for us to Rome for the 19th, but somehow we had to come up with $800 to $900 in cash for an 8 day round-trip economy flight to Rome. Finally, at the last minute on the day we were to leave, we found a bank that advanced us the money on our Visa card, which we rushed back to Mrs. Fetterman. Shortly we were on our way back to the airport with tickets to Rome. We landed there about 6:30 p.m.

As soon as we found our bags and passed customs in the Rome airport, we began looking for Esther. At last we spotted her waving madly in the waiting crowd! Each of us was so very happy to see a familiar looking face in that crowded airport. It seemed full of refugees from eastern communist countries. With special guidance from the Lord, she had found rooms for us at a convent hospice (Casa Nostra), only a short distance from the Vatican. There we would stay and pray and seek and knock on doors and ask to see the Pope!

CHAPTER 18: PREPARING FOR OUR ISRAEL ASSIGNMENT

Several people said to Esther, "You want to see the Pope? Well, good luck, I've been here for two years trying to see him." The Pope could be seen at the great public audiences in a huge Vatican Auditorium on Wednesdays, or at times speaking from his apartment balcony above the huge crowds at St. Peter's Square on Sundays, but to see him personally is something else entirely, almost impossible! No doubt it would require a special invitation, or a special appointment arranged by a Cardinal or some other high Vatican official. Since the Lord had told Esther to speak to the Pope, it began looking as though He would have to make the special appointment, for the closest we would get in that first week, was tickets to the Wednesday public audience and on Sunday with the multitude in St. Peter's square.

We went to the public audience that Wednesday, along with 25,000 other people and quickly saw that it was almost impossible to even get close to him, as he walked down a long closed aisle, to the auditorium stage where he had a special raised seat in front of a large group of Cardinals. As he walked down that long aisle, he was smiling and occasionally reaching over to touch someone's hand or head. There would be hundreds of people reaching out to touch him. Yes sir, it would take a miracle from God for Esther to see him in so short a time.

Our eight days of praying, fasting and seeking were coming to an end. On the 7th day, the Lord gave us a Word of knowledge that our stay would be extended one day! So on the 8th day, when we all went to the airport for Betsy and me to fly back to Tel Aviv, we found the flight had been canceled; we would have to go the following day. It was sort of a one day reprieve for Esther, before she would have to go it alone, and we would have to go back to Israel to try to find some expense money to send her. In fact we were all running out of money by the end of that week. When later we did send her some money, it never reached her, because "The Holy Spirit Bank of Rome" (What a sacrilege!) was on strike!!!. So the Lord by His Holy Spirit led a friend at the American Embassy to bail her out on her last day in Rome.

During that week we had enjoyed touring the Vatican and seeing the beautiful Sistine Chapel and having lunch with Leo, a Vatican radio broadcaster, who questioned Esther's sanity! "How could she really expect such a meeting in such a short time and being such an unknown?"

Two other unusual and somewhat upsetting things happened. The first one was in a nice little restaurant not far from the Vatican, eating Esther's favorite spaghetti meal, when suddenly it dawned on us it was Thanksgiving Day (1979) back in America and this dawning brought visions of turkeys and cranberry sauce and families together and the Puritans praying. What in the world were we doing in Rome on this special day? We looked at each other and said, "Happy Thanksgiving Day, Family, wherever you are!" But we were being made Family in a special way that day in Rome by the Lord--just eating Italian spaghetti!

The other incident grew into a small miracle of God. Someone had invited us to a dinner one evening at an English Seminary. Coming back to our hospice on a very crowded bus about 9 p.m. that night, apparently a professional pick-pocket in the crowd contrived to lift my wallet during the jostling ride. When we arrived near the hospice, I suddenly realized my wallet was gone! Gone, with credit cards, drivers license, and maybe $25 in cash. The bus was still stopped, so we went back and searched through the bus, but no wallet. Somehow, we learned the police station was back in the direction we came from, so we went back on the bus to the Central Police Station. There they told us to come back the next morning to fill out papers. But Esther needed to use the rest room, and apparently at that time of night there was no ladies room available. Finally, a friendly gendarme stood resolutely, with his arms crossed, in front of the gentlemen's room while she made use of that facility. Surely chivalry was not dead!

Praise the Lord, we got back to the hospice just before the doors were locked for the night! The next day we went back to the police station and filled out the necessary report, next to a Chinese couple also filing a report of the wife's purse being snatched by a motor scooter thief. The detective spoke some English and told us there was not much chance of ever seeing the wallet again, but if it was ever found, they would turn it over to the U.S. Embassy which would send it to us in the States. Later we all agreed in prayer asking the Lord to have it returned.

Amazingly, about two months later, it did arrive back at the Little Tabernacle in Baltimore with all the cards, but no cash. The Lord had done it again! Ten years later, I was still using it, but finally had to retire it!

On the ninth day we again went back by bus to the airport, about 30 miles west of Rome, and found our flight to Israel was on schedule, so we tearfully said "Goodbye" to "Little Orphan Esther", and headed to the flight gate for Israel; one of us dropping off a few tracts as we went. (Guess who?!) We found a seat for about a half hour wait, and then we noticed what looked like an American tour group coming in to wait for that same flight. Suddenly we recognized one who came walking by us! Without getting up, we said, "Hello Eula, How are you?"

She looked down and casually said, "Hello", and kept on with her group. Suddenly, she did the biggest double-take you ever saw and came running back to give us big hugs. She said, "I didn't recognize you. This is Rome! What are you doing here? You're supposed to be in Israel!"

CHAPTER 18: PREPARING FOR OUR ISRAEL ASSIGNMENT 301

"You're right, Eula. That's where we are headed right now. We'll explain later why we are in Rome."

She exclaimed, "We kept seeing tracts with the Little Tabernacle name on them and wondered if they ever clean up this place! Your tour would have come through here long ago. So that's how those tracts got here, you left them, just now!" (Actually, none of our tours had ever stopped in Rome.)

It turned out that our seats were together on that plane, and we had a great time sharing with her and others in her group, but could only say that Esther had asked us to come with her for a week in Rome. Esther did not want us to be telling the real objective until the Lord brought it to pass! Which He surely did 8 days later, on Wednesday, Dec. 6, 1979!

THE GREAT HOUSE MOVING OLD 310 THIRD CT. P.C. 9/79
7 MILES AWAY TO LYNN HAVEN, FLA.
BOTTOM SHOWS RENOVATED HOME AT 1414 MISSOURI AVE. 8/81

302 FIRED AGAIN AND AGAIN, PRAISE THE LORD!

DUCKY JOHNSON'S CREW HELPS SEAL ROOF BEFORE STORM

TWO WEARY CARPENTERS DAD AND SON KIRBY

CHIEF CARPENTER WITH WIFE, CAROL AND 2 LITTLE HELPERS: MATTHEW AND PETER,- 9/79

CHAP. 19

OUR RAMOT YEAR IN JERUSALEM

And he said unto me, 'My grace is sufficient for thee; for My strength is made perfect in weakness.' - II Corinthians 12:9

"ONE DAY AT A TIME, SWEET JESUS"

Before we parted from Eula and her tour group at the Ben Gurion Airport, we were invited by the Pastor to visit them at their hotel in East Jerusalem and to share with them the following Sunday about our love for Israel.

After a night's rest at Esther's apartment in Ramot, we went to the bank, where we had deposited the bank check we brought from the States and found we could now withdraw a couple of hundred dollars to send to Esther in Rome. The bank would send it by an inter-bank transfer to the neighborhood bank near Esther. We were told she should have it in a day or two, easy.

Esther went everyday for the rest of her time in Rome, but the bank stayed on strike. The Lord had to use His true Holy Spirit Bank in Heaven to arrange finances another way for her, as said before. It took over three months of "bugging" our bank in Jerusalem before the Italian bank sent the money back! So much for fund transfers to Rome. Thank God, He is able to provide in other ways!

The following Sunday morning rolled around, and we had decided to go to the 9 o'clock English service at the Garden Tomb, which reportedly was very good, and it was! To catch the bus into Jerusalem, we had to leave the apartment on the run without breakfast, and were able to walk the last mile to the Garden. We were not yet familiar on how to make proper bus transfers.

After worship, we had to hike to downtown Jerusalem to do some errands, Sunday being a full business day for the Israelis. Then we had to walk back to East Jerusalem to find Eula's tour group's hotel, which finally we did. All the while still no food that day, and we arrived at the hotel just as they were finishing their lunch. Groan! So they were ready to meet for our sharing time. We had a good meeting with them

304   FIRED AGAIN AND AGAIN, PRAISE THE LORD!

and closed with a couple of the Hebrew songs we had learned, like "Shalom Allechem" (Peace to You), and "Henay Mah Tov" (Behold How Good). After prayer for their group it was time to bid farewell to Eula and her friends and begin again our up and down hike to the nearest bus #35 stop for the ride out to Ramot.

Remember now, that we left our handy little car back in the states, and our little legs were not used to all this up and down walking, and our tummies were used to at least a good Sunday dinner. We must say, to put it mildly, we were nearly exhausted by the time we got on the bus, and almost wondering what in the world we were doing here?

At last the bus came, loaded to the "gunnels" (to use an old sailing expression). We were able to squeeze on, pay our fare, and inch our way to the rear. Someone getting off let Betsy have her seat, and I stood jammed up against the seat, holding on to the hand rail above, trying to look like a veteran at it, and my right knee 'a-killing me'.
So off we went on the 4 to 5 mile round-about, up and down, jam-packed, rough-rider, cow-boy bus drive out to Ramot, with the conversations around us all Hebrew. We certainly were a long way from home, definitely in a foreign land, very weary and hungry!

Nearing Ramot, in my vertical doze, I suddenly realized that the bus radio had changed its tune, to a tune that I was understanding, a tune that was saying something special to us. How could it be?!

I reached down and nudged Betsy, "Listen, Betsy, to the bus radio. They're playing our tune, just for us in English! Hallelujah". Here's what we were hearing:

> "One Day At A Time, Sweet Jesus,[1]
> That's all I'm asking of you,
> Just give me the strength to do every day
> What I have to do-o-o.
> Yesterday's gone, sweet Jesus,
> And tomorrow may never be mine,
> Lord, help me today, show me the way.
> One day at a time." - Marijohn Wilkin

This was December 3, 1979, on the Israel Radio! A song about Jesus! With lyrics! Glory To God! And a special song for us at a moment of great weariness and need. The Lord was telling us that He knew

---

[1] Words and music by Marijohn Wilkin and Kris Kristofferson. Copyright 1973 by Buckhorn Music Publishers, Inc. Used by permission. International copyright secured. All rights secured.

CHAPTER 19: OUR RAMOT YEAR IN JERUSALEM

exactly where we were, how weary we were, and could penetrate all barriers to get us a word of encouragement. We were so grateful, we almost wept as we bounced off the bus and ran up the next big hill to Esther's apartment, totally refreshed by our Lord's loving remembrance and encouragement. Isn't He mighty? That Song is forever a favorite of ours!

"PUT YOUR HAND IN THE HAND OF JESUS"

Some years later, we met in Israel through some beautiful friends, the Hugh McLains, from Zimbabwe (formerly Rhodesia), one of the nicest young men we've ever known. Peter was sound and mature in faith and character and love for Jesus. He had completed his military active duty in the Rhodesian army as a young officer, facing many very dangerous missions. His family owned a large productive fruit farm there. He was spending three months in Israel wanting to help the Christians and Jews as best he could, at the end of a year-long knapsack tour around the world. For some time he did volunteer work for the Christian Embassy in Jerusalem and lived near us on Shimoni St. Some Israelies living on a collective fruit farm (a moshav) in northern Israel, in the Hula Valley, invited him to come to visit them and help trim fruit trees on the farm, which he was delighted to do. Finally, his time was up on the farm and he was heading back to Jerusalem for the last few days to see his friends there, including us, before departing for Zimbabwe, necessarily via England.

The farm family brought him to the main north-south highway to catch the Egged bus south around the Sea of Galilee, down the Jordan River Valley to Jericho, then up to Jerusalem, another rather rough ride. But as he was enjoying the scenic ride down the winding road to the Sea of Galilee, on that Israeli bus sitting next to a young Hassid (an Ultra-orthodox Jew with black hat, black suit, and side-curls), he was startled to hear on the bus radio a very special song, in English, as we had. Peter began hearing this precious song just as they rounded the upper part of the beautiful Sea of Galilee:

> "Put Your Hand In The Hand Of The Man
> Who Rules The Waters;
> Put your hand in the hand of the Man
> Who calms the sea,
> Take a look at yourself,
> And you will look at others differently;
> Put your hand in the hand of the man from
> Galilee.!"

Peter had done exactly that, and His mighty Lord Jesus was blessing Him, too, for blessing His land and His people Israel. Peter looked around at the religious fellow next to him with a big smile and found the young man blocking his ears with his side curls. How desperately sad that the deception, concerning who Jesus was and is, still continues. The evidence of the saving power of Jesus is all around us, even sitting next to you on an Israeli bus and getting a special word of encouragement from our living Lord, even as Peter Coventry was getting that day!

THE WEEPING PHONE CALL FROM ROME

Oh yes, you're wondering whatever happened to Esther back in Rome. We are glad you are wondering and reminding us to get back to that remarkable story. We left her with tearful farewells on November 28 and thought we had sent her some financial help, but no word until late in the day on December 6th. A collect call from one Esther Dorflinger in Rome, will we take it? We sure will! And there she was weeping on the other end of the line and shouting,

"He did it! He did it! The Lord did it!"

"Did what, Esther?"

"He gave the miracle of meeting the Pope personally!"

"You're kidding."

"No I'm not kidding, I was able to get a special ticket from the Bishop we applied to, for the front row on the right side, and after the Pope delivered his speech in the six languages, he came down to pray for the crippled children in front of me. Then he came straight to me and asked who I was!

"I told him, 'A Jewish Believer in Jesus.'

"And he said, 'Bless you my child and your people Israel.'

"I don't know what else he said, but he talked with me several more moments and then seeing the letter I had clutched in my hand he asked, 'Is that for me?'

"I stammered, 'Yes, it is.'

"He said, 'Give it to me, I promise I will read it.'"

She said, "No one believes me, but it really happened!"

We said, "We believe you, Esther! You can tell us all about it when you come."

The next day we met her at Ben Gurion airport and rode back in a sherut with her and another lady coming in from the States trying to catch up with her tour group. All the way back to Jerusalem, Esther was giving us a "blow-by-blow" account of what had happened since we left her in Rome on the 28th. But at this time Esther had no way under the sun to confirm that she had talked to the Pope. None whatever! She needed confirmation and the Lord wonderfully provided it. A little nun in Rome, who had heard Esther speak to a Charismatic group, was passing the Pope's official photographer's shop and "just happened" to look in the window at a display of recent pictures of people taken with the Pope. Lo and behold, there was a beautiful picture of the Pope talking to Esther! She immediately arranged to get a copy and sent it post-haste to Esther in Israel. The Lord had wonderfully provided the confirmation, the proof that she had actually talked with the Pope in just under three weeks after the Lord had sent her to Rome to speak to him.

Later, we were to learn that the Pope had helped many Jews escape during the holocaust and, after becoming Pope, his first audience was given to a Jewish family. Also each week at that time, he played tennis with a good friend, a Jewish man, who happened to be the first-cousin of Esther's high-court case lawyer in Jerusalem, Uri Huppert! Our God can do anything, but fail! Praise His Holy Name!

Sad to say, however, the Vatican and the Roman Catholic Church have never recognized Israel as a bonafide nation, to their great shame and discredit. We believe that God's judgement against them will be heavy. May this Pope help them turn this rejection around to full recognition!

We all went back to Esther's apartment and the next day we helped Pattie catch up with her tour group. She turned out to be the Lord's connection for Esther to meet the leader of the tour group, a Dr. Robinson, and have dinner with the group. We were also included. This tour leader, Dr. Robinson, was a member of the committee in Washington arranging the Presidential Prayer Breakfast in January, who would help obtain an invitation for Esther to represent Israel at the Breakfast and speak to a group of Congressional wives. God's amazing connections never cease!

HEAVENLY CONNECTIONS

All kinds of amazing, heavenly connections were being made during our first month in Jerusalem and that Christmas with Esther.

There was the meeting by Esther with Dr. Robinson's tour group which later resulted in her invitation to the Washington Prayer breakfast. There was the injury to Mrs. Yoder, which required a stay in The Hadassah hospital, and necessitated our daily trips with Mr. Yoder, the distinguished looking, grey-bearded, husband to visit her in the hospital. The meeting with the wounded soldier, Malachi, and sharing with him and his girl friend, "One Day At a Time, Sweet Jesus"! (She said it was on the Israel "Hit Parade" and was her favorite!) The gathering of some 20 precious Believers for that pre-Christmas dinner, two of whom were a special surprise: Russell Moore and Harold Morris from the Southwest Bible College in Birmingham, Alabama.

When Russell called, Esther immediately invited them to come for Christmas dinner with us. Russell was in Israel several years before as part of a Bible study and witnessing team and had met Esther then. Now this courageous young man, given only a few more days to live from the ravages of cancer, moving about with an artificial limb from a recent amputation, determined to fulfill his last wish on earth, to see and express his love for Israel one more time, was here for that pre-Christmas dinner, telling how the Lord was making it possible, with the help of his faithful friend, ex-con Harold Morris. You must read Harold Morris's own amazing story in his book, "Twice Pardoned," published by Focus on The Family. We have permission to quote Chapter 15, "Angels, Brother, Angels", Harold's account of Russell's last visit to Jerusalem.

"ANGELS, BROTHER, ANGELS"[2]
by: Harold Morris

I stared at him, unable to absorb the news. Receiving two life sentences was nothing compared to this. Twelve days to live!

What does one say to someone who learns he is dying when he has just begun? As I looked at Russell - a young man who was sold out to Christ, who studied the Word of God every day, who lived to witness--I could think of nothing to say. Finally, I found my voice,

"Russell," I asked softly, "what are you going to do?"

"I want to do three things before I die," he said. "First, I'll continue my Bible college training because the Word of God is my life. Second, I'd give anything to go with you to a prison and hold a service for the inmates. Third, I must go to Israel. God has called me to that country to witness to the Jews. I want to die there."

Russell attended classes for another week. Growing weaker each day, he asked me to see if the college president would arrange for him to speak to the student body before returning to the hospital. The chapel was packed with students and faculty as Russell challenged us

---

[2] This chapter, "Angels, Brother, Angels," is from Harold Morris' outstanding book "Twice Pardoned," co-authored with Dianne Barker, published by Focus On The Family, copyright 1986. Used with permission.

CHAPTER 19: OUR RAMOT YEAR IN JERUSALEM

never to forsake God's calling.

"Some of you are playing games with God," he said. "When you came here you had a vision and a purpose. But you've lost that direction. You know that you're playing games. It's time to get serious with God."

When he finished, every student and faculty member stood with tear-stained faces. The ovation was for the living Christ, whom Russell had chosen to honor, whether in life or in death. His mother and I helped him leave the stage, and that night he entered the hospital to die.

I visited Russell every day. At his bedside, I'd pretend to search the covers, exclaiming, "There's a leg missing! I think you have cancer!"

He'd laugh and say, "You're different. I really feel comfortable around you." Sometimes in the middle of the night he'd call saying, "Brother, I need to see you. Come minister to me."

Twelve days passed, yet he clung to life. His mother stayed by his side as he underwent chemotherapy and suffered the notorious side effects. He lost his hair and a great deal of weight. At times, visitors were restricted when his white blood count dropped, leaving him susceptible to infection. One day as I started into his room, he stopped me.

"Hold it! My white blood count is down to 800. Brother, before you take another step, please pray that it will double. I believe God will do it if we just pray."

The next morning he called me. "Hey, brother, it didn't double. It tripled!"

During the next few weeks, Russell was in and out of the hospital many times. Although he struggled with pain, he never lost his faith, his fervor for witnessing, or his sense of humor. I was already grieving for him, and one day as we drove through Birmingham, he teased me out of my somber mood.

"Why are you so quiet? Don't be glum. Listen, brother. So what if I die? Just think. I'll be in Heaven! If you have a flat down here, and you're too lazy to change it, I could send a couple of angels down to help. And another thing, I'll have seniority over you when you get there."

Hardly a day went by that he didn't beg me to go to Israel.

"Russell, I can't go. You know I'm on parole. Get your dad or someone else."

"You're it," he said, "You're the only one who can pull it off."

Even if I dared risk violating parole, I didn't have the money to make the trip. Russell had already thought of that. He had an insurance check that would cover most of the cost. Torn between what I wanted to do and what I could do, I prayed. On one of my visits to the hospital,

I met Russell's physician.

"How's he doing?" I asked.

"Not very well," he said. "The right lung is completely gone, and only one-third of the left one remains. I don't know how he's breathing. I'd give him no more that four days to live." I walked to my friend's bedside.

"Russell, if you knew that you only had four days to live, what would you do with your life?"

"I'd go to Israel. I want to die in that country."

"Let's go!" I said, "God, it's up to You," I prayed.

"I love you, brother!" he said, reaching up to hug my neck.

Immediately his health began to improve. He called for the doctor and bargained, "If you'll let me go home, I'll eat vegetables and get strong. I'm going to spend Christmas in Israel!"

The doctor loved Russell as a son and reluctantly agreed to his making the trip. "People will call me a fool for letting him go," he sighed, "And they'll call you a fool for going," he said to me.

"They've called me a fool all my life, but I don't care," I said, "I've made my decision."

He gave detailed instructions about Russell's medical care and asked if I could administer the injection every five hours.

I assured him I knew how to use needles. I had used drugs before I became a Christian, and had given injections to other inmates. He typed a letter authorizing me to carry the drugs and syringes.

"Give this to the captain of the plane and to any authorities who question you," he said. "If a problem arises, tell them to call me collect. I'll be praying for you."

Not all my friends at the Bible college endorsed our plans.

"You will violate parole by leaving the country," a professor pointed out. "And Russell is not physically able to make an eleven-day trip. If that boy dies, you'll be locked up. We don't want that to happen."

I figured that if God hadn't wanted me to go, I would not have received a passport. But I'd obtained one months earlier - before Russell even suggested the trip.

Whenever I discussed my passport with Russell, he smiled knowingly.

"Angels, brother," he said merrily, "Angels!"

The next morning Russell's parents drove us to the airport. Although they realized that they might never see their son alive again, they understood the desire that consumed him, and they did not try to discourage him. As I pushed his wheelchair up the ramp at the Birmingham airport that sunny Sunday morning in December of 1979, his mother hugged us both and said, "Take care of him, Harold."

CHAPTER 19: OUR RAMOT YEAR IN JERUSALEM

"We'll be back," I said, trying to appear confident.

During our flight to New York and our eleven-hour flight to Israel, Russell witnessed to anyone who would listen. Most of the passengers were Jewish, and were drawn to him, curious about his reasons for traveling while so obviously ill. Even flight attendants knelt by his side as he shared God's Word and his reasons for going to Israel. After finishing he'd say,

"You haven't heard anything yet. Listen to his story."

I'd give them round two! At one point during our trip I felt a nudge on my shoulder and turned to find a flight attendant in tears.

"Sir, I'm thankful to God that you and that young boy were on this plane," she said. "I was ready to divorce my husband, but because of that young man, I have recommitted myself to Christ and to my marriage. I had to thank you. Please look after him."

We rented a car as soon as we arrived in Tel Aviv. The doctor had cautioned me that the slightest exercise would exhaust Russell, decreasing his chances for survival. He had stressed that driving was out of the question. But as soon as we rented a car, Russell announced, "I want to drive."

"Take over," I said, and he headed toward Jerusalem forty miles away. We were barely a mile out of Tel Aviv when we passed two young hitchhikers - girls dressed in military uniforms. Russell stopped, and the soldiers climbed into the backseat. One spoke English fluently, having graduated from Boston University. She listened as Russell shared his faith. When we reached her home in Jerusalem, she gave us her phone number and suggested we have dinner together after we had toured some of the cities.

Russell and I found a room at the Moriah Hotel and planned our sightseeing so he would have adequate rest and receive his injections on schedule. Every five hours he filled the syringe and brought it to me, waking me during the night at the appropriate hour.

Wherever we went, people were attracted to Russell. Many approached him on the street, giving him the very thing he wanted - an opportunity to witness. He shared Christ with everyone he met. After two days in Jerusalem, he suggested we return to Tel Aviv. From there we drove to the beautiful city of Haifa, arriving in late afternoon. The strenuous trip had drained Russell's energy, and he seemed to take a turn for the worse. But after resting through the night and eating green vegetables, he began to regain strength.

On the sixth day, Russell woke me at three in the morning and asked me to give him an injection. Handing me the syringe, he said, "Harold, this is the last of the drugs."

"What?" I asked, stunned.

"I was supposed to take one vial every five hours, but the pain was so bad, I've had to double the dose. "There's no more morphine."

I was frantic. By morning Russell was trembling with pain again, and he was spitting up parts of the tumor. I went to see the local druggist. He read the letter from Russell's doctor and said he could not give us the drugs. When I begged him to call Russell's doctor collect, he refused.

I returned to the hotel to call the doctor myself, and when I arrived, I could see that Russell was deteriorating rapidly. When I reached Birmingham on the telephone, the doctor was in surgery. I left a message with Russell's mother to get in touch with the doctor.

By late afternoon, Russell was bleeding from the mouth, spitting up dead tissue, and slipping in and out of consciousness. Desperate, I telephoned several doctors and pleaded for help, but none of them understood the urgency of our situation. I thought of robbing the drugstore, then shoved the thought aside. Desolate, I fell to my knees beside Russell's bed and prayed.

Reading again the letter from Russell's doctor, I noticed for the first time a passage of Scripture he had penned on the top of the page: *"Therefore, whether you eat or drink, or whatever you do, do all to the glory of God"* (I Corinthians 10:31). The words comforted me.

Moments later the telephone rang. It was the druggist, who said that Russell's doctor had called. If I could find a doctor to write a prescription, he would fill it. The druggist gave me the number of a physician who spoke English. He came to the hotel right away.

After examining Russell, the doctor said, "He's dying. He may not live through the night. What are you doing in Israel at a time like this?"

While the doctor gave Russell a series of injections, I repeated the story. The doctor shook his head in amazement.

"Here is enough medication for the night," he said. "I will check on him at eight in the morning. If he is alive, I will see that the druggist gives you all the medication you need."

Through the night I administered Russell's shots and prayed. About 3 A.M. he opened his eyes. I ran to the bed and squeezed his hand. He was thirsty and asked for an orange drink. I hunted the streets of Haifa and finally returned an hour later with the drink. In the morning I bought vegetables for him and bathed him before the doctor arrived. Surprised to find the patient much improved, he went to see the druggist and returned with enough medication for the remainder of our stay in Israel.

After resting for two days, Russell was ready to go again; we headed for the coastal city of Nahariya. Russell phoned a Christian family who had recently moved there from Great Britain, and we were invited to visit. While Russell rested, our hosts' nine-year-old son,

CHAPTER 19: OUR RAMOT YEAR IN JERUSALEM

David, came to me. His eyes were dark with sorrow.

"Why is he dying? It's not fair!"

"Son, there are many things I don't understand," I said. "God's ways are not our ways, and His thoughts aren't ours. Right now I can't tell you why this is happening, but you must trust God. One day we will understand."

"Will you do me a favor?" he asked. "When you go back to the United States, will you call me if Russell dies?"

"I promise," I said.

When it was time to leave, David's father followed us to the car with a Bible in his hand.

"I'd like to share a verse of Scripture with you before you go," he said. The verse he read was I Corinthians 10:31: *"Therefore, whether you eat or drink, or whatever you do, do it all to the glory of God."*

Russell gave me a knowing look and said, "Angels, brother, angels!"

On the way back to Jerusalem we hit a rugged stretch of road going about thirty-five miles per hour. In the middle of nowhere, the car left the road and came to a stop in a rocky area, nearly turning over. Russell was thrown to the floor. I visualized the headline: "Ex-Convict Kills Boy Dying of Cancer in Israel." The engine had stopped on impact, and I was certain the car had sustained heavy damage. But I turned on the ignition, and to my surprise, the motor started. After backing out of the rocks, I looked the car over. There wasn't a dent, and it ran as well as it had before the accident. Again Russell offered an explanation: "Angels, brother, angels!"

The next day, we attended a worship service at the Garden Tomb, believed to be the setting of Christ's resurrection. I bundled Russell up in a blanket to shield him against the early morning chill. Looking toward Golgotha, the rocky hill where Jesus was crucified, Russell spoke softly. "He's real, Harold, He's alive. Tell others that He is alive."

The following day, we were invited to the home of a girl named Esther, whom we had met at the Garden Tomb. There were about twenty-five guests, and several trusted Christ after Russell gave his testimony. As soon as we returned to our hotel, she telephoned.

"You will not believe this," she said. "But tomorrow you and Russell have been invited to the Knesset to visit Yechiel Kadishai. He is the second most powerful man in the country -- Prime Minister Begin's top aide and closest friend!"

How had such an unlikely meeting been arranged? It seems that Esther -- an ordinary girl with courage reminiscent of the Biblical queen -- recognized in Russell such love for Christ that she called Mr. Kadishai. When she explained that Russell had come to Israel because of his great love for the Jewish people, he agreed to meet with us.

Russell stayed awake all night writing two messages from Romans 10 and 11. The next day -- Christmas Eve -- Esther drove us to the Knesset, where we were welcomed warmly by Mr. Kadishai, "Come in I've been expecting you." he said, shaking our hands. As we walked into his office, I noticed a door to the left. Mr. Kadishai pulled a chair close to Russell and sat facing him. Russell unfolded one of the messages he had prepared, opened his Bible, and shared with the Israeli leader about Christ the Messiah.

After a while Mr. Kadishai took the Bible and shared with Russell from the Old Testament. He then presented me with an autographed copy of a book he had written, "Myths and Facts of 1978, A Concise Record of the Arab-Israeli Conflict."

After I related my story and shared my faith in Christ, Mr. Kadishai spoke:. "So you were in prison?" he said, "Menachem Begin was in solitary confinement in Russia. He wrote a book, 'White Nights' detailing his experiences. Mr. Begin chose the title because the desert nights -- viewed from his prison cell -- were never dark."

Mr. Kadishai rose and disappeared through the door I had noticed when we entered the room. In a moment he returned with Menachem Begin!

"May God bless, young man," Mr. Begin said as he shook my hand. Then, turning to Russell, his warm expression changed to shock, at the severity of Russell's condition. He walked over to Russell and extended his hand in friendship.

"May God be with you, young man," Mr. Begin said.

Without a moment's hesitation, Russell reached into his pocket for his second message and handed it to Israel's Prime Minister.

"Mr. Begin, I prepared this for you. If you'll study it, sir, you'll see that Jesus is the Messiah. One day every knee will bow and every tongue confess that He is Lord."

Mr. Begin placed the paper in his pocket and talked with us for a long while. Finally, I said to Mr. Begin, "Thank you, sir, for letting us come today. It is a day we will never forget. But I must share one thing before we leave. When Russell was told he had perhaps only four days to live, I asked what he wanted to do with his life. He said he wanted to come to Israel and to die in this country. He loves you and your people enough that he has come here to die." Mr. Begin wrapped his arms around Russell as a father would embrace his son, and I saw tears in his eyes as he spoke:

"May God be with you, young man, because you are a winner. And one day you will return to Israel." He turned and left the room.

Russell and I returned to our hotel, marveling that God had brought

CHAPTER 19: OUR RAMOT YEAR IN JERUSALEM

such important men into our lives. We spent Christmas Day in Bethlehem, the birthplace of our Saviour. That night we attended a worship service in the field of Boaz. The message, "Mary Had A Little Lamb," rang with meaning. I wrapped my arm around Russell and thought of the life and death of the blessed Lamb of God.

Russell's health continued to decline daily, and he seemed satisfied that he had accomplished what God wanted him to do in Israel. I arranged for an earlier flight home. God had blessed our journey beyond my expectations. Although we had no advanced reservations, He always found a room for us. He protected Russell from diarrhea, which the doctor warned would be deadly in his weakened condition. And He opened numerous opportunities for Russell to share his faith.

Having lived his dream, Russell no longer smiled. On the plane he expended all his energy witnessing. His suffering intensified hour by hour, and although I knew God was in charge, I couldn't understand why He was allowing this. The closer we got to New York, the more distressed I became.

In New York I carried him through the airport like a rag doll and sat him in a chair while I called his mother; he fell asleep. As we arrived in Birmingham at 3 a.m. Russell squeezed my hand weakly and said, "Let's pray."

I'll never forget his words:

"Father, thank You for letting me live my dream. Thank You for bringing me home to see my mother once more. And Father, please bless those who are less fortunate than I am."

I saw that he was crying, and I knew he was praying for me. Russell faced his death with calm serenity while I was distraught. He thought I was less fortunate because I did not see God's hand in his suffering.

Russell lived forty-two days after our arrival back in the United States and I saw him nearly every day. On the morning of February 7, 1980, Russell had been scheduled to speak at the Georgia State Penitentiary. When he realized he didn't have the strength to make it, he urged me to go in his place.

I called the hospital that morning and spoke with him. "Russell, I love you, and I want to thank you for the impact you've had on my life. I've lived many years, but you are so young. If I could, I would take your place and die with honor."

"I know that," Russell whispered. Struggling for breath, he added, "You're a loyal friend, Harold, but never forget this: it's loyalty to Christ that counts."

That was our last conversation. A few hours later, Russell was with Jesus. Through his friendship, I learned that it isn't the length of one's life that counts, but the quality of one's years. God had received more glory from Russell's twenty-two years than from all the time I had lived.

In prison I had learned that loyalty to friends is good, but from Russell I learned that faithfulness to Christ is far more important. Seeing Russell's faith caused mine to grow.

Accepting his death, I saw what man's existence is all about. Romans 1:16 was the theme of his life: *For I am not ashamed of the gospel of Christ, for it is the power of God to salvation for everyone who believes, for the Jew first and also for the Greek.*

That was Russell Moore. His life was woven into the fabric of my being, a continual reminder of what mighty things God can do through the man who is faithful.

(NOTE: This ends the chapter, "Angels, Brother, Angels," from Harold Morris' remarkable book, "TWICE PARDONED." Esther was enabled by the Lord to be in the States for Russell's funeral in Birmingham while here for the Presidential Prayer Breakfast, 1980.)

THE BLACK DOG STORY

THE MIRACLE OF THE MAN WITH THE BLACK DOG - On May 2, 1980

Our friend Edgar Baillie was in Jerusalem with his tour group and had an evening meeting in the American Colony Hotel, attended by some 50 to 60 people. During the early part of the meeting a tall man with a black dog beside him walked in and sat down but, not for long. During a story shared by another visitor, the man with the black dog suddenly got up and left, obviously offended by some remark or other. We all joined in prayer and asked the Lord to help this man, and to open a way of forgiveness and reconciliation. Thereafter, Edgar ministered, and the Lord blessed in many ways.

The following night some six miles away on Ramot mountain, as Esther, Mandi, Barnabas, Betsy and I walked to the corner to catch our ride back to another meeting at the hotel, who walks by in the dark? But the man with the black dog! He recognized us, and we talked briefly. Indeed he had been offended. We apologized and asked him to forgive. He did and ended up asking us to come have coffee in his near-by Ramot apartment. Our ride came and off he went in the dark.

Some three busy weeks later, we were out hiking with our little friend, Rachel, and whom do we meet again? But the man with the black dog! Once more we were invited to visit, and a few nights later, we had a delightful time in his apartment, with cookies and coffee. For

CHAPTER 19: OUR RAMOT YEAR IN JERUSALEM

the most of our hour and a half visit this Jewish man, born in Russia, talked to us about the trial and crucifixion of Jesus--from the Jewish standpoint. Surely the Lord was trying to persuade him to realize that Jesus' crucifixion was for him as well as for us--for the sins of all men. Please pray for this courageous, searching, Israeli intellectual. Our Lord has not run out of miracles! Hallelujah!

Interestingly, the man with the Black Dog was a journalist, a writer of documentaries for TV. During our years in Israel we were to see him 2 or 3 more times in very unexpected moments and have friendly conversations with him, but he seemed to continue feeding himself on the lies and deceptions in modern books declaring Jesus a fraud. At one point he lent us a book called "The Passover Plot", written by a Jewish author supposedly proving that everything Jesus did was part of His extraordinary and brilliant plot to prove himself the Messiah, the final Passover Lamb that takes away the sins of the world. We read it and kept wondering why the author never became a wholehearted believer. It seemed to us that his conclusion was just the opposite of what he was trying to prove.

It reminded us of Civil War General, Lou Wallace, who set out to write a book proving the Bible, Jesus, and Christianity were all frauds and ended with that great epic story, "Ben Hur", proving them all true! General Wallace ended up becoming a real Believer in Jesus, the Bible and Christianity.

There have been many others who have set out to disprove the reality of Jesus and His saving power and have ended up becoming "Bond-Slaves" of our Lord Jesus. Apostle Paul was probably the earliest and greatest example of this. And every true, born-again, humble, faithful, loving servant of Jesus today is prima-facie evidence that Jesus, and His power to save, are amazingly real today and forever! May the Lord still save the man with the black dog. Perhaps we'll see him again on some dark night, walking his dog, but giving us a big hug as a brother in Christ! Still a Jew, but a completed one, a transformed one (I Cor.5:17)!

A REAL QUICK PRAYER AT THE GOOD FENCE

Shortly before leaving for Israel, Betsy and I had attended a Full Gospel Meeting in downtown Baltimore, where the main speaker was a young, Spirit-filled Brethren minister, Dick Green, from Frostburg, Maryland. Amazingly, Dick was saying that God had told him several times that we are moving into the last days, that the coming days would be as in the days of Noah, very evil, and that Dick was to start building a "Noah's Ark" to publicize the day we are in and, in part, fulfill Jesus'

318 FIRED AGAIN AND AGAIN, PRAISE THE LORD!

Words about it as found in Matthew 24. Talk about a monumental task, this was one! The ark was over 400 feet long and at least 75 feet wide! This time it was not to be a floating ark, but a structural replica sitting on a concrete foundation on the side of a mountain in Western Maryland! Dick was convincing in his description of God's call on his life to undertake this huge project and we felt we would like to help him, but we were going to Israel. So, at the end of the meeting, we went up to meet him and tell him we were on our way to live in Israel for a while, if we could ever help him there, please let us know.

So even before we left Baltimore, we received a letter from Dick saying that in February he would be going to England and Germany and was hoping to include Israel in the last part of his journey. Could he and his wife stay with us?

We already knew that Esther was planning to be away on a speaking tour at that time, so we wrote him and told him that we would clear it with her and to come on. There would be ample room for them at her apartment. And they did come!

Now, Israel in February is about like northern Florida, cold, rainy and wet, with a few very nice days interspaced! So in another rented Autobianchi, the four of us began touring Israel as a tiny tour group. The Greens really became our first "private tour group" in Israel. We thoroughly enjoyed going to all the Holy Sites, and attending a number of worship services in Jerusalem with them. Always the trip up north to Nazareth, the Sea of Galilee and the Mount of Beatitudes and on up to the Good Fence at the border of Lebanon was a very special part of such a tour.

After seeing the special sites around the northern part of the Sea of Galilee including Capernaum and the Mt. of Beatitudes, we went up to spend a night at the Horse Farm where our friends, Ray and Virginia Cornwell, live. We wanted the Greens to meet them.

We remember Ray sitting in the restaurant that evening listening to a radio report saying there had been a terrorist attack on the Christian Radio Station, The Voice of Hope, only a few miles away inside of Lebanon. One of the young Christian reporters had been killed. This news was somewhat upsetting to our guests! It caused us all to question our plans to visit the Good Fence at Metulla. But despite the initial misgivings, we headed north the next morning in the overcast and occasional drizzle, determined to make a fast run to the Good Fence and a fast return. Actually Betsy and I knew that the Israeli army along the border was quite capable of handling any real attacks on Metulla, and we also knew at that moment these sporadic attacks were mainly between the Christian Lebanese and the PLO Shiite factions just north of the border. So Betsy and I were not really worried about any bombs

CHAPTER 19: OUR RAMOT YEAR IN JERUSALEM

coming over the fence.

Almost as soon as we got there and were walking from the parking area to the Good Fence observation point, we heard some big guns go "boom-boom" on the other side of the border and a short time later a return "boom-boom'" No doubt the Greens were ready to climb back in the car and "burn rubber" heading south. But Dick's desire to take pictures of the surrounding scenery caused him to come on up to the lookout point. His wife, Lottie, reluctantly came too. While standing at the lookout point, you can look over into Lebanon up the beautiful Valley of The Springs, and we could point out the location of the Radio Station at the far end of the Valley inside Lebanon. At this point, I suggested that we have a quick prayer for the station, the staff, and for the bereaved family of the reporter who had died in the gun fire the night before. So we all joined hands and bowed our heads and, at that moment there was another loud, "BOOM-BOOM."

Lottie stammered, "Ya-ya-yes, a Real Quick Prayer!"

We all broke out laughing and running to the car, Lottie leading the group. Very soon we were rolling south praying as we went!

We've laughed with the Greens a number of times since about that "Quick Prayer" at the Good Fence. The Lord got them safely back to the U.S. and they have continued the slow building of the Ark and The Ark ministry in Frostburg, Md. You would be interested in knowing that because of his obedience in undertaking the building of this Ark-size Church and Conference Center, over several thousand people have been saved, because of the strong warning it gives.

It will take probably $1,000,000 more to finish this "Anchored-On-A-Mountain Ark," but even so it is shouting Jesus' Warning in Matt.24:37-44: *"But as the days of Noah were so shall also the coming of the Son of man be."* America's immorality is far exceeding that of Noah's day--right now! No T.V. or radio then!

Before we leave the "Good Fence" at Lebanon's border, perhaps you would like to know why it is called that--with so much fighting going on on the other side? This is precisely the reason: it was the only gateway to help for South Lebanese Christians. Since the middle 70's South Lebanon was cut off from the rest of the country. They couldn't get medical and economic help. So Israel made a crossing point for the south Lebanese Christians to come across for medical and hospital care and also to work in Israel. Although the factional fighting continues throughout Lebanon and in the south, the "Good Fence" at Metulla is still a powerful benefit to the South Lebanese Christians and forces that still exist. In the early 70's Christians were the majority in Lebanon. Little known to the world, in the last 18 years over 100,000 Christians have been wiped out, perhaps more, by the grim intent and hate-filled actions of Islam to take over by violence and rule the whole land. In May 1988, there was a take-over contest between the Syrian forces, the Iranian-backed Hezbollah forces (radical fundamentalists) and the Lebanese Amal militia in south Beruit, and in south Lebanon. Since then the Syrians have largely taken control with their Russian tanks! Thank God for the Israeli and Christian South Lebanese military buffer zone that's preventing these various Moslem groups from coming across into Israel and wiping out the "Good Fence" forever. At least that's their desire. And thank God for both the "Voice of Hope" radio and the CBN (Christian Broadcast Network) T.V. stations, both now operating from secret locations in South Lebanon. They are still pouring out God's Word and Hope for salvation through Jesus Christ across these strife-torn regions. God's Word does say that Lebanon will also bloom again (Isa. 29:17)! We should pray for these courageous stations and their crews that they can continue and be fully protected by God Almighty!

COFFEE SHOP CONFRONTATION

At the end of a Worship Service the night before we left Baltimore with the tour group to come to stay in Israel with Esther, a friend came up to me and said, "Bro. Sid, you should use this on your trip." It was a handsome blue and silver Star of David with a silver Cross in the middle of it. At the time I was wearing a leather star and cross which I gave him in exchange. A surprise blessing!

This attractive star and cross I wore almost constantly during our stay in Israel, and we were amazed at the almost daily opportunities it brought us to talk to complete strangers about our love for the Jewish Messiah, Jesus, for the Jews and for Israel. For the Arabs too! A great many Jews were delighted to hear this brief testimony of how the love for Jesus led to a love of the Jewish people and His land. Of course many other Jews, mostly the ultra-orthodox, carefully avoided any contact with us.

On a bus one day, a Jewish lady said, "Oh, I'm so sorry, I must get off the bus now, I would love to hear more."

Tough Israeli soldiers would stop and tap the emblem and say, "I like that. That's the way it ought to be." Isn't this what our Lord Jesus came to do, to bring Jew, Arabs and Gentiles together into a great loving family of God through His atonement on the Cross and giving us a "new birth?"

One day in our 6th month in Israel there was a noisy confrontation in a coffee shop about this star and cross. Betsy and I were having to go to the Ministry of Interior to seek to renew our visas for another 3 months, but the office would not be open for another hour. So we

CHAPTER 19: OUR RAMOT YEAR IN JERUSALEM

decided to stop in a coffee shop and get a drink and a piece of pie or cake while waiting. It was one of those sidewalk cafes on Ben Yehuda Street in downtown Jerusalem, probably the busiest business section. When we had finished, I went in to pay the bill and almost immediately the young "kepah" wearing man behind the counter began screaming at me and angrily pointing his finger at the star, saying, "Where did you buy that?"

When confronted like that, I usually try to turn on a friendly smile, and I looked him straight on, grinned and said, "I didn't buy it. A friend gave it to me just before I left the States to bring a tour group to visit Israel with my wife. Do you know what it means?"

He yelled back, "It's no good!"

I called back, "But it is good!"

A lot of people began listening and I continued, "It tells you that because of the love of Jesus, I love Israel and the Jewish people. Now that's good, isn't it?"

And he's still yelling, "That's no good!"

"And on top of that," I said, "Jesus has changed my life, the life of my wife and family, and millions more around the world. He's filled us with love for you and Israel. And we pray for you daily. Now that's good, isn't it?"

And he's still trying to say, "It's no good!"

But his volume is way down and behind him his old man has begun to say, "Dat's goot!"

I went on, "And besides that, this same Jesus is coming back soon again, and He's going to rule the whole earth from Jerusalem, and righteousness and justice and peace will fill the earth."

Now the young man has shut up, but his old man was saying louder, "Dat's goot, dat's goot!"

I grinned again and stuck out my hand and shook the hands of both the young man and his father, saying, "Shalom" and, finally, I was able to pay the bill. Baruch Ha Shem (Bless the Name)!

Interestingly, we might add, quite a number of people had stopped to listen to this confrontation about Jesus and the Star and the Cross. They love watching arguments! Hopefully, many were also convinced that it's good to follow Jesus!

"TUPELO HONEY TO PRIME MINISTER BEGIN'S DEPUTY" and THE HEBREW MEANING OF AMEN!

Before coming to live in Israel, we had read that when Israel's Prime Minister Begin went to Norway to receive the Nobel Peace prize, his chief deputy, Mr. Yechiel Kadishai, had taken the King of Norway a jar of honey from Israel. So in our luggage that November we packed two jars of Florida Tupelo honey, one for our household, and one for Mr. Kadishai. We hoped that somehow we could arrange a visit with him in the Prime Minister's office. Needless to say, our jar was emptied in a couple of months, and it took great restraint for us to stay out of "Mr. Kadishai's honey jar!"

Esther, from her previous contacts with the Prime Minister and Mr. Kadishai, his chief deputy, had been given the phone number of his office. She had suggested we call him ourselves about bringing the Tupelo honey. When I did call I was able to speak directly with Mr. Kadishai and he warmly welcomed us to visit him, described which building to come to and what bus to take to get there. This was an encouraging start.

At last on Thursday, July 17, 1980, the Lord gave us the privilege of visiting Mr. Kadishai in his office adjoining the Prime Minister's in a heavily guarded building not far from the Knesset (Parliament) in Jerusalem. We had hoped to see Prime Minister Begin too, and let the honey be a gift shared with his chief deputy, but Mr. Begin was in the hospital for a heart check-up that day.

Of course the security was tight. We were frisked, and our camera taken away from us. However, after explaining to the chief security guard that Mr. Kadishai might like a picture of "the presentation," he allowed us to take the camera to his office, guided there by a guard.

A secretary directed us to seats in Mr. Kadishai's office and after some ten minutes or so, he arrived, explaining he had been delayed in a committee meeting. He asked his secretary to bring some refreshing lemonade and immediately began expressing his high regard for our Jewish friend, Esther Dorflinger. In 1978 she had presented the Prime Minister and Israel with over $50,000 and a "Love Scroll" from thousands of people in thirty-two countries around the world who gave the gifts and signed the "We Love You Israel Scroll". The Scroll was still kept in a safe in the Prime Minister's office, and a picture of it was on the wall! On that day we told him Esther was in New Zealand speaking on behalf of Israel. Mr. Kadishai then went over to his desk and found souvenir pictures and a program of the Prime Minister's first visit to Egypt which he seemed delighted to give us, and we, honored to receive.

Then we asked if I could present him the gift of Florida honey before a map of Israel while my wife took a picture of us. He nodded, "Of course." As I shook his hand and presented the honey I said, "Mr. Kadishai, we are Christians, and we offer this gift to you and to the Prime Minister as a token of our love for you, for the Jewish people, and for Israel. We want you to know we are praying for you everyday, and

CHAPTER 19: OUR RAMOT YEAR IN JERUSALEM

that millions more, like us, around the world are also praying daily for you."

We could see that his heart was touched as he turned his head slightly, cleared his throat, and with emotion in his voice quietly said, "We know, that's what keeps us going!"

Our answer was a strong "Amen."

He then asked, "Do you know the Hebrew meaning of Amen?"

"We know one meaning, but please tell us the Hebrew meaning," I replied.

A Hebrew lesson followed which we'll never forget and will always cherish.

He continued, "In Hebrew, Amen is spelled with three letters: Aleph, Mem, Nun, the same as your A, M, N. The Aleph stands for Elohim (God); the Mem for Melech (King); the Nun for Naaman (Faithful). So in Hebrew "Amen" really means "OUR GOD IS KING AND HE IS FAITHFUL!

Betsy and I said another emphatic "Amen!"

With that, we thanked him warmly for the visit, the souvenirs, and the special Hebrew lesson. We promised to continue praying for and standing by Israel! And said, "Shalom."

No wonder Israel has survived, and will survive! Keep praying for Israel!

That evening we had the honor of helping a tour group on their evening bus trip to Bethlehem. On the way we shared about our visit with Mr. Kadishai and his Hebrew lesson on "Amen." Coming back to Jerusalem, a young lady from North Carolina shared a song she said The Lord had quickly given her based on the "Amen" story. It's really good! We'll be glad to sing it for you anytime! The lines are simple:

> *"Our God is King and He's Faithful!*
> *Our God is King and He's Faithful!*
> *Our God is King, Our God is King,*
> *Our God is King--Amen!"*

That surely means a lot more to us than the old oft-given definition of "So be it!" THANK YOU, JESUS!

324   FIRED AGAIN AND AGAIN, PRAISE THE LORD!

GREAT FRIENDS OF ISRAEL, RAY AND VIRGINIA

ESTHER WITH RUSSELL: SEE "ANGELS, BROTHER,"(P.308)
MR. BEGIN WAS TOUCHED (P.314)

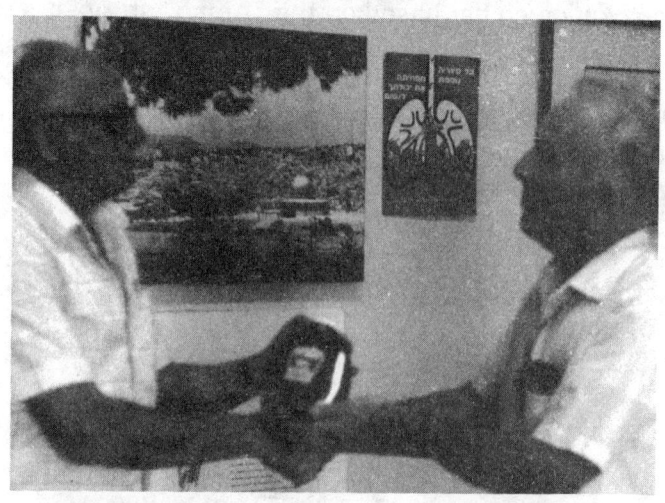

TUPELO HONEY TO MR. KADISHAI, TO ISRAEL WITH LOVE!

CHAP. 20

FROM CONFRONTATIONS TO WARS

He that keepeth Israel shall neither slumber nor sleep. - Psalm 121:4
Pray for the peace of Jerusalem: they shall prosper that love thee.
- Psalm 122:6

CONFRONTATION OF A DIFFERENT SORT - AT YAD VASHEM
About The Nazi Holocaust

During that summer of 1980 we had encouraged as many people as we could to sign up for the fall Solomon tour and said we would be there already, but would meet them at the Tel Aviv airport and tour with them. So eight days after we returned to Israel, and after finding, at the Lord's direction, a tiny "half-star" apartment on the south side of Jerusalem, we came back to the Airport to join up with the in-coming Solomon Tour. We rode the northern circuit with them sharing our experiences and songs and love of Israel. Moshe Dayagi, again, was our able tour guide doing a great job as usual, always adding extras whenever he could as time permitted. But a "dark cloud" was coming!

This unfortunate confrontation took place beside the obelisk of "Yad VaShem," which is Israel's famous memorial to the Nazi Holocaust. It contains some of the most shocking pictorial revelations of the horrors of the Nazi atrocities against the Jews. Outside the main building containing these displays there is a street called the "Avenue of the Righteous Gentiles," memorializing many Gentiles who helped Jews to escape; most were courageous Christians.

On this particular day our group was called over to the obelisk by our tour guide, Moshe, before entering the main building displays, and he proceeded to give us an impassioned speech against Christianity and all Christians for either causing the Holocaust, or allowing it to continue. We know that, for many Jews, Christianity and the Roman Catholic Church are synonymous. They don't seem to recognize there is a huge and very different Protestant Evangelical Church that had nothing to do with the World War II Catholic Pope's failure to condemn Hitler, or try to stop the Holocaust of Jews.

Well, on that particular day, being one of the Christian leaders in our group, my dander rose up real fast, and I felt someone had to make an equally impassioned rebuttal of such total condemnation of all Christians. So I asked for the group's attention and told them I could understand our guide's strong feelings about the Jewish Holocaust, but I felt that he and they should be reminded that I, and millions more of my fellow Americans, gave many years of our lives trying to defeat two powerful enemies at the same time, Germany and Japan, and that hundreds of thousands of our men gave their lives at sea, on land, and in the air to put an end to Hitler, and put an end to the Nazi and Japanese war machines. I stressed the fact that great numbers of these young men, fighting and dying to stop Hitler, were Christians, including my very best friend, Ed Williams. And at least five years of my own life were given to that cause. I would like it to be understood that a lot of us Christians did all we could to stop the Holocaust against the Jews, and that we would do it again, if necessary.

For a time it seemed I had lost the friendship of our guide. He barely spoke to me the rest of the tour, and we could not make contact with him anymore for several months. Finally, we wrote him a letter to his home in Ashkelon saying, "If Mr. Begin and Mr. Sedat could bring Israel and Egypt to a peace treaty, surely he and I should be able to work out some sort of peace agreement and be friends again." Still no word from him.

Some months later, we received a card from Bucharest, Romania, saying, "I'm here on a little friendly tour. Hope all is well. See you soon. Brother Moshe."

By this we knew our peace pact had been signed. Praise the Good Lord for making peace between our friend Moshe and us.

THE "YEVERECHACHA" SONG STORY
WHEN WE TRUST AND OBEY, THE LORD GUIDES ALL THE WAY

It was toward the end of our second stay in Israel. We had been living in our little apartment on Shimoni Street and going three mornings each week to the Moadon HaOleh Hebrew School for new immigrants. We were getting close to the time when we would need to go back to the States for the summer to help at the Little Tabernacle and also to help Betsy's elderly father (Pappy).

Indeed we needed to know whether to get a one-way ticket to the U.S. or a two-way. Did the Lord really want us to come back? It must be time to order the ticket. So on this particular day we knelt to pray together, as usual, this time asking for special guidance and

CHAPTER 20: FROM CONFRONTATION TO WARS

confirmation concerning the Lord's will for us to return or not return.

Getting ready for school, as I was washing my face, I looked over to a scroll near the bathroom door and exclaimed, "Hey Betsy, I can read the Hebrew scroll; it's in the future tense from Ps. 128:5-6: **The Lord will bless thee out of Zion: and thou shalt see the good of Jerusalem all the days of thy life. Yea, thou shalt see thy children's children, and peace upon Israel.**

So we hurried off to catch a bus to school. At midmorning, our class was shifted to join another class, and the teacher told us to practice Hebrew with each other while she wrote some Hebrew verses on the board. Would you believe she was writing Ps.128:5-6? Yes, the same verses on the scroll at our apartment! Then she began teaching us how to sing them in Hebrew. Betsy and I looked at each other in surprise and smiled, realizing that God was again using His Word to confirm our returning to Israel. We will always love to sing those beautiful promises in Hebrew. ("Yeverechecha Ha Shem mitzion"--The Lord shall bless you from Zion.")

At the end of our three months stay in the States, hating so much to leave Pappy alone at his age, we again felt the need to ask the Lord to confirm our return to Israel. It was tough leaving him but he insisted he would be OK. We loaded up our heavy bags and drove the hour and 45 minute trip to Baltimore, planning to arrive on time for the morning worship services at the Little Tabernacle.

There was only one parking place left in front of the Church. As we pulled into it, we noticed the people in the car next to us had just parked too. It was a young minister and his wife and family who had stopped by on their way to their Church, hoping to catch us, before our service began. What a perfect timing of the Lord! They had brought us a farewell love gift. Of course, we thanked them with all our hearts and we thanked God for His perfect timing and confirmation. Praise the Lord! Even our heavy bags got checked from Baltimore to Israel on that trip without any further handling by us in New York. Most unusual! When we trust and obey the Lord will confirm all the way.! Bless the Name of the Lord forever! We just sang Psalm 128:5,6 in Hebrew and it still sounds pretty special! We'll be glad to sing it for you anytime!

There's an old, old hymn that sure helps us know what to do in situations like these, one we learned long ago, called:

"TRUST AND OBEY"
by: Rev. J. H. Sammis

1) *When we walk with the Lord In the light of His word,*
What a glory He sheds on our way;
While we do His good-will, He abides with us still,

And with all who will trust and obey.

Chorus: *Trust and obey, For there's no other way*
To be happy in Jesus But to trust and obey.

2) *Not a shadow can rise, Not a cloud in the skies,*
But His smile quickly drives it away;
Not a doubt nor a fear, Not a sigh nor a tear
Can abide while we trust and obey.

3) *Not a burden we bear, Not a sorrow we share,*
But our toil He doth richly repay,
Not a grief nor a loss, Not a frown nor a cross,
But is blest if we trust and obey.

4) *But we never can prove The delights of His love,*
Until all on the altar we lay;
For the favor He shows, And the joy He bestows,
Are for all who will trust and obey.

5) *Then in fellowship sweet We will sit at His feet,*
Or we'll walk by His side in the way;
What He says we will do, Where He sends we will go,
Never fear, only trust and obey.

"TALITHA CUMI"

Jesus spoke these famous Aramaic words to a lifeless child one day and she actually did rise up--very much alive! He had that power! Amazingly these life-giving words of Jesus, "Talitha Cumi" or "Maid, Arise," are now to be seen in large gold letters in the main business hub of Jerusalem. They are on a monument to a well-known Arab Christian girl's orphanage, once nearby, where now a large office building has been constructed. What a thrill to Believers from all over the world to see Jesus words, "Maid Arise" (Mark 5:35-43), lifted high in the city that rejected and crucified Him. We believe Jesus is saying from Heaven, "ISRAEL, LOOK AGAIN. ARISE AND LIVE THROUGH YOUR MESSIAH!" This monument has become, since 1981 the main point of meeting for Israeli friends in downtown Jerusalem. You often hear, "I'll meet you at "Talitha Cumi"!

To us, it is very interesting that in the last 10 years of Israel's re-existence that, written in 16 inch-high Gold letters at the main business section of its capital city, stand the words of Jesus in Aramaic,

CHAPTER 20: FROM CONFRONTATION TO WARS

"Talitha Cumi," Maid, Wake Up - Arise! And we would add, "for thy Redeemer cometh" (Zech.9:9) again, very soon!"

"AFIKOMEN"

Most significant also is the fact that for nearly 2000 years the Jewish people in their Passover Seder (meal) have been calling the middle matza (they have 3 pieces on the table separated by special napkins) by a Greek word "Afikomen," which literally means "He came!" Few Jewish people know this word is Greek or its real meaning. Most Jewish rabbis explain this word as meaning a "kind of gift," perhaps referring to the fact that the middle piece of matza is broken, hidden, and when found by the children, a piece of "gelt," money, is given to the finder. Then everyone must break off a piece of this middle matza for themselves to eat! That's exactly what the Lord Jesus did for His disciples at the Last Supper, isn't it? It was the Passover Feast (Matt.26:26-29). And what a fantastic gift Jesus (Yeshua), the Saviour, is to the World, to the Jews first and also to us Greeks! (Romans 1:16). Yes, He did come to be their Passover Lamb, and ours, too! The Final and All-Sufficient Sacrifice for the sins of the whole world! Glory to God! Dear Israel, wake up! Dear Jews, wherever you are, wake up! World, Wake Up! Your Messiah and ours came, died for us, rose for us, ascended and is coming again soon to put this old world back into God's Order!

WE GET TO SEE THE SINAI

Near the end of January we enjoyed a 3-day bus trip to Eilat and Sharm El Sheikh at the tip of the Sinai Peninsula with our Ulpan Classmates (our Hebrew School). The Sinai Mountains are huge, barren, breathtaking mountains next to the shore of the Gulf of Eilat with its bright, clear, blue waters, beautiful coral and multi-colored tropical fish. We were able to allay fears and encourage some of the others as we climbed up and down hazardous mountain ravines at King Solomon's copper mines, and were able to get the Eilat police to locate, late at night, the manager of the hostel to open two rooms for some locked-out, weary, travelers (including me). The trip was a wonderful opportunity to demonstrate God's love through Jesus with many Jewish immigrants, really fine folks! Returning late to Jerusalem, so tired, our bags "loaded" with my usual collection of rocks, we tried to catch a cab, but none would stop. Instead, "out of nowhere," an unknown-to-us Israeli "angel" pulled up in his little yellow car and offered to take us home to Shimoni St! Truly sent by the Lord! The

Lord is full of special surprises!!

Out of this trip came Betsy's "adoption" by our dear classmate, Charlotte H., who had had a very harrowing escape from Germany to England just before World War II.

STORY OUT OF THE HOLOCAUST

Most of the fine people in our Ulpan Class were older Jews who had had their own rough times and narrow escapes on their way to Israel. Because their memories of labor camps and prisons, and dying loved ones, were so traumatic, almost none of them ever wanted to look back or talk about those horrible days.

Charlotte H. was fortunate in never being caught to be sent to a labor camp, but her escape from Germany to England required very careful planning and great courage. Reunited with her husband later, they were able to start a successful "military doll" business in England, small dolls dressed in the multitude of British uniform designs and colors.

Another dear friend of ours whom we'll call Naomi, grew up in Poland, her father a learned man in the medical profession. Naomi married an artist. Their ghetto was turned into a German labor camp for making uniforms. Their baby girl was born secretly in the camp. Had it been discovered, they both would have been killed immediately. The baby, too! Somehow they contrived to escape, making their way through Poland, Czechoslovakia, Hungary, fleeing at night on foot, one jump ahead of German patrols, through snow-covered terrains. In Hungary they secured Christian identification papers and eventually escaped to France and later to America. There they found work, were blessed and had another daughter. Her husband died and Naomi learned English as a clerk in Sach's 5th Ave. The first daughter married and went to live in Israel.

Later Naomi immigrated to Israel herself, but she found her own Israeli grandchildren couldn't really believe the things that happened to her and her people back in Poland, nor could they believe about her flight with their own mother when she was a tiny baby. Naomi wanted to get her story written down in good English. Would we help? She was fluent in Polish, French and English (self-taught), but she wanted her story in good English. So we had the honor and privilege of helping Naomi get her fantastic story written down. Throughout her story she would say, "I don't believe in miracles, but that escape (or event) was one!"

We tried to get her to let us print her story (verbatim) with ours, but she politely refused. We hope she won't mind the above sketch under

CHAPTER 20: FROM CONFRONTATION TO WARS 331

a fitting Old Testament Biblical name. We prayed for her several times when she was needing healing from the Lord, and we believe He gave it to her, even though she didn't normally believe in miracles!

THE "ANI SMECHA" TEA PARTY
(I am Happy Tea party)

During the same time, while we were helping Naomi on her story, another classmate, a sweet little French lady who spoke no English, but did speak Polish and a little Hebrew, and who still had the concentration camp number tattooed on her arm, invited Betsy and me and Naomi to her house for a little tea party. We were all trying to learn to speak to each other in Hebrew, so this little tea party at Chaya's apartment would be a real exercise in finding the right words and the right language in which to communicate. But with Naomi present, with her language versatility, there should be no trouble. Chaya served "Ugah" (cake) and coffee, and being French, she had some wine available for those who desired it. (Most Israelis bring out their wine on such occasions!)

We had a good time trying to talk in Hebrew about the various problems and progress we were having in class. Chaya wanted us to hear and sing along with some recorded Israeli songs. We sang the Hebrew songs we had learned in school. Then Betsy and I asked if we could sing a new little Hebrew song which we had just learned from Joy Hjertstedt at the Tabernacle of Praise:

"Ani Smecha Ke Yeshua Iti,
Acshav yeshli chaim hadashim.
Hu noten li, et Ruah Ha Kodesh
Ani Smecha Meod Ki Hu Sheli."

Meaning: "I am happy that Jesus is with me,
Now I have new life,
He gives to me the Holy Spirit,
I'm so happy that Jesus is mine."

They understood the meaning and they said, "Sing it again!" And we did! It was a delightful tea party!

The next day in class during the exercise on "What you did yesterday" (in Hebrew), Naomi said, "We went to a tea party with Sid and Betsy at Chaya's house, and we sang some Hebrew songs."

The teacher asked Betsy, "What did you sing?"

"Havenu Shalom Allechem", "Hiney Ma Tov" and "Yeverechecha." ("We bring peace to you"; "Behold, how good;" "The Lord will bless you.")

She asked us to sing them with the class, which we did.

Then Naomi chimed in with an impish grin, "Oh but, there was another song they sang."

The teacher asked, "What was that, Betsy?"

She replied, "It's a 'notzareme' song, (a Christian song.)"

The teacher said, "That's all right, sing it."

So there in this Hebrew class of 25 Jewish new immigrants we had the privilege of singing about Jesus in Hebrew!! This time the teacher didn't ask us to repeat it! But at least His Name had been lifted up in a beautiful way, thanks to Naomi! Baruch Ha Shem (Bless The Name of the Lord)! And God bless Naomi and her Israeli family!

APPOINTMENT WITH A WAR
The Beginning of Israel's Operation "Peace For Galilee"

On June 3rd, 1982, we felt from the Lord to drive in a little rented car to Northern Israel for 3 days visiting and encouraging Believers in that part of the country, just before our summer trip to the States. Little did we realize the excitement and dangers we were moving into. On the way north along the Jordan Valley, the Lord had us picking up Israeli hitchhikers, talking with them in our limited Hebrew, sharing the Good News of our Messiah and their's, even giving two soldiers Hebrew New Testaments.

It was near sunset when we circled the Western shore of the Sea of Galilee, and began climbing up beyond the Mt. of Beatitudes to Vered HaGalil (the horse ranch) where our dear friends, Ray and Virginia Cornwell and their daughter Mary, live. They have all worked a number of years on the Ranch, and are much beloved by the Jewish Ranch owners, Yudah and Yona.

After a delightful overnight visit with them, we started to go on northward, but remembered we had forgotten to pick up a bag full of tiny Sea-of-Galilee stones for my Israel Stone Creations, so we turned back south toward the Sea, picking up a lady hitchhiker going to Tiberias. She was a teacher at a moshav (a farm community), and she gave Betsy a good grade on her Hebrew. After dropping her off in Tiberias, and gathering the tiny stones at a beach, we again drove northward to Kiryat Shemona arriving in time for a late lunch with our dear friends, Jan and Janice Karnis, who worked at The Voice of Hope Radio Station across the border in Lebanon. Their apartment and town were only about 6 miles south of the border.

After lunch, we drove with them to the fortified border village of Metulla to show another young couple (John and Helen from Eilat) the "Good Fence", the border gate for the Southern Lebanese to jobs and medical help in Israel. Jan identified for us the locations of the PLO

CHAPTER 20: FROM CONFRONTATION TO WARS 333

strongholds in the area at that time: some Moslem Arab villages, and the Beaufort Castle; and then the Christian villages under Major Hadad. Through Pappy's binoculars we could see the radio station and the broadcasting antennas. About 4:45, we were startled to hear and see four Israeli jets going across the border in what I felt was the Beruit direction in Lebanon. We prayed for them, knowing that Syrian-Russian missiles were nearby. On the day before, PLO terrorists had shot and terribly wounded Israel's Ambassador to England, Mr. Argov. This appeared to be Israel's strong retaliation.

Jan and Janice had to hurry back to the apartment in time to record the 5 pm news, before Jan had to go back into Lebanon at 7 pm to work his evening shift at the Voice of Hope radio station. The other couple went with them.

After they left, Bets and I still had no real sense of impending danger. We leisurely drove around tiny Metulla, taking pictures of a man mowing a teeny lawn (unusual in Israel), watching some farm workers just over the border, and then buying ice cream to take back for our after supper dessert with the 2 young couples, a dessert we never got around to! We left Metulla about 5 pm and began listening to the Kol (voice) Israel radio news on the way to Kiryat Shemona. We heard more about the Israeli Ambassador Argov, badly wounded by terrorists in London, and the Israeli air strikes against PLO bases in Lebanon. About 5:20 pm we arrived at Jan and Janice's apartment. Already the PLO rockets were coming in! Security police were riding through town telling the people to go quickly to bomb shelters. Jan and Janice had typed the news, and we prayed with Jan before he left for the station at 6:30 pm. We asked the Lord to keep him completely safe there and back--in Jesus' Name. Also to protect the people of Kiryat Shemona!

The radio reported one shell hitting a jeep and killing the soldier driver on the road we were just on. There was heavy shelling now on Metulla, the border village, with much property damage. A Katyusha rocket completely destroyed a home just two doors from another Voice of Hope Radio announcer in Metulla. Large Israeli artillery pieces along the border were busy as darkness set is. Gun flashes and flares began lighting the dark sky.

After Jan left, we went to the nearby shelters, two stories down under the ground with 3-tier metal bunks. We tried to talk Hebrew with the Israelies, but with their Moroccan accent it was hard for us to understand them. It was Erev Shabbat (Friday evening) and the orthodox Jews had brought their Shabbat meal, and were having the Kiddush (blessing) over the wine and bread, and began sharing all around. Including us! (Very much like Communion!)

Radio reception was bad in the shelter, and it was crowded and very stuffy, no fans working, so we went back to the shelter's entrance to pick up Jan's 8 pm news-cast from The Voice of Hope--and learned he made it safely to the Station. Praise the Lord! Janice asked John and me to pray and ask the Lord for an OK to return to the apartment. We did and the Lord said, "It's all right to return; I am with you." Janice was glad because she wanted to keep hearing her husband's voice at the Station constantly to know he was OK. Most of the PLO shelling was to the north of us, and as Janice said, "If they hit in the middle of Kiryat Shemona, then Israel's army will go into Lebanon."

So we gathered our gear and returned to the apartment for a late supper. The artillery continued intermittent firing. It was good to hear Jan's voice coming in nice and clear from the radio station about 10 miles north in Lebanon. So we listened as he played country-western songs like, "Let There Be Peace In The Valley, " and "It will be Good to Get Home Tonight!" And he prayed for that peace through "Yeshua Hamashiah, the Prince of Peace." We prayed too, and tried to write some letters, but kept going to the windows to see where the shells were falling. About 11:30 we went to bed to try to sleep--with our clothes on.

Suddenly, about 12:45 a.m. we were wakened by a loud "swish-swoosh, boom-boom-boom (Katyushas), like an instant thunderstorm right on top of us! At least 20 missiles had hit close by in the middle of Kiryat Shemona. We were bounced out of bed but not hit--praise God!! We could see the damage, and the fires, and the main power went out in town. Janice ran into the room, yelling, "Katyushas!" We knew already! Then came the uncertainty of not knowing when or where others might hit. However, after more prayer, we felt peace about staying on in the apartment which did have a reinforced security room. And Jan should be coming home soon.

Sure enough a little after 1 o'clock, Jan arrived at the apartment, safe and sound. Praise God! He told us that as he was crossing the border into Lebanon, the Israeli guards tried to persuade him not to go in saying,"Don't you know there's a war on?"

When Jan insisted that he must keep the station on the air, and not give in to the enemy, they let him go saying,

"Well, what kind of flowers do you want on your coffin?"

"None thank you," he replied. "I'm not expecting a coffin."

After his report, we tried to go back to sleep, this time with our shoes on; not that there is time to do anything when the Katyushas hit. Off and on all night the shelling continued, still mostly to the north of town. The Israeli planes kept roaring over, striking PLO targets, and returning.

When morning dawned, the residents came out of their shelters and

CHAPTER 20: FROM CONFRONTATION TO WARS

cautiously surveyed the damage, watchful for downed power lines and unexploded shells. In less than an hour they were told to go back to shelters.

However, we prepared to cross northern Israel to Nahariya on the Mediterranean coast near the Lebanon border, first taking John and Helen to Haifa. Jan and Janice readied for the afternoon shift at the radio station. Again we prayed for each other. As we left Kiryat Shemona we saw much damage in the center of town, only a few blocks from us. A real miracle! No one was injured in the town! Praise The Lord forever!

Driving south and west toward Haifa, we were amazed to see Israel's Army moving on Shabbat! A steady stream of Army tanks, trucks and equipment, troops in buses, were rolling northward - all that day and night. In Haifa we waved to soldiers in a truck and motioned that we were praying for them. They understood and waved their thanks. We saw families saying goodby to their sons, called up, waiting at assembly points, their guns hung over their shoulders, often kippas (yamacha caps) on their heads. And it's Shabbat! Israel was moving against the PLO buildup, finally, with full force. The world should be glad! Most of Israel was!

Nearing Nahariya we stopped at the "Museum of the Holocaust and Resistance." The dear older lady in charge said her younger associate was leaving because her family was in Nahariya. We offered to take her and she said, "Don't go; everybody there is in the bomb shelters. They're under PLO bombing right now!"

When I replied, "We must go to Nahariya; the Lord has told us to go to encourage friends there."

Then the older lady said, as she pointed up, "If He told you, you go. They need you there!" She asked about our Star and Cross and also about the Christian Embassy in Jerusalem. It gave us a brief moment to share. When we asked for more information for our son Brian on the Warsaw Ghetto uprising, she gave us an autographed book. Afterwards we prayed for the Lord to bless her in our Messiah's mighty name.

In Nahariya we found the Believers were trusting in Psalm 91 as their "bomb shelter!" We visited with the Nessims at their apartment. Ruth was taping the Sounds of Israel, including the shelling and Katyusha rockets! While there, her little girl was counting the shells that were bursting in or near the town. She got up to about 35 during our visit of less than an hour. The number went way over 100 before we left Nahariya that night.

After praying with the Nessims, we moved on to the Praise, Prayer and Bible Study meeting at Stan and Ethyl Roberts. The house was packed, all singing the Lord's praises with full trust and faith, while the

PLO artillery shells and Katyushas were falling all around the town. In the Lord, there can be peace in the midst of the battle. Hallelujah! When asked why they weren't in the bomb shelters, they quickly replied, "We are in our Bombshelter--Psalm 91! They were indeed! And God's angels were all around us!

After some three hours with our Lord's precious family there, we heard Stan give his favorite admonition, "Keep Shining," as we headed south to Haifa to pick up Esther at the docks. She was returning on a ferry from Patmos. We then drove back to Jerusalem late that night. All the way, we passed Israeli Army forces moving resolutely northward toward - astonishing victories over their implacable PLO foes. We prayed all the way--for every passing unit.

They would find huge stockpiles of Soviet-made weapons hidden in large tunnels for a planned PLO invasion later that year. The Israelis spent the next three months, June, July and August, hauling these armaments out of Lebanon with giant trucks rolling night and day. In actuality, Israel's so-called invasion of Lebanon in early June 1982 preempted and prevented a huge Soviet-backed Palestinian invasion of Israel.

We believe God's hand was, and is, upon Israel in these modern-day battles. One day we hope the world will appreciate what Israel has done to stop the growth of PLO terrorism in Lebanon against the Christians there and against Israel to the south. Most everyone, except the PLO and their Communist supporters were breathing a sigh of relief and a prayer of thanksgiving for this God-sent liberation effort. Lebanese Christians were certainly thankful!

Back in the bomb shelter one Israeli mother had asked, "Why do we always have to get bombed here when something happens to anger the PLO? Why doesn't our nation or someone do something to stop it?" Well, finally, her little nation, Israel, had done something big, and costly, to bring peace to Galilee and Lebanon! But because of the Islamic hatred of the Jews and the Islamic expansion plans, real lasting peace would not be coming soon.

Sometime later we returned to this northern border town to find a very interesting sight. The Israeli army had captured one of the large artillery guns which had fired on Israel and had it installed in a public square of this border village with this sign on it from Isaiah 54:17:

No weapon that is formed against thee shall prosper; and every tongue that shall rise against thee in judgment thou shalt condemn. This is the heritage of the servants of the Lord and their righteousness is of me, saith the Lord.

We thank God for His mighty angels that watch over us always (Ps.34:7-10), as we trust Him with all our hearts. Our God has not

CHAPTER 20: FROM CONFRONTATION TO WARS

forgotten Israel. (Ps.72:18-19; Ps.121; Rom.9-10-11).

SOME TRUTHS ABOUT ISLAM

The very nature of Islam is expansion, with the teachings of their prophet Mohammed, the Koran in one hand and a sword in the other. The original and continuing nature of Islam is a militant seeking to dominate and conquer the world, even to killing all those infidels who oppose them, which in their eyes includes all non-Islamic people, especially Jews and Christians, who will not submit to Allah and Mohammed. Presently their chief goals are: 1) The complete takeover of Lebanon; 2) The complete recapture of the West Bank and all of Israel and in the process driving both Christians and Jews into the Mediterranean. And 3) The complete spread of Islam throughout Europe, England and the U.S., using their oil riches to build their mosques and centers throughout these lands. Today, Islam is becoming a major force in Europe and Great Britain, and has a very extensive missionary program going in the U.S. We need to wake up! Islam, like Communism, is a complete denial of Jesus Christ, of God's Word, the Bible and of God's plan for the salvation of the world. The Ayatolla Khomeni's pronouncement of the "death penalty" (with millions to be paid the assassin) upon Salman Rushdie for writing a book called "The Satanic Verses" exposing the satanic character and nature of Islam, is prima-facie evidence that Islam itself is not of God but of Satan. Islam right now is using huge grants of money from the key Islamic oil producing nations to missionize the world for Allah, especially the Western Nations!

GOD'S SPECIAL DELIVERY TO THE VOICE OF HOPE RADIO STATION!

Let us tell you another fantastic piece of evidence of God's hand at this time, not only with the Israelies, but also with the Christians broadcasting the Good News of God's Word at the Voice of Hope Radio Station in Southern Lebanon. For over a year the station had needed a special electronic part for a piece of its equipment. Orders had been sent to the States but to no avail. And prayers had been sent up to the Lord. Well, one of those Russian-Syrian war planes was shot down in '82 near the radio station; the tail section fell close by. The station workers pulled the Mig tail onto their porch to examine it. And guess what? The station engineer quickly spotted the needed part there in this Russian plane tail, took it out, placed it in their equipment, and it worked beautifully. Praise The Lord! Forever! He knows how to take care of His people! He even made the enemy bring the needed part to His servants.

With Him nothing is impossible! Just before leaving Israel for the summer, we called our friends who work at the Station to confirm this amazing story. It really did happen! Hopefully the pilot survived by ejection-parachute.

THE PRAYER SHAWL MIRACLE IN LEBANON!

Another beautiful piece of evidence of God's presence with His ancient people, the Jews, was the story carried in the Jerusalem Post early in the war, of the miraculous escape the Lord gave to a young orthodox soldier and his friends traveling in a jeep in the battle zone in Lebanon. They were under fire, but still moving. Suddenly the young orthodox soldier driving the jeep realized the bag containing his prayer shawl, phylacteries and prayer book had fallen out. He quickly stopped and backed up to get his precious bag. As they moved back, a PLO shell landed right where they had been, so they quickly stopped and dove for cover. The next shell demolished the jeep - but the young man and his jeep buddies were not hurt. Praise The Lord forever! The God of Israel still does wondrous things! (Ps. 72:18,19) Surely there were many other instances of God's merciful providence in this war which may or may not be written about in days to come.

Occasionally we find people in America and elsewhere who do not think God's hand is upon this modern day Israel and His People, or even think that present day Israel is a man-made fraud! We strongly reject such foolish thinking and teaching. From the day of its announced Independence as a nation, May 14, 1948, until this day Israel has been attacked by all of its surrounding Arab-Islamic nations and has only survived by the grace of God, the help of God, the plan of God, the miracles of God, and the angels of God. Almost every Israeli soldier who has survived these wars, like Moshe Dayagi, can tell you instance after instance of real miracles of God, which intervened to save them and their nation. Yes, we know that one of the two Super-Power nations has stood with Israel throughout these wars, but have you thought why? It's all because of our foundation on the Word of God and on the faith of Jesus Christ, the Jewish Messiah-Saviour! May God help us continue standing with this little nation and this people. God blesses those who bless Israel and curses those who curse Israel! (Gen.12:1-3) It's that simple!

THE BLUE STRING AND NAIL

In the fall of 1980, on our return to Israel, in obedience to the Lord's direction, we tried to find a small furnished apartment of our own on the

CHAPTER 20: FROM CONFRONTATION TO WARS

south side of Jerusalem. With the help of Esther's friend and our future neighbor, Ruth Weintraub, we were put in touch with an orthodox Jewish landlord who had a couple of apartments on Ruth's street. On a certain day we met him at the apartment, and though very sparsely furnished, with early Israeli "antiques", we soon made our first year's lease on this little-half-star apartment at 32 Shimoni Street. It would be our happy home in Israel for the next five and a half years!

Our new landlord was not new, he was 75 years old, and still an active member of Israel's security forces! This elderly landlord was to become a very close friend, and almost like a dear Jewish Uncle. He would stop by occasionally just for a cup of coffee and cookie visit to talk about Old Testament Scriptures, which often he could quote verbatim in Hebrew. He seemed to love to share in the things of the Lord with us, and would say at times, "I feel The Presence when I'm with you." And each Christmas, without fail, he would bring us a very special Christmas gift. Once it was an antique silver sugar spoon; another time an ancient brass nut-cracker with a Crusader Cross on it; another time it was a candle holder with the Scripture from Proverbs. "The spirit of man is the candle of the Lord." (Prov.20:27). Another time, a lovely silver chalice. He truly blessed us!

One Christmas we met him coming up the sidewalk toward our apartment and he gave us his gift there on the sidewalk. We never will forget what he said to us then, "I want you to know that Christmas means more to me than you realize." Wow!

We replied, "Zev, we surely do believe it. Please accept our deepest thanks and may you have a very special "Hag Sameach" too (Happy Holiday)!"

We never will forget the many times Zev and his wife Ziphora would have us come to visit them with our tour group, large or small, in their 4th floor walk-up apartment in the Old City, where they had a lovely view of the Temple Mount, the Western Wall and the Mount of Olives from their roof. It was always a very happy occasion to sit in their decorated roof-top "succah" (booth) during the Feast of Tabernacles (Booths) and sing the songs of Zion and share Scriptures such as Zech. 8:2-3;21-23; 9:9-10; 14:16-17.

One June before leaving for the States, Zev surprised us with a visit to tell us goodbye and to make sure everything was in order. He was keeping the apartment for us. He said we are like family to him, and he wanted to present us with a long blue thread wrapped around a nail. This symbolized a Jewish legend: "The way the Jews are brought back to Jerusalem is by nailing a nail in the Western Wall ('Wailing Wall'), tying a l-o-n-g blue string to the nail, and the other end to one's belt loop. When one goes to a distant land this string will surely pull him back to Jerusalem!" So we were pulled back, since both our landlord and the Lord wanted us to return!!

We understand too, that an ultra orthodox, militant group called the "Yad LeAchim" (meaning "Hand of the Brothers" - protectors of the faith) called him one day and told him he had to stop renting to us, because we were undesirable Christians, probably "dangerous missionaries," and he told them it was none of their business who he rented to, and hung up on them.

Zev was a 5th generation Jerusalemite, had been shot in the War of Independence, was not afraid of anybody, and at 78 was not about to let some young "whipper-snappers" tell him what to do. Bully for him! And praise God for him! Zev knew that we were more brothers in the Spirit with him than these haters of Christians ever were with him. For doesn't the Word say in I John 4:20. "How can man say he loves God when he hates his brother?" May Zev's blue string and the Good Lord keep pulling us back to Jerusalem. Praise the Name of the Lord! Forever!

IT MUST HAVE BEEN HARD ON OUR KIDS AT CHRISTMAS

It was hard on us to be away from our sons and families, especially at Thanksgiving and Christmas and on their birthdays, but we were far away for six of those seven years doing what we believed the Lord wanted us to be doing, encouraging the Believers in Israel, and encouraging the Jews and Arabs in every way we could. No doubt it was also hard for our boys, never having a home and parents to go home to. It could have been a traumatic experience for them, even though they probably were fully occupied with college and work.

At this moment we are remembering Christmas '82 and trying to recall where our sons were at that time. This is how we remember from afar:

Craig and Ann and their two children, Ginny (7) and Allen (3) were still in Oak Ridge, Tennessee, where Craig was Assistant Principal of a junior high school, and Ann was with the Oak Ridge Association of Universities in Atomic Research. "Our Gang" got together at their home in early August, and had a day at the Knoxville World's Fair. (Islam had a large exhibit there!) Kirby and Carol and their three, Matthew (4), Peter (3) and Betsy (1), were returning to Baltimore from a vacation trip to Oklahoma; and Joe and his wife, Debbie, were returning to Illinois from visiting Debbie's relatives in Georgia. Joe was the Director of Admissions for McMurray College in Jacksonville, Illinois. Chris had been accepted by the University of Tennessee Doctorate program in Bio-Chemistry, with a Teaching Fellowship at U. of T. And Brian was in

CHAPTER 20: FROM CONFRONTATION TO WARS

his 4th year at Maryville College in nearby Maryville, Tennessee.

We did get to see Dusty later in the summer. He had changed jobs and was working with a government agency in Warrington, Va. Betsy's Dad, Pappy, was doing well, praise the Lord, and had gone to Florida for the winter at his apartment near Lake Wales. We talked to him by phone recently, and his first question was, "When are you coming home?" Home to us is wherever the Lord wants us to be serving Him. At this moment, He has us very busy in His vineyard here in Israel. Of course, we get a good case of "homesickness" (as in Pappy's question) for our loved-ones in the U.S.

THE NON-FATAL WAR OF PIES
(A Tongue-in-Cheek War!)

It was Thanksgiving Day in Israel. Esther and several others came to our little apartment for Thanksgiving dinner, another one of Betsy's famous Holiday dinners, without the typical fat American turkey, but a beautiful dinner nonetheless. Especially for old Dad's sake she had also prepared a lovely pecan pie for desert.

Esther, with her "Yankee" ways, stuck her foot in her mouth and said, with proper Yankee snobbery, "We New Englanders always have pumpkin pie at Thanksgiving time." Well, that did it! Nobody talks about my Thanksgiving Pecan Pie like that. The gauntlet was down, "war" was declared! Surely pecan pie, especially Southern Pecan Pie, like the kind my wife makes, far excels pumpkin pie for Thanksgiving dinner, or any dinner for that matter!

Well, Yankee Esther was not disturbed by my dire threats of "war" and my determination to prove the greater excellence of Pecan Pie over pumpkin pie. Not long after she got home that Thanksgiving day she called us, shouting over the phone,

"Guess what? The Lord is on the side of the pumpkin pie! About an hour ago I had a phone call from a friend who said, 'Esther, stay right where you are, don't move. I'm bringing over something just for you.' And do you know she brought over by bus a still-hot pumpkin pie and said it was all mine?"

To which I replied, "Well, Esther, maybe you win the first round, but the "war" is not over. The battle of the pies must go on, until you come to your senses and realize that the Pecan Pie is the greatest."

The next night we were invited to Naomi's daughter's home in Ramot for a delicious Erev Shabbat (Friday evening) dinner, a very lovely vegetarian dinner in a lovely home, with a lovely family, Naomi's daughter, handsome husband and two talented children.

Now you're not going to believe what I'm about to tell you, but at the end of that delicious meal, Naomi's lovely daughter brings in from her kitchen the biggest, yummiest, Pecan Pie you can imagine. It must have been at least 14 or 15 inches across, really the biggest, loveliest Pecan Pie I had ever seen. Well, let me tell you one thing: that dear family and their guests that night set upon that Pecan Pie and almost totally demolished it. It was so lovely, so delicious. We couldn't wait to get home for a phone call. After profuse thanks and goodbyes, we took Naomi to her apartment and soon home we were dialing Esther to report on that super-huge Pecan Pie that we had just enjoyed. Naomi's daughter had no inkling of my preference for Pecan Pies!

Esther yawned in our faces, over the phone of course, "You may be catching up but you will never win over that pumpkin pie that the Lord sent me. The score is tied - - - maybe."

We growled back saying, "The 'war' is still on. You just wait. The Pecan Pies will win yet!"

Well, comes Christmas, and we are invited to the Sidlo Family for Christmas-eve dinner. Now Mrs. Sidlo, from down in Texas, surely is one of the world's finest cooks and her family is among the world's finest people, Jesus People, that is!

Well, I thought I smelled Pecan Pie that night the moment we walked in the door and I peaked in the kitchen. And sure enough there were more pecan pies in that kitchen than I had ever seen in my life. Eileen Sidlo had done it. There stacked in their lumpy, luscious glory was a large mound of crisp, crunchy, bite-size Pecan Pies, like a huge pyramid of Pecan Pies. Wait until we tell that Yankee about this! Anyone that could own that stack of pies would be richer than King Midas himself!

After that lovely, lovely dinner that night, as we were about to depart for our apartment a few blocks away, Mrs. Sidlo brought to me and Betsy as a Christmas present a plate filled with 72 of those lovely little Pecan Pies. Can you believe that? We were loaded with Pecan Pies by a bonafide Master of Pie Baking! When we told Esther about this great event the next day, she immediately and grudgingly accepted defeat and reluctantly declared the Pecan Pie winner of the "War of The Pies." Thus endeth the saga of the "Great Pie War" in Israel.

To keep peace in the family, for Christmas dinner the next day, Betsy made one Pecan Pie and one Pumpkin Pie!! But Brother Sid had a ball giving out bite-size Pecan Pies as Christmas presents that year.

Thank you Lord, for these beautiful Pecan Pie memories! Thanks to Eileen Sidlo, the Pecan Pie won the war! Thanks to Esther for accepting defeat almost sweetly!

Please, no offense meant by this story to all you pumpkin pie lovers. Just reporting the facts of the "war" as it happened!

CHAPTER 20: FROM CONFRONTATION TO WARS 342A

THE "MAID ARISE" MEMORIAL
IN THE HEART OF JERUSALEM

WITH OUR DEAR FRIENDS,
DR. & MRS. KIRCHNER
& MRS. BETTY MCDOWELL

THE BATTLE OF
THE PIES COMES
TO A TRUCE!
Mr. SID, ESTHER
YEHUDIT &
ZIAD'S MOTHER

ESTHER WITH JERUSALEM FRIENDS RUTH & ZEV WEINTRAUB
& HER MOM & DAD, DR. & MRS. KORSON FROM ARIZONA.C.1980

342B   FIRED AGAIN AND AGAIN, PRAISE THE LORD!

SPRINGTIME IN UPPER GALILEE -- IMAGINE FLOWERS EVERYWHERE

OUR BLESSED 1/2 STAR APARTMENT IN JERUSALEM

CHARBEL YUNIS & HIS LOVELY FAMILY IN LEBANON. PICTURE THRU SHELL HOLE!

AT GOOD FENCE LOOKING INTO LEBANON FOR VOICE OF HOPE STATION

CHAP. 21

SEARCH FOR A CHURCH AND OIL

Not forsaking the assembling of ourselves, together, as the manner of some is: but exhorting one another: and so much the more, as ye see the day approaching.   -Hebrews 10:25

LOOKING FOR A CHURCH HOME IN JERUSALEM

Naturally, when we first arrived in Jerusalem to stay awhile in December '79, Betsy and I were very much concerned about having a regular "Church Home" connection, a Body of Believers with whom we could worship, fellowship and work in the service of Jesus Christ. There are not all that many active churches in Jerusalem, (or Israel), some meeting on Shabbat (Saturdays) and some on Sundays. Many of the American Christians gravitate to the active Baptist Congregation in the center of Jerusalem, the one whose main building was burned down by "unknown arsonists" around 1983, usually attributed to the Ultra Orthodox Yad Le Achem boys. A temporary tent-like structure was erected in their parking lot to house their services. But the Pastor there then, a key member of the local ministers' association that had "ostracized" Esther, no doubt had heard of our confronting other members of the council, and never did give us any acceptance or welcome. And we were not Southern Baptist, though we do baptize! We can understand their normal reluctance to recognize and accept ministers from afar, simply because Jerusalem is a magnet attracting all the "religious nuts" in the world, at least all that can get there. And there are many who do!

The Scottish preacher at the Presbyterian Church was quite difficult to understand; the Messianic group did not like Charismatics. But finally, at the suggestion of our dear friends, Wilbur and Betty Presson, who operated a Christian Youth Hostel in Haifa, we found the David & Faith Hjertstedt Fellowship meeting in the Finnish School building and knew right away from the Lord that we had found another Little Tabernacle, a church home called The Tabernacle of Praise. Hallelujah! It was operating on the familiar miracle shoestring, but moving in the gifts of the Spirit, and they gave us a very warm welcome!

A short time later, I was asked to serve as one of the Elders in the congregation, and Betsy with her music abilities, as one of the Praise leaders. The fellowship never grew to any great size, but it was an active, happy and effective one--an interesting mixture of Gentiles, Jews, and Arabs all loving Jesus and learning to love each other! We thoroughly enjoyed our next four years as part of it. At one point when the Hjertstedts took a three months vacation in the States, after Brother David Hjertstedt had been ill, he asked me to serve as the substitute pastor. For varying amounts of time, Wilbur Presson, Bill Watson, Steve Lightle, Paul Kosydar, Reubin Ross, Walt Yarborough and Mike Lambert also served as elders.

In '86 the Hjertstedts completed some 10-12 years of ministry in the Jerusalem area and felt the Lord was sending them "home" to Northwest USA. We all felt that our elder from Texas, a graduate of CFNI (Christ For The Nations), and an oil engineer (who helped Andy SoRelle in his Asher oil project in Israel), was the Lord's choice for a continuing pastor and so Mike Lambert was installed.

Mike and new elders are continuing an effective ministry through the Tabernacle of Praise in Jerusalem, now called the Shekinah Fellowship. (Shekinah refers to the radiance of the Divine Presence!) Praise God forever. Mike and his wife, Helen, who was also President of the Women's Aglow fellowship in Jerusalem, have a Texas size family, two older girls, and three younger boys. They very much need our prayers and support. Praise God, the Little Tabernacle is sending them some regular support, and Mike tries to visit us at the Little Tabernacle whenever he is in the States. We'll never forget those days in that blessed fellowship. May the Lord continue to bless them and empower them by His Holy Spirit to lift up the Blessed Name of Jesus.

Also unforgettable was the anointed singing and piano playing and worship leading by precious Joy Hjertstedt, and the many beautiful songs of Praise, in Hebrew and English, which the Lord gave her in Jerusalem. We hope she will publish a Jerusalem song book some day. After four years away, the Lord sent the Hjertstedts back to their beloved Israel in 1990!!

DIER EL KAMAR

This is the name of a Christian village in the Shouf Mountains southeast of Beirut, Lebanon. It was under constant attack by PLO and Amal Islamic forces during Israel's push into Lebanon against Arafat's PLO forces during 1982-84. God used us and other churches in Jerusalem to reach all the way into those bloody mountains to bring

CHAPTER 21: SEARCH FOR A CHURCH AND OIL 345

some Christmas joy and hope there!

A great privilege was ours from late November 1983 to late February 1984, to substitute for the Pastor of the Tabernacle of Praise, David Hjertstedt, while he and his wife Faith, and daughter Joy, were on a much needed "R & R" vacation in Washington State. Fortunately, there were four fine young men in the small fellowship who took turns helping in the ministry, so the load was not too great. All the services were well attended, and richly blessed by the Lord.

In fact, during that Christmas we had the privilege by God's grace, together with 4 other Jerusalem Churches, plus the Israel Foreign Ministry, and the Israel Fruit & Vegetable Producers Assoc. of getting tons of food sent to help the Christian refugees in South Lebanon, who had been under siege. Sending food to the besieged Christians in Lebanon was initiated by a very courageous, one-armed Christian living frugally in the border village of Metulla, Grant Livingston and his wife Barbara, and Bruce Balfour from Canada, long-time friends of these Christians in Lebanon.

Further, the Lord let us help send all the way to Dier El Kamar in the Shouf Mountains, a Christmas program group of 33 persons in a motley caravan, with gifts of love, joy and hope to some 2500 Christians still trapped by enemy forces.

Because of our responsibilities to the Tabernacle of Praise, Betsy and I did not feel we could join the convoy taking the food and Christmas program into Dier El Kamar. We certainly wanted to! But we did drive up to Metulla with them and pray and wave them through the Good Fence at the Border Gate. As it turned out they were delayed at the Lebanese border an extra day on returning. We, back in Jerusalem, were about to call out the Israeli army, fearing for their safety. When they finally returned 24 hours late, they told us of their exciting passage through the various check-points of the Communist Lebanese factions which were isolating the Christian Villages in the mountains.

They arrived at the besieged Christian town of Dier El Kamar at sunset and were welcomed with open arms by the residents who presented each of the visitors with a rose and a sprig of Lebanese cedar, wrapped in cellophane with the label "Ditez Avec Des Fleurs" (Say it with flowers!). Two wonderful Christmas worship services followed, with praise, testimonies, special music and almost the whole Church raising their hands in response to the invitation to invite Jesus into their hearts! A truly memorable Christmas for them all. There is no way of knowing whether these Christians in their little village in the Shouf Mountains survived that crazy war that surrounded them, and still goes on in parts of Lebanon. One thing we know, they had a happy Christmas Day in 1983, because 33 young Christians from Jerusalem braved extraordinary dangers to reach them with the Love, Joy, Hope, Songs and Story of JESUS! May God grant their full survival!

THE YELLOW BIRD ARRIVES
AND WE GET TO SEE THE EGYPTIAN PYRAMIDS IN THE PROCESS.

After three years of climbing mountains, riding buses, and sometimes renting a little Autobianchi for our circuits to visit the Believers in Israel, to encourage them in the Lord, we began sensing from the Lord that He wanted us to have a little car of our own for these travels. We had heard various stories of how departing workers had left good cars in the care of friends, or given them outright, or for a pittance turned them over to a worthy servant. Could that happen to us? Well, let us share with you how the Lord did provide us with a neat little car.

It wasn't so easy as you will see. We think Israelis must figure that they have enough cars and problems with traffic already; they don't need more cars on the road, especially tourists. But about the first of December we started looking for a car, wanting to have it for all the approaching rainy, cold season! We looked at a new little Autobianchi, 2 doors and just big enough for us, but the salesman acted as though it wasn't available.

Then some friends at the next worship service said they might sell their car to us if they went back to the States in January. Now listen to this. They said they would sell it for just the price of their plane tickets to the States (first-class), half the price of the Autobianchi!! Their car was a Peugeot, four door, hatch back, very compact with very low mileage. For how much? Quite a bargain! The Lord was fixing things, but there was some work for us to do.

On January 10th, Fred (the friend with the car) and I went to the customs office to transfer the title, or so we thought, but found it was impossible now for a tourist to just sell a car, passport to passport, to another tourist. Finally, the custom man said the only way we could do it was by taking the car out of the country. So we got in touch with a man recommended by a friend, who handles such things, a Mr. Davidson. He said not only did the car have to go out of the country, but the new owners would too, since Betsy and I had been more than three months in Israel. Hence the trip to Egypt became necessary, which we'll share later.

Everything was going smoothly we thought. Fred and the man went to Haifa and shipped the car to Cyprus, no problem. Fred and his wife would fly to the States on January 21, and would mail the bill of sale directly to us by airmail, registered, and special delivery! We would go

CHAPTER 21: SEARCH FOR A CHURCH AND OIL

on a three-day trip to Cairo, Egypt in order to get, on our return, a new visa stamp in our passports as tourists, and so be eligible to bring in a car. All this was done. (Something of a charade!)

Then back in Jerusalem we waited, and waited, and waited the arrival of the Bill of Sale. By a series of miracles, we were able to find out, with the help of our good Hebrew speaking neighbor Ruth, that the registered letter had arrived, but the special delivery man had not tried to deliver it, and had sent it back, marked "unknown," to the U.S. by "slow boat!" Davidson, the orthodox Jewish man who was helping us to ship the car, said the same thing had happened to him, and he went to the special post office the next day with me and got the manager there to write a letter, confessing their mistake. With this and other important papers, we went to Haifa that same day, and got the little yellow car (by God's favor) back through the port and custom authorities with permission to keep it in the country for one month! A phone call to the States followed to get Fred to send a zerox copy of the original bill of sale. By plain airmail it arrived on time, and even though our name on the bill of sale was covered up by the registered-letter-receipt (also zeroxed on the copy), because our name was on the registry slip, Davidson was able to get our "yellow Bird" car cleared for a year's stay in Israel!! Hallelujah! "Savlanut" in Israel (Patience) is a must!

So nothing is easy in Israel, but through all that, we became friends with Mr. Davidson and he invited us to the Bar Mitzva of his son!! God has His plan and purpose for everything, if we'll just hang on with enough Savlanut!"

This had all been extra difficult because I had not been feeling up to par. Two bouts with the flu that winter, left me with a hang-on cough. But, praise the Lord, the coughing finally ended and I was "alive" again, with a real car to travel in!

THE EGYPT TRIP

Can we go back a little and tell you about our quick trip to Egypt? We left on January 24th and returned to Israel on the 26th. Our Galilee Tour bus left Jerusalem at 7:30 a.m. and arrived at Raffia, the new border, about 11 a.m. After two hours of border formalities, we went on our way along the northern Sinai coast on an Egyptian bus. The driver, a Mr. Rask (a Moslem with 3 wives and 11 kids--not on the bus!) was a very pleasant man, even with such a long drive from Cairo and back in one day (close to 500 miles total!). The almond trees were in blossom through the Gaza strip. When we passed El Arish, the former border, the drive was beautiful along the Mediterranean with palm trees gracing the beach. Not the same as Miami beach, but there were a few small hotels being built, and a summer palace for President Mubarak, with Bedouin shacks and tents nearby.

Our Egyptian guide, a Coptic Christian, waited to welcome us into Egypt until after we had passed through El Arish, the Biblical division for Egypt and Israel, which was just a wadi. All along the road across the Sinai were more Bedouin shacks and tents. We had to reach the Suez Canal before the last ferryboat at 5 p.m. We arrived about 4:30 to see a long line of waiting trucks and cars. However, our guide must have had special clearance, because we went right on the ferry, no wait. There was no activity on the canal on the way to Cairo. It was getting dark, but on our return crossing we saw a large tanker, really close up. Part of the way from the Suez Canal to Cairo we drove along a smaller canal, where the people were washing dishes, clothes, and themselves in the same water, and some say, drinking it too!! We had taken along two canteens of water, and as warned, were careful not to eat any fresh vegetables or fruits. Praise God, we had no trouble with upset stomachs.

We had reservations in a small, very clean hotel with a convenient room right near the 24 hr. dining room. It was 8:30 p.m. when we arrived in Cairo. Such traffic! They don't seem to believe in traffic lights. And cars come from all directions at once. Somehow, mysteriously, they miss each other! The main streets are real wide, reminded us a bit of Washington, D.C., but the side streets quite narrow, and dirty. I'm sure we didn't see the worst parts of the city where there are so many people, 12 million, plus or minus a few, that some have to live in the graveyards!!

On Tuesday we took a tour of the Great Pyramid, and saw many more in the distance. Somewhat foolishly we climbed up inside the big one on a long narrow stone ascent. A lot of close, cramped climbing. Claustrophobia almost got us! Never again! This was the ramp they slid the Pharoah's coffin up into the closed-in burial room high up in the pyramid. There was little air there. When the guide pointed out the room's center and a peephole for the sun, some people prayed to the sun god, but we stood there and sang softly, "He Is Lord, Jesus is Lord!" Hallelujah! We did two trips in one on that climb, our first and last!! Never, never again!

We saw the Sphinx and the Valley Temple, made with huge blocks of granite. How they ever got them into this desert area and fit them so neatly together without mortar is a marvel! Then the guide took us to see how they make Cleopatra perfume, a tourist trap; and how they make papyrus, most interesting. We were supposed to go to the Cairo museum, but we'd had enough for one day, especially when we had to

CHAPTER 21: SEARCH FOR A CHURCH AND OIL 349

leave the hotel for the return bus trip at 4:30 a.m.!!

On the return trip we just made the ferry as it was leaving the dock at 7:15 a.m. and was our driver happy! He looked back at us, rejoicing with the Arab words for very good - "Kulshi Kwais!" We had no problems getting through the Israeli customs and immigration authorities, which was the purpose for our trip, and were back in Jerusalem at 3:30 p.m--to be greeted by snow!! It was good to fall into bed and sleep a night and a half!!

How did the little car become the "Yellow Bird?" All because of its canary yellow color and "flying" us on many precious visits in Israel. Today, it's still there serving the Lord with another couple who love the Lord and Israel because of Him!.

ANDY SORELLE AND THE ASHER OIL PROJECT

Most people probably know that the little nation of Israel is even today almost totally "oil-less." In the last two or three years (1985-88), according to news reports, there have been some shallow-well findings between the Dead Sea and Ashkelon on the Mediterranean, but nothing of real important commercial value. Israel is still having to obtain oil from Norway, USA and Egypt-- from the wells it had developed in the lower Sinai Peninsula, called the Rodeis Oil Field, now given back to Egypt's control.

Some humorists have kiddingly said that Moses and Joshua must have missed their directions to the Promised Land, and taken a left turn instead of a right turn into Saudi Arabia and the oil riches there. But there are some men, sincere Bible Believers, that understand Deut. 33:24 to mean that one day the lower part of the region assigned to Asher would be very productive in oil. ***And of Asher he said, Let Asher be blessed with children, let him be acceptable to his brethren, and let him dip his foot in oil.*** And of course Israel, as a modern nation, geared to all the mechanical advancements of the age, like buses, cars, planes, farm machinery, tractors, trucks and, yes, tanks, must have a lot of oil for its farming, tourism and factories and its modern and necessary military forces.

One of those men who firmly believes this Word about Asher's foot being dipped in oil is the highly trained and experienced Texas oil man, Andy SoRelle from Houston. Around 1980 or '81, Andy was finally able to gain permission from the Israel government, to fly some of his sophisticated, seismic radiation reading instruments over this region just below Haifa, and to make other topical, ground seismic surveys, and became convinced there was some real oil for Israel under "Asher's foot." Earlier he had helped the Israelis in some of the Rodeis oil discoveries.

After this he was able to secure an oil lease along that part of the Coast and permission to drill. Mike Lambert's father Vick (one of Texas' great oil drillers) was chief engineer on the drilling crew and Mike was his "mud" engineer. Mud is that type of sludge that has to be poured into the drill shaft to lubricate the drill bit. It is constantly recycled and tested.

The whole story one day will be told by Andy, we trust. It's filled with miracle after miracle, with occasional slight signs of oil, through many difficult layers of rock to the depth of 21,428 feet. After having to add some heavy duty pipe, the drill became stuck in oil pitch and rock and the drill pipe broke. Weeks of tedious effort failed to retrieve the broken pipe and drill bit, so after a year and a half of drilling and some 12 million dollars in cost, the whole operation had to shut down. They seemed to be so near to a big "find."

Andy, having been a Full Gospel Business Mens Fellowship leader in Houston, would come up as often as he could to worship with us at the Tabernacle of Praise in Jerusalem. And when they were in a crucial spot, he would ask Pastor David Hjertstedt and the congregation for special prayer.

On two different occasions as we were praying, the Lord gave me two different visions, to my surprise, of what was happening in the hole. The first one showed a geological cross-section of the earth from the shore-line down to the drill-bit. It showed that the bit was reaching down to the base of a huge dome of oil. The top of the dome was south of this point and much closer to the earth's surface. Some months later the second vision related to Andy's request to pray they could reach the oil before 21,000 feet, and the Lord showed me a numerical counter that quickly went up to 22,000 feet and began flashing. It seemed the Lord was saying that to reach oil at that point, Andy's team would have to go down even further. Not knowing anything about oil drilling and not knowing Andy personally, I was reluctant to share these visions with him, but did. He said thanks and went on about his business.

Just before coming back to the States for the summer in 1983, Betsy and I received a call from his precious wife, Maxine, inviting us to come stay with them a few days at the hotel in Tel Aviv where they were, for prayer and encouragement and fellowship. This came from our friendship with Valerie Waller and the Sidloes--and the Lord.

At dinner, the first night with them, we were joined by Andy's American seismic oil-study consultant. While Andy and Maxine were taking overseas phone calls, we shared with this oil geologist about the two visions the Lord had given me, how the Atlit drilling was going

CHAPTER 21: SEARCH FOR A CHURCH AND OIL

down just north of the oil dome into its base. This man immediately said, "That's exactly what my studies showed. Why they drilled as far north as they did, I've never understood." But this fully confirmed the visions!

One of those days Andy blessed us with a trip from Tel Aviv up to the oil drilling site at Atlit. We got to climb on the drill rig and take some pictures (it was not operating at that moment), and Betsy and I got to do a "Joshua March" around the base of the rig. When we ended the march we prayed and sang again the song, "To God Be The Glory." As we were singing, I saw another vision--of oil gushing up out of this well! We told Andy about seeing a vision of oil gushing up from their well and he surprised us by saying, "Oh No, not a gusher! They are hard to control."

Together we prayed for the Lord to shake up the earth and cause the oil to come up anyway. The well geologist, an Israeli, showed us mud samples that he regularly collected, some of them showing faint signs of oil. However, the work had to be shut down, until the Lord provided more funds and directions, and obviously it just was not God's timing to bring forth oil there.

Part of the reason was that, almost immediately, back in the States, Andy needed by-pass heart surgery and, very soon afterwards, surgery for an old stomach ulcer that had ruptured. The Lord was wonderfully merciful to him and brought him through those two deadly situations. Today after finally raising sufficient money to drill again and after negotiating around some Israeli roadblocks, Andy will soon be trying again. May God bless them and give them good success in reaching the oil in Asher's foot for Israel and the Lord!

There was a large news article in the Jerusalem Post, back then, about Andy and the Atlit drilling. A lot of people were ridiculing this effort, based on God's Word as well as on seismic studies. However, we are firm believers that God's promises are sure, His Word is true, and as His Word says, God always has the last laugh! (Psalm 2:1-4). Also we believe that Andy is God's man for this job. Pray much for him.

AN AMAZING SEQUEL

It is not widely known but is absolutely true, that God's Atlit well has already poured out oil on Asher's foot! The drilling was stopped about August 1983, the rig dismantled, and the well pipe received a concrete plug and a heavy-duty cap. Greatly discouraged, Andy and Maxine and their crew all went home; Andy to face the heart and ruptured ulcer surgeries during that winter ('83-'84).

Remember now, we had all prayed that the Lord would even shake up the earth to bring real oil up that pipe some day soon. In the spring of 1984, while convalescing in Houston, and hearing about two earthquakes that crossed the Atlit site, it occurred to Andy to check if anything had happened at the well. He called Jerusalem to his secretary, Valerie Waller, and asked her to get their geologist to go up to Atlit, uncap the well pipe, and see if anything had happened. The geologist went and, when he uncapped the pipe, out poured oil on the ground, equal to four or five barrels of it! We wish he had been prepared to catch the oil. It would have made the most valuable oil souvenirs in the world. It was truly a mighty answer to prayer and the initial fulfillment of God's promise to Jacob's son Asher in Deut.33:24!!!

(To help you to know Andy as a chosen servant of God, and saved by the very hand of God, for finding oil in Israel, please read the following Guidepost Magazine story of Andy as a young fighter pilot in World War II. Used with permission.)

"OUT OF CONTROL"[1] (Andy's Shot-up Plane!)
By: Andrew C. SoRelle, Jr.
Houston, Texas

After the invasion of France in 1944 our outfit, the 48th Fighter Group, 9th Air Force, was one of the first to be moved to Normandy. A steel matted flying strip was laid out for us through apple orchards and hedgerows. We were flying several missions each day in support of our front line troops.

About noon one day in early July, operations received orders to send four Thunderbolts to attack a column of German trucks. It was a typical mission except for one thing: the weather was very bad. The enemy was taking advantage of the weather to retreat, hoping that we would not dare to fly in the prevailing weather conditions.

The four of us took off and stayed low, just beneath the cloud ceiling. Just as we came over the top of a hill, there they were -- trucks and equipment, bumper to bumper, on the highway below. We did not have the advantage of surprise, because after we spotted the convoy we had to circle and return and by that time the enemy was ready for us. Most of the men had scattered into ditches by the roadside. Others

---

[1] Reprinted with permission from Guideposts Magazine. Copyright 1966 by Guideposts Associates, Inc. Carmel, N.Y. 10512. Used with permission of author.

CHAPTER 21: SEARCH FOR A CHURCH AND OIL

had mounted guns and were firing a crossfire through which we were forced to fly. As we made our run it seemed that the whole overcast day was lit up with German tracers.

All of a sudden I felt a heavy jolt to my plane and immediately it went out of control. A German 88-mm shell had ripped a three-foot hole through the left wing.

By a miracle the shell, fused to go off on contact, did not explode. But it did cut the aileron cable. The aileron itself, that all-important tab on the trailing edge of the wing, fell from the plane. I knew in that instant that I had lost my aircraft, 90 percent of my flying control came from the two ailerons, one was gone entirely, and the other was flopping in the wind.

I knew, too, exactly what my plane would do. It would nose down and barrel-roll to the left. Aerodynamically, there was no other possibility and that is precisely what did start to happen. I was only 200 feet from the ground when the roll started. I knew I was going to die. In the seconds that followed I lived an eternity, waiting for the crash.

What happened next, I am told, could not have happened.

Just a few feet from the ground that battle-torn old Thunderbolt snap-rolled. There were no controls on the aircraft with which such a maneuver could be accomplished, and yet it happened. Instead of barrel-rolling, nose down, to the left, I was making a steep climbing turn to the right, just what I needed to do to return to the airstrip.

My plane continued to do the impossible, it flew into the low overcast and leveled out. I could not see the ground. I didn't care! Somehow I had been given a few extra seconds of time and I wanted to get out of that uncontrollable machine as fast as I could. I threw open the canopy and tried to avoid the wildly gyrating stick, as I got loose from all of my harness. I stood up in my seat, just below the slip-stream and tried to go out over the left side of the plane.

But again forces beyond my control took command. Why couldn't I climb out? It was as if I were being physically held back. I looked down into the cockpit - what a mess! My instruments gone, the stick making wild circular movements, and yet my Thunderbolt was flying just as I would have flown it if I had been able. I sat down and buckled up again.

Suddenly I broke out of the overcast and I knew where I was. To my left was the English Channel with barrage balloons, landing craft, warships. And to my right? I looked, knowing what I would see, and there it was. I was approaching my landing strip. I could see the runway just to the right of my plane's nose.

The only control I had left was the tail rudder, which moved the plane right or left. I quickly gave right rudder, which made me do a flat skid that aligned me with the runway. I put the wheels in the down position, and hoped they had dropped: with no instrument panel, I could not tell. With no ailerons the only way I could control the altitude of the aircraft was to cut the throttle: that would make me fall. I chopped the throttle hard and the plane fell away beneath me.

I hit perfectly, right at the beginning of the matted runway. I was going close to 170 miles per hour. The little Thunderbolt bounced violently and dove toward the runway a second time. Again it bounced and almost nosed over. With each new, violent bounce the end of the matting came closer. The very day before I would have plowed into the hedgerows at the end of the runway, but that night the engineers had come in and bulldozed about 200 more yards of runway. My plane hit the new mud and started skidding around and around and finally stopped.

After I turned off the ignition switch, I sat quietly in a supernatural hush. In that silence God became real to me. Audibly, or in my spirit, I heard five clear words, "I have saved your life." I knew I was in the indescribable presence of God. Of course, He was there! He had piloted my plane safely home.

The sirens were screaming across the field. I sat, and listened, and as they raced toward me I knew my friends were going to find a different man in the cockpit of that Thunderbolt from the pilot who had climbed aboard an hour earlier. How could it be otherwise: I no longer belonged to myself at all!

ANDY & MAXINE SORELLE & FRIENDS NEAR ATLIT OIL WELL SITE

CHAP. 21: SEARCH FOR A CHURCH AND OIL   354A

A) ANDY'S ATLIT OIL WELL

B) THE "CLOWN" OPERATOR

C) CORRESPONDENT JAN KARNIS, WIFE JANICE & MIRACLE SON SIMON

D) SOME PRECIOUS MEMBERS OF TABERNACLE OF PRAISE FAMILY

354B   FIRED AGAIN AND AGAIN, PRAISE THE LORD!

OUR TOUR GROUP AT THE MODEL OF THE OLD CITY
WITH FAVORITE GUIDE MOSHE DAYAGI

WITH BROTHER FRANK AND MICAL AT CALVARY, JERUSALEM, 1985

CELEBRATING ESTHER'S FIRST BOOK EDITION
NEXT TO OUR "YELLOW BIRD"

CHAP. 22

A DREAM COME TRUE--PATMOS

The heavens declare the glories of God and the firmament sheweth His handywork.   - Psalm 19:1

Here we are for the sixth time on the famous little Island of Patmos, an island off the western coast of Turkey, so amazingly blessed in the first Century A.D. by the visit of our risen, glorified Saviour Jesus to His beloved John, the Apostle. It still carries an aura of the holiness and glory of that heavenly visit. You should read about this miraculous visit in the first chapter of Revelation. The native Greeks on this Island understand the importance of trying to protect it's name as a holy island, because of Christ's visitation.

Some islands, we are told, are wide open and worldly, but not Patmos. Praise the Lord for that! Almost daily large cruise ships come loaded often with hundreds of tourists most curious to see this special Island. Our landlord also drives one of the several buses that take the tourists up to the huge fortress-like monastery on top of the mountain. Large numbers of devout Christians come to Patmos.

Why have we been here six times? The first three times ('83,'84,'85) were entirely to help Esther come and have the isolation necessary to complete her book, and to help her edit and make corrections also. The very last part of her book was done in Jerusalem, after her typewriter broke down here on the Island. Her excellent book, called "*I Am My Beloved's*" was finally published in Jerusalem in 1985. (By '91 it was in three languages with 22,000 copies distributed!)

The Lord let us come back here in May of '86, when we were "fired" from Israel, to lick our wounds and to begin our book of His many miracles in our lives. He sent us again in '87 and now in '88. Here, there are no distractions of telephone, T.V. or mail call. We have been getting much done, Praise the Lord forever! And we have a deep love for our Greek friends here and in Athens!

356   FIRED AGAIN AND AGAIN, PRAISE THE LORD!

In '84 we wrote a piece about Beautiful, Peaceful Little Patmos. We hope you will enjoy taking the trip with us in it.

- - - - - - - - - -

"BEAUTIFUL, PEACEFUL, LITTLE PATMOS - 1984"
"Let them give glory to the Lord and declare His praise in the Islands." (Isa.42:12)

Jerusalem,
April, 1984

Dear Family and Friends,

Dreaming!

As a child did you dream, as we did, of going to some distant island or land of ancient culture to see and sense that clime, unhurriedly, for a time? And thought, "Oh that can never be. Too far, too costly, no time for that." We've all dreamed those dreams, sparked by precious teachers at home, at church or in school. My mother gave her big family a love for Jesus and the Bible. Love for Israel, the Jews, the Apostles and their writings and travels followed. When we really love and obey Him, our Lord has a marvelous way of making good dreams come true! (Ps.37:4,5; Ro.8:28). Come, join us in another dream-come-true voyage to Patmos.

First Voyage

About this time last year '83, we had the wonderful privilege of going with Esther, one of our "adopted" Jewish daughters, to Athens, Greece, to visit two of her dear friends there and baptize them. After two lovely days, we went on to Patmos on a large sea-ferry, a beautiful 11-hour voyage southeast among the islands of the Aegean Sea. Our objectives were to help Esther with her luggage (including a heavy electric typewriter), to help her find, hopefully, a small apartment for 6 weeks of quiet work on her book manuscript, and to get a bit of rest ourselves. The first night there we were in a little beach-front hotel. The next morning, after prayer and about an hour's search, the Lord led us to a very neat, small apartment. As with most pilgrims, we fell in love with Patmos. You could sense the special serenity and presence of the Lord in this island, no doubt because the Lord chose it for Apostle John's exile and the place to receive the Revelation of Jesus Christ. After only six restful days, wondering if we would ever return to that lovely island, Betsy and I had to leave to meet a tour group of friends coming to Israel. This tour group later visited Patmos also and delivered Esther's mail to her!

Invited Back

Well, Esther worked hard and completed about 200 pages of her book, but still had much more to do. The Lord had her traveling through the summer, fall and winter. No time for the book. This spring she asked if we could go again with her to Athens and Patmos as helpers

CHAPTER 22: A DREAM COME TRUE--PATMOS

and prayer partners. The dear Greek ladies, Nellie and Sophia, also invited us to come, and we felt the Lord's leading to do so. How good of the Lord to let us go again, especially after a month of battle with flu and an ulcerated throat. Both of us were needing a sunny retreat, far from phones and heavy traffic. Going to Patmos isn't all that easy, but when you get there, you find it's worth the effort.

Wrong Ticket

On the Friday before the trip we go to pick up our plane tickets at the Ambassador Travel Agency, in downtown Jerusalem, parking the "Yellow Bird" nearby in a space between other cars, and 10 minutes later when we return, the "Yellow Bird" is gone!! Then we realize we were in a no-parking place, and now there is only an hour before everything closes for the Sabbath. "Ma Laasot?" (What to do?) We have several other errands planned. Can we find the "car-pound?" Wonderfully, the Lord leads us across the street to a taxi-stand and they know all about the problem, and where to take us. With the help of one of them, we are soon out on Hebron Road paying the $25 towing charge and retrieving "Yellow Bird", which we are happy to see is, outwardly, in good shape. A $20 parking ticket must be paid at the post office. This $45 lesson we don't want to repeat! Yet we marvel at the speed and peace the Lord has given us in retrieving the "bird" and helping us get the other errands done that day.

Miracle Repairs

On the day before the trip, March 28, we have more errands to do, including taking Esther's and our baggage to the El Al Airline office for pre-flight check-in. This will give us an extra hour before checking into the airport (35 miles away) at 5 a.m. the next morning, March 29. About noon, riding in the "Yellow Bird," we notice a scraping noise coming from a front wheel, and know right away the disc brakes are gone. (Groan!) Our friend, Matt, who is taking us to the airport and using the car in our absence, will need brakes, too! Jerusalem and Israel are full of hills and mountains! Brakes wear out quickly. Again, what to do?! Who in all Israel would do a brake job by six p.m.? Call Robert, a kind Arab mechanic. His wife says he's not home, but he'll call when he comes in. About 3 p.m. he calls. Yes, he can do it if we bring "Yellow Bird" right away. By 3:30 the "Bird" and I reach his shop - a parking lot across Jerusalem. Keeps his tools and heavy jacks in his car. Sure enough the brakes are gone, so off he goes to buy new parts and in an hour the brakes are replaced, plus new spark plugs, and a parking light is fixed. Bless his heart, his bill is unbelievably low! By five, I'm home helping Betsy finish packing our bags. The Lord has provided another miracle!

A Miracle Key

At 7 p.m. we head toward Ramot on the north side of Jerusalem, to pick up Esther and her heavy luggage. Soon we are back in town at the El Al Office unloading, with a heaven-sent "legal" parking place right in front of the office. A crowd of travelers are checking in their bags; there is a wait, not unusual. Suddenly, Esther remembers that she has locked one of her bags and left the key at her apartment. As we struggle with another key to no avail, a friendly Jewish man next to us says he has several keys - try his! He is wearing a Greek-type fisherman's hat. Praise the Lord, one of his keys works! And all the bags are soon checked in. While thanking the man for the key, mention is made of our going to Athens and Patmos, and that we'll be seeing hats like his. He says he has a little grandson back in Illinois who dearly loves his hat, and he wishes he could find one small enough for him, but he would not get back to Greece this trip. We tell him we will look for one and send it to him. Later, on Patmos we do find a small hat and air-mail it to him. Somewhere there's a happy grandson, and granddad, by the Lord's appointment, wearing Greek fisherman's hats!

The Lord's Healing

After getting Esther home, we felt we had to visit a dear Jewish friend, several miles north of Jerusalem, who had been quite ill. We felt the Lord wanted us to go and anoint him and pray for his healing in the Name of Jesus. We phoned earlier, and he said we could come, even late. When we finally got to his apartment, he and wife warmly greeted us and gave us refreshments. Not only was he in pain from some kind of stomach problem, which the doctors had not been able to diagnose after long stays in the hospital, but his wife was ill too, with an obvious case of flu. Both gladly received the anointing and prayers in Jesus' Name, and we believe both were wonderfully healed by the Lord. They are immigrants from Russia.

Big Hurdle and Flight to Athens

By the time we get home, we have only about 4 hours left to sleep before the alarm buzzes for the run again to Esther's, then to Matt's and then to the airport. Along with our other pieces of hand luggage, we also have the heavy IBM electric typewriter wrapped in a blanket in a suitcase as carry-on luggage!! Thank the Lord for Matt's earlier help, but now comes a big hurdle! Carrying that thing up those plane steps is a tough problem, and the stewardess almost refuses to allow it, but having only a half-filled plane, she relents and stows it under an empty seat. Bless her!

It is a balmy, sunny morning, with some lovely clouds visiting Israel! We enjoy the breakfast on the plane as the Mediterranean Sea and Aegean Island scenes pass below. After only two hours, we are landing

CHAPTER 22: A DREAM COME TRUE--PATMOS 359

in Athens. Now another struggle with that IBM suitcase! After thanking the stewardess, I get about halfway down the steps and here comes a little man running to take the suitcase to the plane-bus for us. Praise the Lord, another angel!! Inside the airport we quickly check through passport control and customs, and on to an airport bank to purchase some Greek drachmas. The Lord leads us to the right place again, for the teller speaks English and kindly calls Nellie at work for us to get specific directions to their house for the taxi man. Soon we are rolling through very crowded and busy Athens to the north-side where their apartment awaits us, the front door key under "You know what!"

Gracious Hostesses

Soon, too, we are all resting (me, sound asleep), waiting to greet Nellie and Sophia when they come home from work. Sophia is a secretary in an oil business; and Nellie is the Greek-English translator for a Christian Greek-American Orphan Relief Society. Needless to say it was a happy reunion for all of us. We share some little gifts which we have brought them, and they welcome us to sit down to a bountiful Greek dinner. During the dinner Nellie tells us that she can't use her car in down-town Athens every day, only every other day, because of the extreme traffic problem. (There are 5 million people in the Athens-Pireaus megalopolis). So tomorrow we may use the car to go some 40 miles southwest to visit ancient Corinth. We had hoped to visit Corinth last year and couldn't. She has remembered! The goodness of the Lord never ceases! That evening there is much sharing, hymn singing, and Greek lessons. And late to bed!

Drive To Corinth

The next morning Nellie and Sophia go to work early; Esther decides to go to town for some needed purchases; and we gird up our courage with prayers and head out of Athens in Nellie's little car (a yellow one too!), going toward Corinth according to the careful directions given to us by Nellie. The highway is a good one and the drive a lovely one along the coast to the Corinthian Canal (a remarkable engineering feat and sight!) Then to new Corinth and directions from a police sergeant to ancient Corinth, a quaint rural village with tourist shops and some Greek temple ruins. All around are fantastic views across flower-covered fields, and to the north across the Bay of Corinth, snow-capped mountains. Now comes a big problem! The key that locks the car is missing! Somehow, it has fallen off the loose key-ring, so we can't lock the car and take the tour through the ruins. A search of the car floor is fruitless, so where could we have lost it? It is also the gas-cap key! Maybe it fell off after we unlocked the car, back in Athens, and is still there by the curb. Oh boy! Rather, Oh Lord, Help! He seems to be saying, "Calm down," and we do.

So we drive part way up a nearby mountain to get an overview of this region where the Apostle Paul spent a year and a half in ministry and to where he sent two of his major letters of guidance to followers of Jesus. On the side of the mountain we stop for a time to read portions of Acts and I Corinthians 13, and have a prayer of thanksgiving for Paul's work in ancient Corinth, and even today!

Then we head back toward Athens, stopping along the way to take pictures of the coast line, still wondering about the "lost" key. Nellie's directions are perfect, we return to her corner and find a convenient parking place near their apartment. Quickly we search the former parking place, but no key. So back to the car and another search of it; this time Success! Down between the seats the wayward key is finally found! Praise the Lord! Our hearts rejoice! So off to the gas station we go to refuel the car. One thing sure, we'll be on the lookout for a more secure key-ring for Nellie. (We did find one for her on Patmos).

Happy Guests

Nellie is already home preparing dinner when we arrive and soon Sophia and Esther come and we share another of their "poli-oreo" (very fine) Greek meals. Afterwards Esther shares about her trips to Poland and Germany. Each night before bedtime, a delicious Greek supper is beautifully served, making us feel like the most important guests in the world, very stuffed, sleepy and happy. Due to their coaching, now we know how to say: "Please and thank you, yes and no, good morning and good evening, okay and goodby" in Greek. Our "mastery" of the language is growing by leaps and bounds!! (Just kidding!)

To the Good Ship Kamiros

On Saturday morning, after a leisurely breakfast, we head for the nearby port of Piraeus in Nellie's little car and a taxi, the taxi leading. After much searching by the taxi driver we finally find the ship, which is also being boarded by hundreds of high schoolers on their spring holiday trip to Rhodes. A porter is found to help get the luggage on the ship, and Nellie and Sophia arrange for us to get some seats in the first class lounge (the cabins are all filled) for the 10-11 hour voyage. After fond goodbyes to dear Nellie and Sophia, we are on our own with those hundreds of bouncing teenagers investigating every nook and cranny of the good ship Kamiros.

The Rhodes Family

An amazing thing is about to happen to us on this ship. Late in the afternoon a nice Greek family with two children come to sit at the table next to us in the ship's lounge. They are friendly and after a time we realize they can speak English as well as Greek, and a little conversation

CHAPTER 22: A DREAM COME TRUE--PATMOS

follows. However, the sun is about to set, and Betsy and Esther want to watch it, so they go out on deck. Later, as I start out to join them, the wife says that her husband, who is out with the children, would like to talk with us more about the Bible when we come back. She says he is very interested in the Bible. This I tell Betsy and Esther as we watch the beautiful sunset. Esther immediately says she feels from the Lord that this man will help with a Greek translation of her book! And sure enough, when we return inside, the conversation soon leads from his study of the Bible and coming to really know Jesus as his Saviour, to how Esther is writing a book about how she, as a Jew, came to believe in Jesus as her Messiah-Saviour. Right away he says that her book should be in Greek, and he has a friend in Rhodes who has the translation and printing facilities to do it. And soon they are inviting us to visit them in Rhodes (they are pharmacists), and we are inviting them to visit us in Jerusalem. Another amazing meeting by the Lord's amazing guidance! Later when a disco develops around us, Nikos is another angel rescuing us in a very noisy situation. Finally, at about 10:45 p.m. we get word that the ship is about to dock briefly at Patmos, so we begin finding our way toward the stern. The ship docks stern first.

Antonios, and Patmos Landing

Esther had written her kind Greek landlord of last year, Antonios Vamvakos, to arrange for apartment accommodations for us and to ask if he would meet the ship (and us) on this date. The little port, called Scala, is a neat white-washed fishing village, with about 200 yards of landing dock or quay. But at night almost none of this is visible as we slowly back toward the dock. Thank goodness, the ship's crew and captain know what they are doing. Soon we hear the stern bridge cables creaking as they lower it to the dock, and suddenly the trucks and cars and people and baggage are pouring out, and in moments, others are flowing in, taking only 4-8 minutes to complete this transfer operation.

His Warm Welcome

Like the other Patmos visitors (and natives), we have moved to the lower deck and are grabbing two bags each and rushing them off, hoping to have time to go back for the others. In the midst of the rush, we catch a glimpse of Antonios carrying off two heavy bags of ours and going back for others, which have to be taken back. Bless his heart--they are not ours! Once on shore with our bags, and that precious IBM typewriter, we pause, catch our breath, and give warm greetings to Antonios. He then helps us load everything into his ancient station wagon (one of the few cars on the island) and takes us up the mountain road to the first bend, to the two little apartments he has for us. Antonios is a very special man with God's hand upon his life. After putting our bags in the rooms, he turns and says that tomorrow is Sunday and no grocery shops will be open, so he will go right then to his house for eggs, crackers and milk for our breakfast. And later in the day we will find a restaurant open. In no time, he returns with ample breakfast fixings! We thank him, and thank him for his great welcome. After he leaves, we have a brief thanksgiving time to the Lord and head for the beds. The boat trip was not rough, but quite cool, and I had gotten very chilled. Now began a night of chills and fever--probably a hangover of the flu bug back in Israel, lasting through the next day.

Sparkling Patmos

So when Antonios comes on Sunday to give us a tour of part of the island, he has only two passengers, Betsy and Esther. I am staying in bed but they tell of their tour with Antonios. Patmos is lushly green and sparkling with many wild flowers, having received unusually heavy spring rains. On the drive Antonios stops to pick lemons from his trees, near Grikou Beach. Olive trees are plentiful, and Antonios tells that several kinds of figs are grown on the island. The fig trees are just leafing out, so no figs yet! After his tour, Esther and Betsy walk downhill to a dockside restaurant for a good lunch and afterwards bring a bountiful dish up for me. A quiet afternoon of sharing, reading and naps, is followed by another trip by Esther and Betsy to the dockside coffee shop where another friend of last year, Stavros, is working and has invited us to come to their opening that evening. People are asking where Betsy's husband is? Later that evening, at the apartment I'm feeling better, and we spend some time praising the Lord together (Betsy using the auto-harp, brought at the request of Nellie and Sophia), reading His Word and praying together.

Rejoicing in The Lord

We're wakened early on Monday morning by the crowing of the roosters, answering each other across the island, the ages-old alarm clock of the world! How wonderful to look out of the kitchen window and see the Apocalypse (the Church over the cave where St. John received The Revelation of Jesus Christ) and above it on top of the mountain in the distance, the famous dark gray Greek Orthodox Monastery of St. John, a huge guardian fortress with the little white-washed houses of the village of Hora nestled around it. Out of our window each morning, you can also see a goat and sheep herder guiding his flocks across the stone walls between the green fields, and hear the sheep bells tinkling musically as they move from field to field. Esther walks to town early this morning to purchase breakfast supplies, and we all enjoy breakfast together in our kitchen area, so she can keep

CHAPTER 22: A DREAM COME TRUE--PATMOS

her typewriter and papers out on the table in her room. After breakfast Esther goes to work on her book, and we relax a while and then walk leisurely to town for errands, breathing deeply the fresh sea air, soaking in the Patmos sunshine, and rejoicing in the Lord to be feeling so much better.

Enter Motorbike!

However, my gimpy right knee starts complaining going down and up the long hill. So I begin thinking maybe there's a motorbike on the island for me. We've noticed some for rent. Last year, while riding one, I took a hard spill on some loose gravel here, so I'm debating. At 66 years, I am not a "spring chicken!" Two days later the knee wins the debate!! For the next six days I ride the groceries and bottled water up that hill on a zippy little motorbike. No spills! Thank The Lord! Betsy and Esther leave the bike riding to me.

Kitchen Vacation For Betsy

But this day, we're walking and Esther will meet us for lunch at the friendly dockside restaurant. We find it quite inexpensive to eat out on Patmos: a delicious dinner for three people, costing only $6 to $8!! (Doubled by 1990!) So our Patmos visit will be a nice vacation from the kitchen for Betsy, too! After lunch we stroll along the dock, watching the small fish in the clear water, the boats, sailors, the tourists,--then slowly up the hill. Antonios comes along and gives us a ride to the apartment! Esther is already there, typing away.

A Small World

So while Esther works hard at writing, we're "working hard" at resting and praying! Late afternoon, back to Scala for supper we all go, then for a cup of special coffee (cappachino) at Stavros' lively coffee shop. To get a seat together, we must ask if we can sit next to a pleasant looking girl reading a book. In the conversation which follows Esther says she is from Israel and the girl shouts, "What?" She is also from Israel--Tel Aviv. We'll call her Miriam. She's a sweet Israeli girl who has been studying in England for three years. We enjoy speaking a little Hebrew and talking of Israel here on this Greek Island! We can sense her tender heart as she relates how she cries each time she drives up to Jerusalem with her family. Since it is getting dark, we express our joy in meeting her and hope to meet again, then take leave to make our climb up the hill, stopping by a bookshop on our way to look for a Greek-English tourist dictionary for Esther. The friendly shopkeeper, recognizing Esther and hearing that she is back to finish her book, and that it may be in Greek, tells Esther that he wants to have her book in his shop when it's finished. We continue our hike up to the apartment under a heavenly ceiling of twinkling stars. Always a special treat, seeing those bright stars and knowing the One who put them there and set their courses!

A Special Word

On Tuesday morning we are thrilled as the Lord directs our attention to Isaiah 42:12: "Let them give glory to the Lord and declare His praise in the islands." So here we are on the Lord's island, by the Lord's direction and provision. With thankful hearts we are determined to fill this island with His praise!

Meeting Friend Aristedes

While Esther continues her work on a new chapter in her book, Betsy and I walk to town to explore the village and do errands. There is sunshine, but a cool wind is blowing. In the narrow street, slowly comes a motor-bike with a man and his little boy riding it. We quickly recognize our friend, Aristedes, the taxi man who was so nice to us last year, and his son, Chris. He stops for a friendly reunion and we inquire about his health and his family. He tells us that since last year, he has had to have two major operations on his back on the island of Rhodes, and the doctors say he'll have to have more. Well, praise God, I sense a strong leading from the Holy Spirit to ask him if we could pray for him and ask the Lord to heal his back. He quietly nods his head, and as we begin to anoint him and lay hands on him and pray for him in the Name of Jesus, right there, he humbly crosses himself, and we believe he received a wonderful healing from the Lord at that moment. We would see him several more times while there and each time he said he was feeling better. When we left the island a week later, late at night, this dear friend was there to see us off, with tears in his eyes. To God be all the praise and glory in Jesus' Name.

A Fish Lunch At Hora

After the errands we walk back up the hill to meet Esther and catch the island's one public bus up the mountain to Hora for a fish lunch in a tiny little restaurant Esther knew about. And as we climb through the village, we come upon our Israeli friend Miriam again, having lunch and reading her book. After the delicious fish and Greek salad lunch, we explore the village a bit, taking pictures of the mountain top views, slowly moving back toward the bus stop for our ride down the mountain. Esther has a box of pecan-filled dates, and says they are for the bus driver, if he recognizes her, but for us if he doesn't. In spite of my love for pecans and dates, he recognizes her warmly, on both bus rides that day. We're glad he got the dates, and we got the friendship!

Prepare A Gift

About this time the Lord tells me to prepare one of the two New Testaments I had at the apartment to offer to Miriam, if she would be interested in reading it. We hope to see her at Stavros' coffee shop that

CHAPTER 22: A DREAM COME TRUE--PATMOS

evening. One Testament is my favorite leather-covered one; the other is a new, green-covered Gideon Testament. This one I make ready to give her. When we return to the dockside coffee shop that evening, she does not show up as we expect. She is leaving Patmos the next evening, and we are taking an all-day boat trip to the island of Samos that day. Probably won't see her again. Too bad. Seems I've missed the Lord in this. But He loves to work out things for His children!

Side-Trip To Samos

Bright and early Wednesday, we head for the dock and the island boat which is loading up with a number of passengers to Samos, a Greek island some 40 miles northeast of Patmos, near the coast of Turkey. Some of the passengers are planning to catch a plane from Samos back to Athens and then on to Europe. It is a pleasant, sunny day, and a pleasant, sunny group; most of us sitting up on the sun deck behind the wheel house, out of the cool wind. The captain's cute little brown dog scurries around from passenger to passenger as sort of a one-dog welcoming committee, happy to receive the pats and affection of all, even sitting in the laps of some. Again it is somewhat startling to find ourselves riding on that beautiful Aegean Sea between mountain-top islands, as part of that dream come true.

Straight Northeast

The boat's course seems to be straight northeast from Patmos and the sea is choppy, but not rough. After about three hours we are near Samos, rounding the jetty into the little harbor of Pithagorion, and soon walking through this quaint fishing village. The people are busy painting and repairing, getting ready for summer vacationers and tourists. After a soft drink in a sidewalk cafe, we buy some picture postcards and then catch a cab to cross the mountain to the northside city and capital of Samos. Turkey can be seen to the east about a mile from the island. Our few words of Greek don't succeed in getting the driver talking in English, so we cross the mountain observing the scenery, which doesn't compare with Patmos (but we are a bit prejudiced by now). The port town of Samos is clean and beautiful with a little central park. Here we have a sunny picnic lunch which Bets had prepared, ending with a Samos ice cream cone. Then another taxi ride back over the mountain to our boat. This taxi man shares a bit more, telling us Samos and Turkey, close neighbors, are big friends, and pointing out the very lovely beaches along the way. At 3 p.m. the returning passengers board the Patmos boat, now somewhat loaded with Samos oranges.

A New Friend

We have only about half as many passengers returning, but we soon make friends with an Australian girl who has been trying to get to

Patmos for several days. This young woman, Idal, who later in our story will be an angel for us, was returning from several months in Russia where she had visited her parents' folks. So we all had much to talk about on our way to Patmos; Esther having had some trips to Russia herself!! With the friendly attentions of the captain's little brown dog, and the steady hands of the captain and crew we made it back to Patmos through some rougher waters for a safe landing in Patmos by 6:30 p.m.

Gift To Miriam

As we come down the gang plank, guess whom we see? Our Israeli friend, Miriam! Her ferry boat doesn't leave until 9 p.m., so we all have supper together: Miriam, Idal and we three. Miriam shares how much she will miss this inspiring island of Patmos, how much she enjoys the writings of St. John!!! This from a young Israeli!! Not expecting to see her again, instead of the little green New Testament, I had my favorite leather-covered one in my pocket. Wanting to obey the Lord, I wrap it in a napkin, and present it to her, saying, "The Lord wants me to give this to you, if you would like it. It's a little book I prize very much." She replies with sincere gratitude: "I'll treasure it; I have wanted one in English for some time. I have a Brit Hadashah (New Testament) in Hebrew which I purchased on Joppa Road in Jerusalem!!" Yes, the Lord wanted her to have the leather one!

Goodbye to Miriam

We walk with Miriam to the ferry to say goodbye. We're hoping to meet her again in Israel!! The big ferry unloads and reloads in 4 minutes!! Esther times them! As they are pulling away from the dock, two cars drive up, their head lights blinking toward the ferry, their horns honking, just a goodbye salute!! It's a special island!! This boat is taking away a very special little Jewish girl, deeply touched by the love of that very special Jewish man named Jesus. We are confident we'll see her again. By the way, she said she had a final exam in her course coming up at the school in England, and that she had received, while on Patmos, the inspiration for her final presentation!

A Motorbike Please!

After this night's trudge up the hill, my cranky right knee is telling me, "Please let's try a motorbike tomorrow." And that's exactly what we do! After breakfast, and seeing Esther off to work at her typewriter, we head to the motorbike shop and our friend, Aristedes, who is helping at the shop this day. After some problems with the first bike, he arranges for a better one (starts nicely). Ah, happy knee! Off we go to take our laundry to a friendly cleaner-shop on the waterfront, to gas up at Patmos' one filling station, then to the post office, bank and grocery errands. Esther meets us for Greek stew and salad lunch with Idal and another Australian. Ah, those Greek cooks!

A Timely Call

After a rest at the apartment (Esther still typing away), we go down to the telephone office with its three public phones to call Nellie and Sophia in Athens to let them know that we would be leaving the island Tuesday night, arriving on the ferry Wednesday morning. It's the right moment for a call! Nellie is in bed in much pain from an abscessed tooth extraction, needing antibiotic injections every eight hours, and very glad for our call. She's wanting prayer for the Lord's help! The next night Esther calls again and she says she is much better. Praise the Lord for His daily miracles and answers to the prayers of His children!

Esther Working Hard

We have noticed, on a back street, a new little Greek Pizza place, so we decide to try it for supper. "Nostimos" (delicious!) In fact it was set up almost like a tiny American pizza shop. Afterwards we again spend a while at Stavros' coffee shop with our friend Idal, then up the hill to the apartment. Each evening before prayer and Bible time, Esther treats us to her day's production in writing. Actually, she is working like a Trojan on a Greek island! And amazingly, the Lord is bringing back many almost forgotten details, so real progress is being made already. Fast approaching is a two or three day job which she has asked me to do; namely, making some careful typing corrections which her proof readers have found necessary in earlier pages of her manuscript. Fortunately, about this time, the rains come again to Patmos, making it appropriate to stay in and proceed with these corrections.

Visiting The Monastery of St. John

The next morning is sunny for a while, so we decide to visit the famous Monastery of St. John on top of the mountain, founded around 1088 by a courageous monk named Christodoulos (means servant of Christ). So after breakfast we catch the 9:30 bus up to the mountain village of Hora, and soon we are climbing the steep paths and steps to the monastery. The huge doors are open, and we begin wandering around inside, hoping to find a guide. We hear the sounds of a worship service in a chapel, and enter briefly. Other tourists arrive and soon a gray-bearded priest motions all of us to follow him to a large room (formerly the dining room, now called the treasure room). He unlocks it and invites us to enter this museum of the past, for a slight fee. A treasure room indeed! It is filled with many interesting religious relics: old embroideries with exquisitely done tiny faces, icons, paintings, frescoes, crosses, chalices, vestments, bishops' staffs and miters, ancient parchments and manuscripts, including part of a fifth century

Gospel of Mark and much more. In a nearby room we see the old bakery, obsolete now, with its ovens and huge kneading trough, big as a casket. By accident, we briefly enter their famous library of ancient documents, reserved for scholars with special permission. Some of the older priests in charge with their great white beards beautifully add to the atmosphere of antiquity of the place!

More on the Mountain

From the top of the monastery a fantastic seascape spreads out on all sides, blue sea and distant islands, and the green hills and fertile fields of Patmos, dotted here and there with tiny white-washed chapels and homes. Antonios tells us that in ancient days when the pirates raided Patmos, the people all rushed to the monastery for safety, and if the pirates tried to break in, they would pour boiling oil on them from the high fortress walls. After this tour of the past with the white-bearded monks of the monastery, we enjoy another fish lunch in the village of Hora, and ride the noon bus back down the mountain. Betsy gets off at the Church of the Apocalypse to enjoy a quiet, woodsy walk down the ancient cobblestone roadway to the apartment. It's beginning to rain again, so I go back on the motor-bike with an umbrella for her!! Esther returns to a full afternoon of work on her book.

A New Song From The Lord

During the next two days with the rains coming frequently, all of us occupy ourselves with inside work. Esther devotes time also to writing a newsletter for us to get printed and mailed from Israel. She gives me turns at the typewriter to begin the long series of manuscript corrections, a laborious job which will not be completed until late Monday.

In spare moments during this whole trip, Betsy and I have been trying to do a careful reading of The Revelation given by our Lord Jesus to John on this island. So while Esther is busy on her newsletter, and I on the corrections, Betsy begins going over St. John's writings again and suddenly, realized the Lord is giving her a beautiful new song, based on Revelation 3:19-20, where He says these amazing, loving words to those lukewarm Laodicean Christians, not primarily to unbelievers: *As many as I love, I rebuke and chasten; be zealous therefore, and repent. Behold, I stand at the door and knock; if any man hear my voice, and open the door, I will come in to him and will sup with him and he with me.* The Lord's message seems to be: "I'm not knocking on the hearts-doors of unbelievers but of believers, calling you to repent and open your hearts and let Me back in to be Lord. You have put Me out of your lives." In His new song our Lord emphasizes in His Word that repentance is the key to restored fellowship with Him!

CHAPTER 22: A DREAM COME TRUE--PATMOS

Song From Jesus!
"Behold I stand at the door and knock and if any man hear my voice,
And open the door of his heart to me, and I will come into him.
As many as I love I rebuke and chasten, be zealous therefore and repent,
And I will sup with you and you will sup with me."

What a tender loving song of warning for today! Oh His patience, love and mercy to us!

Work, Work, Work!

Blue skies and sunshine return Monday. A gardener comes to dig up the gardens around Antonios' apartments. But the corrections are not finished and our time on Patmos is running out. We're to leave tomorrow night about 10 p.m. So, no siesta today! Back to the "grindstone!" Esther, reworking her address files and addressing envelopes for us to fill with the newsletters printed back in Israel; Betsy, writing "Wish you were here" postcards, and keeping the home fires and songs going; and I, still on the tedious process of corrections till the last one is finished in late afternoon! Whew! Praise the Lord! After a quick downhill run for supper and a visit with Stavros, we return for a quiet time in Revelation and a warming cup of cocoa before "Kali Nikta", Goodnight in Greek.

Getting Ready To Leave Lovely Patmos

Our last day on Patmos dawns bright and beautiful. We're so thankful for the privilege the Lord has given us to be here, and are regretting having to leave. Some extra groceries and bottled water must be brought up to Esther, our packing completed, a few more cards and souvenirs purchased, the bike returned, the rent paid, thanks and goodbyes made, the ferry to catch at 10 p.m. -a busy day ahead. We've grown so fond of our Patmos friends. They are asking when we'll be back, and we're saying we hope for a whole month next spring, God willing! We know Esther is in good hands, the Lord's and theirs! And we have work to do back in Israel. So hitch up your spirits and get ready to go!

Farewell Tour With Antonios

In the morning we stop by Antonios' shop to give him our rent, and he tells us that he will be coming by the apartment at 1:30 p.m. to take us on a drive to see the northern part of the island. What a beautiful guy he is! So in the early afternoon Antonios arrives and begins this very special farewell tour telling us about the island, the bays and beaches, and people, and showing us the house in one village of a retired Jewish doctor from Israel, and the U.S., who is the beloved "resident Doctor" for Patmos, who never charges fees for his services to the islanders. Over a very unpaved, winding road we descend to the northern tip of the island to Lambi beach, famous for its deep carpet of smooth multi-colored pebbles. Some of you can guess what happens next! Having forgotten to bring a bag, we all begin filling our pockets with a collection of beautiful stones. Esther gets her feet wet as she reaches in the surf for a special stone! They are especially beautiful when wet! One souvenir shop back in Scala specialized in these polished stones for the tourists, and before the afternoon ends, I'm making some "Patmos Stone Creations" for Antonios, Stavros, and Tony with the "His Stones" label and Scriptures on the bottom, and flying the miniature Israeli flag, no Greek ones available. Don't tell!

" In Summer Patmos He Go Down"

On the way to see a special monastery on the south side of the island, Antonios tells us that the winter population of Patmos is about 2500, but in July and August some 20,000 tourists crowd the island to the point where, as he puts it, "Patmos, he go down!" We ask him if he ever leaves the island on vacation or business and he says, "No, I like it here! My wife goes sometimes to Athens for our knitting and handcraft shop supplies."

In a short time, he has shown us much of this beautiful island, a place where many of us could be very happy to spend our lives, as he is. In his younger days he sailed the world in Greek merchant ships as an engineer. That was enough! In fact, we may have a hard time getting Esther to leave, come the last of May!! How blessed we are to know Antonios, as he drops us off at the apartment, assuring us that he will be back in the evening to take us and our luggage to the Athens ferry. May the Lord bless dear Antonios and his family abundantly!

Another New Song

A few minutes after he leaves, Esther discovers that some of her hanging-on-the-line laundry is missing, some things she had washed in the morning. Then she confesses that the Lord had specifically told her not to do her washing, but to take it all to the friendly little island laundry. She is to spend all her time working on the book. Now Esther is thinking, "But Lord, I only washed a few little things!! -- Maybe someone really needed them!" So after a brief search, Esther and Betsy decide to hike up to the Church of the Apocalypse for a last visit by Betsy. I stay to finish up the "stone creation" gifts. Because a tour group arrives at that time to visit the church, they do get in to see the cave of St. John the Apostle, and as they are hiking back down the mountain, something very special happens. Suddenly Esther asks, "Is there a tune to the Scripture, 'Obedience is better than sacrifice?'"

CHAPTER 22: A DREAM COME TRUE--PATMOS

(I Sam. 15:22). Betsy replies that she doesn't think so. Esther says, "Well now there is, and it goes like this!" She begins singing it to a catchy new tune:

> "*Obedience, is better than sacrifice, and harkening than the fat of the rams!!*"

Repeating it over and over! The Lord has given her a new song, just like that!! Isn't it wonderful how the Lord so lovingly corrects us at times! (Later verse 23 was added.)

> "*For rebellion is as the sin of witchcraft, And stubbornness is as iniquity and idolatry.*"

The Lost Candy Bar!

When they return, the "Stone Creation" gifts are ready, the glue having dried nicely in the sun. So Bets and I busy ourselves making sure everything is packed properly for the voyage back to Pireaus and Athens that night. But "another little calamity" is about to descend. Earlier, we found a little shop that sold Greek-style Mars candy bars (which Esther dearly loves), and bought several to leave with her. Inside one, I carefully hid some money which we know she will need for her food expenses, but there isn't a chance to tell Betsy about that special candy bar left on the table. Later I look for it and can't find it. Yike! I begin thinking perhaps it fell out of my jacket when I took the motorbike back. All through our supper and last coffee time with Stavros and Esther, I'm "sweating out" what's happened to that candy bar? Even go searching for it in the dark side streets where I had walked going home. Coming back from the restroom, Betsy asks Esther, "Where did Sid go?" Esther replies, "He's gone off mumbling something about a lost candy bar, and the boat should be here anytime." Then it dawns on Betsy that the bar she had packed in the camera bag must be the one. Just before the boat arrives, that missing candy bar is finally located and passed on to Esther with the admonition to "Please handle with great care!" Praise the Lord for finding the "Lost Coin," and for all of you who have a loving part in the care and feeding of Esther!!

The Angels Arrive

At some point during this last coffee time, the dear Australian girl, Idal, has come up with her backpack and introduced another Australian named Dick, an engineer, also going on the same boat, and both offering to help us take our luggage aboard ship. Two more of the Lord's special angels. Antonios had earlier dropped off the heavier bags on the quay near the ship's docking point. The "stone creations" were all happily received by our Patmos friends. You'll see one on the cash register at the coffeehouse.

The Blur of Embarkation

About 9:30 p.m. many see the lights of the ship in the distance slowly moving into the little port, and in the dim light of a few street lights, the dock area comes alive with passengers and vehicles maneuvering near the place where the ship's stern ramp will be lowered. The islanders seem to appear suddenly from nowhere; some of them, like Antonios, must have radios to pick up the ships communications with the port. Again we thank Antonios for his tremendous help and hospitality to us and to Esther, and promise to come back next year, God willing and helping us. Here comes Aristedes out of the dark crowd of people for a loving farewell in the Lord. He's just in time, for the ship's stern hawsers are secure, the ramp is down, the trucks, cars, and people are flooding out, and in moments we must join the on-going travelers and vehicles. In the rush on, Betsy follows the Australians carrying our heavy bags, and the next thing I know, they're going up one side of the ship, and I'm, cut off, having to take my bag up the other side. And no goodbye to Esther! I squeeze back to the stern door, next to the ramp, and suddenly someone bangs into me, hugs my neck, and rushes back to the dock. Finally, I realize it was Esther saying goodbye in the blur of embarkation from Patmos!

Heading Out To Sea

Quickly I climb up a deck and find Betsy and those hardy Australian angels. They offer to stay with the bags while we go out to the stern deck to wave and call out fond farewells to Esther, Antonios and Aristedes, still standing on the quay, as the ship slowly heads out to sea. We wave and pray until Patmos and these loved ones are out of sight. Thank God for these precious days on Patmos with these dear people. May the Lord bless them all, and especially help Esther finish her book by the end of May. We don't think the Lord is ready for her to retire to Patmos, as she threatens at times. We will look forward to her return to Israel. This April 10th has been a busy day!

Smooth Night Voyage to Piraeus

We rejoin the Australians and they insist on helping us get the bags upstairs, downstairs, through long passage ways, forward lounges, and downstairs again to the cabin assigned to us in the bow of the ship. Praise God for those two strong young people. Guess what? After a smooth night's voyage, even able to see and hear the waves through our porthole, these young people come to our cabin early the next morning, just as we are ready to repeat that process, and help us do just that!! For the announcement has come that we'll be landing at Piraeus about 8:30 a.m. While coming into the port of Piraeus, we have time to express our deep appreciation to the young Australians and to urge them to really follow Jesus. Soon we were telling them farewell on the

CHAPTER 22: A DREAM COME TRUE--PATMOS

dockside near a taxi stand, and they are off on their own separate journeys, eventually back to Australia. God bless them. After some difficulties, a taxi man is found who will take us to northside Athens to Nellie and Sophia's lovely apartment again, where they have a big breakfast set out for us. After that delightful breakfast, feeling somewhat groggy from the night's voyage, we "crawl" in the beds and sleep soundly for three hours, until the sisters arrive home from work in mid-afternoon.

"Home" In Athens!

What a sweet welcome we get again from Nellie and Sophia! They have those special warm hearts that only the Lord can give. After hearing about part of our voyage and visit on Patmos, they busy themselves preparing another of their princely Greek dinners. Through it we continue to tell of Esther and of all that happened on the island. Sophia is already very excited about her own approaching four day trip to be with Esther on Patmos for Easter, and Nellie says she is very jealous, but cannot go at this time. As they warned us in one of our Patmos-Athens calls, they have many questions and problems in which they need to find the Lord's wisdom and guidance. Also they wish us to make another tape for them with a Bible message and many Gospel songs like the ones their saintly Mother sang with them in their childhood. We will do it -- with the Lord's help.

Happy Fellowship In Jesus

Somewhere during the dinner, Nellie suddenly realizes today, April 11th, is the anniversary of their baptism, when we were with them a year ago, making it for all of us an extra special occasion. We all give thanks to the Lord for the wonderful blessings He has given each of us in this past year. In order to make every moment count, they insist on leaving the dishes alone for now, so that we can enjoy uninterrupted fellowship with them and the Lord. So, sitting in their living room, we spend two hours or more reading Scripture, praying, answering questions, and sharing a message from Revelation 1 that the Lord has put on our hearts, and much impromptu singing of long-ago famous Gospel hymns, with the autoharp by Betsy. What a happy fellowship it is! Betsy brought a song tape for them on the first visit, of Bible choruses in English and Hebrew, which we had made in California, and which they dearly love and often play. This night they record the whole informal session of sharing and singing -- mistakes and all!! As we finish, real late, Nellie asks if we would pray again for the Lord's healing of the lingering tooth extraction infection and pain. We anoint her in the wonderful Name of Jesus, and the Lord gave her immediate relief!! Praise His Holy Name!!

A Greek's Concern For Israel

A sidelight: In the late afternoon her pharmacist came by to give her the antibiotic injection, and he returns again for another injection near midnight. May the Lord bless him for it. They want him to meet their visitors from Israel, and he wants to express to us the heartfelt appreciation and concern of the average Greek citizen for Israel, even though their Greek government has not been very friendly. (Like we found in Egypt). We thank him and let him know that embattled Israel is grateful for all its friends. What a blessed eight hour marathon session of sharing we've had. Nellie's boss is giving her time off in the morning to take us to the airport. "The goodness of the Lord in the land of the living!" (Psalm 27:13)

Fond Farewells

Following a few hours sleep, and a loving farewell breakfast and prayers, we depart in their "Yellow Bird" at 8 a.m. through the heavy Athens traffic for the airport. With hugs and kisses, Sophia drops off near her office, and Nellie continues on to the airport. We can't thank them enough for their extraordinary hospitality to us. May the Lord reward them a hundredfold, and He will!! (Matt. 25:34,35).

What A Blessing

What a blessing and privilege for us to visit again these dear people in Athens and on Patmos. To God be all praise, thanksgiving and glory for every mercy along the way. Like with the brakes giving out at the last moment, there were many difficulties along the way, but the Lord overcame them all. As in the past, He gave us assurance that we were to go, that He would be with us, and that He loves to make good dreams come true.

"THE GREEK SERMON AND THANOS CARBONIS"
The Ex-Communist!

On our first trip to Athens in 1983, we had gone to see the Parthenon and the Acropolis and climbed up on Mars Hill where we sat and read aloud Paul's magnificent sermon to the Athenians in Acts 17. There were some workmen nearby who evidently didn't understand English and paid no attention to us. We should have been speaking in Greek as Paul was. However, a year later Nellie Karakatsani would teach us a short Greek sermon that became quite useful!

On the way to the worship service that Sunday morning at their Evangelical Brethren Church, as we rode along in Nellie's little car, we began asking her how to say certain phrases in Greek. I got out notepaper and pen and began writing probably one of the fastest Greek sermons ever produced!

CHAPTER 22: A DREAM COME TRUE--PATMOS

Good morning - Cali Mera!
Jesus is Risen - Christos Anneste!
Jesus Lives - Christos Zee!
Jesus Saves - Christos Soze!
Jesus is Coming Again - Christos Erhete!
   Soon - Grigora!
Glory to the Lord - Doxa To Theo!
Hallelujah - Hallelujah!

At the Church we were asked by the Minister, Elder Thanos Carbonis, to bring greetings from the Church in Jerusalem. After giving a message in Greek, he introduced me. I said, "Efcaristo," (thanks) and then said in English as he translated, "Shalom, I am delighted and most honored to bring you warm greetings and love from the Church in Jerusalem."

Then, "I would like now to give my special Greek sermon, but after every sentence, I want to ask you to say the Hebrew word, Hallelujah, OK? Endaxi?" (That's Right!) Everybody was smiling and I said, "Cali Mera--Hallelujah; Christos Anneste, Hallelujah; Christos Zee, Hallelujah; Christos Soze, Hallelujah; Christos Erhete, Grigora, Hallelujah; Doxa To Theo, Hallelujah!" They repeated nicely. As I sat down, there was a slight outburst of applause. (Perhaps for the shortness of the "sermon," or the directness of it!) (See above for meanings.)

Afterwards Esther gave her testimony in English of how she found Jesus to be her Messiah and how He sent her to live in Israel; then to travel around the world calling on Christians to live totally for Jesus; to urge them to Stand By Israel. Mr. Carbonis was translating.

Mr. and Mrs. Carbonis had come to Nellie and Sophia's house the night before to check us out for approval to bring these greetings and testimony to their Church, probably the largest evangelical church in Greece with some 25 outlying branches and many ministering elders.

Apparently we passed his inspection. The rest of the evening we spent hearing his testimony of how he, once a rabid communist in the University, had become an on-fire follower of Jesus. It's one of the most interesting stories we've ever heard of the salvation of a rank unbeliever and avowed enemy of religion. We hope that this outstanding preacher-lawyer in Athens will one day soon write his own amazing story for publication in many languages. Many people are still being duped by communism and its twin ideology, Fabian socialism, neither of which solves the bloody sin nature and lostness of man! Or shows he must be born-again from above, as Jesus says in John 3, to become a healthy, Godly person, to produce a healthy, sane society.

A year later in their night service Bro. Carbonis asked me to repeat my Greek Sermon! (Same length!) And while on Patmos that same month, he brought his Bible training group to visit Patmos and we just "happened" to meet them on the mountain near the monastery, where his group was having lunch. Again he asked me to give my short Greek sermon to his class, which I was delighted to do. People seem to like short sermons!! Wonder why? We like it too!

So the little Greek island of Patmos still glows from Jesus' visit in His Risen Glory 1900 years ago! (See Revelation Chapter 1!)

- - - - - - - - - -

ON SEEING A WELSH REVIVAL

Many of us have heard of the great revival of Faith in Wales early in this century. Many thousands of people were saved. Whole villages were cleaned up. God's Word became everything to the Welsh people. One longs to see such revival in our days. Betsy and I did just that in Israel. We got to see a small Welsh revival.

A young lass from Wales by the name of Yvonne came to Israel in the winter of '82-'83, began attending services at the Tabernacle of Praise, got involved with a group of on-fire-for-Jesus young people and was wonderfully saved and filled with the Holy Spirit, and met her future husband (from South Africa) in the fellowship.

She had been an expert hair-dresser on Greek cruise-liners in the Mediterranean, had been to Patmos, even brought her Mom and Dad to Patmos. Her Dad, Geoff (Jeff), almost got left on Patmos while absorbed taking pictures; he heard the ship warning "toot" and had to run pell-mell down the rocky mountain path to catch it!

That winter Yvonne's parents came to Israel for a long dreamed of visit, in fact they almost didn't make it because their plane was caught in a heavy storm over the Mediterranean, struck by lightning twice, ran low on fuel and had to land on the Island of Crete for refueling. We asked them to come have lunch with us one Sunday having been urged by Yvonne to explain to them more about a close walk with Jesus through the Baptism of the Holy Spirit. After lunch we drove to Ein Karem, the village of John the Baptist, on the west side of Jerusalem, down between the mountains where Esther lives today.

In a little outdoor coffee shop, just before sunset, we were telling them about seeing the huge #2 over the Sea of Galilee and how the Lord said it meant His Second coming was very near, tell His people everywhere. Yvonne's father, Geoff, began lighting up like a Christmas tree. He explained that he and Gwyn had just barely made it to Gatwick

CHAPTER 22: A DREAM COME TRUE--PATMOS 377

Airport. In the last seconds someone at the entrance, whether man or angel he didn't know, pointed behind him to a huge #2 sign over a parking lot. "If you leave your van there, you can make it!"

Geoff was realizing that God was connecting the 2's and helping him to yield himself fully to Jesus for the closer walk he needed, and he said, suddenly, "Gee, the Lord can talk to me too! He left Israel shining!! Yup, we got to see a Welsh Revival at sunset in Ein Karem, Israel! They are calling their retirement home in Wales, "Ein Karem"!!

GEOFF MITCHELL'S #2 SIGN AT LUTON AIRPORT IN GREAT BRITAIN, 1983, ON HIS AND GWEN'S JOURNEY TO THEIR OWN WELSH REVIVAL IN JERUSALEM!

THE ORIGINAL # 2 OVER THE SEA OF GALILEE, 1978. THE SIGN OF THE LORD'S SECOND COMING SOON!

378 FIRED AGAIN AND AGAIN, PRAISE THE LORD!

ATHENS PASTOR CARBONIS AND FRIENDS ON PATMOS MOUNTAIN TOP!

FRIEND ARISTEDES EXPERT MECHANIC

SECRETARY BETSY WRITING HAPPILY ON PATMOS

RESTING IN THE PATMOS PEACE!

CHAP. 23

GOD'S LITTLE AND BIG MIRACLES

Eye hath not seen nor ear heard neither hath entered into the heart of man the things which God hath prepared for them that love Him.
- I Corinthians 2:9

Almost everyone alive can recite some or many amazing meetings or connections or coincidences along his life's pilgrimage on this "spaceship" Earth, in which we are given a very fast ride annually around the sun at 17 thousand miles an hour for 70 years more or less, thanks to the goodness of the Lord. Unfortunately most people don't see God's hand of love and directing power in bringing these connections to pass. Personally, we believe those who love, trust and serve Him will see these connections almost daily, if not daily! They are His hand of mercy and of miracles in our life's path. And it sure is exciting to see them!

Here on Patmos, as we write this in May 1988, we have seen several of God's amazing connections in the past three or four days, and we praise and thank Him for everyone of them. No doubt we'll see more on the way back to the States beginning tomorrow and many more in the months to come.

For instance, yesterday morning I began having a strong leading that we needed to call John Christo, who has a house up on the mountain. John had given us his phone number a few days before and asked us to call him about getting together. The Christos grew up partly here, but mostly in Panama City, Florida, our home town, where we knew each other in our high school days. Well, the nudge came from the Lord to call them. So we began trying to ask a kind Greek neighbor lady, to let us use her phone. She had been waving "Cali Mera" ("Good Morning") to us from her porch, and we to her, as we sat there daily on our little balcony, writing. She could not understand our sign language at all and called another neighbor who understood some English. When she knew what we wanted, she waved us over most cordially, insisted on showing us her beautiful home, her Greek needlework, and painting that every lady would dearly love to have to decorate their homes. She shared family pictures with us and then brought us refreshments, caramel custard, a super delight and a delicious Greek sweet called, "Theples."

Finally, we were able to get to her phone and dial the Christo number. Christo himself answered and said, "Hey Sid, thanks for calling. We want you to come up and have dinner with us tonight at 8 p.m. Can you come?"

I said, "Yes indeed, we'd be delighted to come."

"Okay, see you then."

We learned that night that he had asked a local worker to stop by our little apartment down here near the port (we're on the main road up the mountain) and tell us to call him! The man never stopped! But the Lord knew we needed to call him, and so HE told us by His Holy Spirit. Even though the worker never stopped by, our call reached Christo at the exact time he was expecting us to call.

Probably the greatest miracle connection in our lives, a story told earlier, was my 1944 meeting with Betsy for the first time at the Hotel Markham swimming pool in Gulfport, Mississippi. At the first sight of her, the Lord spoke to me and said she was to be my future wife. She was and is, Praise God, now for 42 years. A divine connection? Indeed it was! (In 1991--45 years!)

Another remarkable divine connection was our meeting with Esther in northern Israel, at the ruins of Capernaum, with our tour group in 1977. It was then we heard the Lord say to us, "You're to help this Jewish girl in every way you can. Tell her." And we did. This began a long series of events that led to our living in Israel for over six years. But not until the summer of 1984 did we learn how great a connection of God this had been.

We had come home to the States that summer as usual, to help Pappy and to give Kirby and Carol a good vacation from the Little Tabernacle work. At the same time, Esther had come back to the States to see her parents and her sons. Dr. Korson, her father, had been sick with cancer, and she had gone to try to be of some help to them.

While there in Sun City, Arizona one day out of the blue, she asked her mother, "Mother, do you remember the Monopoly Game?"

"Yes, why do you ask?"

"Do you remember meeting Sid and Betsy in Israel?"

"Yes, indeed!"

"Well, Betsy grew up in Atlantic City in a hotel on the famous corner of Park Place and Boardwalk."

Her mother's tone perked up. "You don't say? What was the name of the hotel?"

Esther replied, "I can't remember."

CHAPTER 23: GOD'S LITTLE AND BIG MIRACLES

Her mother asked, "Could it have been the Marlborough Blenheim Hotel?"

"Yes," Esther replied, "That was it! How did you know?"

"Well," her mother explained, "For 20 years my father (an orthodox Jewish businessman) took us as a family for our vacation in February to the Marlborough Blenheim Hotel. I remember the bridges across the street connecting the two hotels; and the hot and cold running salt water in the bath tubs." Esther was so excited that she called us at Pappy's in southern Maryland to tell us this special discovery about her family's visits to the "M.B".

In a few weeks she came to see us at Pappy's on her return trip to Israel. There she asked him, "Pappy, do you remember a Jewish family from Hartford, Connecticut, who came to 'your' hotel every February for 20 years?"

Pappy replied, "I remember one family who did that who were connected with a large department store."

Esther said, "That was my family! My Grandfather was the manager of it."

"Well," Pappy replied, "The reason I remember them was that they always brought gifts only to Betsy, not to her sisters and brother!"

Betsy still remembers many of the gifts: big dolls, doll furniture, little dolls with porcelain faces, and fancy voile dresses with shirred waists!

Isn't it fantastic that 45 years later, totally oblivious to that amazing connection, we feel from the Lord to tell this unknown-to-us Jewish girl in Israel that the Lord wants us to help her in any way possible!

Truly, her Grandfather had cast his bread upon the waters and 45 years later it was returning to a granddaughter he did not get to see. What a fantastic connection of God to bless His people, and to confirm His Word (Eccl.11:1).

ANOTHER LONG AGO CONNECTION

We were back three mornings a week in Hebrew class, digging hard to learn more of this beloved Biblical language, both written and spoken. To say it's not easy is an understatement! But we also got to renew our friendships with a number of former classmates. After a few classes in October, the man sitting next to us began saying he had seen me somewhere in the past. It turns out that we were in the U.S. Navy on the same base in Corpus Christi, Texas in 1944, in the same barracks, in adjoining bunks. Art, a gifted musician, had been part of the Navy band marching us off to our classes every morning. He remembered me as being quite a serious-minded fellow, intent on doing a good job in the training. God's amazing connections!!

Remember, we mentioned at the beginning of this that we are all traveling on a fantastic spaceship created by God, with all kinds of life support systems built in and perfectly timed in our life-sustaining orbit around the sun, which gives us beautiful seasons and the annual seed-time and harvest. Now, in our day, we have been able to get into the spaceship business in a small way ourselves and we make sure that we can maintain accurate communication with the astronauts and their ships, even to controlling certain mechanical and electronic functions of such ships from the ground. If we, as humans, can create such ships, launch them into space and communicate with them and their inhabitants, surely it's not too much to ask us to believe that the Creator of this spaceship, Earth, that we're on, has our best interest at heart and can surely communicate with and guide us by His Holy Spirit (if we're in a right relationship with Him), and even write for us an Engineer's Guide Book called "The Bible"!

Man's big problem in receiving communications from his true God and Creator, is that in his puffed-up arrogance and so-called brilliance, he is always trying to reach God in his own way or avoid God or deny God or perfect some controllable god-image by which to satisfy his emptiness. So man contrives his own foolish ways: idol worship, astrology, spiritism, transcendental meditation, hedonism, occultism, necromancy; or tower of Babel schemes such as: Humanism, New Ageism, Socialism Communism, Nihilism, ad infinitum!)

As St. Augustine said, "We were made by Thee, oh God, and we are ever restless until we find our way back to Thee." We were made to communicate with God, His Way! The Bible Way--Jesus Way!.

As the Scottish Presbyterians say in their catechism in answer to the question, "What is man's chief end?"

The answer, "Man's chief end is to glorify God and to enjoy Him forever."

Just like our analogy of the spaceship. We'd be awfully dumb to put a spaceship out there with someone in it and we not be able to communicate with them! And the Creator of our spaceship was no dummy either, not by a long way! In fact His ways and wisdom are so much greater than ours. Check I Cor. 1-2; Job 38!

Thank God, He's shown us The Way, The Truth and The Life, JESUS, WHO says that NO MAN comes to the Father, but by Him. And if we come by Him, He will save us, set our feet on The Rock, and give us His Holy Spirit to keep us in constant communication with Himself and His Father. There's no more restlessness in those who come to Him and make that greatest of all connections or reconnections through His Blood and Holy Spirit with the Heavenly Father. Life becomes peaceful, abundant, worthwhile, victorious, delightful, no matter what!

CHAPTER 23: GOD'S LITTLE AND BIG MIRACLES

Hallelujah!!!!!

MIRACLES AT PAPPY'S, SOME LITTLE, SOME BIG!

As all of our sons know, and our grandchildren too, Pappy was a quiet, highly intelligent man, trained and self-trained in a number of fields. He was a lover of the sea and of sailing and was an Army veteran of both World War I and World War II. In the former he had suffered a punctured ear-drum during a mock training battle; during the latter, he need not have served at all, but he volunteered to teach navigation to crash-boat crews of the Army's navy, who picked up downed fliers at sea. He was a Warrant Officer and was serving at a training base in Biloxi, Mississippi, when Betsy and I first met at the Hotel Markham swimming pool in nearby Gulfport, where our famous all-American love story began in 1944, only 47 years ago! (And Pappy suspected I was a Jew even then, from the name!)

Over the years Pappy was to see God's miracle of salvation for our marriage. It was right after that miracle that Pappy pulled me aside and said, "Sid, don't ever forget, honey will get you a lot more bees than vinegar." I understood what he meant. Maybe that was the first big miracle he'd seen, because it took a miracle of God to change things and to save us, as Betsy tells in her account earlier in our book.

He also heard of some of the other miracles of God's deliverance for us in Baltimore. But, normally, he was not given to believing in miracles. Basically he considered himself a Quaker with the same careful keeping of his faith private. The only time Grandma Gin could get him to her Episcopal Church would be for someone's funeral, or maybe for a wedding. One sure thing about Pappy, he dearly loved his family, and in his quiet deliberate way, he proved it over and over. But we all remember one of his favorite and stern expressions was "I never make promises ahead of time!"

During the years there had been many "little" miracles taking place, such as someone dropping a pair of sunglasses overboard at his dock, and then trying to find them six feet down in very murky water. After many attempts, only when I asked the Lord for help, in the next moment He guided my hand directly to the sunglasses. The same thing happened regarding a window-sash anchor weight for his little row boat.

Another day, two of the boys lost the spring out of a favorite stapler, while trying to repair a crab box on his dock. Pappy and most of us thought it was gone forever, but we prayed for His help. In less than a half hour, a small magnet had been borrowed from neighbor Jim Buys, and the magnet had "miraculously pulled" the missing spring up from the muddy bottom!

To Betsy and me, it was no small miracle for us that during all our years in Baltimore and later in those years in Israel, even to his death, Pappy was most generous in his financial help given us. It truly was God's miracle support for us.

But one summer, we were home about September 1982 - when we had heard that Betsy's brother Kirby, Pappy's only son, was desperately sick from alcoholism, and had been warned that he would die soon if he didn't stop drinking. We were helping Pappy as much as we could that summer, about half the time with him and half the time in Baltimore. We distinctly remember talking with Pappy about his dear son's condition, and hearing him say, if he could just get delivered from this thing that would make him (Pappy) believe in miracles.

Pappy's own drinking had been a very serious matter, until about a year before when our son, Craig, had urged him to see if he couldn't do without it, to stop the blackouts Pappy was having after large drinks. "Test it for a week and see if it doesn't help," Craig suggested. Pappy did it and then decided to stop completely. The black-outs stopped! Praise God!

We understood that Betsy's brother Kirby and his wife were understandably not desiring company or visitors at that time. Betsy and I told Pappy we felt the Lord wanted us to fast and to go see them in New Jersey, without an invitation. Pappy said, "Well, I'll be hoping for a miracle." So early the next morning we set out on the five hour drive to Ocean City, N.J., to somehow have prayer with Betsy's brother, Kirby, and his wife, Debbie. They were surprised, but most hospitable. Kirby came in with the ever-present glass in his hands, looking almost like one of our old friends from Baltimore Street. He may not have remembered it, but he too was quite cordial.

We sat down in their recreation room and shared that the reason for our visit was to come to pray for him and ask the Lord to deliver him, and heal him completely. And if he was willing, we should all get on our knees and pray for his deliverance in the Name of Jesus. He was willing! We all got on our knees and we bound the demon of addiction and all the demons of infirmity that go along with it and commanded them out in Jesus' Name. We prayed earnestly for his complete deliverance and healing in the mighty Name of Jesus and we thanked God for it right then!

Afterwards, we got up and went into the dining room for a quick meal that Debbie had prepared for us. Kirby and she sat with us as we ate. We shared how Pappy was doing, and how he was hoping with us for a big miracle for his son.

We were there for only about two hours before heading back to Pappy's home in southern Maryland, arriving about one a.m. The next

CHAPTER 23: GOD'S LITTLE AND BIG MIRACLES 385

morning we shared our great hopes with Pappy that the Lord had heard our prayers and would set Kirby free and heal him. Probably in that same week we were heading back to Israel.

While back in Jerusalem, sometime before Christmas, we heard that Kirby had finally been taken to a hospital and, after two weeks of drying out he was back home, having to use a wheelchair. But the story gets better. He didn't go back to drinking! The cirrhosis of his liver cleared up! And after several months of regaining strength under the loving care of his dear wife, Debbie, he was back on his feet and looking like a new man. That was really a Big Miracle of the Lord that Pappy could believe! How thankful he and all of us were for it! Later, Kirby was a great help to Pappy with his business affairs.

Pappy was to see some more miracles before he went to be with the Lord in March, 1985. One that we had prayed for was that he would get to hear his own son Kirby profess his faith in Jesus Christ. This, Pappy heard at his own hospital bedside one day when a Baptist preacher came by checking on the patients' readiness to meet the Lord. Kirby was visiting Pappy.

The preacher asked Kirby if he believed in Jesus?

Kirby said, "Yes, I believe in Him, but I haven't committed myself to Him completely."

We believe that Pappy, before he departed a short time later, also said, "Have mercy on me too, Jesus." He left peaceably with a smile on his face. The final miracle for Pappy!

AFTER FIVE YEARS A CHRISTMAS WITH OUR PRECIOUS FAMILY

Early in 1984, the Lord told us we could plan to be "home" for a Christmas reunion with our children, grandchildren, and Pappy, for the first time in over five years. We were to write to all of our sons and Pappy to begin setting it up. Sure enough, we were all together, all 17 of us, on Christmas Day, 11 months later. What a happy day! A gift of God's Love in Jesus! Praise the Lord forever for His goodness and mercy to us!

Getting us together for Christmas was no simple matter --for the little birds grow up to be big birds and fly off to different places, including Mama and Daddy bird!!! Fortunately, Betsy's Dad (Pappy) was willing for the flock to "home-in" on his place on St. Leonard's Creek in southern Maryland for a few days before and after Christmas. Bless his heart! (Thanks to many prayers, Betsy's cooking and God's mercy, Pappy seemed to be stronger than before.) Our oldest son, Craig, with his wife, Ann and children, Ginny and Allen, came from Oak Ridge, Tenn. where he was Vice-Principal of a Jr. High School; Pastor son

FIRED AGAIN AND AGAIN, PRAISE THE LORD!

Kirby, his wife, Carol and children, Matthew, Peter and Betsy, came from Baltimore and the Little Tabernacle; Joe and his wife, Debbie, drove some 23 hours from western Illinois where he was a Vice-President of MacMurray College. Sons, Chris and Brian, arrived from Maryville, Tennessee, where Chris was doing a doctoral study and research in Bio-Chemistry at the University of Tennessee, and Brian was working toward his B.A. degree at Maryville College. Brian's Uncle Dusty, whom we informally adopted many years ago at McKim, after a number of years in the Marines, and several years teaching, was then in military intelligence work. He made the short hop from Arlington, Va. Praise God for His great mercy to our little family flock! (P.S.: Pappy survived it all with flying colors at age 85!) Joe got a great group picture of that special event!

GO HOME AND REST BY THE FIRE

Apparently the Pastor of the little congregation that we were members of in Jerusalem sensed that Betsy and I were in great need of rest after several busy months there and a case of flu for me. So, at the close of our last worship service with them, he called us to the front and asked the elders to come join him in prayer for us. After the prayers, Pastor David (Hjertstedt) gave us a strong word of instruction from the Lord to go home, prop our feet up to the fire, and just rest, and rest and rest!! But one thing he didn't explain: How was that fire to keep burning without somebody going out into the woods and cutting firewood, splitting it, hauling it, stacking it, and bringing it into the fire?! Probably had we realized all the frigid air, exercise, and work involved in carrying out that order, we might have been less eager about doing it! But we are so thankful the Lord did let us come to sit by Pappy's fire, and to cut wood for him and for us. It was work, but fun! And plenty cold!! Brrrr!!!

NOT TOTAL HIBERNATION!

Although we had done a lot of happy relaxing by Pappy's fire, our two months in the States had some other pleasant assignments from the Lord. These included frequent ministry at the Little Tabernacle, an Aglow meeting, five home meetings in Baltimore and Washington, sharing at the Woodstock Calvary Assembly of God, and on TV Channel 66 in Virginia about how God is moving in Israel and the Middle East, according to His prophecies and promises in His Word. As always, we were urging Believers to pray for Israel, to visit Israel, and to keep our nation standing with Israel!

CHAPTER 23: GOD'S LITTLE AND BIG MIRACLES

Our stay lasted through most of February; we had a round-trip two-months ticket from Israel. But by then, Pappy seemed to be getting weaker, less active. We hated the thought of leaving him by himself, even though Betsy's sister, Cindy, and brother Kirby and wife Debbie said they would come to be with him at least every other day after we had to leave. I had felt from the Lord that something serious would be happening in a month; Pappy's time could be running out, fast. We tried to get our ticket extended a month, but the airline wouldn't grant it. Betsy was being a very loving and helpful daughter to Pappy, and I was doing all I could to help with maintenance problems and keep the firewood coming in. (Pappy had an oil furnace, but we all loved the warmth of his big fireplace!)

So after we left, Cindy and brother Kirby, and in the last two weeks Betsy's sister Mary who came from England, were all there to help Pappy. Back in Jerusalem when we called Pappy on March 2nd for our mutual wedding anniversary greeting, brother Kirby said Pappy had an upset stomach and couldn't come to the phone. Soon after that came stomach surgery; it wasn't cancer; but a type of blockage. Pappy jokingly said "They took out a dead racoon!"

Seemingly recovering in a nice, nearby nursing home, because he was still so weak and which he seemed to like in spite of his earlier protestations, after lunch on the 27th of March he took a nap and peacefully went on to be with the Lord.

Cindy called us about 11 p.m. that night, which was 6 a.m. the next morning Israeli time. Betsy answered and received the sad news. I was standing beside her, and instantly the Lord gave me a word of Scripture which says of Jesus, **He doeth all things well!** (Mark 7:37). What a comfort! So we immediately began arranging for a two week's round trip ticket back to the States. We were able to be with the family for Pappy's funeral at the historic, rural, little Christ's Episcopal Church on Broom Island Road below Prince Frederick, Md. Rev. Bill Plummer officiated in his loving way. Pappy's casket was borne to his gravesite next to GrandmaGin by his beloved grandsons. All of them would retain long memories of his sailing abilities and his love for Robert Service's "Alaskan Odes" and many other poems which Pappy remembered by heart from his boyhood, including "The Ancient Mariner", "Casey At The Bat", and a family favorite, "The Composite Ghost".

The next morning at breakfast brother Kirby told us of a DREAM he had had, in which Pappy was asking his son Kirby how he could be saved, so he could be with GrandmaGin again. Kirby said with tears in his eyes, "But I couldn't remember how to tell him the way of salvation. And then I woke up."

Betsy said, with tears in her eyes, "Kirby, we've been asking the

388   FIRED AGAIN AND AGAIN, PRAISE THE LORD!

Lord to show Himself to Pappy in some way, and if He can give you a DREAM like that, surely He could give the answer to Pappy in a DREAM, too. Thank you for sharing that with us. We believe he is with GrandmaGin now in Heaven."

One thing is sure, Pappy had lived long enough to hear the plan of salvation and to see several of God's real miracles. He certainly had enjoyed our reading together the book mentioned earlier, "The Light And The Glory," by David Manuel and Peter Marshall, Jr. And Betsy and I will always remember how he loved that old, old hymn called **"The Battle Hymn of The Republic"** by Julia Ward Howe :

> *"Mine eyes have seen the glory of the coming of the The Lord. He is trampling out the vintage where the grapes of wrath are stored; He hath loosed the fateful lightning of His terrible swift sword; His truth is marching on."*
>
> *Chorus:*
> *"Glory, glory, hallelujah, Glory, glory,*
> *Hallelujah, Glory, glory, hallelujah,*
> *His truth is marching on."*
>
> *Verse 4:*
> *"In the beauty of the lilies Christ was born across the sea, With a glory in His bosom that transfigures you and me; As He died to make men holy, let us die to make men free; His truth is marching on."*

GOOD NEWS ABOUT ESTHER'S BOOK

We must confess to bugging Esther relentlessly during 1984 and 1985 about finishing her book, and threatening to withhold food supplies unless she produced 6-10 pages a day. She had to hang a sign outside her apartment saying how many pages completed, so we would know to climb the many steps to her apartment or not, when we came by to check.

Finally, in September of 1985, while we were in the States, we received a phone call from Esther in which she said her entire manuscript would be at the printer's that week (9/10/85), just before she left for her 5th trip to Russia. And her last. She became a "refusenik" from the outside after that trip.

About a month before that she called to say the manuscript was finished! At Last! "But, where is the money to print it!" she asked?

Our answer, "Now the Lord can send the money; He's been waiting

CHAPTER 23: GOD'S LITTLE AND BIG MIRACLES 389

for you to finish the writing. He wasn't going to send it beforehand. Now He can send it!"

Two days later an urgent call came from Jerusalem. It was Esther again saying that a dear German friend was sending the money for printing 5000 copies! This really was a miracle, a big one, of God's amazing provision! Praise God forever! Jehovah Jireh! He is our Provider!! We prayed much for the safe printing and distribution of these books around the world. (And they were!)

Later, we were able to write, "Now It Can Be Told!" The man who made possible the publication of Esther's book was the outstanding German publisher in Berlin, Axel Springer, who went to be with the Lord on Sept.22, 1985, only a month after sending the gift. Axel needed bodyguards and bullet-proof cars in Germany, and elsewhere, because of threats on his life by the KGB and PLO. But he and his wife, Friede, had found a place where they could retreat to from time to time - without guards. There Esther met them, and so did we, and our love for them was instant! There they read Esther's manuscript and offered to publish the book! God's miracle meeting and provision! He was a man of extraordinary ability, courage and faith--and had a personal friendship with many world leaders. Please pray for his dear wife in her deep sorrow. She is a lovely lady, full of humble grace and beauty! She still needs God's special protection and guidance.

In Israel on November 2, 1985 Esther celebrated her son Joe's birthday AND the first printing of her book, "I Am My Beloved's." We all got to see her first copies! It was a long awaited and exciting moment, almost like the celebration of the arrival of a new baby in one's family. It had been a long time coming, but well worth the wait. Those first 5,000 copies in English and German have gone around the world to bless and encourage a multitude with a stronger faith in, love for and walk with Jesus the Jewish Messiah. (By 1992, Esther had distributed, free, over 22,000 copies of her book, now including a Hebrew printing.) We have seen well-worn copies of it that have passed through many hands. May those who have unworn copies begin passing them around. Praise the Lord for helping Esther to complete her book, and Praise The Lord also for the precious German couple, the Axel Springers, who financed her first edition, and for all the others who have helped in later printings. ***Blessed be the Lord God of Israel, who only doeth wondrous things.*** (Ps.72:18,19).

By the way, if any of you are upset or somewhat dismayed by the many times we say Praise The Lord, or Glory to God, or Hallelujah, or Praise His Name, or whatever, please know we do not intend or desire in anyway to offend you. We are mainly talking and writing about the miracles and wonders of God in our lives, and we can't help but exclaim

390   FIRED AGAIN AND AGAIN, PRAISE THE LORD!

from time to time our praise and thanksgiving to Him!. Israel's King David, as a boy shepherd, learned to Praise the Lord at all times of real dangers and enemy attacks. And so he begins his Psalm 34 with these words:

> *I will bless the Lord at all times, His praise shall continually be in my mouth. My soul will make her boast in thee, Lord, the humble will hear thereof and be glad. Oh magnify the Lord with me, And let us exalt His Name together. I sought the Lord and He heard me and delivered me from all my fears.*

Thank God for David and his many, many songs of Praise to God. He has taught us to do the same and we are not ashamed to do it. We love Him and love to praise and thank Him! At all times!

**MIRACLE CHRISTMAS REUNION WITH PAPPY, 12/25/84
SHORTLY BEFORE HIS HOME GOING!**

CHAP. 24

ANOTHER ROUGH FIRING - FROM ISRAEL!

Yea, and all that will live godly in Christ Jesus shall suffer persecution. — II Timothy 3:12

The title of this story fits in with some other experiences we've had in this journey, and we always have to remind ourselves how some of the Lord's other servants had "frequent firing" records: Paul, the writer of so many New Testament Epistles (half the New Testament), probably had the all-time record of firings. We read about it in II Corinthians 4:8-10:

...We are troubled on every side, yet not distressed; we are perplexed but not in despair; Persecuted, but not forsaken; cast down, but not destroyed; Always bearing about in the body the dying of the Lord Jesus, that the life also of Jesus might be made manifest in our body.

II Corinthians 11:23-33: *....Are they ministers of Christ? (I speak as a fool) I am more; in labours more abundant, in stripes above measure, in prisons more frequent, in deaths often. Of the Jews five times received I forty stripes save one. Thrice was I beaten with rods, once was I stoned, thrice I suffered shipwreck, a night and a day I have been in the deep: In journeyings often, in perils of waters, in perils of robbers, in perils by mine own countrymen, in perils by the heathen, in perils in the city, in perils in the wilderness, in perils in the sea, in perils among false brethren; In weariness and painfulness, in watchings often, in hunger and thirst, in fastings often, in cold and nakedness. Beside those things that are without, that which cometh upon me daily, the care of all the churches. Who is weak, and I am not weak? Who is offended, and I burn not? If I must needs glory, I will glory of the things which concern mine infirmities. The God and Father of our Lord Jesus Christ, which is blessed forevermore, knoweth that I lie not. In Damascus the Governor under Aretas the King kept the city of the Damascenes with a garrison, desirous to apprehend me: And through a window in a basket was I let down by the wall, and escaped his hands.*

In the book of Acts he was constantly getting fired, run out of town, beaten, arrested, imprisoned, shipwrecked, hailed before Judges and Kings, apparently a real troublemaker everywhere he went carrying the Gospel. But Paul knew Jesus' warning in one of His final messages just before The Cross in John 15:20 ...*that if they have persecuted me they will also persecute you...,* and in Acts 9:10-16 Ananias tells him that the Lord would show Paul *how great things he must suffer for my name's sake.* And recently Dave Wilkerson has said "What we need today are more troublemakers like Paul" (July '88).

Paul didn't mean to be a troublemaker. Neither have we! The Good News of the Gospel is to bring salvation to those who will repent and receive the atonement of Christ's blood for their sins and deliverance from sin for those who will believe and follow Him. But the bad news is that those who won't believe and receive Jesus Christ will not be saved, but will pay the death penalty for their sins, be lost forever, and go into an everlasting Hell.

So Paul preached the straight Gospel everywhere he went, and as often as not, got fired and run out of town by the Anti-Christ circles. But the Church grew by such fearless preaching: not by milk-toast preachers or the fist-shaking "give-me-my-rights preaching" that we hear a lot of today. His was a gospel of love, but also of love so strong that it was willing to die warning "sinners" there's a Hell-to-pay if we don't repent and turn away from wickedness and unbelief in Jesus, and a Heaven-to-gain if we do! Men and women can gain all of the civil rights in the world by politics, civil strife, "religious" pressures, even military force, and still go straight to Hell. Heavenly rights are gained by faith in Jesus Christ, repentance, rebirth, and reconciliation to God and living in holiness and righteousness as children of God here on earth, as He intended.

But let us tell you how we finally were judged as "DANGEROUS MISSIONARIES" after some six and a half years in Israel and told to get out of the country within 10 days. We did not know at first, when it happened, that we had been judged "Dangerous Missionaries." That was to be learned six months later, when we tried to take a tour group back to Israel, and were arrested at Passport Control at Ben Gurion Airport near Tel Aviv.

COME TO THE MISRAD HAPONIM!

It all began with an official letter, all in Hebrew, to us from the Ministry of Interior about the first of March 1986, requiring us to come immediately to their main office in Jerusalem, bringing our passports

CHAPTER 24: ANOTHER ROUGH FIRING-FROM ISRAEL

with us. Our current visas at that time were to end on March 27th. The letter was addressed to Sid and Betsy Rigell, not to Joseph S. and Elizabeth W. as our passports identified us. However, both our mailbox and the sign on our apartment door showed Sid and Betsy. Naturally we wondered what was up? Were we in for a real surprise?! During our entire stay in Israel, we had been careful not to break the law in any way. No passing out tracts at the Wailing Wall!

At this time Betsy was still attending Hebrew classes three days a week, and we both were continuing to help with the small group of Christian believers, called The Tabernacle of Praise. The letter gave no reason for this surprise order to report to the Interior Ministry office, but we knew it did not bode well, being addressed as it was, and coming not long after this ministry had come under the control of a more extreme orthodox Jewish sect.

Back in early 1980, when we were staying with Esther in Ramot, we had been investigated by the neighborhood council after a radical "Yad Le Achim" (Hand of Brothers) man had charged that we were dangerous missionaries. The council had decided that we were not dangerous missionaries, but strong friends of Israel, or Christian Zionists, and gave their warm approval.

In the fall of '80, Betsy and I moved from the north side of Jerusalem to the south side, at the Lord's direction. We had crowded Esther too much! Now we were enjoying a little apartment on Shimoni Street, with some very good neighbors there, both Jews and Gentiles, and a couple of Arab friends dropping in to see us occasionally.

So here we were with orders to Sid and Betsy Rigell to report to the rulers of visas! During the intervening days we were wondering what terrible sin we had committed. We had been mentioned in Esther's book which was being distributed around late in '85. A couple of years before someone had put Gospels of John, printed in Hebrew, in the mailboxes up and down our street, and we had been accused of doing that, but hadn't. We did think it was a good idea though; it's the greatest piece of Jewish writing in the world today--barring none! Sad to say, probably many of the Jews threw them in the trash. But many may have kept them, secretly!

We remembered several years back when our California friend, Ed Laube, came to Jerusalem seeking to place Gideon Bibles in all the hotels, schools, prisons, and Kibbutzim in Israel. His Gideon Bibles were shipped in and kept in a warehouse somewhere in Jerusalem, and for several weeks he had "a ball" traveling to every corner of Israel boldly distributing the Gideon Bibles, while staying with us! Doesn't everyone know that Bibles are Jewish writings?!

No doubt many of those Bibles were thrown away too, but,

hopefully, many weren't and brought the bright light of the Jewish Messiah, Jesus, to many Jewish hearts. You see Jews don't have to leave their Judaism to be saved. Jesus came to complete the Salvation Plan of God for the Jews, and also the Gentiles by His death as the Lamb of God for our sins, the final great and all-sufficient sacrifice, and proved His power to save by His shed blood and by His resurrection. By His blood means He fulfilled the need for a final perfect sacrifice for sin. That's why the Jew named John the Baptist cried: **Behold the Lamb of God who taketh away the sin of the world.** He knew that Jesus had come to save His people from their sins. Everyone of us has to repent, turn away from our sins, and receive Jesus and His atonement for our sins, to be saved. Jews, when they come to Jesus, are completed in the Salvation Plan that Almighty God sent to us through the Jews and Judaism. (Jn.4:27) .... **Salvation is of the Jews.** The Jews and Gentiles both must convert from sin and unbelief, turn away from sin and unbelief to full belief in Jesus as Saviour, Messiah and Lord! Jews and Judaism are both completed in Jesus!

Interestingly, we are living in a time when Jews are waking up all over the world to this tremendous fact that their salvation comes only through the Jewish Messiah, Jesus. Recently, in May 1988, some 1,200 Messianic Jews, Believers in Jesus, from all over the world (half from Israel) met for a special conference in Jerusalem during Shavuot (Pentecost). It probably was the largest meeting of Believing Jews in Jerusalem since the first century, when there were many thousands in Judea, Samaria, and Galilee. Before the Romans destroyed Jerusalem in 70 A.D. and killed or dispersed the Jews to distant lands, there were hundreds of thousands of Believing Jews in Israel at that time. Recently someone estimated that there are over 6,000 openly Believing Jews in Israel today. This is exciting news and it shows that the Lord is getting many Jews as well as Christians ready for His Soon Return. As He promised! (Matt.25:31; John 14; Acts 1:11).

MR. SHOSHANI'S (X) ON OUR PASSPORTS!

Now back to the story of our enforced departure from Israel! The day arrived quickly for our trip to the Ministry of Interior in downtown Jerusalem. By this time Esther, too, had grown concerned since her book ("I Am My Beloved's") was passing around Jerusalem, and a copy of it reportedly had been given to the brother of the man we must see in the Ministry of Interior. So Esther volunteered to pick us up and take us to the Ministry office. She would wait in a little coffee shop opposite to hear the outcome when we came out after our interview with a Mr. Shoshani on the third floor. After waiting on a number of others to have

CHAPTER 24: ANOTHER ROUGH FIRING-FROM ISRAEL

their visas extended, or not, our number came up and we went into Mr. Shoshani's office with our passports in hand and the official letter "inviting" us to come.

He did not seem friendly at all, but very grim. He seldom was friendly toward anyone, but today he seemed more grim than usual. He was the man who daily decided whether tourists in Israel can extend their stay. He had extended our visa permit a number of times in the past, but we could sense from his grim demeanor that he was about to use his "axe", or pen to "X" us out of Israel.

He took our passports and asked us how long we had been in the country. We explained that we had been going back and forth for a number of years, studying Hebrew and the Bible in Israel, and speaking on behalf of Israel to Christians in the States, and helping to bring tour groups. He gruffly and (mistakenly) said, "We don't need your help!" (Israel needs all the help it can get from Christians and otherwise, and 3-4 billion dollars a year from America's largely Christian taxes.) Well, he immediately came to the last visa stamp in our passports and marked an (X) and a circle around it. He didn't say it, but that (X) meant our stay in Israel was ended.

What he did say was, "You've been too long in Israel on a tourist visa. Why don't you go home for a couple of years." No doubt his computer brain had already figured my age two years hence would be 70, and by then I probably would be unable to come back. We protested and said we loved Israel and wanted to stay in Israel.

He, sensing our sincerity, seemed to relent a bit and said, "Well, bring me five letters of recommendation on the 27th when your present visa expires and we'll see what can be done."

We thanked him and said we would. All the interview had taken place in English. We never tried to use our limited Hebrew in situations of that kind, especially when he was fluent in English. Most of the people in that ministry have to be, it seems.

Outside we made a beeline for the little coffee-shop across the street where Esther was anxiously waiting for us. After discussing all the details over a soft drink, we concluded, somewhat hopefully, that the recommendations we could obtain might change the picture. And since we were only a short distance from a bus stop where we could catch the #22 bus back to Shimoni Street, we thanked her for waiting for us and urged her to head on home herself. She had rented a large house for her family and friends, who were helping distribute her book, east of the Mt. of Olives, the Biblical place called, Bethphage.

Waving, she left for the parking garage, and we turned and walked the few steps to the bus stop, where we were about to have a surprise. As we waited in line to get on the bus, we noticed a properly dressed little man with his brief case getting on the same bus. We had seen this man a number of times in our neighborhood on Shimoni Street and had never said more than a friendly "Shalom" to him before. In fact, he and his wife always seemed quite cool toward us. Once on the street his wife had asked, "Why is it you have so many people coming to your house?"

We answered, "We have many friends here in Israel, and all over the world."

Often she would cross to the other side of the street when she saw us coming. We realized then that they were keeping watch on us and found out later that she and her husband were leaders of a nearby orthodox synagogue and that her husband did special investigative work for the Ministry of Interior! On that day it appeared that he also had just come from the Ministry of Interior and was catching the same bus we were. During the 20 minute bus ride to our exit stop, he did not nod to us or say anything. But just as we stepped down from the bus, he turned and spoke to us in a very friendly manner in English. We felt it was somewhat "put-on."

He said, "Well, how are things with you?"

We were surprised at his "friendliness and interest" on such a day, and I think we answered by using a favorite Hebrew expression, "Ha Col Beseder, Baruch Ha Shem", meaning, "Everything is okay. Bless the Lord." Then we looked around and said, "It's a lovely day, isn't it?"

As he turned and went his way, we wondered if he and his wife had not had a part in turning in an adverse report on Sid and Betsy Rigell, which names they could easily see on our mailbox or apartment door. They did not know our official passport names!

He probably knew that we were to come in to the ministry as the result of his adverse report and was very eager to learn what Mr. Shoshani had decided. We must say that we felt no ill-will toward this little man or his wife. They were simply involved in the age-old effort to "protect" their faith from those Believers who had found the Truth - JESUS REALLY IS THE SAVIOUR OF THE JEWS AND THE GENTILES! Because of the love of Jesus in the Believer's hearts, they also love the Jews and Israel, and are PRIMA-FACIE EVIDENCE that JESUS IS THE MIGHTY REDEEMER and MESSIAH of all who will Believe in Him! Every born-again, Jesus-loving and obeying Believer is absolute evidence of the Messiahship of Jesus (Yeshua)! Sadly, most of their Rabbis are still declaring it to be untrue, despite the evidence to the contrary.

We immediately contacted Zev and Ruth, our Jewish neighbors and faithful friends, to ask them to write a letter of recommendation for us to take to the Ministry of Interior on the 27th. Our dear tour guide, Moshe, down in Ashkelon, said he, too, would be happy to write a letter

CHAPTER 24: ANOTHER ROUGH FIRING-FROM ISRAEL

for us, and our landlord also gladly agreed to write one. Betsy's Hebrew teacher, who had taught us both, said she would be glad to give us one. Mr. Vanderhoeven of the Christian Embassy wrote a very nice letter for us.

Interestingly, our landlord told us to write a letter as from him, and he would put it into Hebrew and sign it. When he saw our first draft, he turned it down as not being strong enough. So he rewrote it saying, "These are the kind of people we need in Israel." Our landlord was the son of a Rabbi, with the heritage of five generations in Jerusalem, and had the sad honor of having lost his only son, an Airforce pilot, in the '67 war. Here we would like to point out that the majority of the Jews we knew were happy to have us live with them in Israel. We are totally opposed to anti-semitism and do not want this account in anyway to encourage it.

Hopefully, we took these letters of recommendation to Mr. Shoshani on March 27th, thinking that surely these would greatly help our case to stay in Israel. However, he hardly looked at them, just stuck them in our file and said we would hear from them in about a week.

LEAVE IN TEN DAYS!

So the following Friday, a week later, another official Ministry of Interior letter arrived in our official names in Hebrew, stating that our request for visa renewal had been denied and we were to leave the country in 10 days. We were quite shocked! It was signed by a higher official, a Mr. Tov. "Tov" in Hebrew means "good", but Mr. Tov didn't seem so good to us at that moment. We determined immediately to go see Mr. Tov and appeal to him for a stay of "execution", and to try to find out what the real reason was behind this sudden expulsion. We also needed more time to close up our little apartment which had become our Israel home; more time to arrange to put our little "yellow bird" car into good hands legally, and we had been invited by two very dear friends to have a part in their wedding on the 27th of April. The Lord had also instructed us to start writing this book. We were to go again to Patmos about May 1st, work on the book (no name yet) as long as we could, and leave there in time to be in the States at the very end of May in order to attend the 50th Reunion of my Bay High School graduation class in Panama City, Florida. Hopefully, we could encourage those who were left to really look to the Lord Jesus for His promise of eternal life. Fifty years was a long time and it would be so good to see these dear friends again.

We had already arranged for our ticket back to the States with a three-week stop over in Greece to enable us to go to Patmos again to begin the writing.

So on the day we needed to go to Mr. Tov, Esther, knowing the location of his office, arranged to take us there. As we approached his office we heard him shouting at someone, apparently on the phone. Finally, he invited us in and told us right off we must leave in 10 days and that we must in the future apply for a visa at the Israel Embassy in Washington, D.C. before attempting to come back. He, too, would give us no reason for this expulsion. He did say we had the wrong kind of visa for being so long in Israel. We said we would be happy to have a temporary or permanent residency visa. He said that was impossible. We knew then that the door to Israel, for some reason, was being slammed shut by Mr. Tov, and his ultra orthodox superiors. However, we appealed to him, for at least an extension of our time until May 1st, saying we had already made plans to leave on that date.

Surprisingly he said, "Well, if you definitely are planning to leave then, I will grant you the extension. Please report back to Mr. Shoshani for him to extend your visas to that date." And he gave us a note to that effect. We thanked him in a friendly manner and reported back to Esther, who again suggested that we might stop by to see her lawyer whose office was nearby, to get his advice on this matter. We were disappointed not to find him in, but his secretary made an appointment for us to see him 2 or 3 days later. Since he had appealed Esther's case successfully, helping her, with God's miracles, to obtain permanent residency in Israel (Read her book, "I AM MY BELOVED'S" to see that exciting victory), we felt that he might give us more hope.

Naturally the inner tensions were building up, and the rumor was flying among the Christians that Sid and Betsy were being kicked out. In fact one morning, Betsy answered the phone to find a dear Jewish lady, a Believer, calling. For years she would call for urgent prayer when she and her husband needed a miracle, and the Lord would hear our collective prayers (as in Matt.18:19) and answer with a miracle. This time she wanted to console us about our forced departure from Israel.

"Look at it spiritually," she said, "Just like Joseph had to order the Egyptians out of the room before he revealed himself to his brothers (Gen.45:1), so the Lord Jesus is having all the Gentiles now leave Israel as He begins to reveal Himself wonderfully to His Jewish brothers."

Thank goodness we had the answer to that already, and Betsy quickly said to her, "But we are not Egyptians! We also are brothers in Jesus Christ by His blood of the New Covenant."

This false teaching had been spreading around Israel and the world for the last year at least. However, we knew that God's Word says,...
He (Jesus) is our peace, who had made both one and has broken down

CHAPTER 24: ANOTHER ROUGH FIRING-FROM ISRAEL

the middle wall of partition between us. (Eph.2:14). Frequently we sang this verse at the Tabernacle of Praise where often were assembled Jews, Arabs, Gentiles, Europeans, Scandinavians, Canadians, Africans, Australians, New Zealanders, Americans, etc. No way would we accept such a false idea in the light of Ephesians and many other Scriptures, including Romans 1:16 ... *I am not ashamed of the Gospel for it's the power of God unto salvation to everyone that believeth, to the Jew first and also to the Greek.* There appears to be a tendency among Jewish Believers to fall into the error of exclusivity and some into the further error of hard-shelled Judaism all over again, back into the Law, and not enjoying the liberty of the Gospel of Jesus as Paul describes it in Galatians 5:1 ...*Stand fast in the Liberty wherewith Christ hath made us free, and be not entangled again with the yoke of bondage.* These tendencies bring with them religious pride and arrogance, not the humility, love, unity and compassion of Jesus Christ.

The morning arrived that we were to go see Mr. Shoshani again. On arising, we knelt to pray for the Lord's wonderful guidance to us through the day, that His will, not ours, be done. Esther was again coming to take us. During breakfast, as sometimes happens, a humorous little jingle popped into my mind: "This is the day for the Shoshani Shakes." As Esther was driving us to the downtown office of the Ministry of Interior, she made two separate, unwise turns in traffic that set off the "shakes"! We arrived before Mr. Shoshani to hear him say that he not only would approve the extension, but that he would give us an extra day. How nice! Then he handed us a piece of paper and told us to write on it that we would abide by these orders and leave the country by said date, and sign our names. Well, I took the paper and pen and started to write and guess what? I had the "Shoshani Shakes" and had to turn it over to Betsy to finish. We bade Mr. Shoshani farewell and left his office for the last time, knowing that our course was set for return to the States via Greece, with little hope in the natural of returning. However, I sensed in my spirit the Lord saying that we would return. Of course we were saddened by the whole situation, having to leave Israel and a lot of dear friends who had become family in the Lord.

Esther then took us to her lawyer, Uri Huppert. He was in and we had a frank discussion of the situation with him. He told us that as far as staying in Israel, we had two strikes against us already! We were Gentiles, and Christians. He urged us not to go to the Israeli Embassy in Washington to seek a visa; they would "stonewall" us forever. But rather arrange with a secular tour company to lead tour groups back to visit both Israel and Egypt, and if there was any problem when we arrived, just call him. He would get us the help needed. And he probably could have, as he was known as one of the outstanding civil rights lawyers in Israel. So we followed his directions. There was only one problem. When we came back the following fall with a tour group, the passport control police arrested us and would not allow us to call him! More about our miracle return later!

THE HECTIC LAST THREE WEEKS

The Israelis often use the expression, "Mah Laasote?" meaning "What To Do?" The Lord had given us three more weeks to get everything tied up neatly to end our stay in Israel. There was our little apartment to clear out, a last circuit of Israel to make, visiting dear friends from Ashkelon to Naharyia, to Metulla, to Vered HaGalil. Also many goodbyes to friends in and around Jerusalem, plus the transfer of the car to new owners, the giving away of many books and household items, and the packing of a few things to leave with Esther, plus paring down our personal luggage to 2 suitcases each! They surely would be 3 full weeks and they were! We were in a tightly zipped daze by that May 1st Olympic flight to Athens. At this point we can't even remember who took us to the airport; we think it was probably Esther and Yehudit, two of the dear people we were Ema and Abba (Mom and Dad) to in Israel.

Let us take you on that last circuit. During those last weeks, we had felt from the Lord that we must make this trip include, if at all possible, among the last contacts within Israel, a contact also with some precious believers in Lebanon, connected with the Voice Of Hope Radio Station. Thanks to Jan Karnis, we had visited them in Lebanon at the station and in their home in 1981 and '82. Through other friends in Israel we obtained their special radio phone number which made possible a direct phone contact to them from Israel. Finally, using that number, we got through to our dear friend Charbel Yunis at his home in Lebanon; he had become the manager of the Voice of Hope. On the night of April 24th, while visiting Nes Amim outside of Naharyia in Northwest Israel, we asked him if he could meet us at the Good Fence at the Border at 1 p.m. the next day. He said he would try. (The border was closed because of Passover week.)

We pulled into that northern border point just above Metulla at 1 p.m. that Friday and went immediately to the nearest guard post. It just so happened that a young Israeli officer was coming in the door at that moment.

We asked, "Do you speak English," not trusting our Hebrew to be fluent enough.

He said, "Yes,"

CHAPTER 24: ANOTHER ROUGH FIRING-FROM ISRAEL

We explained, "We are trying to meet Charbel Yunis, the Manager of the Voice of Hope at 1 p.m."

He said, "Fine, go up to the tourist look-out point and when you see him come to the Fence, wave him around to the Guard Post."

Apparently the young officer realized that we didn't have any authority to wave anybody around, because shortly he sent a tall, lanky, armed soldier after us, at the look-out point, to bring us back and take us through the maze of gates and barbed wire passages and more gates and other guards to the Lebanese side. The soldier's long legs had us short folks running most of the way.

As we approached the gate on the Lebanese side, we looked up and saw behind the gate our smiling Charbel and his whole family, plus a key assistant, all waving vigorously and smiling a great welcome! (They had taken their four children out of school to come to see us.) With three Israeli soldiers guarding us, we all hugged and kissed and had a "glory" meeting right there on the Lebanese side of the border. We had a couple of letters, one for them and one for Francis Rizk, then a sharing time, a praising-the-Lord time, and a prayer and anointing time for the healing of Charbel's wife's eyes in the mighty Name of Jesus! All loud enough for the soldiers to hear, and at least one of them seemed to be enjoying it! All in the space of about 20 minutes. Again hugs and kisses and promises to write and come again to see them in Lebanon as soon as the Lord permits. Thank You Lord, for that very happy reunion!

Then we marched back with the tall, lanky soldier, thanking all of them for letting us see this precious Lebanese family, who have had so much to do with keeping the Voice of Hope alive in Southern Lebanon; through all kinds of dangers and attacks, including the blowing up of the station and killing of a guard and a technician. Charbel said he had prayed for technicians just before this, and the Lord sent him four just in time to help him rebuild the Station quickly in another location. Our God Reigns. Praise Him Forever! Please, please pray for them!

We were to hear about a year later, from Charbel, that the Lord had indeed healed his wife's eyes very quickly after our combined border prayer meeting, under the watchful eyes of the armed Israeli guards. The Lord was watching, hearing and answering too! Praise His Holy Name! "Dear Lord, please continue to bless and protect Charbel and his brave family and associates in their extraordinarily courageous Christian broadcast work in South Lebanon. In Jesus' Name!"

During those last special days in Israel, there were the Easter-time services at the Tabernacle of Praise, the welcoming back to Israel of Pastor David and Faith Hjertstedt, making the last visits with many wonderful friends; two Passover dinners (Seders), one with our landlord, and one at Nes Amim (A Christian kibbutz in Northern Israel.) There was and one at Nes Amim (A Christian kibbutz in Northern Israel.) There was a farewell dinner held at Pastor Hjertstedt's apartment for us by the Tabernacle of Praise, during which time two young people put on a hilarious skit mimicking Betsy and me in our daily lives, all expressing their love and appreciation for us. How we love and appreciate them!

Many reminded us of prayers we had prayed with them, and how the Lord had given wonderful miracles to them, or someone they had asked prayer for. Erika, a little Jewish woman remembered a prayer at a bus stop one day for a young Jewish man that she was concerned about, and how the Lord had speedily answered his need. What his need was, we never knew, however Erika knew, God knew and we were agreeing with her to ask boldly in the Name of Jesus for that need to be met, and it was. Erika was probably the boldest witness for Jesus in all of Jerusalem, and was always telling people in many languages about Yeshua, her Saviour. She frequently would ask us to pray with her for some miracle need. To God be all the Glory, Praise and Thanksgiving!

Another testimony that evening was from a dear English woman who had worked as a "Nanny" for a doctor and his family on Shimoni Street, not far from where we lived. She was caring for a precious set of twins, about 10 months old. One day she was rolling the babies in a stroller by our apartment as we were just coming in. Seeing her and the babies, we had stopped to talk with her and noticed one of the twins had an awful birthmark on her lower lip. These were Jewish babies, but knowing that our Lord Jesus was Jewish and brought healing and salvation to the Jews first, we asked if it was possible for us to pray for the little girl's healing.

She said, "Yes, please do it." We reached down quickly and laid hands on the little baby and quickly prayed for the miracle of healing in Jesus' Name. (The Lord tells us in Mark 16:18...***That in His Name those who believe may lay hands on the sick and they shall recover.***

At this party many months later, we learned for the first time that the little baby was totally healed by the Lord about a month after this prayer! The horrible birthmark was completely gone! Praise His Holy Name forever! To Him be all the Glory and Honor forever!

Before leaving Israel we had the great honor of participating in a very unique wedding of two special friends, Barbara Jones and Barnabas Krockmal. When the happy day arrived, April 27, 1986, the Lord had provided some five ministers, including Barbara's father, to be present and have parts in their wedding! Barnabas was a research scientist at the Hebrew University, and Barbara, one of the Lord's sweetest and kindest servants and singers ever created. Bless them Lord! And the Lord led us to ask them to be the new proud owners of our little "yellow bird," at a heavenly price, since they had no other transportation.

SPECIAL PEOPLE WE WANTED TO SAY GOODBYE TO:

BEARDED JOHN

One of the most tragic stories concerning a Jewish Believer we've ever come upon involved a little man with a long white beard, whom we knew during most of our years in Israel. He was in his 70's and we came to think of him as Bearded John. Throughout all kinds of weather, John would somehow manage to get to the Church meetings on the east side of Jerusalem toward Bethlehem, often walking miles to get there. Brother David, or ourselves, or someone in our congregation, would always try to arrange to take him home to a mental institution where he lived on the far west side of Jerusalem. John not only could speak English, fluent Hebrew, Greek, Arabic, Spanish, Italian and Russian, but said he knew eight languages in all.

He said he was born on the island of Rhodes, and had become a believer in Jesus in his youth, and had come to Israel during the British Protectorate, before Israel became a nation. Early on, as is said today, he had married a Jewish girl who also became a believer and was killed because of it according to his account. Later he took another wife, had two sons, and when they, his wife and her relatives, discovered that John was a sincere believer in Jesus, they had him committed to a mental institution, where he had been at this time some 30 years or more. John had a medley of old-time Christian hymns that he loved to sing on our way home from Church meetings. Sometimes John's clothes would be almost unbearably ripe or smelly and we would have to admonish him to get the institution to provide him some clean clothes, or members of the congregation would do it. Now and then old John would tell us about "witnessing" to fellow inmates and praying with them to be saved before they died. So like many other saints, "Bearded John" had become the Lord's unbitter servant within a mental institution.

Reminds us of a friend in Nepal by the name of Prem Pradham, who suffered some 14 years in prisons and, while there, won so many fellow prisoners and guards to the Lord that they stopped putting him in prison. Today he's been honored by the Government as a special citizen of Napal, directs a large Christian School and orphanage, and has adopted hundreds of orphan children as his own. Hardships could not quench his love for Jesus nor his light! The Lord Himself will honor them both with, *Well done thou good and faithful servant, thou hast been faithful over a few things, I will make thee ruler over many things: enter thou into the joy of thy Lord.* (Matt.25:23)

MICHAEL

One day I stopped at a filling station and the attendant, after filling up the "Yellow Bird" with petrol and receiving my payment in shekels, looked at the Star of David and Cross that I was wearing, and in a very friendly way said, "Hey, I like that, that's the way it ought to be -- together."

I said, "Yes indeed, we are followers of Jesus, the Jewish Messiah and have a great love for Israel and the Jewish people, because of Him."

He replied, "I would like to have one like that. Could you get me one?"

"I think I have another one, not exactly like it, however. This one was given to me by a friend back in the States from Georgia, USA. I'll look for the other one, and bring it back to you in the next few days."

"Hey, I too am from Georgia! USSR! I would like it much."

Sure enough, stuck away in a drawer in the apartment was another Star and Cross together. I put it in a small box, wrapped it and took it back to his filling station, which was only a few blocks away. He thanked me and said he would keep it in a safe place. We became warm friends with him and his family and shared a number of meals together. He told us he came from Tbilisi in Soviet Georgia and had many Christian friends there.

Once Esther came back from Russia with some slides of his home town and when we showed them to him and his wife, he almost climbed into the screen, he was so excited. He had one great hope that one day soon, after some 18 years away from Russia, his precious relatives still there, including his mother, he could go back to visit them. We asked the Lord to give him his heart's desire and we understand his great hope came true in 1987!

His little daughter was born on Christmas day, and they often set up a small Christmas tree on her birthday in their apartment to celebrate both birthdays, his daughter's and Jesus'! Some of the orthodox didn't like it, but he said, "It was none of their business how he believed!" He's working in a different job now, but we always try to go by to see them and encourage them in their faith in the God of Israel and His Messiah Son whenever we can.

A MESSIANIC FAMILY

In Northern Israel lives a family of Jewish Believers who have suffered much persecution and discrimination, but have been steadfast and unmoved in their faith, and have steadfastly refused to "cut and run". Like the parents, the children have courageously stood up for their faith in Jesus as their Jewish Messiah, as their Saviour. We deeply love and honor them.

At least three of the children have been serving in the Israeli Armed Forces. The oldest daughter, whom we had the privilege of praying for and seeing receive the Baptism in the Holy Spirit, was assigned to duty in South Lebanon when Israel occupied that area. She was a real prayer warrior and would tell the patrols that she would be praying for them when they went out, that the Lord would protect them and bring them back safely. Eventually they all were asking her to cover them with her prayers, and she was asked by some of the officers to come meet with them to explain her faith, which she did, gaining at least their admiration and respect, if not their acceptance. The last we heard of this dear young Jewish girl, she was serving in another Army Post in Northern Israel and still being a prayer warrior as well. May the Good Lord bless her and her family mightily. They have all been a bright blessing to Israel and worthy of high honor and appreciation, as courageous servants of the Lord. Their example has been an inspiration to many!

OTHER FRIENDS

Space does not permit us to tell all we would like to say about the many dear friends we had in Israel such as the Weintraubs, Gat Rimons, Dayagis, McClains, Mike and Helen Lambert, the Watsons, the Hjertstedts, Avi, Chaya, and Suzanne, Yehudit and Yacov, Schlomo and Yael, Ilan and Cheryl, Jan and Janice and their miracle son, Simon, Jeanne, Dennis and Magus, Al and Margaret, Lev and Hava, the Ojedas, Chamarras, and the black man from Ghana and his family, Esther Sorensen, Wolfgang and Jennie, Mary and Ann Marie Chanslor, Merika, Ziad and Majed, Meri, Kos and Carla, Betty and Paul, Tony and Marta, Valerie and the Sidloes, Erika, and so many others we met and loved and were greatly blessed by.

We've said all the farewells we could squeeze into our last three weeks in Israel, including a very special Seder at our Landlord's home. The "Yellow Bird" found a good home. The apartment was in good hands until the end of our rent period. The major household items had been distributed or assigned, the last circuit had been made even to that special border visit with our precious Lebanese friends, our tickets ready, our suitcases packed, and we called ahead to our Athens friends, the Karakatsanis, to see if they could put us up and call Antonios for our Patmos apartment and obtain the ferry tickets for us. They could! God bless them!

Esther and Yehudet came to pick us up to go to the airport for our tearful and possibly last farewell to them and Israel. Then we were on our way to Athens to see our dear friends, the Karakatsanis, who welcomed us new "refugees" with open arms, entertained us royally, and helped us on our way to Patmos, where Antonios met us with his usual huge, happy welcome! We were Fired Again, but still Praising the Lord!

We would have two weeks before Esther, her son Joe, Lev and Hava were coming from Israel, Merika and her friend from Finland, all coming to meet these mutual friends on Patmos. So after resting for a day or two and attending a special Greek Easter service on the mountain, we dug in for long daily sessions of writing. We had to spend at least two days or more searching through our memory banks making some kind of usable lists and outlines to guide the chronology of our story and writing.

As usual late each day, we would spend some time going up to St. John's cave to study the Book of Revelation. By the time the visitors came on the 15th, the writing was well underway; and by the end of our stay, we had completed over 110 pages. Rough draft that is! Praise the Lord for another precious time on Patmos, for some progress in writing the story of His miracles in our lives, and for two new songs to Betsy from Revelation. They were from:

Rev. 12:10-11...*Now is come salvation and strength, and the kingdom of our God, and the power of his Christ: for the accuser of our brethren is cast down, which accused them before our God day and night. And they overcame him by the blood of the Lamb, and by the word of their testimony: and they loved not their lives unto the death, for the accuser of our brethren is cast down.*

And Rev. 14:6-7:... *And I saw another angel fly in the midst of heaven, having the everlasting gospel to preach to every nation and people on the earth, saying with a loud voice, Fear God, give glory unto Him, for the hour of His judgment is come, and worship Him who made the heaven and the earth, the sea and the fountains of waters.*

You must get Betsy to play and sing them for you! Both are powerful and for today!

DEAR NELLIE & SOPHIA IN ATHENS, GREECE

CHAPTER 24: ANOTHER ROUGH FIRING-FROM ISRAEL

Andre Crouch's song, "THROUGH IT ALL", sure helps in the rough times, when we get "Fired" and shaken like that.

THROUGH IT ALL[1]

BY Andre Crouch

I've had many tears and sorrows;
I've had questions for tomorrow;
There've been times I didn't know right from wrong;
But in ev'ry situation God gave blessed consolation
That my trials come to only make me strong.

Chorus:
Through it all, Through it all,
Oh I've learned to trust in Jesus,
I've learned to trust in God.
Through it all, Through it all
Oh I've learned to depend upon His Word.

I've been to lots of places,
And I've seen a lot of faces;
There've been times I felt so all alone;
But in my lonely hours, yes, those precious lonely hours,
Jesus let me know that I was His own.

I thank God for the mountains,
And I thank Him for the valleys;
I thank Him for the storms He brought me through;
For if I'd never had a problem,
I wouldn't know that He could solve them,
I'd never know what faith in God could do.

---

[1] © Copyright 1971 by Manna Music, Inc., 25510 Ave. Stanford, Suite 101, Valencia, Ca. 91355, International Copyright Secured. All Rights Reserved. Used with permission.

408 FIRED AGAIN AND AGAIN, PRAISE THE LORD!

B & B NEWLYWEDS IN ISRAEL

IBRAHAM'S "COLD DRINK SERVICE"

JOY, FAITH & PASTOR DAVID HJERTSTEDT

SARAH & JULIE IN SUCCAH

OUR ISRAELI LANDLORD, ZEV & WIFE, ZIPPORAH IN THEIR SUCCAH

CAPTURED PLO GUN (SEE ISA.54:17) "NO WEAPON THAT IS FORMED AGAINST ISRAEL SHALL PROSPER"

CHAP. 25

FROM PATMOS TO A WHIRLWIND SUMMER IN THE STATES

And we know that all things work together for good to them that love God, to them who are the called according to His purpose.
- Romans 8:28

Patmos in May is such a peaceful, pastoral, and pleasant island that one not only falls in love with it, but becomes glued to it, with no desire to leave. But leave we must, with Lev and Hava and Joe joining us for the overnight ferry ride northwest to Piraeus and Athens. They are going back to Israel. We remember that Lev and Hava stayed awake most of the night on the ferry writing letters to family and friends for us to mail for them in New York the next day.

As we landed in Piraeus early the next morning, Joe ran ahead to locate a taxi for the ride to the airport; they needed to make a beeline to the airport to catch their plane. Ours was later so we weren't in any hurry. In a few minutes they came back with the "great" news that Joe does not have his plane ticket. It's back on Patmos with Esther his mother, and they need us to go with them to help Joe get another ticket. Well, we couldn't take Joe to the States with us and couldn't leave him in Athens, so off we went, all of us jammed in a little taxi at what seemed to be 90 miles an hour, weaving through Athens traffic, trying to get to the plane on time. Although Joe was booked on the El Al flight, the airline clerk insisted he must have the original ticket or buy another one. All our pleading availed nothing, so reluctantly, we pulled out our credit card. This was going against my Scottish grain! It's one of those places where one must grit and grin and bear it and say, "Praise The Lord, anyhow! He'll make it up!" So off they went to Israel and off we went to wait for our Olympic flight to the States. Never a dull moment in the service of the Lord!

The Lord knew Kirby and Carol were weary and needed a break from

410   FIRED AGAIN AND AGAIN, PRAISE THE LORD!

inner-city ministry, after doing a trojan job for nearly seven long years. With the help of the young men who had continued in the Turn-Around-With-Jesus-Home, established in 1974 in the 1501 building, they had prepared an apartment for us in the 1503 building, and had completed 1505, for use by the Lighthouse Youth Ministry group, including an all new 2-floor apartment for the resident director and his family in the rear of 1505 E. Baltimore Street. Kirby was also doing construction work to support his family, as well as carrying the full preaching load and care of the Church. The Lord had arranged to send us home (get us fired!) just in time to bring them relief, and for them to begin a well-deserved sabbatical leave. They had labored faithfully for seven long years at the Little Tabernacle and were quite ready for relief. We and the Little Tabernacle can never thank them enough for their faithfulness during those years of our absence.

All this shows how true Romans 8:28 is: **All things work together for good to them who love the Lord, who are the called according to His purpose.**

Kirby, Carol and their four little ones awaited us at the B.W.I. airport in Baltimore. What a treat to see them all, including our latest grandson, "Little Luke", who was destined to blossom into one of the most smiling, loving, hugging little boys you ever did see! Like all our grandchildren, of course!

After a night with them in the old home place at 615 Colorado Ave, we were taken by Kirby to southern Maryland to see Betsy's brother and his wife, Debbie, who were now the proud owners of Pappy's St. Leonard Creek home, "The Bight." They had graciously kept our Ford Escort over the winter in their garage, while we were overseas, and on the morrow we were pushing on to Panama City, Florida for the 50th anniversary of my High School graduation class. Praise God! He was letting us have this opportunity and joy of seeing these dear classmates of long ago. Fifty years is a long time between hellos, handshakes and hugs! And what a joy it was to see them all! Most of the class had survived those 50 years, but a few were missing from the toll of time and wars, including my best friend in "Bay" High, Ed Williams, who gave his life in W.W.II along with many, many others putting a stop to Hitler and his Holocaust.

Since Betsy and I had come the longest distance (from Israel and Greece), we received the Long Distance prize of a toy airplane. And also a nice ballpoint pen, the reason for which escapes me, but we both have enjoyed using it. Our thanks to the Reunion Committee.

As part of the program that night, Mr. Alan Douglas showed some ancient news films of events in Panama City during the 20's and 30's, one of which showed a clip of the Panama Grammar School graduation class of 1932. There in the middle was a grinning little character (me) overshadowed by a real tall female classmate. If I remember rightly, I was still at the age when a boy needed to keep girls as far away as possible! The modern "birds and bees" teaching programs were unheard of at that time, and the world was far better off without them! They have only led to an astonishing undermining of the moral character and fabric of our schools and nation!

I'd been asked to give the Invocation or opening prayer at the Reunion, so Betsy and I were seated at the head table. While this film was being rewound and another reel threaded, there was an awkward space of time in which we felt led to ask the class President and M.C. Wilford Varn, if we could share an interesting little song called, "Hallelujah Anyhow" ("Praise The Lord Anyhow"), as a filler. He hesitated for a moment but finally said, "Okay." So we quickly went to the mike and shared that we would like to sing a song which we had found to contain a real secret for life's pilgrimage, including those difficult situations we face from time to time. So we sang "Hallelujah Anyhow" for them. (They were kind to us--no tomatoes or rocks were thrown!) The words are:

1) "When you're in the valley deep and low,
   Friends so true and blue where do they go?
   If you want to see your troubles fly,
   Then just sing this song and hold your head up high!
Chorus) "Hallelujah Anyhow!
   Never going to let my troubles get me down.
   Whatever problems life may bring,
   I'll hold my head up high and sing,
   Hallelujah anyhow!
2) "Once I read about a man named Job,
   Trials and afflictions laid him low.
   His wife said why don't you curse God and die?
   But instead he shouted with his head up high.
3) "Now I see a jail house dark and cold,
   And inside two preachers strong and bold,(Paul & Silas)
   They said why should we sit down here and cry?
   So they sang this song and held their heads up high."

Sunday morning breakfast was to be the final event of the Reunion and naturally we had a struggle with that. We felt the Lord would want us to be at our boyhood home Church for the Sunday morning worship, but we also felt that He would have us attend the breakfast to be able to talk with a number of our old classmates we had missed talking with the night before. So we made our way out to the restaurant at Grand Lagoon and had another pleasant time renewing these old friendships (Betsy took care of the breakfast eating, while I went around and talked with the old classmates.) Saying those "Goodbyes" was real hard!

We were able to leave in time to get to the last part of the morning worship, arriving in the balcony just as they were singing the last hymn before the sermon, a hymn that I had dearly loved in my boyhood in that Church, "I'll Go Where You Want Me To Go, Dear Lord; I'll Be What You want Me To Be." It was being sung on Heaven's special timing! Yes, tears flowed!

"U F O"
UNIDENTIFIED FLOATING OBJECT
(KNEE OPERATION)

During this time (1986), because of old knee injuries which had become painful intermittently, I had begun using a cane occasionally to help me take some weight especially off of my right knee. It seemed to have some kind of floating object in the knee joint that was making the knee feel like its gears were stripped. Both knees had been injured some 43 years before, but the right knee apparently was needing surgery real soon. About three or four years before this, we had a Baltimore specialist examine it, and take x-rays to try to locate this UFO (unidentified floating object). It was there then, but for some reason he failed to locate it. Must have thought I was kidding!

Back in Baltimore, we went to him again and this time his x-rays succeeded in locating the problem. He operated and removed the floating object and identified it as a piece of cartilage that had grown to about 1½" long, 1" wide, and ½" thick. He said the joint was quite battered (old news!) and might need replacement one day soon. What a relief to get that UFO out of the joint. Only by God's grace had I gotten this far without the operation. Today the knee is not working as smoothly as one would like it, but it's working, without the pain, thanks to the good Lord and the good surgeon, Dr. Johnson.

As soon as we got back to Baltimore after the reunion, we also began inviting people to go back to tour Israel with us that fall, also for the Christian Celebration of the Feast of Tabernacles sponsored by the Christian Embassy. We were following the Israeli lawyer's advice, and more importantly the Lord's leading. We made plans with the secular tour company, Galilee Tours, with offices both in Israel and in New York.

By September the Lord had given us a group of 25 people from all over the country including 4 ministers: Bro. Harold Wallace, Bro. Bob Garrett, myself and Bro. Arthur Bonhomme, the former Ambassador

CHAPTER 25: FROM PATMOS TO A WHIRLWIND SUMMER

from Haiti to the U.S., now living and ministering in Washington, D.C.

During this time too, Kirby and Carol were on vacation and making plans for a rapid move back to their beloved Tulsa. The Elders and the Church had agreed that they should be on leave with pay (which wasn't much) for the next year in appreciation for their faithfulness to the Lord and to His Church for the past 7 years. This would help them to get resettled in Tulsa, and the Church would also help them with their moving expenses.

Before they left we were offered a lot of Pappy's old furniture by Betsy's brother, and Pastor Kirby was able to rent a Ryder truck and with help from Peter and Matthew and the Youth Home, to bring it up to the Little Tabernacle to help outfit the third floor apartment which we and the Wallaces would be using.

MIRACLE HELP AT LTC AFTER OUR RETURN FROM ISRAEL

That summer of '86 was a kaleidoscope of interesting changes, events, assignments, appointments, mercies and miracles of the Lord. Looking back one could almost write a small book about it. At 68 years of age and Betsy 9 years younger, we were having to get back into the full-time Little Tabernacle harness; reassuring the congregation that the Church would continue strongly; doing all we could to help Kirby and Carol rest up and make the transition back to Tulsa; helping to get the third floor apartment fully furnished and livable, not only for ourselves, but also for the Wallaces whom we had invited by letter from Patmos to come make their base with us, if they needed it; begin recruiting for a Fall tour group back to Israel; making a flying trip to Houston, Dallas and Odessa; planning some special services among other things, plus much more; and somewhere along the way having that UFO removed from my knee.

Two new elders with their wives, Bob and Andrea Vinson, and Bob and Peggy Smith plus Rev. Harold and Judy Wallace added much strength to the congregation during these transition months. It's amazing that at the time we sent the letter offering help to the Wallaces, they were in North Carolina in something of the same situation that we were in years before in South Carolina! They were being persecuted and forced out of that area because of their long-time concern for and openness to minister to the blacks as well as the whites.

Certainly our letter was a Godsend, right on time! And we felt the Lord would want us to give them a home with us, as Sissy and Walter had done for us in 1955 in Panama City, Florida.

John Monk, who was directing the Lighthouse Ministry for young

414   FIRED AGAIN AND AGAIN, PRAISE THE LORD!

men next door in our 1505 building, along with the LTC Elders, including Bob Schloer, would be able to carry on the preaching services while we led that Fall Tour back to Israel.

That summer in July we were scheduled to spend several days at a mission conference in Odessa, Texas, sponsored by a group called The Promised Land, led by Mrs. Rita Glasscock. This group, because of our friends, James and Judith Hathaway, had been praying for us and helping us for many years. And we very much wanted to keep our speaking engagement with them. But on the way down, we thought we ought to have a brief stop by Houston to see Andy and Maxine SoRelle, and also Avi and Chaya Mizrachi and their daughter, Suzanne, in Dallas at CFNI (Christ For The Nations Institute).

We had to leave on a Sunday afternoon for Houston, arriving there an hour late, due to flight delays, but Andy and Maxine were still at the airport, Praise The Lord. They took us directly to the John Osteen Church that evening, especially to request prayer for Joe Wilkinson, my longtime Delta pilot friend down in Georgia, who was suffering from cancer. After the service, Andy took us not to his home but to one of the fanciest hotels we had ever been in, to check us in and have dinner with us before going on to their home. They came back to have lunch with us the next day and took us to our flight to Dallas and Odessa. Coming from our "digs" on Baltimore Street on Sunday afternoon to that elite hotel was a quantum leap, leaving us feeling more than somewhat out of our realm. It was a joy to see the SoRelles again and to be with them for that short time. We deeply appreciate their treating us to that special night and day in Houston.

Our visits in Odessa with the precious Promised Land group and with the Hathaways were super blessings in both instances, as was the visit on the way home with the Mizrachis at CFNI in Dallas. All in one week, and back to earth we came to Baltimore Street! Betsy and I got to see our first working oil field; from a distance it looked like a scattered bunch of big chickens slowly "pecking away" at the earth! Up and down! Up and down! Those big pumps go!

A SPECIAL ARAB NAMED IBRAHIM

There is a special providence of God always happening in the lives of His people as they travel through life, and as God wills, from country to country. This is as true as day following night, as His rainbows following rains and storms. Nearly everywhere God's people and servants go, if they are wide awake, they will be meeting special people of like precious faith and love. We've seen this happen in every place we have visited so far. Many of you have seen it happen to you, over

CHAPTER 25: FROM PATMOS TO A WHIRLWIND SUMMER

and over again.

The Lord has His special people serving Him in every corner of the world, in low places and high. This was especially true in Israel, where we were privileged to meet bright servants of the Lord from all over the world, and many precious servants right in the land of Israel, and a number in Lebanon. Some of the most dedicated Arab Christians we met in Northern Israel in Kefar Josef, in Nazaraeth and in Turon, and a few in Jerusalem and Bethlehem.

But there's one in Jerusalem who had been especially dedicated to the Lord as a baby and had grown up to be one of the best friends and fellow workers the Jewish people ever had, and the Arabs, and the Christians, and the tourists, too! Ibraham's grandfather had lived to be 147 years old (no kidding!) and was written up in one of the National Geographic Magazine decades back during the British mandate time. Ibraham showed us very proudly an ancient copy of this story. Even today, he has relatives that are over 100, still trudging up and down the mountains to work in the old city of Jerusalem! "Such hardy people" show that regular walking, up and down The Mount of Olives, can be good for your health!

We first met Ibraham at the Baptist Congregation in Jerusalem. He was and is ever smiling, cheerful, and helpful, a small man about my size, who has a house and family on the Mt. of Olives, just over the crest on the eastern slope. He has a large family of eight children, a kindly wife, and several other family members living with him in very small quarters. He supports all of them by working with a telephone cable-laying crew made up of Jews and Arabs, who think of themselves as a working team.

Despite being small in size, Ibraham is a strong, intelligent and compassionate man. There is no telling how many people he has helped, even in the middle of the night, in bad weather, and even when in financial need himself. Most of his children are miracle children, because after his first child died, the doctors warned him that his wife could have no more children. Now they have eight well behaved, growing (some grown) stairsteps. He too knows about grit and God's grace!

We came to know him "early on" in our stay in Israel. He would come often to the meetings at the Tabernacle Of Praise. I would always give him a big hug and tell others that this was my twin brother in the Lord and "We always see eye to eye!" Ibraham would also attend worship services at several of the other congregations in Jerusalem, always available to lend a helping hand, whether it was to move a stove or refrigerator, or take a sick person to the hospital at midnight. Most of the time he had no transportation of his own, but he always knew how to find some, using whatever language needed, whether Arabic, Hebrew, English, Russian, or whatever!

"Dear Lord, please bless and protect our dear friend Ibraham and his family on The Mt. of Olives."

WATCH AND PRAY

Often during the Feast of Tabernacles, Ibraham would borrow a friend's donkey to ride in the parade of Christians celebrating the Feast of Tabernacles. Sometimes this parade would begin at the Intercontinental Hotel at the southern end of the Mt. of Olives as hundreds of Christians, carrying banners of love for the Lord, and Israel, wound down a very, very steep road that led by the Garden of Gethesemane, then across the Kidron Valley at St. Stephens Church, then along the road below the ancient Eastern Gate, on around the Temple Mount Wall to the Dung Gate and into the Western Wall area for the final Praise Time To The Lord.

My brother, Frank, and his wife, Mical, had accompanied us back to Israel that September and were with us for the Feast of Tabernacles. Because of Frank's and my gimpy knees, we rode in our little Yellow Bird (the Peugeot car we had at that time) to a parking place opposite St. Stephen's Church to wait for the marchers to come down the Mt. of Olives on their way to the Western Wall. We had dropped Betsy and Mical up on top of the Mountain to march down with the group. The police were there directing the flow of traffic along this road out of Jerusalem which led eastward down to Jericho and the Dead Sea.

The parade of marchers was about half way by us, as we stood on the corner waving and cheering them on, when here comes Betsy and Mical to join us and almost immediately here comes Ibraham--on his donkey. He coaxed his donkey over to where we were and I introduced him to my brother Frank and his wife Mical. Ibraham immediately began pulling out cans of cold sodas from his donkey bags and insisting on giving us four of them. We told him we only needed two, but he insisted on leaving us the four and took off to catch up with the parade. That guy, generous to a fault, as they say! At about this moment, a young French woman, who had been staying in the apartment above the St. Stephen's Church with other friends of ours, came through the crowd to our corner and urgently asked for prayer for healing of her back which had been giving her a lot of trouble.

Immediately we agreed to pray for her right there on the corner and set the cans of soda on the stone wall close behind us. We joined hands with her and all closed our eyes and prayed earnestly for the young lady's healing in the Name of our Lord Jesus. We had opened one

CHAPTER 25: FROM PATMOS TO A WHIRLWIND SUMMER 417

of the drinks before we set them all down on the wall to pray, and guess what? After praying and thanking the Lord for hearing our prayer for the young lady, we opened our eyes and turned to pick up the drinks and, lo and behold, three drinks were gone!! The thief had left us the opened one! That one was really enough for us all, but we did learn another meaning of the Lord's admonition, when He said, "**Watch and Pray**"! (Matt.24:41). There are times, perhaps many times, when we should keep our eyes open when we are praying. Thank You, Lord, for another good lesson on how to pray! And thank You, Lord, for Ibraham's great thoughtfulness and generosity, and for healing the woman's back!

Once, to help a family from the Outer Banks of North Carolina who wanted to stay in Jerusalem for a long visit, Ibraham arranged to make a new door through a wall in his small place to make them a separate living space. Sometime later this dear family from North Carolina arranged for Ibraham, his wife and two oldest children to come to stay with them for a while in the United States. The two older children stayed on to attend schools and Ibraham returned to Israel with his wife after traveling by faith through some 25 states, visiting friends he had met in Israel. In his bags he had brought several kilos of stones from The Holy Land, to give his Christian friends and hosts a little piece of Israel as a Thank You Gift.

The unexpected happened. His older daughter fell in love with a Christian U.S.Coast Guardsman while living in North Carolina, and sent back word that she was going to marry him. And she did!

When the word got around among the 'Muktars', the Arab Islamic leaders on the Mt. of Olives, where several thousand Arab Moslems live, problems for Ibraham began to develop. This is where the nitty-gritty about Islam set in, the Sharia or Law of Islam!

We were told that these Moslem leaders said to Ibraham that his daughter, supposedly a Moslem girl, could not marry a Christian. That he was to call and tell her to stop it or come home. If she didn't, Islamic law required that the father or oldest son be sent to kill her. A Moslem man may marry a Christian, but a Moslem girl cannot marry outside that faith, and no Moslem can leave that faith without being subject to the penalty of death. Keeps Islam growing! The Sword of Islam is no joke!

One day, in the fall of '86, just after my knee surgery, we received a phone call from the Richmond, Va. bus station from Ibraham asking us to meet him that afternoon at the Baltimore bus station. Surprise! Ibraham is in the U.S.A.! We did so and brought him to the Little Tabernacle to spend the night with us. He was in great distress because he couldn't get in touch with his daughter and was convinced that she was not answering his phone calls because she was afraid that he had been sent to kill her. He said, "That's what they told me to do, but I have come with my suitcase full of wedding gifts for my daughter from me and my family."

Finally the next morning, Betsy was able to reach the daughter in the Outer Banks, who explained that the phone lines had been down because of a storm, but it was true that she was afraid that her father had come to kill her according to the Islamic law. We knew this law to be true because just the year before in September '85, U.S. newspapers reported the same thing had happened to a daughter in an Arab family in Los Angeles who had decided to become Christian. The oldest brother was sent to kill her on the school ground and after doing so, quickly fled by plane to an Arab nation on the Persian Gulf.

Praise the Lord, in a long distance call from Baltimore, on that morning, Betsy was able to convince the daughter that her father had come in love and peace and wanted only to bring wedding gifts to her. She finally agreed to talk with her Dad. They made plans to meet in the Outer Banks. And they did, joyfully!

Ibraham was able to return safely to Jerusalem to continue on into the winter his work laying telephone cable and also his remarkable custom of helping people in need, wherever he met them.

Three things that the Islamic faith does not teach are love, forgiveness, and mercy especially for anyone outside of Islam. Because he had been dedicated to the Lord by a Christian nun as a baby, the Lord had helped Ibraham come to know all three of these graces. But because he and all his people were members of an Arab Moslem community, he had had to submerge his faith in Jesus Christ to prevent deadly harm coming to his family and himself.

There's no way of knowing whether the Islamic leaders out of retribution for Ibraham's refusal to carry out the "death penalty" on his daughter that Islam requires, staged this accident or not. But the following winter or spring, he was suddenly pinned under a huge telephone cable spool falling on him, badly injuring his legs. Could have easily killed him.

Over the years he and his family have been a tremendous help to Esther and her sons as they lived on Mt. Bethphage, a short distance east of the Mt. of Olives. Esther told us that he had suffered terribly from these injuries and had several operations trying to save his legs, but in spite of the pain, he continued to help her and others whenever he could. We saw him briefly in October 1990 and he was almost completely recovered. Praise and thank God.

There's no way of knowing whether that accident was an intentional effort to kill him or not. We suspect it was, but the true God and Father of our Lord Jesus Christ would not allow it.

CHAPTER 25: FROM PATMOS TO A WHIRLWIND SUMMER

Islam cannot be of God, for God Is Love according to Jesus in (John 3:16, and I John 4:7,8). And we've told many times that the Arabic written around the Gold Dome of the Mosque of Omar on the old Jewish Temple Mount, quoting the Koran, says that "Allah is God, Mohammad is his chief prophet; the Koran is his true word; and he has no son and has no need of a son." This is a total denial of the Salvation Plan of the God of Abraham, Isaac and Jacob through the substitutionary (Passover) Death and Resurrection of His Only Begotten Son, JESUS CHRIST--and a devilish attempt to substitute a religion with a false prophet, with a sword of vengeance, filled with anger and hatred toward the Jews and Christians. The fact that those two mosques are sitting on the most Holy Site of Judaism, and violent murderous outbreaks take place at the slightest suggestion that Islam leave that Jewish Holy site and go back to Mecca where it came from, clearly proves its usurping nature. And, finally, there is absolutely no historical record that Mohammad ever came to the Holy Land on his white charger and rose to Heaven from that Mount. It is all unholy fiction, and a rank counterfeit, attempting to substitute a hate-filled religion with a sword for the true faith that God planned and carried out in Jerusalem through the Cross of Jesus Christ, His Only Son, for the salvation of mankind--Jews, Gentiles, and Arabs! How the gullible world is being deceived! Recent experiences with the rabid Islamic leaders such as Khomeni, Saddam Hussein, Assad of Syria, and the Hezballah of Lebanon (and their hostages) should illustrate the unbenign nature of Islam.

Please pray for Ibraham and his family and for a multitude more of the Arabs and Jews to know the TRUE SAVIOUR AND MESSIAH, JESUS, THE ANOINTED SON OF GOD!

Quite an amazing summer. We finally got out of it! Praise The Lord!

THE TEMPLE MOUNT ON MT. MORIAH

420   FIRED AGAIN AND AGAIN, PRAISE THE LORD!

SOME OF OUR WONDERFUL FRIENDS ON PATMOS

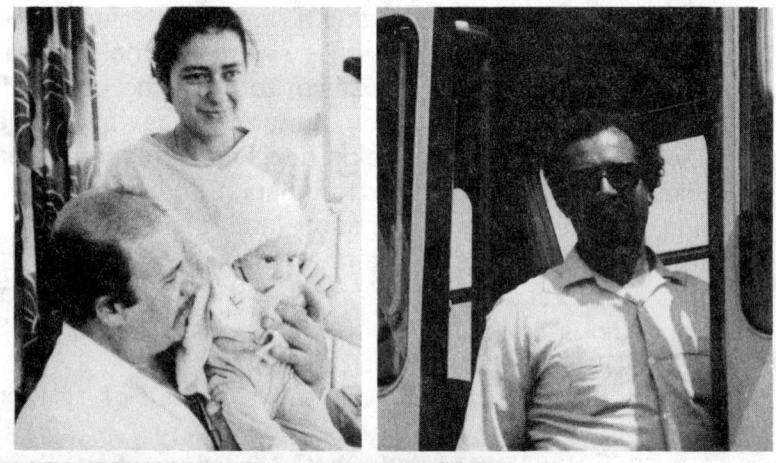

CHAP. 26

DANGEROUS MISSIONARIES ARRESTED

IN ISRAEL!

For our light affliction, which is but for a moment, worketh for us a far more exceeding and eternal weight of glory. - II Corinthians 4:17
For with God all things are possible. - Mark 10:27b

Since we had been thoroughly blackballed and expelled from Israel in May,1986, Betsy and I knew that we were likely to run into some kind of trouble getting back into Israel, when we showed up with this tour group without the prior visa from the Israel Embassy in Washington. But we knew what the Israeli lawyer had said, "Don't do it. They'll stonewall you forever!" So we were hoping to be able to reach him when we returned. Normally American tourists do not need visas in advance of coming to Israel. Israel, Greece, England and other nations usually stamp the passport of a tourist with an allotted time to stay in the country when he arrives. In Israel it's 3 months, unless, as in our case, a computer's red light starts flashing.

Just before our tour group was to leave, we lifted up a special desire to the Lord, saying, "Lord we sure would like this tour to be recorded on film, the video kind. Could that be possible?" We left the petition in the Lord's hands. When the day of our departure from Baltimore arrived a good part of our group met at B.W.I. (Baltimore Washington International Airport) to fly as a group to the Kennedy Airport in N.Y. where we would meet the rest of our group for the flight to Israel. Guess what? The Lord had directed our dear Jewish brother, Len Winter, a retired Army Major, to pick up a new video camera, film and instruction book 3 days before and begin learning its secrets! Here he was at BWI already recording our departure and doing a great job! He and his wife, Barbara, were real treasures on the tour! Throughout the next 14 days, Len was steadily doing his video job, getting excellent results, acting like a veteran cameraman.

Our Pan Am plane had over 300 Christian Pilgrims eagerly looking forward to their visit to the Holy Land. We had a brief stopover, going and coming, at the DeGaulle Airport outside of Paris and had a delightful time singing the Lord's praises and songs of Israel in the airport lounge during the wait. There was a lot of musical talent in our group and in the whole group. Bob Garrett treated the pilgrims to a remarkable trumpet solo in the Paris Airport--without the trumpet! Apparently it's a musical secret known only to him and a few others, especially his sons. All of Bob's family, Mom, Dad, four sons and one daughter are great musicians and singers and love the Lord. What a joy to know them and tour with them.

As we were nearing Israel, I told Betsy that I must go up to where our co-host, Rev.Harold Wallace, was seated and quietly alert him to what possibly could happen to Betsy and me at the Ben Gurion Airport; that we could be pulled out of line, put under arrest and sent back home on the next flight. He, with the help of the other ministers, was to lead the group on through the tour and bring them safely home with the Lord's great help. I had not told him before because I didn't believe it would help in anyway!

The plane landed at Ben Gurion Airport, probably around 5 p.m.; the passengers rode buses from the plane to the main terminal entrance to passport control. With hundreds of people arriving, usually there are some dozen or more passport check officers in booths, before which the tourists have to line up and pass through.

We made sure all our people were going through all right, then Betsy and I presented our new passports to the immigration officer, a lady. (Our old passports, with the (X), providentially had expired in August and so we had to acquire new ones). She entered our passport numbers and names in the computer, and apparently began getting the red light. A policeman nearby was calmly summoned by the lady and he came and told us to come with him to the police office. Gulp! We knew we were in trouble! Big trouble!

We told the Senior police officer we were leaders of a group that was already inside, and we needed to speak with our co-leaders to tell them what was happening. So he sent a young policeman with us to alert the leaders, and to get our bags. He allowed us to open one of the suitcases to transfer some of the things we had for Esther, who was then waiting outside, hoping and praying that we could get through.

I began telling Betsy, "Altidagi, Betsy, (Hebrew for don't worry). The Lord will find someway to get us through." Back in the police office, we asked why we were being detained, and at first they would say only that the Ministry of Interior would not allow us to come in, and that we were to be sent back to the U.S. on the next plane leaving early the next morning. We would be held in police custody until then. We asked

CHAPTER 26: DANGEROUS MISSIONARIES ARRESTED

if we could make a phone call to our lawyer in Jerusalem. The officer said, "No, no calls permitted except to the American Embassy." It was already about 6 p.m., and we knew there would be little chance of finding anyone except a Marine guard on duty at the Embassy. Another way had to be found.

About this time another large tour group came in from another plane, in the midst of which was Hela Brand, one of the heads of the Tour company in New York we had been dealing with. Perhaps Hela could help. She came rushing over to talk to the police in Hebrew about us but could not prevail on them to change their minds. She had to go on through with her group. Gloom settles! Betsy and I both probably looked as if we had lost our last friend by this time, but I kept saying, "Altidagi, Betsy, the Lord will find a way!"

About this time we were able to pursuade the police to tell us what their readout from the Ministry of Interior said was the real reason we couldn't enter Israel. They said, "It's because you're DANGEROUS MISSIONARIES!" Really I don't think they believed it!

Suddenly, a well dressed Israeli came up to us and said, "The other leaders of your group asked me to come back to see you and talk to the police and try to get you out." He said his name was Zvi Givati. He was helping the Christian Embassy welcome the Christian Tour Groups. He left us with the words, "Don't worry, let me see if I can work out something." Apparently, after hearing from the police why we were being held, he went back to our tour leaders to tell them the situation wasn't good. They immediately began putting some heavy pressure on him. Former Ambassador Bonhomme showed Zvi a copy of a Voice Magazine, showing him shaking hands with President Johnson. And he assured Zvi that he still had many powerful contacts in Washington. A dear friend from Texas, Margaret Baker, pulled out her Gold Presidential Card, indicating she had influence in the Reagan administration. And Bro. Wallace said, The White House will hear about this immediately, and furthermore, if they are not released right away, our whole tour group will go back to the States with them!

Mr. Givati then came back to see us in the police office and said, "You have some pretty important people in your group don't you?"

We said, "We sure do!"

He said, "Well, let me try to make some phone calls."

In a few minutes he came back saying there was no one on duty at the Ministry of Interior when he called. Then, he said, "I'll try something else." He returned and talked to the police and in a few minutes he came to us and said, "I've arranged for you to be in my custody for the next two weeks--if you promise to leave Israel at the end of your tour with your group." Praise God!

Wow! We said, "We gladly make that promise!" Later we learned that the last call he tried to make was to the General in charge of the military region in which the airport was located. He was sure this General (who was his brother) would okay our entry, if Zvi would take full responsibility. However, he could not reach his brother so he decided to go back to the police, use some "hutzpah", and persuade the police that "an international incident was about to be caused." "These people have influence all the way to the White House, and as a retired General myself, I will be glad to take care of them, and prevent this."

The police officer quickly agreed and released us into his custody for two weeks! Hallelujah! Zvi has a super desire to build goodwill between the Jews and the Christians. After nearly two hours, we were set free! "Thank You, Lord!"

We told the police thanks for their concern and said "Shalom." After thanking Zvi and assuring him we would check in with him often at the Convention Center in Jerusalem, we went out to our tour bus, which our co-leaders had stubbornly held at the airport until our release. Before getting on the bus we had a brief, thankful reunion with Esther! The Lord had worked a wonderful miracle and had overruled Satan's plan to keep us out of the land. Praise His holy name forever!

We saw our "Angel" Zvi Givati, the retired General, many times during the next two weeks, and became very good friends with him and his wife. They were eventually to come to the States in the Spring of 1989 to stay and speak at the Little Tabernacle, and many other places around the nation. Bro. Len Winter was not allowed to video our arrest as he was trying to, but before the tour was over he did get a great segment showing General Zvi and his wife, Esther, expressing their gratitude on behalf of Israel for the thousands of Christians who had come to the Feast of Tabernacles Celebration to bless Israel. What special angels they are!

By the end of the year we were working again with Galilee Tours for a Spring tour back to Israel!

Soon after the October tour, we sat down to our little typewriter and wrote the head of the Ministry of Interior a strong letter of protest concerning our arrest in October 1986 at Ben Gurion Airport. It went as follows:

LETTER OF PROTEST

1503 E. Baltimore St.
Baltimore, Md. 21231 USA
December 5, 1986

The Honorable Mr. Peretz
Ministry of Interior
Jerusalem, Israel

CHAPTER 26: DANGEROUS MISSIONARIES ARRESTED

Dear Mr. Peretz,

Recently on October 14, 1986, while leading an American tour group of 25 Christian pilgrims to the Celebration of the Feast of Tabernacles, sponsored by the Christian Embassy in Jerusalem, my wife and I were stopped at the Ben Gurion Airport passport control and told we could not enter and would be sent back to the States on the next flight. We were shocked! Finally, we were told it was because we were "missionaries." To be stopped and held in custody like this, after bringing other tour groups and helping with many others over the past 10 years, was most embarrassing and unjust. My wife and I have had a deep love for the Jewish people and Israel for decades and have been calling on our fellow Christians and political leaders to stand by Israel for a long time.

Fortunately, there were some very important people with our group, with access to the White House, who interceded for us, and arranged for our release after about 1 1/2 hours, based on our agreement to leave Israel at the end of the 15 day tour. Of course, we did this.

For the past few years, as pensioners, we have stayed on in Israel for several months each year, studying Hebrew and trying to be goodwill friends to all we met in Israel. We were breaking no laws, and never were accused of such. We never were there as "missionaries", but were there as a retired couple, occasionally meeting with tour groups we had encouraged to come to visit Israel.

Finally, last April we were called into your ministry and surprised to be asked to leave the country by Mr. Shoshani, who stated we had been there "too long on a tourist visa." Each year we had returned to the States for several months to encourage many others to tour Israel, and to urge strong resistance against the evil of anti-semitism.

Since we have a proven record of friendship and love for Israel, and for the Jewish people,* and since in our stays in Israel we were fully law abiding, never accused of any crime, and since we have been long helpful in bringing tour groups to Israel, we respectfully request that our names be fully cleared for entry to your beloved Israel for the purpose of bringing a tour in March and October, 1987.

We've been asked by Galilee Tours to bring a tour group to Israel under their direction in March 17-26, 1987. Therefore, we will need your approval and clearance as soon as possible in order to enlist a good group for this tour.

We thank you for your kind assistance in this matter.

With all good wishes to you,

Yours Very Truly,
Joseph S. & Elizabeth W. Rigell

*(Including three injuries in WW II in America's efforts to stop the Nazis and the Holocaust.)
JSR/ewr

We also sent copies of it to General Zvi Givati, John Vanderhoven, Mrs. Axel Springer, and the head of her publishing company in Germany, Ernst Kramer. Ernst had sent us a letter suggesting he might be able to offer some help since the Springer Company and Foundation in Berlin, Germany had long-time influential connections with Israel. He wrote a short letter saying, "Let's see what we can do to open Pandora's box." Mrs. Springer, who had become a very dear friend, also had an apartment in Jerusalem, and very highly placed Israeli friends.

We were not at all sure we would get a reply from the Ministry of Interior but, some time in January, a letter arrived from them, from a top deputy, all in official Hebrew. It took us a couple of days to translate everything, but we did quickly recognize some of the words, one being "Taute" (mistake) at the Ben Gurion Airport! Praise God, it looked like an apology, and so it was as you see in the following translation. We called a friend of ours, Irv Weintraub, a professor at Towson State University, a Hebrew scholar, and brother to our friend and neighbor Zev in Jerusalem, and asked him if he would come and double check our translation. He said he would be glad to and he came down early one Sunday morning and went over the Hebrew letter and our translation. He found only one phrase that needed reworking.

Ministry of Interior
January, 1987   Honored Mr. Joseph & Elizabeth Rigell
                                                          Baltimore
                                                          Honored Sir,

The Subject: Your Entrance to Israel
Document - Your letter from day, Dec. 5, '86
In the beginning let me express my apologies on the happenings with your arrival to Israel on 14 October, 1986.
It became clear to me, after inspection, that the border inspecting officer stopped your entrance in error, in the framework of the action to clarify details concerning people who are staying illegally in Israel.
When this error was discovered, and much to my sadness only after the event, your entrance was authorized. I repeat and express my sadness and my apologies on that which happened.
     In Much Honor,
     Mr. Bar Levi, Senior Advisor to the Minister

The Lord had worked another miracle! We sent copies of this most

CHAPTER 26: DANGEROUS MISSIONARIES ARRESTED

unusual letter to the other people involved, with our great thanksgiving to the Lord and to them.

We felt the Lord wanted us to check the "door to Israel" again fairly soon after the "apology letter," so we began recruiting a group for the March tour 1987, again with Galilee Tours. We wrote our "Angel Zvi" concerning our tour and time of arrival and asked if he could possibly meet us at the airport. As our group of fourteen unloaded from the plane-bus at the airport entrance to the Passport Control officials, there stood smiling Zvi outside the entrance, saying, "Haven't I met you somewhere before? I have three "VIP" passes; get someone else, give me your passports, follow me, and I'll take you through." What an "Angel" the Lord had given us! We grabbed one of our tour members and gave our passports to Zvi and went through faster than ever before! Our "Angel Zvi" was very much on duty. Praise The Lord for him!

The next tour group was the Fall of '87. Another lovely group--put together by the Lord! Again we notified Zvi and again he was at the airport to welcome the Christian tour groups from all over the world on behalf of the Christian Embassy. These groups were coming again to join Israel in celebrating the Feast of Tabernacles. (See Zech. 14:16).

As we arrived at the Passport Control officers, we could see Zvi way on the other side of the huge room at the welcome booth, near the baggage carrousels, but he was making no move to come to greet us or assist. Did he not get our letter? It turned out that he had personally checked the Ministry of Interior and found that we were no longer on their blacklist, so he was letting us come through on our own. And we did, with no problem! Then we had another happy reunion with him at the welcome booth and a number of other contacts with him during the tour. Isn't the Lord good?! We'll praise His Holy Name forever! With His Holy Saints and Angels above!

A SPECIAL SAINT ABOVE - SHARON!

One of those saints above, a lovely and talented young Jewish Believer, named Sharon, had so wanted to go to Israel with us on that March '87 tour. Her twin sister Gwen and mother, Eunice, and Gwen's stepson, Brian, did go. Sharon was desperately ill with Hodgkin's disease (a type of cancer). In spite of her chemotherapy treatments, she was believing the Lord would work a miracle for her to go. But, alas, her husband vetoed it. The Lord had a greater tour waiting for precious Sharon.

We left BWI on Purim. This is the Jewish celebration of the their deliverance by the Lord through Queen Esther and her Uncle Mordecai from a death decree during their captivity in Persia under King

Ahasuerus and the evil Prime Minister Haman. Haman had planned the extermination of the Jews especially out of hatred for Mordecai. After Queen Esther and the Jews fasted three days without food or water, evil Haman was exposed by Esther and was hung on the same gallows on which he had planned to hang Mordecai.

Then King Ahasuerus ordered that the God of the Jews be declared the God of all Persia. Quite a story! (Read "Esther" in your Bible!) The Jewish people always read this story during Purim and they all celebrate the deliverance of the Jews by the Lord.

Sharon, weak and pale, but bright with love, came to see our Tour group off at the airport, bringing a bag of Purim treats for each of our pilgrims! Such a trooper she was! Her battle against that disease continued for weeks after our return. Her doctors and nurses at John Hopkins did all they could for her. So many prayers went to God's throne for Sharon. But the Lord had something better for her. (Phil.1:23-24). Leaving a loving family and two handsome little sons, precious Sharon went on to be a Special Saint in God's Heaven!

After she went on to be with the Lord, her sister Gwen brought us Sharon's small Bible in which Gwen had inscribed and drawn a picture of a little heart-shaped pillow with arms outstretched and the words inside: "We love you this much!" It was just like the pillow Sharon had given us earlier in the summer! We loved them that much, too!

THE 1987 TOUR AND ISRAEL'S TERRIBLE DROUGHT

After our angel friend, Zvi, let us come in on our own with the fall tour group of 1987, we had a moment to look at the latest visa stamp on our passport, and sure enough it showed the standard three months stay allowed for most tourists. Of course we were delighted to see this. We really were off the "black list," and no doubt could come again and receive a similar three month stay.

For sensitive Christian tourists, the most blessed and inspiring places in Israel are Bethlehem, Bethany, Jerusalem, Nazareth and the area around the northern end of the Sea of Galilee. On our first tour to Israel, ten years ago, we had a Spirit-filled Arab Christian guide just for Bethlehem to whom we posed the question, "What, to you, is the most holy site in all of Israel?"

He thought a moment and said, "I guess it would have to be the Sea of Galilee; no one can build a shrine over it and call it his!" A great answer!

This he said after almost drowning in the Sea of Galilee just a few days before when someone began falling overboard from one of the tourist boats. He immediately jumped in to help, forgetting one

CHAPTER 26: DANGEROUS MISSIONARIES ARRESTED 429

important matter: he didn't know how to swim! The sailors got them out okay, but he was half drowned. Had to spend a night in a hospital! A courageous man but not so wise in this instance.

When we returned to the Sea of Galilee on the '87 tour, we found that the sea level had dropped 10 feet from a three-year drought; the worst in modern Israel's 40-year history. Even before we left Israel in May 1986, the shoreline had receded at least 200 feet, which interestingly led to the discovery of the ribs of an ancient sunken fishing boat. Using the latest time-dating techniques, the Israeli scientists concluded that the boat dated back to the time of Jesus. Some bright reporter, either misinformed or with "tongue in cheek," announced, "This may have been the boat in which Jesus came to Israel!" The scientists carefully proceeded to excavate the ancient boat from the mud, build a flotation device around and under it, dig a channel to float it to shore, and today it's in its own boat house on the edge of the Sea, preserved in a large "tub" filled with chemicals to prevent deterioration. Tourists can view it through a long glass wall at Kibbutz Nof Ginossar. The boat is something like 25 feet long and 8 feet wide, said to be typical in size and construction to the first century fishing boat design.

We need to remind ourselves and the world that the Sea of Galilee is the major water source for the whole nation of Israel. Its supply streams flow from the south side of Mt. Herman and the Golan Heights, making it necessary to control and guard these areas at all times.

The day that we were at the Sea, our whole overall group, (some 300 Christians) filled up two modern Sea of Galilee tourist boats when we crossed the Sea from Tiberias to Capernaum. About halfway across with a calm sea, the ships' captains, at our request, stopped the boats side by side, lashed them together, for us to have a Praise and Worship service right there in the middle of the Sea of Galilee. (It's quite common for Christian pilgrims to do this.) Different leaders shared Bible readings and meaningful messages from the Lord to us. There were many praise songs with musical instruments. There were trumpets, autoharps, tambourines, guitars, and quite a gathering of followers of Jesus singing His praises on that special Sea that, no doubt, He loved and still loves very much. This Sea of Galilee service ended with special prayers that the Lord would stop the drought, and send bountiful rains, plus strong warnings of heavy judgments if Israel and America do not repent of the terrible evils that are sweeping both nations, and turn back to God and His Word and His Son Jesus Christ, the Jewish Messiah and Saviour.

The following warning was brought forth again, which had been given to us at the Little Tabernacle just before the tour:"CALL MY PEOPLE TO SOLEMN FASTING, PRAYER AND REPENTANCE

THROUGHOUT THE LAND TO TURN THIS NATION BACK TO MY WAY OF HOLINESS AND RIGHTEOUSNESS. CALL THIS NATION TO TURN AWAY FROM THE HORRIBLE EVILS THAT ARE PRESENT IN THE LAND. THE HOLOCAUST OF INFANTS IS GROSS EVIL! I'VE HEARD THE CRIES OF OVER 20 MILLION INFANTS MURDERED IN COLD BLOOD DURING THE LAST 14 YEARS, AND I WARN YOU, SAITH THE LORD, THAT AMERICA WILL BE DESTROYED, TOTALLY DESTROYED, IN LESS THAN 10 YEARS IF THIS INFANT HOLOCAUST IS NOT STOPPED SOON! REMEMBER MY WORD WHICH I GAVE TO MY PEOPLE LONG AGO IN II CHRON.7:14, AND DO IT! THIS IS YOUR ONLY HOPE." (See Rev. 13 & 14).

Well, guess what happened the next day? After a wonderful time on the Sea of Galilee, at Capernaum, Mt. of Beatitudes, touring the Golan Heights, and visiting the coastal town of Nahariya, we were on our way back to Tel Aviv, stopping at Megiddo, an ancient fort of King Solomon next to the great Jezreel Valley where the end-time war of Armageddon will be fought. The sky had become overcast and soon it began to sprinkle. Most of the tour group climbed to the top of the tell[1] for the tour guide's lecture which was cut short by the increasing rain. They all ran down into the underground tunnel which led to an ancient spring and came out of the small mountain into more rain. By the time they got back to the bus, which was moved around the mountain, most of our people were soaking wet, but happy as they could be! Yes, happy and praising God with all their might for He was sending His early rains to break the drought in answer to our prayers, and Israel's!

When you have a Church tour group such as ours traveling to Israel, they are apt to break forth in praise songs at the drop of rain! Nutty but fun people! We're remembering a song for rain that Barbara Winters sang at the Sea of Galilee as we saw Israel's terrible need for rain in October '86:

"Send down the rain Lord, Send down the rain,
Send down the latter rain.
We need the rain, Lord, we need the rain,
We need the latter rain.
"There's healing in the rain, Lord, healing in the rain,
Healing in the latter rain,
So send down the rain, Lord, send down the rain,
Send down the latter rain."

Praise the Name of the Lord. He hears our daily prayers.

---

[1] An artificial mound consisting of the accumulated remains of ancient settlements.

CHAPTER 26: DANGEROUS MISSIONARIES ARRESTED

SHEEP PATHS ON THE MOUNTAINS OF ISRAEL

Throughout our tours to Israel, and several years of living there, we have described many scenes in that now beautiful and blooming land, restored by God. A Jewish people restored to their land, and a land restored to great beauty and productivity by the hand of God through hard-working Jewish immigrants. A Scripture verse that always thrills us is Psalm 102:16 which says that, when the Lord shall build up Zion, He shall appear in all his glory! See the beautiful context: Ps.102:12-22:

> *But thou, O Lord, shalt endure for ever; and Thy remembrance unto all generations.*
> *Thou shalt arise and have mercy upon Zion: for the time to favour her, yea, the set time is come.*
> *For Thy servants take pleasure in her stones, and favour the dust thereof.*
> *So the heathen shall fear the name of the Lord, and all the kings of the earth Thy glory.*
> *When the Lord shall build up Zion, He shall appear in His glory.*
> *He will regard the prayer of the destitute and not despise their prayer.*
> *This shall be written for the generation to come: and the people which shall be created shall praise the Lord.*
> *For He hath looked down from the height of His sanctuary; from heaven did the Lord behold the earth;*
> *To hear the groaning of the prisoner; to loose those that are appointed to death;*
> *To declare the name of the Lord in Zion, and His praise in Jerusalem.*
> *When the people are gathered together, and the kingdoms, to serve the Lord.* (Psalm 102:12-22)

Here we see the Psalmist gives a prophecy that Almighty God will have mercy upon Zion and favor her at a set time, that his servants will take pleasure in His stones and favor the dust thereof; that the heathen will fear the name of the Lord; and earthly kings will fear God's glory; that the Lord will build up Zion and then appear in His glory. (His Return is quite soon, for Zion has been and is being remarkably rebuilt!) And notice that this is written for a generation to come, a generation created to praise the Lord. We are now in such a generation as never before. In our generation those that love the Lord and His coming are praising Him as never before! In greater numbers! Hallelujah!

So as we tour Israel, we are so privileged to see the rebuilding of Zion, of Israel, throughout its length and width. One sees beautiful wheat farms, vineyards, fruit orchards, citrus groves, "truck" farms, dairies, fish "farms," olive and banana groves, forests, new and old industries, schools, colleges, military bases, housing developments and new settlements--all evidences of a vigorous land and people. There are also signs of old things and ways, such as the occasional Bedouin tents with their flocks of sheep and goats. And donkeys!

Paradoxically, among the truly beautiful scenes in Israel are the starkly, barren, brown and yellow mountains east of Jerusalem going down to Jericho and to the Dead Sea (some 20 miles east of Jerusalem), even far down to Eilat. Perhaps the most beautiful pictures we've seen of these mountains were made by a precious Jewish girl, saved by Yeshua, on our first tour to Israel. We wish we had her whole series to show you right now.

Eventually, it was to dawn on us that these mountains had a peculiar series of horizontal markings on them all the way down to Jericho. We began wondering what caused those horizontal indentations. Were they signs of erosion or some kind of paths? Finally, we realized that these horizontal lines must be paths made by sheep and goats grazing on the side of these mountains during the rainy season in the winter and spring, when they are, for a very short period, green with grass.

Our first tour guide, Moshe, told us how he had been in such a desert region when the first drops of rain came and he had watched the grass springing up out of the ground, growing rapidly, blooming a tiny flower and making seed all in a 24-hour period. He told us this in all seriousness, saying this is how it is when grass grows in the barren mountains and deserts to the east and south of Jerusalem, and of course in the Sinai Desert to the southwest.

We asked Moshe if those streaks along the sides of the mountains were made by the sheep and goats during the short grass-growing season? Always on the way down to Jericho you see some ancient Bedouin tents with their ever-present flocks of goats and sheep (and some donkeys) nearby. Moshe agreed that these were the paths made by the grazing sheep and goats and donkeys. However, Betsy asked if they could have been made by eons of water erosion. Always a gentleman, Moshe replied, "Perhaps some of it is by erosion."

For a long time Betsy could not be persuaded that the sheep and goats made those paths. It took a lot of convincing!

With many other tours and tour guides, Avi, Joseph, Moshe, and Gershon, we would ask that question of the guides, including two friends who had been sheepherders, Paul and Dave. All said those

CHAPTER 26: DANGEROUS MISSIONARIES ARRESTED 433

horizontal paths had to be made by the sheep and goats grazing on those mountains. Finally, after about the umteenth guide's confirmation, Ema (Mama) Betsy gave up and said, "I believe!" She's now a Believer, not a doubter, not only in grits, but also in the sheep paths on the mountains in the Judean Wilderness!

Many times, coming back up to Jerusalem from the Dead Sea and Jericho, we would see those flocks of sheep and goats grazing and moving horizontally along those rocky mountain slopes, till finally one day she became a real Believer, we hope! To make all those paths it did take centuries and countless sheep to do it. They've had the time! Baruch Ha Shem! (Bless the Name of the Lord!)

Aren't we glad we know the Great Shepherd of human sheep? His name is JESUS! (John 10; Ps.23; Ps.100; Hebrews 13:20-21).

WE SPENT MANY HAPPY HOURS WITH THESE BEAUTIFUL BELIEVERS - AND NOT JUST BECAUSE EILEEN SIDLO MAKES THE TASTIEST PECAN PIE-LETS IN ALL THE WORLD!

TEXANS-VALERIE WALLER & THE SMILING SIDLOS IN JERUSALEM

434 FIRED AGAIN AND AGAIN, PRAISE THE LORD!

ON THE WAY TO B & B'S WEDDING - 1986

COURAGEOUS FRANCIS RIZK OF LEBANON & JAN VANDERHOEVEN OF ISRAEL

OUR "ANGELS" ESTHER AND ZVI GIVATI

CHAP. 27

SOME YUMMY STORIES

Delight thyself also in the Lord; and He shall give thee the desires of thine heart. — Psalm 37:4

"HONEYOLOGY"

We would like to call this section Honeyology! Many of you already know about our special love for honey, called "devash" in Hebrew and "mele" in Greek.

My mother's father, whom we called "Papa" and from whom my given names came, was a lover of honey, the Bible and the Lord! One of my earliest childhood memories was eating at Papa's table at Ashford, Alabama and seeing a small glass pitcher of honey always on the table. At the main meals almost always there would be beautiful browned-top, homemade biscuits, still hot from the oven. Papa would always end his meal with one or two of these biscuits open on his plate with beautiful homemade butter spread on them, and then honey poured over that. But sometimes he would pour the honey in the plate and stir the butter into the honey as sort of a honey-butter paste to spread on his biscuits. That was his favorite way of ending a meal. To him it was most satisfying, after which he had no need of cookies or cake or any other sweets; his meal was complete with that lovely honey-butter-biscuit combination. That's when I learned to love honey, eating at my Grandfather's table. But it was a special kind of honey!

Sometime, probably during the '20's, on a fishing trip to the Dead Lakes in Florida's "panhandle" near Wewahitchka, he and his son DeWitt discovered that super-special honey called "Tupelo", which is found nowhere else in the world. It is collected by bee keepers in that region in only two weeks in the spring, the first two weeks in May, when the tupelo trees are blooming along the river banks of the area. (See the account at the end of this section by our friend veteran beekeeper, Mr. L.L.Lanier, on how they do it.)

The years went by, but the taste and love for Tupelo honey were never lost. Whenever we went back to Panama City from the North we would always search for a supply of Tupelo honey for our table back in Baltimore, or wherever we were living, including Israel. You remember the story in Chapter 19 about how we presented Prime Minister Begin's chief deputy, Mr. Kadeshai, a jar of this honey as an expression of our love for Israel and learned from him the Hebrew meaning of "Amen"--"Our God is King and He is Faithful!" In very recent times the Lord has had us presenting this honey to the Governors of all 50 states, as we shared God's Solemn Warnings of Coming Judgement on America. (See Chapter 28).

In fact each year when we went back to Israel at the end of our summer work in Baltimore, we would always try to have a large plastic jar of Tupelo honey in our bags. Or more! You may be asking why in the world would someone take honey to Israel? Isn't it supposed to be a land flowing with milk and honey? Yes, indeed, Israel's honey (devash) is quite excellent honey and the production of it has grown greatly since about 1880, at the time of the first Allyah (Going up to Israel) from Europe. When the Jewish people first started to return to their ancient land to begin establishing farms along the Coast from Ashkelon to Naharyia and from Tiberias and the Hula Valley to Metulla, and throughout the Valley of Megiddo, they needed bees to pollinate the fruit trees and crops that they were bringing back to the land after 1900 years of devastation, especially by the Turks and Islam in the last 400 years.

God had begun moving on many Jewish hearts to go back to their ancient land. Other "allyah" waves of immigrants came in the early decades of this century, all of which eventually led to the establishment of Israel as a re-born nation in 1948, and the immediate declaration of war by all the Islamic nations surrounding the tiny newborn nation.

God's Word, which is sweeter than the honeycomb and more to be desired than much fine gold, as we're told in Psalm 19:10, also tells us that God will fight for His ancient people and He has. (Ps.121:4). At least five more wars have erupted against Israel since '48, and with God's mighty help and intervention, little Israel still stands very strong! The USA was founded by the Pilgrims and Puritans to be a lover of the God of Israel, of the Bible, of Jesus the Messiah and to be a channel of the Gospel of God's Salvation to the world through His Son Jesus, the Way, the Truth and the Life, (Jn.14:6); the Only Way of Salvation (Acts 4:12). The United States, because of this spiritual heritage, has been God's main and most powerful friend to Israel. May God help us ever to be such a friend.

Little Israel has become not only the defender of freedom in the Middle East, but also the very Bread Basket of the Middle East,

CHAPTER 27: SOME YUMMY STORIES

supplying mountains of food to all her Arab neighbors, even while most of them refuse to recognize her and make peace with her. Yet, Israel continues, by God's grace to bloom and blossom like a rose, (Isaiah 35:1), and to flow with milk and honey,(Exodus 3:8).

It is important that we mention a couple of thoughts found in Proverbs and Isaiah:

Proverbs 24:13 ....*My son eat thou honey because it is good and the honeycomb because it is sweet to thy taste.*

Proverbs 25:27.... *It is not good to eat (too) much honey: so for men to search their own glory is not glory.*

Isaiah 7:15 ...*Immanuel, Butter and honey shall he eat that he may know to refuse the evil and choose the good.*

And let's remind ourselves that it is a key food that helped John the Baptist (along with locusts) to survive in the desert when he was preaching for repentance and revival in Israel and preparing the way for the Messiah to come. (Matt.3:4)

Amazingly, after Jesus' Resurrection, He appeared to His disciples in an Upper Room there in Jerusalem and they were fearful and doubtful that He could be real, even though they could see Him and hear Him speak to them. To prove His reality, Jesus asked them to give Him something to eat and they gave Him some fish and honeycomb.

(Luke 24:42-43)... *And they gave him a piece of a broiled fish, and of a honeycomb. And he took it and did eat before them.* This was sweet proof!

Natural food advisers also say a bit of honey and honeycomb will help to prevent allergies from the various pollens of one's region. No doubt, there's real truth in this.

Our Lord Jesus also has given us a life blessing commandment that is filled with "Heavenly Honey" (pure love) in John 15:12-14. There He tells us, "*This is my commandment that ye love one another as I have loved you. Greater love hath no man than this, that a man lay down his life for his friends. Ye are my friends if ye do whatsoever I command you.*"

Perhaps you recall earlier in the book how Betsy's Dad (Pappy) once gave me some special advice when she and I were having relationship problems. He said, "Sid, here's a piece of truth you need: you'll get a lot more bees with honey than with vinegar," meaning your marriage will be happier if you will be very loving toward your wife at all times. This is also true of the Lord's teaching in the Sermon on the Mount, where He gives us the recipe for a truly God-blessed life in the Beatitudes, (Matt.5:1-12, Matt.7:2), and even to loving our enemies. (Matt.5:44).

There are stories through the centuries of Christians being assisted to escape further persecution and death because they obeyed the Lord

Jesus and showed love to their captors! Remember Paul and Silas and the jailer! And Prem Pradham in Napal in our day!

So now you know something about honeyology and why old Dad loves honey! And how he learned a hard lesson!

TUPELO HONEY FROM TUPELO TREES
By Mr. L.L. Lanier, Wewahitchka, Florida 32465

"Tupelo honey is produced from the tupelo gum tree which grows profusely along the Chipola and Apalachicola rivers of northwest Florida. Here in the river swamps this honey is produced in a unique fashion. Bee hives are placed on elevated platforms along the river's edge, from which during April and May the bees fan out through the surrounding Tupelo-blossom-laden swamps and return with their precious treasure. This river valley is the only place in the world where Tupelo honey is produced commercially.

"Real Tupelo honey is light amber in color, light golden with a greenish cast. The flavor is delicious, distinctive, a choice table grade honey. Good white tupelo, unmixed with other honeys, will not granulate. Due to the high levulose content it does not granulate and due to this high levulose, low dextrose ratio, diabetic patients have been permitted by their physicians to eat Tupelo honey. Average analysis: levulose 44.03%, dextrose 29.98%.

"Black tupelo, ti-ti, black gum, willow, and several other honey plants bloom in advance of white tupelo and are used to build up bee colony strength and stores. Since these sources produce a less desirable, darker honey, which will granulate, the product is sold as a bakery grade honey. Some stores are selling a honey labeled Tupelo which is as dark as the bakery grade honey. Possibly it is just that or a blend which is a cheaper honey for which the buyer may be paying a premium price.

"The important point which we wish to make here is that all honey that is being labeled Tupelo is not top quality Tupelo as the bees make it and as skilled beekeepers produce it. Some honey may be very light in color and could very well have a high percentage of gallberry. Gallberry blooms right after Tupelo. The honey is attractive, as it is a light white honey, but it is not Tupelo and will soon granulate. Some honey is labeled Tupelo and wild flower. In this case the buyer has no guarantee of just how much real Tupelo he may be getting.

"Fine Tupelo is more expensive because it costs more to produce this excellent specialty honey. To gain access to the river locations where the honey is produced requires expensive labor and equipment. In order to get fine, unmixed Tupelo honey, colonies must be stripped of all stores just as the white Tupelo bloom begins. The bees must have clean combs in which to place the Tupelo honey. Then the new crop must be removed before it can be mixed with additional honey sources. The timing of these operations is critical and years of experience are needed to produce a fine product that will certify as Tupelo honey."

- - - - - - - - - -

"GRITSOLOGY"

Now is the time to tell you why our family loves Grits! One of our longtime sayings is that "Grits and Honey Saved the South!" Of course with the Lord's great mercy, mighty love and help, the South has been able to recover and rebuild from the terrible devastation that took place during the Civil War, especially during General Sherman's vengeful march through the South. It was a war that never should have taken place, but it did, and the whole nation suffered its greatest losses of any war before or since. As a point of interest my grandfather, Wm. Henry Rigell was a Confederate soldier in the 10th Regiment of the Georgia Militia as a teenager.

Most of the old timers who lived through reconstruction days after the Civil War were pretty much all gone by the time I had reached an age in the middle '30's to be interested in those days. I do remember some, including my grandmother, Munny, and my mother, Mamma, who would say that those were very dark, sad and difficult times, which people just don't like to talk about. They survived on corn bread and molasses and some fat back (unsliced bacon meat) at times. My grandparents kept a cow and chickens in their barn-yard there in Ashford, Alabama, for fresh milk and butter and eggs for almost as long as they lived. "Honey" in those olden days was not a common delicacy, but sugar cane syrup was. Honey on the table arrived much later when times improved.

One of the delights of visiting the Grandparents in those "olden days" was to have a big breakfast of Grits, bacon, eggs, and biscuits with a huge glass of milk straight from the cow, cooled overnight in the old ice box, and with fresh butter mixed into the Grits or sometimes a spoonful of "red-eye" gravy (ham gravy) in the middle of your large serving of Grits. Um-m-m boy good! Made a "young sprout" get up and go into all kinds of adventures there on the little farm or in that little farm town.

One Christmas Dad and Mom took their big family by train from Milligan, Fla., where Dad had a small sawmill, back to their old home in Ashford, Ala. to be with the Grandparents. Dad, being quite a hunter and fisherman himself, had decided that we younger boys were old enough to begin learning about guns, so he gave us all "B-B" guns for Christmas along with one of those little tubes of "B-B" lead pellets for ammunition and target practice. Dad apparently had not thought the whole thing through, or else he didn't realize how mischievous his younger sons could be.

No more than two days had passed before Al and Frank and myself had become the "wild gunmen" of that little town. We probably would have held up a bank, had we not known already that stealing was distinctly out. But we did proceed to shoot out many glass panes from a neighbor's old hot house, the back window of a passing Model"T" Ford, and then ended up shooting at each other from behind trees. It was war, for a while! At last brother Al got hit squarely between the eyes! Praise God, it was between, not in! Instantly a noticeable marble-size bruise popped up! That really scared and "sobered" us up. The most sobering thing of all was shortly thereafter, we had to face the music for our misdeeds. Dad was a severe but just judge who carried out swiftly his own paddling sentence himself, which we knew we deserved and never forgot. The problem today is the abysmal lack of such clear and speedy punishment for crimes. When we were eventualy allowed to use the "B-B" guns again, strictly on probation, they were to be used only for those circular bull's-eye targets you made on a piece of paper or in the woods while hunting bears and tigers and elephants of which there were none in our region! Maybe some bears, but they were far away! Rabbits and squirrels were fairgame but much too fast.

Oh yes, this story was about Gritsology wasn't it? So as boys we learned to love Grits and corn pones and syrup (later honey).
I remember those very delicious corn bread patties (or pones) that Betsy would bake until they were puffed up and crisp and you would put butter inside, and would eat them like they were better than almost anything. She learned how to make these corn pones from my mother who learned it from my father's mother, when Mom was a young bride. As a matter of fact those corn pones were simply another use of corn meal, which also gives us Grits!

How blessed our family is to have gotten in on the ground floor of learning about that great secret food that the South discovered, next to the Word of God, to rebuild and build on!

Even today and throughout much of this Century travelers through the South, stopping at hotels and motels, will very often find themselves with a serving of Grits with their eggs, bacon and toast breakfast, often with a little puddle of butter already in it. Many of our own guests here at the Little Tabernacle will often look surprised at their serving of Grits and ask, "What is it? How do I eat it?" And we could answer that it's

CHAPTER 27: SOME YUMMY STORIES 441

"Manna," which is Hebrew for that question "What is it?" - food from Heaven! We generally tell them it's ground corn which is eaten just like corn on the cob, with butter, salt and pepper on it. Only with Grits the corn is off the cob and ground up already.

In 1979, when we had accepted the invitation to come stay in Israel with Esther and to go on circuit from time-to-time to encourage the Believers in Israel, we had to make careful plans for the stay and what we would need. Of course we (at least I) included Grits in our luggage, plus a request to friends to include Grits in their "care packages". While living with Esther in Ramot, we would often enjoy a Grits breakfast and try not to be insulted when Esther would turn her nose up at the idea of eating Grits.

"That's what you feed horses, isn't it," she would say! She was somewhat of a true Yankee from New England, and like a true Yankee she looked with disdain at the name and idea of Grits being a staple food for humans.

I would kid her about it, saying, "All of Israel needs to be converted to Grits to survive!" But secretly, I was not upset by her reluctance to eat it, for it extended our limited supply. At that time we had not found Grits in Israel. In true Yankee fashion she thought it should be eaten, if one must, with sugar and cream, which is something of a sacrilege in the South or "assur" (the Hebrew word for forbidden).

The next year when we began living in our own little apartment on the southside of Jerusalem on Shimoni Street, we were delighted to have neighbor Ruthie to come over for a Grits breakfast on mornings when we were not going to Hebrew class. She soon began liking the Grits and was a great help to us in our Hebrew lessons. One might say we exchanged Grits for Hebrew; and she was our first convert to Grits! She was already a Believer in Jesus as her Messiah. More good news coming up!

Not long afterwards, Betsy was shopping in a friendly neighborhood grocery when she learned that a plastic bag containing what, in Hebrew read "corn flour," turned out to be what looked like a package of yellow Grits. She brought it home and tried it and, "Voila" or "Heney," "Behold" it was "Yellow Israeli Grits!" That was a day of rejoicing! We no longer had to import our Grits from America or carefully ration our supply. We could have Grits morning, noon and night, for breakfast, lunch and dinner, if we pleased! From then on many guests from near and far had the great privilege of a Betsy Breakfast with Yellow Grits, white yolked eggs (at that time the Israeli eggs looked very pale) and thin slices of "Nockneek" (Israeli beef salami), which would cook up almost like "goy" bacon. Our big food problem was solved since a goodly Grits breakfast was for a long time the mainstay of my day.

Many friends not only enjoyed those Betsy Breakfasts with Grits, but they kept coming back for more Grits and more love of the Lord. Most everyone has heard of the expression people use after they have finally come through a long period of hard times and they say it was "by grit and by grace". Grandma Munny used it, referring to the years after the Civil War when her large family came through those days by "Grit" (real courage, hard, hard work), and God's Grace (mercy). Mamma used it concerning her years through tragedies and sicknesses, through the depression years and teaching years at monthly wages that would be ludicrous today, "By Grit and By God's Grace"! No government welfare programs in those days! No one expected it! No one demanded it, except the Socialists and Communists who began creeping into our nation from Europe.

The dictionary says "Grit, is a small rough hard particle, as of sand, stone, etc; A resolute spirit; courageous determination and pluck." And "Grits" are from coarsely ground corn. Our years in the South, in the service, in the ministry, our many years in Baltimore and those six plus years in Israel, were all accomplished by God's Grace and the courage He gives through Jesus. We could also call it by "Grit and Grits and God's Grace!" Mostly the latter!

THREE YUMMY STORIES

Almost everyone we've ever met will have a special yen for a certain food at times. I remember being stationed on San Clemente Island, 70 miles off the coast of California, in summer of 1945, training there in a very special Naval Airforce electronic countermeasure school on one end of the Island. On the other end of the island was a Navy ship-bombardment range. When they bombed that end, we'd bounce on the other end, well at least we'd feel it. In the middle of the island was a small airfield that we used for training. One particular day at noon chow, I came down the chow-line with my tray and the cooks were plopping the food on in their own inimitable way and, lo and behold, I saw some real fresh sliced cucumbers. My tummy turned a double flip and said, "I want a bunch of those cucumbers!" What a joy to see something green and fresh like that! This gives you an idea of how you and your tummy can have a special yen for and respond to some particular food.

Back in the middle '70's during our visit with my family in Panama City, Betsy and I were asked by my oldest sister, Sissy, to go out to the beach area, and pray for her daughter, Judy Beth, who was in the last month of her pregnancy, and was having to spend much of the time in

CHAPTER 27: SOME YUMMY STORIES

bed. All along on that trip from Baltimore we had seen several kinds of summer fruits, peaches, watermelons, grapes, pears, and I had begun having a very strong yen for some cold, sliced fresh fruit.

By the way, I should say these stories are intended to indicate that God knows all about these things. And if we are doing that which pleases Him, He will fix it! I say this unashamedly! Betsy and I will tell you He'll do it for the big things, too! We have seen Him do it over and over. Praise His Holy Name!

So on that day of our visit to our niece's home, she was indeed in bed, and very expectant! There, "resting" on top of the little one soon-to-come, was a large bowl of mixed, sliced fresh fruit, a large bowl! We chatted for a few minutes, and I kept hoping she would offer me a spoon to help her with her chopped fruit. She didn't and we kept quiet. After a bit, we anointed her and prayed the Lord would give her and the baby a safe and easy delivery. And the Lord did a few days later! But still no chopped fruit! I must admit that I had not literally asked the Lord for even a small bowl of chopped fruit.

The next day we were to visit a dear Jewish friend serving time in the Eglin Federal Prison at Ft. Walton Beach, west of Panama City. This dear man was serving a short sentence for something illegal he had done before he became a Believer in Jesus. His wife and children were coming over from Pensacola to meet us for that afternoon visit. What a joy it was to see them all there that day in the prison picnic area. His wife had brought a large blanket and a large picnic basket filled with goodies. We all sat on the blanket in a circle and his wife opened up the basket and the first thing you could see was a huge tupperware bowl of chopped fruit with individual serving dishes next to it. Well, my tummy jumped for joy again as she served me the first dish! The Lord had heard that special yen and met it even inside a prison, admittingly a low security prison, into which a large picnic basket loaded with chopped-up fruit could come!

Before this dear friend had left for that prison, the Lord had given us an encouraging word for him that, like Joseph of old (in Egypt), he would find favor with the warden of the prison, and he had! As we understand it, he'd been put in charge of receiving goods for the prison and had his own office and desk. A couple of fellow prisoners told us that he had also become the unofficial chaplain of the prison and was leading Bible Studies and helping the men to get saved and filled with the Holy Spirit. Praise God that the Lord had him put in prison to help those men find the Way, the Truth and the Life, JESUS! No doubt that prison hated to see our friend leave not long afterwards. We know the Lord is continuing to bless and use him, his wife and his family in His service. Joseph became a mighty servant of the Lord, too!

Now some of you know about my penchant, or love, for pecan pies, about which we wrote in the Battle Of The Pies in Israel. We came home one summer from Israel, and soon Esther followed to arrange for one of her trips to Russia in Washington, D.C. I never will forget our taking her to Washington, D.C. to make these arrangements. At lunch time we began looking for a place to eat, and for some strange reason, I had a yen for a piece of pecan pie. Just then we passed a restaurant with a display of pies in the window, and under a piece of pecan pie in the window was the price tag of $2.65. Poof! There went my yen! No true southern boy with a depression upbringing will ever spend that much for one piece of pie, even his favorite, pecan pie!

We did find a more reasonable place to get a hot dog not far away. However, way down in South Georgia at Fern Armstrong and Phyllis Johnson's home, the Lord did provide not only a beautiful piece of pecan pie, but a lovely cake tin filled to the brim with lucious shelled pecan halves, for more pecan pies back in Baltimore. How blessed can one be! The Lord is so good!

A YEARNING FOR WAFFLES

But probably the most interesting tale of how the Lord met a special food yen, was the summer we were home from Israel and on the way south to visit friends and family in an AMC Pacer lent to us by Mel and Julie Meadows in Virginia. Then it started: I began having a yearning for waffles! This also had been a longtime favorite for breakfast. In Israel we did not yet have a waffle iron, but occasionally the Pastor's wife, Faith Hjertstedt, would invite the elders and their wives to their home for a waffle meal. Her waffles were super!

But now we were a long way from Israel and the "big waffle attack" was on. It seemed throughout the two week trip south that we would see "Waffle House" signs, but either not at the right time, or we'd miss the exit. Wife Betsy knew about my desire for waffles, but we both held our peace when we were guests of friends and family; we did not announce this big waffle attack, and no one seemed to sense it.

So on the way back north, we finally saw a waffle house sign just south of Atlanta, and I said to Betsy, "Don't let us miss the exit." And we didn't. But as soon as we turned off at the exit, we suddenly realized that this was the exit that would take us to the apartment of a young couple who had once lived with us in Baltimore at the "Turn-Around-With-Jesus-Home", Betty Jean and Joe Bob, who had just had their first baby. We had to forego the waffle to try to see them. When we called Bob, he was home for lunch just a few more minutes, so we had to go straight to their apartment. We had a wonderful reunion with them, and an opportunity to pray for them and their baby.

CHAPTER 27: SOME YUMMY STORIES

Then back to Rt. 75 to speed north toward Oak Ridge, Tenn. We had to be there for a 6 pm dinner with our sons, Chris and Brian, who would meet us at son Craig and Ann's home. Having missed both breakfast and lunch, we arrived on time and quite hungry. They had barbecued chicken that night which suited us fine.

The next morning after a cereal breakfast, we needed to head straight back to Virginia to return the Pacer car to the Meadows. Arriving there at dusk, we felt we had to give the car a wash. So we found a "do-it-yourself" car wash. This was our first experience with one of these gadgets, and the last user had turned it off at half cycle. When we put our coins in, the machine was activated, the hose jumped off the hook, spraying everything in sight, including us! We finally subdued it, and got the car washed. It was the wettest and most hilarious car wash we'd ever done!

After a short drive we arrived at the Meadows home with a clean car, but somewhat bedraggled ourselves. Julie gave us snacks and sent us off to bed in their lovely home. The next morning she came to Betsy with the following apologetic announcement: "Betsy I'm running a little low on eggs, and I'm out of bacon. Would you and Pastor Sid mind having waffles?? I just bought a good used waffle iron last week, and I'd like to try it out!"

Betsy smiled a happy and knowing smile and said, "That would be just great! My husband has had a yen for them the whole trip! This is the Lord's doing, and it's marvelous in our eyes, and yummy to our tummies! Thank You Lord." How about that? The Lord never fails! Even to provide a waffle when needed.

Someone might say these special yen-fillers were simply accidents, but let me share with you a great truth that we have learned in our walk with the Lord Jesus. "Nothing happens by accident when you walk with Him. Our Lord has everything perfectly planned and timed: He meets every need out of His riches in glory." (Matt. 6:33; Phil.4:19; Ps. 37:3-5)....*Trust in the Lord and do good, so shall thou dwell in the land, and verily thou shalt be fed. Delight thyself also in the Lord; and he shall give thee the desires of thine heart. Commit thy way unto the Lord, trust also in Him and He shall bring it to pass.*

Speaking of waffle irons, let us share with you how the Lord arranged for us to have our own waffle iron in our tiny Shimoni Street apartment in Jerusalem. Late that year, in November, David Hjertstedt, the pastor of the Tabernacle of Praise in Jerusalem, desperately needed a three months rest time in the States, as mentioned earlier. So the Elders and congregation cooperated in helping him, his wife Faith and daughter Joy to go, and I and the other elders were left in charge.

The three months would go by rapidly and for the most part

smoothly. Right after Christmas, Betsy and I received a phone call from our dear friend, Joan Zaher, in Los Angeles, California, saying, "Our fellowship has a young man named Mark Bruno, coming to Jerusalem right after the first of the year. He'll have a large red duffle bag to bring for you. What do you want us to put in it?"

We named a number of things which were needed by us and others, and added, "If you can find someone with a waffle iron which they seldom use, put it in too! We'll be most grateful."

And sure enough Mark brought that big red duffle bag, loaded with all kinds of goodies, which we shared around. There in the midst was a lovely waffle iron together with the needed voltage transformer. What a beautiful sight! Thank you, Lord! And thank you, Joan and Mark, and the gracious anonymous waffle iron donor wherever you are. We're the happy owners of a real "live" waffle iron!

But the story doesn't end there. Toward the end of February we received word to meet the returning Pastor and his family at Ben Gurion Airport. Others joined us at the airport to welcome them back to Israel. Faith Hjertstedt confided in Betsy that they had brought back a special gift for us, knowing how we "ooh-h-ed and aah-h-ed" about her waffles, a waffle iron!

As Betsy and I drove back up toward Jerusalem in the little Yellow Bird, she told me about the appreciation gift that the Hjertstedts had brought back for us. Boy! That makes for a problem! Now what do we do with two waffle irons?! So as we drove along the expressway up toward Jerusalem, we prayed and asked the Lord to guide us in exactly what to do. Immediately the Lord answered, "It's simple, tell them the truth!" We thought, "Okay Lord, we'll do exactly that."

A few days later they invited us over to their apartment for a report on how things had gone and were going with the Church. All during the meeting there was a nicely wrapped package (about the size of a waffle iron) sitting on their coffee table.

So after our report and refreshments, they picked up this "mysterious" package and presented it to us saying, "We want you to know how much we appreciate what you both have done for the Church in our absence, and knowing how much you love waffles, we have brought you, all the way from U.S.A., this waffle iron!!"

Now, the moment of truth!

Smiling, we said, "Well we want you to know that it's been a real privilege to serve the Tabernacle of Praise these three months in your absence, and we appreciate so much this gift. We thank you very, very much for it. But we have a confession to make: During your absence, Joan Zaher in California arranged to send us one early in January, and it won't be really kosher for us to have two. Perhaps you know

CHAPTER 27: SOME YUMMY STORIES

someone else who needs one?"

Then Faith spoke up quickly and said, "That's very interesting. Our old waffle iron here seems to be on its last legs! Perhaps we could...."

With huge grins and a joyful flourish we returned the lovely waffle iron that had just been given to us to Faith's hands with these words, "In that case, it gives us great pleasure to give you this new waffle iron which has just arrived from the States. May it be used for many more waffles for hungry people in the Lord's service right here in Jerusalem! Praise the Lord forever!"

"LORD, WAS THERE ANYTHING GOOD DONE IN OUR YEARS AT MCKIM?"

This question came up early one Sunday morning, in the summer of 1984, about 14 years after we had left the McKim work on Baltimore Street. Betsy and I were home from Israel and were spending a good part of the time with her aging Father who, at 84, needed care and companionship, even though he wouldn't admit it! But each Sunday we would get up early to drive to Baltimore for the morning and the evening services and drive the 80 miles back to Pappy's between 11 p.m. and 1 a.m. that night.

On that particular Sunday morning, as we drove into East Baltimore passing the Flag House Court high rise apartment buildings, from which hundreds of youngsters had come to participate in the McKim clubs, athletics, summer Bible School and other activities during our 14 years there, we softly verbalized this question up to the Lord: "Lord, was there any lasting good done in those years at McKim?"

Little did we know at that moment that, before the day was out, the Lord would clearly answer that question. And there's nothing wrong with wondering if one's hard work for the Lord had borne lasting fruit in His Kingdom and for His Glory. We went on to the Little Tabernacle for a beautiful morning worship service.

Afterwards we would go with Kirby and Carol and the Grandchildren and one or two of the young men still at the TAWJH[1], or some other Church members or visitors, to Roy Rogers for lunch, then back to the Little Tabernacle for an afternoon nap in the "prophets" room on the second floor before the evening service.

That afternoon, knowing we had to drive back to southern Maryland after the evening service, we stopped at the Amoco station on Fayette and Central Ave. to fill our gas tank before the trip that night. This

---

[1] Turn Around With Jesus Home

station has about 5 different pump "islands" and we went to the end one. For some reason, I asked Betsy to take the money to the cashier (paying first is required) while I waited ready to pump when the cashier turned on the pump.

While Betsy was waiting in line to pay for the gas, this nice looking young black man behind her in line asked, "Aren't you, Miss Betsy?" (Now remember this is only about six hours after we asked the Lord if there was any good done in the McKim years, and this filling station is only a block from McKim Center!)

When Betsy replied, "Yes, who are you?"

He said, "I'm Michael Partlow. Don't you remember, from McKim? I used to be on the wrestling team and our family came to the Center and participated in the programs."

Betsy asked about his family and what he was doing and was he still living for the Lord?

Michael replied that he was married, had a good job, lived in the suburbs and was attending Church regularly!"

Betsy said, "I know Mr. Sid wants to see you; he's right over there."

So Michael came over and greeted me as warmly as he had Betsy, kind of like long-lost-kin-folks! And in Jesus we are brothers in the Lord! We urged Michael to keep on walking with Jesus, abiding in Jesus, and bearing good fruit for the Father's glory! (John 15).

So, through this dear young black man, the Lord had speedily answered our early morning prayer. Something real good had been done in those years. Later, in the next three or four years, the Lord would let us see many others who had come through those years and had become sound Christians under His keeping, nurturing and guiding power. We plant, Apollos waters, but "God gives the increase." To Him be all the praise and glory, always!

Michael Partlow, Charles Dorsey, Ray Tillery, Dwight Warren, Bobby Franklin and all you other guys and girls, we pray that you are following Jesus all the way from here to Heaven. We appreciate so much the love and appreciation that many of you have shown us for the encouragement we gave you in Jesus during your early years. Be faithful to Him and He will bring you through.

ANOTHER GOOD REPORT!

At the very moment we were finishing the story above, John Monk came to the room where we were working and said there was a lady named Ruth at the door asking for us. Not knowing any Ruth recently, we went downstairs wondering who it could be. Perhaps you've guessed it already. It was a dear lady named Ruth Livesay whose family lived near McKim in the Flag House Courts in the 60's and who had

CHAPTER 27: SOME YUMMY STORIES

stopped by to see if we were still in this part of the world. We were so happy to see her and to hear about her eight children, all grown, most of them married, giving her eleven grandchildren. How we enjoyed talking about the old times at McKim Center. She had been such a great help, working with the girls club program and the nursery school. Several of her sons have served honorably in the Army overseas, and Billy soon will retire after 23 years of service.

We must tell you a little story about Billy when he was 3 years old, and intensely desiring to go with the other Flag House Court children to our Christian Nursery school. His mother asked us if we would let him come with her other children to see if he really was old enough. Well, Billy cried the whole time for about 3 days. Finally, it was too much and we had to send a note asking his mother to keep him home until he grew up a bit and was no longer a baby.

The next Monday, I was driving the little VW school bus around the Project to pick up the nursery school children. Just as I finished picking them up, I looked across the street and there was Billy on the sidewalk wagging his finger at me, calling me over. He was demanding an immediate face to face conference.

So leaving the bus I crossed the street to him and said, "Good morning, Billy. How are you? What can I do for you?"

He didn't answer any of my questions. He looked up at me, shook his finger toward my face and said, "OO dutty-bum, oo!"

I said, "When you are a little older, Billy, we'll be glad to have you come back." And he did come back and did real well! Praise The Lord.

So the day we were writing all this story, the Lord sent in a tremendous confirmation through this dear mother, who reared that big family against heavy odds, and made a really valuable contribution of her time and efforts to help many others during those days. Her husband, Al, worked for many years as a trusted and faithful driver of the Rummage Shop truck. We're so thankful to the Lord for bringing Mrs. Livesay by to say to us, "Yes, Sir, there was a lot of good done in those years! Just look at my family!" Thank you, Lord!

Since this visit Ruth had recommitted her life to the Lord and had the blessed experience of being brought back from the dead, not once but twice!!

One Sunday afternoon she called Betsy at the Little Tabernacle: "Miss Betsy, this is Ruth. I was brought into Church Home Hospital on Friday DOA (Dead on Arrival!). I had stopped breathing and my heart had stopped. During this time I felt like I was going through a tunnel, but there was no fear!! At the end of the tunnel there stood Jesus, so bright and shining! He didn't speak to me with his mouth, but he told me much with His eyes! I asked Him if I could come back for there was much work to do here with my family. With His eyes, He agreed, and let me come back through the tunnel. Always before, Miss Betsy, I had had a terrible fear of dying. But now I know there is nothing to be afraid of when you know Jesus!!"

Miss Ruth was able to share this testimony for several months, and was reading the Word daily and growing in the love of JESUS! After five months back among the living, Ruth was much better prepared to go when her heart stopped the third time, her last call to Heaven!

"WALLACES MIRACLE CAR"

Have you ever wanted a car that would last and last and last and last? Most of us do want such a car, but very few ever find one. We must tell you about one like that which we were privileged to drive two summers. Each June when we came back from Israel to the States, we needed to find some kind of car to use for the three months while helping our Preacher son Kirby at the Little Tabernacle Church, helping Betsy's Dad, Pappy, at the Bight (in his 80's), and making necessary trips down the East Coast and west to Tennessee.

One summer on our first Sunday back, our friend Eula Pecora asked us what we would be using for a car. We said we didn't know, but the Lord would provide. Not long after Church she and her husband showed up with her second car and keys to it! It kept us going for much of the summer.

Other times dear friends, The Meadows in Warrington, Va., lent us an AMC Hornet and another time a station wagon; another time the Dudleys in North Carolina lent us a great big diesel station wagon (the "choo-choo"). We are everlastingly grateful to them all for their wonderful help.

But there's one car we haven't mentioned. We came home as usual in June and Evangelist Harold Wallace was with us on our first Sunday back at the Little Tabernacle. After preaching the message, Bro. Wallace asked Betsy and me to come up, he wanted to pray for us. He thanked the Lord for our safe return from Israel and asked the Lord's special blessings upon us for the summer work, and also that the Lord would please provide us with a good car for our summer travel needs: "In fact, Lord, I ask You to give them a new car for their use this summer."

At that moment we didn't realize that Brother Wallace had just recently acquired a new car which he had been needing himself for several years. In a day or so, Bro. Wallace headed back to his home in Burgaw, N. C. A few days later, we received a surprise phone call from

CHAPTER 27: SOME YUMMY STORIES

him saying, "When I prayed that prayer for a new car for you a few days ago, the Lord immediately said to me, 'How about your car, Harold?' So my wife Judy will be bringing 'your new car' up tomorrow. Please see that she gets on a bus heading home right away." We gulped, thanked him profusely and said, "Okay!"

Judy did bring it and went back on the bus right away. We had full use of this brand new Toyota Station Wagon for that summer and I believe the next summer too! Often Bro. Harold had to use a bicycle for transportation there in his hometown, while we were using his new Toyota! He really wanted to do this for the Lord's sake--and ours. And the Lord has rewarded him with a truly miracle car!

By December 1988, that blessed little Toyota was still running fine, had gone over 330,000 miles with very little repair, still looked almost new and was still serving the Lord. Still going in '91!

That, no doubt, is the best way to have a very blessed miracle car!

Speaking of cars, early in 1988 the Lord blessed us for a week with an unusual car. For sometime Betsy and I had felt the need to visit some long ago friends and relatives in the southern part of Florida, in the Tampa-St. Petersburg area. Our 42nd wedding anniversary was coming up on March 2nd, and, after checking with the airlines, we found the most economical way we could do it was to fly to Tampa, rent a budget car for a week, visit with those friends and relatives in that area, then drive northwest to Panama City for two or three days with our friends and relatives there. We would drop off our rented car and fly back to Baltimore from there.

When getting our plane tickets, we had reserved a compact car for a week and earlier had called long-time friends, Sam and Mary Lona Davis in Tampa, to see if we could see them that Saturday evening. Of course we could; they would meet us at the airport to guide us to their home in Tampa. Sam was a retired forester and during W.W.II and the Korean conflict was a highly decorated Navy pilot. Sure enough they were waiting for us at the airport and proceeded with us to get our baggage and over to the car rental desk.

There the young lady told me, "I'm sorry, Sir, but we are out of compact cars. Would you mind something larger at the same price?"

Kiddingly, I allowed that would be quite all right, "How about a Lincoln Continental?"

And she said, "Well, we don't have any Lincoln Continentals, but would a Lincoln Town car be all right?"

I cleared my throat and said, "I reckon that would do!" Those words I was soon to regret. Outside, night was already falling, and with the keys in hand I went searching through this huge covered parking lot for the car. Finally, I found it. Seemingly all the attendants were busy somewhere else. I got in that "monster" and quickly found I didn't have the slightest idea of how to get lights on, or get it properly going. It seemed to have almost as many buttons, switches and levers as a "747"! After finally getting "the monster" started, then I succeeded in getting lost in that garage going the wrong way. Betsy and the Davis's didn't know what a miracle it was that I finally showed up at the airport entrance some 20-30 minutes later, all in one frazzled piece!

After a pleasant night with the Davis's, attending Church and having lunch with them the next day, we were on our way to visit all those other folks we needed to see, riding in this fancy Lincoln car! I must say that my precious wife of 42 years enjoyed her ride in that very comfortable car for that week, but I for one was never so glad to turn a rented car in without a scratch (Praise God!) at the end of that week when we left it at the Panama City airport to fly home. And another thing, I am so happy, I don't have and don't need one of those fancy cars, which some big TV evangelists seem to love, to their shame.

Thank God for the little Ford Escort that He's given us to do our traveling for Him in. He sure taught us a lesson on being careful what we say--and what we ride in!

- - - - - - - - - -

LETTER TO GRANDCHILDREN

Patmos, Greece
May 14, 1988

Dear Ginny, Allen, Matthew, Peter, Betsy and Little Luke,

Your Grandmother, Softa, and Granddad, Sabba, have been permitted by the Lord to come for the 6th time to this famous little Island called Patmos in the Aegean Sea, south-east of the mainland of Greece, and about 35 miles west of the Turkish coast, for those of you who are studying world geography. This island is famous entirely because it is the place where Jesus in His Risen, Glorified Form (remarkably described in Revelation 1:13-18) came down to give very important Revelations to Apostle John concerning certain seven churches, and concerning end-time events yet to come in the world.

Softa and I first came here when we were living in Israel, by plane from there to Athens and from Athens to Patmos by a large ferry boat. We came then with Esther Dorflinger, a Jewish Believer, to help her find a place where she could start writing her book. Perhaps you've seen a copy of it in your home called, "I Am My Beloved's", which means I belong completely to Jesus with all my love and life. That was in 1983.

A very nice little apartment for Esther and ourselves in the harbor village of Skala was soon found with the Lord's great help. In '84 and '85 we came again with her to help finance the visits, and also to help

CHAPTER 27: SOME YUMMY STORIES 453

edit and make corrections in her manuscript. During this time several people began urging us to start writing our own book, to tell of God's many miracle blessings in our lives.

So in 1986, when we had to leave Israel because someone had reported that we were "Dangerous Missionaries", we felt the Lord wanted us to come to Patmos to rest a moment and to begin writing "Our Book". How old were we? I'll tell this much: I was 68; Softa, much younger! We had three beautiful, quiet weeks in the same little #2 apartment where we can look across the harbor to the sea and on to other Greek islands. On the other side we look up the side of the beautiful mountain to the Church of the Apocalypse, and near it a Greek Orthodox Seminary (for training young priests). On top of the mountain we see the fortress-like monastery of St. John, built in the 10th Century with the village of Hora gathered around its priestly skirts, (massive walls).

We came back last year ('87) from Baltimore to write for another 3 weeks and to visit our many dear friends here. They're special!

Having no phone or TV, we can devote full-time to writing. Our neighbors speak only Greek and we speak very "lego" (little) Greek, so no interruptions here. Our landlord, Antonios Vamvakos, is a very kindly Greek man who loves the Lord and us, and loves Patmos, as if it were his very own. Once he sailed on Greek merchant ships as an engineer all over the world, including to America, but now he wants only to stay on the Island with his wife and daughter, Katarina and Kassandra. Kassandra is near your age, Ginny. Antonios tells us not to come in July and August because of the flood of tourists, 15,000-20,000! As he says, "So many, Patmos, he go down."

Nearby on the mountain side are little Greek homes, all white and, frequently, a little white chapel in the woods or on a rocky hill near a house. We are told that there are some 365 chapels on the Island, one for each day of the year, something like family chapels that the priests have the duty to hold a service in, once a year.

In the symphony of sounds around us you can hear the tinkle of the bells on the sheep and goats, a few cows, roosters crowing near and far, an occasional donkey braying, and the ever present crows cawing. These crows have black wings with greyish brown bodies, different from their U.S. cousins, but the same purpose, famous for robbing gardens. Many sparrows a-tweeting and a-chirping all the day! Oh yes, many seagulls sailing gracefully overhead, and a few dogs a-barking in the night.

This afternoon there's another sound, the flip-flop of runners, school kids, running a 4 kilometer race from the school up the mountain and back down to the harbor. We have a ringside seat under our grapevine porch to watch them huffing and puffing by in all shapes and sizes, first one group and then another, perspiring greatly. It's been a hot afternoon. Later we found out that our landlord's daughter, Kassandra, had come in second in the race!! A real honor for a 12 year old! Today is Saturday the 14th of May. Softa and I went to the port village to mail some postcards and to get food supplies for our pantry for the weekend. Almost every day the village is full of tourists that come in all kinds of ships from near and far to visit this special Island that the Lord himself once visited in a spectacular way!

Guess whom we met among the natives and tourists? Two brothers from Panama City, Florida, who once lived here for a time back in the '30's with their grandparents up on the mountain. John and A.I. Christo have been rebuilding an old house on the mountain for themselves. They asked us to have a fish lunch with them at the port, and we did, a delightful time. We hope to see them again before we leave about 10 days from now to go back to Baltimore. (Later, they did invite us to their mountain-top home for dinner of Patmos rabbit! Great! And a fantastic view of the surrounding sea and neighboring islands from their roof look-out!)

A very funny thing happened about 1:30 a.m. Friday morning. Perhaps you have heard about bombings, on TV or in newspapers. Recently in the news there have been reports of bombings in Beirut and on Cyprus, and some threats by that man called Arafat (the PLO leader) that he would be bombing various American targets. Mr. Reagan, our President, has sent him word, "He'd better not!" Well, at 1:30 A.M., Friday morning I was awakened by what sounded like a bomb going off right in or under our apartment! Wow, what a loud sound!!! Boy, did I sit straight up in the bed, wondering what's happening? Almost expecting the ceiling to fall in on us! It was a shocking and frightening moment. When nothing fell, I eased out of bed and began looking around, searching for the cause of the terrible explosion and could not find anything, not a thing, no sign of damage. Finally Softa, who had not been blown out of bed, raised up in bed and said, "Why don't you go back to sleep? Everything is all right. You must have been dreaming." Well, if it was a dream, it was a most realistic one. So I went back to bed, still wondering and shaking my head, and dropped off to sleep again. Oh yes, I forgot to tell you, there was also a kind of windstorm during the night and some shutters on the next apartment had been banging away, eerily, most of the night, like setting the stage for the explosion or a visit by "Dracula!".

Well, Softa waked me up at a reasonable hour to tell me she thought she had discovered what had exploded!

"Aha! What was it?" I asked wonderingly.

CHAPTER 27: SOME YUMMY STORIES

She replied, "I believe the large frying pan that was sitting on top of a stack of dishes had fallen over into the metal sink."

Still not quite believing, I said,"Go make that frying pan fall again into the metal sink." She did, and that big old frying pan made that big old explosion again! Really!! The great mystery explosion was solved! And no one was hurt! Boy, was I glad!!!

It was so good to see you at the reunion. Just wish we could have had more time together. Maybe we can all be together again in July in Tennessee! Hope So!

Much Love in Jesus,
Sabba and Softa

P.S: One of the most interesting sights on Patmos in May is to see the small, beautiful fields of ripened wheat, golden in color, waving in the strong island breezes. Then about the middle of May you see the weather-hewn farmer and his helper cutting the wheat with a hand scythe and stacking it in bundles. One farmer near our apartment did have small mowing machine, with two helpers, one sweeping the grain into the machine, and the other stacking the grain, while he pushed the mower. An ancient farming scene changing slowly day by day.

LEE NELSON'S LETTER

Thanksgiving 1989

Dear Pastor Sid and Betsy,

I greet you in the spirit of Thanksgiving and with a warm heart full of the Love of Jesus for you all precious ones in Baltimore at the Little Tab. I have you all in my heart and prayer. Pastor Sid and Sister Betsy I am so thankful to God and our Lord Jesus Christ and to you precious ones for training and teaching me in the ways and Word of God by your good example. The Little Tabernacle has a very special place in my heart and life. It was there I got rooted and grounded in God; it was there I really saw the love of God in action for the first time. So you can see why I love you all and thank God for giving me such wonderful spiritual parents and good example of faith and love and forgiveness.

Pastor Sid and Betsy, you are highly esteemed in my heart and mind and on this Thanksgiving Day I wanted to say thanks for every love, patience, all of your kindness to me and the chance to get rooted and grounded in His (God's)Love, and Word!

As for me I am doing great. I am now attending Rhema Bible Training Center and it's a blessing and gift from our good God. I haven't gotten married yet but me and God are working on that.

So my precious Little Tabernacle family, I pray that you have a blessed and wonderful thanksgiving in our Lord Jesus Christ. I love you and appreciate all you are doing with and for God.

In His Love,
Lee Nelson

Lee lived at the Turn-Around-With-Jesus-Home for several years. John Warrington had led him to the Lord when Lee was in the Baltimore City Jail.* Lee even went on our first trip to Israel with us, and we have a picture of him astride a camel on the Mt. of Olives. Later Lee worked with Pastor Kirby and helped in the Church regularly. He moved to Tulsa, Oklahoma and as you can see is growing in the Lord!

That's a letter to be thankful for! Praise God for it and for Lee's love and his "Hanging on to JESUS!"and JESUS' Hanging on to Lee!

* There are many kinds of Jails! We've all been in some of them! There are jails with iron bars, but also jails without bars. Such are: jails of hatred, lust, envy, greed, unforgiveness, grudges, lying, pride, arrogance, prejudice, self-pity, jealousy, self righteousness, false religions, drugs, occult beliefs, witchcraft, etc. JESUS came to set us free from all these jails, too! Praise His Mighty Name!!!

LEE NELSON WITH HIS CAB IN TULSA, CHRISTMAS, 1989

CHAP. 28

BIBLE PROPHECIES AND WARNINGS

Surely the Lord God will do nothing but He revealeth His secret unto His servants the prophets. — Amos 3:7

Howbeit when He the Spirit of truth is come He will guide you into all truth, for He shall not speak of Himself but whatsoever He shall hear, that shall He speak, and He will shew you things to come.
— John 16:13

STUDYING BIBLICAL PROPHECIES IN JERUSALEM

A Christian student, whatever age, living for a time in Jerusalem and seeing the amazing rebirth of the Land, the people, the industries, the agriculture and the blooming of Israel on every side as prophesied by Isaiah, and other prophets, cannot help but become interested in seeing what other prophecies from The Book are being fulfilled in our time. This began happening to us on our first tour in 1977, when we first glimpsed the remarkable rebirth and rebuilding of Israel. So we continued to observe and study with more tours, and over six years of living in Jerusalem, making notes along the way. What follows is a list of definite Bible Prophecies we believe are being fulfilled in our time.

There are many serious Bible students who also think that nearly all the Bible Prophecies concerning the return of the Lord Jesus have been fulfilled or are being fulfilled now. If so, this certainly makes His return imminent, as indicated in the story we told of that huge #2 written in the sky over the Sea of Galilee in 1978. When we asked the Lord what the "2" meant, He said (via the Holy Spirit as in John 16:13): *IT MEANS MY 2ND COMING IS VERY NEAR TELL MY PEOPLE EVERYWHERE!*

Each prophecy fulfilled is a miracle of God. No doubt there are others, unseen or overlooked, so this list is not meant to be absolutely final. Nor is it in a set order. Also there are many prophecies yet to come to pass, such as those about Armageddon, The Beast and Anti-

Christ in Jerusalem, The "666" forced numbering, The 144,000, The Invasion of the Kings of the East, Christ's actual Return, The Millennium, The New Jerusalem; all forecast in Revelation!

BIBLE PROPHECIES BEING FULFILLED IN OUR TIME
Jerusalem, Israel, 1986 (revised 1991)

1. Abraham And Descendants To Be Greatly Blessed! Genesis 12:1-3 *...Now the Lord had said unto Abram, Get thee out of thy country, and from thy kindred, and from thy father's house, unto a land that I will shew thee: And I will make of thee a great nation, and I will bless thee, and make thy name great, and thou shalt be a blessing: And I will bless them that bless thee, and curse him that curseth thee; and in thee shall all families of the earth be blessed.* Abraham, the revered Father of the Jews, became a very great blessing to all the Earth through JESUS and the Bible! Nations that have blessed Israel have been blessed (U.S.A. for one), those who have cursed Israel, have been cursed and their empires disintegrated. (Rome, Spain, Germany, England.) Each of these nations once ruled far flung empires, but lost them after they, in various ways, did harm to God's ancient people. Germany and England in this century.

2. The Rise Of The Arabs As Descendants Of Abraham's Son By Hagar--Ishmael! In the prophecies concerning Arabs in Genesis 16:10-12; 17:20, God says Ishmael will be as a wild man, his hand against every man, and every man's hand against him, and he shall dwell in the presence of all his brethren and God will make him fruitful, he will beget 12 princes, and make of him a great nation. Ishmael in our modern day not only is the progenitor of all the Arab nations but of Mohammed and Islam in its anti-Jew and anti-Christian world-domination theology. But, amazingly, the Arabs are blessed with incredible oil riches to carry out their programs. Almost all of the 6-700 Moslem mosques in America have been built with the oil riches! "Ishmael" is still denying the claims of the Jewish people to the God-given covenants to Abraham, Isaac, and Jacob, and later to and through Jesus. But it is true that God's promise of special blessings to Abraham's son by Hagar has been fulfilled in our day.

3. Return Of The Jews To Their Homeland!- Ezekiel 34:13; 36:24; 37:12, 21-23; 39:22-29; Zech.8:7-8; Jer.16:14,15; 23:7-8; 30:3,10-11; 31:10; Amos 9:14-15, and others such as Gen.17:7-8. The New Exodus from the Soviet Union and Ethiopia is a major and startling fulfillment. Hallelujah! And Baruch Ha Shem! (Bless The Name!)

CHAPTER 28: BIBLE PROPHECIES AND WARNINGS 459

4. Israel, The Nation, Re-established In 1948! A Nation Born In A Day, May 14, 1948! - Isaiah 66:8; Amos 9:14-15; Luke 2:34. This was an amazing event!

5. Revival Of Hebrew As A Spoken Language! - Zephaniah 3:9 -"betok" (in truth.) (Betsy and I had the privilege of learning to read, write and speak basic Hebrew in an "Ulpan" in Jerusalem in 1980-85!). It's a tough one to learn!

6. Jerusalem Reunited Under Complete Jewish Control! June 6, 1967. What a day of rejoicing that was! **No longer trodden down under Gentile feet**. - Luke 21:24.

7. Rebuilding Of Zion! - Psalm 102:12-22; Isaiah 62:1-3. Incredible! Verse 16 in Psalm 102 makes a remarkable promise: **When the Lord shall build up Zion, He shall appear in His glory!** Who is rebuilding Zion (Israel)? Who works miracles? It's the Lord who is doing it!

8. Israel's Desert Blooming! - Isaiah 35:1. Incredible! Wish we had space for an album of pictures! The story is told of Mark Twain on a pilgrimage to the Holy Land in 1869, on seeing that bleak and desolate land said, "Palestine sits in sackcloth and ashes. Over it broods the spell of a curse that has withered its fields and fettered its energies...and renowned Jerusalem, itself the stateliest name in history, has lost its ancient grandeur and is become a pauper village." He felt there was no hope of it blooming again. How wrong he was!

9. Israel's Fruit Being Sent To All Parts Of The World! - Isaiah 27:6. (Millions of crates shipped each year. Includes oranges, grapefruit, melons, grapes, bananas and avocados!)

10. Plowmen Overtaking The Reaper In Israel! - Amos 9:13 - Several crops per year! Thousands of tons exported! Irrigation greatly developed!

11. Gentiles Coming To Help Israel, Especially Christians! - Isaiah 49:22; 60:10; 61:5. This has happened in many ways all during the return of the Jews to Israel and still is happening.

12. Nations In League Against Israel! - See passages about Gog and Magog in Ezekiel 38, 39; and Zech. 12:1-9. Jerusalem becomes a cup of trembling and a burdensome stone for all people, Zech. 12:1-3. All nations are coming against Jerusalem (by way of the UN), opposing

Israel's legislation that all of Jerusalem is its permanent Capital, since about July 1980, and nearly all countries removing their embassies from Jerusalem; for Israel's bombing of Iraq's atomic installation in 1981, which was to build bombs to destroy Israel, as admitted by Iraq's President Saddam Hussein; and for moving (1982) against the PLO operations in Lebanon, which literally prevented a massive invasion of Israel, which was then being prepared by PLO Islamic terrorists and communists from many nations fully aided and directed by the Soviets. Plus the "shellacking" Israel gave the Syrian-Soviet Airforce in 1982; plus Israel's refusal to give up the West Bank and Gaza for a PLO state in its very heart or to return the Golan Heights to Syria; plus the terrible humiliation to Islam and the Soviets in the rapid defeat of Saddam Hussein in Desert Storm in 1991. Both powers will seek revenge; this is inevitable! Against Israel and the U.S.A. By 1995, probably!

13. The Rise Of Gog--Russia, Soviet Union, Ezek.38:2. Russia became a nation in the 1700's; the Soviet Union, in 1917! Finally allowing Jews to return to Israel in growing numbers, 1985-92! Longtime "Dictatorship of The Proletariat" (The Workers) (?), committed to atheism and so totally without God's blessing and the wisdom of His Word!

14. God's Condemnation Of Gog For Her Actions! Ezek.38:3. Already the Lord tells us through Ezekiel that He is against these Anti-Israel forces, will destroy 5/6th of them, after bringing them forth with "hooks" -- that the whole world may know He alone is Lord.

15. Hooks In The Mouth Of Gog! - Ezekiel 38:3-4. Armageddon is just around the corner. Ezek. 37-39; Rev.16:16, Zech.12:3,9. Mid-East oil, hatred for returned Jews, and the refounded State of Israel make up three pronged hooks for God to pull Russia and her largely Moslem army, and her allies, toward military confrontations ending in Armageddon - soon. The humiliating defeat of Syrian-Soviet planes, tanks, and anti-aircraft missiles in 1982, and again defeat in the Iraq-Soviet 1990-91 attempt to take over all the Mid-East oil, starting with Kuwait, greatly increases Soviet-Syrian-Islamic-PLO determination to build up again their end-time league and annihilation plans against Israel. Israel's bountiful food supply is a big hook too. Syria has been heavily rearmed with 2 billion worth of improved Scud-type missiles from North Korea, intended for "enemy" Israel. Paid for by our "friend" Saudi Arabia! Israel must stay on guard! And so must we!

16. Invasion To Be Turned Back! Ezek. 38:4. "*I will turn thee back*.." The Soviets along with the PLO and Syria were turned back in 1982 by

CHAPTER 28: BIBLE PROPHECIES AND WARNINGS

the Peace for Galilee strike by the Israelies, who were warned of massive invasion plan by these forces. The Soviets were involved in building up Syria and Iraq and were humiliated in their effort to gain control of Middle East Oil, in order to so cripple the western nations.

17. God Predicts Soviet (Russia's) Preparations! Ezek. 38:7 *"Be thou prepared and prepare for thyself and all thy company that are assembled unto thee..."* The Soviets have used and will continue to prepare and use many other people in their push toward world domination. Soviet ships have been supplying not only Cuba and Nicaragua but also Ethiopia, Libya, Syria, Iran, Lebanon, the PLO, Jordan, Egypt, parts of South Africa (The ANC and Mandela) plus a number of others. This includes training their military forces for war, such as their thousands of military advisers in Iraq before and during Desert Storm.

18. A Larger Attack On Israel Is Coming! Ezek. 38:9 Russia and her Arab Muslim allies will in the near future attack Israel like a storm. This is a soon coming event in which God says in Ezek. 38:16 *And I will bring thee against my land, that the heathen may know me when I shall be sanctified in thee, oh Gog, before their eyes. ...Thus will I magnify myself and sanctify myself and I will be known in the eyes of many nations and they shall know that I am the Lord.* Ezek. 38:23.

The Lord goes on to say in Ezek. 39:1-4 that He will spare only one sixth of the invading forces. Their armaments He will cause to fall out of their hands and Russia and her Allies will be destroyed upon the mountains of Israel.

In Ezek.39:6 *I will send a fire on Magog and among them that dwell carelessly in the isles; and they shall know that I am the Lord.* In the 7th verse He says, *So will I make my holy name known in the midst of my people....*

19. Rise Of China, With An Army Of 200 Million Today! Rev.16:12-16; 9:16. Russia and others now wooing China! And the U.S.A. is also! This huge army one day will move westward on highways being prepared today!

20. The Revived Roman Empire! - Daniel 2; 7:23-24; Rev.17:12-17. Ten nations of Western Europe have formed into the European Economic Community (E.E.C.), Greece becoming the 10th nation in January 1981, and moving rapidly toward a "United Europe" in 1992! The European Economic Community of Nations (now 12) have their own Parliament meeting in Brussels, Belgium. A most powerful and ominous economic force forming! To be a major player in Mid-East affairs.

21. Peace With Egypt! - Isaiah 19 - It has been quite shaky at times but it's still intact after nearly twelve years! Effected by Mr. Sadat of Egypt and Mr. Begin of Israel and Mr. Carter of the U.S. in 1979 in the Camp David Accords.

22. The Old City Of Jerusalem Is Being Beautifully Rebuilt! The ancient ruins of the earliest City of David have been excavated and are viewable; the south slope of the Temple Mount has been thoroughly excavated. - Psalm 102:16; Amos 9:11b.

23. Signs In The Heavens And Distress Of Nations! - Matt.24:29. Luke 21:25. God is giving many such signs today: great storms, fires, tornadoes, typhoons--and allowing great distress of nations. The newly discovered hole in the Ozone layer, the AIDS plague; Runaway Crimes, Drug addictions, Abortions and other Murders!

24. Growing Perplexity Among Nations! - Luke 21:25. In their inability to bring order, to solve economic problems, to stop the proliferation of arms, hatreds, crime, diseases and in America the break-down of education. Stage set for a super World Leader!

25. Wars, Earthquakes And Famines! - Matt.24:7. All these are increasing at an incredible rate in our day. Droughts and hunger in many lands. Millions dying each year, thousands each day.

26. As In The Days Of Noah! - Matt.24:37. Even an Ark of Warning is being built near Frostburg, Md., USA; same size as Noah's, but of concrete and wood, not just wood! The original, it is said, has been found on Mt. Ararat in our day.

27. Promise To Lebanon To Hear The Words Of The Book! Happening via the "Voice of Hope" Radio station, and CBN TV in South Lebanon. Lebanon one day will be freed to bloom again as an ally of Israel, Isaiah 29:17-18; 35:1-2. However, Lebanon has, in effect, now become a "protectorate" of Syria in 1991 with U.S. acquiescence!

28. Sin Abounding And The Love Of Many Waxing Cold! - Matt.24:12 - Leading to great apostasy in the Church - when abominations to God are approved by man, such as abortions (first degree murder of real babies), the elimination of capital punishment for real murderers, support of communist (godless) revolutions, support of the removal of prayer and Bible reading from our schools. (Deut.6:1-10; II Tim. 3:14-17). Putting World-Peace-Now ahead of God's Peace through Jesus Now,

CHAPTER 28: BIBLE PROPHECIES AND WARNINGS 463

approving homo-sexuality, even "ordaining" them. The Scriptures old and new, totally reject this form of sexuality as a gross evil and a demonic perversion of God's creation. The Bible gives them no hope unless they repent and turn away from it just like murderers, thieves, adulterers, liars, etc., must repent and turn away from their sinful lifestyles. God has mercy on those who will repent. (Lev.18:22, 29-30; Ro.1:21-32; I Cor.6:9-10; II Tim. 3:1-7; Rev. 21:8).

29. Famine Of hearing The Word Of God! - Amos 8:11. Bible reading and prayer taken from America's schools and elsewhere, and the "Bloody" Gospel no longer heard in mainline churches, most of which are dying - marked with "ICHABOD" - God's glory and power are gone.

30. "Great Falling Away Has Begun! Matt.24:12. II Thess.2:3. Jesus warned against backsliding in Luke 9:62 and John 15. Apostle Paul warns against it in Gal.5:4; Heb.2:3; 3:14; and Apostle Peter warns against it in II Pet.2:20-22. Anyone who deliberately turns away from and denies the Lord Jesus or who lives hypocritically in disobedience to Him, not bearing good fruit for the Father's glory, will be lost. Polls of denominations show all kinds of unbelief in them. One major Presbyterian Church has lost nearly half of its membership in the last 30 years. Smaller Presbyterian denominations remaining true to the Word of God are still growing.

31. Mark of Beast Is Ready! - Rev. 13,14. This "666" number is easily seen in many ways today in actual numbers on credit cards, car tags, and in the international products code stripes. For information on this write to Dr. Mary Relfe, P.O. Box 4038, Montgomery, Alabama 36104, USA. DON'T TAKE THE MARK!

32. Third Temple Preparations Exist In Jerusalem Today Among The Ultra-Orthodox! Includes a new corner-stone ready to be laid, new priestly garments made and Cohanim (priests) being trained. (Ezekiel 40-46) No more blood-sacrifice for Israel (Hosea 3:4) on Yom Kippur, the Day of Atonement. For Israel has had no true blood sacrifices since about 70 A.D. when the Romans completely destroyed the Temple in Jerusalem, as prophesied by Jesus (Mark 13:2), Who knew He had come to be the FINAL, PERFECT, ETERNAL BLOOD SACRIFICE FOR THE SINS OF THE JEWS -- AND FOR US ALL. (Heb. 10:12; I Cor.5:7).

33. God's Spirit Of Grace And Supplications Coming Upon The House of David Today! (Zech.12:10). All over the world, this is happening! Jewish people are waking up and believing in JESUS as their Messiah-

Saviour! In Israel too!

34. Evil Being Called Good, and Good Called Evil! - Isa.5:20-21; Matt.24:12. Check your TV--if you can stand to turn it on! It's full proof!

35. Knowledge Shall Be Increased! - Daniel 12:4. Today because of computers, scientific knowledge is increasing by leaps and bounds. Also through wide travel, instant communications and TV, plus satellites and space explorations. But knowing God's Word is the greatest knowledge one can ever have!

36. God Is Helping Israel Today! - Isaiah 41:8-16; Rom.11. Especially with U.S.A. backing and financial support - mainly taxes from Christians in America, a nation founded on the Bible and the Gospel of JESUS! (But now in denial, thanks to our Supreme Court, the ACLU, Mrs. O'Hair, New Agers, Humanists etc.) Eph.6:12.

37. Spiritual Comfort Is Being Given To Israel By Many Of God's True Servants And Saints! Isaiah 40. The courageous work of the Christian Embassy in Jerusalem illustrates this!

38. Asher Dips His Foot In Oil! - Deut.33:24. Moses prophesied that the tribe of Asher would dip its feet in oil. This was fulfilled in the summer of 1984 when several barrels of oil poured out on Asher's land-foot at Atlit below Haifa, when Andy SoRelle's "failed" deep-well pipe was uncapped. The Lord sovereignly fulfilled this prophecy by causing the oil to flow up 21,000 feet of pipe by shifting the earth's crust with two earthquakes! To God be all the glory! This information came to light in May 1989. Pray the Lord to have Andy cleared soon for further drilling in "Asher's Foot." Andy confirmed this to us personally! Also plans to drill again early in "92.

39. This Gospel Of Jesus Christ And His Kingdom Is Being Preached Throughout The World For A Witness To All Nations Today! (Matt.24:14). By radio and TV satellites!!! By CBN, TBN, and others expanding rapidly. (Rev. 14:6-7). By Bibles and tracts printed in native tongues and by bold evangelists going into every corner of the Nations. In spite of the quacks, critics, crooks and persecutions. Prem Pradham in Nepal! Our Dr. Jerry and Ginny Kirshner in Singapore and China!

40. False prophets, False Christs, Almost Everywhere! - Matt.24:24. One of them gave 88 reasons why Jesus was coming for His Church in

CHAPTER 28: BIBLE PROPHECIES AND WARNINGS 465

September 1988! Others claim to be Christ already returned. Blasphemers are abounding, too.

41. Increasing Persecution of Christians! Millions killed in this century; about 300,000 per year! Matt.5:10-12; Jn.15:18-27; II Tim.3:12; Rev. 13:7. But we have His wonderful promise that nothing can separate us from the Love of Christ or Himself. Ro.8:35-39. That He will make everything work out for our good, Ro.8:28, and He will never leave us nor forsake us! Matt.28:20; Heb.13:5b.

42. Chernobyl = Wormwood! Rev.8:10-11. Huge area in Russia and surrounding countries, (people, towns, cities), covered in radiation poison--"made bitter" and deadly!

43. Euphrates Dries Up! - Rev.16:12! Caused by Russian-built dam in Syria, temporarily cutting off the water. Iraq screamed and the Soviets turned the water back on! Will happen again in days to come!

44. The Jews Persecuted By Rome, Spain, Germany, etc.! Fulfilling Luke 21:24. The Holocaust of 6 million Jews by Nazi Germany is vividly depicted at the "Yad Vashem" in Jerusalem. Heartbreaking to view.

45. The Jews Will Meet God In The Desert! - Rev.12:6,14. Much new housing for the Russian Jews being built in desolate areas. When Gog and Magog come down on Israel, she will find refuge in the wilderness, as in the Negev desert! Also in Petra, Jordan.

46. Babylon Revived In Our Day! Daniel 4:4. Saddam Hussein has claimed to be Nebuchadnezzar reincarnated and has been rebuilding Babylon!

47. The Last Days Look! - II Tim.3:1-4 gives the evil picture! With all our so-called advances in education, religion and sciences, the human race grows more and more evil, not better; more blood-thirsty and wicked the world over. I Tim. 4:1-2 tells how in the last days many shall leave the faith; being seduced by evil spirits and doctrines of devils, becoming lying hypocrites, having seared, burned out, consciences.

48. Jesus Is Still Building His Mighty Church And *The Gates Of Hell Will Not Prevail Against It!* Matt. 16:18. It is true that the church is being belittled and maligned by the mockers and the anti-Christ forces among us. Their voices are growing but, Praise God, the true Church of Jesus

Christ is growing stronger every day, even in the U.S.A. Acts 2:17-18 is happening today, praise God: *And it shall come to pass in the last days, saith God, I will pour out of my spirit upon all flesh....*

49. Our Lord Jesus Is Coming Back Soon!! But not on a day or date set by a man - only by The Heavenly Father. *When you see these things come to pass, look up for your redemption draweth nigh.* - Ps. 102:16, Luke 21:28.

50. The Enemy Is Coming In Like A Flood! - Isaiah 59:19. A flood of satanic evil! But God is Lifting Up His Standard - JESUS! The Holy Spirit today is giving God's Word and Son JESUS a huge lift-up all across the world (in USSR, China, India, Africa). Spirit-filled Churches and missions are lifting up The Son in singing: *Even so, come, Lord Jesus.* (Rev. 22:20)

51. Men's Hearts Failing Them For FEAR! Making heart disease and failure America's biggest killer! (Luke 21:26).

52. Peace Now Being Shouted and Sought At Any Price! I Thess. 5:1-3: *When they say peace and safety, then cometh sudden destruction.* Peace, increasingly, is in short supply! Real Peace is only found in the Yoke and Vine and Rock of Jesus! (Matt. 11:28-30; John 15; Matt 7:24-25). World peace by men is not possible!

So, dear ones, let's be JESUS' Wise and Faithful Servants, looking to HIM (Matt. 24:44-45; Hebrews 12:1-6), for our daily orders and for that *Peace of God which passes all understanding, (that) shall keep your hearts and minds through Christ Jesus!* (Phil.4:7).

MADE DEAR FRIENDS BY JESUS! (See pages 23 & 93)

GOD'S SOLEMN WARNINGS

Righteousness exalteth a nation, but sin is a reproach to any people.
— Proverbs 14:34

ANOTHER WARNING TO AMERICA

This chilling warning came in a worship service at the Little Tabernacle in early October 1987 by the Holy Spirit to Pastor Rigell in the midst of the Sermon message for that day. Here it is:

GOD'S CHILLING WARNING

"Call My people to solemn fasting, praying and repentance throughout the Land to turn this nation back to My Way of holiness and righteousness. Call this nation to turn away from the horrible evils that are present in the Land. THE HOLOCAUST OF INFANTS IS GROSS EVIL! I've heard the cries of over 20 million infants murdered in cold blood during the last 14 years, and I warn you, saith the Lord, that America will be destroyed, totally destroyed, in less than 10 years if this INFANT HOLOCAUST is not stopped soon! Remember my Word which I gave to my people long ago in II Chron. 7:14 and do it! This is your only hope." (Over 30 million U.S. babies brutally murdered by 1992!)

This Warning desperately needs to be put in the hands of our President, ALL Supreme Court Justices, Senators, Congressmen, Governors, Legislators, Mayors and ALL the Ministers in the land. God has promised to forgive and heal the land if God's people will do what He tells us to do in that famous verse of Scripture in II Chronicles 7:14. This will be our next job: Trying to warn our nation like Jonah did Nineveh, to repent and turn back to God. May there be no whales on the way!

While we are writing here on Patmos in May of 1988, we are also studying carefully the Book of Revelation which tells of Jesus calling, over and over, for repentance in the churches. Toward the end of these great Revelations, most of which are to take place in our day, when great plagues and judgments begin to fall, such as aids, cancer, heart attacks, wars, famines, earthquakes, droughts, huge forest fires, and storms, even huge hail from heaven, weighing up to 100 lbs., a terribly sad sentence is repeated several times after these judgments come: *And they blasphemed the God of heaven...and repented not of their deeds.* (Rev. 16:11).

We recall that two years ago (1986) when we came to Patmos after

Betsy: *And I saw another angel fly in the midst of heaven, having the Everlasting Gospel to preach to every nation and people on the earth, saying with a loud voice: "FEAR GOD, GIVE GLORY UNTO HIM, FOR THE HOUR OF HIS JUDGMENT IS COME AND WORSHIP HIM WHO MADE THE HEAVEN AND THE EARTH, THE SEA AND THE FOUNTAIN OF WATERS."*

We felt at that time that the Lord was saying: "GET BUSY WARNING MY PEOPLE." Then came the warning concerning the Abomination of Abortions in 1987, that they must be stopped or else--Great Judgment on America! By the end of 1988 we were hearing Col. Myrl Allinder's warning that the Pentagon's top echelon of strategic planners were convinced of Soviet plans for a first strike against America, probably between 1993-95.

We were then reminded of Dave Wilkerson's book, "Set The Trumpet To Thy Mouth" (1985), prophetically warning of America's destruction in one hour, soon to come, if America did not wake up and turn back to God.

In September a surprising message came to us from Sweden from our dear friend, Rocky Schmit, a North Dakota farm boy who became a Marine, saw some of the worst of the Vietnam War, returned to attempt with other revolutionary-minded vets to burn down Washington, D.C. He was then a rabid Jew hater, drug user, fugitive, but somehow he met Mighty JESUS in Greece, like Saul of Tarsus, became a lover of JESUS, the JEWS and ISRAEL. He lived in Israel several years as a kibbutz hand, married a Swedish girl, had several children, and now lives in Sweden, working as a farrier (a horseshoer), always longing to return to Israel. Dear, tough, humble, devoted to JESUS, Rocky has long prayed and wept for America. His transcribed tape message which follows soon will warmly touch your heart and warn you deeply.

Early in 1989, after visiting with Col. Myrl Allinder in Florida, we felt constrained to print out the "Warning Letter" to give and send to political and religious leaders across the land. This letter warns prophetically that God's awesome judgment on America, has begun already (AIDS, fires, earthquakes, storms), and will increase if America does not: 1) turn back to God, to His Word and prayer, as in our beginnings; 2) If America does not stop the Horrible Holocaust of Babies (we're worse than the Nazis), and 3) If America does not Stand By Israel!

The first place we were led to give out these WARNINGS was at a Christian Leadership Conference in Ridgecrest, N.C. in May 1989, as we were returning from son Chris and Julie's wedding in Maryville, Tenn.

CHAPTER 28: BIBLE PROPHECIES AND WARNINGS 469

Several hundred Church leaders were there. With the Lord's amazing help we were able to get the Warning Letters into the hands of the key leaders early on, but nothing, not the slightest mention was made of it at the conference. Ignored? Yes, indeed! But we spread the WARNINGS directly as we met the people.

These stony rejections could have caused a screeching halt to the whole Mission had the Lord not done two things: (1) He showed us Jeremiah 1:17, **That we were not to be dismayed at their faces,** or rejections. And (2) in July, while driving down Interstate 81 on the way to Col. Allinder's ordination in Harrisonburg, Virginia, Betsy heard from the Lord for herself. She was driving while I was napping. As she drives she loves to sing to the Lord and pray. She asked the Lord for some reassurance about The Warning Mission we were embarking on. He spoke to her from Acts 10:20, **Go with him, doubting nothing!** Such a tremendous reassurance and direction from the Lord! And she did go gladly, praise God, to 50 states! 30,033 miles by air, including Hawaii; 14,825 miles by car! Over 12 months!

After the Ridgecrest Conference we rushed back to Baltimore to attend the Maryland Governor's Prayer Breakfast and to give him a copy of these Warnings and to ask for an appointment. Gov. Schaefer, whom we've known for a long time, told us, "Just call my appointment secretary, she'll arrange it." And we called and called and called. She finally gave us an appointment with an assistant. But we had wanted to tell him personally what Col. Allinder had told us the Governors urgently need to do, in the face of a possible Soviet first strike soon: Each state needs to establish, as soon as possible a carefully shielded defense communication system that would survive a nuclear blast.

We tried to get these Warnings to the Governor through a close friend of his, Charlie Benton, also was a longtime friend of ours. Mr. Benton gave us a 45 minute appointment in his Annapolis office. Apparently, he did get the Warning to the Governor, for later we learned that in his 1990 budget was a request for 3.7 million dollars for an underground shelter and communication center. For this we are thankful.

Mr. Benton is a very fine Christian man and also secretary of finance and budget for the State of Maryland. Along with several Bibles in his office, he has a wall plaque expressing his own number one rule of life: **Seek ye first the kingdom of God and His righteousness and all these things will be added unto you.** (Matt.6:33).

Later, in 1990, sixteen Maryland State Senators courageously filibustered a wide-open abortion bill to death! Perhaps there is hope for Maryland yet! But in 1991, Maryland's legislature finally rammed through the most liberal abortion bill in America and Governor Schaefer signed it within the hour, calling the bill "the right thing to do!" The Governor at that moment signed the death warrant for 40,000 Maryland babies (in one year!), but it's probable he also signed his own blood-soaked ticket to Hell if he does not repent and stop these murders! May God help us to reverse this gross evil by a referendum in 1992.

There have been many other warnings in recent years including one by our dear friend, Don Odon, during his last visit to the Little Tabernacle in March of 1989, shortly before he left for his Heavenly Home. He quoted Jude 14,15: *And Enoch also, the seventh from Adam, prophesied of these, saying Behold, the Lord cometh with ten thousands of his saints, to execute judgment upon all and to convince all that are ungodly among them of all their ungodly deeds which they have ungodly committed, and of all their hard speeches which ungodly sinners have spoken against Him.*

One of the most extraordinary warnings concerning a final judgment by invasion and destruction of America is contained in a piece called "Washington's Vision," General George Washington, that is! President Washington was a devout servant of Jesus Christ, a real man of prayer and dedication to God's Word and Way. We believe this account of his vision is authentic and timely.

After these warnings we will give an account of how the Lord enabled us to personally deliver God's Solemn Warning to every State Capital, to all the Governors, at least their deputies or secretaries, Lt. Governors, Sec. of State, Attorneys General, Supreme Court Justices, State House and Senate leaders and many Mayors and Ministers!

ROCKY SCHMIT'S TAPE MESSAGE TO THE LITTLE TABERNACLE WITH WARNING TO AMERICA

September '88

Well, here we go. Shalom, Brother Sid and Sister Betsy, and all the brothers and sisters at the Little Tabernacle. Been thinking about you tonight. It's midnight in Tidahome, Sweden. This is your brother, Rocky. Can't sleep. The Lord's been holding me awake with the Word here. It's the same old Word from Isaiah. I shared it with you once before, from the 56th chapter there. The prophet says, *His watchmen are blind, they are all ignorant, they are all dumb dogs, they cannot bark; sleeping, lying down, loving to slumber. Yea, they are greedy dogs which can never have enough, and they are shepherds that cannot understand; they all look to their own way, everyone for his gain, from his quarter.* (Isaiah 56:10,11).

Outside I hear a dog barking. Oh-h, the Lord wouldn't let me sleep tonight. He's been dealing with me these last days about, about warning people, in love, before things hit them.

I got a pretty hard lesson just two days ago here. I was up in a cherry tree picking cherries. My boys and a little neighbor boy were playing out in the yard. I heard them all jump in the car. We've got a beat-up old Volvo here. They were playing, having a good time. You know I felt so strong that I should tell them to get out of the car. You know I don't mind them playing in that old car, it's an old wreck. I shoe horses over here, and a horse drug some barbed wire two times around the car, and scratched it up pretty bad, so I'm not worried about the boys hurting the car. I was like arguing with myself when I was up there in the cherry tree, picking these cherries. It was like, you know, I was saying, "Let them have their fun. What's wrong with you, Rocky? Why should you tell them to get out of the car?"

Well, what I didn't know was that their Mother had told them, just a short time previously, that they shouldn't play in the car. I hadn't heard that. But I was being very bugged up there in the cherry tree. It almost felt like the Lord was telling me to tell them to get out of the car. Well, while I was pushing this out of my head, trying to tell myself to let them have fun, and I was just trying to go on peacefully picking cherries up there, I hear a SCREAM, and I know it's coming from the car, and I come down out of the cherry tree so fast, and I run over to the car, and there's my little boy with his hand stuck in the door. The little neighbor boy had slammed the door right on his little fingers and he was stuck there. To make that part of the story short, I opened the door, looked at his hand, and it was all purple, and the blood blisters and everything. I just praised the Lord anyhow, and put him in the car. The little tyke, he's five years old, he's tough, but he was crying pretty hard, and I took off for the emergency room in the local hospital, which is about 30 kilometers away. We got there and they did some x-rays, and his fingers weren't crushed, praise the Lord, and the Doctor said we were very lucky.

The point is, I was up in the cherry tree, and Somebody was telling me to tell those boys not to be playing down there in the car. If I'd done my job as a Daddy, and just shouted down from the tree, "Boys get out of that car," they would have gotten out of the car. But I resisted the word I was getting from the Lord, and my little boy suffered.

Brothers and sisters, I've been getting a word about America here for some years. It began when we were living in Jerusalem. The Lord sent us back to America as a family, my wife and I and our children. We travelled from the East Coast to the West Coast. Part of the Word was to warn every Jewish brother and sister we met that something very dark was going to happen in America toward the Jewish people. And that they'd better make plans to go back to Israel now.

The other part of the Word had to do with a dream I had when I was still in Jerusalem. At that time I was spending a lot of time in the Gates of the Old City of Jerusalem, carving Scriptures in stones. One night I had a dream about the city of Chicago. I've never had a dream like this. I was walking in the downtown area of Chicago, the area called "The Loop," in the dream. There was nothing there, Brothers and Sisters, it was like those big buildings, those skyscrapers, the whole "Loop" area, everything was just melted. It was just rubble! There was nothing standing, I was going up and down where the streets were supposed to be, it was eery, there were no people, there was nothing there. I found one little building standing. It was a little store-front Church with a neon sign over it, "The Church of the Nazarene". That was the only thing standing there. That's all there was to the dream that I could remember.

But it was right after I had this dream, I was in the Jaffa Gate of the Old City of Jerusalem, carving **Pray For The Peace of Jerusalem** (Psalm 122:6), in a big paving stone. Two Arab boys, they were in their early 20's, just came by and started talking to me. A lot of people came by and talked to me at that time. It was a wonderful time to witness about Jesus, and His love. These young men stopped and asked me about the Scripture, and started talking about God. Now these men, they love God, they called Him, Allah. They were Moslems; I might say they were very evangelical Moslems. They were in an Arab University at a place called Bier Zeit, and they were always trying to evangelize the Marxists in the University and were having their share of troubles doing that! They didn't have any revelation yet about Jesus. They knew He was the Messiah, but apparently they still had the Moslem blindness about the details of His life. They believed He'll come back again. The one man told me he was going to Chicago in just a few weeks, to study medicine. He asked me about Chicago, and I said, well I just had a dream about Chicago. He wanted to hear the dream, so I started to tell him the dream. He got very excited, he said, "Wait a minute, wait a minute! I've had the same dream!" Then he proceeded to finish the dream that I had started to tell! He ended up by saying, "The only thing that I saw standing there was some kind of a little Church." Apparently it was the same little thing that I had seen, The Church of the Nazarene.

"Now Father, I don't know really why you've asked me to share this again with the Brothers and Sisters. But it's very, very clear to me that I am supposed to do this. I see this tape is starting to run down, I believe You would have me share with them a little more of why this has been so impressed on my heart. Father, Oh Father, thank you for

CHAPTER 28: BIBLE PROPHECIES AND WARNINGS

that Moslem boy, and how you're dealing with his heart by your Holy Spirit, and how You gave him this dream. You showed him that he could have something in common with a Christian. You showed him that Jesus is the Messiah. You want to show him also that He is Your Son. We pray for all the Moslems that are in America right now. Oh, Father, that Your Holy Spirit would deal with them, that Christian people would be open, Oh God, to witness to them, to love them, in the Name of Jesus. Father, that there could be a great harvest again in America, before these terrible things that People are seeing in the Spirit, before they come. Oh, God, we pray that there could be such a move, such a return to You in America, that You could do what You did with Nineveh, that You could postpone or cancel the fiery judgment! Oh God, that You could, Oh Father, that You could change these things that You have to do with Your perfect righteousness. Ah Father."

Before this tape runs out, I should share with you why this thing about Chicago came back again. I was driving with my boys to pick up my daughter, Gabriella, at a summer camp. Our old Volvo stopped Sunday afternoon on a big highway here. Just stopped dead. Now my boys being as they are, they said, "Well, Pappa, pray." So we prayed and the car started again. It was wonderful, I didn't have to pay any 300 crowns to get it towed off the big highway. It went further on towards this camp we were going to, but then it died again. It stopped right in front of a little country store. The store was closed, but just as I got out and opened up the hood and puttered with the engine a little bit, the owner came along and opened up, which was wonderful, because I could telephone from there to somebody at the camp to come to get me. While I was waiting for these people to come to get us, I talked with this man. He was from Iraq, from Baghdad, and he was a little bit fed up with Sweden. He was going to move to America, to Chicago, and he asked me what I thought about it! If Chicago would be a good opportunity for his family? Well, I was in one of these moods where I just didn't feel like sharing that I'd had a dream about Chicago and I saw total destruction. I held that inside, I talked very materialistically with him, about the wonderful opportunities in America, about how the taxes were about half as high as in Sweden, etc. etc. I left him with that and wished him good luck in America.

Well, I felt so condemned when our friends came and picked us up and took us to the camp. We switched batteries in the car, and I drove our car after them, and all the way to the camp, I was thinking, I should have told this guy the dream, I should have told him, I should have told him. You know the Lord didn't leave me alone, until I promised Him that on the way home I would stop at that little store. So I promised the Lord that on the way back, if the store was open, I would tell the man the dream.

I see the tape is running out here, but just to make it short, I didn't go directly back to that store, after I picked up my little girl. I took the kids swimming instead to a lake in another direction. We were in swimming, and I brought my little boy out of the water, and I bumped into a man who was bringing his little boy into the water. Now there were hundreds of people on this particular beach on a Sunday afternoon, and who do you suppose it was I bumped into? I didn't recognize him right away, because he didn't have his glasses on, but he recognized me. It was the man that had the store, who was on his way to Chicago.

Now, I knew he wasn't a Moslem. I knew that in the Spirit. I said, "You're a Christian, aren't you? You're Assyrian. That's right he was Christian from the Assyrian Church. He was the backslider in his family. His father was a priest, his grandfather was some kind of a priest or a bishop, and his brothers were deacons, or something in the Assyrian Church. He was open to the Lord! We sat down on the sand there and I shared this dream with him. It shook him up a little bit, and he is going much more prayerfully to Chicago. But it all shook me up even more.

This is why I knew when the dogs barked tonight, that I had to share this with you."

AS PROMISED EARLIER: GEORGE WASHINGTON'S VISION

George Washington was born on February 22, 1732. Few military figures in history ever faced misery and deprivation as did Washington and his forces at Valley Forge in the winter of 1777-1778. But three years later British General Charles Cornwallis surrendered to Washington at Yorktown to end the American Revolutionary War.

The following is a well-documented account of a vision General Washington had at Valley Forge.

ANTHONY SHERMAN

More than a century ago a Mr. Wesley Bradshaw published an article in which he quoted Anthony Sherman, who was an officer with General George Washington at Valley Forge.

Bradshaw's original article was reprinted in the National Tribune, Vol. 4, No. 12, for December, 1880. He told of the last time he saw Anthony Sherman, and these are Bradshaw's words: "The last time I ever saw Anthony Sherman was on the fourth of July, 1859, in Independence Square. He was then ninety-nine years old, and becoming very feeble. But though so old, his dimming eyes rekindled as he gazed upon Independence Hall, which he came to visit once more.

CHAPTER 28: BIBLE PROPHECIES AND WARNINGS

"Let us go into the hall," he said. "I want to tell you of an incident of Washington's life - one which no one alive knows of except myself, and, if you live you will, before long, see it verified.

"From the opening of the Revolution we experienced all phases of fortune, now good and now ill, one time victorious and another conquered. The darkest period we had, I think, was when Washington after several reverses, retreated to Valley Forge, where he resolved to pass the winter of 1777. Ah! I have often seen the tears coursing down our dear commander's care-worn cheeks, as he would be conversing with a confidential officer about the condition of his poor soldiers. You have doubtless heard the story of Washington's going into the thicket to pray. Well, it was not only true, but he used often to pray in secret for aid and comfort from God, the interposition of whose Divine Providence brought us safely through the darkest days of tribulation.

"One day, I remember it well, the chilly winds whistled through the leafless trees. Though the sky was cloudless and the sun shone brightly, he remained in his quarters nearly all the afternoon alone. When he came out I noticed that his face was a shade paler than usual, and there seemed to be something on his mind of more than ordinary importance. Returning just after dusk, he dispatched an orderly to the quarters of the officer I mention who is presently in attendance. After a preliminary conversation of about half an hour, Washington, gazing upon his companion with that strange look of dignity which only he alone could command, said to the latter:

WASHINGTON'S VISION

"'I do not know whether it is owing to the anxiety of my mind, or what, but this afternoon as I was sitting at this table engaged in preparing a dispatch, something seemed to disturb me. Looking up, I beheld standing opposite me a singularly beautiful female. So astonished was I, for I had given strict orders not to be disturbed, that it was some moments before I found language to inquire into the cause of her presence. A second, a third, and even a fourth time did I repeat my question, but received no answer from my mysterious visitor except a slight raising of her eyes. By this time I felt strange sensations spreading through me. I would have risen but the riveted gaze of the being before me rendered volition impossible. I assayed once more to address her, but my tongue had become useless. Even thought itself had become paralyzed. A new influence, mysterious, potent, irresistible, took possession of me. All I could do was to gaze steadily vacantly at my unknown visitant.

"Gradually the surrounding atmosphere seemed as though becoming filled with sensations, and luminous. Everything about me seemed to rarefy, the mysterious visitor herself becoming more airy and yet more distinct to my sight than ever before. I now began to feel as one dying, or rather to experience the sensations which I have sometimes imagined accompany dissolution. I did not think, I did not reason, I did not move; all were alike impossible. I was only conscious of gazing fixedly, vacantly at my companion.

THE FIRST PERIL

"Presently I heard a voice saying, 'Son of the Republic, look and learn,' while at the same time my visitor extended her arm eastwardly. I now behold a heavy white vapor at some distance rising fold upon fold. This gradually dissipated, and I looked upon a strange scene. Before me lay spread out in one vast plain all the countries of the world--Europe, Asia, Africa, and America. I saw rolling and tossing between Europe and America the billows of the Atlantic, and between Asia and America lay the Pacific. 'Son of the Republic,' said the same mysterious voice as before, 'Look and learn.' At that moment I beheld a dark, shadowy being, like an angel, standing, or rather floating in mid-air, between Europe and America. Dipping water out of the ocean in the hollow of each hand, he sprinkled some upon America with his right hand, while with his left hand he cast some on Europe. Immediately a cloud raised from these countries, and joined in mid-ocean. For a while it remained stationary, and then moved slowly westward, until it enveloped America in its murky folds. Sharp flashes of lightning gleamed through it at intervals, and I heard the smothered groans and cries of the American people.

"A second time the angel dipped water from the ocean, and sprinkled it out as before. The dark cloud was then drawn back to the ocean, in whose heaving billows it sank from view.

THE GROWTH OF AMERICA

"A third time I heard the mysterious voice saying, 'Son of the Republic, look and learn.' I cast my eyes upon America and behold villages and towns and cities springing up one after another until the whole land from the Atlantic to the Pacific was dotted with them. Again, I heard the mysterious voice say, 'Son of the Republic, the end of the century cometh, look and learn.'

THE SECOND PERIL

"At this the dark shadowy angel turned his face southward, and from Africa I saw an ill-omened specter approach our land. It flitted slowly over every town and city of the latter. The inhabitants presently set themselves in battle array against each other. As I continued looking I saw a bright angel, on whose brow rested a crown of light, on which was traced the word "Union," bearing the American flag which he placed between the divided nation, and said, "Remember ye are

CHAPTER 28: BIBLE PROPHECIES AND WARNINGS

brethren." Instantly, the inhabitants, casting away their weapons became friends once more, and united around the National Standard.

THE THIRD PERIL

"And again I heard the mysterious voice saying, 'Son of the Republic, look and learn.' At this the dark, shadowy angel placed a trumpet to his mouth, and blew three distinct blasts; he sprinkled it upon Europe, Asia, and Africa. Then my eyes beheld a fearful scene: from each of these countries arose thick, black clouds that were soon joined into one. And throughout this mass there gleamed a dark red light by which I saw hordes of armed men, who, moving by with the cloud, marched by land and sailed by sea to America, which country was enveloped in the volume of cloud. And I dimly saw these vast armies devastate the whole country and burn the villages, towns and cities that I beheld springing up. As my ears listened to the thundering of the cannon, clashing of swords, and the shouts and cries of millions in mortal combat, I heard again the mysterious voice saying, 'Son of the Republic, look and learn.' When the voice had ceased, the dark shadowy angel placed his trumpet once more to his mouth, and blew a long and fearful blast.

"Instantly a light as of a thousand suns shone down from above me, and pierced and broke into fragments the dark cloud which enveloped America. At that same moment the angel upon whose head still shone the word "Union," and who bore our national flag in one hand and a sword in the other, descended from the heavens attended by legions of white spirits. These immediately joined the inhabitants of America, who I perceived were well-nigh overcome, but who immediately taking courage again, closed up their broken ranks and renewed the battle. Again, amid the fearful noise of the conflict, I heard the mysterious voice saying, 'Son of the Republic, look and learn.' As the voice ceased, the shadowy angel for the last time dipped water from the ocean and sprinkled it upon America. Instantly the dark cloud rolled back, together with the armies it had brought, leaving the inhabitants of the land victorious.

FINAL PEACE

"Then once more I beheld the villages, towns and cities springing up where I had seen them before, while the bright angel, planting the azure standard he had brought in the midst of them, cried with a loud voice: "While the stars remain, and the heavens send down dew upon the earth, so long shall the Union last." And taking from his brow the crown on which blazoned the word "Union," he placed it upon the Standard while the people, kneeling down, said, "Amen."

"The scene instantly began to fade and dissolve, and I at last saw nothing but the rising, curling vapor I at first beheld. This also disappearing I found myself once more gazing upon the mysterious visitor, who, in the same voice I had heard before, said, 'Son of the Republic, what you have seen is thus interpreted: Three great perils will come upon the Republic. The most fearful is the third passing which the whole world united shall not prevail against her. Let every child of the Republic learn to live for his God, his land and Union.' With these words the vision vanished, and I started from my seat and felt that I had seen a vision wherein had been shown to me the birth, progress, and destiny of the United States."

A WORD OF WARNING

Anthony Sherman climaxed his recollection of Washington's words by saying, "Such, my friends, were the words I heard from Washington's own lips, and America will do well to profit by them."

Thomas Jefferson once said of our first President: "His integrity was the most pure, his justice the most flexible, I have ever known. He was, indeed, in every sense of the word, a wise, a good and a great man."

INTERPRETATION OF THE VISION

These three perils which George Washington saw all took place on American soil.

Peril 1: Was no doubt the revolutionary war which still continued for three years after the Lord gave Washington the vision. There was much suffering, but not as intense as the other perils which were yet to come.

Peril 2: The ill-omened spectre coming from Africa points towards slavery as the issue of a terrible civil conflict when the nation was divided and brothers fought brothers.

Peril 3: The last and most terrible of all, clearly predicts hordes of enemies from Europe, Asia and Africa, armed for mortal combat. A red light accompanies these terrible invaders -- indicating they are no doubt Communists. They come by air (the cloud), land (perhaps via Canada) and sea. They devastate all of America, destroying cities, towns and villages. Millions are engaged in mortal conflict. Just when all seems lost, divine intervention from heaven, angels and saints descend to assist the inhabitants of America to close their ranks and win the final victory.

A special warning is given by the Angel of the Union to Americans: "LET EVERY CHILD OF THE REPUBLIC LEARN TO LIVE FOR HIS GOD, HIS LAND, AND UNION." This is an indication that in the last peril patriotism, the love of country, and respect for our constitution and our faith in God will be in great jeopardy. Already we find this to be the case. May God help us to heed the warning of the guardian Angel of America -- before it's too late!

The two World Wars and the Korean and Vietnam wars were never

CHAPTER 28: BIBLE PROPHECIES AND WARNINGS

shown to Washington. Probably because they were not fought on American soil.[1]

GOD'S WARNING MISSION TO AMERICA

How were we to do The Warning Mission? "Fifty States is a lot of territory," we thought. "Do we find a motor home, Lord? Our car is over four years old and we've had much trouble with it this year." We even looked at some motor homes, and found them to be very expensive! So we prayed more! Soon we felt the Lord saying, "Take a U.S. map, make CIRCLES of a few states, fly to a key city, rent a car, circle the State Capitols, and fly home." Sounded great! The cost? Far, far less than a motor home! Time consumed, far less! Wear and tear on us, far less! The Lord knows how to economize and how to do the job! Praise His Holy Name! The cost: just under $15,000, which the Lord provided in time. Praise His Holy Name!

While "cooling our heels" trying to see the Governor of Maryland in 1989, we made day trips to Washington, D.C. to take the Warnings to the U.S. Senators. In two summer weeks we visited 62 Senators offices. Never got to speak with even one Senator! A few favorable responses from assistants, but most were cool, cold, or stony cold!

One day while leaving a Senator's office we almost bumped into two well-dressed men coming in, one quite tall and definitely familiar looking. Suddenly, we realized it was that famous movie star, "What's-His-Name?" For the life of me I couldn't think of it, but I stuck out my hand and shook his hand warmly saying, "We're so pleased to see you; this is my wife, Betsy." He nodded, smiling. The other man quickly ushered him on past and Betsy and I were left walking down the hall wondering to ourselves who in the world was that movie star. Then it dawned on us! It was the long time movie great, Jimmy Stewart, who was in Washington that day publicizing a book of poetry he had just written, so the papers reported. No Senators, but ONE movie great!

We mailed the Warnings to the other 38 senators, the 435 congressman, as well as to the Supreme Court Justices, President, Vice President and their wives and the Cabinet, as well as the Maryland State Senators and Legislators. May God grant that a great number of these leaders personally read and took seriously these Warnings. America's whole future depends upon heeding them!

---

[1] Reprinted from: End-Time Handmaidens, Inc. Engeltal, P.O. Box 447, Jasper, Ark. 72641 - with permission.

The Supreme Court's July 1989 decision in the Missouri-Webster case, in effect giving the States more room to limit abortions, made going to the States most urgent. America's future depends on stopping this Holocaust of Babies! So on August 2, 1989, we began the EIGHT CIRCLES OF STATES, ending in January, 1990. Oh, how the Lord was with us!

- THE FIRST CIRCLE OF STATES was to 4 nearby states as a "Trial Run" - to the capitals of Maryland, Delaware, New Jersey, and Pennsylvania. Since the Governors seemed always too busy, we realized that seeking appointments with 50 governors could last forever. So we must go to their offices "Cold Turkey" and try to present at least a secretary or deputy with The Warning. The same with Senators!

The Lord reminded us of the visit to the Prime Minister's office in Israel, and the part that tupelo honey played in that blessed visit. So we sent off an urgent message to our dear Tupelo friends, the Laniers, in Wewahitchka, Florida to begin supplying us with some 50 "Tupelo honey bears," which they did. Then we had printed a goodly quantity of the "Tupelo Honey and Amen Story" to share with each Governor, along with the Special Warning letters addressed to each State official and off we went to the capitals. (The book, The World Almanac, was a great help!)

- THE SECOND CIRCLE OF STATES was the 7 New England ones: starting at Albany, N.Y. to Conn., R.I., Mass., Maine, and Vermont with side trips to Plymouth Rock, Ragged Mountain Camp and Kennebunkport. We did catch the governor of Vermont for a brief 2 minutes.

- THE THIRD CIRCLE was the 9 Southeastern states: Va., N.C., S.C., Ga., Fla., Ala., Miss., Tenn., W.Va. We did this circle also in our car

- THE FOURTH CIRCLE was 6 states from Columbus, Ohio to Ky., Ind., Ill., Wisc., Michigan and back to Columbus.

- After this came a BIG SIDE TRIP with our tour group to CIRCLE ISRAEL for two weeks. Soon after our return we left for the seven northern midwestern states.

- THE FIFTH CIRCLE OF STATES: Missouri, Kan. Neb. Iowa, Minn. and North and South Dakota. The landing point was Kansas City, Kan.

- THE SIXTH CIRCLE, and longest, was 7 states in the Southwest starting at Phoenix, Arizona to Sacramento, California, through Donner Pass to Carson City, Nevada, east to Salt Lake City, Utah, further east to Cheyenne, Wyoming, south to Denver, Colorado, southwest to Santa Fe, New Mexico and back to Phoenix by way of Flagstaff, some 3600 miles in two weeks, and then back to Baltimore for a speaking date.

Early in December when we were halfway through our southwestern circle of states, the Holy Spirit reminded us that this would be a good

CHAPTER 28: BIBLE PROPHECIES AND WARNINGS 481

time to be giving out the "Jesus Jingle Bells" song, which beautifully magnifies the Name of Jesus at Christmas time. This reminder came when we were in Salt Lake City. The next morning, a Monday, Betsy quickly wrote out the words and off to the copy shop we went, printing some 300 copies. Then like Johnny Appleseed we started planting them in every place we could, starting in Salt Lake City.

Next in Cheyenne, Wyoming, the Secretary of State overheard us singing it in her office, and asked, "What are you trying to do? Put Christ back in Christmas?"

We replied, "We sure are, and to get the Bible and prayer back in schools."

She said, "Well, I believe in the separation of Church and state." But she later admitted that she too had had prayer in her school, a parochial school.

The rest of the Christmas season, even into the New Year, we had a "ball" singing "Jesus Jingle Bells" in the thirteen remaining capitals we visited. We would get people to join us along the way in impromptu song sessions. Fanatical? You might think so. We don't. People think it's all right to scream and holler at a baseball or football game, or sing loudly their highschool and college songs, which have no heavenly connections. It seems to us much more important to sing even publicly the praises of Him Who is our Heavenly Connection. Usually, "A fanatic is just someone who loves Jesus more than you do." Many years ago we learned a real fanatical song some of you may want to use sometime. It goes like this:

"Hoorah for JESUS, Hoorah for JESUS!
Someone's in the stands shouting, Hoorah for JESUS!
One, two, three, four, who you going to yell for?
JESUS, that's who! Rah, Rah, Rah!" (Repeat)

Too bad there aren't more such fanatics! Five days later we were on our way to -- THE SEVENTH CIRCLE of 4, beginning at Austin, Texas, to Baton Rouge, Louisiana, Little Rock, Arkansas, and Oklahoma City, Oklahoma, and a Christmas stop with our son Kirby and his family in Tulsa.

- THE EIGHTH CIRCLE of the far northwest started December 30, 1989 in Seattle, Washington, then to Oregon's capital, Salem, back to Olympia, Washington where we saw our second Governor. Also saw many dear friends, awesome mountains, deserts, snows, heavy winds, and big tumbleweeds!

OUR "JUMP" TO ALASKA landed us in Fairbanks (-18 degrees F.), Anchorage, Sitka and Ketchican, but not in Juneau, the Capital. Bad weather prevented us. Disappointed, we came back to Seattle, and flew on to Helena, Montana and Boise, Idaho - nice visits in these capitals.

We had to postpone Hawaii and head back to Baltimore because I had a bad case of bronchitis with fever, and a "busted" tooth. Praise the Lord, we had reached 49 states, and 48 Capitals! Juneau and Honolulu must wait. However, we sent their Governors by mail the sample of Tupelo honey and THE SOLEMN WARNING FROM THE LORD! Later, in Dec. 1990, with God's great help we made it to Hawaii for four days of Warning Work in the 50th State.

OBSERVATIONS FROM WARNING MISSION

"Thanks Letters" came from the Governor of Hawaii and some 17 other Governors, including an especially strong PRO-LIFE letter from the courageous Governor of California, Gov. George Deukmejian. However, we did see many miracle mercies and beauties of God's power and love throughout this beautiful land. Yes, God has blessed America! But we're polluting the land--with innocent blood of over 100,000 unborn babies per month--all PREMEDITATED MURDERS--UNPUNISHED!!

Out of 48 states we got to see only two Governors, but did see a large number of other key people, and many believers who would take The Warnings to their churches and communities.

The politicians across the land, for the most part seem almost totally resistant to taking a stand on the abortion issue and to be wishing it would somehow quietly go away. Only a few times, and praise the Lord for them, did we find a politician willing to take an open and firm stand against the killing of unborn babies. It is clear evidence that America has lost its moral and spiritual backbone and has come to believe in the deceptions of Satan, such as that presented by the U.S. Supreme Court Justices in 1973--that a woman has "a right to kill" the "fetus" (the living child) which she has conceived, regardless of the circumstances. Neither age, nor poverty, nor unwillingness to bear a child, should give that right to kill, ever.

Not only were the politicians running scared to take a righteous stand, but were earnestly seeking politically safe compromises, such as the Governors of Connecticut, Idaho and Maryland.

Governor O'Brian of Connecticut signed into law a liberal abortion bill passed by their legislature, all the while saying he was opposed. Gov. Andrus of Idaho vetoed a strong anti-abortion bill passed by his courageous legislature while saying he too was opposed to abortion. How sad in both cases, since both men had the finest opportunity to be true God-fearing statesmen, guarding the constitutional rights of children (including the unborn). And they "blew" it badly. So did Maryland's Gov. Schaefer in 1990, when he signed a very liberal abortion law only minutes after its passage -- thus condemning 40,000 babies (in one

CHAPTER 28: BIBLE PROPHECIES AND WARNINGS   483

year) to death!!!

Several of the key legislators in Boise, Idaho assured us that they would never approve a pro-abortion legislation for their state. They did pass a strong pro-life bill only to have it vetoed by Governor Andrus who wanted to be elected for his fourth term the next fall (1990). It was too late in the session for them to override his veto!

One other thing we observed in the journey was that the over-spending and excessive taxation bug seems to have bit many of the states. Several of the states are building new capitol buildings where the old ones seemed totally adequate. The taxing and spending disease has spread wildly across the nation. Massive public programs require massive public taxation. The states, like the national government, need to wake up and stop spending us into bankruptcy.

At one point during our nationwide Warning Journey we heard that the Governors were all attending a Presidential Conference on Education at the University of Virginia. We remember watching very avidly the TV news of that conference and hearing some of the articulate Governors' summations on the problems of education in America. The former Secretary of Education, Mr. Bennett, was there and we noticed he almost "let the cat out of the bag" when he made a comment about the decay of the schools since 1963. Remember that was the year that our unnoble Supreme Court pronounced God's Bible unwelcome in the schools of America!

Today it is almost a crime (if not one) to have a Bible on a teacher's desk or even in the library of our schools. The Book that was the moral Foundation and Backbone of America has become THE MISSING LINK in any plan of recovery. How sadly America falls! As the man in the Lt. Governor's office in Atlanta added when we said America has thrown out the Manufacturer's Handbook, GOD'S WORD, "YES, AND THE MANUFACTURER'S WARRANTY HAS RUN OUT!" SO IT WILL BE UNTIL "THE BOOK" FINDS ITS WAY BACK TO THOSE TEACHERS' DESKS AND TO THE TOP OF THE REQUIRED READING LIST IN AMERICA'S SCHOOLS.

Psalm 119:105 says it so clearly: *Thy Word is a lamp unto my feet and a light unto my path.* And Psalm 127:1 should tell the President and all his men the SECRET TO REBUILDING OUR EDUCATIONAL SYSTEM: *Except God builds the house* (including the schools), *they labor in vain who build it. And except God watches the city, the watchman* (police and army) *watch in vain.*

Anyone who is ignorant of God's Word, The Bible, is to be pitied for he has missed the greatest wisdom the world has ever known; and he is doomed to blind stumbling regardless the secular degrees attained!

- - - - - - - - -

FIRED AGAIN AND AGAIN, PRAISE THE LORD!

BROADCAST THROUGHOUT AMERICA!
DR. BILLY GRAHAM GIVES A SIMILAR WARNING!

LITTLE TABERNACLE CHURCH
1503 E. Baltimore St., Balt. Md. 21231
March 9, 1990

"THREE VERY STRONG WARNINGS TO AMERICA"

I. THE WARNING BY COLONEL MYRL ALLINDER (USMC-RET.), In November 1988:"WE HAVE 7 YEARS REMAINING...SOMETIME BETWEEN 1993-1995 - THE USSR WILL DESTROY OUR NUCLEAR WEAPONS AND OUR MILITARY...AND THE SOVIET IS POISED." Glasnost and perestroika notwithstanding!

_ At a 3-hour private meeting with Col. Allinder in Clearwater, Fla. on March 1, 1989, this highly decorated fighter pilot, and later one of 8 top "Strategic Planners" for the Navy Department, emphatically repeated to us this warning re the Soviet intentions as determined from all our Intelligence Sources. He described their ability to destroy our electrical and communication systems with a series of 8-10 hydrogen bombs (!), positioned 150 miles above the U.S.A., which would burn out all exposed electrical systems in America!

II. "GOD'S CHILLING WARNING, October 4, 1987: "CALL MY PEOPLE TO SOLEMN FASTING, PRAYING AND REPENTANCE THROUGHOUT THE LAND TO TURN THIS NATION BACK TO MY WAY OF HOLINESS AND RIGHTEOUSNESS. CALL THIS NATION TO TURN AWAY FROM THE HORRIBLE EVILS THAT ARE PRESENT IN THE LAND. THE HOLOCAUST OF INFANTS IS GROSS EVIL! I'VE HEARD THE CRIES OF OVER 20 MILLION (now over 30 million) INFANTS MURDERED IN COLD BLOOD DURING THE LAST 14 YEARS (now 19, AND I WARN YOU, SAITH THE LORD, THAT AMERICA WILL BE DESTROYED, TOTALLY DESTROYED, IN LESS THAN 10 YEARS IF THIS INFANT HOLOCAUST IS NOT STOPPED SOON! REMEMBER MY WORD WHICH I GAVE TO MY PEOPLE LONG AGO IN II CHRON. 7:14, AND DO IT! THIS IS YOUR ONLY HOPE." (By the Holy Spirit to Pastor Rigell at the Little Tabernacle Church in Baltimore, Md.)

III. THE WARNING BY DAVID WILKERSON in his 1985 Book,"SET THE TRUMPET TO THY MOUTH". In Chap. 1,"THE DESTRUCTION OF AMERICA", he warns us that America is to be destroyed by fire! Very few will escape this sudden destruction. In a surprise attack, using hydrogen bombs, as Col. Allinder warns, the enemy will destroy America in one hour. Our nation will be no more. David goes on to say it will happen because America has sinned against God's greatest light, THE GOSPEL LIGHT. As we have been saying for over 10 years, so David says, God's judgment will fall on America because of the floods of evil we have allowed to flow freely in the land, such as: murdering of millions of babies, allowing all kinds of perverted sex, corruption, drunkenness, drug abuse, ungodliness, rampant divorce and adultery, pornography, molestations of children, cheatings, robbings, dirty movies and T.V., and widespread approval of occult practices.

"IN ONE HOUR IT WILL ALL BE OVER." He pleads for America to repent. The Biblical city of Nineveh repented after the warning by Jonah and was spared by God! See Jonah 3, Jude v.14-15, and Rev.14:6-7. With Col. Allinder and David Wilkerson, we weep and pray that America will heed GOD'S STRONG WARNINGS SOON AND LIVE, NOT DIE. Sodom and Gomorrah didn't repent and perished!

In His Great Love, Joseph S. & Elizabeth Rigell

P.S.: These are just 3 of many very strong warnings concerning the SOON COMING JUDGMENTS OF GOD upon America received in the past 3 years from God-fearing men. "Wake up, America, your time is fast running out." *"Blessed is the nation whose God is the Lord; and the people whom He hath chosen for His own inheritance."* (Ps.33:12) *"The wicked shall be turned into hell, and all nations that forget God."* (Psalm 9:17)

CHAPTER 28: BIBLE PROPHECIES AND WARNINGS

WARNING LETTER TO GOVERNORS AND STATE OFFICIALS:

Date of visit during 1990

Dear Governor,

Since the Bible and Prayer were thrown out of our schools in 1962-3, our schools have decayed badly! Since God's law against the murder of babies was thrown out in 1973, all "HELL" has broken loose in America! Each year over 1 ½ million babies are being ripped apart in "abortions by choice" - all pre-meditated murders! We're far worse than the Nazis, AND DESERVE THE SAME JUDGMENT!

Our nation is plagued with other terrible crimes, street drugs, murders and sex-diseases, making us ready for God's fire and brimstone, like Sodom. Through earthquakes, fires, storms and plagues, ALMIGHTY GOD IS WARNING AMERICA OF DEVASTATING, FIERY JUDGMENTS COMING VERY SOON.

My wife and I have served the Lord for 40 years, largely in Inner-city ministry with delinquents, gangs, addicts, ex-addicts, and the poor in Baltimore. In 1989, the Lord is sending us across America with the enclosed WARNINGS. We hope to reach all the states and many key officials.

GOD'S TERRIBLE JUDGMENT ON AMERICA WILL COME SOON IF WE DO NOT: (1) TURN BACK TO HIM, TO HIS WORD, AND HONOR HIM AS OUR FOUNDING FATHERS DID, (2) STOP THE HOLOCAUST OF BABIES--ABORTIONS, and (3) STAND BY ISRAEL.

PLEASE, TAKE THESE WARNINGS SERIOUSLY - see page 2. They are not from "wild-eyed kooks", but are sent from God through three of His courageous servants, with long ministries of fidelity to God and to our nation. God's Word says He will show His Servants things to come.(Amos 3:7 & John 16:13.)

We plead with you TO HELP AMERICA TO TURN BACK TO GOD as set forth in our FOUNDING BOOK, THE BIBLE, (Deuteronomy 6:1-12; 2 Timothy 3:14-17); TO STOP THE UNGODLY HOLOCAUST OF BABIES (all first-degree murders) (Psalm 106:37-38; Proverbs 24:11-12); and TO STAND BY ISRAEL in her struggle to survive, (Gen.12:3; Ps.102:16; Zech.12:3,9; Rom.11).

GOD'S WORD IS CLEAR: "The wicked shall be turned into hell, and all the nations that forget God." (Psalm 9:17) "Righteousness exalteth a nation: but sin is a reproach to any people." (Proverbs 14:34). "Blessed is the nation whose God is the Lord." (Psalm 33:12). "Except the Lord build the house, they labour in vain that build it: except the Lord keep the city, the watchman waketh but in vain."(Psalm 127:1). This applies to our schools also! All of the first 15 colleges in America were founded to train Ministers and teachers of God's Word? No wonder God blessed our nation!

You hold a key role in the future of our Nation. We are praying you will choose life, not death, for us! (Deut. 30:14-19).

In God's Service,
Joseph S. & Elizabeth Rigell,
Pastor Emeritus
Little Tabernacle Church
Baltimore, Md. 21231

486   FIRED AGAIN AND AGAIN, PRAISE THE LORD!

PRESENTING HONEY & WARNING TO GOVERNOR GARDNER, WASHINGTON STATE

MISSOURI CAPITOL, JEFFERSON CITY, OCT.31,'89

TV APPEARANCE WITH BLACKIE GONZALES, SANTE FE, 12/1/89

CHAP. 29

THREE GREAT MEN OF FAITH

Now faith is the substance of things hoped for, the evidence of things not seen. For by it the elders obtained a good report.
- Hebrews 11:1-2

During our lives a great concern has been the gradual depreciation of the importance of our Christian faith in America in the fields of education, ethics, politics, economics, journalism, the media, and among the leaders of our nation. We've seen the decided increase of resistance to spiritual matters and high moral values in almost every direction we look. The trend has been to reject or disparage anything relating to the Old Time Religion that centered in Jesus Christ and His Cross. The Anti-Christ, anti-morality spirit has grown amazingly. The "Enemy" really has come in like a flood. (Isaiah 59:19; Matt.24:12).

Along with others, we wondered about the founders of our nation. Didn't they have a vital faith in God and in Jesus Christ as His Son and our Saviour? Wasn't this nation founded on the Word of God, the Bible, and the mighty saving knowledge of salvation through Jesus Christ? We remembered that the schools of our childhood still had prayer and Bible reading daily in the classroom. But that ended in 1962 & '63.

So we began researching our history again and found that almost every recorded landing on these shores was made by explorers or settlers who came ashore, planted a cross on the beach and knelt to thank Almighty God in the Name of Jesus Christ for the safe voyage and for His continued protection and provisions.

The Pilgrims had begun their long journey by kneeling on the dock at Delftshaven, England, to ask God's blessings, and ended it several months later in the winter of 1620 by kneeling at Plymouth Rock to thank Almighty God, the God of Israel for their safe arrival after great perils at sea. They humbly asked for His great help in establishing in this new land a people who would love and serve Him and extend the Gospel of His Son, Jesus Christ, throughout the whole of it.

We learned that those first settlers in this "new" world realized clearly they needed both basic and higher education for their children, and they began establishing Christian schools and colleges, especially to train ministers and teachers of God's Word. All the original Ivy League colleges were so founded, and a hundred more!

Many other ministers and leaders have been equally concerned, equally appalled at the grave deterioration in the moral fabric and foundation of our nation. A number of excellent books have been written on the subject, of which we mention a few that have been most meaningful to us: "The Light And The Glory", by Peter Marshall, Jr. and David Manuel; "America's Dates With Destiny", by Pat Robertson; "The Myth of Separation" by David Barton; "Milestones To Immortality" by Dr. Watson F. Pindell.

In the following pages we wish to share with you a few nuggets of inspiration we have gleaned from the lives of Christopher Columbus, George Washington and Abraham Lincoln. This is done chiefly to help our own grandchildren, and others, to know that our nation was founded on the Solid Rock of Faith in the God of Israel, in His Holy Word, the Bible, and in His Holy Son, Jesus Christ, whom He sent to be our Saviour--if we would love and follow Him. America must turn back to God's Word soon in repentance or be lost, first in the hell of man's own making, AND in the one already made by God for those who reject His Word, His Way, and His Warning to turn back!

CHRISTOPHER COLUMBUS-CHRIST-BEARER

Christopher Columbus was born in Genoa, Italy about 1446 into a family of wool carders and weavers, a trade which Christopher and his brother, Bartolomeo, learned well. However, they were more interested in the maritime world of sailing explorations, navigation, and map making. In fact they became expert cartographers and were employed in this field in Lisbon, Portugal. Their studies of Marco Polo's travels and others, plus sailing on trading ships to West Africa and England led them to dream of sailing westward in a daring voyage to reach the East Indies and Cipango (Japan).

Columbus went to the rulers of Portugal, England, and Spain with his "dream," spending eight years trying to get some ruler or patron to finance him. His proposal was for three ships, well provisioned, costing around 1/3 of a million dollars, in today's monetary terms. Quite an ambitious dream! But it was an 8 year struggle!

Finally, with the help of some highly placed God-fearing friends, and after many disappointments, his mission was approved by Queen Isabella and King Ferdinand of Spain. Columbus had become convinced that God had reserved for Ferdinand and Isabella of Spain the honor of sending forth the expedition that would bring the Gospel to

CHAPTER 29: THREE GREAT MEN OF FAITH

undiscovered lands. The King and Queen after hearing Columbus' proposal to discover new lands for the glory of God and His Church, and to spread the Gospel of the Holy Saviour to the ends of the earth, finally agreed to back his plan. They were doing it in gratitude to God for His help to their Spanish forces in finally defeating the Moors (Moslems) who had controlled southern Spain for several centuries.

The next eight months were spent by Columbus in happy preparation for the expedition, and on August 3, 1492, Columbus knelt on the dock in the pre-dawn to receive Holy Communion. Shortly, "In The Name of Jesus," Columbus and his three ships, Santa Maria, Pinta and Nina, and some 90 crewmen, set sail westward toward a totally new world. In 1992 America and Spain will celebrate this amazing journey!

[1]"The first days of the voyage could not have gone more smoothly. Their sails filled with the sea breeze, the great red crusader's crosses on them were thrust forward, as if going on before.

"They reached Grand Canary Island on August 9, reprovisioned and made repairs, and finally launched out to the west into the unknown on September 8.

"These were beautiful days--a following sea under azure skies, fresh winds billowing the white sails, flying fish and petrels skimming the waves. As the three small vessels sailed on, the succession of days settled into a familiar rhythm, with each new dawn being greeted by one of the ship's boys singing:

Blessed be the light of day and the Holy Cross, we say;
and the Lord of Veritie, and the Holy Trinity.
Blessed be th' immortal soul, and the Lord who keeps it whole.
Blessed be the light of day, and He who sends the night away.

"And yet, with the light of each new day, they sailed farther and farther out into waters where no man had ever ventured before. And gradually, suspicion and fear began to dog their wake. None of them had ever been farther than three hundred miles offshore; now they were well over three thousand, and still going...

"After 31 straight days of heading almost due west from the Canaries, the mood of their crews was ugly. The Pinzon brothers, captains of the Pinta and the Nina, were convinced that if they continued one day further on their present course, they would have mutiny on their hands. They demanded a meeting with Columbus.

---

[1] From "The Light and The Glory," by Peter Marshall and David Manuel, copyright 1977 by Peter J. Marshall, Jr. and David B. Manuel, Jr. Used by permission of Fleming H. Revell Company.

"Reluctantly, Columbus turned from the window to face the Pinzon brothers--and reality. He consented to turn back. He had no choice, really. But he extracted one more promise from them: three additional days. If they had not sighted land by the twelfth, they would come about and head home. Not at all sure they had three days of goodwill remaining, the Pinzon brothers left.

"We can imagine Columbus sitting alone in his cabin, after their departure, staring at the last entry in his journal, the quill pen motionless in his hand. Outside, the masts groaned--she was pulling well, he thought. Not that it mattered any more. It was all over. The specter of defeat seemed to stand by his side, resting a bony hand on his shoulder. Columbus shuddered. Glancing down, he noticed that he had absently written his name. Christopher-Christo-ferens. Christ-bearer......

"But three days were still three days! And God was still God! He was the God who had answered his prayers so often in the past, sometimes at the last moment, when all hope was gone and only a miracle could save the situation. Columbus must have prayed then as he had never prayed before.

"The next morning, his journal records that during the previous twenty-four hours they had made an incredible fifty-nine leagues[2], more than they had covered on all but one day of the whole voyage! In fact, so fast were they now sailing that the men on the Santa Maria grew more alarmed than ever at how rapidly they were widening the distance from their homeland. For the first time the crew openly challenged their commander. According to the historian Las Casas, who personally knew Columbus: 'The Admiral reassured them as best he could, holding out to them bright hopes of the gains which they would make, and adding that it was useless to complain, since he was going to the Indies and must pursue his course until, with the help of the Lord, he found them.'

"This could hardly have been reassuring. Their mood must have been blacker than ever. An even greater miracle was needed.

"On the morning of October eleventh, as they continued to fly along, aboard the Pinta a great shout went up: a reed was sighted and a small piece of wood that had unmistakably been shaped by a man. And over on the Nina, this news was answered with the sighting of a small twig with flowers on it. These sure signs of land instantly transformed the mood of the three ships into the happiest they had been in weeks!

"The prize for the first person to sight land was an annuity of ten

---

[2] A league is estimated to be about 3 miles!

CHAPTER 29: THREE GREAT MEN OF FAITH

thousand maravedis[3], and now the men were clamoring to take turns aloft as lookouts. The ships seemed to be racing one another, with first one and then another forging into the lead. As night fell, instead of taking in sail, they elected to plunge on into the darkness at an almost reckless pace, luminescent foam curling up from their bows. At 10:00 p.m., Columbus and one of the sailors simultaneously sighted a tiny light, far ahead of them.

"As Las Casas retells it from Columbus's journal, 'It was like a small wax candle being raised and lowered. Few thought that this was an indication of land, but the Admiral was certain that they were near land.' Whatever the light was, Columbus took it as a strong encouragement from the Lord to press on as fast as possible.

"At 2:00 a.m., with less than four hours remaining before the dawn of the third and final day, aboard the Pinta the electrifying cry at last rang out: 'Tierra! Tierra!' The lookout had spied what appeared to be a low white cliff shining in the moonlight, and Martin Pinzon confirmed the sighting by firing a cannon as a signal. Land!

"Immediately they took in sail and turned south, staying well offshore, to avoid piling up on the barrier reefs. The remaining hours until daybreak they felt their way along cautiously. One can imagine Columbus's prayers now, as full of passion as before, but overflowing with gratitude.

"They reached the southern tip of the island, just as the sun rose above the blue horizon on their larboard beam. A new day was dawning, a new era for mankind. The fears and aches of weeks at sea seemed like nothing at all now. In every heart was dawning an awareness of the enormity of what they had accomplished--and the awe of it was overwhelming! Whereas, at the time of the first sighting, there had been laughing and dancing, now they were silent, as every eye followed the coastline slowly unfolding before them, glowing in the morning sun.....

"Columbus was the first to set foot on dry land, carrying the royal standard, with the brothers Pinzon directly behind him, bearing a huge white banner with a green cross and the crowned initials of Ferdinand and Isabella on either side of it. The men kissed the white coral beach, which was almost too bright to look at in the noonday sun. Then their eyes filled with tears, as they knelt and bowed their heads. Columbus christened the island San Salvador--'Holy Saviour'--and prayed: "O Lord, Almighty and everlasting God, by Thy Holy Word Thou hast created the heaven, and the earth, and the sea; blessed and glorified be Thy Name, and praised be Thy Majesty, which hath deigned

---

[3] Ten Thousand Maravedis equals about $1,600 U.S. 1977 dollars.

to use us, Thy humble servants, that Thy Holy Name may be proclaimed in this second part of the earth.'....

"On every island at which they stopped, Columbus had his men erect a large wooden cross 'as a token of Jesus Christ our Lord, and in honor of the Christian faith.' Almost always, they found the inhabitants peaceful, innocent, and trusting, and the Admiral gave strict orders that they were not to be molested or maltreated in any way. He had determined that their own reputation, which was obviously preceding them through the islands, would be as favorable as possible."

After losing the Santa Maria on Hispanola and becoming separated from the Pinta in a huge storm, Columbus barely made it back to Spain with one ship, the Nina, to receive great acclaim and honors from the King and Queen. After giving them the report of his remarkable discoveries, illustrated by many valuable artifacts, Columbus and the Sovereigns all fell on their knees to thank God for His bountiful mercy, and all sang the "Te Deum" with tears flowing! He would lead three other voyages for them. However, he eventually lost favor and would become a broken and embittered man, his health badly weakened, his sailing days over, his last days spent fretting over not receiving his proper share of the gold coming from the Indies.

Finally, on Ascension Day, 1506, Columbus, a very old man at 53, realizing his life was ebbing away, received the final Sacrament of The Church and prayed the prayer of Jesus, "Father, into Thy hands I commend my spirit." The famous Admiral of the Ocean departed for another world, a heavenly one!

---------- --

Christopher Columbus, a very courageous sea captain, a man dedicated to taking the Light of Jesus westward to fulfill the dream God had given him, though detoured by pride and greed at times, had sailed on and on, often on his knees amidst the great storms to reach the desired havens, to reach a New World. We all owe him much honor! (Author's note).

The following poem about Columbus was not an easy one to find. It was finally located through friends in what people often call "A Pure Coincidence!" Praise The Lord for His "Little Miracles!" The reason why we wanted to include it in our book goes back 44 years to Dr. J. McDowell Richards' orientation address to Columbia Seminary student body in 1948, my first year there. Dr. Richards, the Seminary President, ended his message with this inspiring poem. At least to one student! His text probably was Phil. 3:14

.....I press toward the mark for the prize of the high calling of God in Christ Jesus.

CHAPTER 29: THREE GREAT MEN OF FAITH

COLUMBUS

Behind him lay the gray Azores, Behind the Gates of Hercules;
Before him not the ghost of shores; Before him only shoreless seas.
The good mate said: "Now must we pray, For lo! the very stars are gone.
Brave Adm'r'l, speak! What shall I say?"
"Why, say: 'Sail on! sail on! and on!'"

My men grow mutinous day by day:
My men grow ghastly, wan and weak.
The stout mate thought of home; a spray
Of salt wave washed his swarthy cheek.
"What shall I say, brave Adm'r'l, say,
If we sight naught but seas at dawn?"
"Why, you shall say at break of day: "Sail on! sail on! sail on! and on!"

They sailed and sailed, as winds might blow,
Until at last the blanched mate said:
"Why now not even God would know Should I and all my men fall dead.
These very winds forget their way,
For God from these dread seas is gone.
Now speak, brave Adm'r'l, speak and say....."
He said: "Sail on! sail on! and on!"

They sailed. They sailed. Then spake the mate:
"This mad sea shows his teeth tonight.
He curls his lip, he lies in wait, He lifts his teeth as if to bite!
Brave Adm'r'l, say but one good word:
What shall we do, when hope is gone?"
The words leapt like a leaping sword: "Sail on! sail on! sail on! and on!"

Then pale and worn, he paced his deck,
And peered through darkness. Ah, that night
Of all dark nights! And then a speck--A light! A light! At last a light!
It grew, a starlit flag unfurled! It grew to be Time's burst of dawn.
He gained a world; he gave that world
Its grandest lesson: "On! sail on!

Taken from "THE MODERN BOOK OF AMERICAN VERSE"

By Joaquin Miller

FIRED AGAIN AND AGAIN, PRAISE THE LORD!

GEORGE WASHINGTON[4]

The Continental Congress desperately needed a mature and courageous man to lead the relatively unskilled militias of the colonies against the British after the early battles of Lexington, Concord and Bunker's Hill. The American Minute men had acquitted themselves well in their first battles with the British Redcoats. However they needed someone with skilled overall military leadership. George Washington had become an outstanding and courageous officer in the Virginia militia and early-on had offered to lead a force of 1,000 men at his own expense to face the British in Boston. At the Continental Congress it was both John Adams and Ben Franklin who persuaded the Congress to unanimously choose George Washington to become the Commander in Chief of the new Continental Army.

Washington reluctantly accepted the appointment closing with these words:

"'I beg it to be remembered by every gentleman in this room that I this day declare with the utmost sincerity that I do not think myself equal to the command I am honored with.' (At 43, Washington was lifted into unwanted prominence!)

"On the morning of June 23, 1775, as word of the victory of the Battle of Bunker Hill was about to reach Philadelphia, a throng of admirers assembled around Washington. He was about to leave to take command of the Continental Army at Cambridge. His extraordinary popularity with ordinary people was a phenomenon which would remain constant throughout Washington's life in public service. He was a quiet man, not given to easy back-slapping friendships. And his popularity, when he was made aware of it at all, surprised and astonished him-- which only served to draw people to him all the more.

"Because of this humility and this popularity, and because of a truly supernatural gift of wisdom, he evoked jealousy from his colleagues in Congress and in the military. But the affection of the people never wavered. And this morning, the tall, firm-jawed, blue-eyed Virginian was positively resplendent in his brand-new general's uniform with its blue coat and cream-colored breeches and waistcoat. Embarrassed at the fuss being made over him by the gathering of officers and delegates and the band playing in his honor, Washington quickly swung up into the saddle, waved good-bye, and set off at a brisk trot.

---

[4] From "The Light and the Glory" by Peter Marshall and David Manuel, copyright 1977 by Peter J. Marshall, Jr. and David B. Manuel, Jr. Used by permission of Fleming H. Revell Company.

CHAPTER 29: THREE GREAT MEN OF FAITH

"Who was this statuesque horseman who was riding off into the destiny of every American? Much controversy among historians has raged about him, but in the hearts of ordinary Americans, he has shared the place of top affection with only one other President. Surprisingly little is known about Washington's boyhood, and stories like the one about the cherry tree seem to be apocryphal attempts to fill the void. We were especially curious about him, in the light of the controversy which we found in the history books of the nineteenth century. Some enthusiastic Christians claimed that Washington was a committed Christian, while arch-conservatives pointed out that these enthusiasts were prone to claim that anyone who had ever alluded to God was a believer. They noted that Washington referred to God in such general terms as Divine Providence and Heaven, which smacked to them of the deism that was at that time making such incursions.

"It was an important question, because in the three centuries of American history which this book covers, only three other men played as pivotal a role as that of George Washington -- Columbus, Winthrop, and Whitefield. In the lives of all three, the measuring rods of their ability to carry out their divine callings had been: TRUST in Him, sacrifice, and selflessness.

"'By chance' we stumbled across an old book, out of print for more than half a century, which provided many of the answers. We found it on a rainy Tuesday, in the stacks of the Yale Divinity School Library. It was written by a man named William Johnson, and it bore the title, *George Washington, the Christian*.

"What we came upon inside ranked in excitement with the discovery of Columbus's heaven-sent rebuke. When he was about twenty, George Washington filled 24 pages of a little manuscript book with some of the most beautiful prayers we have ever read. All of them were written out in his own hand, and he titled the little book 'Daily Sacrifice.' The first entry was subtitled 'Sunday Morning' and contained these words:

"*Let my heart, therefore, gracious God, be so affected with the glory and majesty of (Thine honor) that I may not do mine own works, but wait on Thee, and discharge those weighty duties which Thou requirest of me...*

"And in the next entry, 'Sunday Evening,' are these words:

"*O most glorious God...I acknowledge and confess my faults, in the weak and imperfect performance of the duties of this day. I have called on Thee for pardon and forgiveness of sins, but so coldly and carelessly that my prayers are become my sin and stand in need of pardon. I have heard Thy holy Word, but with such deadness of spirit that I have been an unprofitable and forgetful hearer...But, O God, who* art rich in mercy and plenteous in redemption, mark not, I beseech Thee, what I have done amiss; remember that I am but dust, and remit my transgressions, negligences and ignorances, and cover them all with the absolute obedience of Thy dear Son, that those sacrifices (of repentance, praise and thanksgiving) which I have offered may be accepted by Thee, in and for the sacrifice of Jesus Christ offered upon the Cross for me.

"In Monday Morning's entry, young Washington had written:

"Direct my thoughts, words and work, wash away my sins in the immaculate Blood of the Lamb, and purge my heart by Thy Holy Spirit...daily frame me more and more into the likeness of Thy Son Jesus Christ.

"And in Monday Evening's:

"Thou gavest thy Son to die for me: and hast given me assurance of salvation, upon my repentance and sincerely endeavoring to conform my life to His holy precepts and example.

"The man who wrote these words was no Deist[5], but a very devout Christian.

"His mother had been a strong source of spiritual life in his early years. On the day he left home to begin a lifetime of serving his country, she said to him: 'Remember that God only is our sure trust. To Him, I commend you.' and then she added, 'My son, neglect not the duty of secret prayer.' The extensive notes on the margins of his prayer-filled notebook indicate that Washington heeded this advice. His discipline of private prayer was to stand him in good stead in the years to come.

"Entering the Virginia militia as a young officer, Washington distinguished himself in combat during the French and Indian Wars. One of the campaigns in which he served included the Battle of the Monongahela, July 9, 1755. In this action, the British forces were decimated, and his commanding officer, General Edward Braddock, was killed. Fifteen years after this battle, Washington and his life-long friend Dr. Craik were exploring wilderness territory in the Western Reserve. Near the junction of the Kanawha and Ohio Rivers, a band of Indians came to them with an interpreter. The leader of the band was an old and venerable chief, who wished to have words with Washington. A council fire was kindled, and this is what the chief said:

---

[5] Deist is defined as: 1) One who believes in the existence of a God on the evidence of reason and nature only, with rejection of supernatural revelation.

2) One who believes in a God who created the world but has since remained indifferent to his creation.

CHAPTER 29: THREE GREAT MEN OF FAITH 497

"'I am a chief and ruler over my tribes. My influence extends to the waters of the great lakes, and to the far blue mountains. I traveled a long and weary path, that I might see the young warrior of the great battle. It was on the day when the white man's blood mixed with the streams of our forest, that I first beheld this chief. I called to my young men and said: "Mark yon tall and daring warrior? He is not of the red-coat tribe--he hath an Indian's wisdom, and his warriors fight as we do-- himself alone is exposed. Quick let your aim be certain, and he dies.' Our rifles were leveled, rifles which, but for him, knew not how to miss....'Twas all in vain; a power mightier far than we shielded him from harm. He cannot die in battle. I am old, and soon shall be gathered to the great council fire of my fathers in the land of shades, but ere I go, there is something that bids me speak in the voice of prophecy: Listen! The Great Spirit protects that man, and guides his destinies--he will become the chief of nations and a people yet unborn will hail him as the founder of a mighty empire.'

"Confirmation of this episode can be found in Bancroft's definitive nineteenth-century history of th United States. And at that same battle, according to other sources, as well as Washington's journal, the 23 year old colonel had two horses shot out from under him and four musket balls pass through his coat. There was nothing wrong with the Indians' marksmanship!

"'Death,' wrote Washington to his brother, Jack, 'Was leveling my companions on every side of me, but by the all-powerful dispensations of Providence, I have been protected.' This conviction was further shared by Samuel Davies, the famous Virginia clergyman, who wrote. 'To the public, I point out that heroic youth....whom I cannot but hope Providence has preserved in so signal a manner for some important service to his country.' Indeed, such was Washigton's fame that across the ocean, Lord Halifax was to ask, 'Who is Mr. Washington? I know nothing of him, but that they say he behaved in Braddock's action as bravely as if he really loved the whistling of bullets.'

"This was God's man, chosen for the hour of America's greatest crisis."....

(When he arrived at Cambridge he found that the gathering of the American militias gave the atmosphere of a happy jamboree rather than a military encampment.) ......"But leaving was impossible, and Washington knew it. For he was a man under authority--God's and Country's--and his life was not his own.

"Because he had spent his life under authority, Washington knew firsthand the value of discipline and obedience. He had been disciplining himself for years, and now by the example he set, it was clear that he expected his officers to do the same, That meant that officers were expected to be present at all inspections, assemblies, meals, and other functions on time, and in correct uniform. And while he did not require them to rise at 4:30 a.m., as he sometimes did, they were to curb their own foul language forthwith....

"But he was willing to do whatever he felt God would have him do, regardless of what it would cost him in reputation or popularity.

"Thus the change in the attitude of the Continental Army, that summer of 1775, was rapid and dramatic. The day after Washington formally took command, the following general order was issued:

"'The General most earnestly requires and expects a due observance of those articles of war established for the government of the army, which forbid profane cursing, swearing and drunkenness. And in like manner, he requires and expects of all officers and soldiers not engaged in actual duty, a punctual attendance of Divine services, to implore the blessing of Heaven upon the means used for our safety and defense.'"

(The lowest point for the new nation came in the winter of 1777 when the Patriot forces almost froze or starved or died of diseases at Valley Forge, Pa.).

But "This, then was the miracle of Valley Forge. That the men endured was indeed amazing to all who knew of their circumstances. But the reason they endured--the reason they believed in God's deliverance--was simple: they could believe, because their General did believe.

"Washington made no secret of his Christian faith. In His general order calling for divine services every Sunday, he said: 'To the distinguished character of a Patriot, it should be our highest glory to add the more distinguished character of a Christian.' And others, such as the pastor of a nearby Lutheran church, Henry Muhlenberg, would note his faith with approval:

"'I heard a fine example today, namely, that His Excellency General Washington rode around among his army yesterday and admonished each and every one to fear God, to put away the wickedness that has set in and become so general, and to practice the Christian virtues. From all appearances, this gentleman does not belong to the so-called world of society, for he respects God's Word, believes in the atonement through Christ, and bears himself in humility and gentleness. Therefore, the Lord God has also singularly, yea, marvelously, preserved him from harm in the midst of countless perils, ambuscades, fatigues, etc., and has hitherto graciously held him in His hand as a chosen vessel.'"

Through 6 long years against almost insurmountable odds,

CHAPTER 29: THREE GREAT MEN OF FAITH

discouragements, dangers from the enemy, and jealousies and treasons from within, Washington resolutely led the newly birthed nation of 13 former British colonies to victory in October 1781 at the surrender of the British General Cornwallis at Yorktown, Virginia. -------Through the formulation of a durable, God-inspired Constitution, led daily in prayer at the urging of the oldest delegate, Ben Franklin (see "The Turning Point" following these accounts). -------Through two unanimously elected terms as president from 1789 to his retirement in March 1797. ------- And, finally, to his untimely death from pneumonia, December 14, 1799 at age 67 at his beloved home, Mt. Vernon, on the Potomac. Surely this God-fearing man had earned this nation's lasting appreciation and honor expressed in the saying, "First in war, First in peace, First in the hearts of his countrymen." Yes, by the grace of Almighty God he had led this nation to a noble beginning, honoring God, his Son Jesus Christ and His Holy Word!

One of the most remarkable stories of God's many providences for Washington and his American forces has to do with a Jewish man who greatly helped in the Revolution and went in debt doing it. We had heard this for a long time but didn't know his name or details.

Finally, we called a dear Jewish friend, Educator and Hebrew scholar, Dr. Louis Kaplan, here in Baltimore, who knew immediately the name of the Jewish patriot, Haym Salomon, and referred us to the local Jewish Historical Society. We warmly credit them for this story.

AN AMAZING JEWISH PATRIOT

Haym Salomon helped finance Washington's army and secure America's independence. Haym was a gentlemen of precision and integrity, an immigrant from Poland, who quickly established his devotion to the cause of American Liberty, and energetically aided the efforts to finance the war. He was born is Lissa, Poland in 1740. As a youth he had to flee Poland. He learned several languages on his way to America where he made his home in N.Y.

He chose without hesitation to devote his energies and resources to American independence knowing that in the emerging nation, Jews would have the privilege of participating in public life and at the same time would have religious freedom. He helped to lay the foundation to what would become a nation of nations.

In 1776 the British arrested him in New York and after a term in the provost prison he was rearrested and sentenced to death as a spy--- on charges that he had received orders from General Washington to burn their fleets and destroy their storehouses, which he attempted to execute to their great injury and damage. He escaped with a bribe of gold, being aided in escape from prison by a friend of Gen. McDougall and a group of patriots, "The Sons of Liberty." In N.Y. he helped French and American prisoners to escape. After escaping from British occupation he went to Philadelphia and became a patriotic merchant and successful broker.

In Philadelphia financier Robert Morris noted Haym's financial skills and linguistic ability. France and Holland were ready and willing to lend money to the Revolutionary cause. Haym conducted negotiations which made possible for Americans to buy weapons, food, uniforms and pay to maintain civilian and military morale. Salomon made loans without charge.

He died on January 6, 1785 at age 45, leaving his pregnant wife and 3 children seriously in debt. Most of his holdings were in depreciating government notes, about $353,744.45, never repaid. Fortunately his young wife would remarry and be well cared for.
Baruch Ha Shem!

This is another instance of the truth of God's Word in Ecclesiastes 11:1

....Cast thy bread upon the waters, for thou shall find it after many days.

God has returned a mountain of bread to feed Haym's Jewish people here and in Israel since those early days!!! Again, Baruch Ha Shem!

ON THE WARNING MISSION - MR. SID TRIED OUT OHIO GOVERNOR'S MUSEUM-PIECE DESK! HE WISHED HE COULD PROCLAIM A DAY OF PRAYER AND FASTING FOR THE NATION TO STOP ALL ABORTIONS SINCE ALL OF THEM ARE PREMEDITATED, 1ST DEGREE MURDERS OF INNOCENT BABIES WHO HAVE THE CONSTITUTIONAL RIGHT TO LIFE; TO RETURN THE BIBLE AND PRAYER TO ALL OUR SCHOOLS; AND TO STAND BY ISRAEL IN HER STRUGGLE FOR SURVIVAL!

CHAPTER 29: THREE GREAT MEN OF FAITH 501

THE TURNING POINT[6]
By: John S. Kelley

It was hot and humid in Philadelphia. The Pennsylvania State House, later to be known as Independence Hall, was filled with the best minds from 12 of the 13 newly independent American States. (Only Rhode Island was not represented.)

They had assembled daily since May 14, (1787) to hammer out a Constitution to give national meaning to the Declaration of Independence signed 11 years earlier.

But it was now June 28, and the Constitutional Convention had creaked almost to a stop. Even under the able leadership of General George Washington, the convention was in danger of arguing itself to death. There had been wrangling and disagreement on nearly every point. William Few, one of four delegates from Georgia, described that morning of June 28 as "an awful and critical moment. If the convention had then adjourned," he said, "the dissolution of the union of the States seemed inevitable."

A voice broke a momentary silence. It was that of Benjamin Franklin, Pennsylvania's elder statesman-inventor and the oldest of the delegates at 81. He had said little these past days, but now he turned to George Washington. With the curious round eyeglasses he had invented himself sitting low on his nose, he said: "In this situation of this assembly, groping as it were in the dark to find political truth, and scarce able to distinguish it when presented to us, how has it happened, Sir, that we have not hitherto once thought of humbly applying to the Father of lights to illuminate our understandings?"

Franklin reminded the delegates they were sitting in the very room where the Continental Congress had offered prayers at the beginning of the Revolutionary War. "Our prayers, Sir, were heard, and they were graciously answered," said Franklin. "All of us who were engaged in the struggle must have observed frequent instances of a superintending providence in our favor..."And have we now forgotten that powerful Friend?....I have lived a long time, Sir, and the longer I live, the more convincing proofs I see of this truth--that God governs in the affairs of men."

The delegates listened intently as the great statesman continued: "I firmly believe that without His concurring aid we shall succeed in this political building no better than the builders of Babel. And what is worse, mankind may hereafter from this unfortunate instance despair of establishing governments by human wisdom and leave it to chance, war, and conquest. I therefore beg leave to move that henceforth prayers imploring the assistance of heaven and its blessings on our deliberations be held in this assembly every morning before we proceed to business."

The Convention was stunned and embarrassed. Franklin's motion was quickly seconded, but dissenting voices were heard once again in the historic hall. Some argued there was no money to pay a chaplain. Alexander Hamilton warned that holding prayers might lead the public to believe the convention was a failure. Finally Edmund Randolph, governor of Virginia, proposed that a special sermon be preached on July 4, and that from then on prayers be used. It was settled.

The convention, brought by Franklin's wisdom to an awareness of its need for strengths which the delegates did not possess, went on. The great Constitution gradually became a living document. On September 17, 1787, it was signed by all but three of the delegates. Ratification by the States was completed the following year. A nation had been born.

---

[6] Copyright 1974 by The General Council of the Assemblies of God in the Pentecostal Evangel". Used with permission.

ABRAHAM LINCOLN

In Dr. Watson F. Pindell's book, "Milestones To Immortality," about "The Pilgrimage of Abraham Lincoln," there is an introduction by Dr. D. James Kennedy, senior minister of Coral Ridge Presbyterian Church in Ft. Lauderdale, Florida. Dr. Kennedy says, "I do not believe it is possible to understand Lincoln to any depth unless we understand something of the spiritual quest and spiritual discovery of his life. It has well been said he was mastered by one book and that book was the Bible."

We desire in the next few pages, quoting from Dr. Pindell's book, to show that, although at times Lincoln seemed to be a skeptic, "he could never escape the spiritual influence of his mother and her love of God and the Bible." And Dr. Kennedy adds that "Lincoln's melancholy and emptiness was ended at Gettysburg, when Lincoln said in a personal letter that as he looked out over those thousands of white crosses, he 'then and there consecrated his heart to Christ,' and there he found the peace which had so long eluded him. His spiritual discovery is clearly felt in the majestic cadence of his Second Inaugural Address."

Dr. Pindell also quotes Joseph W. Alsop in a recent speech at Franklin and Marshall College which shows an amazing fact about Lincoln: "It would be an immense gain if all professors of American History were required to get most of the Bible by heart as Lincoln did."

In many ways Abraham Lincoln, like Christopher Columbus and George Washington before him, was another strange giant of a man raised up by God's hand to achieve something very great in God's plan for mankind. Columbus, under God's hand, opened up a New World; Washington, under God's hand, birthed a New Nation into freedom; Lincoln, by God's hand, would keep that New Nation from splitting forever, and set a race free from slavery.

Frontier Life

Lincoln was born near Hodgenville, Ky. on February 12, 1809 to Thomas and Nancy Lincoln, two hardy pioneers on the log-cabin frontier of America at that time. Thomas, as a boy, had seen his own father killed in their cornfield by marauding Indians in a sneak attack. Nancy, taller and heavier than average, faithfully read her Bible, and served her family. Abraham attended school at the age of 6 with his sister Sarah, both having been taught their letters by their mother, both making excellent progress in reading and writing. By the age of 7, "Abraham shared with his sister in the Bible readings conducted in the cabin on those Sundays when preaching was not available at the Little Mount

CHAPTER 29: THREE GREAT MEN OF FAITH

Separate Baptist Church." The family was led regularly by Thomas Lincoln in this prayer before each meal: "Fit and prepare us for humble service, we beg for Christ's sake. Amen."

In 1816, in Abraham's 8th year, Thomas Lincoln moved his family 100 miles north into Indiana, where land titles were sure and where the state did not permit slavery. Like other pioneers of the day they built their own log cabins for homes often with dirt floors and wooden windows. Fortunately, Thomas Lincoln was a good carpenter. Because of Abraham's rapid gain in reading and writing he became the family's official scribe in correspondence with friends back in Kentucky.

Nancy Hanks Lincoln became ill in 1818 with a malady caused by spoiled milk for which there was no known remedy at that time. She knew that she was going to die and called her children to her side and told them to be good and kind to their father, to one another, and to the world. She expressed the hope that they might live as they had been taught by her to live: to love and reverence God. Her coffin was fashioned by Thomas Lincoln using pegs which Abraham whittled to hold the boards together. Some time after the burial a grave-side sermon of salvation, hope and comfort was preached by the Rev. David Elkin of the little Baptist Church they had attended in Kentucky.

After more than a year, Thomas was able to marry a warmhearted widow, with three children of her own, Sally Bush Johnston, whom they had known in the Hodgenville area. With a passion for order and cleanliness she soon revolutionized the housekeeping process of the family and the appearance of Abraham and Sally.

Before his step-mother's coming, Abraham's books were the *Bible*, *Dilworth's Speller* and *Aesop's Fables*. Now she added *Webster's Speller*, *Robinson Crusoe* and the *Arabian Nights*. Another book acquired about this time was *Pilgrim's Progress*. Abraham was constantly reading aloud from these books to the family gathered around the fire. He almost knew them by heart. Special passages he would write down on a board, or a paper if he had it, keeping a scrapbook of these treasures. Three other books acquired at the time were quite influential on him: *Life of George Washington* by Mason Weems, *Autobiography of Benjamin Franklin,* and *Lessons in Elocution* by William Scott. His thirst for knowledge seemed unquenchable!

Abraham went again to school briefly at the age of 11, hiking 9 miles each way. His total schooling, including the months in Kentucky, hardly amounted to a full year, but the lack of formal schooling did not prevent him from continuing his search for knowledge. Eventually, like George Washington, he would study surveying and become proficient in it. He also began studying debating and then the serious study of law. He had an obsession about books, saying, "The things I want to know are in books; my best friend is the man who will get me a book I have never read." "There is something peculiarsome about Abe," his friends would say about his love of books.

Although tough as nails from hard work in farming, rail splitting and excelling in the roughest of sports with the roughest of young men, he never drank intoxicants nor used tobacco. He was seldom profane and never blasphemous. His step-mother said, "Abe was the best boy I ever saw, or ever expect to see. He never told me a lie." His personal integrity, truthfulness, honesty and kind heart were virtues traced to his father, Thomas. Although he worked hard for his father and for neighbors, it became clear that farming was not his first love. "My father taught me to do farm work, but he didn't teach me to love it," he often said.

At 19 Abraham and a friend steered a flatboat loaded with farm produce to New Orleans for the princely sum of $8 a month, plus his passage back. A dangerous and demanding adventure it was, for a distance of 1222 miles. It took 3 months and he earned $24 which went to his father, as required in those days.

In March 1830, not long after Abraham's 21st birthday, the Lincolns moved 200 miles westward to Macon County, Ill., and the next year they moved 100 miles southeast to Coles County. At 22, now legally free of giving his wages to his father, Abraham left home to do another flatboat trip to New Orleans. He returned to New Salem, a growing town outside of Springfield, Ill., to undertake making a living for himself. At this time he cast his first ballot and made speeches for Whig party candidates. The man whose flatboat Lincoln had guided to New Orleans, employed him as a clerk in his general store. This store owner, Denton Offutt, was a great booster of Lincoln's, telling everyone that Lincoln knew more than any man in the United States! "Someday," Offut said, "he will be the President of this country!" Further he said, "He can outrun and outwrestle any man in Sangamon County."

Early Political Awakening

At the age of 23, in March 1830, he became a candidate for the State legislature! He had joined a debating society in 1830 also and was making influential friends, one of whom encouraged him to begin the study of law.

In appearance Lincoln at this time was rugged, slender, broad-shouldered, and 6 feet 4 inches tall. Amiable and self assured and wise for his years. For his candidacy, he wrote a remarkable piece on principles of education, general improvements and limitations on interest rates, which appeared in the *Sangamo Journal*, the erudition of which

CHAPTER 29: THREE GREAT MEN OF FAITH

would do credit to a college graduate. Lincoln lost the election, running eighth among thirteen, but had found the field of service that intrigued him.

In the three months before the election he served in a militia call-up to face an Indian attack scare, (The Black Hawks). The men in his company chose him to be their captain, a great honor he always felt. The only bloodshed was from massive attacks by swarms of mosquitoes!

With his friend, Wm. Berry, Lincoln joined in partnership to buy Offutt's general store. This venture failed two years later when Berry died, leaving the store $1,100 in debt (a great amount of money in those days!) Lincoln assumed the burden to repay the debt (which he called his "National Debt") earning him the nickname of "Honest Abe." This nickname was proved true in the past as a clerk for Offutt. When Abraham made a mistake in change or weight of a purchase, after work he would walk many miles to repay 6 1/4 cents or deliver a quarter pound of tea he felt due for his own mistake. Out of work and out of money, but not out of friends, Lincoln was urged by his friend, John Calhoun, the surveyor of Sangamon County, to study the book, *The Theory and Practice of Surveying*, and he would make him his deputy. In six weeks intense study he fully mastered the book and got the job!

In the spring of 1834, at age 25, Lincoln ran again for the State Legislature and was successful. A Whig state leader, John T. Stewart, admired young Lincoln and encouraged him to study law, lending him books with which to begin. He persevered in his study of law, eventually purchasing a set of Blackstone's *Commentaries on the Laws of England* at an auction. On September 9, 1836, age 27, he passed his oral bar examination which gave him the privilege of hanging out his shingle, "*A. Lincoln, Attorney-at-Law!*"

He finally paid off his "National Debt" through very hard work and the help of many friends. He turned his full efforts to the learning and practice of law and steadily improved his performance, through three partnerships, eventually becoming one of the best trial lawyers in Illinois. Among his talents were: "A keen sense of justice, a magnetic personality, an uncanny mastery of convincing speech, tact, and the gift of presenting complex matters in simple terms."

After an up and down courtship with Mary Todd, a young lady from a high social and finishing school background, and nine years younger, Lincoln and she were married, Nov. 4, 1842. Mary had earlier avowed that she was determined to marry a man who would one day be President, and she did!

In 1846, after 4 terms in the Illinois legislature, Lincoln ran for Congress. His opponent accused him of being an infidel and a scoffer at Christianity. In a handbill dated July 31, 1846, Lincoln answered the charges this way: "That I am not a member of any Christian Church is true; but I have never denied the truth of the Scriptures; and I have never spoken with intentional disrespect of religion in general....

"Probably it is to be my lot to go on in a twilight, feeling and reasoning my way through life, as questioning, doubting Thomas did. But in my poor, maimed, withered way, I bear with me as I go on a seeking spirit of desire for a faith that was with him of old time, who, in his need, as I in mine, exclaimed, 'Help Thou my unbelief.'

"Lincoln here defined himself as a seeker after truth who had found the Scriptures helpful in his search. For comfort he had the sure promise, **Seek and ye shall find.** (Luke 11:9). His faith in Christ became evident in succeeding years."

Finding The Truth

In 1850 the death of his 4 year old son Willie left Lincoln inconsolable. The minister who preached the funeral sermon, the Rev. James Smith, proved a great help to the Lincolns. Smith, a Scotsman, had bested a leading atheist in a 3 week debate in April, 1841. Out of this he published in 2 volumes his defense for the Scriptures, called *The Christian's Defence*. Lincoln acquired the set and undertook a lawyer-like investigation of the Bible. Later he told his brother-in-law, Ninian Edwards: "I have been reading a work of Dr. Smith on the evidences of the Christian religion, and have heard him preach and converse on the subject and am now convinced as to the truth of Christianity."

One result of his study was his wife Mary becoming a member of Smith's Presbyterian Church and her renting a pew in the Lincoln name. Although Lincoln did not become a member, he frequently attended the Sunday morning service when he was in town. Lincoln had his own ideas of what preaching ought to be. He reportedly said, 'I do not like to hear cut and dried sermons. When I hear a man preach I like to see him act as if he were fighting bees!'

When his father, Thomas Lincoln, was dying in early January 1851, Lincoln wrote to his step-brother, "I sincerely hope that father may recover his health, but at all events, tell him to remember to call upon and confide in our great and good Merciful Maker, Who will not turn away from him in any extremity. He notes the fall of a sparrow and numbers the hairs of our heads, and He will not forget the dying man and his trust in Him."

"One day he received a summons to prepare the will of a dying woman. He drove out to her home in the country, his young friend Gilbert J. Greene accompanying him to act as witness. Facing death, the expiring woman expressed her faith in God. She spoke of His faithfulness to her all her life. Lincoln was deeply impressed. 'Your faith in Christ is true and strong. You are to be congratulated on passing through life so usefully and into the life beyond so hopefully.'

"The woman asked him to read a few verses from the Bible at her side. Instead, he simply quoted from memory part of the 23rd Psalm, **Though I walk through the valley of the shadow of death I will fear no evil, for thou art with me; thy rod and thy staff they comfort me.** Again, without taking the Bible, he repeated such verses as, **Let not your heart be troubled; ye believe in God, believe also in me,** and **In my Father's house are many mansion; if it were not so I would have told you. I go to prepare a place for you.** (John 14:1-2). He then recited the words of the hymn, 'Rock of Ages.'"

"On the return trip to Lincoln's office Greene said to him, 'You have acted as a pastor as well as an attorney today.'"

"Lincoln replied, 'God and eternity and heaven were very near me today.'"

His Sense of Humor

"Lincoln's ever-present sense of humor often came to the surface under surprising circumstances. In answer to an inquiry of a New York firm that asked him for a report on the financial standing of an acquaintance, he replied: 'Yours of the 10th received. First of all, he has a wife and a baby; together they ought to be worth $500,000 to any man. Secondly, he has an office in which there is a table worth $2.50 and three chairs worth say, $1.00. Last of all, there is in one corner a large rat-hole which will bear looking into!'"

His Ten Guidelines

"Over the years Lincoln accumulated a store of wisdom which he expressed in his **Ten Guidelines**. They are:
1. *You cannot bring about prosperity by discouraging thrift.*
2. *You cannot help small men by tearing down big men.*
3. *You cannot strengthen the weak by weakening the strong.*
4. *You cannot lift the wage earner by pulling down the wage payer.*
5. *You cannot help the poor by destroying the rich.*
6. *You cannot keep out of trouble by spending more than your income.*
7. *You cannot further the brotherhood of men by inciting class hatred.*
8. *You cannot establish security on borrowed money.*
9. *You cannot build character and courage by taking away a man's initiative and independence.*
10. *You cannot help men permanently by doing for them what they should and could do for themselves.*"

No doubt Lincoln felt these were some additional rules of life that would be complimentary to the 10 Commandments of God which he knew so well and by heart.

Against Slavery

"At the formation of the Federal Union there had been general agreement that slavery was an evil to be suppressed rather then a good to be encouraged. Evidence of this feeling was the unanimous sentiment at the Constitutional Convention to abolish the African slave trade in 1808."

Lincoln was very much against slavery and the spread of it. And in the middle 1850's began speaking out against the spread of this evil saying, "No man is good enough to govern another man without that man's consent."

The "Republican Party," founded in Wisconsin in 1854, came into Illinois in 1856 and Abe Lincoln soon became its state leader. In a race against Stephen A. Douglas, Lincoln as the Republican candidate, made these memorable remarks: "A house divided against itself cannot stand. I believe that this government cannot endure permanently half slave and half free. I do not expect the Union to be dissolved--I do not expect the house to fall--but I do expect it will cease to be divided..." In his opinion the Federal and State Governments should work together to restrain the spread of slavery. At the end of the Douglas debates, Lincoln's turn for rebuttal came and he showed his quick sense of humor by taking off his coat, handing it to a young man and saying with a smile, "Here, you hold my clothes while I stone Stephen." (A reference to Paul in the Bible.) Lincoln out-polled Douglas by over 5,000 votes, but an apportionment system in the legislature voted Douglas the election 54 to 46. Lincoln's humor still held in this frustrating loss. "He summed up his feelings in the wry statement of the boy who stubbed his toe. 'It hurts too much to laugh and I am too big to cry.'"

The debates over the slavery and states rights questions greatly increased across the land. Lincoln became the major spokesman of the Republican Party against the spread of slavery and against secession over it, and its nominee for President.

Elected President!

So in 1860 Lincoln was elected as President of the nation, a badly fractured nation over those questions. Thurlow Weed, an Albany newspaper editor, came to interview Lincoln concerning the political problems facing the nation. "He told his friends, 'Lincoln talked without restraint, but I never heard him use a profane or indecent word, or tell a story that might not be repeated in the presence of ladies.'"

In those days the President would be inaugurated on March 4, so

CHAPTER 29: THREE GREAT MEN OF FAITH

on February 21, 1861, Lincoln and his family took the train at Springfield, Ill., with their destination Washington, D.C. In a cold drizzle he bade the gathered well wishers farewell: "Friends, no one who has never been in a like position can understand my feelings at this hour nor the oppressive sadness I feel at this parting.

"For more than a quarter century I have lived among you, and during that time I have received nothing but kindness at your hands. Here the most sacred trusts of earth were assumed; here all my children were born and here one of them lies buried. To you, dear friends, I owe all that I have, all that I am. All the strange checkered past seems to crowd now upon my mind.

"Today I leave you; I go to assume a task more difficult than that which devolved upon General Washington. Unless the great God who assisted him shall be with me and aid me, I must fail. But if the same Omniscient Mind and the same Almighty Arm that directed and protected him shall guide and support me, I shall not fail; I shall succeed.

"Trusting in Him, who can go with me, and remain with you and be everywhere for good, let us confidently hope that all will yet be well. To His care commending you, as I hope in your prayers you will commend me, I bid you an affectionate farewell."

His Humor Questioned!

"Lincoln's humor was not always understood. It was a necessary therapy for his fits of depression. It was a device to 'whistle down sadness,' as his friend Judge David Davis put the matter. Lincoln said, 'I laugh because I must not weep--that is all, that is all.' He remarked on another occasion: 'I tell you the truth when I say that a funny story, if it has the element of genuine wit, has the same effect on me that I suppose a good square drink of whiskey has on an old toper; it puts new life into me.'"

Uphill Path!

On March 4, 1861, Lincoln made his First Inaugural Address, carefully reasoned and persuasive, pointing to slavery as immoral and secession as the essence of anarchy. "His clarity, candor, and loftiness of purpose made him a hard man to resist. Although his path led uphill all the way, his spirit never faltered."

Even as Lincoln was being inaugurated, 7 southern states had already seceded and formed the Confederate States of America, electing Jefferson Davis of Mississippi as President of the Confederacy, with a new constitution making slavery a legal part of their economy and states rights were made supreme.

In the north, Lincoln and his cabinet were facing much uncertainty and confusion. Many were questioning if Lincoln had the statesmanship necessary to handle this momentous crisis?

"Soon after settling in the White House, the Lincolns rented a pew in the New York Avenue Presbyterian Church, where Mrs. Lincoln became a member. The whole family regularly attended the Sunday morning service. During prayer by the minister, Dr. Phineas D. Gurley, Lincoln also stood in an attitude of reverence, although it was customary for the congregation to remain seated! (A stained glass window of this church now shows a tall figure reverently standing as the minister prays while the congregation remains seated.)

Today we know that Lincoln, with God's help, did have the qualities necessary for this great crisis!

Later a Presbyterian elder recalled his privilege of being seated not far from Mr. Lincoln at Sunday services for a year and a half and described his attitude as always that of an earnest and devout worshiper. Lincoln was a serious Church goer and seeker after God rather than a church member.

"Lincoln also attended the midweek service! To avoid pestering office-seekers and contractors, he gave up sitting with the congregation. He entered by a side door and sat in the minister's darkened study with the door ajar that led to the prayer meeting. Here he could be a silent listener to the prayers offered by the congregation. Lincoln always found that listening to people talking to God was a greater source of strength than listening to people talking about God. To make him comfortable, Dr. Gurley had a large divan made to accommodate Lincoln's unusual length of leg, for which the average chair made no allowance. (This divan can be seen today at the church.)"

The War Begins

Lincoln faced profound problems of office-seekers, of appointing responsible people such as ambassadors, of selecting men to be heads of departments, at the same time dealing with the breakup of the Union. As he surveyed the scramble for office in a government that was disintegrating, Lincoln remarked, "I feel like a man whose house has caught fire at one end and yet he is renting rooms at the other."

Then came the first shots of the war: Confederate forces fired on Federal troops at Ft. Sumter in the Charleston, S.C. harbor. And so the war was on. In August 1861 at the request of a joint House and Senate committee, the President issued an executive proclamation for "a day of public humiliation, prayer, and fasting to be observed by the people of the United States." He would call for prayer many times!

"In his proclamation Lincoln said: 'It is fit and becoming in all

CHAPTER 29: THREE GREAT MEN OF FAITH

people, at all times, to acknowledge and revere the Supreme Government of God; to bow in humble submission to his chastisement; to confess and deplore their sins and transgressions in the full conviction that the fear of the Lord is the beginning of wisdom; and to pray, with all fervency and contrition for the pardon of their past offenses, and for a blessing upon their present and prospective action."

We must say that Lincoln was too honest a man to ever call the people to do something he didn't believe in.

"The first ten months in the White House were one long nightmare for Lincoln. Favor-seekers hounded him incessantly, war stresses strained every part of the nation, and success proved elusive. Trying to keep a country united in which one vociferous group insisted on the abolition of slavery while an equally noisy faction shouted that slavery should be untouched, taxed him to the limits of his patience and his powers."

And besides all this Lincoln was having economic difficulties as well as political ones. Getting his generals and armies organized and moving into action were part of the overall problems. Someone wanted him to fire U.S. Grant for a temporary tactical failure and probably because he was known to be a heavy drinker.

"Lincoln listened silently to all the arguments offered as to why he should relieve Grant from his command. Finally, he gathered himself up in his chair and said with impressive earnestness: 'I cannot spare this man--he fights!'"

"I am in no boastful mood. I shall not do more than I can; but I shall do all that I can to save the government, which is my sworn duty as well as my personal inclination. I shall do nothing in malice. What I deal with is too vast for malicious dealing."

"He remarked to an observer, 'I do the very best I know how--the very best I can; and I mean to keep doing so until the end. If the end brings me out all right, what is said against me will not amount to anything. If the end brings me out wrong, ten angels swearing I was right would make no difference.'"

A basic principle he set for himself was this, "I shall correct errors when shown to be errors, and I shall adopt new views as fast as they shall appear to be true views." Always his primary purpose was to preserve the Union.

The battles of minds and guns were not going well for Lincoln in June of 1862, but he courageously wrote, "I expect to maintain this contest until successful or until I die, or am conquered, or my term expires, or Congress or the country forsakes me."

Without consulting his cabinet Lincoln drew up an Emancipation Proclamation that called for the freeing of all slaves, January 1, 1863.

Lincoln's political enemies were enraged and called his Emancipation Proclamation, "Lincoln's Thunderbolt."

Observe The Sabbath!

"Another notable document came out of the White House in November 1862. It was headed, 'General Order Respecting the Observance of the Sabbath Day in the Army and the Navy.' The order read, 'The President, Commander-in-chief of the Army and Navy, desires and enjoins the orderly observance of the Sabbath by the officers and men in the military and naval services. The importance for man and beast of the prescribed weekly rest, the sacred rights of Christian soldiers and sailors, a becoming deference to the best sentiment of a Christian people, and a due regard for the Divine will, demand that Sunday labor in the army and navy be reduced to the measure of strict necessity. The discipline and character of the national forces should not suffer, nor the cause they defend be imperiled by the profanation of the day or the name of the Most High.'"

Although Lincoln may not have written this document, obviously it expressed his will or he would have changed it before he signed it.

No matter the seriousness of the topic or the situation, Lincoln could often turn up a humorous anecdote. "One that he enjoyed had to do with a man who had entered the theater just as the curtain went up. So interested was he in the stage performance that he put his tall silk hat, open side up, on the seat next to him. He failed to notice a very stout woman approaching this seat. She sat down on his tall silk hat. There was a crunching noise. The owner of the flattened hat reached for it as the stout woman hastily arose. He looked sorrowfully at his ruined hat, then looked reproachfully at the woman. 'Madam, I could have told you my hat would not fit you before you tried it on!'"

A Congressman, during these sorrowful days, found the President reading a bit of nonsense by Artemus Ward, one of his favorite humorists. Resentfully he asked the President how he could indulge in such levity? "Then, as Arnold told the story, the President threw down the book, tears streamed down his cheeks, and his whole frame shook as he burst forth, 'Mr. Arnold, if I could not get momentary respite from the crushing burden I am constantly carrying, my heart would break!' Arnold belatedly understood that laughter and humor were at times the mask behind which Lincoln hid his grief."

Finally, in the summer of 1863, the Union began seeing signs of victory and was rejoicing over triumphs at Gettysburg and Vicksburg and elsewhere. Not long after the horrendous losses on both sides at Gettysburg, a memorial committee arranged for Edward Everett, a famous orator, to give the main address. Many other dignitaries were invited. "Two weeks before the occasion Lincoln received a letter saying, 'It is our desire that after the oration, you, as Chief Executive of the nation, formally set apart the grounds to their sacred use by a few appropriate remarks.' Everett spoke for nearly two hours before giving way to Lincoln. In less than two minutes the President delivered his Gettysburg classic. His address is a living witness to the truth that a speech need not be everlasting to be immortal! Surely, these two hundred and sixty-seven words will stir men's hearts to the end of recorded time.

THE GETTYSBURG ADDRESS

"Fourscore and seven years ago, our fathers brought forth on this continent a new nation, conceived in liberty and dedicated to the proposition that all men are created equal.

"Now we are engaged in a great civil war, testing whether that nation--or any nation, so conceived and so dedicated--can long endure.

"We are met on a great battlefield of that war. We are met to dedicate a portion of it as the final resting place of those who have given their lives that that nation might live.

"It is altogether fitting and proper that we should do this.

"But, in a larger sense, we cannot dedicate, we cannot consecrate, we cannot hallow this ground. The brave men, living and dead, who struggled here, have consecrated it far above our poor power to add or subtract.

"The world will little note nor long remember what we say here; but it can never forget what they did here.

"It is for us, the living, rather, to be dedicated to the unfinished work that they who fought here have thus far so nobly advanced. It is rather for us to be here dedicated to the task remaining before us; that from these honored dead, we take increased devotion to that cause for which they gave the last full measure of devotion; that we here highly resolve that these dead shall not have died in vain; that this nation, under God, shall have a new birth of freedom; and that government of the people, by the people, for the people, shall not perish from the earth."

Some antagonistic reporters called the President's remarks silly and shameful. But the reporter for the Chicago Tribune wired: "The dedication remarks of President Lincoln will live among the annals of man." The Springfield Republican gave its approval: "His little speech is a perfect gem; deep in feeling, compact in thought and expression, and tasteful and elegant in every word and comma."

At the White House, Lincoln devoted a great deal of time to meeting citizens with special requests during 2-3 hours each weekday. A Miss Wentwoth asked for permission to record the interviews with other petitioners and the President agreed. "The following incident is one among many that she took down and eventually published in "Putnam's Magazine" for November 1870.

'Your petition is granted,' said the President.

'Oh, President Lincoln! I believe that you are a Christian. I thank God for it. I will pray for you every day with my whole heart.'

'I have need of your prayers,' said Lincoln soberly. 'I have need of all the prayers that can be offered for me.'

'Oh, Mr. Lincoln, that is the Christian spirit--that is faith in Jesus! Oh, let me hear you say that you believe in Him!'

'I do,' was the solemn answer. 'I believe in my Saviour.'"

In early June 1864, at The Republican Convention in Baltimore Lincoln was renominated without opposition to run for the Presidency.

That summer Joshua Speed came to visit Lincoln at the Soldiers Home, 3 miles from the White House, the summer home for the Lincolns which afforded some relief from the heat. "As Speed entered the living room he saw Lincoln intently reading his Bible. Approaching him, Speed said with some sarcasm, 'I am glad to see you are profitably engaged.'

"'Yes,' agreed Lincoln quietly, 'I am profitably engaged.'

"'Well,' asserted Speed, more in surprise than in anger, 'If you have recovered from your skepticism, I am sorry that I have not.'

"Lincoln arose, looked Speed earnestly in the face, and placing his hand on his shoulder, said emphatically, 'You are wrong, Speed; take all of this book upon reason that you can, and the balance on faith, and you will live and die a happier man.'"

In a letter of September 4, 1864, Lincoln showed how persistently he looked to God. This letter was written to Mrs. Eliza Gurney, a Quaker woman, who had previously prayed with him in the White House:

CHAPTER 29: THREE GREAT MEN OF FAITH

"In all it has been your purpose to strengthen my reliance on God. I am much indebted to the good Christian people of the country for their constant prayers and consolations, and to no one more than yourself. The purposes of the Almighty are perfect, and thus prevail, though we erring mortals may fail to accurately perceive them in advance. We hoped for a happy termination of this terrible war long before this; but God knows best, and has ruled otherwise. We shall yet acknowledge His wisdom, and our own error therein. Meanwhile we must work earnestly in the best lights He gives us, trusting that so working still conduces to the great end he ordains. Surely He intends some great good to follow this mighty convulsion, which no mortal could make and no mortal could stay."

"My enemies pretend I am now carrying on this war for the sole purpose of abolition. So long as I am President, it shall be carried on for the purpose of restoring the Union. But no human power can subdue this rebellion without the use of the emancipation policy, and every other policy calculated to weaken the moral and physical forces of the rebellion...Let my enemies prove to the country that the destruction of slavery is not necessary to a restoration of the Union. I will abide the result."

To a candidate for Lt. Governor of Illinois on the Union ticket, he passed on a pledge of devotion to the Union cause with these words, "I will tell you what the people want. They want and must have success. But whether that comes or not, I shall stay right here and do my duty. Here I shall be. And they may come and hang me on that tree (pointing out of the window), but God helping me, I shall never desert my post."

"Lincoln summed up the whole matter of reelection in a brief farmer's proverb: 'I am reminded in this connection of a story of an Old Dutch farmer who remarked to a companion once that it was not best to swap horses when crossing a stream!'"

The Democrats of that day well nigh exhausted the English language of epithets against Lincoln in condemning his alleged faults, calling him at least 20 horrible, abusive, slanderous names.

"Early in September 1864, the black people of Baltimore presented Lincoln with an ornate, gold-decorated Bible as an expression of their respect and affection. Lincoln's response gave a clear indication of his unreserved acceptance of the Bible as the Word of God. He wrote: 'In regard to this great book I have but to say it is the best gift God has given to man. All the good Saviour gave to this world was communicated through this book. But for it we would not know right from wrong. All things most desirable for man's welfare, here and hereafter, are to be found portrayed in it. To you I return my most sincere thanks for the elegant copy of the great Book of God which you present.'"

"In Lincoln's defense, Edwin L. Godkin, reporting in the London Daily News said, 'I never heard of his uttering or writing one word to show that these shameless attacks aroused in him a single angry impulse. How many men of high breeding and culture are there who would pass through a similar ordeal with as much credit?'"

Election day, November 8, 1864 finally arrived and Lincoln's majority was in excess of 400,000, and a total electoral college vote of 212 against 21 for McClellan.

"A semi-humorous note on Lincoln's re-election came in a report of an incident in Middletown, Connecticut. Torchlighters parading past the house of a clergyman read a transparency: 'The angel of the Lord called unto Abraham out of heaven a second time.'" (Genesis 22:15).

"William C. Bryant capsulized the reasons for Lincoln's reelection in these words: 'The plain people believed Lincoln honest, the rich people believed him safe, the soldiers believed him their friend, the religious people believed him God's choice, and even the scoundrels believed it profitable to use his cloak.'"

"A disenchanted Confederate said,'This war was got up drunk but they will have to settle it sober!'"

"Following his re-election Lincoln said a few things to his friend Noah Brooks that are worth repeating. 'I have been driven many times upon my knees by the overwhelming conviction that I had nowhere else to go.' Another acknowledgment of his need of God occurred in his statement to this same friend: 'I should be the most presumptuous blockhead upon this footstool if I for one day thought I could discharge the duties which have come upon me since I came into this place without the aid and enlightenment of One who is wiser and stronger than all others.' Dependence upon God was an enlightening experience for the Lincoln of the White House."

That Lincoln's spiritual pilgrimage and search had brought him into a sound and saving faith in Jesus Christ, and in his Heavenly Father and ours, is clearly seen in the several references to God's Word in his SECOND INAUGURAL ADDRESS on March 4, 1865. (It is considered by many the most Christian state paper ever written by an American

CHAPTER 29: THREE GREAT MEN OF FAITH 517

President!):

"Both parties deprecated war; but one of them would make war rather than let the nation survive, and the other would accept war rather than let it perish. And the war came...

"Neither party expected for the war the magnitude or the duration which it has already attained. Neither anticipated that the cause of the conflict might cease with, or even before, the conflict itself should cease. Each looked for an easier triumph, and a result less fundamental and astounding. Both read the same Bible, and pray to the same God; and each invoke His aid against the other. It may seem strange that any men should dare to ask a just God's assistance in wringing their bread from the sweat of other men's faces (Genesis 3:19); **but let us *judge not, that we be not judged.*** (Matthew 7:1). The prayers of both could not be answered--that of neither has been answered fully.

"The Almighty has His own purposes. ***Woe unto the world because of offenses! for it must needs be that offenses come; but woe to that man by whom the offense cometh.*** (Matthew 18:7). If we shall suppose that American slavery is one of those offenses which, in the providence of God, must come, but which having continued through His appointed time, He now wills to remove, and that He gives to both North and South this terrible war, as the woe due to those by whom the offenses came, shall we discern therein any departure from those divine attributes which believers in a living God always ascribe to Him?

"Fondly do we hope--fervently do we pray--that this mighty scourge of war may speedily pass away. Yet, if God wills that it continue until all the wealth piled by the bondman's two hundred and fifty years of unrequited toil shall be sunk, and until every drop of blood drawn by the lash shall be paid by another drawn by the sword, as was said three thousand years ago, so still it must be said, ***The judgments of the Lord are true and righteous altogether.*** (Psalms 19:9)

"With malice toward none; with charity for all; with firmness in the right as God gives us to see the right, let us strive to finish the work we are in; to bind up the nation's wounds; to care for him who shall have borne the battle and for his widow and his orphan--to do all which may achieve and cherish a just and lasting peace among ourselves, and with all nations."

This address is inscribed along with the Gettysburg address in the Lincoln Memorial in our nation's Capital, Washington, D.C. Praise The Lord!

As Joshua Speed arrived to visit Lincoln for the last time at the White House, two ladies were expressing their exuberant gratitude to the President. "Lincoln remarked to his friend, 'Speed, when I die, I want it said of me by those who know me best, that I always plucked a thistle and planted a flower when I thought a flower would grow.'"[7]

During another grave national crisis, Mr. Lincoln responded with true wisdom when he said, "Sir, my concern is not whether God is on our side; my great concern is to be on God's side!"[8]

Amazingly, in a dream in the first week of April 1865, one month after his second inauguration, Mr. Lincoln came downstairs at the White House and found a coffin holding a corpse with the face covered. He asked the soldier on guard, "Who is dead in the White House?"

The shocking reply was, "The President. He was killed by an assassin!"

Loud mourning awakened him from the dream, and he could sleep no more that night! He told his wife and bodyguard of it!

He had received 80 letters threatening death and two bullets had passed through his tall hat during his presidency. His trust and hope was in the Lord Jesus Christ. He had God's peace in his heart when, in Ford's Theater on April 14, 1865, Good Friday, his life was taken by the cowardly assassin, John Wilkes Booth. How fitting--he gave his life on the day we remember as the day our Lord Jesus gave His. Lincoln had followed his Lord in final sacrifice. (John 15:13)

What a debt of honor, love and appreciation America owes this man and his memory! Thank God for Abe Lincoln.

---

[7] The many quotes in this section on Lincoln are from "MILESTONES TO IMMORTALITY: The Pilgrimage of Abraham Lincoln," by Watson F. Pindell, copyright 1988, published by Role Models, Inc. 4505 Fitch Ave., Baltimore, Md. 21236, used with permission.

[8] From page 295 "THE LIGHT AND THE GLORY", by Peter Marshall and David Manuel.

CHAPTER 29: THREE GREAT MEN OF FAITH 519

THANK YOU, LORD, FOR THEIR FAITH!

And so we end this brief, but we trust profitable, search for the Guiding Faith of our Founding Fathers. May all who read this book of our Pilgrimage either have THIS FAITH NOW or TURN TO IT QUICKLY. *So then* (saving) *Faith comes by hearing, and hearing by the Word of God.* (Rom.10:17). *But what saith it? The word is nigh thee, even in thy mouth, and in thy heart: that is, the word of faith, which we preach; That if thou shalt confess with thy mouth the Lord Jesus and shall believe in thine heart that God hath raised him from the dead, thou shalt be saved. For with the heart man believeth unto righteousness; and with the mouth confession is made unto salvation. For the Scripture saith, Whosoever believeth on him shall not be ashamed. For there is no difference between the Jew and the Greek; for the same Lord over all is rich unto all that call upon him. For whosoever shall call upon the name of the Lord shall be saved.* (Romans 10:8-13) *But without faith it is impossible to please Him; for he that cometh to God must believe that He is, and that He is a rewarder of them that diligently seek Him.* Hebrews 11:6. *And they said, Believe on the Lord Jesus Christ, and thou shalt be saved, and thy house.* (Acts 16:31). His Name is JESUS! For He came to save us from our sins and reconcile us to our Heavenly Father! "Thank You, Lord, for THIS FAITH that was in our Founding Fathers!"

FAITH OF OUR FATHERS
By: Frederick W. Faber

1. Faith of our fathers! living still
   Inspite of dungeon, fire and sword:
   O how our hearts beat high with joy
   Whene're we hear that glorious word!
   Faith of our fathers! holy faith!
   We will be true to thee till death!

2. Our fathers, chained in prisons dark,
   Were still in heart and conscience free;
   How sweet would be their children's fate,
   If they, like them, could die for thee!
   Faith of our fathers! holy faith!
   We would be true to thee till death!

4. Faith of our fathers! we will love
   Both friend and foe in all our strife,
   And preach thee, too, as love knows how,
   By kindly words and virtuous life:
   Faith of our fathers! holy faith!
   We will be true to thee till death!

520 FIRED AGAIN AND AGAIN, PRAISE THE LORD!

"RETIRING" 1989 AFTER 40 YEARS IN THE MINISTRY

PASTOR JOHN, THE WALLACES, JACK CHAPMAN & GIVATIS JOIN PASTOR EMERITUS SID IN 3RD FLOOR APT.

2 SPECIAL "GRANDDAUGHTERS"
JENNIFER SMITH & SARAH ESTES

"THE MIRACLE TWINS"
DIEDRE & JOSEPH JOHNSON

CHAP. 30

"NOT FINISHED JUST BEGUN"

RETIRING AND REFIRING

My son, forget not my law, but let thine heart keep my commandments: For length of days and long life and peace shall they add to thee. - Proverbs 3:1,2
With long life will I satisfy him and show him my salvation.
- Psalm 91:16

70TH BIRTHDAY AND PRAYER FOR SOMEONE TO CARRY ON AT THE LITTLE TABERNACLE

The year 1988 was a special year of Thanksgiving for us, for its very first day marked the completion for me of 70 years of vigorous and victorious life through many trials and tribulations, by God's Grace, on His planet Earth! As a child I had heard and was taught the Scriptures above and many more about God's desire to give long life to those who love Him, and His commandments. Like King David, and the Apostle Paul, I have loved Him and His mighty Son JESUS since my youth, but, like both of them, there were times when I grievously broke His commandments. Also like David in Psalm 51 and Apostle Paul in Romans 7:14-8:2, I wept on my knees before the Lord confessing my sins, and pleading for forgiveness and deliverance. And He mercifully forgave and cleansed me of my sins, and delivered me from them! Praise His Holy Name forever! He does not want us continuing in a sinful state but in a righteous state! (Rom.6:18,22).

God loved us so much that He sent Jesus to pay the death penalty for our sins, and in resurrection power to yoke us to Himself and lead us into righteous living with victory over sin, over self, over the world, over the devil and all his demons, over death and Hell--to always cause us to triumph in Christ Jesus (II Cor. 2:14,15)! He makes everything work out for our good, as we abide in JESUS and follow His purpose; He proves to us that nothing can separate us from HIS LOVE in JESUS !!!!!(Romans 8:28,38,39). How we thank Him and praise His Holy Name! How we love to sing His praises in His Word! In such Scriptures as:

Ps.23:6 - *Surely goodness and mercy shall follow me all the days of my life and I will dwell in the house of the Lord forever!*

Ps.34:1-4 - *I will bless the Lord at all times, His praise shall continually be in my mouth! My soul shall make her boast in the Lord; the humble shall hear thereof and be glad....*

Ps. 63:3 - *Thy loving kindness is better than life, my lips shall praise Thee. Thus will I bless Thee ...I will lift up my hands in Thy name.*

Ps. 100 - *Make a joyful noise unto the Lord, all ye lands....*

Ps. 103:1-3- *Bless the Lord, O my soul: and all that is within me bless His holy name.*

Isaiah 40:31 - *They that wait upon the Lord shall renew their strength...*

Matt.6:33 - *Seek ye first the kingdom of God, and His righteousness and all these things shall be added unto you,!* **Hallelujah!**

Yes, some would say that there are thousands, even millions of people who have lived 70 years, and much more, without this faith, apparently making it on their own, and without this vaunted help of JESUS. Well, they've made it only by God's Grace (whether they know it or not), for as Paul said to the Athenians, *"In Him we live and move and have our being."* (Acts 17:28). Without repentance and faith in God and in His Son JESUS---"The Lamb of God that taketh away the sin of the world" -- the final great sacrifice for mankind's sin (John 1:29; 3:35,36) -- they go on into eternity to face God's judgment on their own, with no assurance at all of forgiveness and salvation. Man willfully does this, but it is not what God wants (Jn.3:16,17). God would have no man to perish but have all to come to Repentance AND Salvation (II Peter 3:9).

Two of the saddest verses in the Bible relate to rejection of God and His Son JESUS:

Because that, when they knew God, they glorified him not as God, neither were thankful: but became vain in their imaginations, and their foolish heart was darkened. (Romans 1:21)

From that time many of his disciples went back, and walked no more with him. (John 6:66)

This Scripture should wake up a great number of people to our

CHAPTER 30: NOT FINISHED JUST BEGUN! 523

need to get hooked up to the eternal Life and Power Source, JESUS, and begin saying,

I am not ashamed of the Gospel of Christ, for it is the power of salvation to all those who believe, to the Jew first and also to the Greek. (Romans 1:16)

Psalm 100 is a very special Thanksgiving Psalm which ends with: *Enter into His Gates with Thanksgiving and into His courts with praise, be thankful unto Him and bless His Name. For the Lord is good, His mercy is everlasting; and His truth endureth to all generations.*

Our hearts were filled with overwhelming thanksgiving and praise to God for His everlasting mercies and His ever enduring Truth, JESUS!

On January 1, 1988, together with the Little Tabernacle Church and a host of friends, we celebrated God's goodness and mercy through 70 years, and, God willing and helping, we'll celebrate His loving care and tender mercies for yet more birthdays. (Already 4 more!). There have been many trials and dangers, rejections, and persecutions, storms and adverse winds through the years, but the Lord has delivered us, and has been with us all the way, as He promised us in the Old and New Testaments. We give Him all the praise and glory and Thanksgiving in the precious Name of JESUS! Amen!

At the beginning of 1988, Betsy and I intensified our prayers to the Lord to raise up a courageous and anointed younger man to help carry on the Little Tabernacle work as well as to strengthen the eldership and membership for His continuing service into the future. A careful transition was needed.

Some months earlier in 1987, the Lord specifically spoke to our hearts concerning His choice of the pastoral successor, and we in turn spoke to the young man at least two times about the calling of God on his life to the Little Tabernacle. Because of the nature of the Little Tabernacle ministry, a successor pastor would need to have a passionate love and devotion to Jesus, a deep concern for the people of the Inner City, and for all races; must have a soul-winner's heart, great courage, and a deep love for Israel; and a wife who was equally dedicated. He should also come and begin working in the Church as an assistant some time prior to being given the pastoral responsibilities.

At this time the young man and his wife and two sons were attending a large suburban church, although he had been earlier on the staff of the Lighthouse Ministry next door. We knew that Pastor Kirby felt the same way about this young man. Now we must wait on the Lord. Months passed. Finally, on a Sunday morning in February 1988, "right out of the blue," the young man, John Monk and his wife Terri and sons, Little John and Michael, showed up for worship. During the Testimony time, John stood up and announced that the Lord had told him and his family to come be a part of the Little Tabernacle Church.

At that time he was supporting his family through construction work. But on a Monday morning, early in June, he came to the Little Tabernacle asking for prayer. Unexpectedly, he had just been laid off from his work. As they say in Israel, "Mah laasote" (What to do?). We did pray, and the Lord quickly answered, "Put him to work at the Little Tabernacle; I will provide." And He has. His income has been quite low, but there's been food on his table and many other blessings for him, his family and the Little Tabernacle. Assigned many dirty maintenance jobs (as tests) along with regular praise and worship leading, John more than passed his "exams"!

So as we faced 1989, we rejoiced with great gladness and thanksgiving for the Lord's great miracle blessings to us--and over the prospect that in our 33rd year in Baltimore, the Lord had already provided an humble, dedicated and anointed young man of God, "tried under fire", to replace us beginning in May of '89, to carry on His work at the Little Tabernacle, a work that has reached into distant lands, as well as throughout Baltimore and the United States. To God be all the praise, glory, thanksgiving and honor in the mighty NAME of JESUS! Amen!

If any one thing can be said about our now 36 years in Baltimore and part in Israel, it would be that they have been FILLED to overflowing with God's mercies, miracles and love as we have lifted up His Son JESUS! There's no wonder why we love, praise and thank Him so! He's been with us all the way as promised!

Hopefully, this chronicle of God's mercies and miracles will be printed early in 1992 during my 75th year on God's Space Ship Earth-- by His Amazing Grace!

HOW AND WHERE ARE OUR SONS TODAY?

As Mom Betsy and I near the end of this account of our journey together, with and for the Lord Jesus, there may be some who will wonder again what's the news of our sons, especially since they all were "graduated" from us by 1979, and it's now 1992.

Well, our oldest son Craig, who reminded us of a little "Judge" as a small boy, is now the principal of a large elementary school, Willow Brook, in Oak Ridge Tennessee, and has a precious family: wife Ann, and daughter Ginny in the 11th grade and son Allen in the 7th. Ann has pursued a career in personnel management at Oak Ridge Associated Universities. They thoroughly enjoy being Tennesseans.

CHAPTER 30: NOT FINISHED JUST BEGUN!

Second son, Kirby, with his wife Carol and their four children, returned to Tulsa, Oklahoma late in 1986 after pastoring the Little Tabernacle Church in Baltimore during the years we were in Israel. In Tulsa, Kirby is continuing in construction work and Bible teaching in the Tulsa Christian Fellowship. Carol is working as a head nurse in the Pediatric Intensive care unit of a Tulsa hospital, having recently completed her R.N.degree! Matthew, Peter, Betsy and Little Luke are doing very well in a Christian school. Little Luke spends his time keeping everybody cheered with his happy smile.

Third son, Joe, has just completed work as Director of Admissions at St. Andrews College in Laurinberg, North Carolina. He began helping in this department at Maryville College, went to Phillips University in Enid Oklahoma as Assistant Director of Admissions, then to MacMurray College in Jacksonville, Illinois as Director of Admissions and from there to Western Maryland College. He has done an excellent job for each of these schools in which he has worked. He loves to play tennis and golf whenever he can.

Our fourth son Christopher, born on October 4, 1957, the day that "Spudnik" went up, also attended Maryville College, as did Craig, Joe, Dusty and Brian. Afterwards he obtained his PhD in Bio-Chemistry at the University of Tennessee in Knoxville. He is working for the Environmental Testing Company in Knoxville and is married (since May 20, 1989) to Julie Smith of Oak Ridge. They have just received their first "bundle of joy," Laura Emily, red headed like her mother Julie. Chris always said he planned to be head of General Motors; so it will be interesting to see how this works out. GM needs real help now!

Son Brian, also a Maryville College graduate, continues to live near the college and works for the First Tennessee Bank Operations Center in Alcoa, Tennessee. Loves Tennessee too!

Brian's Uncle Dusty, who "adopted" us as his family, lives in Arlington Va., does intelligence work for the Government, was a Marine in Vietnam; continues in a Special Ready Reserve Paratroop unit. Always telling us to stay away from the Middle East!

We thank God for each of these our precious sons, and for God's Hand upon their lives. We thank Him also for Ma and Pa Eggert of Maryville, for their love and great help to our sons in letting them "rent" their old farm-house for a token and their handyman work all their college years and beyond!

> ***Children are an heritage of the Lord: and the fruit of the womb is his reward.*** - Psalm 127:3
> ***Children's children are the crown of old men!*** Pro.17:6
> Thank You, Lord, for our crown of seven!

RIGELL FAMILY TREE

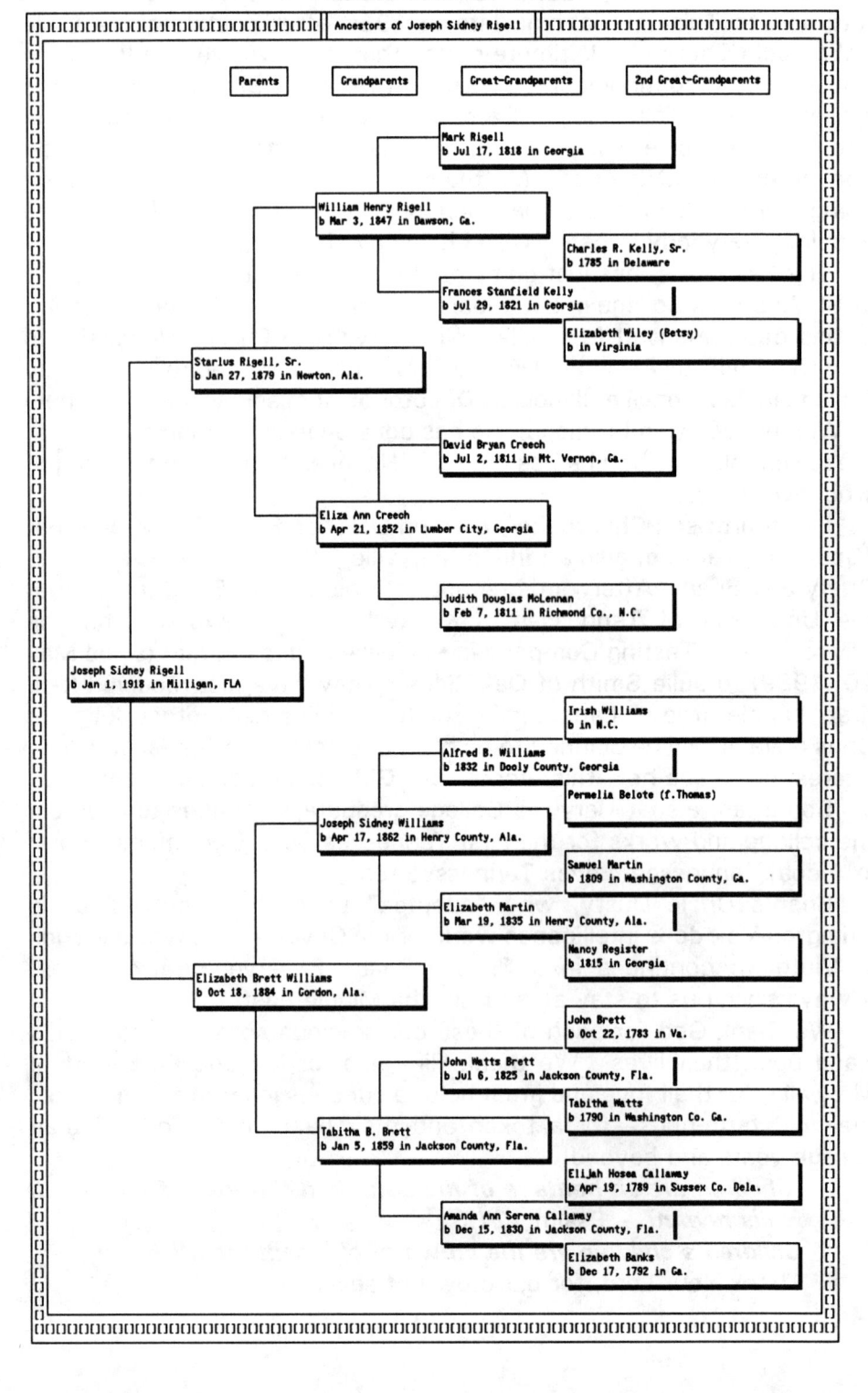

Ancestors of Joseph Sidney Rigell

Parents | Grandparents | Great-Grandparents | 2nd Great-Grandparents

- **Joseph Sidney Rigell**
  b Jan 1, 1918 in Milligan, FLA
  - **Starlus Rigell, Sr.**
    b Jan 27, 1879 in Newton, Ala.
    - **William Henry Rigell**
      b Mar 3, 1847 in Dawson, Ga.
      - **Mark Rigell**
        b Jul 17, 1818 in Georgia
      - **Frances Stanfield Kelly**
        b Jul 29, 1821 in Georgia
        - **Charles R. Kelly, Sr.**
          b 1785 in Delaware
        - **Elizabeth Wiley (Betsy)**
          b in Virginia
    - **Eliza Ann Creech**
      b Apr 21, 1852 in Lumber City, Georgia
      - **David Bryan Creech**
        b Jul 2, 1811 in Mt. Vernon, Ga.
      - **Judith Douglas McLennan**
        b Feb 7, 1811 in Richmond Co., N.C.
  - **Elizabeth Brett Williams**
    b Oct 18, 1884 in Gordon, Ala.
    - **Joseph Sidney Williams**
      b Apr 17, 1862 in Henry County, Ala.
      - **Alfred B. Williams**
        b 1832 in Dooly County, Georgia
        - **Irish Williams**
          b in N.C.
        - **Permelia Belote (f.Thomas)**
      - **Elizabeth Martin**
        b Mar 19, 1835 in Henry County, Ala.
        - **Samuel Martin**
          b 1809 in Washington County, Ga.
        - **Nancy Register**
          b 1815 in Georgia
    - **Tabitha B. Brett**
      b Jan 5, 1859 in Jackson County, Fla.
      - **John Watts Brett**
        b Jul 6, 1825 in Jackson County, Fla.
        - **John Brett**
          b Oct 22, 1783 in Va.
        - **Tabitha Watts**
          b 1790 in Washington Co. Ga.
      - **Amanda Ann Serena Callaway**
        b Dec 15, 1830 in Jackson County, Fla.
        - **Elijah Hosea Callaway**
          b Apr 19, 1789 in Sussex Co. Dela.
        - **Elizabeth Banks**
          b Dec 17, 1792 in Ga.

CHAPTER 30: NOT FINISHED JUST BEGUN!

WHITE FAMILY TREE

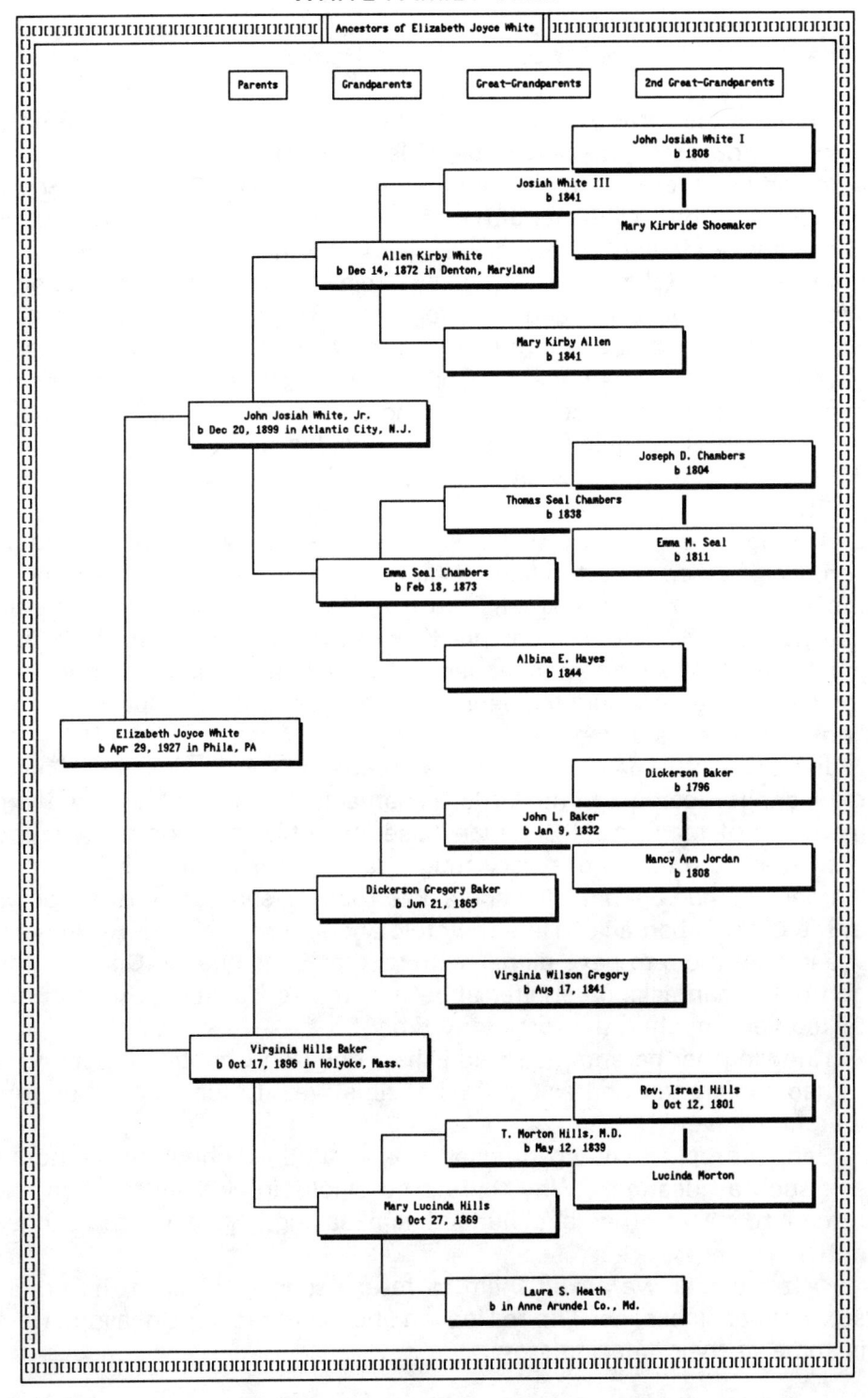

Ancestors of Elizabeth Joyce White

Parents — **Grandparents** — **Great-Grandparents** — **2nd Great-Grandparents**

- **Elizabeth Joyce White** b Apr 29, 1927 in Phila, PA
  - **John Josiah White, Jr.** b Dec 20, 1899 in Atlantic City, N.J.
    - **Allen Kirby White** b Dec 14, 1872 in Denton, Maryland
      - **Josiah White III** b 1841
        - John Josiah White I b 1808
        - Mary Kirbride Shoemaker
      - Mary Kirby Allen b 1841
    - **Emma Seal Chambers** b Feb 18, 1873
      - **Thomas Seal Chambers** b 1838
        - Joseph D. Chambers b 1804
        - Emma M. Seal b 1811
      - Albina E. Hayes b 1844
  - **Virginia Hills Baker** b Oct 17, 1896 in Holyoke, Mass.
    - **Dickerson Gregory Baker** b Jun 21, 1865
      - **John L. Baker** b Jan 9, 1832
        - Dickerson Baker b 1796
        - Nancy Ann Jordan b 1808
      - Virginia Wilson Gregory b Aug 17, 1841
    - **Mary Lucinda Hills** b Oct 27, 1869
      - **T. Morton Hills, M.D.** b May 12, 1839
        - Rev. Israel Hills b Oct 12, 1801
        - Lucinda Morton
      - Laura S. Heath b in Anne Arundel Co., Md.

JENNIFER'S TRIP TO HEAVEN

(The Story of her Cancer Battle, Trip to Heaven and Visit with Jesus)

It was in the early '70's when we first met the Smiths. Jessie Smith, a widow and a real prayer-warrior, called us for prayer for her son, Tom, who had been terribly crushed on the job between two trucks. A sharp metal projection on the rear of the cement truck cut a deep slice into his chest and abdomen. He was in shock trauma at the University of Maryland Hospital in Baltimore. Only a minister could get in to see him. Would I go to visit him and pray for him? Of course I would and did. He was in very bad shape, not expected to make it. And he wasn't saved. But by the grace of God and many prayers, after several operations and a long recovery time, he eventually was able to go back to work. Still he didn't immediately turn his heart to the Lord, but Jessie and all of us knew God had spared his life and we praised God for it.

Through the years we would see Jessie Smith and another miracle son, Gary, when we attended Bel Air Full Gospel meetings. Gary, once thought to be a slow learner from a birth injury, received wonderful healing from the Lord, has completed Bible School, and holds a full-time job driving a Bel Air street sweeper! Later we heard requests for prayers for her little granddaughter Jennifer, who had cancer. But we didn't know any details at that time.

In early 1990 Tommy, Cathy, their teenaged son Patrick and 10 year old Jennifer came to the Little Tabernacle to church. They were members of the Central Christian Assembly of God which really stood with them through those very rough days fighting cancer. Then we learned she had been healed and asked them to share their testimonies at the Little Tabernacle. Here they told about Jennifer's trip to Heaven! We invited them to have dinner with us that Sunday after Church, and gently I began asking Jennifer about her trip to Heaven. She had not talked very much in the testimony time.

Knowing her parents had said it happened on Christmas morning, I turned to Jennifer and asked: "What time was it, Jennifer, when you were in Heaven?"

Jennifer replied with a surprised look as though I should know not to ask such a question, "Why there's no clocks in Heaven!" Then she turned to her brother and nudged him saying, "And no telephones either!"

After dinner we asked them to return soon to give us the whole story of her illness, her Trip to Heaven and her miraculous healing. Here is some of their amazing story:

CHAPTER 30: NOT FINISHED JUST BEGUN!

When Jennifer first got sick, Tommy and Cathy were separated. Cathy had noticed some knots on Jennifer's left side, and she would complain now and then of tremendous pain in her shoulder. This was in 1986 when she was six years old.

After seeing several doctors, and having tests at a hospital, they were referred to Johns Hopkins where the doctors told Tommy and Cathy that Jennifer had a tumor the size of a grapefruit, and that they believed it was attached to several of her organs, her heart, her lungs, and said she had about a 20% chance to live. What a terrible shock!

Even though Cathy was backslidden at the time, and Tom was a fresh new Christian, Cathy told the doctors that they were going to see the power of prayer. They went to the Chapel at Hopkins, and wept before the Lord, "went to pieces," one said! There Cathy rededicated her life to the Lord.

The Doctors scheduled a biopsy for the following day. Tommy's pastors and praying family and friends gathered. Tommy was able to stay with Jennifer while waiting for the surgery and had a long time of prayer, during which the Lord told him they were going to remove the tumor. The knots already felt like they had shrunk when they wheeled Jennifer into the operating room. Sure enough they removed a tumor the size of a grapefruit that was entangled around 2 ½ ribs and one half of the left lung. However, they would need to operate again in 2 weeks on the other lung.

Her brother Patrick waited as close to the operating room as possible the whole time of the operations. Whenever Jennifer was home from the hospital they would always carry her, literally, to The Central Christian Assembly of God on Sundays for prayer. The Sunday before the second operation the Lord spoke with a very reassuring prophecy of how He had greater miracles to do through Jennifer's illness, that He had brought them back together for a reason and that they should give Him all the praise, honor and glory.

However, the second operation was worse than the first! They installed a "Hickman" in Jennifer's chest for the chemotherapy treatments, which were to begin in four days. To each operation Jennifer took a friend, her "Teddy". The nurses even dressed him up like a doctor. We asked to see Teddy, but they said he was flat now; squashed from being slept on so much.

The chemo made her deathly sick; all she did was vomit, vomit, vomit! Jennifer asked, "Why do you come to the hospital to get sick? I thought you came to get better!" They told them Jennifer would probably have to take chemo for two years. They also gave her radiation treatments which burned her up from the inside; she went down to 28 pounds.

Just before Christmas 1986, she was in the hospital with a fever of 105, resting on a refrigerated bed! On Christmas eve her fever had gone down to 103, and apparently her white blood count was up, so the hospital urged them to take her home for Christmas, no doubt believing it would be her last.

Her mother said, "She was so sick, like a rag doll, so skinny, it would hurt her for us to hold her, so we pushed her around in a kitchen chair with wheels, where she curled up in a fetal position. Christmas day she got up to open her presents, but she was so sick, she just went back to bed and went to sleep."

At 10:10 a.m. Christmas morning their Pastor, Rev. Terry Kirk, called and wanted to know how and where Jennifer was. Another brother, Gary Kern, had called him and said he was on his way to take his mother a Christmas gift, and the Lord made him stop his truck and start interceding for Jennifer. At this time Jennifer waked up and started screaming for her mother, "Mommy, Mommy!"

Cathy ran into the bedroom.

She looked at Cathy and cried, "I died, I died, I died and went to Heaven."

Cathy said, "No you didn't, Jenny, you were right here all the time!"

Jennifer replied, "No, I had this dream, and I died and I went to Heaven." The rest of the day she was miserable, but her fever had broken when she waked up from the "dream!"

The following Sunday when they went to Church, Gary Kern came to them and told them that in his praying for Jennifer, he saw a vision of the death angel come and try to take her, and the Lord drove him off with a sword. In between Christmas Day and that Sunday, Jennifer had told them the same thing.

Cathy continued, "All Christmas Day she didn't speak about her trip to Heaven, but between Friday and Sunday she drew pictures and told us that this had happened. So when Gary told us this, we looked at each other and said, 'She really did go to Heaven!' But she didn't really open up until sometime later.

"We were in a doctor's office, looking at a Children's Bible Story book, and when Jennifer looked at the picture of Heaven, she said, 'Mom, that's not what it looks like.'"

When we asked Jennifer to tell us what Heaven was like she said, "When I died, I woke up at the gate, and Jesus asked me if I wanted to come in, but He didn't talk very much. He took my hand, and I got to pet a lion. We went past this beautiful place and it was all golden and there was a lot of steps with angels going up and down. There was an angel playing a harp and there were flowers all around. Jesus took me up to this special place, and then the devil saw me and he tried to take

CHAPTER 30: NOT FINISHED JUST BEGUN!

me, and Jesus took a sword and hit him with it. And then He told him to be gone, and he was gone. Then Jesus took me to the gate and let me come back home."

Later, two other times while Jennifer was still sick, Jesus came to her: once He came and sat on her bed. He was BIG! And once she was talking to Him in her sleep!

Pastor Kirk came to them and said the Lord had showed him that they were hindering God's Spirit to heal Jennifer by their unbelief. They had seen so many children dying in the hospital, with whom they had become real close and it was pulling them down. They had to make a stand on Jesus, and thank God for healing her, and turn their heads away from anything else. And from that day Jennifer started getting stronger everyday. Of 17 children in her oncology section, Jennifer is the only survivor! Praise Jesus for her survival!

In May of 1987 they took Jennifer to Disney World, on her "Make A Wish" trip given to any child with a life threatening disease. She was still weak, thin and had lost all her hair.

After a year and a half of chemo, it still looked like there was a spot on her lung, but it turned out to be fluid caused by the operation, which the doctor drained. Soon after that, they stopped the chemo treatments and Jennifer was healed! Wish you could see her now, such a healthy looking 11 year old. All thanks and praise to God in Jesus' Name!

A very important note: Whenever they would bring Jennifer into or out of the hospital, she would ask them to take her by the big statue of Jesus in the old entrance foyer to Johns Hopkins Hospital. (See Chapter 12, page 187). There Jennifer would reach over to caress His feet, putting her finger in the nail hole, and looking up, tell Jesus she loved Him! Jesus is her Best Friend, even better than Teddy!

Today Jennifer calls us her good friends too. How blessed we are to know a little girl who has been to Heaven and walked and talked with Jesus! She wants everyone to know that JESUS IS REAL, that HE DOES HEAL, and that HEAVEN IS REAL too!!!

THE LOST STAR AND CROSS

For those of you who have persevered almost to the end with us (of the book, that is), we want to share with you a remarkable story of an incident, a near "heart-breaker," that took place during our last visit to Patmos in 1990, where we struggled to finish more of the manuscript for this book.

Patmos is the place where we started our book five years ago when we were "Fired" from Israel. But eleven years ago, the night before leaving Baltimore to go to live for a time in Israel, a friend gave me a beautiful blue-enamel Star of David with silver edges and a silver Cross in its center, which emblem I wore constantly for those six and a half years in Israel, and wherever else we have been. Many, many people have stopped me to ask what it means, giving me wonderful opportunities to witness to JESUS as our Jewish Messiah and Saviour (See Chapter 19, "Coffee Shop Confrontation on Ben Yehudah Street", page 320). Tough Israeli Army soldiers would ask about it, and more than one of them tapped it with his finger and said, "Yes, that's the way it ought to be." Over the eleven years this star and cross emblem has given us hundreds of such opportunities to share our love for JESUS and our love for the Jewish people, whom many people in the world seem determined to hate. Like that soldier, we've said many times, "Christians and the Jewish people go together whether they like it or not." We get equally hated by the Anti-Christ and the Anti-Jewish forces in the world, such as: Communism, Islam, Humanism and New Ageism.

Well, let's get back to the near "tragic incident" on Patmos many months ago. On that day Betsy was putting some of my clothes in the bathroom; I was still in my pajamas, trying to wake up. (You know she's the "early bird" and I'm the "midnight owl.") Suddenly something fell out of the shirt, making a tingling noise when it hit. She looked all around in the tiny bathroom for whatever it was and found nothing. Knowing I carry all kinds of junk in my pockets, she wasn't too concerned; it could have been a nail or a screw!. To help her, I even swept the floor in there and couldn't find anything, still not realizing what was missing.

After breakfast, needing some gas in the motorbike, I went around the harbor to the one little filling station where I had been once before. The rugged Greek attendant welcomed me in Greek and pointed to my chest apparently asking where the Star and Cross emblem was. He made me realize that I didn't have it on. Most of the people in the village of Scala where we were staying had seen me wearing it.

CHAPTER 30: NOT FINISHED JUST BEGUN! 533

So I went back immediately to our neatly furnished little apartment #2 to search for it, now realizing what probably had fallen from my shirt pocket. Again Betsy and I began looking high and low for the Star and Cross. I remembered putting it in my shirt pocket the night before, so obviously what had fallen out in the bathroom must have been the Star and Cross, and it must have fallen straight into the toilet. Sad to say, it had been flushed a number of times since that tinkling sound had been heard. Even so, Betsy fished around with the commode brush and found nothing!

Gloom settled in like when Casey struck out and Mudville lost in that famous epic baseball game of yore, "Casey at the Bat" (one of Pappy's favorite poems which he could quote almost verbatim).

We prayed about it, almost wept about it, but we both felt that the Star and Cross emblem was gone forever. "Mah LaaSote?" "What to do?" as they say in Israel. "Pappa", as many Patmians call me there on the island, would not have his identifying emblem as he rode his motorbike around the village. Could we get one made in a local shop? Betsy even went and asked two jewelry shops. No way! I even started whittling on a small, thin, piece of white pine, found somewhere, cutting out in relief a star and a cross, which by using our blue and red felt pens made a fair substitute. However, it wasn't the real thing.

The Lord kept reminding Betsy that He had recently come behind us, making miraculous corrections for us in small and big things, like finding the candy bar on Patmos, (the one in which we had hidden some money for Esther), and finding the diamond which fell out of Betsy's ring and was missing for a week. He reminded us again of the Scripture in Isaiah 52:12, which says that He is our rereward! (Our rearguard). He would use this for His glory in some way as in Romans 8:28 where He promises to **Make all things work together for good to them that love God, to them who are the called according to His purpose.**

The day was fast ending and the pall of this loss was heavy, but we were still believing that somehow the Lord would work it out. We were wondering if this was an indication of an end of an era, perhaps the ending of our connection with Israel. No way could we believe it. I had taken a lot of criticism for wearing it over the years from almost all sides, especially from certain people who have judged the Star of David to be a cultish symbol, about which I would remind our readers that Satan has used almost every good symbol, including the Cross, in his dirty work. The Cross itself is a symbol of what our Lord has done for us, and the Star a symbol of a very courageous nation and people.

Well, guess what? About 11 o'clock that evening as Betsy was preparing for bed, she took another look at the contour of the toilet plumbing, and saw there was a distinct downward bend in the pipe before it rose up to exit. Screwing up her courage she reached her little hand down into this pocket, and started screaming and weeping at the same time. Yes sir, she had found the Star and Cross and chain! They had not been swept away into the Agean Sea after all! A thorough cleansing of the Star and Cross restored it to sparkle again in our daily rounds!

All praise, honor, glory and thanksgiving to Almighty God for coming behind, for being with us all the way, and having miracles for us when they are needed! If He can come behind and make up for our mistakes in the little things, He can do it in the big things too. As we walk with the Lord, trusting and obeying Him, there will be many more little and big miracles all the way to Heaven. We'll praise and thank Him forever. Hallelujah!

SONGS FROM PATMOS

Mom Betsy and I would be greatly remiss if we did not share with you about the nine beautiful songs that the Lord revealed to her on Patmos.

Most everyone in the family already knows that the Lord has given Mom Betsy a lovely voice and a heart for receiving and singing Scripture songs. Years before we ever went to Patmos the Lord gave her a bouncy little song based on Proverbs 3:5-8 which surely tells us a sure-fire method for receiving God's guidance for which path to take in our lives, how to be healthy, and how to prosper God's Way. Those verses are:

Trust in the Lord with all thine heart: lean not to thine understanding. In all thy ways acknowledge him, and he shall direct thy paths. Be not wise in thine own eyes: fear the Lord, and depart from evil. It shall be health to thy navel, and marrow to thy bones. (Proverbs 3:5-8)

But let's go back to Patmos. Our first trip to Patmos occurred in April 1983 while we were living in Jerusalem. Esther wanted us to go see her dear friends in Athens, Nellie and Sophia Karakatsani, and to help her go on to Patmos with all her notes and her electric typewriter to continue work on her book. After arriving on Patmos and finding simple accommodations at Antonios Vamvakos' apartments, we settled in to help Esther in reading and re-reading and correcting her

CHAPTER 30: NOT FINISHED JUST BEGUN! 535

manuscript.[1] Late each afternoon we walked down to the port for a Greek supper or a cup of "cappuccino" (coffee with whipped cream).

On subsequent trips, late each afternoon, Betsy and I would climb halfway up the mountain to the Church of the Apocalypse for a time of reading the Book of Revelation, given by JESUS to His Apostle John, who was a prisoner of the Romans there. Tradition says, this occurred in a cave now covered by the Church building. We would pray and ask the Lord to open our understanding to His Revelation and to give Betsy the music to some of the verses during our stay on the Island, usually about 10 days or 2 weeks.

The first lovely song, as mentioned in the previous Patmos chapter, and as given to Betsy was based on Revelation 3:19-20:

(1)... *Behold, I stand at the door, and knock; and if any man hear my voice, and open the door of his heart to me, and I will come in to him. As many as I love, I rebuke and chasten: be zealous therefore and repent, and I will sup with you and you will sup with me.*

The next one was based on Revelation 5:9-10:

(2)... *And they sang a new song, saying Thou art worthy to take the book and open the seals thereof: for thou was slain, and hast redeemed us to God by thy blood out of every kindred, tongue and nation. And hast made us unto our God kings and priests; and we shall reign on the earth. Oh worthy is the Lamb.*

And again in 1986 the words to Revelation 14:6-7 which are written in a plaque on the wall of the Cave where St. John received the Revelation.

(3)... *And I saw another angel fly in the midst of heaven, having the everlasting Gospel to preach to every nation and people on the earth, Saying with a loud voice, Fear God, give glory unto Him, for the hour of His judgment is come, and worship him that made heaven and earth, the sea and the fountain of waters.*

In 1987 the Lord gave the tunes to the following Revelation Scriptures, Revelation 12:10-11:

(4)... *Now is come salvation, and strength, and the kingdom of our God, and the power of His Christ: for the accuser of our brethren is cast down, which accused them before our God day and night. And they overcame him by the blood of the Lamb, and by the word of their testimony; and they loved not their lives unto the death, for the accuser of our brethren is cast down.*

---

[1] "I Am My Beloved's", by Esther Dorflinger, published 1985 in Jerusalem, Israel.

And Revelation 22:20 & 17:

(5)... *Even so Lord Jesus come quickly, even so Lord Jesus come, He which testifieth saith, Surely I come quickly, even so Lord Jesus come. The Spirit and the bride say Come. And let him that heareth say Come, and he that is thirsty and whosoever will, freely drink the water of life.*

The following year, 1988, Revelation 14:13:

(6)... *And I heard a voice from heaven saying unto me, Write, Blessed are the dead which die in the Lord from henceforth: yea, saith the Spirit, that they may rest from their labors; and their works do follow them, who die in the Lord.*

And Revelation 7:9,10,14:

(7)... *After this I beheld, and lo, a great multitude, which no man could number, of all nations and kindreds, and people and tongues, stood before the throne, and before the Lamb, clothed with white robes, and palms in their hands; And cried with a loud voice saying, Salvation to our God which sitteth upon the throne, and to the Lamb, Salvation to our God which sitteth upon the throne and unto the Lamb....These are they which came out of great tribulation and have washed their robes, and made them white in the blood of the Lamb, and cried with a loud voice saying, Salvation to our God which sitteth upon the throne and to the Lamb....(Repeat).*

Then in 1990 from Revelation 5:11-14:

(8)...*And I beheld, and I heard the voice of many angels round about the throne and the beasts and the elders: and the number of them was ten thousand times ten thousand, and thousands of thousands: Saying with a loud voice, Worthy is the Lamb that was slain to receive power, and riches, and wisdom, and strength, and honour, and glory, and blessing. And every creature in heaven, and on the earth, under the earth, and such as are in the sea, and all that are in them, heard I saying, Blessing, and honour and glory and power, be unto him that sitteth upon the throne, and unto the Lamb for ever and ever. And the four beasts said, Amen. And the four and twenty elders fell down and worshipped him that liveth for ever and ever.*

And Revelation 17:14:

(9)...*And they that are with him are called chosen and faithful, called chosen and faithful to the Lord of lords. And they that are with him are called chosen and faithful, called chosen and faithful to the King of Kings. These shall make war with the Lamb, and the Lamb shall overcome them: for he is the Lord of lords and the King of Kings...*

We were so blessed by the Lord to visit some of his dear people in Athens and on Patmos seven times, to encourage the Believers there as well as to study, pray and to write in the last four visits. Each time the

CHAPTER 30: NOT FINISHED JUST BEGUN!   537

Lord would give Betsy at least one song, sometimes two, not always at the Cave, but while on the Island. We've already told you how there is still a sense of the Lord's glory and presence on the Island because of His glorified visit to Apostle John there.

There are at least seven other Revelation songs that Mom Betsy knows and we will try to make sure that they are recorded as she plays them on her autoharp. Anyone desiring a copy of these tremendously anointed and inspiring songs may write us for it.

The other Revelation songs are:

Rev. 1:18 *I am He that liveth and was dead...*
Rev. 2:7 *Him that overcometh will eat of the tree of life...*
Rev. 3:12 *Him that overcometh will I make a pillar
          in the temple of my God...*
Rev. 4:11 *Thou art worthy, Thou art worthy...*
Rev. 11:17,15: *We give thee thanks, Lord God Almighty...*
Rev. 15:3,4: *And they sang the song of Moses...*
Rev. 15:3,4: *Great and marvelous are thy works...*
Rev. 17:14: *King of kings and Lord of lords...*
Rev. 21:3,4: *Behold the tabernacle of God is with men...*

All of this may seem rather bland without the music, and rightly so. If it were possible, we would have the melodies recorded, with the sounds of Betsy's voice on these pages, so that as you read the Scriptures, you'd also be hearing the songs in all their beauty.

DECLARING THE WONDROUS WORKS OF THE LORD

Early on in this writing venture, our purpose and desire was to **declare the wondrous works of the Lord** (Ps.26:7; Ps.71:17-19; Ps.105:1-3) which we have seen and experienced in our lives, during our long mercy-filled journey together. Throughout, we've tried to tell many exciting (at least to us) stories of the miracle-working hand of God, stories of little miracles and big miracles, of small wonders and large wonders. Please know we are not implying that somehow God owed us a constant flow of wonders. Not by any means!

We've wanted only to show that the goodness and mercy of the Lord really follow those who make the Lord God of Israel their Shepherd (Ps.23). This also means the Lord Jesus Christ, the Great Shepherd of the sheep (Jn.10:11-15)! In Psalm 23:6 David says, **Goodness and mercy shall follow me all our days of my life, and I shall dwell in the house of the Lord forever.** The Hebrew word for "follow" is "chase after!" That makes it even "gooder"!

The Psalmist David, understanding the life of a shepherd boy, surely grasped the love and power and mercy of our Heavenly Shepherd--called the Great Shepherd of our souls in Hebrews 13:21,22 and called our Good Shepherd in John 10:11. Glory to God, nothing can take us out of His hands as we trust Him and obey His Word and Voice. And finally, we give Him all the praise and glory and thanksgiving for these wonders, just as we thank Him for every beautiful sunrise and sunset He has given us to see in this journey. *Surely the heavens declare His glory and the firmament shows His handiwork.* (Ps.19:1). So will we throughout eternity. Like the disciples in Luke 10:17-20, we've seen the wonders of His Love and Power, but are reminded by JESUS that the best part is to know that our names are written down by HIM in Heaven. *Rejoice not that the spirits are subject to you, but that your names are written in heaven.* Luke 10:20

Through JESUS we can KNOW THAT WE ARE SAVED, as Apostle John over and over and over again confirms in His first letter to His "little children". Like the song says: "Oh the wonder of it all, just to think that God loves me," and has made possible through JESUS an abundant life here and eternal life with Him, hereafter! In Mark 11:22-26 our LORD JESUS said that if we would really have faith in God and pray without any doubting, with constant forgiveness in our hearts, we too shall see a constant flow of miracles, mercies for others and for ourselves. He said it, too, in Matt.21:22 *And all things whatsoever you shall ask in prayer, believing, you shall receive.*

The Apostle John in John 16:23,24 quotes the LORD JESUS saying, *Verily, verily I say unto you whatsoever you have asked the Father in my name, He will give it you. Hitherto have you asked nothing in my name: ask and ye shall receive, that your joy may be full.*

FUNDAMENTALISTS

Over the years we've been thoroughly damned for being fundamentalists. So have many, many others. The world will always be damning Christian fundamentalists, those who remain faithful to the Bible, God's powerful revelation to mankind. Chuck Colson, a former tough Marine officer, who served prison time for his role in the Watergate fiasco which triggered the "political assassination" of President Nixon, met Jesus in prison and was truly "BORN AGAIN". He wrote a very successful book by that name, and has established the outstanding Prison Fellowship Ministry. Chuck became a "fundamentalist" and writes how he is honored to be called one. What he says about that subject follows.

CHAPTER 30: NOT FINISHED JUST BEGUN!

"THE SCARLET F"[2]
By: Chuck Colson

According to a recent article in the New York Times I am a totalitarian theocrat. The authors implied that I am anxious and confused about my faith, given to apocalyptic visions, possibly a sadist, and basically opposed to fiction, psychology, journalism, and assertive women.

In other words, according to the author's definition, a fundamentalist.

At least I was mentioned in good company. James Dobson came under attack in the same article as a potential child abuser with sadistic tendencies.

The article was a scathing indictment of Bible-Believing Christians and full of misinformation. Had the authors bothered to read my work, they would have known that I am anything but a theocrat. (I devoted much of "Kingdoms in Conflict" to critiquing that movement.) But never let it be said that journalistic integrity stood in the way of social commentary.

I'll admit that there may be, among believers, people with all kinds of problems, prejudices, and odd notions. But what does that prove? There are people with kooky ideas among the ranks of liberals, Republicans, school teachers, and the editors of book review pages.

But the article's irresponsible labeling seems to me symptomatic of the growing tendency to substitute symbols and slogans for reason and argument in public discourse.

These days when you call someone a fundamentalist, you lump that person together with Shiite Muslims, the Ayatollah Khomeini, and the stereotypical backwoods bigot who stomps about angrily thumping his Bible. Call someone a fundamentalist and there's no argument: Your victim is hung without trial.

Another example: Episcopal Bishop John Shelby Spong released a book recently in which he asserted that the apostle Paul was a homosexual. In a "Today Show" interview, Spong explained his mission, captured in his book's title: "Rescuing The Bible from Fundamentalism." His interviewer nodded obligingly--though probably neither she nor one in a hundred viewers had the foggiest notion what fundamentalism really means. No, everyone just knows it's a bad word--so Bishop Spong comes across as a hero for rescuing us from it.

Well, I for one am tired of seeing a perfectly good word twisted and used to beat Bible-believing Christians bloody.

The time has come to set the record straight: Fundamentalism simply means adherence to the fundamental facts--in this case the fundamental facts of Christianity. And understanding the history of this term is critical to understanding fundamentalism today.

Fundamentalism rose out of a controversy at the end of the nineteenth century when evolution science and so-called higher biblical criticism began to challenge prevailing assumptions about biblical authority. This assault on orthodoxy affected even the great religious institutions of the day. Princeton Theological Seminary, for example, issued a statement of faith calling doctrines such as the Virgin Birth and the inerrancy of Scripture mere "theories."

Meanwhile workers were leaving their farms for the sweatshops and assembly

---

[2] From Another Point of View in April 1991 edition of the monthly newsletter of Prison Fellowship "Jubilee". Used with permission.

lines of urban industry, creating new ethical and social crises. A lively "social gospel"--strong on good intentions, but weak on biblical doctrine --emerged.

The first orthodox response to these developments came in 1910 when a group of pastors and lay people published a series of slim volumes titled "The Fundamentals." These booklets defined what had been the non-negotiables of the faith since the writing of the Apostles' Creed.

The word fundamentalist first appeared publicly a decade later when a conservative Baptist newspaper used it to describe those ready "to do battle royal for the Fundamentals."

Those fundamentals have been generally understood over the years to embrace five points: (1) the infallibility of Scripture; (2) the deity of Christ; (3) the Virgin Birth and miracles of Christ; (4) Christ's substitutionary death; (5) Christ's physical resurrection and eventual return.

These are still the backbone of orthodox Christianity. If a fundamentalist is simply one who claims these truths, then there are fundamentalists in every church and denomination-- Catholic, Presbyterian, Baptist, or Brethren. Every believing Christian is a fundamentalist.

Tragically, Christians have been taken in by distortions of the term. I recently heard a pastor warn his flock against falling away from the faith and getting involved in "sex, drugs, and fundamentalist sects." In much of the church's intramural battling, Christians have used the word against one another.

Admittedly, as the years have passed, the term had been used to describe certain separatist movements, anti-intellectualism, and legalism. It's been confused, misunderstood, and maligned. But enough is enough. It is time for orthodox believers to recapture this word for its original meaning.

Fundamentalism, in its classical sense, ought to be a badge of honor, not a slur of shame. The great distinctions in our world today are not between "fundamentalist sects" and some truer Christianity. The divisions are between those who know the Christ of the Gospels and those who prefer to make God in their own image; according to their own notions of modernism.

It is along those battle lines that I take my stand! The world may scoff, but you can call me a fundamentalist any time.

-Chuck Colson is chairman of PF (Prison Fellowship) and Author of "Born Again" and other Christian writings.

SELECTIONS FROM OUR FAVORITE DAILY DEVOTIONALS

Many sincere Christians in our day have long made it a habit in their daily devotions not only to read portions of the Bible along with their daily prayers but also add a reading of a selection from a devotional booklet giving helpful commentary on the Scripture.

It is interesting to note that as a little boy Abraham Lincoln's mother regularly read her Bible and helped her children learn to read it too. In their family Bible, published in 1799, was a statement by a Bible professor in Switzerland saying, "The Scriptures are the most valuable

CHAPTER 30: NOT FINISHED JUST BEGUN!

blessings God ever bestowed upon us except the sending of His Son into the world. They are a treasury containing everything that can make us truly rich and truly happy."

George Washington's mother urged him, as he was leaving home for militia service, to remember faithfully to engage in daily prayer and Bible reading.

There are many devotional booklets available today, but two that Betsy and I have thoroughly enjoyed and that have helped to strengthen our devotion and walk with Jesus are: "My Utmost For His Highest" by Oswald Chambers, an English Bible scholar in the early part of this century, and "Renewed Day By Day" by A. W. Tozer, a true servant of God also in the early part of this century, in Chicago, who believed with Paul that though his outer man was perishing, the Lord was renewing day by day his inner-man (II Cor. 4:16).

Our dear friend, Jim Elmore, the late director of the McKim Boys Haven, first recommended Oswald Chamber's book to us many years ago. Though he had never been to a Seminary, Jim knew Jesus and His Scriptures far better than we did. Jim had met Jesus at the end of World War II in a Pauline conversion experience in Berlin, and had a similar passionate love and devotion to Jesus as did Apostle Paul!

Dr. Tozer's book of daily devotions was recommended to us by my brother Frank a number of years ago, and we have found it tremendously helpful, for Tozer like Oswald often gives us the spiritual jolt or insight we need from day to day.

We hope you will enjoy the four selections and will go out soon to a Christian Book Shop and get yourself copies of both to go along with your Bible studies and prayer times. You'll be glad you did! They cannot, nor should, ever take the place of your Bible readings, but will help you enjoy your Bible more.

Thy word is lamp unto my feet, and a light unto my path. -Ps.119:105

But continue thou in the things which thou has learned and hast been assured of, knowing of whom thou has learned them. And that from a child thou hast known the Holy Scriptures, which are able to make thee wise unto salvation through faith which is in Christ Jesus. All Scripture is given by inspiration of God, and is profitable for doctrine, for reproof, for correction, for instruction in righteousness. That the man of God may be perfect thoroughly furnished unto all good works. II Tim.3:14-17

THE TEST OF LOYALTY - by Oswald Chambers[3]

And we know that all things work together for good to them that love God.

-Romans 8:28

It is only the loyal soul who believes that God engineers circumstances. We take such liberty with our circumstances, we do not believe God engineers them, although we say we do; we treat the things that happen as if they were engineered by men. To be faithful in every circumstance means that we have only one loyalty, and that is to our Lord. Suddenly God breaks up a particular set of circumstances, and the realization comes that we have been disloyal to Him by not recognizing that He had ordered them; we never saw what He was after, and that particular thing will never be repeated all the days of our life. The test of loyalty always comes just there. If we learn to worship God in the trying circumstances, He will alter them in two seconds when He chooses.

Loyalty to Jesus Christ is the thing that we "stick at" to-day. We will be loyal to work, to service, to anything, but do not ask us to be loyal to Jesus Christ. Many Christians are intensely impatient of talking about loyalty to Jesus. Our Lord is dethroned more emphatically by Christian workers than by the world. God is made a machine for blessing men, and Jesus Christ is made a Worker among workers.

The idea is not that we do work for God, but that we are so loyal to Him that He can do His work through us, "I reckon on you for extreme service, with no complaining on your part and no explanation on Mine." God wants to use us as He used His own Son.

THE NEVER-FAILING GOD - by Oswald Chambers

For He hath said, I will never leave thee, nor forsake thee.

Heb.13:5

What line does my thought take? Does it turn to what God says or to what I fear? Am I learning to say not what God says, but to say something after I have heard what He says? "He hath said, I will never leave thee, nor forsake thee. So that we may boldly say, The Lord is my helper, and I will not fear what man shall do unto me."

"I will in no wise fail thee" -- not for all my sin and selfishness and stubbornness and waywardness. Have I really let God say to me that He will never fail me? If I have listened to this say-so of God's, then let me listen again.

"Neither will I in any wise forsake thee." Sometimes it is not difficulty that makes me think God will forsake me, but drudgery. There is no Hill Difficulty to climb, no vision given, nothing wonderful or beautiful, just the commonplace day in and day out--can I hear God's say-so in these things?

We have the idea that God is going to do some exceptional thing, that He is preparing and fitting us for some extraordinary thing bye and bye, but as we go on in grace we find that God is glorifying Himself here and now, in the present minute. If we have God's say-so behind us, the most amazing strength comes, and we learn to sing in the ordinary days and ways.

---

[3] These quotations are from MY UTMOST FOR HIS HIGHEST by Oswald Chambers. Copyright (c) 1935 by Dodd Mead & Co. Copyright renewed (c) 1963 by Oswald Chambers Publications Association, Ltd. Used by permission of Discovery House Publishers, Box 3566, Grand Rapids, Mi. 49501.

CHAPTER 30: NOT FINISHED JUST BEGUN!

DO NOT HOPE TO WIN THE LOST BY BEING AGREEABLE[4]
By: A. W. Tozer

Watch ye, stand fast in the faith, quit you like men, be strong.
- I Cor.16:13

In our day, religion may be very precious to some persons, but hardly important enough to cause division or risk hurting anyone's feelings! In all our discussions there must never be any trace of intolerance, we are reminded; but obviously we forget that the most fervent devotees of tolerance are invariably intolerant of everyone who speaks about God with certainty. And there must be no bigotry--which is the name given to spiritual assurance by those who do not enjoy it.

The desire to please may be commendable enough under certain circumstances, but when pleasing men means displeasing God it is an unqualified evil and should have no place in the Christian's heart. To be right with God has often meant to be in trouble with men. This is such a common truth that one hesitates to mention it, yet it appears to have been overlooked by the majority of Christians today.

There is a notion abroad that to win a man we must agree with him. Actually, the exact opposite is true! The man who is going in a wrong direction will never be set right by the affable religionist who falls into step beside him and goes the same way. Someone must place himself across the path and insist that the straying man turn around and go in the right direction.

DO NOT LAUGH AT SOMETHING GOD TAKES SERIOUSLY
By: A. W. Tozer

...Their conscience also bearing witness, and their thoughts the meanwhile accusing or else excusing one another.
- Romans 2:15

One way the devil has of getting rid of things is to make jokes about them--and one of the sick jokes you hear is that the conscience is that part of you which makes you sorry when you get caught!

There are some things that are not the proper objects of humor, and one of them is conscience. That power of conscience that God has set in the human breast can suddenly isolate a soul, and hang it between heaven and hell, as lonely as if God had never created but one soul--that's not a joking matter.

Remember the conscience is always on God's side--always on God's side! It judges conduct in the light of the moral law, and as the Scripture says, excuses or accuses. The Light that lighted every man that comes into the world is not a joking matter. The eternal, universal presence of the luminous Christ is not a joking matter.

Joke about politics if you must joke--they are usually funny, anyway. But don't joke about God and don't joke about conscience, nor death, nor life, nor love, nor the cross, nor prayer.

There is legitimate humor in our lives, and I think it is in us by the gift of God. Your sense of humor does not have to dry up and die. There's plenty to laugh at in the world--but be sure you don't laugh at something that God takes seriously. Conscience is one of those things.

---

[4] "DO NOT HOPE TO WIN THE LOST BY BEING AGREEABLE" and "DO NOT LAUGH AT SOMETHING GOD TAKES SERIOUSLY" by A. W. Tozer, are taken from *Renewed Day by Day*, compiled by Gerald B. Smith, Copyright 1980 by Christian Publications. Used with permission.

FIRED AGAIN AND AGAIN, PRAISE THE LORD!

TWO OF OUR FAVORITE HYMNS

THE SOLID ROCK
By: Edward Mote

1) My hope is built on nothing less Than Jesus' blood and righteousness;
   I dare not trust the sweetest frame, But wholly lean on Jesus' name.
Chorus:
   On Christ. the solid Rock, I stand;
   All other ground is sinking sand,
   All other ground is sinking sand.
2) When darkness veils His lovely face, I rest on His unchanging grace;
   In every high and stormy gale, My anchor holds within the veil.
3) His oath, His covenant, His blood. Support me in the whelming flood;
   When all around my soul gives way, He then is all my hope and stay.
4) When He shall come with trumpet sound, Oh, may I then in Him be found;
   Dressed in His righteousness alone, Faultless to stand before the throne.

AMAZING GRACE
By: John Newton

1) Amazing grace how sweet the sound, that saved a wretch like me!
   I once was lost, but now am found, Was blind, but now I see.
2) Twas grace that taught my heart to fear, And grace my fears relieved;
   How precious did that grace appear The hour I first believed!
3) Thro' many dangers, toils and snares, I have already come;
   'tis grace hath bro't me safe thus far and grace will lead me home.
4) When we've been there ten thousand years, Bright shining as the sun,
   We've no less days to sing God's praise Than when we first begun.
   Praise God, Praise God.......

OTHERS WE DEARLY LOVE:
What A Friend We Have In Jesus!
How Great Thou Art!
Blessed Assurance.
Joy To The World!
More Like The Master.
The Old Rugged Cross.
Beneath The Cross of Jesus.
He Lives!
Revive Us Again.
Anywhere With Jesus.
To God Be The Glory!

CHAPTER 30: NOT FINISHED JUST BEGUN! 545

POSTSCRIPT

No claim is made that our ministry was better or more fruitful than any other. Most ministries have their successes and failures, and most faithful ministers deserve more appreciation for perseverance and persistence in spite of opposition and hard knocks. Jesus never said that following Him would be easy; He warned of the opposite--that the Way of The Cross includes rejection and persecution. (Jn.15:18-21).

But if we really abide in Him, we would see good fruit borne for the Father's glory, not for ours. So we have told our story, and we trust there has been much good fruit borne for the Father's glory and for the lifting up of the Name of JESUS, in this increasingly polluted and rebellious world. (Ps.71:17-18; Pro.3:1-3; Jn.12:32; Jn.15).

Many times we have thought of Abraham Lincoln's famous reply regarding his critics during his Civil War years: "I do the very best I know how--the very best I can; and I mean to keep doing so until the end. If the end brings me out all right, what is said against me will not amount to anything. If the end brings me out wrong, ten angels swearing I was right would make no difference." (See page 511).

Many times we have received deep encouragement from JESUS in Matthew 5:11-12:

Blessed are ye when men shall revile you, and persecute you, and say all manner of evil against you falsely, for my sake. Rejoice, and be exceeding glad: for great is your reward in Heaven: for so persecuted they the prophets which were before you.

Don't forget, our LORD JESUS plainly tells us He will RETURN TO JERUSALEM (Acts 1:11; Rev.1:7) and will rule the earth with justice, peace, and holiness abounding. All the works and workers of evil will be defeated! This old world will become a NEW WORLD! Living will become GOOD again, as it was in the beginning. (Gen.1:31). It will be truly the New World Order--made by God's Man and men!

It behooves all of us to heed JESUS' WARNINGS in Matthew 24, Mark 13, and Luke 21, to believe them, to recognize the absolute accuracy and certain fulfillment of HIS PROPHECIES, to be praying without ceasing, to be ready and looking for His Return, to be faithfully loving, obeying and serving Him as good stewards. And singing the Revelation song *EVEN SO COME, LORD JESUS!* (Rev.22:20).

His Return will be seen by all the tribes of the earth and probably will be the greatest of God's wonders for earthlings. It will happen soon!! (Matt.24:27-30; Luke 21:27; Acts 1:11). Let's all be Ready!

If not now READY, it's time to get READY. Get on **The Jesus Track**

(Jn.14:6), **The Jesus Rock** (Matt.7:24), **The Jesus Vine** (Jn.15), and **In Jesus' Yoke** (Matt.11:28-30). Then you'll be really READY! Sorry there are no other tracks to Abundant Life here or to Heaven hereafter!

I am the door: by me if any man enter in, he shall be saved, and shall go in and out and find pasture. The thief (Satan) comes only to steal, and to kill, and to destroy: I am come that they might have life, and that they might have it more abundantly. I am the good shepherd: the good shepherd gives his life for the sheep.
-John 10:9-11

Neither is there salvation in any other: for there is none other name under heaven given among men, whereby we must be saved. *-Acts 4:12*

Just come to JESUS, repenting of sins (on knees--with tears), asking Him to forgive and save. You will be blessed beyond your finest dreams! As Oswald Chambers says, we all need a personal, passionate devotion to the Lord JESUS CHRIST! (I Cor.2:9-10). Receiving JESUS means LIFE; Rejecting Him means DEATH AND HELL! We dare not ignore what Jesus says of Himself:

THE "I AMS" OF JESUS!
1. I AM THE BREAD OF LIFE, THE LIVING BREAD (Jn.6:35,48,51)!
2. I AM THE LIGHT OF THE WORLD (Jn.8:12)!
3. I AM HE (The MESSIAH) (Jn.8:24, 28; 13:19)!
4. I AM (Before Abraham) (Jn.8:58)!
5. I AM THE DOOR OF THE SHEEP (Jn.10:7,9)!
6. I AM THE GOOD SHEPHERD (Jn.10:11,14)!
7. I AM THE SON OF GOD (Jn.10:36)!
8. I AM THE RESURRECTION, AND THE LIFE (Jn.11:25)!
9. I AM THE WAY, THE TRUTH, AND THE LIFE (Jn.14:6)! (NO MAN COMES TO THE FATHER BUT BY ME!)
10. I AM THE TRUE VINE (Jn.15:1-11)! (WITHOUT ME YOU CAN DO NOTHING!)
11. I AM JESUS (Acts 9:5; 22:8; 26:15)!
12. I AM ALPHA AND OMEGA, THE BEGINNING AND THE ENDING; THE FIRST AND THE LAST (Rev.1:8,11,17; 21:6; 22:13)!
13. I AM HE THAT LIVETH AND WAS DEAD AND BEHOLD I AM ALIVE FOREVERMORE, AMEN; AND **HAVE THE KEYS OF HELL AND OF DEATH** (Rev.1:18)!
14. I AM THE ROOT AND OFFSPRING OF DAVID AND THE BRIGHT AND MORNING STAR (Rev.22:16)!

CHAPTER 30: NOT FINISHED JUST BEGUN! 547

Also America has some big decisions to make--to be saved! AMERICA WILL BE FINISHED BY OR BEFORE 1995 IF (1) WE DON'T REPENT AND TURN BACK TO GOD, AND IN THE FEAR AND LOVE OF GOD (both emotions named in Deuteronomy 6) PUT GOD'S WORD, THE BIBLE AND PRAYER, BACK INTO OUR SCHOOLS; (2) IF WE DON'T STOP THE HORRIBLE SLAUGHTER OF BABIES IN THE ABORTION (HORROR!) CHAMBERS OF AMERICA (Some 40,000 killed in Maryland alone in 1991 - over 1½ million in the U.S.!); and (3) IF WE DON'T STAND BY GOD'S SPECIAL LAND AND PEOPLE, ISRAEL!

> God says: ***And it shall come to pass in that day, that I will seek to destroy all the nations that come against Jerusalem.*** (Zechariah 12:3,9).

Our only hope is to do with great courage the above 3 steps as we obey God's Orders in the II Chronicles 7:14:

> *If my people who are called by my name will humble themselves and pray and seek my face, and turn from their wicked ways, then will I hear from heaven, forgive their sins, and heal their land.*

The demon spirits of MURDER are loose in our land because "we" threw out the MAJOR MORAL RESTRAINTS, GOD'S WORD and COMMANDMENTS in 1963, and PRAYER to Him in 1962, and have soaked our land in innocent blood, some 30 million babies killed in cold blood and thrown into garbage dumps since 1973!

ALMIGHTY GOD WILL SURELY AVENGE THESE MURDERS! Their innocent blood cries to Him day and night! If it's alright for doctors and pregnant women to kill babies, what's to restrain the other pagans? NO ONE HAS THAT RIGHT!!! NO WOMAN HAS THE RIGHT TO CHOOSE TO KILL A BABY!!! NO SUPREME COURT OR GOVERNOR HAS THAT RIGHT!!! AMERICA, PLEASE WAKE UP! YOUR TIME IS ALMOST GONE!!

The 30,000 nuclear missiles still in the hands of Yeltsin (Russia) and others will be used to punish America if we don't obey God. It will only take 12 to 15 of them to knock the U.S.A. completely out! The Russians, etc., have been deeply humiliated by America, and basically they (the hardliners), plus Islam, hate us enough to plan revenge and retaliation soon. NUCLEAR SUBS OFFSHORE CAN EASILY DO IT!

America must stay alert, prepared and right with God, if we're to survive! There's no hope for us if we don't do these things. Neither is there hope for the public schools of America until our Founding God, His

Word and Real Prayer are the foundation and honored participants in them again. WE MUST INVITE GOD BACK INTO THE SCHOOLS OF AMERICA!!!

Eternity is ahead, but God willing, we have more work to do for the Lord here before He calls us home. He has told us we must do a SECOND WARNING MISSION to all the States this year - 1992. (See page 479). So we really are "NOT FINISHED, JUST BEGUN!" Pray for us! PLEASE HELP IN WARNING OUR NATION.

Finally, we thank God for all the precious friends and family who have blessed us in this long journey. If we have ever hurt you in any way, please forgive! And we certainly forgive those who may have hurt us in the Firings! In spite of the jolts and jams, we've known the "Joy of Jesus" all the way! Praise HIS Name! As in John 15:11-14:

"These things have I spoken unto you, that my joy might remain in you, and that your joy might be full. This is my commandment, That ye love one another, as I have loved you, greater love hath no man than this, that a man lay down his life for his friends. You are my friends, if ye do whatsoever I command you."

- - - - - - - - - -

SEVEN STEPS TO SALVATION

Men still cry, "What must I do to be saved?" The Bible provides a clear answer.

1. Acknowledge "For all have sinned and come short of the glory of God" (Romans 3:23). "God be merciful to me a sinner" (Luke 18:13).

2. Repent "Except ye repent, ye shall all likewise perish" (Luke 13:3). "Repent ye therefore, and be converted, that your sins may be blotted out" (Acts 3:19).

3. Confess "If we confess our sins, he is faithful and just to forgive us our sins,and to cleanse us from all unrighteousness" (I John 1:9). "If thou shalt confess with thy mouth the Lord Jesus, and shalt believe in thine heart that God hath raised him from the dead, thou shalt be saved" Romans 10:9).

4. Forsake "Let the wicked forsake his way, and the unrighteous man his thoughts; and let him return unto the Lord...for He will abundantly pardon" (Isaiah 55:7).

5. Believe "For God so loved the world, that He gave His only begotten Son, that whosoever believeth in Him should not perish, but have everlasting life" (John 3:16). "He that believeth and is baptized shall be saved; but he that believeth not shall be damned" (Mark 16:16)

6. Receive "He came unto His own, and His own received Him not. But as many as received Him, to them gave He power to become the sons of God, even to them that believe on His name" (John 1:11,12).

7. Pray Now! Give your heart to Jesus by praying this prayer (on your knees if possible): "Dear Lord Jesus, I believe you died for my sins and I ask your forgiveness. I receive you now as my personal Saviour and invite you to direct my life from this day forward. Fill me with your Holy Spirit and help me to fill myself with your Holy Word that I may live for you throughout this life. Amen." **Find a Bible Believing and Teaching Church to serve the Lord in!**

CHAPTER 30: NOT FINISHED JUST BEGUN! 549

THE LORD'S LITTLE TABERNACLE COMPLEX
LTC CHAPEL IS BEHIND THESE BUILDINGS

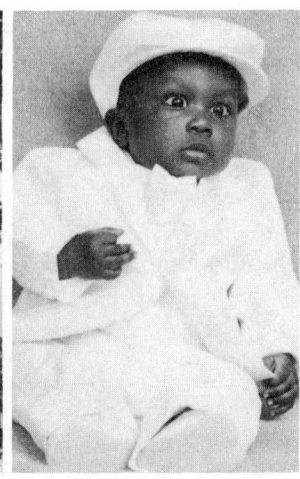

LITTLE JOSEPH
NOT ABORTED! PTL!

STEPPING DOWN AFTER 33 YEARS   NEW PASTOR JOHN MONK AND HIS FAMILY
CHARLOTTE SCHLOER & HER ELDER BOB - ONE OF THE FINEST COPS IN THE WORLD

JOHN WARRINGTON
FINE STREET EVANGELIST

550 FIRED AGAIN AND AGAIN, PRAISE THE LORD!

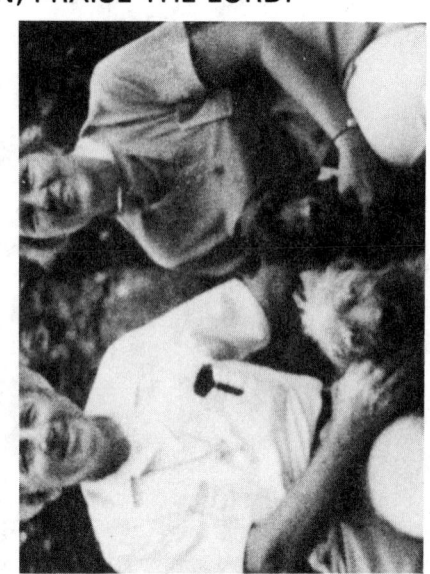

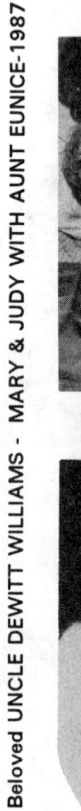

TOP: CHARLIE, MARY, JUDY, BETSY, & FRANK
BOT: DICK, NANCY & SID, FAMILY REUNION-1981
FAITHFUL DOGS, NICKEL & PEACHES-1979

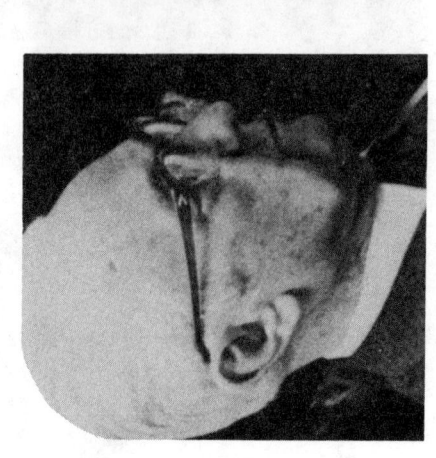

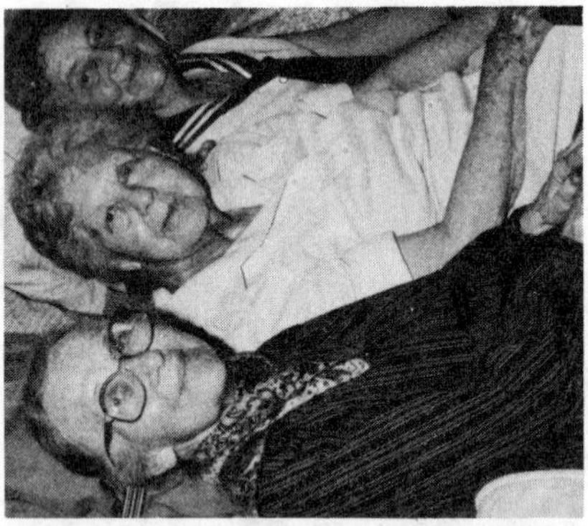

MARY, BETSY, CINDY & KIRBY WHITE-1985
Beloved UNCLE DEWITT WILLIAMS - MARY & JUDY WITH AUNT EUNICE-1987

FIRED AGAIN AND AGAIN, PRAISE THE LORD!

PANAMA CITY, FLA.-- "BAY HIGH" GRADUATION CLASS - 1936

ARMY AIR FORCE PRIMARY FLIGHT SCHOOL, AMERICUS, GA. - JUNE 1941

FIRED AGAIN AND AGAIN, PRAISE THE LORD!

CHAPTER INDEXES

Preface - "A GOOD NAME"

PAGE   PART I
1. Chap 1: "THE EARLY YEARS"
   Two Special Friends
   Our First Hurricane
   Challenged!
   Lost In A Great Swamp!
   A Cold Winter's Night Decision
21. Chap. 2: FROM PEACE TO WAR TO WEDDING
   The Take-Off Crash
   The Other Knee Blows Up!
   Boot Camp-Mustard Gas-
     Facing Death-Total Commitment!
   The Great Surprise in Gulfport!
   Another Surprise - In Corpus Christi
   Happy Days Ahead - P-T-L!
41. Chap. 3: GETTING ON THE LORD'S COURSE
   A Summer of Shark Fishing!
   The Mayor's Boat House Disappears
   The First Lesson At Seminary
   Extra Work and Another Close Call
   Picture Pages (52A & 52)B
53. Chap. 4: SEMINARY GRADUATION TO CONFRONTATIONS
   A Couple To Be Married?
   More About Mom!
   Our Move to Chester And The Second Firing!
65. Chap. 5: FROM SPIRITUAL LIMBO TO GHETTO
   Heading North to Princeton
   The Miracle Apartment in Hopewell
   Baby Joe Pushed Off Cliff
   Invited to McKim

PART II
75. Chap. 6: MCKIM DAYS (OR DAZE)
   Some McKim History
   Dusty Arrives
   God Provides A Home
   The Hell-Bound Flags
   The Gang Attacks
   Gang Leader Invades Office
   A Real Miracle For JR's Little Boy
   Wonderful Community Center Workers
   The Home-Grown Future Director
   Our Italian Restaurant Friend
   Two Special Street Friends
   The David Yankelov Story
101. Chap. 7: THE WAR ON POVERTY AND OTHER WARS
   Cast-iron Stomach, Special Audit
   The Great Psychiatrist
   The Dead-End Conference In Cincinnati
   Picture pages (114A & 114B)
115. Chap. 8: AN UNEXPECTED WAR - OR THIRD FIRING
   My Betsy Leaves Me
   Betsy Tells Her Background
   A Very Difficult Story
125. Chap. 9: FROM THE RACE RIOTS TO TWO MORE FIRINGS
   Palm Sunday Riots - 1968
   The Louisville Shout-down
   Carl's Funeral
   Brian's Arrival
   The Near Self-Massacre on Memorial Day
   Our First Joshua March - July 1969
   The Axe Falls at McKim
   The Old Factory Becomes A Christian Center
   Fired Again, Praise The Lord

PART III
147. Chap. 10: THE LITTLE TABERNACLE ARISES
   God's Long Distance Call via Florida
   The Traffic Light Healing
   Another Traffic Light Miracle
   The Last Upper Room Service in The Old Factory
   "How Great Thou Art"
   The Search Begins For Another Home for The Little Tabernacle
   The Amazing Funeral Honorarium
   The Conference with the Einspruchs - Jesse's Part
   Our Next Tent, The Old Barber School
   Kitty's Dream
   Miracles in The Store Front
   Amazing Prophecy Given by the Holy Spirit through Linda Requard
   Gin's Request Granted!
167. Chap. 11: THE FREBURGER STORY
   Exciting Adventures Ahead
   A Journey Into Faith
   Others Share The Journey
   "Where'er I Go"
181. Chap. 12: MIRACLE CONTRACT AND GOLDEN KEY
   At Long Last The Golden Key
   Debbie Comes To Washington - Debbie's Letter
   The Unexpected Invitation

FIRED AGAIN AND AGAIN, PRAISE THE LORD!

The Big Picture of Jesus Finds a Home
The Huge Statue of Jesus at Johns Hopkins
Johns Hopkins Read Out Of Meeting
The Unexpected Call From The Bus Station
A Rebel Boy Delivered
Jesus '73 Camp and the Tornado Turns Away

199. **Chap.13: MOM'S HOME-GOING; SON'S HOME-COMING!**
Life With Papa And The No-Good Farm Miracle
The Lord's Warning Message To A Popular Minister
The Lord's Miracle Method Of Artificial Respiration
News Events for 1974 -
A Tiny Taste of a Newsletter
The Angels Came And Lifted Mom Up To Heaven!
A Remarkable Story At The Funeral Home
Our Own Missing Son Returns - Hallelujah!
Jesus Is Real
You Can't Block God Out! (Another Rebel Called Home)

PART IV

225. **Chap.14: MORE MIRACLES OF JESUS**
Dashing Through The Snow
A Christian TV station for Baltimore?
The Strange Snow Fall
Jesus Piggy-Bank Miracle
A Very Special Christmas - 1975

237. **Chap. 15: GOD'S SOLEMN WARNING TO THE CHURCH**
The Solemn Warning to the Presbyterian Church,
"Moment of Truth" by Demos Shakarian
1776-1976 - 200th Birthday of our Country!
Dr. Karl Barth's Reply
But America Throws Out The Bible and Prayer!
Another Godless & Subversive Organization
The Von-Trapp Family
Early Warning Through Agathe

249. **Chap. 16: AN AMAZING YEAR-1977- THE CALL TO ISRAEL**
The Christmas that Wouldn't Turn Off
Happy Birthday, Jesus
Before Israel, Meet Edgar Baillie
Before Israel Comes Don Odon's School of The Prophets
You Are Part Of God's LTC Miracle
They That Wait Upon The Lord
Our First Ride High Up to Israel

265. **Chap. 17: THE ISRAEL CONNECTION GROWS**
Esther Comes To Baltimore
Brother Sid Needs an Operation & Betsy's Diamond Disappears
Our Second Tour To Israel
Our Macedonian Call
On Finding Emmaus
Return To Israel Confirmed in England.

285. **Chap. 18: PREPARATION FOR OUR ISRAEL ASSIGNMENT**
The Great House Moving of '79
Finding Fishing Worms - The Old Timey Way!
It Wasn't Easy Being A Preacher's Kid
The Heavenly Anointing Oil Miracle

PART V

303. **Chap. 19: OUR RAMOT YEAR IN JERUSALEM**
"One Day At A Time, Sweet Jesus"
"Put Your Hand in the Hand of Jesus"
The Weeping Phone Call from Rome
Heavenly Connections
"Angels, Brother, Angels":..Russell Moore - Harold Morris
The Black Dog Story
A Real Quick Prayer At the Good Fence
Coffee Shop Confrontation
Tupelo Honey to Prime Minister Begin's Deputy
The Hebrew Meaning of Amen!

325. **Chap. 20: FROM CONFRONTATION TO WARS**
Confrontation of A Different Sort at Yad Vashem.
The "Yeverechacha" Song Story
When We Trust and Obey the Lord Guides All the Way
Talitha Cumi, Afikomen, We Get to See Sinai
Story out of the Holocaust
The "Ani Smecha" Tea Party
Appointment With A War
"Operation Peace For Galilee"
Some Truths About Islam
God's Special Delivery to the Voice Of Hope Radio Station
The Prayer Shawl Miracle in Lebanon
The Blue String and Nail
It Must Have Been Hard on our Kids
The Non-Fatal War of Pies !
Picture Pages (342A & 342B)

FIRED AGAIN AND AGAIN, PRAISE THE LORD!

343. Chap. 21: SEARCH FOR A CHURCH AND OIL
  Looking For A Church Home In Jerusalem
  Dier El Kamar
  The Yellow Bird Arrives and We Get to See the Egyptian Pyramids
  The Egypt Trip
  Andy SoRelle and The Asher Oil Well
  An Amazing Sequel
  "Out of Control" (Andy's Shot-up Plane!)
  Picture Pages (354A & 354B)
355. Chap. 22: A DREAM COME TRUE ON - PATMOS
  Beautiful, Peaceful, Little Patmos - 1984
  The Greek Sermon and Thanos Carbonis
  On Seeing A Welsh Revival

PART VI

379. Chap. 23: GOD'S LITTLE AND BIG MIRACLES
  God's Miracle Connections
  Another Long Ago Connection.
  Miracles at Pappy's, Some Little, Some Big!
  After Five Years, Christmas with our Precious Family.
  Go Home and Rest By The Fire.
  Not Total Hibernation
  Good News About Esther's Book
391. Chap. 24: ANOTHER ROUGH FIRING- FROM ISRAEL
  Come To The Misrad Haponim!
  Mr. Shoshani's (X) On Our Passports
  Leave In Ten Days!
  The Hectic Last Three Weeks
  Special People We Wanted to say Goodby to: Bearded John, Michael, A Messianic Family, etc.
409. Chap. 25: FROM PATMOS TO A WHIRLWIND SUMMER
  "U F O," Unidentified Floating Object. (Knee Operation)
  Miracle Help at LTC After Our Return From Israel
  A Special Arab Named Ibraham
  Watch and Pray
457. Chap. 26: DANGEROUS MISSIONARIES ARRESTED
  Arrested at Passpot Control.
  A Special Saint Above- Sharon
  The 1987 Tour and Israel's Terrible Drought
  Sheep Paths on The Mountains of Israel

435. Chap. 27: SOME YUMMY STORIES
  Honeyology.
  Gritsology
  Three Yummy Stories - Chopped Fruits, Waffles, pecan pies!
  "Lord was there Anything Good Done In Our Years At McKim?"
  Another Good Report
  Wallace's Miracle Car
  Letter To Grandchildren
  Lee Nelson's Letter

PART VII

457. Chap. 28: BIBLE PROPHECIES AND WARNINGS.
  Studying Biblical Prophecies
  Bible Prophecies Being Fulfilled
  God's Solemn Warnings,
  Another Warning to America,
  God's Chilling Warning
  Rocky Schmit's Tape To The Little Tabernacle with Warning To America.
  As Promised Earlier: George Washington's Vision
  God's Warning Mission To America
  Observations From Warning Mission
487. Chap. 29: THREE GREAT MEN OF FAITH
  Christopher Columbus-Christ-Bearer
  George Washington
  An Amazing Jewish Patriot
  The Turning Point
  Abraham Lincoln
  Thank You, Lord, for Their Faith
521. Chap. 30: RETIRING & REFIRING "NOT FINISHED JUST BEGUN"
  70th Birthday and Prayer For Someone To Carry On At LTC
  How And Where Are Our Sons Today?
  Family Trees
  Jennifer's "Trip To Heaven"
  The Lost Star and Cross
  Songs From Patmos
  Declaring The Wondrous Works Of The Lord
  The Scarlet F - by Colson
  Selections From Our Favorite Daily Devotionals
  Two of Our Favorite Hymns
  Postscript
  Seven Steps To Salvation!
  Picture pages
  Chapter Index